Procurement and Supply Chain Management

Pearson

At Pearson, we have a simple mission: to help people make more of their lives through learning.

We combine innovative learning technology with trusted content and educational expertise to provide engaging and effective learning experiences that serve people wherever and whenever they are learning.

From classroom to boardroom, our curriculum materials, digital learning tools and testing programmes help to educate millions of people worldwide – more than any other private enterprise.

Every day our work helps learning flourish, and wherever learning flourishes, so do people.

To learn more, please visit us at **www.pearson.com/uk**

Tenth Edition

Procurement and Supply Chain Management

KENNETH LYSONS
MA, MEd, PhD, Dipl.PA, Ac.Dip.Ed.,
DMS, FCIS, FCIPS, FInst M, MILT

BRIAN FARRINGTON
BSc(Econ), MSc, PhD, FCIPS

Pearson

Harlow, England • London • New York • Boston • San Francisco • Toronto • Sydney
Dubai • Singapore • Hong Kong • Tokyo • Seoul • Taipei • New Delhi
Cape Town • São Paulo • Mexico City • Madrid • Amsterdam • Munich • Paris • Milan

PEARSON EDUCATION LIMITED
KAO Two
KAO Park
Harlow CM17 9SR
United Kingdom
Tel: +44 (0)1279 623623
Web: www.pearson.com/uk

First published 1981 (print)
Tenth edition published 2020 (print and electronic)

Contains public sector information licensed under the Open Government Licence (OGL) v3.0.
http://www.nationalarchives.gov.uk/doc/open-government-licence/version/3/

Contains Parliamentary information licensed under the Open Parliament Licence (OPL) v3.0.
http://www.parliament.uk/site-information/copyright/open-parliament-licence/

Pearson Education is not responsible for the content of third-party internet sites.

ISBN: 978-1-292-31791-5 (print)
       978-1-292-31793-9 (PDF)
       978-1-292-31795-3 (ePub)

British Library Cataloguing-in-Publication Data
A catalogue record for the print edition is available from the British Library

Library of Congress Cataloging-in-Publication Data
Names: Lysons, Kenneth, author. | Farrington, Brian, author.
Title: Procurement and supply chain management / Kenneth Lysons, MA, MEd,
   PhD, Dipl.PA, Ac.Dip.Ed., DMS, FCIS, FCIPS, FInst M, MILT, Brian
   Farrington, BSc(Econ), MSc, PhD, FCIPS.
Other titles: Purchasing and supply chain management.
Description: Tenth Edition. | Hoboken : Pearson, 2020.
Identifiers: LCCN 2019051789 | ISBN 9781292317915 (paperback) | ISBN
   9781292317939 (pdf) | ISBN 9781292317953 (epub)
Subjects: LCSH: Purchasing. | Business logistics.
Classification: LCC HF5437 .L97 2020 | DDC 658.7/2—dc23
LC record available at https://lccn.loc.gov/2019051789

10 9 8 7 6 5 4 3 2 1
24 23 22 21 20

Cover: Rob Whitworth 2012/Alamy Stock Photo

Print edition typeset in 10/12pt Goudy Old Style MT Pro by SPi Gobal
Printed in Slovakia by Neografia

NOTE THAT ANY PAGE CROSS REFERENCES REFER TO THE PRINT EDITION

Dedications

I dedicate this book to my family. They mean everything to me. In particular, to Joyce, my wife, who has unstintingly supported me throughout my career. She is without comparison.

I also dedicate this book to the memory of Kenneth Lysons. Ken's devoted wife, Audrey, and their family continue to be a source of inspiration to me. This relationship has extended over many years and is greatly valued.

Brian Farrington

Contents

Supporting resources

Visit **go.pearson.com/uk/he/resources** to find valuable online resources

For Instructors:
- Comprehensive Instructor's Manual containing teaching tips and notes on case studies for each chapter
- Downloadable PowerPoint slides containing figures from the book

For more information please contact your local Pearson Education sales representative or visit **go.pearson.com/uk/he/resources**

Preface

Dr Brian Farrington is the author of the tenth edition of this acclaimed book. The output of any book is influenced by many sources, including:

- professional feedback from lecturers at Universities and Colleges; their views are invaluable
- the Chartered Institute of Procurement and Supply's education syllabus and the Institute's continual quest to enhance standards
- legal challenges to procurement decisions
- emphasis on environmental and socially responsible procurement
- feedback from learners and practitioners
- the author's international consultancy experience
- the recognition that a procurement specialist has to exercise the highest moral and ethical standards and that some fall short
- the challenge presented by cyber security.

There are two new chapters, thanks to the foresight of Pearson.

Public Sector Procurement is a new chapter, recognising the public sector's impact on the global economy. Public accountability means that scrutiny of decisions is far more open than the private sector.

Sustainability and Socially Responsible Procurement is a new chapter, recognising that this is a highly challenging global issue wherein procurement has great influence. More initiatives are necessary.

There has been a serious recasting of much of the content. There is an unrivalled opportunity for procurement specialists to manage risk, finance and corporate performance. The author seeks to instil in all procurement specialists the fact that effective and innovative procurement pays a significant part in the management of economies and corporate performance.

Acknowledgements

Writing a book of this complexity requires the support, advice and patience of many people. The challenges, frustrations and achievements are never solely down to the author. I am indebted to many organisations and people who have materially assisted. By exception, Joe Anwyll, has provided me with constant professional opportunities and challenges. These have kept me focused.

Sandra Small has, again, risen to every challenge I have faced her with. The changes made to this edition have presented Sandra with severe timescales and technical issues. She has risen to these with unquestionable diligence and expertise.

Joyce, my wife, has tolerated, with the utmost goodwill, my absolute focus on getting the tenth edition of the book finished to meet an exacting deadline.

It would be remiss not to acknowledge the 'new' relationship with the Pearson team in India. The help and support of Bincy Menon, Agnibesh Das and Vinay Agnihotri have been vital. It can truly be said to have been an experience! Louise Attwood's attention to detail during the copyediting process has ensured the book is of the highest quality.

Publisher's acknowledgements

Text Credit(s):

4 CIPS Australia Pty Ltd: The Definition of Procurement, CIPS Australia Pty Ltd; **5 Investopedia:** Supply Chain Management, Investopedia, www.investopedia.com; **5 Techopedia:** Supply Chain Management, Techopedia, www.techopedia.com; **7 Penguin Random House:** Marrian, J., 'Market characteristics of industrial goals and buyers', in Wilson, A. (ed.), *The Marketing of Industrial Products*, Hutchinson, London, UK, 1965, p. 11; **8 Earlsgate Press:** Lamming, R., 'The future of purchasing: developing lean supply', in Lamming, R., and Cox, A., (eds), *Strategic Procurement Management in the 1990s*, Earlsgate Press, UK, 1985, p. 40; **13 Pearson Education:** Syson, R., *Improving Purchasing Performance*, Pitman, 1992, pp. 254–5; **17–18 CAPS Research:** Carter, P. L. and Ogden, J. A., *The World Class Purchasing and Supply Organisation: Identifying the Characteristics*, Center for Advanced Purchasing Studies, University of Arizona. Reprinted with permission from CAPS Research; **19 Pearson Education:** Saunders, M., *Strategic Purchasing and Supply Chain Management*, Pitman, UK, 1994, p. 11; **21–22 Pearson Education:** Syson, R., *Improving Purchasing Performance*, Pitman, UK, 1992, pp. 254–5; **22 Elsevier:** Farmer, D., 'Organisation for purchasing', *Purchasing and Supply Management*, February, 1990, pp. 23–7; **23 Oxford University Press:** Carr-Saunders, A. M. and Wilson, P. A., *The Professions*, Oxford University Press, UK, 1928; **25 National Association of Presort Mailers:** Whittington, E., 'Will the Last Buyer Please Stand Up!', Proceedings NAPM 84 Annual Conference, May 1999; **32 Pearson Education:** Chopra, S. and Meindl, P., *Supply Chain Management. Strategy, Planning & Operation*, 6th edn, Pearson Global Edition, Pearson Education Ltd, Harlow, UK, 2018; **32 McGraw-Hill Education:** Ohmae, K., *The Mind of the Strategist*, McGraw-Hill, New York, USA, 1982; **32 Pearson Education:** Mintzberg, H., 'Five Ps for strategy' in Mintzberg, H., Lampel, J., Quinn, J. G. and Ghoshal, S. (eds) *The Strategy Process*, Prentice Hall, Upper Saddle River, New Jersey, USA, 2003, pp. 3–10; **33 Pearson Education:** Mintzberg, H., 'Five Ps for strategy' in Mintzberg, H., Lampel, J., Quinn, J. G. and Ghoshal, S. (eds) *The Strategy Process*, Prentice Hall, Upper Saddle River, New Jersey, USA, 2003, p. 9; **37 Macmillan Publishers:** David, F. R., *Concepts of Strategic Management*, Macmillan, New York, USA, 1991, p. 4; **38 Pearson Education:** Hax, A. C. and Majluf, N. S., *The Strategy Concept and Process*, Prentice Hall, Upper Saddle River, New Jersey, USA, 1999, p. 416; **40 Harvard Business School Publishing:** Kraljic, P., Purchasing must become supply management, *Harvard Business Review*, Sept/Oct, 1983, p. 110; **41 University of Wolverhampton:** Worral, L., Strategic analysis: a scientific art, Occasional paper No. OP001/98, University of Wolverhampton, 27 May 1998; **42 Mentor Books:** Brown, A. and Weiner, E., *Super Managing: How to Harness Change for Personal and Organisational Success*, Mentor Books, 1985, p. ix; **42 University of Boras:** Choo, C. W., 'Environmental scanning as information seeking and organisational learning', *Information Research*, Vol. 7, No. 1, October, 2001; **45 Harvard Business School Publishing:** ICMA, *Management Accounting 2000: Official Terminology*: www.icmacentre.ac.uk, 2000; **45 Public Service Commission of Canada:** Lawrence, E., 'Srategic thinking' paper prepared for the research Directorate Public Service Commission of Canada, 27 April, 1999; **46 Pearson Education:** Mintzberg, H., 'Five Ps for strategy' in Mintzberg, H., Lampel, J., Quinn, J. G. and

Ghoshal, S. (eds) *The Strategy Process*, Prentice Hall, Upper Saddle River, New Jersey, USA, 2003, p. 124; **46 Elsevier:** Carr, A. S. and Smeltzer, L. R., 'An empirically based definition of strategic purchasing', *European Journal of Purchasing and Supply Management*, Vol. 3, 1997, pp. 199–207; **49 Pearson Education:** Rumelt, R. P., 'Evaluating business strategy' in Mintzberg, H., Lampel, J., Quinn, J. G. and Ghoshal, S. *The Strategy Process*, Prentice Hall, 2003, p. 81; **51–52 Organisation for Economic Co-operation and Development:** Risk Management and Corporate Governance OECD (2014); **54 Harvard Business School Publishing:** Kraljic, P., 'Purchasing must become supply management', *Harvard Business Review*, Sept/Oct, 1983, p. 110; **55 Elsevier:** Nellove, R. and Söderquist, K., 'Portfolio approaches to procurement', *Long Range Planning*, Vol. 33, 2000, pp. 245–67; **57 John Wiley & Sons, Inc:** Gelderman, C. J. and van Weele, A. J., 'Strategic direction through purchasing portfolio management: a case study', *International Journal of Supply Chain Management*, Vol. 38, spring, 2002, pp. 30–8; **71 Nort Atlantic Treaty Organization:** NATO, *Logistics Handbook*, 1997, paras 103–4; **71 Council of Supply Chain Management Professionals:** Logistics Management, Council of Supply Chain Management Professionals, cscmp.org; **72 Council of Logistics Management:** Council of Logistics Management Professionals USA, 12 February 1998; **72 NATO:** NATO, Logistics Handbook, 1997, paragraph 104; **74 Institute for Regional Security Ltd:** Australian Defence Logistics. The need to enable and equip Logistics Transformation. Kokoda Paper No. 19, June 2014. Waters & Blackburn Kokoda; **75 High Court of England and Wales:** DHL Supply Chain Ltd v Secretary of State for Health and Social Care [2018] EWHC 2213 (TCC); **76–77 Reverse Logistics Executive Council:** Rogers, D. S. and Tibben-Lemke, R., *Going Backwards: Reverse Logistics Trends and Practices*, Reverse Logistics Executive Council, Pittsburgh, USA; **78 Pearson Education:** Atken, J., quoted in Christopher, M., Logistics and Supply Chain Management, 2nd edn, Pearson Education, Harlow, UK, 1998, p. 19; **79 Emerald Publishing Limited:** Cooper, M. C., Lambert, D. M. and Pugh, J. D., 'Supply chain management – more than a new name for logistics', *International Journal of Logistics Management*, Vol. 8, No. 1, 1997, pp. 1–4; **79 Simon & Schuster:** Porter, M. E., *Competitive Advantage*, Free Press, 1985, p. 3; **83 The Global Supply Chain Forum:** Adapted from Lambert, D. M., Cooper, M. C. and Pagh, J. D., 'Supply chain management: implementation, issues and research opportunities', *The International Journal of Logistics Management*, Vol. 9, No. 2, 1998, p. 2; **85 Emerald Publishing Limited:** Chee Yew Wong, Skipworth, H., Godsell, J. and Achimugu, N., 'Towards a theory of supply chain alignment enablers: a systematic literature review', *Supply Chain Management*, Vol 17, Issue 4, 2012, pp. 419–437; **88 Cranfield School of Management:** Cranfield University School of Management, Supply chain vulnerability, Final Report, 2002, pp. 35–7; **94 Simon & Schuster:** Porter, M. E., *Competitive Advantage*, Free Press, 1985, pp. 118 and 162–3; **95 Taylor & Francis:** Cudahy, G., 'The impact of pricing on supply chains' in Gattorna, J. L. (ed.) *Gower Handbook of Supply Chain Management*, 5th edn, Gower, UK, 2003, pp. 62–75; **97 Gartner, Inc:** www.gartner.com; **104 Pearson Education:** Mintzberg, H., *The Structure of Organisations*, Prentice Hall, 1979, p. 2; **104 Harvard Business School Publishing:** Kotter, J. P. *Leading Change*, Harvard Business School Press. Boston, MA, USA, p. 169; **105 Harvard Business School Publishing:** The main ideas about core competences were developed by Prahalad, C. K. and Hamel, G., in a series of articles in the *Harvard Business Review*, Vol. 88, 1990, and in their book *The Core Competence of the Corporation*, Harvard Business Press, Brighton, Massachusetts, USA, 1990; **106 Faculty of Technical Sciences:** Grinnel, S. and Apple, H. P., 'When two bosses are better than one', *Machine Design*, 9 January, 1975, p. 86; **109 University of Michigan:** French, P., Jr. and Raven, B., 'The basis of social power' in Cartwright, D. (ed.), *Studies in Social Power*, Michigan Institute for Social Research, 1959; **110 Pearson Education:** Mintzberg, H., *The Structure of Organisations*, Prentice Hall, Upper Saddle River, New Jersey, USA, 1979, p. 2; **112 Simon & Schuster:** Quinn, J. B., *Intelligent Enterprise*, Free Press, New York, USA, 1992; **112 Deloitte:** The organisation of the future: Arriving now. Deloitte Insights (2017), www.2.deloitte.com; **113 John Wiley & Sons, Inc:** Ford, D., Gadde, L-E., Hakansson, H. and Snehota, I., *Managing Business Relationships*, 2nd edn, John Wiley, Hoboken, New Jersey, USA, 2003, p. 18; **118 Rambam Health Care Campus:** Teich, S. T. and Faddoul, F. F., 'Lean management – the journey from Toyota to Healthcare', *Rambam Maimonides Medical Journal*, April 4 (2), 2013; **120 Emerald Publishing Limited:** Toni, A. D. and Tonchia, S., 'Lean organisation, management by process and performance measurement', *International Journal of Operations and Production Management*, Vol. 16, No. 2, 1996, pp. 221–236; **121 Van Nostrand Reinhold:** Goldman, S. L., Nagel, R. N. and Preiss, K., *Agile Competitors and Virtual Organisations: Strategies for Enriching the Customer*, Van Nostrand Reinhold, New York, 1995; **121 McGraw-Hill Education:** Bowersox, D. J., Class, D. J. and Cooper, M. B., *Supply Chain Logistics Management*, International edition, McGraw-Hill, 2002, pp. 16–19; **122 Emerald Publishing Limited:** Van Hoek, R., 'Reconfiguring the supply chain to implement postponed manufacturing', *International Journal of Logistics Management*, Vol. 9, No. 1, 1998, pp. 1223–47; **122 Martin Christopher:** Christopher, M., Managing the global supply chain in an uncertain world, India Infoline Business School at: www.Indiainfoline.com/bisc/gscm.html, pp. 1–5; **123 International Group for Lean Construction:** Hoekstra, S. and Romme, J., *Integral Logistics Structures: Developing Customer-orientated Goods Flow*, McGraw-Hill, quoted in Naim, M., Naylor, J. and Barlow, J., 'Developing lean and agile supply chains in the UK housebuilding industry', Proceedings IGLC-7, 26–28 July 1999, University of California, pp. 159–68; **123 Supply Chain Sustainability School:** Supply Chain Mapping Guidance Protocol (2017). Version 1. May www.supplychainschool.co.uk; **125 John Wiley & Sons, Inc:** Gardner, J. T. and Cooper, M. C., 'Strategic supply chain mapping approaches', *Journal of Business Logistics*, Vol. 24, No. 2, 2003, pp. 37–64; **125 Emerald Publishing Limited:** Gardner, J. T. and Cooper, M. C., 'Strategic supply chain mapping approaches', *Journal of Business Logistics*, Vol. 24, No. 2, 2003, pp. 37–64; **126 Emerald Publishing Limited:** Scott, C. and Nestbrook, R., 'New strategic tools for supply chain management', *International Journal of Physical Distribution & Logistics Management* Vol. 21, No. 1, 1991; **129 Thomson Reuters Corporation:** Hellriegel, D., Slocum, J. W. and Woodman, R. W., *Organisational Behaviour*, West Publishing, 1986, p. 340; **129 Penguin Random House:** Handy, C., *Understanding Organisations*, 4th edn, Penguin, 1993; **130 HarperCollins:** Lewin, K., *Field Theory in Social Science*, Harper & Row, USA, 1951; **131 Aberdeen Group.Inc:** Collins, D., *Organisational Change*, Routledge, 1998. The authors are indebted to Harty, C., 'Do n-step guides for change work'? CIPS Knowledge in Action series, for the information contained in this section; **134 Organisation for Economic Co-operation and Development:** CCNM/SIGMA/PUMA, Centralised and Decentralised Public Procurement, 108, 2000, p. 5; **134 Institute for Supply Management, Inc:** Institute of Supply Management (USA), Glossary of Key Supply Management Terms, see ISM website: www.ism.ws; **135 Pearson Education:** Torrington, D. and Hall, L., *Personnel Management*, Prentice Hall, Upper Saddle River, New Jersey, USA, 1991, p. 208; **136 Harvard Business School Publishing:** Sobek, I. I., Durward, K., Liker, J. K. and Ward, A. C., 'Another look at how Toyota integrates product development', *Harvard Business Review*, Vol. 76.4, July/August, 1998, p. 36; **142 Hachette Book Group:** Klein, W. C. and Murphy, D. C., *Policies: Concept in Organisational*

Guidance. Little-Brown, Boston, USA, 1973, p. 2; **142–143 Crossrail Limited:** Crossrail Procurement Policy Document Number CR/QMS/PROC/POL/1101; **149 Government Accountability Office:** International Electronic Commerce. Definitions and Policy Implications, GAO-02-404; **149 Taylor & Francis:** Zwass, V., 'Electronic commerce: structures and issues', *International Journal of Electronic Commerce*, Vol. 1, No. 1., Fall, 1996, pp. 3–23; **149 Taylor & Francis:** Hackbarth, G. and Kettinger, W. J., 'Building an E- business strategy', *Information Systems Management*, Vol. 17, 2000, p. 78; **149 McGraw-Hill Education:** Greenstein, M. and Feinmann, T., *Electronic Commerce Security, Risk Management & Control*, Irwin McGraw-Hill, Boston, 2000; **153 Pearson Education:** Kalakota, R. and Robinson, M., *E-business 2.0*, 2nd edn, Addison Wesley, Boston, USA, 2001, p. 310; **155–156 McGraw-Hill Education:** Killen, K. H. and Kamauff, J. W., *Managing Purchasing*, Irwin, 1995, p. 60; **156 Elsevier:** Monczka, R. M. and Carter, J. R., 'Implementation of electronic data interchange', *Journal of Purchasing and Supply Management*, Summer, 1998, pp. 2–9; **157 National Computing Centre:** National Computing Centre, 'The impact of e-purchasing on supply chain management', *My IT Adviser*, 17 September, 2002; **159 Taylor & Francis:** Adapted from Ronchi, Stefano, *The Internet and the Customer Supplier Relationship*, Ashgate, 2003, p. 48; **163 Intergraf:** International confederation for printing and allied industries, 'E-Auctions – Code of Conduct', March 2005; **163–164 Intergraf:** Reprinted with permission from International confederation for printing and allied industries, 'E-Auctions – Code of Conduct', March 2005; **170 KnowledgeBrief:** e-Procurement Best Practice Guideline, July 2003, www. knowledgebrief.com; **174 Sourcing Industry Group:** Sourcing Industry Group, How to create a Playbook for a best-in-class Supplier Lifecycle Program, www.sig.org, 2015; **184 AIRCC Publishing:** Used with permission from AIRCC Publishing. *International Journal of Managing Value and Supply Chains (IJMVSC)*, Vol. 6, No. 4, December 2015; **187 Institute for Collaborative Working:** The Partner – May 2017, Used with permission from Institute for Collaborative Working, p. 58; **190–191 PricewaterhouseCoopers:** PWC Detailed SRM maturity model; **193 Elsevier:** Cox, A., 'Regional competence and strategic procurement management', *European Journal of Purchasing and Supply Management*, Vol. 2, No. 1, 1996, p. 64; **198 RAND Corporation:** The RAND Corporation is a non-profit institution that helps improve decision making through research and analysis. https:www.rand.org; **199 Institute for Supply Management/W.P. Carey School of Business:** Adapted from Krause and Handfield, 1999. Reprinted with permission from the publisher, Institute for Supply Management and W.P. Carey School of Business at Arizona State University.; **200 Institute for Supply Management, Inc:** Mitchell, L. K., 'Breaking up is hard to do – how to end a supplier relationship', ISM resource article at: www.ism.ws/ResourceArticles/cpoomitchell.cfm; **201–202 Institute for Supply Management, Inc:** Campbell, P. and Pollard, W. M., 'Ending a supplier relationship', *Inside Supply Management*, September 2002, pp. 33–8; **203 Richard Chesterman:** The Honourable Richard Chesterman 40 RFD QC; **209 The Incorporated Council of Law Reporting for England & Wales:** New Zealand Shipping Co Ltd v AM Satter Awaite & Co Ltd [1975] AC 154 Reprinted with permission from ICLR.; **209 Court of Appeal:** Blackpool and Fylde Aero Club Ltd v Blackpool Borough Council [1990] W&R 1195.Court of Appeal; **209–210 Court of Appeal:** Pickfords Ltd v Celestica Ltd [2003] EWCA CIV 1741 (19th November 2003); **210 UK Department of Transport:** UK Department of Transport in an Invitation to Tender for the Thames Link, Southern and Great Northern Franchise, included at 4.6 validity of Bids; **212 High Court of England and Wales:** Transformers & Rectifiers Ltd v Needs Ltd [2015] EWHC 2689 (TCC); **213 Pearson Education:** Elliot, C. and Quinn, F., *Elliott and Quinn Contract Law*,

Pearson, Harlow, UK, 2019; **213 The National Archives:** The Sale of Goods Act (1979) Section 2(1); **213 The National Archives:** The Sale of Goods Act (1979) section 13(1); **214 The National Archives:** The Sale of Goods Act (1979) section 14(2); **214 The National Archives:** The Sale of Goods Act (1979) section 14(3); **214 The National Archives:** Supply of Goods and Services Act (1982)section 13; **214 The National Archives:** Supply of Goods and Services Act (1982) section 14(1); **214 The National Archives:** Supply of Goods and Services Act (1982) section 15(1); **214 The National Archives:** UCTA (1977)section 13; **214 The Incorporated Council of Law Reporting for England & Wales:** Lloyds Bank Ltd v Bundy [1975] QB.326. CA Reprinted with permission from ICLR.; **215 High Court of England and Wales:** FG Wilson (Engineering) Ltd v John Holt & Company (Liverpool) Ltd [2012] EWHC 2477 (Comm); **215 House of Lords:** Curries v Misa [1875] LR10 Ex153, 162; **215–216 Thomson Reuters:** Peel, E., *Treitel The Law of Contract.* Sweet and Maxwell, London, UK, 2007; **216 The National Archives:** The Companies Act (2006) section 39(1); **216 High Court of England and Wales:** CRJ Services Ltd v Lanstar Ltd (Ha CSG Lanstar) [2011] EWHC 972 (TCC); **217 Michael Burton:** Mr Justice Burton; **217 The Incorporated Council of Law Reporting for England & Wales:** Butler Machine Tools Co Ltd v Ex-Cell-O Corpn (England) Ltd, [1979] 1 WLR 401 Reprinted with permission from ICLR.; **217 The National Archives:** Sale of Goods Act (1979); **217 High Court of England and Wales:** Thermal Energy Construction Ltd v AE & E Lantjes UK Ltd [2009] EWHC 408 (TCC); **218 High Court of England and Wales:** MW High Tech Projects UK Ltd v Haase Environmental Consulting GmbH [2015]152 (TCC); **218 High Court of England and Wales:** Requirements of Clause 11 (11.3); **218 The National Archives:** The Misrepresentation Act (1967) Section 2(1); **219 High Court of England and Wales:** Kingspan Environmental & Ors v Borealis A/s & Anor [2012] EWHC 1147 (Comm); **220 High Court of England and Wales:** Bluewater Energy Services BV v Mercon Steel Structures BV & Ors [2014] EWHC 2132; **220 Sir Vivian Arthur Ramsey:** Hon MR JUSTICE RAMSEY; **221 High Court of England and Wales:** TSG Building Services PLC v South Anglia Housing Ltd [2013] EWHC 1151 (TCC); **221 Robert Akenhead:** Mr Justice Akenhead at para 51; **222 Pearson Education:** Elliot, C. and Quinn, F., *Elliott and Quinn Contract Law*, Pearson, Harlow, UK, 2015, p. 326; **224 The Incorporated Council of Law Reporting for England & Wales:** Aluminium Industrie Vaasen BV v Romalpa Aluminium Ltd [1976] 1 WLR 676 Reprinted with permission from ICLR.; **224 Guildhall Chambers:** Professor Gerald McMeel and Stefan Ramel. *Retention of Title – A thorn in the side?* Guildhall Chambers, June 2009; **224 High Court of England and Wales:** Professor Gerald McMeel and Stefan Ramel. *Retention of Title – A thorn in the side?* Guildhall Chambers, June 2009; **225–226 High Court of England and Wales:** Diamond Build Ltd v Clapham Park Homes Ltd [2008] EWHC 1439 (TCC); **227 High Court of England and Wales:** Trustees of Ampleforth Abbey Trust v Turner & Townsend Project Management Ltd [2012] EWHC 2137 (TCC); **228 High Court of England and Wales:** Tandrin Aviation Holdings Ltd v Aero Toy Store LLC & Anor [2010] EWHC 40; **228 Nicholas Hamblen:** Mr Justice Hamblen; **228 High Court of England and Wales:** Bluewater Energy Services BV v Mercan Steel Structures BV & Ors [2014] EWHC 2132; **229 High Court of England and Wales:** Alfred McAlpine Capital Projects Ltd v Tilebox Ltd [2005] EWHC 281 (TCC) 25 February; **229 The Incorporated Council of Law Reporting for England & Wales:** Lord Dunedin in Dunlop Pneumatic Tyre Company v New Garage and Motor Company Ltd [1915] AC 79 Reprinted with permission from ICLR.; **235 International Organization for Standardization:** ISO 8402. Reprinted with permission; **235 Mentor Books:** Crosby,

P. B. (1980) *Quality Is Free*, Mentor Books, 1980, p. 15; **235 McGraw-Hill Education:** Juran, J. M., *Quality Control Handbook*, 3rd edn, McGraw-Hill, 1974, section 2, p. 27; **236 Pearson Education:** Logothetis, N., *Managing Total Quality*, Prentice Hall, Upper Saddle River, New Jersey, USA, 1991, pp. 216–17; **238 DTI:** DTI, *Total Quality Management and Effective Leadership*, London, UK, 1991, p. 8; **238 Thomson Reuters Corporation:** Evans, J. R., *Applied Production and Operations Management*, Southwestern Publishing, Tennessee, USA, 4th edn, 1993, p. 837; **239 Elsevier:** Zaire, M. *Total Quality Management for Engineers*, Woodhead Publishing, Cambridge, UK, 1991, p. 193; **243 The National Archives:** Supply and Sales of Goods Act (1994) (SSGA); **248 The National Archives:** The Public Contracts Regulations (2015); **251 Vanguard Management Systems Ltd:** ISO9001 (2015); **253 BSI:** BS EN ISO 8402 (1995), section 3.4, p. 25; **257 Asian Productivity Organisation,:** Taguchi, G., *Introduction to Quality Engineering*, Asian Productivity Organisation, 1986, p. 1; **262 Ford Motor Company Ltd:** Ford Motor Co. Ltd, *Failure Mode and Effects Analysis Handbook*, Ford Motor Co. Ltd Dearborn, MI, 1992, p. 22; **268 McGraw-Hill Education:** Lawrence D. Miles, whose book *Techniques of Value Analysis and Engineering*, McGraw-Hill Education, 1972; **276 McGraw-Hill Education:** Miles, D., *Techniques of Value and Value Engineering*, 3rd edn, McGraw-Hill, 1989, p. 243; **282 Added Value Logistics:** Institute of Logistics and Transport, How to Manage Inventory Effectively, Added Value Publication Ltd, Altrincham, UK, 2003, p. 94; **282 National Audit Office:** NAO(2012–13) Report HC 190 Session; **283 U.S. Government Accountability Office:** GAO-18-658 VA Pharmacy Inventory Management; **284 Pitman Publishing Ltd:** Compton, H. K. and Jessop, D., *Dictionary of Purchasing and Supply Management*, Pitman, 1989, p. 135; **308 APICS:** The Association for Operation Management (APICS), Chicago, Illinois. Founded in 1957 as the American Production and Inventory Control Society. Association for Supply Chain Management (APICS), Used by permission; **312 Harvard Business School Publishing:** Hayes, R. H. and Pisano, G. P., 'Beyond world class: the new manufacturing strategy', *Harvard Business Review*, January–February 1994, p. 75; **323 Dow Jones-Irwin:** Vollman, T. E., Berry, W. L. and Whybark, C. D., *Manufacturing Control Systems*, 2nd edn, Irwin, 1988, p. 788; **326–327 Pearson Education:** Chopra, S. and Meindl, P., *Supply Chain Management*, Prentice Hall, 2001, p. 247; **331 U.S. General Services Administration:** The USA, GSA (General Services Administration); **336 The Chartered Institute of Purchasing & Supply:** CIPS Knowledge Works, e-sourcing: www.cips.org; **338 Business Intelligence Limited:** Waller, A., quoted by Lascelles, D., *Managing the E-supply Chain*, Business Intelligence, 2001, p. 19; **343 John Wiley & Sons, Inc:** Buffa, E. S. and Kakesh, K. S., *Modern Production Operations Management*, 5th edn, John Wiley, 1987, p. 548; **351 Knowledge Transfer:** ITIL www.knowledgetransfer.net/dictionary/ITIL/en/Service_Level_Agreement; **354 Oxford Economics:** Oxford Economics Final Report April (2011) The Size of the UK outsourcing market – across the private and public sectors; **358 Perkins:** Perkins, B., *Computer World*, 22 November, 2003; **367 Institute for Supply Management, Inc:** Humbert, X. P. and Passarelli, C. P. M., 'Outsourcing: avoiding the hazards and pitfalls', Paper presented at the NAPM International Conference, 4–7 May, 1997; **368 Partnership Sourcing Ltd:** Partnership Sourcing Ltd, *Making Partnerships Happen*: www.psicbi.com; **369 John Wiley & Sons, Inc:** Knemeyer, A. M., Corsi, T. M. and Murphy, P. R., 'Logistics outsourcing relationships: customer perspectives', *Journal of Business Logistics*, Vol. 24, No. 1, 2003, pp. 77–101; **373 Partnership Sourcing Ltd:** PSL *Creating Service Partnerships*, Partnership Sourcing Ltd, 1993, p. 7; **376 John Wiley & Sons, Inc:** Ramsay, J., 'The case against purchasing partnerships', *International Journal of Purchasing and Materials Management*, Fall, 1996, pp. 13–24; **379 The National**

Archives: Trade Marks Act (1994); **381 Transparency International:** , 'Defence Offsets – Addressing the risks of corruption & raising transparency', *Transparency International*, Published April 2010, www.treansparency.org; **383 European Union:** Article 85(1) of the EEC Treaty; **383 John Wiley & Sons, Inc:** E.C. Journal, 84–28.8, 1968; **383 Brundtland Commission:** World Commission on Environment and Development, 1987; **384 Pearson Education:** Webster, F. E. and Wind, Y. J., *Organisational Buying Behaviour*, Prentice Hall, 1972, pp. 33–7; **385 Association for Consumer Research:** Bristor, J. M. and Ryan, M. S., 'The buying centre is dead, long live the buying centre', *Advances in Consumable Research*, Vol. 4, 1987, pp. 255–8; **394 Pearson Education:** Nagle, T. T., Hogan, J. E. and Zale, J. *The Strategy and Tactics of Pricing. A Guide to Growing More Profitably*, Pearson Education Limited, Harlow, UK, 5th edn, 2014, p. 1; **395 McGraw-Hill Education:** Leighton, D. S. R., *International Marketing*, McGraw Hill, New York, USA; **395 McGraw-Hill Education:** Leenders, M. R., Fearson, H. E. and England, W. B. *Purchasing & Materials Management*, R D Irwin Inc., Homewood, Illinois, USA, 1980; **395 John Wiley & Sons, Inc:** Winkler, J., *Winkler on Marketing Planning*, Wiley & Sons, Hoboken, USA, 1973; **395 McGraw-Hill Education:** Ammer, D. S., *Materials Management*, RD Irwin, 1968; **395 US Government Accountability Office:** Best Practices for Estimating and Managing Program Costs, Applied Research and Methods, US Government Accountability Office (GAO) July 2007; **401 The International Society of Parametric Analysts:** *Parametric Estimating Handbook*, Fourth Edition – April 2008; **403 Cambridge University Press:** Luke 14:28.29, King James version bible, Cambridge University Press; **403–404 The International Society of Parametric Analysts:** *Parametric Estimating Handbook*, Fourth Edition – April 2008; **404 National Aeronautics and Space Administration:** NASA Cost Estimating Handbook Version 4.0. February 2015. NASA CEHv4.0; **408 High Court of Justice:** SRCL Ltd v The National Health Service Commissioning Board (NHS) [2018] EWHC 1985 (TCC) (27 July); **416 Office of Fair Trading:** Office of Fair Trading Decisions CA98/03/2013; **416 Office of Fair Trading:** Case CE/9248–10, 6th December 2013; **426 Auditor General for Wales:** Public Procurement in Wales. Auditor General for Wales – Archwilydd Cyffredinol Cymmr, October 2017; **429 Oxford Brookes University:** The Institute of Public Care, Oxford Brookes University, https://ipc.brookes.ac.uk. Used with permission; **430 House of Commons Library:** House of Commons (Standing Order No 148); **430 House of Commons Library:** House of Commons Library. Briefing Paper Number 6029, 19 September 2018, Public Procurement and Contracts; **430 Public Accounts Committee:** Public Accounts Committee, Contracting out public services to the private sector. Feburary 2014; **431 Lichfield City Council:** Adapted from Lichfield City Council, www.lichfield.gov.uk; **432 The National Archives:** Duncan Dallas. Public Procurement thresholds 2018/2019 in England, Wales and Northern Ireland, January 4; **435 Thomson Reuters Corporation:** Public Sector Blog (22.04.15). publicsectorblog.practicallaw.com. Used with permission from Thomson Reuters Corporation; **439 High Court of England and Wales:** Woods Building Services v Milton Keynes Council [2015] EWHC 2011 (TCC); **222–223 Peter Coulson:** Mr Justice Coulson at paragraph 5; **440–441 Royal Courts of Justice:** Resource (NI) v Northern Ireland Courts & Tribunals [2011] NIQB 121 18.11.11; **441 High Court of England and Wales:** At para 147 of the judgment is Mr Justice Coulson's rescoring of the two bids Neutral Citation Number: [2015] EWHC 2011 (TCC); **443–444 Commonwealth of Australia:** ANAO (2017–18) Report No 6, The Management of Risk by Public Sector Entities, Australian National Audit Office. Used with permission from Commonwealth of Australia; **445 United States Department of Justice:** Department of Justice U.S. Attorney's Office Press Release, 23 September 2016,

Southern District of Florida; **445 Corruption and Crime Commission:** Corruption and Crime Commission – New Zealand Report on Fraud and Corruption in Procurement in WA Health: Dealing with the Risks. 12 June 2014; **446 Courts of New Zealand:** High Court of New Zealand Decisions. The Queen v Paul Kenneth Rose and Jane Clare Rose. R v Rose [2016] NZHC 1109 (25 May 2016); **447 Commonwealth of Australia:** The Australian Criminal Intelligence Commissions Administration of the Biometric Identification Services Project, Auditor-General Report (2018–19) No 24, Performance Audit; **451 European Union:** *Buying Green! A Handbook on Green Public Procurement*, 3rd edn. European Commission, Brussels, Belgium, 2016; **453 United States Environmental Protection Agency:** Sustainable Manufacturing, United States Environmental Protection Agency, https://epa.gov; **454 Willmott Dixon:** Used with permission form The Willmott Dixon Holdings Ltd, https://www.willmotdixon.co.uk; **457–458 Milton Keynes Council:** A Social Value toolkit for Milton Keynes Council (2015) Version 1.0 April https://www.milton-keynes.gov.uk; **458 International Organization for Standardization:** ISO 14001, Key benefits, International Organization for Standardization; **458–459 International Organization for Standardization:** Sustainable procurement— Guidance, Achats responsables—Lignes directrices, International standard ISO 20400, First edition 2017-04. http://gpp.golocal-ukraine.com/wp-content/uploads/ISO_20400_2017E-Character_PDF_document.pdf; **460–462 National Audit Office:** Used with permission from National Audit Office. Addressing the environmental impacts of government procurement, HC 420 Session 2008–2009, 29 April 2009; **463 Brighton & Hove City Council:** Suppliers Guide to completing the Pre-Qualification Questionnaire (PQQ) https://www.brighton-hove.gov.uk; **463 Action Sustainability:** Supply Chain Sustainability Schools Performance Measurement Special Interest Group (May 2016) Recommended pre-qualification questions. Copyright © Action Sustainability 2017. Used by permissions. Retrieved from https://www.supplychainschool.co.uk; **464–465 Business for Social Responsibility:** Business for Social Responsibility (2018) New Models for Sustainable Procurement, February, www.bsr.org; **465–466 European Union:** *Buying Green! A Handbook on Green Public Procurement.* 3rd edn. European Commission, Brussels, Belgium, 2016; **466 European Union:** Council of the European Union, Analysis of the final compromise text with a view to agreement, Brussels 18 February 2019; **467–468 ENGIE:** Clause on ethics and social and environmental responsibility, (2018) www.engie.com. Used with permission; **469 International Labour Organization:** International Labour Organisation, *Tripartite Declaration of Principles concerning Multinational Enterprises and Social Policy (MNE Declaration)*, 5th edition. International Labour Organisation, Geneva, Switzerland, 2017; **476 John Wiley & Sons, Inc:** Meredith, J. R. and Mantel, S. J., *Project Management: A Managerial Approach.* 6th edn, John Wiley & Sons, Hoboken, USA, 2006; **477 Pearson Education:** Vaidyanathan, L., *Project Management, Process. Technology and Practice.* Pearson International Edition. Pearson, Harlow, UK, 2013; **477 Association for Project Management:** Association for Project Management. Summerleys Road. Princes Risborough Bucks HP27 9LE; **477 ILX Group:** PRINCE2®; **487 Association for Project Management:** Association for Project Management http://www.org.uk; **487 The Australian Government Publishing Service:** Guidelines for Managing Risk in the Australian Public Service, MAB/MIAC No.22, 1996; **487 Commonwealth of Australia:** The Australian Diplomatic Communications Network – Project Management, anao.gov.au; **489 Association for Project Management:** A Guide to Project Auditing. Association for Project Management 13.07.18; **489 National Audit Office:** Report by the Comptroller and Auditor General. HC 408. Session (2017–2019) 11October 2017; **494 Pearson**

Education: Adapted from Vaidyanathan, L., *Project Management, Process. Technology and Practice.* Pearson International Edition. Pearson, Harlow, UK, 2013; **497 U.S. Department of Transportation:** US Department of Transportation. Cost Plus Percentage of Cost Contracts, http://www.fta.dot.gov/13057_6115.html; **498–499 FIDIC:** FIDIC, http://www.I.fidic.org/resources/contracts; **499 Institution of Engineering and Technology:** Institution of Engineering and Technology, https://www2.theiet.org/resources/books; **500 Institution of Chemical Engineers:** Institution of Chemical Engineers, http://www.icheme.org; **500 Association of Consultant Architects:** Association of Consultant Architects, http://www.acarchitects.co.uk; **504 John Wiley & Sons, Inc:** Birou, L. H., and Fawcett, S. E., 'International purchasing benefits and requirements and challenges', *International Journal of Purchasing and Supply*, Jan.,1993, pp. 22–5; **504 John Wiley & Sons, Inc:** Trent, R.J., and Monczka, R.M., 'International purchasing and global sourcing: what are the differences?', *Journal of supply Chain Management*, November, 2003; **504 John Wiley & Sons, Inc:** Rexta, N., and Miyamo, T., 'International sourcing: an Australian perspective', *ISM Resource Article*, Winter, 2000; **507 Pearson Education:** Griffin, R. W. and Pustay, M. W., *International Business. A Management Perspective.* Global Edition. Pearson Education Ltd, Harlow, UK, 2003; **508–509 Pearson Education:** Ferraro. G., *The Cultural Dimension of International Business.* Prentice Hall, Upper Saddle River, New Jersey, USA, 2010; **511 International Chamber of Commerce:** The International Chamber of Commerce (ICC); **511 Corporate compliance insights:** Corporate compliance insights, 'Incoterms Rules – How they can improve your Company's compliance, reduce your risk and maximise your profit'. 21 January 2013, www.corporatecomplianceinsights.com; **514 International Chamber of Commerce:** Incoterms® 2010; **518 Jamric Press International:** Foley, J.F., *The Global Entrepreneur: Taking Your Business International*, Jamme Press International, 2nd edn, 2004; **519 Willmott Kevin:** Willmott, K., 'Understanding the freight business', in as 3 above, pp. 203–4; **520 Government of Ireland:** Bills of Exchange Act (1882), section 3(1); **521 SITPRO:** As 18 above – SITPRO is the UKs Trade Facilitation Agency, supported by the DTI; **521 Taylor & Francis:** Yasvas, B.F., and Freed, R., 'An economic rationale for countertrade', *The International Trade Journal*, Vol. XV, No. 2, Summer, 2001, pp. 127–56; **537 Elsevier:** Rubin, J. Z. and Brown, B. R., *The Social Psychology of Bargaining and Negotiation*, Academic Press, 1975; **537 Code of Personnel Management:** Gottschal, R. A. W., 'The background to the negotiating process' in Torrington, D., *Code of Personnel Management*, Gower, 1979; **537 Pitman Publishing Ltd:** Lysons, C. K., *Modified Version of Definition in Purchasing*, 3rd edn, Pitman, 1993; **543 The National Archives:** The Misrepresentation Act (1967) Section 2(1); **553 Penguin Random House:** Fisher, R. and Ury, W., *Getting to Yes*, Penguin, 1983; **553 Harvard Business School Publishing:** Galinsky, A. D., *Negotiation Strategy: Should You Make the First Offer?* Harvard Business School, 2004; **560 Harvard Business School Publishing:** Ertel, Danny, 'Turning negotiation into a corporate capability', *Harvard Business Review*, May–June, 1999, pp. 55–70; **563 Cambridge University Press:** McCarthy, W., 'The role of power and principle in getting to yes', in Breslin, J. W. and Rubin, J. Z., *Negotiation Theory and Practice*, Cambridge University Press, 1991, pp. 115–22; **568 The World Bank:** The World Bank, *Procurement Guidance – Contract Management General Principles*, 1st edn, The World Bank, Washington DC, USA, September 2017; **574 Commonwealth of Australia:** Australian National Audit Office (ANAO), *The Better Practice Guide*, ANAO, Canberra, Australia, 2012; **574 Commonwealth of Australia:** Reprinted with permission from the ANAO, Better Practice Guide; **575–578 Commonwealth of Australia:** Reprinted with permission from the ANAO, Developing and Managing

Contracts-Australian Essay, www.australianessay.com; **578 Southwark Council:** Southwark Council Report of Housing & Community Safety Scrutiny Sub-Committee (2011) February; **599 Institute for Supply Management, Inc:** Aljian, G. W., *Purchasing Handbook*, National Association of Purchasing Management, 1958, section 16.1; **600 Springer:** Van Nostrand, *Dictionary of Business and Finance*, Van Nostrand, London, 1980; **600 Thomson Reuters Corporation:** Barfield, J. T., Raibon, C. A. and Kinney, M. R., *Cost Accounting*, West Publishing, 1994, p. 709; **600 Inland Revenue Department:** Definition provided by the Inland Revenue; **617 Telegraph Media Group:** Buffett, W., 'Apocalypse is nigh: Buffett tells Berkshire Faithful', *Money Telegraph*, 4 April 2005; **621 Department for Business, Energy & Industrial Strategy:** Department for Business, Energy & Industrial Strategy UK Energy in Brief, 2018; **623 UK Energy Research Centre:** UK Energy Research Centre. The UKs Global Gas Challenge, Research report, November 2014; **632 CAPS Research:** Fearon, M. E. and Bales, W. A., *Purchasing of Non-traditional Goods and Services*, Center for Advanced Purchasing Studies, USA, focus study executive summary, 1995; **634 Institute for Supply Management, Inc:** Duffy, R. J. and Flynn, A. E., 'Services purchases: not your typical grind', *Inside Supply Management*, Vol. 14, No. 9, p. 28; **635 Institute for Supply Management, Inc:** ISM, 'Glossary of Key Supply Management Terms': www.ism.ws; **640 Institute for Defense Analyses:** Winner, R. L., Pennel, J. P., Bertrams, H. E. and Slusarczuk, M. M., 'The role of concurrent engineering in weapon system acquisition', *IDA Report R-338*, AD-A203 615, 1988; **644, 646 Massachusetts Institute of Technology:** Handfield, R. B., Krause, D. R., Scannell, T. V. and Monczka, P. M., 'Avoid the pitfalls in supplier development', *Sloan Management Review*, winter, 2000, pp. 37–48; **646 HarperCollins:** Fearon, H., *Purchasing Research, Concepts and Current Practice*, American Management Association, 1976, p. 5; **652 Taylor & Francis:** Kydos, W., *Measuring, Managing and Maximising Performance*, Productivity Press, Boca Raton, Florida, USA, 1991, p. 17; **652 Springer:** Van Weele, A. J., *Purchasing Management*, Chapman and Hall, 1995, pp. 201–2; **654 Pearson Education:** Scheuing, E. E., *Purchasing Management*, Prentice Hall, Upper Saddle River, New Jersey, USA, 1989, p. 137; **661–662 Harvard Business School Publishing:** Robert Kaplan and David Norton of the Harvard Business School, 1990; **665 Cambridge University Press:** Robertson, D. C. and Rymon, T., 'Purchasing agents deceptive behaviour: a randomised response technique study', *Business Ethics Quarterly*, Vol. 11, No. 3, 2001, pp. 455–79; **665 The Chartered Institute of Purchasing & Supply:** CIPS, E-ethics: position on practice guide, prepared by the CIPS Consulting Group: www.cips.org; **665 IPMM:** IPMM Forum at: www.ipmm.ie/ipmm_forum/viewmessages.cfm; **670 SAGE Publications:** Badaracco, J. L. Jr and Webb, A. P., 'Business ethics – a view from the trenches', *California Management Review*, Vol. 37, No. 2, Winter, 1995, pp. 64–79; **670 Chartered Institute of Management Accountants:** CIMA, *Fraud Risk Management: A Guide to Good Practice*, Chartered Institute of Management Accountants, London, UK, 2008; **677 United States Government:** Cybersecurity Procurement Language for Energy Delivery Systems. ESCSWG. April 2014. es-pl@energetics.com; **679 U.S. Department of Commerce:** Supply Chain Risk Management Practices for Federal Information Systems and Organisations, April 2015. The publication is available free from: http://dx.doi.org/10.6028/NIST.SP. 800–161; **690–691 The Chartered Institute of Purchasing & Supply:** Code of ethics, CIPS Council (2009), 11 March. All rights reserved, The Chartered Institute of Purchasing & Supply (CIPS), 2020 www.cips.org; **692–693 The Chartered Institute of Purchasing & Supply:** CIPS Code of Conduct, CIPS Global Board of Trustees on (2013) 10 September. All rights reserved, The Chartered Institute of Purchasing & Supply (CIPS), 2020 www.cips.org.

Plan of the book

Part 1 Introduction and strategy				
Chapter 1 The scope and influence of procurement	Chapter 2 Strategic procurement	Chapter 3 Logistics and supply chains	Chapter 4 Organisational and supply chain structures	Chapter 5 Procurement policies, procedures and support tools

Part 2 Strategy, tactics and operations 1: Procurement factors					
Chapter 6 Supplier relationships and partnering	Chapter 7 Legal and contractual management	Chapter 8 Quality management, service and product innovation	Chapter 9 Matching supply with demand	Chapter 10 Sourcing and the management of suppliers	Chapter 11 Purchase price management and long-term cost-in-use

Part 3 Public sector procurement and sustainable procurement	
Chapter 12 Public sector procurement	Chapter 13 Sustainability and socially responsible procurement

Part 4 Strategy, tactics and operations 2: Operation and strategic performance	
Chapter 14 Project procurement and risk management	Chapter 15 Global sourcing

Part 5 Strategy, tactics and operations 3: Negotiation skills, contract management, category and world class procurement			
Chapter 16 Negotiation skills, practice and business benefits	Chapter 17 Contract management	Chapter 18 Category and commodity procurement	Chapter 19 World-class procurement to enhance business performance

Part 1

Introduction and strategy

Chapter 1

The scope and influence of procurement

Learning outcomes

This chapter aims to provide an understanding of:

- how to define procurement
- how to define supply chain management
- strategic roles of procurement
- procurement as organisational buying
- the strategic scope of procurement
- integrated supply chain management
- procurement and change
- world-class procurement
- the status of procurement and supply management
- reflections of procurement positioning in business
- the scope of procurement in the public sector

Key ideas

- Procurement as a function, process, supply or value chain link, a relationship, discipline and profession.
- Procurement as a strategic business activity.
- Definitions of purchasing, procurement and supply chain.
- Globalisation, information technology, changing production and management philosophies as factors in the evolution of procurement.
- Characteristics of world-class procurement.
- Leverage, focus and professionalism as factors contributing to the status of procurement within an organisation.
- Procurement as a business change agent.
- Procurement as a key influencer on business decisions.

Introduction

The first edition of this book was published in 1981. This, the tenth edition, is published in 2020. The procurement profession has achieved some notable successes. These include:

- it is recognised by many as a profession
- a dramatic improvement in academic standards and research
- active involvement at a corporate strategy level
- career opportunities on an international basis
- Chartered Institute of Procurement & Supply impact on standards
- wide-ranging, positive initiatives to deliver corporate goals.

Despite the successes, there remain critical allegations related to facets of procurement performance where failures are apparent. These include:

- absence of long-term strategies to support corporate goals
- an inability to play a decisive role on major projects, including ICT and construction
- a failure to impose robust contract terms and conditions on suppliers and contractors
- an inability to conduct due diligence and to identify high level risks in the supply chain
- inadequate involvement and influence on contract management activities
- an inability to adequately evaluate procurement workloads and staff to meet the forward business challenges.

Throughout this book, procurement is the focus term, recognising that the function has other descriptors, including purchasing and buying.

The author is resolute in his belief that procurement warrants corporate recognition. The key purposes of the book are to inform, motivate and convince our readers that the highest personal standards and knowledge impact on performance.

1.1 How to define procurement

CIPS Australia[1] motivated a debate on an agreed procurement lexicon. The following statements were proposed:

> Procurement is the business management function that ensures identification, sourcing, access and management of the external resources that an organisation needs or may need to fulfil its strategic objectives.

> Procurement exists to explore supply market opportunities and to implement resourcing strategies that deliver the best possible supply outcome to the organisation, its stakeholders and customers.

> Procurement applies the science and art of external resource and supply management through a body of knowledge interpreted by competent practitioners and professionals.

The author offers two more definitions of procurement.

> Procurement is a pro-active, strategic corporate activity to ensure a continuing supply of goods and services to enable world-class organisational performance.

> Procurement manages supply chain risks through effective negotiation of contracts, cost and price models, quality and other essential supply characteristics.

1.2 How to define supply chain management (SCM)

Investopedia[2] define supply chain management (SCM) as 'Supply chain management is the management of the flow of goods and services and includes all processes that transform raw materials into final products. It involves the active streamlining of a business's supply-side activities to maximise customer value and gain a competitive advantage in the market place.'

Techopedia[3] define SCM as 'The management and oversight of a product from its origin until it is consumed. SCM involves the flow of materials, finances and information. This includes product design, planning, execution, monitoring and control.'

1.3 Strategic roles of procurement

The strategic ability and contribution of procurement is the differentiator that sets the function apart from a transactional modus operandi. Boeing, in developing its 787 Dreamliner, expanded the role of procurement from outsourcing parts to outsourcing entire subsections. It has been estimated that nearly all of the jet's design and fabrication, along with some 40 per cent of the estimated $8 billion in development costs, is being outsourced to subcontractors.

1.3.1 Due diligence

Due diligence is a structured methodology to help determine that a supplier has the necessary qualities to become a partner of the buying organisation. The term 'due diligence' is more usually associated with financial reviews in takeover situations. Within a procurement context it includes consideration of the supplier's:

- financial robustness, including working capital
- competence and availability of key personnel resources
- reliance and extent of sub-contracting
- history of legal disputes and litigious actions
- experience of partnering relationships
- existence of a robust 5-year business plan
- history of insurance claims
- IT system robustness.

Conducting due diligence requires specialist knowledge and skills. It also requires liaison and collaboration with in-house specialists in areas including finance, legal and security.

1.3.2 Risk management of the supply chain

Identifying supply chain risks and developing acceptable risk mitigation strategies is a hallmark of a strategically focused procurement operation. All supply chain risks fall into one of three categories:

1 Those risks that only the supplier can manage
2 Those risks that only the buying organisation can manage
3 Those risks that must be jointly managed by the supplier and the buying organisation.

Examples of risks that fall into category 1 are:

- Having a robust business continuity plan
- Ability to match resource planning to programme deliverables
- Contractual relationships with sub-contractors
- Design, inspection and testing
- Having available sufficient working capital
- Through-life product support.

1.3.3 Relationship management

The adversarial way of business life is an outdated concept, a fact that some procurement operations need to realise. The skill of managing relationships with key strategic suppliers necessitates attention to, for example:

- conducting regular blame free reviews of contracts
- a joint commitment to continuous improvement
- sharing long-term business goals
- active involvement of senior people at both organisations
- negotiations based on genuine business objectives
- the provision of accurate and timely business and contract management data.

1.3.4 Continuous improvement of supplier performance

All sectors of the economy have competitive challenges, sometimes from off-shore organisations. The procurement community have a strategic role to motivate suppliers to continually improve their performance. The performance on long-term contracts can be incentivised to reward the supplier's investment and initiatives. The contract can require continuous improvement as an obligation. In some situations, the buying organisation may jointly invest in new technology, providing the supplier agrees to appropriate ownership of intellectual property and perhaps licensing upon payment of a royalty on sales.

1.3.5 The supplier's investment in 'right first time'

An organisation's reputation for quality is a prime business consideration. The law courts regularly try cases where non-compliance with the specification is at issue. Suppliers have expert knowledge, or should have, of the goods or services they provide. The supplier can add value to a procurement by ensuring that the specified quality can be satisfied or exceeded. The supplier can also advise on through-life costs, maintenance support, inspection and testing and continuous improvement. When the procurement specialist is engaged in pre-qualification processes there should be a penetrating analysis of the bidder's quality management attributes.

1.3.6 The supplier's investment in inventory

The rapid business approach to just-in-time has focused attention on who pays for inventory in the supply chain pipeline. Buying organisations are naïve to believe this is a 'free of charge' service willingly entered into by the supplier. There are costs involved, including strategic warehousing facilities, distribution network costs, danger of product changes, working capital costs and so on. The concept of consignment stock is a proven concept in manufacturing, with some suppliers very adept of completely satisfying the buyer's needs for line side stock.

1.3.7 The supplier's investment in procurement expertise

It is a strange phenomenon that when buyers visit potential suppliers they often fail to probe the supplier's investment in procurement expertise. When the author engages with clients engaged in a tendering exercise and the supplier makes a presentation, it is most unlikely that there will be a procurement specialist on their team. Why? It can only be concluded that their procurement operation is not seen as contributing to a competitive edge.

1.4 Procurement as organisational buying

Organisational buyers have been defined by Marrian[4] as:

> Those buyers of goods and services for the specific purpose of industrial or agricultural production or for use in the operation or conduct of a plant, business, institution, profession or service.

Organisational buyers are those who buy on behalf of an organisation rather than for individual or family use or consumption. Organisational buyers can, as shown in Table 1.1, be considered to belong to one of four buying groups, each of which can be further subdivided.

Some of the categories in Table 1.1 may overlap. Thus, in the National Health Service, some supplies may be bought centrally by government agencies, regionally by health authorities and locally by hospitals themselves.

Table 1.1 A typology of organisational buyers

Types of organisation	Characteristics	Examples
Industrial/producer organisations	Purchase of goods and services for some tangible production and commercially significant purpose	Manufacturers: primary (extractive) producers – agriculture, forestry, fishing, horticulture, mining
Intermediate organisations	Purchase of goods and services for resale or for facilitating the resale of other goods in the industrial or ultimate consumer markets	Distributors, dealers, wholesalers, retailers, banks, hotels and service traders
Government and public-sector organisations	Purchase of goods and services for resale or use by organisations providing a service, often tangible, and not always commercially significant at national, regional and local levels	Central and local government, public utilities
Institutions	Purchase of goods and services for institutions that buy independently on their own behalf	Schools, colleges, hospitals, voluntary organisations

1.4.1 Procurement as supplier management

Supplier management may be defined as:

> That aspect of procurement concerned with rationalising the supplier base and selecting, coordinating, appraising the performance of and developing the potential of suppliers and, where appropriate, building long-term collaborative relationships.

Supplier management is a more strategic and cross-functional activity than 'buying', which is transactionally and commercially biased. The relationship between procurement purchasing and supplier management is shown in Figure 1.1.

1.4.2 Purchasing as external resource management

The following is the view of Lamming:[5]

> The new strategic function will probably not be called purchasing – that is much too limited a word. The connotations of purse strings and spending money have no relevance to the setting up and management of strategic interfirm relationships. This task is concerned with ensuring the correct external resources are in place to complement the internal resources. Perhaps 'external resource managers' is a term that future purchasing managers will adopt.

Figure 1.1 The relationship between procurement, supplier management and purchasing

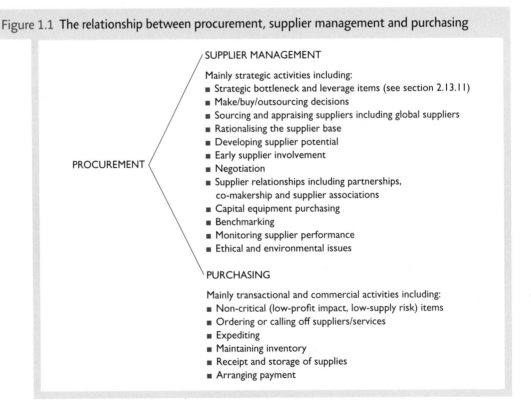

PROCUREMENT

SUPPLIER MANAGEMENT

Mainly strategic activities including:
- Strategic bottleneck and leverage items (see section 2.13.11)
- Make/buy/outsourcing decisions
- Sourcing and appraising suppliers including global suppliers
- Rationalising the supplier base
- Developing supplier potential
- Early supplier involvement
- Negotiation
- Supplier relationships including partnerships, co-makership and supplier associations
- Capital equipment purchasing
- Benchmarking
- Monitoring supplier performance
- Ethical and environmental issues

PURCHASING

Mainly transactional and commercial activities including:
- Non-critical (low-profit impact, low-supply risk) items
- Ordering or calling off suppliers/services
- Expediting
- Maintaining inventory
- Receipt and storage of supplies
- Arranging payment

1.5 The strategic scope of procurement

The strategic scope of procurement will vary according to the nature of the organisation's business activities. The author has consulted in, for example, a gold mining organisation and an international deep-sea communication cable laying organisation. The strategic variables were quite different. The principles of strategic scope are illustrated by Figure 1.2.

Each of the key areas shown in Figure 1.2 is analysed and shown in tabular form in Tables 1.2 to 1.7. Table 1.2 provides indicative areas of financial strategic considerations including the corporate strategic relevance. All the considerations and relevance are pertinent to procurement decision making. Table 1.3 concentrates on the legal strategic considerations of important relevance to procurement decisions making. Table 1.4 examines supply chain risks, including the corporate strategic relevance. All these considerations should be within the scope of procurement influence and action. Table 1.5 deals with operational strategic matters again emphasizing the areas in which procurement can play a major role. Table 1.6 raises the technology strategic considerations, outlining the potential scope and influence of procurement. Table 1.7 deals with managing obstacles to change and emphasizes the continuing potential influencing skills of procurement specialists.

1.5.1 Finance – strategic scope of procurement

Table 1.2 provides indicative areas of financial strategic considerations for procurement.

Figure 1.2 Strategic scope of procurement – key areas

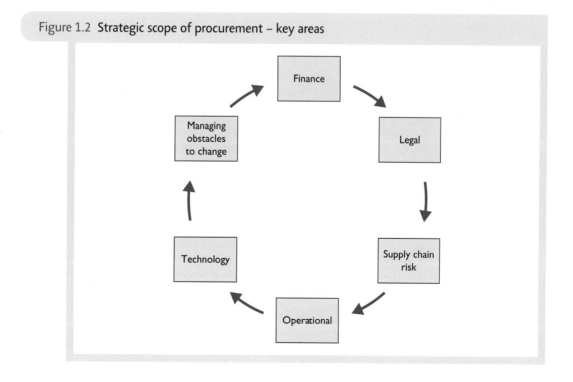

Table 1.2 Indicative areas of financial strategic considerations for procurement

Financial strategic consideration	Corporate strategic relevance
1 Supplier payment terms	Cash flow
2 Bought in price of goods & services	Competitiveness in market place
3 Contract termination costs	Provision for termination costs
4 Currency fluctuations impacting on bought in price of goods & services	Decision to forward buy currency
5 Delivery late on goods, services and for projects	Product launch/payment of damages to customers
6 Changes in scope of specification	Impact on selling prices
7 Payment of supplier 'up-front' fees	Vulnerability if no guarantee in place
8 Late payment to suppliers	Supplier applies 'stop' on deliveries

1.5.2 Legal – strategic scope of procurement

Table 1.3 provides indicative areas of legal strategic considerations for procurement.

1.5.3 Supply chain risk – strategic scope of procurement

Table 1.4 provides indicative areas of supply chain strategic considerations for procurement.

Table 1.3 Indicative areas of legal strategic considerations for procurement

Legal strategic considerations	Corporate strategic relevance
1 Apply buying organisation procurement Terms & Conditions	Supplier's obligations and liabilities very clear
2 Product liability accountability	Reduces corporate exposure to product liability claims
3 Clarity of specifications	Management of quality standards
4 Apply damages for suppliers' non-performance	Resistance of claims for corporate non-performance
5 Bank/parent company guarantees	Provides safeguards for specified events
6 Supplier's insurance provision	Management of risk exposure
7 Supplier's key personnel provision	Reduces risk associated with knowledge and skills provision
8 Jurisdiction	No exposure to off-shore jurisdictions

Table 1.4 Indicative areas of supply chain strategic considerations for procurement

Supply chain risk strategic considerations	Corporate strategic relevance
1 Single, dual or multiple sourcing strategy	Continuity of supply and competitive forces
2 Extent of off-shore sourcing	Exposure to supply chains
3 Financial failure of strategic supplier(s)	Idiosyncrasies Cost of resourcing and delay in supply of goods and services
4 Force majeure events	Delays to supply
5 Contract management effectiveness	Early warning of supply chain issues
6 Business continuity safeguards	Exposure to serious delays in provision of goods and services
7 Supplier conflict of interest	Exposure to secret/confidential data disclosure
8 Cost of goods and services	Exposure to margin erosion

1.5.4 Operational – strategic scope of procurement

Table 1.5 provides indicative areas of operational strategic considerations for procurement.

1.5.5 Technology – strategic scope of procurement

Table 1.6 provides indicative areas of technology strategic considerations for procurement.

1.5.6 Managing obstacles to change – strategic scope of procurement

Table 1.7 provides indicative areas related to managing obstacles to change considerations for procurement.

Table 1.5 Indicative areas of operational strategic considerations for procurement.

Operational strategic consideration	Corporate strategic relevance
1 Forecasting future demand for goods and services	Continuity of supply and long-term contracts in place
2 Accurate up-to-date data on inventory and supply	Production and service planning
3 Procurement and supply chain IT systems robustness	Provision and management of data
4 Quality management	Guarantee of high-quality goods and services
5 Make or Buy strategy	Known reliance and risks using third parties for supply of essential strategic goods and services
6 Supplier partnering	Absence of adversarial supplier relationships
7 Authority to enter into contracts with third parties	Procurement control of contractual commitments, including delegated authority for emergency purchases
8 Field failures of products – emergency responses	Reputational management

Table 1.6 Indicative areas of technology strategic considerations for procurement

Technology strategic considerations	Corporate strategic relevance
1 Conduct continuous procurement research into technology improvements	Awareness of technology improvements/new technology available
2 Supplier obligations for continuous improvement	Ensure technology supply is not static
3 Financial investment with strategic suppliers to enhance technology	Joint development of technology with potential benefits of joint IPR ownership
4 Management of Intellectual Property Rights	Minimise risk from IPR hostage scenarios
5 Availability of supplier IPR products and services when new products/services are introduced	Continuity of supply
6 Supplier guarantee/warranty provision	Reputational management
7 Early supplier engagement in our technology research and development	Partnering collaboration
8 Supplier promotional support for new technology introduction	Financial assistance with new technology launch
9 Political environment	Awareness of political environments in end markets
10 Outsourcing to access high-cost technology	Manage cost of introducing new technology

Table 1.7 Indicative areas related to managing obstacles to change considerations for procurement

Managing obstacles to change strategic consideration	Corporate strategic relevance
1 Avoiding fixation on existing suppliers	Competitive forces applied to market supply
2 Ensuring product samples are robustly tested	Alternative source of supply
3 Avoidance of malpractice with existing suppliers	Robust audit processes
4 Management customer preferences	Promotion of new/enhanced products
5 Right to terminate contracts for convenience	Flexibility for changing suppliers
6 Willingness to increase annual performance obligations	Continuous improvement
7 Change in buyer's category management portfolio	Persistent strategy review on sourcing strategies
8 Relevant use of small/medium enterprises	Social responsibilities

1.6 Integrated supply chain management

Procurement and supply chain management reflects a growing emphasis concerning the strategic business importance of suppliers. Supplier relationships are gradually shifting from an adversarial approach to a more cooperative approach with selected suppliers. The activities that the modern procurement organisation must undertake require a different mindset than that traditionally adopted. Supplier development, partnering, supplier–design involvement, the use of full-service suppliers, lifecycle costing, long-term supplier contracts and relationships, strategic cost management and integrated Internet linkages and shared databases are now seen as ways to create new value within the supply chain. Procurement is attracting high-quality people who aspire to senior business positions once they have established their credibility in dealing with challenging procurement scenarios.

Three conclusions may be reached about this new era. First, the reshaping of the role of procurement in the modern economy has been necessary in response to the challenges presented by worldwide competition and rapidly changing technology and customer expectations. Second, the overall business impact of the procurement function is increasing, particularly for firms that compete in business environments characterised by worldwide competition and rapid change. Third, procurement must continue to become more sensitive to, and integrated with customer requirements, as well as with operations, logistics, human resources, finance, accounting, marketing and information systems. This evolution will take time to occur fully, but the integration is inevitable.

The above has been adapted from an article in *Solar Energy Market Express*.[6] Fearon[7] gives a more detailed exposition of professional development and published literature in his historical evolution of the procurement function.

The author has identified seven strategic stages of development that procurement must pass through to become a competitive weapon in the battle for markets (see Table 1.8).

Other attempts to trace the evolution of procurement are those of Syson[8] and Morris and Calantone[9] who each identify three stages. Syson refers to 'the changing focus of procurement as it evolves from a purely clerical routine activity to a commercial stage in which the emphasis is on cost savings and finally a proactive strategic function concerned with materials or logistics management.' Morris and Calantone differentiate between (i) clerical, (ii) 'asset management' and profitability and (iii) 'core-strategic' function stages.

Jones,[10] however, criticises the above approaches on two grounds. First, they are non-operational and merely indicate the stage of development of procurement activity, the criteria for which may differ from one procurement organisation to another. Second, the models have a restricted number of development measurement variables. In an attempt to remedy those deficiencies Jones suggests a five-stage development model using 18 measurement criteria. The five stages of procurement development measured on a scale of 1–5 are shown in Table 1.9.

The procurement profile shown in Figure 1.3 enables the stage of development reached by a particular organisation to be identified and assessed on a scale of 1–5. The profile also indicates areas where further development is required, as measured in the 18 criteria shown in Figure 1.3 Appropriate strategies to meet identified shortcomings can then be devised.

Table 1.8 Procurement and supply chain strategic phases – Farrington model

Stage	Strategic description
Stage 1 'Traditional'	Procurement & Supply Chain (PCS) are treated as disparate activities, hence there is no unified strategic approach, nor is there a 'function' strategy. There is no exposure or liaison with corporate strategy development or operational application. This exposes the organisation to significant risks, supply delays, contractual non-performance and passive responsiveness to other function instructions.
Stage 2 'Awakening'	PSC managers have a rudimentary awareness of strategic planning and have attempted to change strategic direction where vital goods and services are concerned. There will be no positive change unless the Board of Directors agree and support new strategic actions that will have their support. Learning & development is a requirement. The costs of change are unknown.

Table 1.8 *Continued*

Stage	Strategic description
Stage 3 **'Implementation'**	PSC have been designated as activities where collaboration/integration will be positive in all operational and financial respects. There is a comprehensive plan for strategic change, linked to defined objectives and timescales. The intent is to, initially, focus on strategic suppliers, giving careful thought to long-term contracts and partnering behaviour.
Stage 4 **'Systems development'**	It is recognised that PSC management requires comprehensive, timely and accurate data. Accordingly, project funding is available to integrate PSC systems with appropriate corporate systems. The new systems will be designed to link wherever possible with strategic suppliers' systems with the aim of enabling continuous supplier performance. In-house ICT have PSC as a vital customer, warranting the highest level of support in accordance with KPIs.
Stage 5 **'Leadership'**	PSC are recognised as strategic leaders in key commodity groups. Learning & development and recruitment strategies ensure strategic leadership is evident and that exacting performance is achieved. PSC have a strategic involvement when corporate strategy is considered in the short, medium and long-term.
Stage 6 **'Global reach'**	The PSC has global reach and has in place long-term strategic contracts that include logistics, cost-management, continuous improvement, partnering behaviour, active supply market research, quality management, environmental management and cutting-edge technology.
Stage 7 **'Standards challenge'**	The PSC performance is under constant review against known thought leaders and best-in-class. PSC management demonstrate continuous performance achievements. The high-level reviews include supplier performance against contractual obligations and strategic one-off projects. There is interchange between corporate departmental heads thereby ensuring the broadest understanding of PSC challenges and opportunities.

Table 1.9 Procurement development stages and performance capabilities

Stage of development	Capabilities	Estimated organisational contribution
Stage 1 Infant	Fragmented procurement	None or low
Stage 2 Awakening	Realisation of savings potential	Clerical efficiency. Small savings via consolidation 2–5 per cent
Stage 3 Developing	Control and development of procurement price/negotiation capabilities	Cost reduction 5–10 per cent
Stage 4 Mature	80/20 recognised Specialist buyers Cost reductions Commencement of supplier base management	Cost reduction 10–20 per cent Acquisition costs 1–10 per cent
Stage 5 Advanced	Devolution of procurement Strong central control Supply chain management	Cost reduction 25 per cent Cost of ownership Acquisition cost and supply chain management 30 per cent + Leverage buying Global sourcing Understanding and practice of acquisition cost and cost of ownership

Figure 1.3 **Purchasing profile analysis**

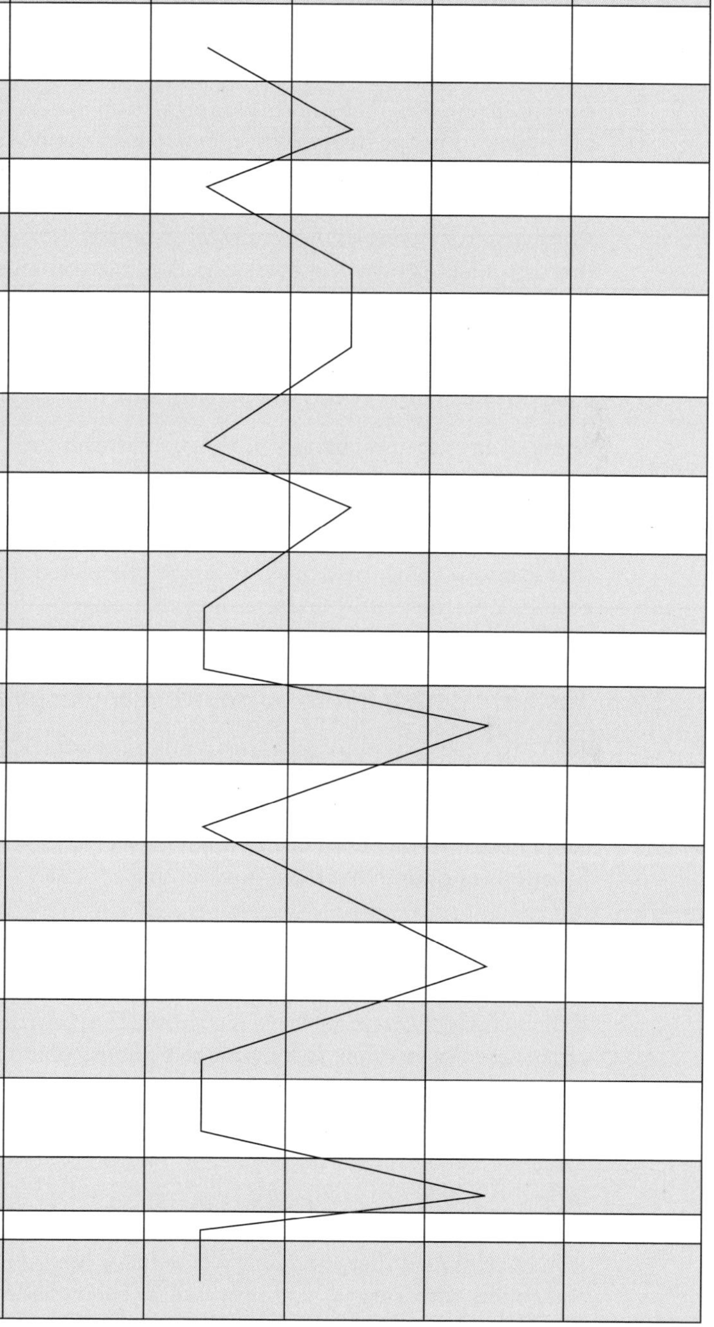

Measurement area	Stage of development				
	1 Infant	2 Awakening	3 Developing	4 Mature	5 Advanced
Activity breakdown analysis					
Purchasing organisational structure					
Purchasing services					
Function position in the business					
Extent of training/ development of buyer					
Relative remuneration levels					
Measurement of purchasing performance					
Standard of information systems					
Computer technology					
Standard of operating procedures					
Interface development (buying centre)					
Buying process involvement					
Buyer characteristics/ development					
Degree of purchasing specialism					
Supplier interface development					
Policy on ethics					
Hospitality					
Quality of buyer–supplier relationship					

1.7 Procurement and change

There are a number of drivers influencing and demanding changes in procurement, including those detailed in the following sections.

1.7.1 The challenge to manage escalating costs in purchasing goods and services

In the twenty-first century a number of pressures on costs manifested themselves. Not the least of these has been the volatility in the cost of oil, feeding its way into most supply chain costs. The continuing escalation of acts of terrorism, culture tensions, displacement of people from Africa, tensions in the EU all impact on costs and economic confidence. The related impact on the cost of living and consequent demands for wage increases are signs of potentially troubling times. The traditional emerging economies supplying, for example, the retail sector cannot escape the pressure on costs, noting that this sector has its own cost pressures. Adding to all this is the impact of difficulties in the financial services sector, making the cost and availability of capital a factor in investment decisions and availability of working capital.

1.7.2 The public sector focus on driving out inefficiencies in public expenditure

Some of the greatest changes in procurement in the 1990s and early in the twenty-first century have been in public expenditure. The large amounts of spend in central and local government have often been tackled through the aggregation of requirements. While significant improvements in procurement have been made there remain challenges to further improve value for money. It can be postulated that procurement will have to adapt across departmental boundaries and that classic silos of procurement will have to be abolished.

1.7.3 The increasing trend to outsource manufacture and services

There has been a rapidly growing trend to outsource a wide range of manufacturing and service delivery. This trend has challenged procurement departments to improve their management of tender processes, due diligence, negotiation with different cultures, managing outsourced contracts and applying open book methodologies. Procurement as a function is not immune from outsourcing actions.

1.7.4 The recognition that procurement is a significant contributor to corporate efficiency

Enlightened organisations have recognised that procurement can contribute to corporate efficiency. An example is long-range business planning which requires input on long-range costs, availability of strategic materials and supplies, supply chain developments and trends in service delivery; for example, voice recognition technology as an anti-fraud measure.

1.7.5 The positive impact of global sourcing

It may be argued that the retail sector has a long-standing expertise in global sourcing and coping with long-range supply issues. Their challenge includes responding to fashion changes and a cycle of product selection for the seasons of the year. The challenge for other buyers is their ability to find excellent suppliers wherever they are in the world. International airlines have used global sources to provide equipment and services. The challenges for procurement include how to structure their organisation. It is not uncommon for retailers to set up a buying and supply organisation in the Far East.

1.7.6 The enhanced use of information technology and e-procurement

The IT revolution has impacted on procurement. What developments lie ahead? The drivers for change in procurement must surely include the objective of eradicating paper. In one procurement process each tender document weighed in excess of six kilograms. The resultant tenders were heavier! Secure networks that facilitate a whole electronic procurement system, through to payment, is a far-reaching objective for the global economy. E-procurement is in its relative infancy with relatively few reverse auctions, electronic tendering and knowledge storage and gathering strategies.

1.7.7 The redressing of procurement power

Many suppliers have grown by acquisition and have assumed to themselves a power that has affected buyer's pricing, output allocation and other restrictive practices. The procurement profession has been relatively unsuccessful in countering this power, for example by forming effective buying clubs, although the public sector has taken significant initiatives in setting up consortia.

1.7.8 The challenge to outdated traditional practices

It is always difficult to look within. The procurement profession itself must challenge outdated traditional practices. A movement from transactional operations to strategic activities would be desirable in many organisations. Defensive posturing that involves keeping stakeholders in the dark by denying them access to information, for example, the status of tendering processes, is unprofessional. An effective challenge to traditional practices would be useful in the construction sector where quantity surveyors handle the complete procurement cycle to the total exclusion of procurement specialists.

1.8 World-class procurement

The term 'world class' was popularised by the book *World Class Manufacturing* by Schonberger,[11] published in 1986. Schonberger defined world-class manufacturing as analogous to the Olympic motto '*citius, altius, fortius*' (translated as faster, higher, stronger). The world-class manufacturing equivalent is continual and rapid improvement.

Twelve characteristics of world-class supplier management were identified by the Center for Advanced Procurement Studies,[12] namely the following:

- *Commitment to total quality management (TQM).*
- *Commitment to just-in-time (JIT).*
- *Commitment to total cycle time reduction.*

- *Long-range strategic plans* that are multidimensional and fully integrated with the overall corporate plan, including the organisation's supply strategy, and related to customers' needs.
- *Supplier relationships*, including networks, partnerships and alliances. Relationships include such matters as supply base rationalisation and the segmentation of suppliers as 'strategic', 'preferred' and 'arm's length'. Relationships with strategic suppliers include a high level of trust, shared risks and rewards, sharing of data and supplier involvement in product improvement.
- *Strategic cost management* – this involves a total life acquisition approach to evaluating bids and the use of IT to support a paperless and seamless procurement process across the whole supply chain.
- *Performance measurements*, including regular benchmarking with and across industries. Performance measures are developed in consultation with customers, other organisational units and suppliers.
- *Training and professional development*, including identification of required skills for higher-level procurement posts and the maintenance of employee skills inventories.
- *Service excellence* – procurement is proactive, anticipates customers' needs and demonstrates flexibility.
- *Corporate social responsibility*, especially regarding ethical, environmental and safety issues and support of local suppliers.
- *Learning* – world-class procurement recognises that learning and education are critical factors in continuous improvement.
- *Management and leadership* – although listed last, this is probably the key factor. Procurement executives earn and enjoy top management support and recognise the importance of transformational change. Such leaders have vision, foster open communications, treat others with respect and develop the potential of both their staff and suppliers.

Ultimately, world-class procurement depends on trading with world-class suppliers. World-class suppliers will tend to mirror the characteristics of world-class procurement listed above. Research reported by Minahan[13] indicates that, to be considered 'world class' suppliers must excel in such areas as competitive pricing, quality and lead times; these attributes are 'just the price of entry to get into the game'. The research identified the following three characteristics of world-class suppliers:

- *continuous improvement* – world-class suppliers have a formal and proven commitment to achieve year-on-year products and process improvements
- *technology and innovation* – world-class suppliers are technology leaders in their respective industries, providing customers with next-generation technologies and a 'leg-up' on their competition
- *adaptability* – world-class suppliers are willing to invest in new equipment, develop new technologies and rework their businesses to better support the strategies of their customers.

World-class supplier management is therefore concerned with:

- searching for suppliers with the above characteristics or the potential to achieve them

- providing such suppliers with specifications of the purchaser's expectations relating to products and services and agreeing how supplier performance will be measured against expectations
- recognising outstanding supplier performance by such means as the award of long-term contracts and sharing the benefits of collaborative innovation or performance that enhance the purchaser's competitiveness.

Strategic procurement partnerships are partnerships of equals in which suppliers are regarded as a source of the competitive edge responsible for a major share of product costs. As Saunders[14] rightly observes:

> For a firm to reach world class standards in serving its own customers, it is vital to achieve world class standards in controlling its network of suppliers.

1.9 The status of procurement and supply management (PSM)

Within a particular organisation the status of PSM is influenced by leverage, focus and professionalism.

1.9.1 Leverage

Traditionally, leverage of procurement has been focused on enhancing profitability. This is relevant in a manufacturing or purchase for resale context, but is irrelevant for procurement in a central and local government environment where procurement has a direct impact on the quality of public services being offered. The same can be said of procuring goods and services for the National Health Service.

The greatest scope for savings lies in the areas of greatest expenditure. For many organisations these areas are labour and materials. Labour is usually outside the scope of procurement unless outsourcing activities are being considered. Within this context, outsourcing call centres to the Far East has reduced some labour costs by more than 20 per cent for European-based organisations. Similarly, when labour is outsourced within Europe under TUPE (Transfer of Undertakings Protection of Employment) regulations, labour costs have also been reduced by more than 20 per cent. This is achieved by finding smarter ways of working and redeploying the labour to other roles. There is also the factor of the labour becoming more productive by using advanced IT systems. These cost improvements require a short-term investment by the new provider of services.

Expenditure on materials and services that are purchased from third parties is where professional buyers must demonstrate their effectiveness in obtaining value for money. The benefits can be highlighted in organisations driven by the profit motive. It is the case that:

- assuming other variables remain constant, every pound saved on procurement is a pound of profit
- for many reasons, such as increased defects or poorer deliveries, a pound off the purchase price does not necessarily represent a pound of profit
- when purchases form a high proportion of total costs, a modest saving on bought-out items will result in a similar contribution to profits as would a substantial increase in

sales; so, as shown below, a 4 per cent reduction in purchase costs makes the same contribution to profits as a 20 per cent expansion in turnover.

Sales			
Then	Now	Increase	Extra profit
£	£	%	£
100,000	120,000	20	2000 (assuming 10 per cent on turnover)
Procurement			
50,000	48,000	−4 (i.e. a saving)	2000

This argument must, however, be used carefully.

- Cost reduction can be counter-profitable if the result is lower quality or higher expenditure on production.
- The total cost of ownership (TCO) approach emphasises that not just the purchase price but also all costs associated with the acquisition, use and maintenance of an item should be considered.
- As the proportion of expenditure on supplies and the complexity of bought-out items varies widely from organisation to organisation, it follows that there will be a corresponding variance in the contribution of procurement to profitability.

The profit contribution may be low, for example, in the pharmaceutical industry where the ingredients of a patent medicine can be insignificant compared with the costs of marketing the product. Conversely, it will be significant in the motor vehicle industry where the proportion of material costs to total factory costs is high.

Procurement as a factor in profitability is likely to be critical where:

- bought-out items form a high proportion of total expenditure
- short-run prices fluctuate
- judgments relating to innovation and fashion are involved
- markets for the finished product are highly competitive.

Procurement will be less critical, though still important, where:

- bought-out items form a small proportion of total expenditure
- prices are relatively stable
- there is an absence of innovation in operations.

Within non-manufacturing organisations the savings resulting from value-for-money efficiency procurement may allow increased expenditure in other areas.

1.9.2 Focus

Syson[15] states that the position of procurement within a particular organisation depends on whether the focus of the function is transactional, commercial or strategic. Each of these foci is appropriate to sustaining commercial advantage for different types of enterprise: 'in terms of effectiveness, the key question is whether the correct focus exists. In terms of efficiency, how well are the key tasks discharged?' Over time, the focus of procurement may, as shown in Figures 1.4 and 1.5, change from transactional to a procedure perspective. The more procurement becomes involved in commercial and strategic areas, the greater will be its effectiveness and consequent standing within the organisation.

In Figures 1.4 and 1.5 it will be noticed that as PSM moves from a transactional to a pro-activity focus, performance measures also change from efficiency to effectiveness.

■ *Efficiency* is a measure of how well or productively resources are used to achieve a goal.

■ *Effectiveness* is a measure of the appropriateness of the goals the organisation is pursuing and of the degree to which those goals are achieved.

Syson[16] refers to the level of the procurement department, implying that the level at which procurement is placed in a hierarchical structure reveals its status within that

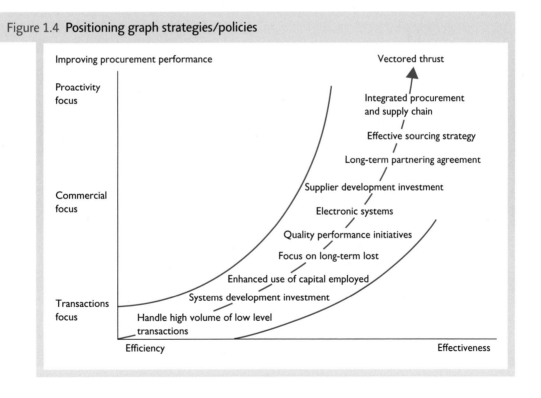

Figure 1.4 **Positioning graph strategies/policies**

Figure 1.5 Positioning graph: measures of performance.

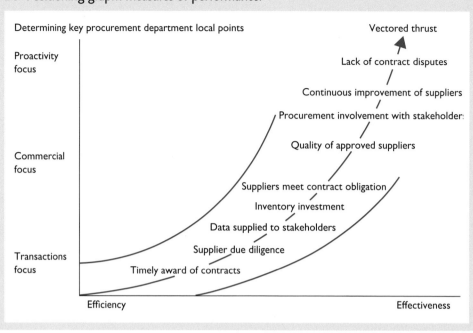

company. From a different perspective, broadly similar considerations will apply in determining the recognition given to procurement by other supply chain members.

A somewhat different approach to determining the internal status of procurement is provided by the three laws propounded by Farmer:[17]

1 Procurement increases in perceived importance in direct relationship with the reduction in length of the product lifecycle times.

2 Procurement is perceived to be important when the business concerned interfaces significantly with a volatile market(s).

3 Procurement is important whenever the organisation concerned spends a significant proportion of its income on procurement goods and services in order to allow it to do business.

Empirically, the importance of procurement both organisationally and within the supply chain is indicated by structural and influential factors.

Structural factors

These include:

■ the job title of the executive responsible for PSM
■ to whom and at what level the executive in charge of PSM reports
■ the total spend for which PSM is responsible
■ the financial limits placed on PSM staff to commit the undertaking without recourse to higher authority
■ the committees on which PSM staff are represented.

Influential factors

Ibarra[18] has identified network centrality, power and innovative involvement as important influential factors in the determination of status.

Network centrality, like formal authority, implies a high position in a status hierarchy and also varying degrees of access to and control over valued resources. As stated in section 3.2.1, procurement is frequently a key activity in materials management. Procurement is also central in supply chains, as indicated in section 3.10.

Power may be considered from two aspects: the sources of power and the use of power. The sources of power are briefly considered in section 4.1.4. The use of power may be defined as the ability to affect outcomes.

The executives in charge of PSM may have all the five sources of power identified by French and Raven in section 4.1.4. Executives also derive power from having access to information or occupying a boundary-spanning position that links organisations' internal networks to external suppliers and information sources.

Innovative involvement, as Ibarra shows, may be either administrative or technical and may itself be an indicator of power as any change in the status quo requires an individual to use power and mobilise support, information and material resources to overcome resistance to change. Persons with a high position in the organisation are more likely to be successful innovators than those further down with less or little power.

Technical innovators are directly related to the primary work activity of an organisation and include the introduction of new products, services and production technologies.

Administrative innovations involve changes in structure and administrative processes and are more directly related to internal management than the other types of innovation. Kanter's[19] observation that 'corporate entrepreneurs have often to pull in what they need for their innovation from other departments or areas, from peers over whom they have no authority and who have the choice about whether or not to ante up their knowledge, support or resources to invest in or help the innovator' is of relevance to both supply chain management and the centrality of procurement within it.

The status of PSM in any organisation depends on two key factors. First, the ability to impact positively on the bottom line of corporate strategic planning and, second, recognition by PSM of the value of its contribution to profitability and competitive advantage and being able to market that contribution to top management and other supply chain members.

1.9.3 Professionalism

As long ago as 1928, Carr-Saunders and Wilson[20] made a distinction between professionalism and professionalisation. *Professionalism* is traditionally associated with certain attributes, including:

- skill based on theoretical knowledge
- prolonged training and education
- demonstration of competence by means of tests and examinations
- adherence to a code of professional ethics.

Professionalisation is associated with the development of associations that seek to establish minimum qualifications for entrance to a professional practice or activity, enforce appropriate rules and norms of conduct among the members of the professional group and raise the status of the professional group in the wider society. Thus, attempts to raise the external perception of procurement have included:

- the establishment of institutions concerned with promoting the concept of 'professional' procurement, such as the Chartered Institute of Procurement and Supply (CIPS) in the UK and the Institute of Supply Management (ISM) in the USA (in 2004, over 42 national procurement associations were affiliated to the International Federation of Procurement and Materials Management)
- the development of undergraduate and postgraduate courses with a procurement content
- the establishment of 'chairs' in procurement or logistics at some universities
- research into PSM and related fields
- the publication of textbooks and specialist journals relating to procurement, such as *Supply Management (UK)*, *European Procurement Management* and the *International Journal of Procurement and Supply Management*, as well as, in the logistics field, *Logistics Focus* and the *International Journal of Logistics*
- published codes of ethics (see Appendices 1 and 2).

Notwithstanding the enhanced status of procurement in the UK by the granting in 1992 of a Royal Charter to the then Institute of Purchasing and Supply, the occupation has to surmount difficulties in its quest for professional status.

Such difficulties include:

- no regulation of entry – it is not necessary to have a professional qualification in procurement to enter the occupation
- procurement practitioners are at all levels of evolution, so those with only an operational or transactional knowledge of procurement might experience difficulty in moving to strategic procurement
- limited powers to enforce ethical standards.

The general problem, however, is what constitutes the academic content. Procurement is a hybrid subject that draws heavily on other disciplines to build its knowledge base. Such disciplines include accounting, economics, ethics, information technology, marketing, management and psychology.

Even the study of subjects such as negotiation can be enhanced by knowledge of the approaches to negotiation in such fields as politics and industrial relations.

Cox[21] regards much contemporary academic work relating to procurement as 'unscientific', characterised by uncritical accounts of what procurement practitioners do, untheoretical research and the development of 'fads and short-term fixes'. Such academic work is often regarded as irrelevant by procurement practitioners. Cox therefore calls for a proactive, scientific approach to the academic study of procurement. He believes that such an approach will involve the use of systematic theory to provide general laws and the application of deductive and inductive reasoning to respectively 'construct optional procurement strategies based on "fit for purpose" awareness of business and market processes and indicate the optional role for procurement in business'.

The change in emphasis from procurement as a reactive administrative activity to one that is proactive and strategic has resulted in numerous lists of the skills and attributes that procurement staff should possess in order to maximise their contribution to the achievement of organisational goals.

In a client survey, in Europe (2018) by Farrington[22] the following ten procurement areas were identified as most relevant at a corporate level:

1 Management of supply chain risks
2 Access to latest technology
3 Competitive purchase prices
4 Effective supplier relationship management
5 Timely decision making
6 Cash flow
7 Demonstrable procurement skills
8 Forecasting of forward procurement prices
9 Zero defects on incoming goods and services
10 Contribution to corporate strategy.

A study, by Giunipero and Pearcy[23] based on a review of relevant literature and a rating by 136 procurement/supply management professionals identified 32 skills required of a world-class purchaser. These skills were categorised under seven headings:

1 Strategic
2 Process management
3 Team
4 Decision making
5 Behavioural
6 Negotiation
7 Quantitative.

Examples of strategic, behavioural and quantitative skills are:

Strategic skills	Behavioural skills	Quantitative skills
Strategic thinking	Interpersonal/communication	Computational
Supply base research	Risk-taking/entrepreneurship	Technical
Structuring supplier relationships	Creativity	Blueprint reading
Technology planning	Inquisitiveness	Specification development
Supplier cost targeting		

Whittington[24] has stated that 'the buying task as we know it will disappear . . . Organisationally, procurement will often find itself in a place called "distribution functionality" or "strategic supply" located where the customer is'. She also believes that the procurement professional of the future will be concerned with three types of tasks:

- *facilitating* that is, team leadership and providing the 'proper blending and use of all necessary skills'
- *contract negotiating and developing* that is, procurement people – this will still be required – to write and negotiate advantageous contracts for the organisation
- *technical expertise (computer skills)* that is, the challenges of procurement on the Net and funding products in the world of cyberspace as well as other EDI tasks.

This view is supported by Lamming (see section 1.4.2) and others. In the Kolchin study referred to above, almost two-thirds of the respondents believed that the designation of procurement would change. The three most cited new names were 'supply management', 'sourcing management' and 'logistics'.

1.10 Reflections on procurement positioning in business

Procurement specialists should, at all times, question the progress being made by procurement and its positioning in business. There is a plethora of academic studies, independent reviews by audit authorities and consultancy organisations linking their findings to the subliminal message that procurement can make things a lot better.

Volvo have said: 'The awarding of business to a supplier is one of the most important decisions made by Volvo Purchasing. It directly impacts our ability to deliver to the customer, remain competitive and deliver future developments through projects'. This statement puts the role of procurement in a very positive corporate context. Procurement is in control of its destiny. The highest standards of professional practice, personal standards of procurement staff and delivering positive corporate change are necessary facets of success.

1.11 The scope of procurement in the public sector

Public sector procurement is the subject of Chapter 12. Within the public sector there are nuances when compared with the private sector. The scope of public sector procurement includes:

- compliance with the organisations 'standing orders'
- compliance with all regulatory requirements
- ensuring competition is founded on ethical standards
- public visibility of procurement processes and contract awards
- issuing invitations to tender and pre-qualification documentation
- exposing cost drivers behind the contract price
- negotiation
- providing expert advice to ministers, officials and appointed representatives
- contract management
- achieving supplier's compliance with goods and service specifications.

Discussion questions

1.1 Procurement often lacks a strategic focus and, in consequence, is viewed as an administrative function. Do you agree? Why?

1.2 Taking one example of 'an important purchase' in your organisation, prepare a flow chart showing the processes involved in procuring that purchase. Can you then identify the decision points?

1.3 Name four procurement risks that exist in your organisation.

1.4 What do you believe will be the business challenges facing procurement over the next decade?

1.5 In what significant ways does public sector procurement differ from private sector procurement?

1.6 There are major advantages transferring technical specialists into procurement whereby they can add their expertise to commercial decisions. Would you agree with this? Why?

1.7 How does procurement contribute to managing corporate risks?

1.8 Many procurement actions are conducted electronically. What do you foresee as the next major development in this regard? When you answer this, think about reverse auctions and their impact on negotiation of price and cost.

1.9 Would it be true that when procurement is effectively organised and operated the balance of power can never be with a supplier?

1.10 In what ways is it helpful for a buyer to have technical knowledge of the categories they procure?

1.11 Do long-term contracts present less, equal or more risk to a buying organisation than short term contracts?

References

[1] CIPS Australia Pty Ltd.

[2] www.investopedia.com.

[3] www.techopedia.com.

[4] Marrian, J., 'Market characteristics of industrial goals and buyers', in Wilson, A. (ed.), *The Marketing of Industrial Products*, Hutchinson, London, UK, 1965, p. 11.

[5] Lamming, R., 'The future of purchasing: developing lean supply', in Lamming, R. and Cox, A. (eds), *Strategic Procurement Management in the 1990s*, Earlsgate Press, UK, 1985, p. 40.

[6] *Solar Energy Market Express*.

[7] Fearon, Harold, Center for Advanced Purchasing Studies, Emeritus.

[8] Syson, R., *Improving Purchasing Performance*, Pitman, 1992, pp. 254–5.

[9] Morris, N. and Calantone, R. J., 'Redefining the purchasing function', *International Journal of Purchasing and Materials Management*, Fall, 1992.

[10] Jones, D. M., 'Development models', *Supply Management*, 18 March, 1999. The authors are particularly grateful to Dr Jones for the use of Figures 1.6 and 1.7.

[11] Schonberger, R. J., *World Class Manufacturing: The Next Decade: Building Power, Strength and Value*, Free Press, New York, USA, 1986.

[12] Carter, P. L. and Ogden, J. A., *The World Class Purchasing and Supply Organisation: Identifying the Characteristics*, Center for Advanced Purchasing Studies, University of Arizona.

[13] Minahan, T., 'What makes a supplier world class?', *Purchasing On Line*, 13 August, 1988.

[14] Saunders, M., *Strategic Purchasing and Supply Chain Management*, Pitman, UK, 1994, p. 11.

[15] Syson, R., as 14 above.

[16] Syson, R., as 14 above.

[17] Farmer, D., 'Organisation for purchasing', *Purchasing and Supply Management*, February, 1990, pp. 23–7.

[18] Ibarra, H., 'Network centrality, power and innovation involvement, determinants of technical and administrative power', *Academy of Management Journal*, Vol. 36 (3), June, 1993, pp. 471–502.

[19] Kanter, R. M., 'When a thousand flowers bloom' in Staw, B. M., and Cummings, L. L. (eds), *Research in Organisational Behaviour*, Vol. 10, 1988, p. 189.

[20] Carr-Saunders, A. M. and Wilson, P. A., *The Professions*, Oxford University Press, UK, 1928.

[21] Cox, A., 'Relational competence and strategic procurement management', *European Journal of Purchasing and Supply Management*, 1996, Vol. 2 (1), pp. 57–70.

[22] Farrington, B., Client Survey. www.brianfarrington.com.

[23] Giunipero, L. C. and Pearcy, D. H., 'World class purchasing skills: an empirical investigation', *Journal of Supply Chain Management*, 2000, Vol.26 (4), pp. 4–13.

[24] Whittington, E., 'Will the last buyer please stand up!', Proceedings NAPM 84 Annual Conference, May 1999.

Chapter 2

Strategic procurement

Learning outcomes

With reference, where applicable, to business and procurement, this chapter aims
to provide an understanding of:

- strategic thinking
- what is strategy?
- strategy development
- levels of organisational strategy
- corporate strategy
- growth strategies
- business-level strategy
- strategic management
- strategic analysis
- important environmental factors
- internal scrutiny
- strategy formulation
- the evaluation of alternative strategies
- strategy implementation
- post-implementation evaluation, control and review
- strategic procurement and supply chain process models

Key ideas

- Strategies are a key ingredient of business success.
- Mintzberg, Johnson and Scholes and the definitions of strategy.
- Mintzberg's ten schools of strategic development.
- Rational planning, incremental and emergent views of strategy.
- Growth, stability, combination and retrenchment strategies.
- Strategic procurement and procurement strategy.
- Environmental and internal scanning to strengthen strategic formulation and challenge.

- Linking procurement strategies to corporate strategic objectives.
- Critical success factors.
- Vision and mission statements and business, procurement and supply objectives.
- Lifecycles, scenario planning, cost–benefit, profitability and risk analysis as approaches to the evaluation of strategies.
- Portfolio planning with special reference to Kraljic and Kamann.
- Policies and strategy implementation plans.
- The CIPS procurement and supply chain model.

Introduction

Procurement occurs within a corporate environment, wherein there will be a long-term business strategy. Procurement also occurs in relatively small organisations, sometimes on a single site. In many of these situations, long-term business planning may not exist, or if it does, it will be at a superficial level. Understanding and contributing to delivery of the strategy is a vital driver for procurement. Wheelen and Hunger[1] have produced a checklist for conducting a strategic audit of a corporation. Within the 'Internal Environment: Strengths and Weaknesses' is a checklist for 'Operations and Logistics'. It is an excellent prompt for procurement specialists (noting carefully that they use the term 'purchasing') and consists of the following:

a What are the corporations' current manufacturing/service objectives, strategies, policies and programmes?

   i. Are they clearly stated or merely implied from performance or budgets?

   ii. Are they consistent with the corporation's mission, objectives, strategies and policies and with internal and external environments?

b What are the type and extent of operations capabilities of the corporation? How much is done domestically versus internationally? Is the amount of outsourcing appropriate to be competitive? Is purchasing being handled appropriately? Are suppliers and distributors operating in an environmentally sustainable manner? Which products have the highest and lowest profit margins?

   i. If the corporation is product-oriented, consider plant facilities, type of manufacturing system (continuous mass production, intermittent job shop, or flexible manufacturing), age and type of equipment, degree and role of automation and/or robots, plant capacities and utilisation, productivity ratings, and availability and type of transportation.

   ii. If the corporation is service-oriented, consider service facilities (hospital, theatre or school buildings), type of operations systems (continuous service over time to the same clientele or intermittent service over time to various clientele), age and type of supporting equipment, degree and role of automation and use of mass communication devices (diagnostic machinery, video machines), facility capacities and utilisation rates, efficiency ratings of professional and service personnel, and availability and type of transportation to bring service staff and clientele together.

c Are manufacturing or service facilities vulnerable to natural disasters, local or national strikes, reduction or limitation of resources from suppliers, substantial cost increases of materials, or nationalisation by governments?

d Is there an appropriate mix of people and machines (in manufacturing firms) or of support staff to professionals (in service firms)?

e How well does the corporation perform relative to the competition? Is it balancing inventory costs (warehousing) with logistical costs (just-in-time)? Consider costs per unit of labour, material and overhead; downtime; inventory control management and scheduling of service staff; production ratings; facility utilisation percentages; and number of clients successfully treated by category (of service firm) or percentage of orders shipped on time (if product firm).

    i. What trends emerge from this analysis?

    ii. What impact have these trends had on past performance and how might these trends affect future performance?

    iii. Does this analysis support the corporation's past and pending strategic decisions?

    iv. Do operations provide the company with a competitive advantage?

f Are operations managers using appropriate concepts and techniques to evaluate and improve current performance? Consider cost systems, quality control and reliability systems, inventory control management, personnel scheduling, total quality management (TQM), learning curves, safety programmes and engineering programmes that can improve efficiency of manufacturing or of service.

g Do operations adjust to the conditions in each country in which it has facilities?

h Do operations consider environmental sustainability when making decisions?

i What is the role of the operations manager in the strategic management process?

A critic of Wheelen and Hunger would point to the paucity of procurements' inclusion in 'Operations and Logistics'. Dr Farrington has developed SPA (strategic procurement audit) to test procurement's ability to withstand an SPA. The top 12 facets are:

1 Does a comprehensive procurement strategy exist?

2 Is there a linkage between the corporate and procurement strategies?

3 Is there a global dimension to procurement?

4 How is supply guaranteed in times of shortage?

5 How are long-term contract prices forecast and managed?

6 Is the procurement strategy founded on expert supply chain knowledge?

7 Does outsourcing feature in the strategy?

8 How is genuine partnering behaviour incorporated in the strategy?

9 How are single sourced supply situations evaluated for risk?

10 What are the strategic provisions for inventory in our contracts?

11 Have all intellectual property considerations been taken into account?

12 At what frequency is the strategy reviewed, and who is involved in the review?

2.1 Strategic fit between the supply chain and competitive strategies

Chopra and Meindl[2] logically argue that:

> a competitive strategy will specify, either explicitly or implicitly, one or more customer segments that a company hopes to satisfy. To achieve strategic fit, a company must ensure that its supply chain capabilities support its ability to satisfy the needs of the targeted customer segments. There are three basic steps to achieving this strategic fit, namely:
>
> 1 Understanding the customer and supply chain uncertainty
> 2 Understanding the supply chain capabilities
> 3 Achieving strategic fit.

2.2 What is strategy?

Strategy, derived from the Greek word *strategia*, means 'generalship'. Ohmae[3] argued that 'what business strategy is all about is, in a word, competitive advantage. The sole purpose of strategic planning is to enable a company to gain, as efficiently as possible, a sustainable edge over its competitors. Corporate strategy thus implies an attempt to alter a company's strength relative to that of its competitors in the most efficient way.' In the public sector, the strategy is concerned with providing a range of public services that deliver value for money, with all that this implies.

2.2.1 Definitions – Mintzberg

Mintzberg[4] observes that the word 'strategy' 'has long been used implicitly in different ways even if it has been traditionally used in only one'. He provides five different definitions of strategy: plan, ploy, pattern, position and perspective.

1 As a *plan*, strategy is some sort of consciously intended course of action, a guideline (or set of guidelines) to deal with a situation. From this perspective, strategy is concerned with how leaders try to provide organisational direction and predetermined courses of action. It is also concerned with cognition (knowing), or how plans or intentions are initially conceived in the human brain.

2 As a *ploy*, strategy is a specific manoeuvre intended to outwit an opponent or competitor.

3 As a *pattern*, strategy is a stream of actions demonstrating consistency in behaviour, whether intended or not intended.

4 As a *position*, strategy is a means of locating an organisation in an environment. The positional approach sees strategy as 'a mediating force by which organisations find and protect their positions or "niches" in order to meet, avoid or subvert competition in the external environment'.

5 As a *perspective*, strategy is a concept or ingrained way of perceiving the world. Mintzberg points out that 'strategy in this respect is to the organisation what personality is to the individual' – that is, distinct ways of working deriving from the culture or ideology of the undertaking that become the shared norms, values and determinants of the behaviour of the people who collectively form the organisation.

Mintzberg's five definitions help us to avoid attaching simplistic meanings to strategy. As he observes:[5]

> Strategy is not just a notion of how to deal with an enemy or set of competitors in a market. . .

> A good deal of confusion. . . stems from contradictory and ill-defined uses of the term strategy. By explicating and using various definitions, we may thereby enrich our ability to understand and manage the processes by which strategies form.

2.3 Strategy development

2.3.1 Mintzberg's ten schools

Mintzberg *et al.*[6] have identified ten 'schools' that have appeared at different stages in the development of strategic development, which they classify under three headings: prescriptive, descriptive and configuration.

Prescriptive schools are concerned with how strategies *should* be formulated, rather than how they actually are. Mintzberg's three prescriptive schools are shown in Table 2.1.

Descriptive schools are concerned with representing how, in reality, strategies are formulated rather than how they 'ought' to be made. Mintzberg's six descriptive schools are shown in Table 2.2.

The *configuration school* emphasises two aspects of strategy. The first describes 'organisational states' and their surroundings as *configurations*. An organisation 'state' implies entrenched behaviour. Configurations are therefore relatively stable clusters of characteristics relating to a particular school. Thus, 'planning' is predominant in mechanistic conditions of relative stability and 'entrepreneurship' in more dynamic configurations of start-up and turnaround. The configuration school, therefore, can integrate the preceding nine schools as it recognises that each school represents a particular configuration contingent on its time and context.

The second aspect is concerned with *transformation*. The configuration school sees strategy formation as a process of transformation or 'shaking loose' entrenched behaviour so that the organisation can make the transformation or development to a new state or configuration. The key to strategic management, therefore, is to sustain stability but periodically recognise the need for change to a new configuration.

Table 2.1 Mintzberg's prescriptive schools of strategy formation

Designation	Strategy formation process
The design school	Strategy making as a process of *conception* – that is, abstract thinking or reflective activity. Strategy making is an acquired, not a natural or intuitive, skill and must be learned formally
The planning school	Strategy formation as a *formal* process – that is, a course of action or procedures
The positioning school	Strategy formation as an *analytical* process – that is, strategy formation is the selection of generic, specifically common, identifiable positions in the marketplace based on analytical calculations

Table 2.2 **Mintzberg's descriptive schools of strategy formation**

Designation	Strategy formation process
The entrepreneurial school	Strategy formation as a *visionary* process – that is, strategy exists in the mind of the leader as a vision of the organisation's long-term future
The cognitive school	Strategy formation as a *mental* process – that is, strategy formation takes place in the mind of the strategist as a process of perceiving, knowing and conceiving the environment in an objective way, distinct from emotion or volition
The learning school	Strategy formation as an *emergent* process of learning over time, in which, at the limit, formulation and implementation become indistinguishable
The power school	Strategy formation as a process of *negotiation* – that is, strategy is shaped by political games involving transient interests and coalitions of those holding internal or external power who seek to arrive at a consensus on strategy by means of persuasion, bargaining and sometimes direct confrontation
The cultural school	Strategy formation as a *collective* process – that is, strategy formation is a process of social interaction based on beliefs and understandings shared by organisational members
The environmental school	Strategy formation as a *reactive* process – that is, adapting to the environment rather than by initiating changes in the environment

2.3.2 Strategic drift

Market types have an impact on procurement; a phenomenon not always recognised.

(i) Slow-cycle markets are those in which products have strongly shielded positions where competitive pressures do not easily penetrate the firm's sources of strategic competitiveness. This is described as a monopoly position, such as that held by IBM for many years.

The impact on procurement may be:

- no pressure to negotiate prices to drive down costs
- tolerance of suppliers who fail to innovate
- insistence that suppliers comply with specifications without challenge
- buyers trapped in traditional procurement practices.

(ii) Standard-cycle markets where business strategy and organisation are designed to serve high-volume or mass markets. The likely focus is on market control as in the automobile and appliance industries. Market dominance is achieved through capital investment, superior learning and the use of expert resources. Eventually, competition is attracted by high profits. Examples are Coca-Cola, Ford and Boeing.

The impact of market dominance on procurement may be:

- long-term contracts with static scheduled deliveries
- reliance on large-scale suppliers
- narrow concentration of buyers on category procurement
- complacent procurement behaviour based on power positioning.

(iii) Fast-cycle markets are characterised by perpetual innovation and shorter product cycles. When a dominant firm fears competition, they seek to counter attack before the competitive advantage is eroded. An example of fast-cycle markets is Komatsu challenging Caterpillar's dominance.

The impact on procurement may be:

- a challenge to continually seek supplier's innovation
- application of value engineering
- aggressive negotiation for cost reduction
- constantly changing supplier base.

World-class procurement is founded on a recognition that, regardless of the market type, procurement must challenge suppliers to provide continuous improvement, drive out unnecessary costs and invest in relationship management.

2.4 Levels of organisational strategy

As shown in Figure 2.1, in a typical large, diversified business, strategies are formulated, evaluated and implemented at three levels.

For non-diversified undertakings and those with only one line of business, corporate and business strategies are normally synonymous.

2.5 Corporate strategy

Generally, corporate strategies are concerned with:

- determining what business(es) the enterprise should be in to maximise profitability
- deciding 'grand' strategies (see below)
- determining the 'values' of the enterprise and how it is to be managed.

Figure 2.1 Levels of organisational strategy

- coordinating and managing major resources and relationships between the enterprise, its markets, competitors, allies and other environmental factors
- deciding on business locations and structures.

Because corporate strategies provide long-term direction, they change infrequently. Corporate strategies are usually less specific than those at lower levels and, consequently, are more difficult to evaluate.

2.6 Growth strategies

These are adopted when an organisation seeks to expand its relative market share by increasing its level of operations. Growth strategies can be classified as shown in Figure 2.2.

2.6.1 Integration strategies

Vertical integration strategies reflect the extent to which an organisation expands *upstream* into industries that provide inputs (*backward integration*), such as a car manufacturer acquiring a steel rolling mill, or *downstream* (*forward integration*) into industries that distribute the organisation's products, such as a car manufacturer acquiring a car distribution chain.

Backward integration

Backward integration seeks to ensure continuity of supplies by owning or controlling suppliers. David[7] has identified the following conditions that might cause an organisation to adopt a backward integration strategy, all of which have procurement and supply applications:

- when an organisation's present suppliers are especially expensive, unreliable or incapable of meeting the firm's needs for parts, components, assemblies or raw materials
- when the number of suppliers is few and the number of competitors is many

Figure 2.2 **Growth strategies**

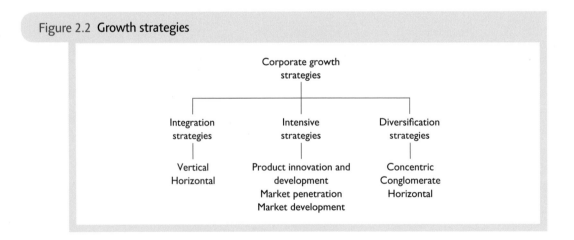

- when an organisation competes in an industry that is growing rapidly (in a declining industry, vertical and horizontal strategies reduce an organisation's ability to diversify)
- when an organisation has both the capital and human resources needed to manage the new business of supplying its own raw materials
- when the advantages of stable prices are particularly important (this is a factor because an organisation can stabilise the cost of its raw materials and the associated price of its product via backward integration)
- when present suppliers have high profit margins, which suggest that the business of supplying products or services in the given industry is a worthwhile venture
- when an organisation needs to acquire a needed resource quickly.

A further important factor may be:

- to reduce dependence on suppliers of critical components.

Forward integration

Forward integration can:

- avoid dependence on distributors who have no particular allegiance to a particular brand or product and tend to 'push' items that yield the highest profits
- provide production with stable, continuous and predictable demand requirements
- provide cost savings by eliminating intermediaries or distributors.

Some disadvantages of vertical integration include:

- difficulties in balancing capacity at each stage of the supply chain as the efficient scale of operation of each link in the supply chain can vary, so, when internal capacity is inadequate to supply the next stage it will be necessary to supply the deficiency by buying out and, conversely, excessive capacity gives rise to the need to dispose of the surplus
- high investment in technology and development may inhibit innovation and change due to the need to redesign, retool and retrain.

Backward or forward integration often call for highly diversified skills and abilities, such as manufacturing, transport and distribution, which require different business capabilities.

For the above reasons, many manufacturers – particularly in car and food manufacture – have abandoned vertical integration in favour of:

- outsourcing
- tiering of suppliers, e.g. Tier 1 supply direct to original equipment manufacturer (OEM)
- long-term partnerships or joint-venture agreements with suppliers
- *Keiretsu* strategies (*Keiretsu* is the Japanese word for 'affiliated chain' and such chains comprise mutual alliances that extend across the entire supply chain of suppliers, manufacturers, assemblers, transporters and distributors)
- the creation of virtual companies that use suppliers on an 'as needed' basis.

Horizontal integration

Horizontal integration focuses on expanding operations by acquiring other enterprises operating in the same industry or merging with competitors. Examples of horizontal integration are mergers, acquisitions and takeovers aimed at:

- reducing competition
- increasing economics of scale
- transferring and integrating resources and competences.

2.7 Business-level strategy

A strategic business unit (SBU) has been defined[8] as:

> An operating unit or planning focus that groups a distinct set of products or services that are sold to a uniform set of customers facing a well-defined set of competitors.

Generally, business-level strategies are concerned with:

- coordinating and integrating unit strategies so that they are consistent with corporate strategies
- developing the distinctive competences and competitive advantages of each unit
- identifying product market niches and developing strategies for competing in each
- monitoring products and markets so that strategies conform to the needs of product markets at their current state of development.

The selection of a business strategy involves answering the strategic question 'How are we going to compete in this particular business area?'

One approach to business-level strategy is the competitive strategy of Michael Porter.[9]

2.7.1 Porter's competitive strategy

Competitive strategies are based on some combination of quality, service, cost and time. Porter's typology identifies three strategies that can be used to give SBUs a competitive advantage.

- *Cost leadership* – operating efficiencies so that an organisation is the low-cost producer in its industry. This is effective when:
  - the market comprises many price-sensitive buyers
  - there are few ways to achieve product differentiation
  - buyers are indifferent regarding brands (Coke *v* Pepsi).

  Some potential threats to this strategy are that:
  - competitors may imitate this strategy, thus driving profits down
  - competitors may discover technological breakthroughs
  - buyer preferences may be influenced by differentiating factors other than price (see also section 3.8.1).

- *Differentiation* – attempting to develop products that are regarded industry-wide as unique (see also section 3.8.2).

■ *Focus* – concentration on a specific market segment and within that segment attempts to achieve either a cost advantage or differentiation. Because of their narrow market focus, firms adopting a focus strategy have lower volumes and therefore less bargaining power with their suppliers.

2.7.2 Functional strategies

These are concerned with the formulation of strategies relating to the main areas or activities that constitute a business – procurement, finance, research and development, marketing, production/manufacturing, human resources and logistics/distribution.

Functional strategies are expected to derive from and be consistent with corporate and business strategies and are primarily concerned with:

■ ensuring that the skills and competencies of functional specialists are utilised effectively

■ integrating activities within the functional/operating area, such as procurement and marketing

■ providing information and expertise that can be utilised in the formulation of corporate and business strategies.

The selection of functional strategies involves answering the strategic question 'How can we best apply functional expertise to serve the business needs of the SBU or organisation?'

Strategic procurement and procurement strategy

Strategic procurement is the linking of procurement to corporate or business strategies.[10] Some comparisons between procurement at the corporate and functional levels are shown in Table 2.3.

Some procurement decisions, such as those relating to the acquisition of capital equipment, outsourcing and entering into long-term partnership alliances, are generally made at the corporate/business level, often on the basis of information or recommendations from procurement at functional or operational levels. As stated in Chapter 1, the extent to which procurement is involved in the formation of organisational strategies is largely dependent on the extent to which procurement is perceived by top management as contributing to competitive advantage. The procurement executive who reports directly to

Table 2.3 Procurement strategy at corporate and functional levels

Corporate/business level	Functional/operational level
Formulated at higher levels in the hierarchy	Taken at lower levels in the hierarchy
Emphasise procurement effectiveness based on widespread environmental scanning. Some of this information will be communicated upwards from functional level	Emphasise procurement efficiency based on information from a more limited environmental scanning. Some information obtained from suppliers etc. may be communicated upwards
Corporate strategy must be communicated downwards	Integrated with corporate strategies so far as these are communicated and understood
Focused on issues impacting future long-term procurement requirements and problems	Focused on issues impacting current tactical procurement requirements and problems

the chief executive is clearly in a stronger position to influence organisational strategy than one lower in the hierarchy who reports to a materials or logistics manager. Irrespective of their level of reporting, procurement staff should contribute to corporate strategy by the provision of supply market intelligence on the basis of which decisions can be made and to competitive advantage by improving the effectiveness of the function. Kraljic[11] states that a company's need for a supply strategy depends on:

- the strategic importance of procurement in terms of the value added by the product line and the percentage of materials in total costs
- the complexity of the supply market, gauged by supply scarcity, pace of technology and/or materials substitution, entry barriers, logistics cost or complexity and monopoly or oligopoly condition.

Kraljic claims that:

By assessing the company's situation in terms of these two variables, top management and senior purchasing executives can determine the type of supply strategy the company needs both to exploit its purchasing power vis-à-vis important suppliers and reduce its risk to an acceptable minimum.

2.7.3 Procurement strategy

Procurement strategy relates to the specific actions that procurement may take to achieve the objectives of the business. Some examples are shown in Table 2.4.

Table 2.4 Procurement strategy examples

Situation	Solution
A manufacturing company keeps failing to win work in the Far East because they cannot guarantee 'local content' by purchasing goods in the local Far East market	Revision of procurement strategy to include sourcing study in the Far East with the deliberate aim of purchasing at least 30 per cent of goods in Far East market
An international airline with a 'Buy British' strategy is not providing internationally competitive sources of supply, thereby reducing financial operating margins	Revision of procurement strategy to actively research international supply markets and locate new sources that offer competitive prices and world-class supply
Corporate procurement failing to meet the specific needs of SBUs where each SBU Managing Director is accountable for R.O.C.E. (Return on Capital Employed)	Revision of procurement strategy and organisation to create SBU procurement whose sole focus will be the SBU profitability
There are insufficient funds to refresh IT platform and lack of IT strategic and operational skills	Adopt an outsourcing strategy through which a credible third party will refresh the IT platform and IT support services, having accepted stringent contractual obligations for a long-term contract
An international financial institution has corporate procurement but use of the corporate agreements is not mandatory. Each operating company makes its own arrangements on key 'commodity' purchases, including travel	Corporate procurement briefs all locations of the benefits of corporate agreements and makes their use mandatory
An Atomic Electricity Generating organisation tenders, every year, the supply of scaffolding and specialist engineering support services	Agree that a long-term strategy through the tendering and award of a 5–7-year contract in return for static pricing and contract performance

2.7.4 Global procurement strategy

This is discussed in Chapter 15.

2.8 Strategic management

Strategic management, as shown in Figure 2.3, refers to the processes of strategic analysis, formulation, evaluation, implementation, control and review.

2.9 Strategic analysis

A useful definition is:[12]

> Developing a theoretically informed understanding of the environment in which the organisation is operating together with an understanding of the organisation's interaction with its environment in order to improve organisational efficiency and effectiveness by increasing the organisation's capacity to deploy and redeploy its resources intelligently.

The tools of strategic analysis include environmental scanning, Porter analysis, scenario analysis, organisational appraisal, critical success analysis, gap and strengths, weaknesses, opportunities, threats (SWOT) analysis.

2.9.1 Environmental scanning

Some writers regard 'the environment' as relating to all factors relevant to strategic management that are outside the boundaries of a particular organisation. Others think of the environment as encompassing both external and internal environments.

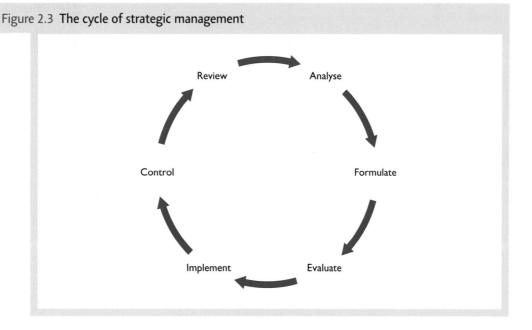

Figure 2.3 **The cycle of strategic management**

Environmental scanning has been described as 'a kind of radar to scan the world systematically and signal the new, or unexpected, the major and minor'.[13] Choo[14] states that organisations monitor their environments to:

> understand the external forces of change so that they may develop effective responses which secure or improve their position in the future. They scan to avoid surprises, identify threats and opportunities, gain competitive advantage and improve short-term and long-term planning.

2.10 Important environmental factors

Important external environmental factors relating to the strategy of an organisation are sector, industry and macro-environmental.

2.10.1 Sector

Sector relates to whether the enterprise is located in the private, public or voluntary sectors of the economy.

The *private sector* includes single traders, partnerships and companies owned by private investors. There is a wide variety of such undertakings that can be loosely classified according to their primary function into:

- *primary*, or extractive, organisations, such as agriculture, mining, fishing
- *secondary*, or manufacturing and assembly, organisations, such as food or car manufacturers
- *tertiary*, or distributive, organisations, concerned with the physical distribution of goods from producers to consumers, such as transport, wholesalers, retailers or providers of services, such as schools, hospitals.

The *public sector* in the United Kingdom comprises national government, local government, government-owned and controlled agencies and corporations and monetary institutions. The armed forces and the National Health Service commits large amounts of expenditure to their activities.

The *voluntary sector* describes bodies that are independent of government and business and are non-profit making, such as charities and churches.

Because of the wide variety of enterprises, some writers prefer to use the term 'organisational' in preference to 'corporate' strategy. Sector factors influence strategic management both at the organisational and functional levels.

At both levels, strategy is influenced by the underlying philosophy of the sector. Thus, what is known as the public–private paradox emphasises that, while business and government have much in common, ultimately they are different. Public-sector and private-sector procurement members of staff, for example, do many of the same things and are both increasingly focused on competitiveness. There are, however, substantial differences that, as shown in Table 2.5, help to determine their respective procurement strategies.

2.10.2 Industry

An industry can be defined as a group of companies within a sector offering products or services that are close substitutes for each other.

Table 2.5 Comparison of some public-sector and private-sector factors relating to procurement strategies

Factor	Public sector	Private sector
Aims	To provide the end users, members of the general public, with what they need when they need it and at the best value for money	To provide the enterprise with supplies that will enable it to achieve competitive advantage via positioning, cost and differentiation
Profit	Value for money spent irrespective of profit	Value for money spent commensurate with and as a contribution to profitability
Accountability	Procurement officers in central and local government are accountable and subject to audits for the spending of public money	Private procurement is accountable to the shareholders or owners of the undertaking for the spending of private money
Transparency	In the context of public procurement, transparency refers to the ability of all interested parties to know and understand how public procurement is managed	In the context of private procurement, the requirement for transparency is confined to those directly concerned, such as customers, suppliers and similar stakeholders
Procedures	In the interests of transparency, public procurement procedures are characterised by: ■ well-defined regulations and procedures open to public scrutiny, such as standing orders, EU directives ■ clear standardised tender documents and information ■ equal opportunity for all in the bidding process	Fewer standardised procedures and greater flexibility on the part of procurement staff to make unilateral strategic decisions than in the public sector

Rivalry among competitors is central to the forces contributing to industrial competitiveness. It is important to understand, therefore, the factors that contribute to the attractiveness and competitiveness of an enterprise within the industry.

In a practical context, there is evidence that in the short term the enterprise can consider:

- selective tendering using penetration pricing as the strategy
- focusing on buying organisations who desire change from non-performing suppliers
- offering attractive delayed payment options to help buyer's cash flow
- aiming sales efforts to displace 'weak' suppliers
- promoting new systems to aid continuous improvement
- heavily investing in R & D to create new products/services
- radical changes to service delivery
- targeting the public sector outsourcing market where initial investment is required for replacement of legacy systems.

2.10.3 Macro-environmental factors

These are the changes in the political, economic, social, technological, environmental and legal environments that directly or indirectly affect the organisation, both sector and industry-wise, as well as nationally and globally. These can be recalled by the mnemonic PESTEL:

- **P**olitical – the role of government, that is, regulator or participator, political ideology
- **E**conomic – gross domestic product (GDP), labour rates, monetary and fiscal policies
- **S**ocial – social trends, socio-economic groupings, value systems, ethics
- **T**echnological – changes, rates of technological change, costs and savings, patents
- **E**nvironmental – 'Green' considerations, disposal of products, atmospheric factors
- **L**egal – laws relating to competition, employment, the environment, consumer protection.

2.11 Internal scrutiny

This, in effect, is the internal scanning of resources, culture, value chains, structure and critical success factors.

2.11.1 Resources

Resources commonly identified are:

- *Money* enables an organisation to have the maximum choice between alternatives. An important aspect of money is liquidity or ready availability. Too much money tied up in plant or stocks may limit the ability of an enterprise to take advantage of opportunities.
- *Physical facilities* include plant and machinery. Important strategic factors are location, life, flexibility or alternative uses and the dangers of obsolescence. Such factors influence decisions regarding whether to buy or hire facilities or outsource some operations.
- *Human resources* include the specialised competences of the workforce and how easily specific attributes can be acquired or replaced. A further factor is the extent to which human resources can be replaced by technology. Non-availability of resources may limit the achievement of corporate goals and lead to the search for alternative means of acquiring them, such as via partnership agreements or outsourcing. Other resources, including patents and reputation, may provide an organisation with a competitive advantage over rivals in the same industry.
- *IT resources* facilitate rapid communication between the organisation and its external contacts, including suppliers and customers, in addition to being a source of intelligence.

2.11.2 Culture

Culture is 'the way things are done round here'. Procurement is a vital part of an organisation's culture. The way in which procurement conducts itself will impact on the organisation's reputation. Examples of world-class procurement actions that enhance an organisation's reputation include:

- conducting tender processes in a transparent manner
- providing opportunities for small companies to win contracts
- conducting negotiations in a professional manner
- not engaging in criminal or dubious personal/business practices

- adopting the highest ethical standards
- paying supplier's invoices on time
- not manipulating contracts to gain unfair price advantage.

2.11.3 Value chains and structure

These are dealt with in Chapters 3 and 4 respectively.

2.11.4 Critical success factors (CSFs)

A CSF has been defined as:[15]

> An element of organisational activity which is central to its future success. Critical success factors may change over time and may include such items as product quality, employee attitudes, manufacturing flexibility and brand awareness.

In the design of new products, the early involvement of suppliers may be a critical success factor.

CSFs are linked to key tasks and priorities. *Key tasks* are what must be done to ensure that each critical success factor is achieved. *Priorities* indicate the order in which key tasks are performed.

Some critical success factors relating to procurement strategies include:

- total quality management
- tailored supply chains for specific categories
- just-in-time deliveries with strategic emergency inventory availability
- total cycle time reduction
- world-class supplier relationships
- complete visibility of the cost drivers on strategic purchases
- e-procurement platforms
- KPIs in place for the procurement department
- training and development of procurement staff and stakeholders
- environmental, product safety and ethical standards.

Procurement must have the objective of performing at the highest level to deliver a competitive edge to their organisation.

2.12 Strategy formulation

As we have seen, strategies can be formulated by a process of rational planning or may emerge incrementally. These two approaches are sometimes presented as conflicting, based on the concept that strategic planning is inimical to creative thinking. Instead, however, the two approaches should be seen as complementary. As Lawrence[16] observes:

> The essential point . . . is that strategic thinking and strategic planning are both necessary and none is adequate without the other, in an effective strategy making regime. The real challenge is how to transform today's planning process in a way that incorporates, rather than undermines strategic thinking.

Strategy formulation at corporate, business and functional levels relates to the:

■ formulation of a vision statement

■ preparation of a mission statement

■ derivation of objectives

■ application of SWOT analysis.

2.12.1 Vision statements

Vision, from a strategic aspect, has been defined as:[17]

> A mental representation of strategy created or at least expressed in the head of the leader. That vision serves both as an inspiration and a sense of what needs to be done.

Such a vision is often the starting point for strategy formulation. The vision must, however, be communicated to others in a mission statement.

A vision statement articulates a realistic, credible and positive projection of the future state of an organisation or functions or operations within that operation.

A typical vision statement for the procurement activity might be:

> To develop, as part of an integrated supply chain, world class procurement strategies, policies, procedures and personnel to ensure that, by means of effective sourcing, competitive advantage is achieved by, for example, lowered supplies costs, commensurate with quality, shortened supply cycles and good supplier relationships.

2.12.2 Objectives

Objectives are explicit statements of the results the organisation wishes to achieve. Corporate and business objectives are medium-term to long-term, strategic and general and usually cover growth, profitability, technology, products and markets. Functional or operational objectives are short-term, tactical and specific. Thus, 'elements of strategy at a higher management level become objectives at a lower one'.[18]

As we saw earlier, the classic definition of the overall procurement task is:

> To obtain materials of the right *quality* in the right *quantity* from the right *source* delivering to the right *place* at the right *time* at the right *price*.

This definition is somewhat simplistic and, sadly, perpetuated, for the following reasons:

■ the term 'right' is situational – each company will define 'right' differently

■ what is 'right' will change as the overall procurement context and environment change

■ the above rights must be consistent with corporate goals and objectives from which functional/operating goals and objectives are derived

■ in practice, some rights are irreconcilable – for example, it may be possible to obtain the right quality, but not the right price as 'the best suppliers are often the busiest but also the most expensive'

■ procurement objectives have therefore to be balanced according to overall corporate strategy and requirements at a given time; as shown in Table 2.6, procurement objectives derive from corporate objectives.

Table 2.6 Procurement and corporate objectives

Business objectives	Procurement and supply objectives
A statement of the position the organisation is aiming for in its markets, including market share	The objective of providing the quantity and quality of supplies required by the market share and market positioning objectives
A key objective of, say, moving out of speciality markets and entering volume markets	A key objective of developing new, larger suppliers and materials flow systems more geared to larger numbers of fewer parts while keeping the total inventory volume low
A key objective to build new businesses that will generate positive cash flow as well as reasonable profits	Contribute to cash flow improvement by means of lower average inventory and by negotiating smaller delivery lots and/or longer payment terms
A plan to develop some specific new products or services	A plan to develop appropriate suppliers
An overall production/capacity plan, including an overall policy on make or buy	A plan to develop systems that integrate capacity planning and/or procurement planning, together with the policy on make or buy and partnering relationships
A plan to introduce a cost reduction programme	A plan to introduce supplies standardisation, supplier reduction programmes and e-procurement
A financial plan, setting out in broad terms how the proposed capital expenditure is to be financed, together with an outline timescale and an order in which the objectives need to be achieved	A financial plan, setting out broadly the profit contribution expected from procurement and supply, together with the time in which it should be achieved and the priorities of the objectives

2.12.3 SWOT analysis

Environmental scanning and internal scrutiny described earlier in this chapter provide the intelligence for a SWOT (strengths, weaknesses, opportunities and threats) analysis. Figure 2.4 indicates that some form of SWOT analysis or matrix is an essential preliminary step in the formulation of strategies designed to convert the inspirations expressed in vision and mission statements into realities and ensure that the objectives are achieved.
In Figure 2.4:

- S → O *strategies* are those that seek to utilise organisational strengths to exploit external opportunities
- W → O *strategies* are those that seek to rectify organisational weaknesses so that external opportunities can be exploited
- S → T *strategies* are those that utilise organisational strengths to reduce vulnerability to external threats
- W → T *strategies* establish defensive plans to prevent organisational weaknesses from being highly vulnerable to external threats.

SWOT analysis can be undertaken at all three organisational levels – corporate, business and functional. An example of a SWOT analysis leading to some possible W → T

Figure 2.4 SWOT matrix

		Internal scrutiny	
		What are our *strengths*?	What are our *weaknesses*?
Scanning the internal environment	What are the *opportunities* we can exploit?	S → O strategies	W → O strategies
	What are the *threats* affecting our business?	S → T strategies	W → T strategies

strategies is where the organisation is under some threat as the manufacture of a major product requires the purchase of a highly sensitive raw material for which there is a high demand and few suppliers. In such a case, the SWOT/TOWS matrix may be used, as shown in Figure 2.5.

SWOT analysis has been criticised on the grounds that, in practice, such exercises are often poorly structured, hastily conducted and result in vague and inconsistent lists of subjective factors reflecting the interests and prejudices of the proposers. Such criticisms can be countered by:

■ *making the analysis a group process* in which the free flow of ideas is encouraged

■ *the use of qualifiers* requires the movers of statements for inclusion in the analysis to give reasons, so, instead of just saying 'too much reliance on one supplier', the proposer would be required to add 'because the supplier takes our business for granted and we are possibly paying more than necessary'.

Figure 2.5 SWOT analysis applied to a supplies situation

STRENGTHS	WEAKNESSES
■ Purchasing power ■ Regular demand ■ Purchasing probity and goodwill	■ Highly sensitive imported material
THREATS	OPPORTUNITIES
■ Competition for the material from competitors ■ Few suppliers ■ Exchange rates	■ Alternative materials ■ Possibility of vertical integration with a supplier ■ Outsourcing ■ Partnerships ■ Virtual company formation

2.13 The evaluation of alternative strategies

In a given situation, there are normally several alternative strategies that are available. The aim is to evaluate several strategic options – including a 'do nothing' or 'do the minimum' option, which, where appropriate, may be included, even if it is unacceptable in operational terms.

Rumelt[19] identifies four principles that can be applied to strategic evaluation:

- *consistency* – the strategy must not present mutually inconsistent policies
- *consonance* – the strategy must represent an adaptive response to the external environment and the critical changes occurring within it
- *advantage* – the strategy must provide for the creation and/or maintenance of a competitive advantage in the selected area of authority
- *feasibility* – the strategy must neither overtax available resources nor create insoluble problems.

An alternative set of criteria is that a given strategy should, first, meet the requirements of a given situation, second, provide sustainable competitive advantage and, third, improve company performance.

2.13.1 Methods of strategy evaluation

There are several possible approaches to choosing a strategy that meets the above criteria. Porter's positional approach to strategy formation is simply the selection of one of three generic positions based on an analysis of the organisation's position in the environment.

Other important approaches include lifecycle analysis, scenario planning, return analysis, profitability analysis, risk analysis, resource deployment analysis, non-financial factor appraisal and portfolio planning and analysis.

2.13.2 Lifecycle analysis

This is based on the concept that all products in their original, unmodified form have a finite lifespan, as shown in Figure 2.6.

Figure 2.6 Product lifecycle

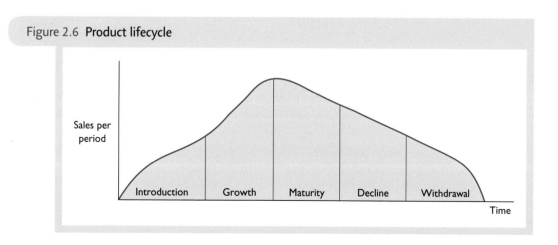

The product lifecycle or Gopertz curve plots the actual or potential sales of a new product over time and shows the stages of development – growth, maturity, decline and eventual withdrawal. Important aspects of product lifecycles are:

- *their length* – from development to withdrawal, which may be short with products subject to rapid technological advances
- *their shape* – not all products have the same shape to their curve; so-called high learning, low learning, fashion and fad products have different curves reflecting different marketing strategies
- *the product* – this can vary depending on whether the product lifecycle applies to a *class* (that is, the entire product category or industry), a *form* (that is, variations within the class) or a *brand*.

From the strategic aspect, the lifecycle approach has become increasingly important for the following reasons:

- *environmental factors* – such as the relative environmental performance of a product, as in the case of purchasing packaging, paper and the subsequent management of waste
- *durability factors* – such as competition between substitute commodity products – aluminium and steel in the car industry, for example
- *obsolescence* – with regard to capital equipment, which may be a factor in deciding to adopt an outsourcing strategy
- *changing demand* – this concept of the product lifecycle helps marketing managers to recognise both that products may need to be continually changed to prevent sales decline and that there is a need to formulate marketing strategies to stimulate demand; this strategy may impact procurement strategies, such as how far in advance to place orders for materials or components that are likely to change.

2.13.3 Scenario planning

Scenario planning consists of developing a conceptual forecast of the future based on given assumptions. Thus, by starting with different assumptions, different future scenarios can be presented. The assumptions can be based on the examination of trends relating to economic, political and social factors that may affect corporate objectives and supply and demand forecasts. Planning therefore involves deciding which scenario is most likely to occur and devising appropriate strategies for it. An example is examining how the prices of sensitive commodities, such as gold, change in the scenarios of glut and shortage.

2.13.4 Return analysis

Return analysis – the returns likely to accrue from the adoption of a particular strategy – may be done by such means as cost–benefit analysis or profitability analysis.

Cost–benefit analysis may be defined as:

> A comparison between the costs of the resources used, plus any other costs imposed by an activity (such as pollution, environmental damage) and the value of the financial and non-financial benefits derived.

Cost–benefit analysis often involves a consideration of trade-offs. Thus, when considering which of several alternative materials or components to use, a number of cost–benefit trade-offs need to be considered. Generally, increased quality means increased prices and, ultimately, increased costs. The decision on which to specify must therefore attempt to balance the interrelationships of cost, quality and projected selling prices with company objectives relating to sales quantities and profitability.

2.13.5 Business profitability

Procurement is motivated to understand suppliers' profits, not least to assure themselves that the supplier will remain in business. Profit is an emotive subject simply because there is no 'right' profit for a supplier to achieve. Monitoring the financial press gives indications of large organisations and business sectors being impacted by a variety of circumstances. Some examples follow (taken from press reports during research for this edition of the book):

- Airlines slash profit forecast as costs soar – Airlines' fuel costs this year are forecast to rise by nearly 30%
- Jack Daniel's maker cuts profit forecast on trade war
- Retail giant Next has hiked its profit outlook after an unusual spell of sunny weather spurred demand for T-shirts and picnic sets
- Honeywell raises 2018 profit forecast – reflected strength in its end markets
- EasyJet lifts profit forecast as rivals falter
- BMW shares dived up to 6% citing the chaos caused by new European fuel efficiency rules and worries about the possible disruption from tariff disputes.

Some key determinants of profit are:

- the pricing strategy, considering pricing options such as full cost, penetration and skimming
- fixed costs – those unavoidable regardless of volume produced
- variable costs – energy is a prime example
- sales volume – impacted by customer loyalty, marketing success and quality characteristics
- cost of debt – high borrowings at penal rates of interest has major impact on profitability
- inventory – impacts on working capital.

2.13.6 Risk analysis

Some degree of corporate risk will always exist. Typically, the words 'catastrophic' and 'material' are used to highlight the issue. However, risk is a more complex business issue. Consideration of the following three comments provides a sharp focus.

> 'While risk-taking is a fundamental driving force in business and entrepreneurship, the cost of risk management failures is still often underestimated, both internally and externally, including the cost in terms of management time needed to rectify the situation. Corporate governance should therefore ensure that risks are understood, managed, and, when appropriate, communicated'.[20]

> 'There is scope to make risk governance standards more operational, without narrowing their flexibility to apply them to different companies and situations'.[21]

'Perhaps one of the greatest shocks from the financial crisis has been the widespread failure of risk management. In many cases risk was not managed on an enterprise basis and not adjusted to corporate strategy.'[22]

These comments are from the Organisation for Economic Cooperation and Development (OECD) sixth peer review based on the OECD Principles of Corporate Governance. The peer review process is designed to facilitate effective implementation of the OECD Principles and to assist market participants, regulators and policy makers.

At a simplistic level, from a strategic perspective, a risk is something that may have an impact on the achievement of objectives. A comprehensive insight into corporate risks can be gained by accessing the United States Securities and Exchange Commission FORM 10-K required pursuant to Section 13 or 15(d) of the Securities Exchange Act of 1934.

In respect of the fiscal year ended 31 December 2013, the Coca-Cola Company reported the following risk factors:

- obesity concerns may reduce demand for some of our products
- water scarcity and poor quality could negatively impact the Coca-Cola system's production costs and capacity
- if we do not anticipate and address evolving consumer preference, our business could suffer
- increased competition and capabilities in the marketplace could hurt our business
- product safety and quality concerns, including concerns related to perceived artificiality of ingredients, could negatively affect our business
- increased demand for food products and decreased agricultural productivity may negatively affect our business
- changes in the retail landscape or the loss of key retail or foodservice customers could adversely affect our financial performance
- if we are unable to expand our operations in emerging and developing markets, our growth rate could be negatively affected
- fluctuations in foreign currency rates could affect our financial results
- if interest rates increase, our net income could be negatively affected
- we rely on our bottling partners for a significant portion of our business; if we are unable to maintain good relationships with our bottling partners, our business could suffer
- if our bottling partners' financial conditions deteriorates, our business and financial results could be affected
- increases in income tax rates, changes in income tax laws or unfavourable resolution of tax matters could have a material adverse impact on our financial results
- increased or new indirect taxes in the United States or in one or more of our other major markets could negatively affect our business
- increase in the cost, disruption of supply or shortage of energy or fuels could affect our profitability
- increase in the cost, disruption of supply or shortage of ingredients, other raw materials or packaging materials could harm our business.

There are 20 more risks in the FORM 10K. It is strongly suggested by the author that readers study these in order to gain a comprehensive insight into corporate risk exposure.

2.13.7 Resource deployment analysis

Resource deployment analysis is the assessment of the likely effect on key resources of adopting a particular strategy. Thus, a decision whether or not to adopt an outsourcing strategy with regard to a support service will be preceded by an analysis of the effects on tangible and intangible resources, including finance, human resources, competitive advantage and growth.

2.13.8 Non-financial factor appraisal

When making strategic decisions, it is important to consider such non-financial aspects as:

- enhancement (or otherwise) of the organisational image
- effects on suppliers, customers, competitors and the general public
- environmental and ethical factors
- the likelihood of change, development, obsolescence
- staff and union reaction to the strategy
- ethical implications of the proposed strategy.

2.13.9 Portfolio planning and analysis

Portfolio planning and analysis aim to assist with strategic decisions as to where to invest scarce organisational resources among a number of competing business opportunities. This approach is analogous to an investment manager deciding which shares to buy with the aim of creating a portfolio designed to meet a given investment strategy, such as achieving growth or providing income.

2.13.10 The BCG portfolio

One of the most popular portfolio approaches is the Boston Consulting Group (BCG) matrix. This approach to strategy formulation analyses business opportunities according to market growth rate and market share. As shown in Figure 2.7, based on these criteria, businesses can be categorised as:

- *stars* – businesses with high market share and high growth
- *cash cows* – businesses with high market share and low growth
- *question marks* – businesses with low market share and high growth
- *dogs* – businesses with low market share and low growth.

The BCG matrix can be used to decide what strategy(ies) to adopt at all three strategic organisational levels: corporate, business and functional/operational.

2.13.11 Procurement portfolio management

In 1983, Kraljic[23] introduced the first portfolio approach for use in procurement and supply management, although a similar 'matrix' was described by Fisher[24] in 1970.

Figure 2.7 Corporate strategies within the BCG matrix

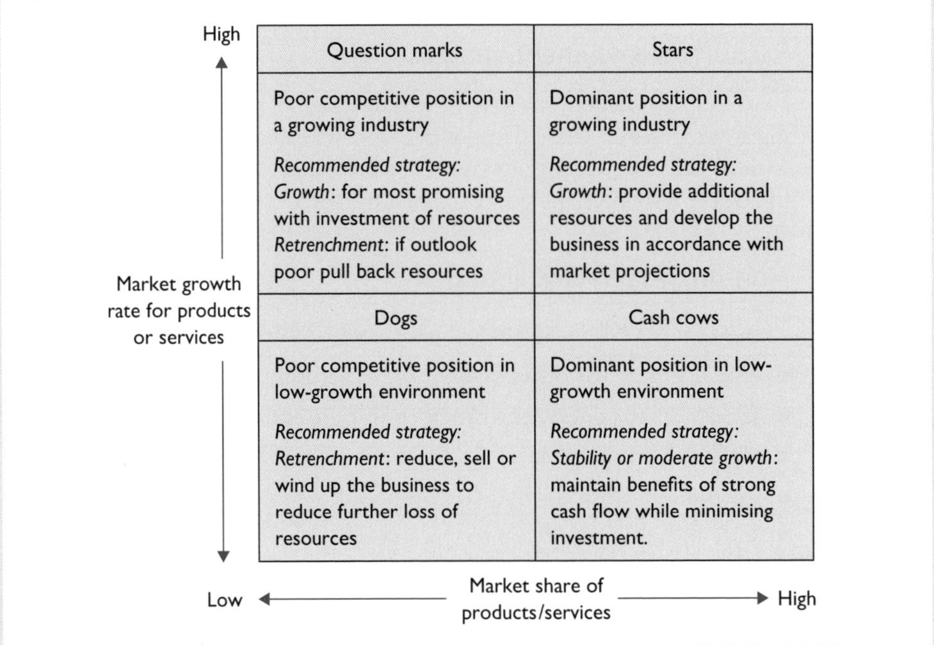

	Question marks	Stars
High ↑	Poor competitive position in a growing industry	Dominant position in a growing industry
	Recommended strategy: *Growth*: for most promising with investment of resources *Retrenchment*: if outlook poor pull back resources	*Recommended strategy:* *Growth*: provide additional resources and develop the business in accordance with market projections
Market growth rate for products or services	Dogs	Cash cows
	Poor competitive position in low-growth environment	Dominant position in low-growth environment
↓	*Recommended strategy:* *Retrenchment*: reduce, sell or wind up the business to reduce further loss of resources	*Recommended strategy:* *Stability or moderate growth*: maintain benefits of strong cash flow while minimising investment.

Low ←——————— Market share of products/services ————→ High

Kraljic's starting premise is that:

Threats of resource depletion and raw materials scarcity, political turbulence and government intervention in supply markets, intensified competition and accelerating technological changes have ended the days of no surprises. As dozens of companies have learned, supply and demand patterns can be upset virtually overnight.

The Kraljic portfolio aims to guide managers so that they can recognise the weakness of their organisation and formulate strategies for guarding against supplies disruption.

Kraljic states that the *profit impact* of a given supply item can be defined in terms of:

■ volume purchased
■ percentage of total cost
■ impact on product quality or business growth.

Supply risk for that item is assessed in terms of availability:

■ availability
■ number of suppliers
■ competitive demand
■ make-or-buy opportunities
■ storage risks
■ substitution opportunities.

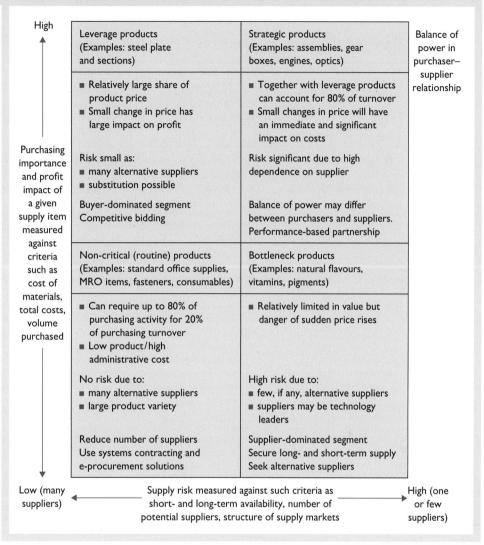

Figure 2.8 The Krajic portfolio matrix (adapted)

These profits and risk factors enable all purchased items to be assigned to one of the four quadrants shown in Figure 2.8.

Nellove and Söderquist[25] state that all portfolio approaches to procurement involve three common steps:

1 analysis of the products and their classification
2 analysis of the supplier relationships required to deliver the products
3 action plans to match product requirements to supplier relationships.

Thus, the steps for the use of the matrix in Figure 2.8 are:

■ list all purchases in descending value order
■ analyse the risk and market complexity of each purchase

- position each item on the matrix accordingly
- periodically, decide whether or not to move a particular purchase to an alternative quadrant.

The aims and possible tasks associated with each quadrant are shown in Table 2.7.

Table 2.7 Aims, tasks and information associated with each procurement focus

Procurement focus	Aims	Main tasks	Required information
Leverage aims (high profit impact, low supply risk)	■ Obtain best short-term deal ■ Maximise cost savings	■ Ensure suppliers are aware that they are in a competitive situation ■ Group similar items together to increase value and quality for quantity discounts ■ Utilise blanket orders but keep contract terms relatively short (1–2 years) ■ Search for alternative products/suppliers ■ Negotiate value-added arrangements – VMI, JIT, storage ■ Consider moving into strategic quadrant	■ Good market data ■ Short-term to medium-term demand planning ■ Accurate vendor data ■ Price/transport rate forecasts
Strategic items (high profit impact, high supply risk)	■ Maximise cost reductions ■ Minimise risk ■ Create competitive advantage ■ Create mutual commitment to long-term relationships	■ Prepare accurate forecasts of future requirements ■ Carefully analyse supply risk ■ Seek long-term supplier/partnering agreements (3–5 years) with built-in arrangements for continuous improvement and performance measurement ■ Consider joint ventures with selected suppliers and customers to gain competitive advantage ■ Take prompt action to rectify slipping performance ■ Possibly move purchasing back into leverage quadrant until confidence restored	■ Highly detailed market data ■ Long-term supply and demand trend information ■ Good competitive intelligence ■ Industry cost curves
Non-critical (routine) items (low profit impact, low supply risk)	■ Reduce administrative procedures and costs ■ Eliminate complexity ■ Improve operational efficiency	■ Simplify requisitioning, buying and payment ■ Standardise where possible ■ Consolidate and buy from consortia ■ Encourage direct ordering by users/internal customers against call-off contracts ■ Use e-procurement ■ Consider clustering into leverage quadrant	■ Good market overview ■ Short-term demand forecast ■ Economic order quantity ■ Inventory levels
Bottleneck items (low-profit items, high supply risk)	■ Reduce costs ■ Secure short-term and long-term supply	■ Forecast future requirements as accurately as possible ■ Consolidate purchases to secure leverage ■ Determine importance attached to purchases by supplier ■ See if specification measures – buffer stocks, consigned stocks, transportation ■ Search for alternative products/supplies ■ Contract to reduce risk	■ Medium-term demand/supply forecasts ■ Very good market data ■ Inventory costs ■ Maintenance plans

Gelderman and van Weele[26] point out that 'in general little is known about *the actual use* of purchasing portfolio models or how purchasing professionals position commodities and suppliers into the portfolio and develop strategies from its use'. To gain insights into such issues, we interviewed a limited number of executives and purchasing professionals employed by a large Dutch chemical company. The interviewees were selected for their experience in the use of portfolio models in actual purchasing situations. Their findings in relation to the company DSM may be summarised as follows.

Basic

- Generally matrix movements follow a clockwise pattern from bottleneck to non-critical; non-critical to leverage; leverage to strategic.
- DSM works on the principle that the non-critical and bottleneck quadrants should be as empty as possible.

Bottleneck items

For processed materials, a key question is whether standardisation is possible, permitting movement to the leverage quadrant.

Where standardisation is not possible, approaches reported are:

- capacity deals, concentrating purchases with one supplier
- obtaining a better bottleneck position by reducing supply risk on the one hand and obtaining a better negotiating position on the other
- 'staying in the corner and making the best of it' by keeping stocks, hedging, broadening the specification, searching for alternative suppliers and so on.

Many non-critical (MRO) and equipment items are 'bottleneck' due to over specification. Less complicated and more generic specifications allow 'pooling' of purchases across units/groups and consequent movement from the bottleneck quadrant to the non-critical one and/or non-critical to the leverage quadrant.

Non-critical items

At DSM, the main products are office supplies and services. As stated above, the main considerations influencing movement to the leverage quadrant are standardisation and pooling. Where pooling is not an option, purchase cards are useful for individual non-strategic commodities.

Leverage items

DSM distinguishes between 'strategic partnerships' and 'partnerships of convenience'.

Only a limited number of supplies qualify for movement from the leverage to the strategic quadrant, which is feasible when:

- the supplier has proper capabilities for co-design
- the purchaser (DSM) is prepared to spend time on supplier development
- the purchaser has sufficient levels of trust in the supplier at all organisational levels.

When a supplier does not qualify as a strategic supplier, the focus is on efficiency and cost reduction rather than design optimisation.

Partnerships can be either technology (joint venture, co-development, concurrent engineering) or logistics-driven (JIT). The latter are regarded as 'partnerships of convenience' or tactical solutions to tactical problems and reside in the leverage quadrant.

Strategic items

Successful strategic partnerships are rare and DSM policy is to reduce or restrict dependence on the supplier involved. Partnerships, over time, may become unsatisfactory or the supplier does not wish to be involved in joint development.

With underachieving partners, DSM may adopt such approaches as supplier development, making the product less complicated and developing new suppliers.

Conclusions

While recognising the limitation of their investigation, Geldermann and van Weele concluded that:

■ the portfolio approach is helpful in positioning commodities/supplies in different matrix quadrants

■ the pre-eminent value of the approach is in helping procurement practitioners to move commodities/suppliers around specific quadrants to reduce dependence on specific suppliers

■ the Kraljic portfolio is 'an effective tool for discussing, visualising and illustrating the possibilities of differentiated procurement strategies. . . it is a powerful tool for coordinating procurement strategies among various, fairly autonomous business units'.

In addition, the Kraljic categories provide a useful way of classifying purchases by total spend under each heading.

2.14 Strategy implementation

Strategy implementation is concerned with converting a strategic plan into action and doing what needs to be done to achieve the targeted strategic goals and objectives. The principal differences between strategy formulation and strategy implementation are shown in Table 2.8.

Strategy implementation should be seen as a learning process from which all organisational levels can benefit.

Table 2.8 **Contrasts between strategy formulation and implementation**

Strategy formulation	Strategy implementation
The positioning of forces before the action	Management of forces during the action
Focuses on effectiveness	Focuses on efficiency
Is primarily an intellectual process	Is primarily an operational process
Requires good initiative and analytical skills	Requires special motivation and leadership skills
Requires coordination of a few individuals	Requires coordination of many people

2.14.1 The main stages of strategy implementation

1 Communicate strategic plans to all who have not been involved in their formulation. Good communication helps to avoid negative reactions, particularly where strategies involve significant change.
2 Obtain commitment from those concerned. This involves disclosure and discussion in consultative processes, such as meetings and team briefings.
3 Framing policies and procedures.
4 Setting operational targets and objectives and ensuring that these are related to corporate objectives.
5 Assigning responsibilities and commensurate authority to individuals and teams for the achievement of objectives.
6 Changing organisational structures, where necessary.
7 Allocation of resources and agreeing budgets.
8 Providing employees with required training.
9 Constantly monitoring the success or otherwise of strategies and making required revisions.

Resource allocation and policies are important aspects of the above activities. Organisational structures are considered in Chapter 4 and procedures in Chapter 6.

2.14.2 Resource allocation

In most organisations the financial, physical, human and technological resources allocated to a function/activity will be reduced to quantitative terms and expressed in budgets or financial statements of the resources needed to achieve specific objectives or implement a formulated strategy.

2.14.3 Policies

Policies are instruments for strategy implementation. A policy is:

> a body of principles, expressed or implied, laid down to direct an enterprise towards its objectives and guide executives in decision making.

Policies are mandatory and must be adhered to by all people and activities throughout the organisation.

It is useful to consider the advantages of policy generally and policies for procurement specifically.

The advantages of policies

At corporate, functional and operational levels, policies have the following advantages:

- corporate policies provide guidelines to executives when formulating functional and operating strategies
- policies provide authority based on principle and/or precedent for a given course of action
- they provide a basis for management control, allow coordination across organisational units and reduce the time managers spend making decisions

- they provide management by exception, providing guidelines for routine actions, so a new decision is required only in exceptional circumstances
- they lead to uniformity of procedures and consistency in thought and action.

Procurement policies

Toyota Procurement Policy

Our policy is to seek the purchase of goods and services from suppliers that enhance positive impacts on the environment and society whilst meeting our business requirements. By incorporating social, environmental and ethical considerations into procurement decisions we endeavour to make a positive contribution to the environment and society.

Hitachi Procurement Policy

Partnership policy	At Hitachi we fully realise the value of developing trusting relationships with our valued suppliers.
Our open-door policy	Regardless of whether a supplier is a domestic or overseas company, we do our utmost to insure free competition.
Fair business relationship policy	It is our policy to always maintain a fair business relationship with all of our suppliers.
Selection of suppliers policy	We evaluate and select suppliers based upon criteria such as quality, price, lead time, quality of management, technical standards and abilities.
Our policy for sharing information and maintaining confidentiality	We attend to all suppliers' offers sincerely, and are willing to offer necessary information to suppliers. At the same time, we realise that suppliers' offers supply us with confidential and sensitive information. We always endeavour to maintain and keep such information strictly confidential.

Asian Infrastructure Investment Bank Procurement Policy

The Procurement Policy in AIIB projects aims to support recipients to achieving the successful implementation of bank-financed projects through efficient, fair, ethical and transparent procurement processes that optimise both value-for-money and social and environmental sustainability, which governs the procurement of goods, works, non-consulting services and consulting services for all bank-financed projects.

Policy statements can be written in relation to virtually every aspect of procurement activity. Other important areas for which policy statements may be prepared include:

- procurement authority – who may purchase and limitations on authority
- use of purchasing cards
- procurement of capital equipment
- environmental policies
- disposal of waste and surplus

- buying from small and medium-sized enterprises (SMEs) and local purchasing
- e-procurement
- ethical policies.

In general, the procurement policies of individual organisations should conform to three basic principles:

- procurement policies should aim to select and procure, in an economically rational manner, the best possible goods and services available
- suppliers worldwide should be eligible to participate in procurement transactions on open, fair and transparent principles and easy-to-understand, simple procedures
- procurement transactions have an important contribution to make to society worldwide – for example, corporate procurement practices should consider the effective preservation of natural resources and protection of the environment.

Procurement policies are usually specified in a procurement manual that should be regularly revised. The policies may be varied to meet an exceptional situation, such as a breakdown in supplies, but this should only be done on the authority of the executive who has ultimate responsibility for procurement.

2.14.4 An example of a strategy implementation plan

An example of a public-sector organisation plan is shown in Figure 2.9. The 11 headings of the plan can easily be adapted to the requirements of a private-sector enterprise.

2.15 Post-implementation evaluation, control and review

This is concerned with verifying the degree to which implemented strategies are fulfilling the mission and objectives of the organisation. Evaluation differs from control. Post-implementation evaluation can apply the principles listed in section 2.12 above. Spekman[27] states that the objective of evaluation is to enable procurement managers to understand both the process and result of strategic planning and offers the following list of evaluation criteria:

- Internal consistency
  - Are the procurement strategies mutually achievable?
  - Do they address corporate/division objectives?
  - Do they reinforce each other? Is there synergy?
  - Do the strategies focus on crucial procurement issues?
- Environmental fit
  - Do the procurement strategies exploit environmental opportunities?
  - Do they deal with external threats?
- Resource fit
  - Can the strategies be carried out in the light of resource constraints?
  - Is the timing consistent with the department's and/or business's ability to adapt to the change?

Figure 2.9 An example of a strategy implementation plan.

Aims
To support the achievement of the council's key objectives and allow concentration of more resources, both financial and staff time, on delivering core tasks. This will be done by securing best value for money, reducing or managing risk and modernising related business processes by adopting best practice procurement techniques for all bought-in external goods and services.
Objectives
1 Take a *strategic overview* of corporate procurement. ■ Undertake portfolio analysis to identify key spend areas and supplies. ■ Identify scope for aggregation of demand into large/corporate contracts. ■ Identify scope for collaborative arrangements. ■ Identify the procurement community within BFBC. ■ Create procurement performance measures against agreed baseline. ■ Prepare an annual report to the executive board. 2 Establish procurement as specific element in *corporate and departmental planning process.* ■ Incorporate council's procurement strategy and this implementation plan into the council's annual policy and performance plan. ■ Establish procurement strategy/plan for each individual department as part of annual service plans. ■ Review plans annually in normal planning process. 3 Adopt a commercial approach, in line with *best value principles*, to all procurement decisions. ■ Evaluate all bids on quality as well as whole life costs whenever appropriate. ■ Review procurement processes and contract regulations (and keep them under review). ■ Prepare process guide in the form of a procurement manual and best practice toolkit with standard documentation and procedures to help department staff. ■ Ensure, in addition, that departments have access to professional advice/involvement wherever needed. 4 Development scope for *e-procurement.* ■ Forge links with neighbouring authorities to identify scope for collaborative procurement and establishment of local e-marketplace. ■ Ensure new contracts incorporate requirements for e-trading wherever possible. ■ Identify scope for e-tendering and e-auctions. 5 Commit to principles of *sustainability and ethical procurement* where these can be achieved within the terms of best value principles. ■ Develop appropriate best practice guidance with staff. 6 Simplify *business processes.* ■ Establish framework agreements for high-volume/low-value goods and services. ■ Prepare process guide in the form of a procurement manual and best practice toolkit with standard documentation and procedures to help departmental staff. ■ Ensure effective interfaces with other council systems and processes. 7 Improve *communications* with markets. ■ Publish annual procurement plan/programme of forthcoming contracts. ■ Identify markets that do not deliver optimum performance and seek to develop/manage them to better effect. ■ Identify opportunities for greater partnerships working/collaboration with suppliers/markets. ■ Initiate development programme with major suppliers and partners. 8 Ensure availability of appropriate *training and guidance* for all staff involved in procurement (including schools). ■ Undertake procurement skills gap analysis. ■ Develop training programme, buying in expertise as required. ■ Prepare procurement guidance reference manual covering principles and processes and summarised mini guide. ■ Prepare detailed best practice toolkit with standardised documentation. 9 The *organisation of procurement* will remain unchanged but: ■ Improve communications with staff and schools. ■ Develop feedback system for identifying lessons learnt from individual procurement exercises and sharing best practice. ■ Ensure clarity in all guidance issued (use plain English). 10 Ensure all suppliers are treated fairly and openly in the awarding of council contracts. ■ Prepare ethical code as part of procurement manual and integrate with council's code of conduct. 11 Commit to *continuous improvement* of all procurement practices and procedures. ■ Regularly review contracts regulations, procurement manual and toolkit. ■ Initiate benchmarking review of procurement and refresh biannually. ■ Establish and monitor key performance indicators for procurement.

This figure is reproduced by kind permission of Rob Atkins and the Bracknell Forest (UK) Borough Council

- Communication and implementation
    - Are the strategies understood by key implementers?
    - Is there organisational commitment?
    - Is there sufficient managerial capability to support effective procurement planning?

The control process involves four stages, as shown in Figure 2.10. Setting standards is not easy, owing to the multitude of possibilities.

Normally, specific performance standards can be grouped under four headings:

- service to internal and external customers
- contributors to the competitive advantage of other elements in the supply chain
- staff effectiveness and efficiency
- financial measures – that is, cost reductions, conformity to budgets.

Performance measurement, as applied to the procurement function, is considered in Chapter 17.

Johnson and Scholes[28] state that, in reviewing strategic options, it is important to distinguish between three interrelated aspects of any strategy. The typical procurement strategies/tactics or contributions for each of the three aspects of strategic development are shown in Table 2.9.

2.16 Strategic procurement and supply chain process models

2.16.1 What are models?

Models are representations of real objects or situations. A model aeroplane, for example, is a representation of the real thing. Physical replicas are referred to as *iconic models*. Alternatively, we can have models that are physical in form but do not have the same appearance as the things that they purport to represent. These are known as *analogue models*. A thermometer, which represents temperature, is an analogue model. Today,

Figure 2.10 **Steps in the control process**

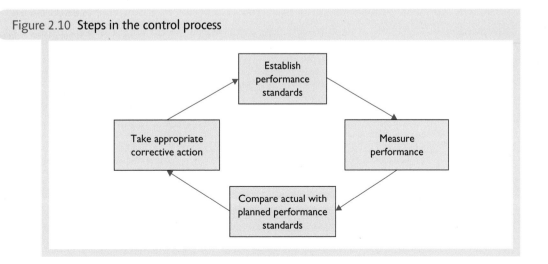

Table 2.9 Typical aspects of procurement strategies, tactics or contributions to corporate development strategies

Aspects of strategic development	Typical purchasing strategies/tactics contributions
Generic strategy (the basis on which the organisation will compete or sustain excellence)	
Cost leadership	Lower purchase costs achieved by consolidation of purchases, single sourcing, global procurement. Reduction in costs of purchasing system and administration. Value for money spent. Logistical contributions to competitive advantage. Buying sub-assemblies in lieu of components, etc.
Differentiation	Involvement of suppliers in product design and development, value analysis, total quality management, alternative materials. Stimulation of technological developments in one supplier market, etc.
Focus	Location of specialist suppliers, make-or-buy decision for specialist components, subcontracting, outsourcing, etc.
Alternative strategy directions in which the organisation may choose to develop	
Do nothing	
Withdrawal	Running down/disposal of inventory. Negotiating contract cancellations, etc.
Consolidation	Moving to standard/generic materials/components to increase potential use. Negotiation of limited period contracts, etc.
Market penetration	Provision of information regarding competitors, price volatility, unused capacity in the supplier market. Negotiation of contracts with options for increased supply or stocking of inventory at suppliers, etc.
Product development	Liaison with design and production. Partnership sourcing; supplier appraisal. Negotiation regarding ownership of jigs and tools for bought-out items. Timing of supply deliveries. MRP II. Value engineering, etc.
Market development	Liaison with marketing. Partnership sourcing, specifying packaging and shipping instructions. Identification of vital points in the supply/value chain
Diversification	Supply considerations, such as effect on set-up costs and productions runs. Purchasing quantity considerations. Promotion of interchangeability of materials and components, etc.
Alternative methods by which any direction of development may be advanced	
Internal development	Organisational aspects of purchasing. Recruitment or development of purchasing staff. Integration of purchasing into materials management or logistics
Acquisition	Corporate level issues relating to: ■ backward integration – activities concerned with securing inputs, such as raw materials by acquisition of supplies ■ forward integration – activities concerned with securing outputs, such as acquisition of distribution channels, transport undertakings, etc. ■ horizontal integration – activities complementary to those currently undertaken, such as consortia, franchising, licensing or agency and outsourcing agreements

computers are used to simulate situations and provide answers to 'What if . . . ?' questions. In general, models can be classified as:

- *mathematical* – these represent a problem by a system of symbols and mathematical relationships or expression (the formulae used in Chapter 9 are of this type)
- *non-mathematical* – these can take the form of charts, diagrams and similar visual representations that communicate information.

2.16.2 The CIPS Procurement and Supply Management model

Much of what has been discussed in this chapter is admirably summarised in the Chartered Institute of Procurement and Supply (CIPS) Procurement and Supply Management model.[29] This is a generic representation of an organisation and shows where procurement and supply management fit into it at both strategic and operational levels. The model shows where the organisation's procurement and supply management strategy fits in, too, what it covers and how it can be implemented. The model shows the high-level stages of procurement and supply management activity and key steps at each stage. The model can also be used by procurement and supply management practitioners to explain to colleagues where their role fits into their organisation and what it covers.

The overall CIPS model is shown in Figure 2.11.

The model shows how organisational vision, mission, values and corporate strategy are derived from environmental factors, such as the government, customers, competitors, stakeholders and other external influences, and an evaluation of organisational competences.

The model also shows how purchasing strategies interface with and are related to other organisational functions/activities such as R&D, finance, marketing and technical ICT strategies.

The aspects of procurement indicated under the headings of strategic sourcing analysis, proactive demand management and acquisition pre-contract and post contract are dealt with in appropriate chapters of this book.

2.16.3 Other procurement models

Other procurement models include the Ministry of Defence's acquisition management system (AMS), the supply chain operations reference (SCOR) and the European Federation of Quality Management (EFQM) model. All these can be accessed on the Internet.

2.16.4 Supply chain strategic leadership

This facet of strategic leadership is highlighted by CIPS.[30] It explores that one of the key functions of leaders in procurement and supply is to lead (as well as manage) the supply chain.

- Motivating and inspiring supply chain partners to offer above-compliance levels of service, innovation, support and value addition.
- Utilising motivational and relationship-maintaining influencing approaches (e.g. contract incentives, gain sharing, role modelling, supplier development) to change perceptions, attitudes and behaviours, where required to correct problems or shortfalls in performance or conduct.

Figure 2.11 The CIPS procurement and supply management model

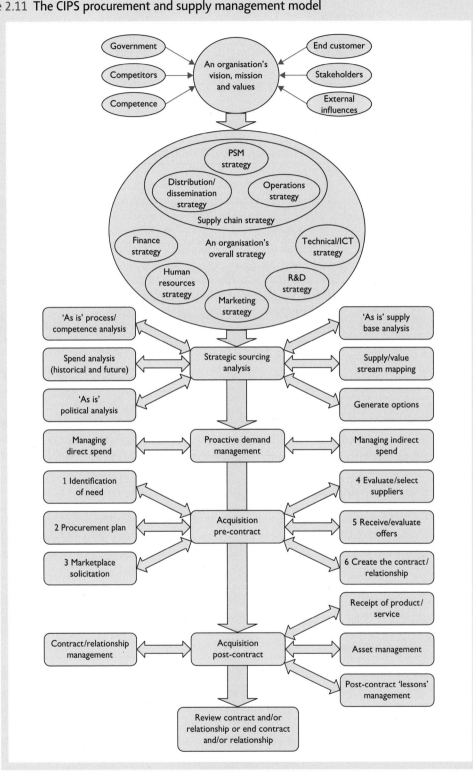

- Mobilising and developing resources and capabilities within the supply chain (e.g. through supplier forums, best practice sharing, motivation and quality circles, benchmarking, supplier development and knowledge management) in support of development and improvement: continuous value addition, reduction in waste and costs, process or performance improvement and/or supply innovation.

- Introducing changes (to contracts, relationships, processes and systems) in a constructive, supportive relationship-maintaining and – where possible – collaborative manner: maximising the acceptability and quality of change plans.

- Facilitating collaboration and alliance-building between stakeholders in the supply network, in support of improvement and development: emphasising shared goals and mutual benefit; resolving potentially divergent or conflicting interests; encouraging best practice and ideas sharing; and so on.

- Leading by example in desired standards of conduct and performance (such as ethical trading or corporate social responsibility policy).

- Utilising influence (including market power, incentives and rewards) to encourage the raising of standards in the supply chain (especially in regard to minimum acceptable labour and environmental standards in globalised supply chains).

Discussion questions

2.1 Define 'strategy' and link the definition to the procurement strategy within your organisation.

2.2 Give two examples to demonstrate that a procurement strategy can be directly integrated with the organisation's strategy and long-term business plan.

2.3 If you were faced with the proposition that a procurement strategy is irrelevant to modern business because market forces will always dictate where the balance of power is at any time, how would you explain that while market forces are at work a procurement strategy is essential?

2.4 How can a long-term procurement strategy be adapted to accommodate short-term supply market opportunities that arise?

2.5 What impact does government legislation have on procurement strategies?

2.6 Thinking about the organisation in which you are employed or have knowledge of, list up to three examples under each of the following headings:
   - key strengths
   - key weaknesses
   - key opportunities
   - key threats.

2.7 List some of the issues in strategic management for (i) small firms, and (ii) multinational corporations.

2.8 Choo points out that organisations engage in environmental scanning to understand the forces of change. What should procurement departments consider to ensure they monitor supply markets to understand the forces of change?

2.9 Macro-environmental factors impact on procurement strategies. Using the PESTEL approach, what steps should a procurement operation take to ensure it monitors the legal impact on its strategies?

2.10 Procurement strategies require attention to supply chain risks. Can you give examples of six risks that only a supplier can manage and six risks that must be managed jointly by the supplier and buyer?

2.11 In Kraljic's purchasing portfolio, under which headings, 'leverage', 'routine' and 'bottleneck', would you place the following items?
    (a) chemical supplies for glass manufacture
    (b) steel
    (c) cleaning materials
    (d) security services
    (e) bottling equipment for a brewery.

2.12 Your Sales Director has said that your products are now uncompetitive in world markets and a cost reduction of 20 per cent is required on purchased goods and services. The existing purchasing strategy is such that only European suppliers are used. How would you reconsider the existing strategy and formulate an alternative?

References

[1] Wheelen, T. L. and Hunger, J. D., *Strategic Audit of a Corporation*, Wheelen & Hunger Associates, 1982 and 2005.

[2] Chopra, S. and Meindl, P. *Supply Chain Management. Strategy, Planning & Operation*, 6th edn, Pearson Global Edition, Pearson Education Ltd, Harlow, UK, 2018.

[3] Ohmae, K., *The Mind of the Strategist*, McGraw-Hill, New York, USA, 1982.

[4] Mintzberg, H., 'Five Ps for strategy' in Mintzberg, H., Lampel, J., Quinn, J. G. and Ghoshal, S. (eds) *The Strategy Process*, Prentice Hall, Upper Saddle River, New Jersey, USA, 2003, pp. 3–10.

[5] As 4 above, p. 9

[6] Mintzberg, H., Ahlstrand, B. and Lampel, J., *Strategy Safari*, Prentice Hall, Upper Saddle River, New Jersey, USA, 1998, pp. 1–21.

[7] David, F. R., *Concepts of Strategic Management*, Macmillan, New York, USA, 1991, p. 4.

[8] Hax, A. C. and Majluf, N. S., *The Strategy Concept and Process*, Prentice Hall, Upper Saddle River, New Jersey, USA, 1999, p. 416.

[9] Porter, M., *Competitive Strategy: Techniques for Analysing, Industries and Competitors*, Macmillan, New York, USA, 1980.

[10] Carr, A. S. and Smeltzer, L. R., 'An empirically based definition of strategic purchasing', *European Journal of Purchasing and Supply Management*, Vol. 3, 1997, pp. 199–207.

[11] Kraljic, P., 'Purchasing must become supply management', *Harvard Business Review*, Sept/Oct, 1983, p. 110.

[12] Worral, L., 'Strategic analysis: a scientific art', Occasional paper No. OP001/98, University of Wolverhampton, 27 May, 1998.

[13] Brown, A. and Weiner, E., *Supermanaging: How to Harness Change for Personal and Organisational Success*, Mentor Books, 1985, p. ix.

[14] Choo, C. W., 'Environmental scanning as information seeking and organisational learning', *Information Research*, Vol. 7, No. 1, October, 2001.

[15] ICMA, *Management Accounting 2000: Official Terminology*: www.icmacentre.ac.uk.

[16] Lawrence, E., 'Strategic thinking' paper prepared for the research Directorate Public Service Commission of Canada, 27 April, 1999.

[17] As 4 above, p. 124.

[18] As 11 above.

[19] Rumelt, R. P., 'Evaluating business strategy' in Mintzberg *et al.*, as 3 above, p. 81.

[20] Risk Management and Corporate Governance OECD 2014.

[21] Same as 21 above.

[22] Same as 22 above.

[23] As 12 above, pp. 109–17.

[24] Fisher, L., *Industrial Marketing: An Analytical Approach to Planning and Execution*, Brandon Systems Press, UK, 1970.

[25] Nellove, R. and Söderquist, K., 'Portfolio approaches to procurement', *Long Range Planning*, Vol. 33, 2000, pp. 245–67.

[26] Gelderman, C. J. and van Weele, A. J., 'Strategic direction through purchasing portfolio management: a case study', *International Journal of Supply Chain Management*, Vol. 38, spring, 2002, pp. 30–8.

[27] Spekman, R. E., 'A strategic approach to procurement planning', *Journal of Purchasing and Supply Management*, spring, 1989, pp. 3–9.

[28] Johnson, G. and Scholes, K., *Exploring Corporate Strategy Text and Cases*, 3rd edn, Prentice Hall, Upper Saddle River, New Jersey, USA, 1993, pp. 203–43.

[29] CIPS, procurement and supply management model. Full details of this model are shown on the CIPS website: www.cips.org

[30] Corporate and Business Strategy. The Official CIPS Course Book Chartered Institute of Purchasing & Supply.

Chapter 3

Logistics and supply chains

Learning outcomes

This chapter aims to provide an understanding of:

- what is logistics?
- materials, logistics and distribution management
- reverse logistics
- supply chains
- supply chain management (SCM)
- supply chain vulnerability
- value chains
- value chain analysis
- supply chain optimisation
- procurement positioning within supply chain management

Key ideas

- Military and non-military logistics to support operations at optimum cost.
- The scope of materials and physical distribution management (MM and PDM).
- Total systems management, trade-offs, cooperative planning and manufacturing techniques as important logistics concepts.
- Reverse logistics scope and influence.
- Networks, linkages, processes, value and the ultimate 'customer' as key supply chain characteristics.
- Infrastructure, technology, strategic alliances, software and human resource management (HRM) as key supply chain enablers.
- External and internal supply chain risks.
- Porter's and Hine's value chain model.
- Cost and differentiation as a means to competitive advantage.
- Objectives and factors in supply chain optimisation.
- Supply chain relationship management.

Introduction

Procurement is increasingly considered within the wider context of supply chains. Logistics, however, is a much older term. It is therefore appropriate that the present chapter should begin with a consideration of logistics.

We next define the terms 'supply chain' and 'supply chain management' (SCM) and identify some types of supply chains, the processes that comprise supply chain management and the enablers via which SCM is implemented. An aspect of SCM that has only recently received serious attention is supply chain vulnerability.

The chapter ends with a consideration of supply chain optimisation, the impact of SCM on traditional purchasing and some contributions of purchasing to the supply chain management field.

3.1 What is logistics?

3.1.1 Military logistics

The supply chain approach developed from logistics. Logistics, initially a military term dating from the Napoleonic Wars, refers to the technique of moving and quartering armies – that is, quartermasters' work. The scope of logistics in a military sense is reflected in the definition adopted by NATO:[1]

> The science of planning and carrying out the movement and maintenance of forces. In its most comprehensive sense the aspects of military operations which deal with:
>
> (a) design and development, acquisition, storage, transport, distribution, maintenance, evacuation and disposition of materiel (materiel: equipment in its widest sense including vehicles, weapons, ammunition, fuel, etc.);
>
> (b) transport of personnel;
>
> (c) acquisition of construction, maintenance, operation and disposition of facilities;
>
> (d) acquisition or furnishing of services; and
>
> (e) medical and health service support.

NATO also distinguishes between two important aspects of logistics: acquisition logistics and operational logistics (Figure 3.1).

3.1.2 Non-military applications of logistics

Non-military applications of logistics, although generally less complicated, still cover the same ground, as indicated by the following definitions:

> The Council of Supply Chain Management Professionals (CSCMP)[2] define logistics management as 'that part of supply chain management that plans, implements and controls the efficient, effective forward and reverses flow and storage of goods, services and related information between the point of origin and point of consumption in order to meet customers' requirements.'

> The European Logistics Association defines logistics as 'the organisation, planning, control and execution of the goods flow from development and purchasing, through production and

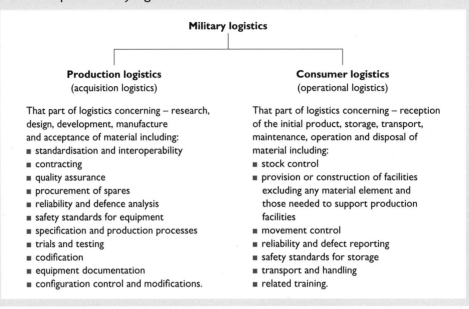

Figure 3.1 **The scope of military logistics**

Military logistics

Production logistics
(acquisition logistics)

That part of logistics concerning – research, design, development, manufacture and acceptance of material including:
- standardisation and interoperability
- contracting
- quality assurance
- procurement of spares
- reliability and defence analysis
- safety standards for equipment
- specification and production processes
- trials and testing
- codification
- equipment documentation
- configuration control and modifications.

Consumer logistics
(operational logistics)

That part of logistics concerning – reception of the initial product, storage, transport, maintenance, operation and disposal of material including:
- stock control
- provision or construction of facilities excluding any material element and those needed to support production facilities
- movement control
- reliability and defect reporting
- safety standards for storage
- transport and handling
- related training.

Source: NATO, *Logistics Handbook*, 1997, paragraph 104

distribution, to the final customer in order to satisfy the requirement of the market at minimum costs and capital use.'

3.2 Materials, logistics and distribution management

As shown in Figure 3.2, logistics comprises both materials management and physical distribution management.

3.2.1 Materials management

Materials management (MM) is concerned with the flow of materials to and from production or manufacturing and has been defined as:[3]

> The planning, organisation and control of all aspects of inventory embracing procurement, warehousing, work-in-progress and distribution of finished goods.

Some aspects of MM that may be included under the heading 'Materials flow' are listed in Table 3.1.

The factors influencing the activities assigned to MM include the following:

- procurement is frequently the 'key' activity
- production planning and control may be assigned to MM or the manufacturing function where this is separate – the former tends to apply when production is materials orientated, such as in an assembly factory; the latter when production is machine/process orientated.

Figure 3.2 Scope of logistics management

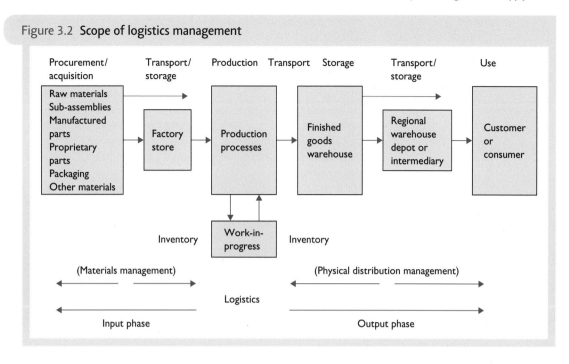

Table 3.1 Materials flow activities

Materials flow	Typical activities
Planning	Preparation of materials budgets, product research and development, value engineering and analysis, standardisation of specifications
Procurement	Determining order quantities, processing works and stores requisitions, issuing enquiries, evaluating quotations, supplier appraisal, negotiation, placing contracts, progressing deliveries, certifying payments, vendor rating, supplier and contract management
Storage	Stores location, layout and equipment, mechanical handling, stores classification, coding and cataloguing, receipt of purchased items, inspection, storage or return, stock and store safety and security, stock integrity and rotation, stores environment management, issuing to production, providing cost data, stock records and verification, recycling or disposal of obsolete, surplus or scrap material
Production control	Forward ordering arrangements for materials, preparing production schedules and sequences, issuing orders to production, emergency action to meet material shortages, make-or-buy decisions, quality and reliability feedback and adjustment of supplies flow to production line or sales trend

3.2.2 Distribution management

The physical movement and delivery of goods and services to customers is a key objective of supply chain management. It is important for procurement to recognise their potential role in assisting distribution management to be highly efficient and cost effective.

Procurement should have a strategic role in defining the distribution strategy. Corporately, the strategy will be either:

(i) own the assets (buildings, equipment and transport vehicles, or some of the assets)

(ii) lease or rent assets

(iii) outsource distribution in its entirety.

The distribution strategy is impacted by: economic factors, channels of distribution and their location, service centres and warehouses locations, and the nature of the goods or services. For example, there are noticeable differences between the distribution of perishable goods and engineering parts and equipment.

In addition to the distribution strategy, warehouse operations, stock management and transport planning are other components of the strategy.

The area of stock management is a key consideration wherein procurement can have a major impact. They can advise on such matters as:

- negotiating consignment stock at key locations, including the client's premises
- negotiating lead times and contract terms and conditions when lead times not met
- negotiating minimum order quantities
- negotiating virtual inventory management.

3.2.3 Logistics

The term logistics has its origins in military and defence organisations. Defence logistics has been defined[4] as 'Defence Logistics acquires the resources for military operations, positions those resources where they are needed, sustains them throughout the conduct of operations and redeploys and generates them. It can be defined broadly as "the science of planning and carrying out the movement and maintenance of forces".'

It is postulated that, in the above context, logistics encompasses four generic processes as follows:

1 Requirements determination – establishing what is needed, in what quantity and quality, when and where.
2 Acquisition (for procurement) – buying the supplies and services and other resources needed to meet the requirements that have been determined
3 Distribution – moving the resources acquired to their place of use, which includes the supply tasks of collecting, storing, protecting and issuing resources
4 Conservation – deriving the greatest value from all resources, specifically by caring for them through the maintenance tasks of servicing, inspection, repairing, modifying and overhauling.

The author recognises that confusion exists about the differences between logistics and supply chain management. More will be explained in section 3.4 but it may be noted here that logistics is the backbone on which supply chains are driven. In a commercial organisation logistics includes managing the flow of goods and supplies involving information, data and documentation between two or more entities. It is, in consequence, 'narrower' than supply chain management.

In 2018 the UK Department of Health & Social Care awarded a £730 million NHS logistics contract to Unipart Logistics. Unipart's responsibilities include delivering medical devices and hospital consumables – other than medicine – to NHS trusts;

warehousing; inventory management; order processing and delivery. The previous supplier DHL Supply Chain Limited went to the High Court[5] to appeal against contract award. DHL lost the case.

The logistics services were described as:

(i) management of existing logistics services, including transport, inventory management and site facilities

(ii) provision of inbound logistics and inter-depot trucking services

(iii) support for expansion of logistics services to meet projected increased demand

(iv) provision for home and community delivery services for continence products (and potentially other products), on behalf of the NHS, to residential homes, care homes, domestic premises and any NHS-funded providers of community health care services.

3.2.4 Cooperative planning

This can work forwards to customers and backwards to suppliers. The change from product-orientated to customer-orientated supply chains and, thus, faster supply resources, can provide customers with alternatives such as make to stock, make to order and finish to order. Conversely, from the inward supply side, effective, cooperative planning may relate to zero defects, on-time delivery, shared products and information exchanges relating to such matters as shared specifications, design support, multiyear commitments and technology exchange. Overall, both suppliers and customers can benefit from reduced costs of inventory, capacity, order handling and administration. Cooperative planning utilises, as appropriate, manufacturing and scheduling techniques, including the following:

- Manufacturing techniques
  - computer-aided design (CAD)
  - computer integrated manufacture (CIM)
  - flexible manufacturing systems (FMS)
  - materials requirement planning (MRP)
  - manufacturing resources planning (MRP II)
  - optimised production technology (OPT)
  - strategic lead time management (STM).

- Scheduling techniques
  - just-in-time (JIT)
  - materials requirement planning (MRP)
  - manufacturing resources planning (MRP II)
  - enterprise resource planning (ERP).

This can be explained by the cost–value curve shown in Figure 3.3.

1 The lowest cost value is at the procurement stage when supplies are purchased.
2 During transportation of supplies, value remains low because little capital is invested until raw materials and components enter production – the only costs incurred relate to acquisition and holding.

Figure 3.3 **The added value aspect of logistics**

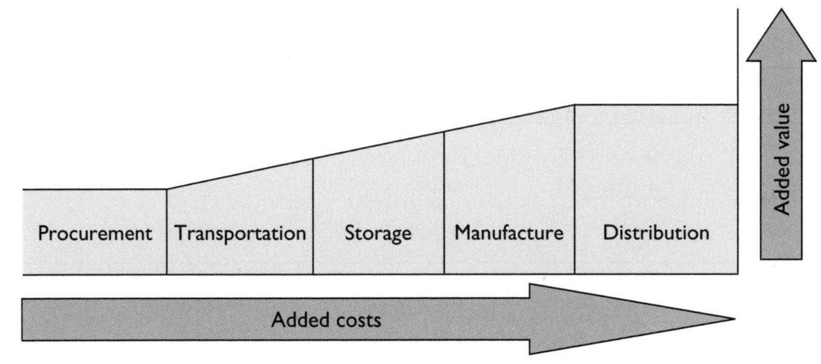

3 The curve becomes steeper as raw materials and components are gradually incorporated into the final product. This is because of accumulated manufacturing costs and increasing interest costs that reflect the value of capital invested.

4 The curve becomes flatter (but not flat) at the end of the production process because no more manufacturing costs apply. The value added in distributing must exceed its cost at the macro level otherwise the manufacturer would supply an ex-works product. However, on an item basis they may choose to add a figure for distribution that is less than its unit cost. This increased value may be seen in the form of greater total sales. At this stage the invested capital is at its highest value and the cost of stocking finished goods instead of selling them involves higher opportunity costs than holding the initial supplies. This shows why the logistician is, if anything, more concerned with PDM than MM as the potential for cost reduction is the highest at this point of the total supply chain. Cost reduction by speeding flows of materials, work-in-progress and finished products is not the only concern of the logistician. Logistics management involves two flows. The first, as stated above, is the flow of materials and work-in-progress across the organisation to the ultimate customer. The second, as shown in Figure 3.4, is a reverse flow of information, in the form of orders or other indicators on which future demand forecasts can be based.

Logistics management may be regarded as a subsystem of the larger enterprise or a system of which procurement, manufacturing, storage and transportation are sub-systems. In essence, logistics is a way of thinking about planning and synchronising related activities. Figure 3.4 also shows how logistics management crosses conventional functions.

3.3 Reverse logistics

Rogers and Tibben-Lemke[6] have defined reverse logistics as:

> The process of planning, implementing and controlling the efficient, cost-effective flow of raw materials, in process inventory, finished goods and related information from the point of consumption to the point of origin for the purpose of recapturing value or proper disposal.

Figure 3.4 Materials, products and information flows across an organisation

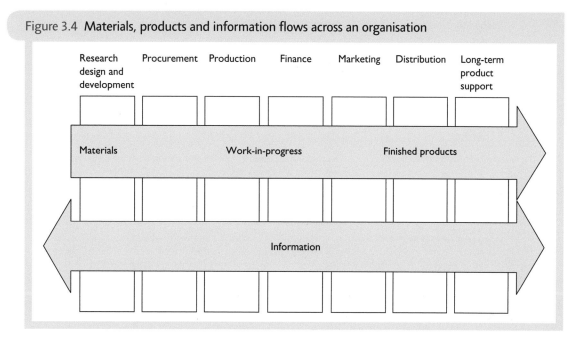

Reverse logistics requires comprehensive strategies and policies to ensure corporate processes adequately serve the business and enhance its reputation. The reverse logistics considerations will vary from business to business. For example, a catalogue retailer will tend to have a simpler set-up, than a manufacturer of engineering capital equipment sold around the world. Table 3.2 shows some key reverse logistic considerations and their business implications.

Procurement has many roles in reverse logistics. These roles potentially include:

- negotiating contracts with third parties
- monitoring legislative changes
- activating inventory management policies
- considering outsourcing of transportation and warehousing
- negotiating supplier product warranties
- ensuring IT contracts have appropriate resource times and fix
- dealing with environment matters, e.g. scrap disposal
- supporting field service specialists.

3.4 Supply chains

3.4.1 Definitions

There are many definitions of the term 'supply chain', of which the following is typical:[7]

> A supply chain is that network of organisations that are involved, through upstream and downstream linkages, in the different processes and activities that produce value in the form of products and services in the hands of the ultimate customer or consumer.

Table 3.2 Some key reverse logistic considerations and their business implications

	Reverse logistics considerations	Business implication
1	IT system provision	An IT system capable of tracking sales, returns and customer service actions
2	Business drivers	These will include economic, legislative and corporate citizenship motivations and necessities
3	Customer service and help-desk	A responsive customer service who are versed in the range of solutions that may be offered to clients
4	Warranty management	A system capable of tracking warranty expiry dates, linking this to potential repair/replacement policy
5	Third party supplier commitment	A contractual agreement committing third-party suppliers to all facets of reverse logistics
6	Repair, replacement, refurbishment and scrap policies	A decision rationale for dealing with different solutions to deal with faulty goods or services
7	Repackage and resell	A strategy for retailers to deal with returned goods that are not faulty
8	Spare parts inventory and location	Availability of spare parts inventory to satisfy customer demands; this may include consignment inventory
9	Claims management requirements and timescales	Contractual safeguards to prevent wrongful claims and unachievable corrective timescales
10	Returns logistics	Engagement, or not of third-party logistics providers and provision of intermediate warehouses
11	Field service provision	Provision of field service specialists with client focused response times
12	Financial write-down policy	Planning for write-downs and impact on bottom-line forecasts
13	Environmental management	Recycle, landfill or other disposal of unwanted products

The above definition emphasises the following key characteristics of supply chains:

■ *Supply chains are 'networks'* – traditionally, supply chains were loosely linked associations of discrete businesses. The network concept implies some coordination of 'cow to customer' processes and relationships. An alternative definition is that a supply chain is:

A network of connected and interdependent organisations mutually and cooperatively working together to control, manage and improve the flow of materials and information from suppliers to end users.[8]

Networks are further considered in section 4.3.

■ *Supply chain linkages are upstream and downstream – upstream* means 'against the current' and relates to the relationships between an enterprise and its suppliers and suppliers' suppliers. *Downstream* is 'with the current' and relates to the relationship between an enterprise and its customers. There can also be *upstream–downstream*, as is the case with organisations that have returnable containers, pallets, drums and so on or trade-in products.

■ *Linkages* – the coordination of supply chain processes and relationships. A supply chain is only as strong as its weakest link.

■ *Processes* – in the context of a business, a process is defined by Cooper et al.[9] as:

> A specific ordering of work activities across a time and place with a beginning and an end and clearly identified inputs and outputs, a structure of action.

From a procurement standpoint, the processes that comprise the supply chain are shown in Figure 3.5. From a supplier's standpoint the processes are shown in Figure 3.6.

■ *Value* is defined by Porter[10] as 'what buyers are willing to pay'. Superior value stems from offering lower prices for equivalent benefits or providing unique benefits that more than offset a higher price.

■ *The ultimate customer* – a customer is simply the recipient of the goods or services that result from all the processes and activities of the supply chain. A function or subsystem can be the customer of the preceding or succeeding link in a supply chain.

Customers may be either internal or external. The definition refers to the 'ultimate customer or consumer' so that the supply chain may extend beyond the customer from whom the direct order for goods or services emanates.

3.4.2 Types of supply chains

Supply chains can be classified in numerous ways. An organisation such as a food retailer will have many types of supply chains reflecting differences in products, services, production and distribution methods, customer–supplier relationships and information flows. Supply chains may be roughly classified according to four customer–supplier characteristics and also in relation to virtuality, scope, service, complexity, products, purpose and value.

Figure 3.5 **Supplier chain processes from a procurement perspective**

Search	Acquire	Use	Maintain	Dispose

Figure 3.6 **Supply chain processes from a supplier's perspective**

Research	Design	Manufacture or provide	Sell	Service

Customer–supplier characteristics

These may give rise to:

- *concentrated chains* found in businesses such as the automotive industry that have:
  - few customers but many suppliers
  - customers with demanding requirements
  - EDI systems or a requirement for JIT deliveries.

- batch manufacture chains that have:
  - many customers and many suppliers
  - complicated relationship webs – an undertaking with which an enterprise is in contact may, at different times, be a customer, supplier, competitor or ally.

- retail and distribution chains that have:
  - many customers but relatively few suppliers
  - customised methods, such as vendor-managed inventory (VMI) of facilitating dealings with suppliers.

- *service chains* that implement the mission statements of organisations such as hospitals libraries and banks concerned with the delivery of services, books, information and financial services or restaurants and cinemas delivering food and entertainment, for example – essentially service chains are not different from manufacturing chains as every service involves people, something physical (an asset or part of something performed), an action and a time element.

Other characteristics

- *Virtuality* – virtual is the opposite of real. Thus, a 'virtual' enterprise is the counterpart of a real, tangible business. As Christopher[11] states, 'a virtual supply chain is, in effect, a series of relationships between partners that is based upon the value-added exchanges of information'. In a virtual supply chain, information replaces the need for inventories. A mail-order business may have no inventory and simply call for supplies from the manufacturer when orders are received from customers.

- *Scope* – supply chains may be local, regional and international in scope. Some suppliers of gas, such as BP, for example, have the ability to put together delivery chains to bring gas supplies from Trinidad to Spain, from Siberia to China and from North Africa to Southern Europe.

- *Complexity* – the author has encountered three degrees of supply chain complexity, as outlined below:
  - Coach builder – simplistic supply chain. This is the simplest form of supply chain for procurement to manage as shown in Figure 3.7.
  - Racing car manufacturer – multi-dimensional supply chain as shown in Figure 3.8.
  - Public sector organisation – outsourced strategic services as shown in Figure 3.9.

- *Purpose* – a distinction can be made between *efficient* and *responsive* supply chains. *Efficient* supply chains are primarily concerned with reducing the cost of operations, as in lean supply chains. These work best when forecast accuracy is high and product

Figure 3.7 **Simplistic supply chain**

Supplier of G.R.P panels ←→ Buyer ←→ Private & Public sector customers

Figure 3.8 **Extended supply chain**

Suppliers of raw materials, components and assemblies ←→ Strategic suppliers ←→ Buyer ←→ International dealership ←→ Private customers

Figure 3.9 **Ultimate supply chain**

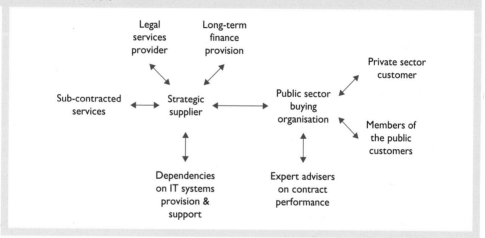

variety low. *Responsive* supply chains are primarily concerned with minimising the delivery cycle time, as in agile supply chains. These work best when forecast accuracy is low and product variety high.

- *Products* – supply chains vary widely according to the end product. Examples are build-to-forecast and build-to-order supply chains and ones for innovative and functional products (see section 4.3.2).
- *Value chains* – these are dealt with later in the present chapter.

3.5 Supply chain management (SCM)

There is no universally agreed definition of SCM. Mentzer *et al.*[12] state that the many published definitions can be classified into three categories – a management philosophy, implementation of a management philosophy and a set of management processes.

SCM as a management philosophy

Mentzer *et al.* suggest that, as a management philosophy, SCM has the following three characteristics:

- a systems approach to viewing the supply chain as a whole and managing the total flow of goods inventory from the supplier to the ultimate consumers
- a strategic orientation towards cooperative efforts to synchronise and converge intra-firm and interfirm operational and strategic capabilities into a unified whole
- a customer focus to create unique and individualised sources of customer value, leading to customer satisfaction.

SCM as a set of activities to implement a management philosophy

The seven activities listed below as essential to the implementation of a management philosophy are:

- integrated behaviour
- mutually shared information
- mutually shared risks and rewards
- cooperation
- the same goal and same focus on serving customers
- integration of processes
- partners to build and maintain long-term relationships.

These activities are implied in the following list of SCM objectives:

- the integration of both internal and external competencies
- the building of alliances, relationships and trust throughout the supply system
- the reduction of costs and improvement of profit margins
- the maximisation of return on assets (net income after expenses/interests)
- the facilitation of innovation and the synchronisation of supply chain processes
- the optimisation of the delivery of products, services, information and finance both upstream and downstream and across internal and external boundaries.

SCM as a set of management processes

As shown by Figure 3.10, Farrington lists ten SCM processes that are essential for an effective Corporate Supply Chain Strategy.

Each of these ten processes is briefly described below

- *Corporate Supply Chain Strategy.* In the absence of a defined and agreed corporate supply chain strategy it is very unlikely if there will be an effective supply chain operation. The strategy will require collaboration between competing forces for finance, resources, working capital and accountability for performance. For example, the strategy may require investment in inventory in various parts of a country or the world. Who will fund the investment? Some key customers may be prepared to invest in definitive inventory providing it is available to satisfy unscheduled demand.
- *Integration with Strategic Customers at both Technical and Relationship levels.* Strategic customers are the life blood of the survival of a business. The technical compatibility

Figure 3.10 Supply chain management: integrated corporate vision of business processes

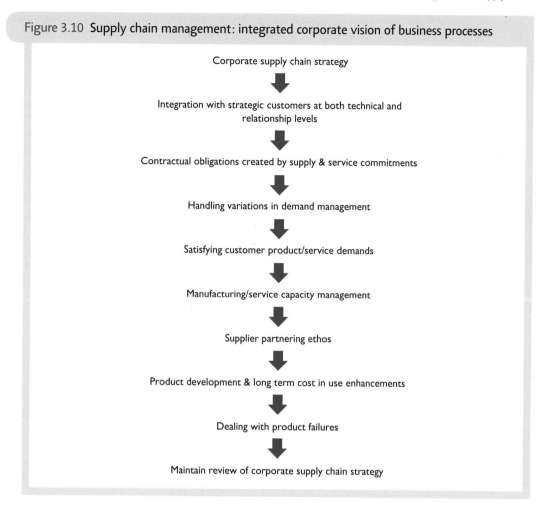

Corporate supply chain strategy

Integration with strategic customers at both technical and relationship levels

Contractual obligations created by supply & service commitments

Handling variations in demand management

Satisfying customer product/service demands

Manufacturing/service capacity management

Supplier partnering ethos

Product development & long term cost in use enhancements

Dealing with product failures

Maintain review of corporate supply chain strategy

of systems is a key requirement. To understand this compatibility will require an investment in time and probably finance. The ability to establish and maintain effective relationships between the parties is never easy to achieve. It has been said that all relationships begin with the best of intentions but people change, circumstances change and markets change. All this places pressure on overall relationships.

■ *Contractual Obligations created by Supply & Service Commitments.* Words are easily expressed, however some contract obligations are more difficult to satisfy. The supply chain strategy requires all contractual obligations to be mutually agreed. These obligations must be capable of being measured, reported and regularly discussed. An inability of any member of the supply chain to meet one obligation can impact negatively on many relationships. Service commitment are mentioned here to emphasise the need to maintain a skilled workforce in sufficient numbers to satisfy the obligations.

■ *Handling Variations in Demand Management.* It is inevitable that there will be variations in demand management. The corporate supply chain strategy must give active consideration to this facet. One solution is to have strategic safety stock, although there is a working capital consideration here. Another solution is to have pre-signed off suppliers on a 'purchase in emergency scenario'. This may require an investment in tooling. Another alternative is to have an agreed 'stock bond' held at a key customer with pre-determined timescales when the stock bond' must be used. These issues can be time consuming negotiations but offer a unique opportunity to convince key customers that there are positive solutions.

■ *Satisfying Customer Product/Service Demands.* This will require an expert process to handle incoming orders/instructions from a variety of customers, each with their own unique manner of placing demands on suppliers. Some of these demands may be issued through agents, other national representatives and varied systems requirements. Those in-house people who handle the incoming demands have a vital role to play in ensuring that there are no delays in managing the demand inputs in a timely and accurate manner. The demand may include complex shipping transportation requirements to remote locations around the world.

■ *Manufacturing/Service Capacity Management.* This is the ultimate dilemma for many organisations. Do they plan on the basis of existing capacity demands or do they seek to forecast future demand and plan manufacturing/service capacity on that basis? A leading question is 'who in the business is accountable for future demand forecasts?' In one client of the author the answer would be sales/marketing. What happens when they get the forecast completely wrong and capacity has been created? The Finance Director could be faced with redundancy payments; HR faced with industrial unrest; procurement faced with terminating contracts; media faced with adverse media reactions and so on. The supply chain strategy must embrace all alternative options for creating capacity and for effectively managing that capacity.

■ *Supplier Partnering Ethos.* Procurement is a key player in this scenario. Partnering does not come easy to many organisations. It is a culture that is in direct opposition to a culture of blame and hostility. True partnering requires an investment in time and resources to ensure both parties are true believers in partnering. For example, one deal was in its final stages of negotiation when the Finance Director of a new strategic supplier point blank refused to agree to 'open book costings' and the buyer's 'right of audit.' When asked to explain the difficulties the response was that 'it demonstrated a lack of trust on the part of the buying organisation.' Careful explanation had to be given to say that 'costs' had a mutual impact of respective profitability and that ' right of audit' was two way and demonstrated openness where there could be respective benefits. These are only two examples of this scenario but a complete chapter could be written on this subject alone.

■ *Product Development & Long Term Cost In Use Enhancements.* A supply chain strategy will embrace product development and long term cost in use enhancements. All products and many services have a 'shelf life' and when this expires, if nothing is done, competitors have their opportunity to attack a market sector. There has to be an investment in product development, underwritten by investing in staff with new approaches to both problem solving and understanding technological potential. The 'Green' agenda is an excellent case in point, where 'greening' can offer tremendous social, business and financial benefits to a wide range of interested parties. The long term cost in use calculation son projects is not at the forefront of many deliberations on investment, particularly when bidders will not commit to long-term cost in use calculations.

■ *Dealing with Product Failures.* The author has been engaged in business situations where products have failed in service and a supplier has not had the competence or ability to find an acceptable short term solution. Imagine an aircraft on a remote airstrip where a safety critical item fails. The aircraft cannot fly again until the part arrives and is fitted. In a similar vein, imagine there is a problem in a chemical formulation in respect of a medicine. That medicine cannot be used until the formulation is corrected, tested and approved by the necessary authorities. The supplier's deniability that it is not their problem will not be of help to the buying organisation. There must be an effective quality management regime in place and a convincing process for dealing with product failures.

■ *Maintain Review of Corporate Supply Chain Strategy.* It is a fatalistic prediction to conclude that a current supply chain strategy is a long term solution. Market demands can change in a matter of months. There are examples within the retail sector, airline sector, catering and construction where events have turned supply chain matters on their heads. It has led to bankruptcies, thousands of workers being displaced in the economy, major projects abandoned or delayed for years. An effective corporate board of directors will ensure that the supply chain strategy is constantly reviewed and revised as necessary.

3.5.1 SCM enablers and barriers

Research by Marien[13] identified four key enablers if SCM was to be successful. The enablers were organisational infrastructure, technology, strategic alliances and human resource management. Although these enablers remain relevant, they are somewhat simplistic given the rapid development and globalisation of supply chains.

Wong *et al.*[14] produced a very informative paper in which they conducted a literature review and produced six supply chain enabler constructs, namely:

■ organisational structure

■ internal relational behaviour

■ customer relational behaviour

■ top management support

■ information sharing

■ business performance management system.

Through his consultancy assignments, the author has had active involvement in creating and developing complex supply chains. These supply chains included a South Korean manufacturer supplying a European client with products in the client's markets in Europe, Australia, USA, Canada, Argentina and other locations. The author has developed the Farrington Supply Chain Enabler Model to provide a checklist that may apply, with additions to meet specific supply chain scenarios. The checklist is shown in Table 3.3.

It is absolutely necessary to determine how the supply chain will be managed. There is comprehensive evidence of contract management failures where there is a one-on-one relationship. Supply chains are complex and an investment in their management is a strategic necessity.

There are potential barriers to the success of supply chains. The barriers can be summarised under six headings, namely:

■ regulatory and political considerations

■ lack of top management commitment

■ reluctance to share information with partners

	Table 3.3 Farrington Supply Chain Enabler Model
1	Transportation considerations – overland, airfreight, sea cargo
2	Warehousing locations and ownership
3	Reverse logistics
4	Customer order cycle time
5	In-stock and safety stock considerations
6	Investment creating the supply chain
7	Time-to-market
8	Outsourcing relationship management
9	IT systems and compatibility with supply chain
10	Procurement capability
11	Product/service modifications
12	Contractual KPIs for supply chain
13	Leveraging technology to enhance visibility and communications
14	Relationship structures
15	Obsolescence
16	Implications of supply chain failures

- incomparable information systems
- incomparable corporate structures
- globalisation challenges.

3.5.2 Software as an SCM enabler

Four essential software supply chain requirements are connectivity, integration, visibility and responsiveness.

- *Connectivity* is the ability to exchange information with external supply chain partners in a timely, responsible and usable format that facilitates inter-organisational collaboration.
- *Integration* is the process of combining or coordinating separate functions, processors or producers and enabling them to interact in a seamless manner.
- *Visibility* is the ability to access or view pertinent data or information as it relates to logistics and the supply chain.

■ *Responsiveness* is the ability to react quickly to customers' needs or specifications by delivering a product of the right quality, at the right time, in the right place, at the lowest possible cost. System availability is 24/7.

Initially, software providers specialised in either management planning or execution applications, as shown in Figure 3.11

The current emphasis is on the creation of software that integrates each of the software types shown in Figure 3.11 and deals with the supply chain as a continuous process rather than as individual stages. Thus, enterprise resource management (ERP) may be defined as:

> A software solution that addresses the enterprise's needs, taking the process view of an organisation to meet the organisational goals by tightly integrating all functions of an enterprise.

The core ERP subsystems are sales and marketing master scheduling, materials requirements planning (MRP), capacity requirements planning (CRP), bills of materials, procurement, shop floor control, accounts payable and receivable and logistics.

Leading ERP vendors have either purchased or partnered with advanced planning and scheduling (APS) vendors and have developed Internet versions of their supply chain offerings. Internet supply chains cause the walls between internal and external supply chains to break down. Enterprise application integration (EAI) enables providers to convert their entire suites of enterprise applications into e-business applications and provide a framework that ties businesses electronically to their customers, suppliers, electronic trading communities and business partners. Such suites offer several advantages, including that:

■ an integrated suite presents a single view to the user from screen to screen and information is stored in a single database and the rekeying of information from one system into another is eliminated

■ a single database provides a tighter integration of business processes

■ maintenance is cheaper and upgrades easier when there is only one system to upgrade and one supplier to deal with

■ for the above reasons, connectivity, integration, visibility and responsiveness are essential attributes of supply chain software.

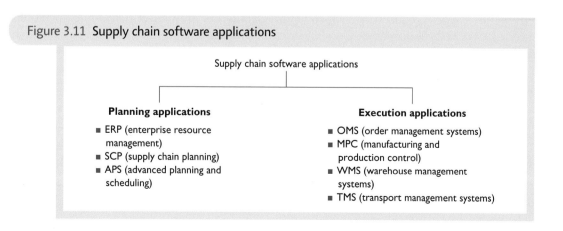

Figure 3.11 **Supply chain software applications**

3.6 Supply chain vulnerability

Supply chains are vulnerable due to both external and internal risks.

External risks are those attributed to environmental, economic, political and social causes, such as storms, earthquakes, terrorism, strikes, wars, embargoes and computer viruses.

Internal risks are those attributable to interactions between organisations in the supply chain. A Cranfield University report[15] identifies five categories of supply chain risk:

- *Lack of ownership* due to the blurring of boundaries between buying and supplying organisations arising from factors such as outsourcing and the creation of complicated networks of business relationships with confused lines of responsibilities.
- *Chaos risks* due to mistrust and distorted information throughout the supply chain. An example is the so-called 'bullwhip' effect, in which fluctuations in orders increase as they move upstream from retailers to manufacturers to suppliers.
- *Decision risks* due to chaos that makes it impossible to make the right decision for every player in the supply chain.
- *JIT relationship risks* due to the fact that an enterprise has little capacity or stock in reserve to cater for disruptions in the supply chain due to late deliveries, such as transport breakdowns.
- *Inertia risks* due to a general lack of responsiveness by customers or suppliers to changing environmental conditions and market signals with consequential inability to react to competition moves or market opportunities.

To the above may be added:

- *supplier base reduction*, especially single sourcing in which an enterprise is dependent on one supplier
- *globalisation* in which advantages of sourcing abroad may be offset by extended lead times, transport difficulties and political events
- *acquisitions, mergers and similar alliances* that may reduce supply chain availability.

The Cranfield report observes that 'supply chain risk management starts with the identification and assessment of likely risks and their possible impact on operations'. To assess risk exposure, the company must identify not only direct risks to its operations, such as the loss of critical raw materials or process capability, but also the potential causes of those risks at every significant link along the supply chain.

The report also lists ten ways in which to manage supply chain risk. The first three of these measures run counter to current supply chain trends:

- *diversification* – multiple sourcing
- *stockpiling* – use of inventory as a buffer against all eventualities
- *redundancy* – maintaining excess production, storage, handling and transport capacity
- *insurance* – against losses caused by supply chain disruption
- *supplier selection* – more careful assessment of supplier capability and risks of dealing with particular suppliers
- *supplier development* – working closely with suppliers, sharing information and collaboration initiatives

- *contractual obligation* – imposing legal obligations with stiff penalties for non-delivery
- *collaborative initiatives* – spreading risk among grouped companies on an ad hoc basis or as part of a trade association
- *rationalisation of the product range* – companies, particularly distributors, may wish to exclude products with supply problems from their product ranges
- *localised sourcing* – reduction of risks arising from congested transport networks or intermodal transport transfer by shortening transport distances.

3.7 Value chains

Supply chains and value chains are synonymous. A value chain is:

> a linear map of the way in which value is added by means of a process from raw materials to finished delivered product (including service after delivery).

Important value chain models have been developed by Porter and Hines.

3.7.1 Porter's value chain model

Porter states that the activities of a business can be classified into five primary and four support activities, each of which will potentially contribute to competitive advantage. The activities, shown in Figure 3.12, comprise the value chain.

The five *primary* activities are as follows.

- *Inbound logistics* – all activities linked to receiving, handling and storing inputs into the production system, including warehousing, transport and stock control.

Figure 3.12 Porter's supply chain

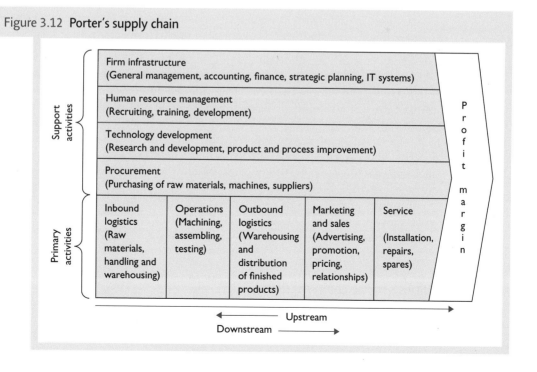

89

- *Operations* – all activities involved in the transformation of inputs to outputs as the final product(s). In a manufacturing enterprise, these would include production, assembly, quality control and packaging. In a service industry, these include all activities involved in providing the service, such as advice, correspondence and preparation of documents by a legal firm.

- *Outbound logistics* – activities involved in moving the output from operations to the end user, including finished goods warehousing, order processing, order picking and packing, shipping, transport, maintenance of a dealer or distribution network.

- *Marketing and sales* – activities involved in informing potential customers about the product, persuading them to buy and enabling them to do so, including advertising, promotion, market research and dealer/distributor support.

- *Service* – activities involved in the provision of services to buyers offered as part of the purchase agreement, including installation, spare parts delivery, maintenance and repair, technical assistance, buyers' enquiries and complaints.

The four *support* activities for the above primary activities are the following:

- *Firm infrastructure* or general administration – including activities, costs and assets relating to general management safety and security, management information systems and the formation of strategic alliances.

- *Human resource management* – all the activities involved in recruiting, hiring, training, developing and compensating the people in an organisation.

- *Technology development* – activities relating to product design and improvement of production processes and resource utilisation, including research and development, process design improvement, computer software, computer-aided design and engineering and development of computerised support systems.

- *Procurement* – all activities involved in acquiring resource inputs to the primary activities, including the purchase of fuel, energy, raw materials, components, sub-assemblies, merchandise and consumable items from external vendors.

The word 'margin' on the right side of the Figure 3.12 indicates that the enterprise obtains a profit margin that is more than the cost of each of the individual activities or subsystems that comprise the value chain. Viewed differently, the end customer is readier to pay more for a product or service than the total cost of all the value chain activities or subsystems.

Linkages are the means by which the interdependent parts of the value chain – both internal and external – are joined together. Such linkages take place when one element affects the costs or effectiveness of another element in the value chain. Thus, intranets and the Internet are useful linkages as they may reduce the cost of supply chain administration. Linkages require coordination. Ensuring that products are delivered on time, for example, requires the coordination of operations (production), outbound logistics and service activities. Linkages are considered further in section 4.3, on networks.

3.7.2 Hines's value chain model

Writing in 1993, Peter Hines[16] recognised that Porter made two valuable contributions to our understanding of value chain systems.

First, Porter places a major emphasis on the materials management value-adding mechanism, raising the subject to a strategic level in the minds of senior executives. Second, he places the customer in an important position in the supply chain.

3.7.3 A critique of Porter

Hines also identified three major problems with Porter's model:

1 Neither Porter nor the firms discussed concede that consumer satisfaction – not company profit – should be their primary objective. The focus of Porter's model is on the profit margin of each enterprise, not the consumer's satisfaction.
2 Although Porter acknowledges the importance of integration, his model shows a rather divided network, both within the company and between the different organisations in the supply chain.
3 Hines believes that the wrong functions are highlighted as being important in Porter's primary and support activities.

Hines suggests that the above three criticisms result from the fact that Porter's model is based solely on American cases 'without reference to more innovative Japanese enterprises'. Porter's conclusions may therefore 'prove inappropriate for companies facing the challenges of the twenty-first century with the prospect of an array of more developed competitors. Indeed in some cases close adherence to Porter's methodology may prevent firms from further continual development'.

3.7.4 Alternative models

To correct the above problems, Hines offered two models:

■ a *micro* integrated materials value pipeline
■ a *macro* ten forces partnership model.

The main contrasts between the Porter and Hines models are summarised in Table 3.2. The following are the important features of Hines's model.

■ The value chain points in the opposite direction to that in Porter's model, emphasising differences in both objectives and processes.
■ Demand is determined by collective customer-defined price levels.
■ Primary functions in each of the separate firms in the value chain must be integrated and 'traditional arm's length external barriers and internal divisions broken down'. The emphasis is on collaboration rather than competition.
■ Key primary functions and secondary activities differ, as shown in Table 3.4. The significance of each of the secondary activities identified by Hines is, briefly, as follows:

  – Activity-based costing (ABC) enables the exact cost of products and the benefits of activities such as *kaizen* and value analysis to be ascertained. By allocating costs to activities rather than functions, we can identify the true costs involved in delivering the product. A simpler method of value chain analysis is to call the price charged to the customer at the end of the supply chain 100 per cent and,

Table 3.4 Porter's and Hines's models contrasted

	Porter	Hines
Principal objective	Profitability	Consumer satisfaction
Processes	Push system	Pull system
Structure and direction	Series of chains linking firms pointing from raw materials source to customer	One large flow pointing from consumer to raw material source
Primary activities	Inbound logistics, operations, outbound logistics, marketing and sales service	Teams concerned with marketing, materials, engineering, quality, R&D and design
Secondary (support) activities	Firm infrastructure, HRM, technology development, procurement	Activity-based costing (ABC), HRM/training/education, TQM, EDI, profit

by working backwards, ascertain the cost of each supply activity. ABC enables the most serious non-value-adding problems to be identified first and addressed promptly.

- Human resources management (HRM) – especially employee training and education – facilitates effectiveness, efficiency and proactive thinking.
- Total quality management (TQM) provides a culture for all network members.
- Electronic data interchange (EDI) together with intranets, extranets and so on, all facilitate quick response to customers' requirements and draw network members closer together.
- Profit should be roughly equalised between network members and result from reducing total production and consumption costs to below what consumers are willing to pay for products meeting their specifications.

3.8 Value chain analysis

Value chain analysis is concerned with a detailed examination of each subsystem in a supply chain and every activity within these subsystems with a view to delivering maximum value at the least possible total cost, thereby enhancing value and synergy throughout the entire chain.

Porter[17] states that there are two ways in which an enterprise can obtain a sustained competitive advantage: first, cost and, second, differentiation.

3.8.1 Cost

Cost analysis with regard to value chains is performed by assigning costs to the value chain activities. The approach of activity-based costing (ABC) is, as stated above, of particular relevance in this context.

Porter identifies ten major cost drivers that determine the value or cost of activities:

- *Economies or diseconomies of scale* – fixed costs spread over a large volume of production are more cost-effective than producing small quantities of an item. Diseconomies of scale in procurement can occur if large requirements meet an inelastic supply, forcing up input prices.

- *Learning and spillovers* – learning can reduce costs and can spill over from one industry to another via suppliers, ex-employees and reports of representatives.

- *Capacity utilisation* – changes in the level of capacity utilisation will involve costs of expanding or contracting.

- *Linkages between activities* – the cost or value of an activity is frequently affected by how other activities are performed. Linkages with suppliers centre on the suppliers' product design characteristics, such as service and quality. The way in which a supplier performs activities within the value chain can raise or lower the purchaser's costs.

- *Interrelationships* – sharing a value activity with another business unit can reduce costs. Certain raw materials can be procured more cheaply by combining units' requirements.

- *Degree of vertical integration* – every value activity employs or can employ purchased inputs and thus poses integration choices. The cost of an outbound logistics activity may vary depending on whether or not the enterprise owns its own vehicles.

- *Timing of market entry* – an enterprise may gain an advantage from being the first to take a particular action.

- *Firm's policy of cost or differentiation* – the cost of a value activity is always affected by policy choices a firm makes independently of other cost drivers. Policy choices reflect a firm's strategy and often deliberate trade-offs between cost and differentiation.

- *Geographic location* – location relative to suppliers is an important factor in inbound logistical cost.

- *Institutional factors* – government regulations, taxation, unionisation, tariffs and levies constitute major cost drivers.

An enterprise that controls the above drivers better than its rivals will secure a competitive advantage over them.

A cost advantage can also be gained by reconfiguring the value chain so that it is significantly different from those of competitors. Such reconfigured chains can derive from differing production processes, automation, direct instead of indirect sales, new raw materials or distribution channels and shifting the location of facilities relative to suppliers and customers.

3.8.2 Differentiation

Porter[18] states that a firm differentiates itself from its competitors when it provides something unique that is valuable to buyers beyond simply offering a new price. A differentiation advantage can be obtained either by enhancing the sources of uniqueness or reconfiguring the value chain.

The drivers of uniqueness are often similar to the cost drivers listed above and include:

- *policy choices* – about what activities to perform and how to perform them, such as what product features to include, services to provide, technology to employ or quality of outputs
- *linkages between activities* – such as delivery time, which is often influenced not only by outbound logistics but also by the speed of order processing
- *timing* – being the first to adopt a product image may pre-empt others doing so
- *location* – convenience of use for customers and other such factors
- *interrelationships* – sharing technologies or sales effort, for example
- *learning and spillovers* – learning how to perform an activity better; Porter observes that only proprietary learning leads to sustainable differentiation
- *integration* – providing a service in-house instead of leaving it to suppliers may mean that the organisation is the only one to offer the service or provide the service in a unique way
- *scale* – large-scale operations can allow an activity to be performed in a unique way not possible at a smaller volume
- *institutional factors* – good union relationships may avoid losses in production time due to strikes and so on.

Reconfiguring a value chain to create uniqueness can involve devising a new distribution chain or selling approach, forward integration to eliminate channels of distribution, backward integration to enhance quality and the adoption of new production technologies.

3.8.3 The main steps in value chain analysis

Porter[19] provides lists of the main steps in strategic cost analysis and differentiation analysis.

For *strategic cost analysis* these steps are:

1. identify the appropriate value chain and assign costs and assets to it
2. diagnose the cost drivers of each value activity and how they interact
3. identify competitors' value chains and determine the relative costs to competitors and the sources of cost difference
4. develop a strategy to lower your relative cost position by controlling cost drivers or reconfiguring the value chain and/or downstream value
5. ensure that cost reduction efforts do not erode differentiation or make a conscious choice to do so
6. test the cost reduction strategy for sustainability.

3.9 Supply chain optimisation

Supply chain optimisation is different from SCM. The latter concentrates on controlling the various elements in the supply chain. Optimisation is about removing the non-value-added steps that have infiltrated or been designed into the link of processes that constitutes a particular supply chain. Optimisation is concerned with the removal of supply chain inefficiencies and has been defined as:

> the management of complicated supply chains in their entirety with the objectives of synchronising all value-adding production and distribution activities and the elimination of such activities that do not add value.

3.9.1 The objectives of supply chain optimisation

The above definition emphasises the importance of:

- synchronising all value-adding production and distributing activities
- eliminating activities that do not add value.

Other objectives include the following:

- *Providing the highest possible levels of customer service* – research shows a strong relationship between customer satisfaction and customer loyalty. Customer service levels should aim to create delighted customers by exceeding customers' expectations. Such expectations include responsiveness and value.

- *Achieving cost-effectiveness* – cost-effectiveness is also referred to as value for money and may be expressed as a ratio:

$$\frac{\text{Value of benefit received}}{\text{Cost of the benefit}}$$

- *Achieving maximum productivity from resources expended or assets employed* – productivity is also a ratio, relating outputs to one or more inputs. An increase in output per unit of input is an increase in productivity. Thus, the total productivity of a supply chain is:

$$\frac{\text{Total output}}{\text{Total input}}$$

The challenge is to increase the value of output relative to the cost of input. Productivity also increases when the same output is achieved with less input.

- *Optimising enterprise profits* – Cudahy[20] points out that 'the logic and aim of enterprise profit optimisation (EPO) is the simultaneous optimisation of the supply and demand sides of a business both within an enterprise and throughout its trading network. Thus by simultaneously improving operational efficiency and achieving profitable growth, EPO can enhance revenue and thereby complement cost reduction and asset productivity as a means of enhancing profitability.'

Cudahy states that the introduction of a pricing and revenue optimisation (PRO) system involves the following four basic steps:

- *Step 1: Segmenting the market* – identifying from historical transaction data the selection of groups of people who will be most receptive to a product. Frequent segmentation methods include demographic variables, such as age, sex, race, income and occupation, and psychographic variables, such as lifestyle, activities, interests and opinions.

– *Step 2: Calculating customer demand* – use of pricing software to predict how a customer or micro segment will respond to products and prices based on current market and other conditions.

– *Step 3: Optimising prices* – this is concerned with deciding what prices to offer to a particular customer to maximise a particular profit objective, market share or other strategic goals. Based on an analysis of cost, demand, market position, price elasticity and competitive pressures, it recommends optimum – not lowest – prices to achieve these goals.

– *Step 4: Recalibrating prices* – this is the fine-tuning of prices to customer buying behaviour.

Cudahy observes that pricing and revenue optimisation are not about competing on price but extracting the maximum value from a company's products and capacity.

■ *Achieving maximum time compression* – time compression is an important aspect in achieving customer satisfaction, cost-effectiveness and productivity. Wilding[21] rightly observes that while cost and transfer price comparisons are open to a variety of interpretations, time is a common measure across all supply chain partners. Speeding up the flow of materials downstream and the flow of information upstream increases productivity, provides competitive advantage by virtue of rapidly responding to customers' requirements and eliminates non-value-adding process time. Beesley[22] claims that at least 95 per cent of process time is accounted for by non-value-adding activities. Time compression has applications for all aspects of the supply chain but is of particular importance as, unlike material, time wasted cannot be replaced. In general, non-value-adding activities relating to time can be categorised as:

– queueing time – materials waiting to be processed

– rework time – rectifying errors

– time wasted due to managerial decisions (or indecisions)

– cost of inventory in the supply chain.

Regarding inventory, Beesley claims 'as a general rule the volume of inventory held in a supply chain is proportional to the length of time expressed as the total time to customer'. If the supply chain is compressed work-in-progress, cycle and buffer stocks are reduced, with consequent lower overhead, capital and operating costs.

3.9.2 Factors in supply chain optimisation

The important factors in supply chain optimisation are described below.

Reduction of uncertainty

Davis[23] refers to 'three distinct sources of uncertainty that plague supply chains':

■ *suppliers* – failure to fulfil delivery promises

■ *manufacturing* – machine breakdowns, computer foul-ups that route materials to the wrong place and so on

■ *customers* – uncertainty regarding order quantities and the 'bullwhip' effect or increase in demand variability further up the supply chain, e-orders from distributors fluctuating more than retail rates, which are fairly uniform.

All of the above increase inventory. Inventory exists as a simple insurance against uncertainty of supply. Reduction of uncertainty – by means of reliable, accurate and valid forecasts, the study of demand trends and use of statistical methods – can optimise the supply chain by avoiding holding excess stock and, conversely, delay in responding to customers' demands due to stockouts.

Collaboration

Optimisation is normally most likely to be achieved by collaboration between cross-functional teams within the organisation and customers and suppliers external to it. Such collaboration may optimise product and process design and customers' and suppliers' satisfaction.

Benchmarking

Gartner[24] have an approach to benchmarking facets of supply chain performance, as detailed below:

- order to ship (days)
- order to delivery (days)
- perfect order – OTIF (%)
- days of raw material (days)
- days of work-in-progress (days)
- days of finished goods (days)
- value of total inventory (% of sales)
- direct material cost (% of sales)
- supplier receipts – on time (%)
- supplier receipts – passing quality (%)
- plant utilisation (%)
- demand forecast error (%)
- NPD time – concept to shipment (months)
- New product introduction forecast error (%)
- Transportation costs (% of sales)
- warehouse and DC costs (% of sales)
- inventory obsolescence (% of inventory value)

Key performance indicators (KPIs)

KPIs express abstract supply chain objectives in financial or physical units for the purpose of comparison. Data relating to various functions, processes or activities is assembled, quantified and transformed into physical or financial information that can be used to compare results – often against benchmarks – and then measure relative performance. Thus, the performance of both suppliers and customer with regard to delivery of orders on time can be expressed as a percentage of the orders placed. KPIs, considered in detail in section 10.9.2, can provide not only objectives to achieve but also the motivation to achieve or better the required performance.

Leadership

The impetus for supply chain optimisation and world class SCM must either derive from or have the support of top management. This requires two-way communication between top management and the senior managers responsible either for the integrated supply chain or functions and processes within it. Important leadership characteristics are the ability to articulate the vision of an optimised supply chain to other team members, set and motivate the team to achieve goals, innovate and introduce change, nurture the competences of team members, foster a culture of continuous learning and improvement and display high levels of personal integrity.

Actions to improve supply chain performance

Davis[25] suggests a number of actions that can be used to improve supply chain performance and reduce vulnerability to demand uncertainty in both products and processes.

For products, these actions include the use of standard components and sub-assemblies, lower tolerances, fewer product offerings and the production of a generic product.

For processes, typical actions may be to reward suppliers' performance, subcontract, inbound freight handling, remove bottlenecks, introduce self-managed work teams and devise improved forecasting techniques.

The strategic, tactical and operational level decision-making processes should all be influenced by the search for supply chain optimisation. Strategies also lead to structures, as described in Chapter 4.

3.10 Procurement positioning within supply chain management

There is little clarity on the positioning of procurement within supply chain management. There is no clarity on 'functional' activities. What is Materials Management, Logistics, Purchasing, Procurement, Inventory Management or Supply Chain Management? The fact is they, each, are what an organisation wants them to be!

Regardless of the 'activity title' a business, at the highest level, needs to determine how all third-party expenditure and the related business consequences, will be effectively managed. To this end, procurement must engage, as a minimum in:

- supply market research
- managing contractual risk
- negotiating product and service delivery KPIs
- managing working capital invested in inventory
- managing environmental issues
- auditing the effectiveness of the supply chain components
- handling supplier performance default
- managing continuous improvement on supply chain inputs
- quality management of purchased goods and services
- supply chain relationship management.

3.10.1 Rationalisation roles

These roles are 'all the numerous day-to-day activities performed to decrease costs successively' and are of three types.

- Discovering what needs to be purchased and where:
  - determining specifications for purchased goods and services in association with design, production, transportation and other supply chain functions
  - providing critical information to strategic managers on materials, prices, availability and supplier issues
  - selecting and rationalising the number of first-tier suppliers
  - advising on make-or-buy decisions, outsourcing, leasing and similar strategies
  - ensuring that suppliers meet performance expectations with regard to price, quality and delivery
  - evaluating the benefits and dangers of global sourcing
  - forging relationships and long-term partnerships with key suppliers
  - endeavouring to obtain maximum possible value from all suppliers by implementing value management, analysis and engineering.

- Rationalisation of logistics:
  - locating suppliers so that the least possible interruption is likely to occur to JIT and similar delivery arrangements
  - negotiating the best possible contracts and arrangements for transportation and distribution
  - undertaking responsibility for reverse logistics and the disposal of scrap and surplus by environmentally acceptable means
  - providing suppliers with accurate forecasts of requirements and facilitating such approaches as JIT and MRP.

- Rationalisation of procurement routines, procedures and policies:
  - involvement in the selection of appropriate supply chain packages and the reduction of procurement costs via e-procurement
  - involvement in the design of all procurement and supply chain structures
  - ensuring that staff receive appropriate training in general management, SCM and special aspects of procurement
  - monitoring the ethical aspects of procurement
  - measuring all aspects of supply chain and procurement performance.

3.10.2 Development roles

These involve coordinating the internal R&D activities of the purchaser with those of suppliers. Research by McGinnis and Vallopra[26] has shown that early supplier involvement in new product development contributes to competitive advantage in the areas of new products, time-to-market, achieving high quality, cost advantages, sales and profits. Supplier involvement is more likely in the design of manufactured than non-manufactured products, though it can apply to both. In general, enterprises that focus on upstream product specification and design activities where they can best use their resources will want to outsource downstream activities where they are not cost-effective or less competent than specialised suppliers, such as component manufacture, so that suppliers will have greater roles to play in these areas. Important procurement roles in supplier involvement in product development include participation in cross-functional product development teams, the identification of suppliers capable of contributing and supplier development and monitoring.

Discussion questions

3.1   Why is logistics so important to an international airline?

3.2   Comment on how logistics impacts upon:
    (a) a retail organisation selling from a catalogue
    (b) a cruise line operator
    (c) a construction company with projects in Europe and the Middle East.

3.3   A trade-off is where an increased cost in one area is more than offset by a cost reduction in another, so that the whole system benefits. Within the concept of logistics, where may the conflicts occur when the procurement department wants to purchase in bulk to obtain aggregated discounts and rebates? Consider in your answer the role of procurement, finance, warehousing and transport.

3.4   The environmental aspects of waste management and disposal have a very high profile in many countries. If you consider the next decade, what initiatives can be taken by procurement to stimulate more reverse logistics activities?

3.5   Map out a supply chain for a Formula 1 racing team.

3.6   A manufacturing company has a strategic raw material supplied from the only source in the world. That source is located in a country that is subjected to the harshest environment for four months of each year. This is ice and snow that makes internal transport impossible during that time. How would you identify the risks created by this phenomenon and what other related risks arise?

3.7   What, if any, are the differences between a supply chain and a 'pipeline'? If there are differences, are there problems that could occur with pipelines and not supply chains and vice versa?

3.8   Taking an example of a key purchase in your organisation, draw a process map of the supply chain, estimating what each process adds in cost and time.

3.9   A manufacturer of high energy generation equipment has decided to cease production and exit the market for this equipment. What, in your opinion are the top four supply chain implications and impact?

3.10 If you were asked to take a procurement initiative to incentivise suppliers to reduce your inventory, shorten supply cycles and reduce purchase costs, what factors would you include for:

(a) those things that could be improved within your organisation?

(b) those things that could be improved by the suppliers?

3.11 What are the business implications of high-quality supply chain relationships? Can these relationships be measured and if so, how?

References

[1] NATO, *Logistics Handbook*, 1997, paras 103–4.

[2] cscmp.org.

[3] Council of Logistics Management Professionals USA, 12 February 1998.

[4] Australian Defence Logistics. The need to enable and equip Logistics Transformation. Kokoda Paper No. 19, June 2014. Waters & BlackburnKokoda.

[5] DHL Supply Chain Ltd v Secretary of State for Health and Social Care [2018] EWHC 2213 (TCC).

[6] Rogers, D. S. and Tibben-Lemke, R., *Going Backwards: Reverse Logistics Trends and Practices*, Reverse Logistics Executive Council, Pittsburgh, USA.

[7] As 6 above.

[8] Atken, J., quoted in Christopher, M., *Logistics and Supply Chain Management*, 2nd edn, Pearson Education, Harlow, UK, 1998, p. 19.

[9] Cooper, M. C., Lambert, D. M. and Pugh, J. D., 'Supply Chain Management – more than a new name for logistics', *International Journal of Logistics Management*, Vol. 8, No. 1, 1997, pp. 1–4.

[10] Porter, M. E., *Competitive Advantage*, Free Press, New York, USA, 1985, p. 3.

[11] Christopher, M., as 8 above, p. 266.

[12] Mentzer, J.T., De-Witt, W., Keebler, J.S., Soonhong, M., Nix, N. W., Smith, C.D., and Zacharia, Z.G., 'Defining supply chain management', *Journal of Business Logistics*, Vol. 22, No. 2, 2001.

[13] Marien, E. J., 'The four supply chain enablers', *Supply Chain Management Review*, Vol. 4, No. 1, March/April 2000.

[14] Chee Yew Wong, Skipworth, H., Godsell, J. and Achimugu, N., 'Towards a theory of supply chain alignment enablers: a systematic literature review', *Supply Chain Management*, Vol 17, Issue 4, pp 419–437, 2012.

[15] Cranfield University School of Management, 'Supply chain vulnerability', Final Report, 2002, pp. 35–7.

[16] Hines, P., 'Integrated materials management: the value chain redefined', *International Journal of Logistics Management*, Vol. 4, No. 1, 1993, pp. 13–22.

[17] As 10 above, pp. 62–118.

[18] As 10 above, pp. 119–63.

[19] As 10 above, pp. 118 and 162–3.

[20] Cudahy, G., 'The impact of pricing on supply chains' in Gattorna, J. L. (ed.) *Gower Handbook of Supply Chain Management*, 5th edn, 2003, Gower, UK, pp. 62–75.

[21] Wilding, R., 'Supply chain optimisation: using the three "Ts" to enhance value and reduce costs', *IFAMM Global Briefing*, 2004, pp. 18–19.

22 Beesley, A. T., 'Time compression: new source of competitiveness in the supply chain', *Logistics Focus*, June, 1995, pp. 24–5.

23 Davis, T., 'Effective supply chain management', *Sloan Management Review*, summer, 1993, pp. 35–45.

24 www.gartner.com.

25 As 25 above.

26 McGinnis, M. A. and Vallopra, R. H., 'Purchasing and supplier involvement' in *New Product Development and Production/Operations Process Development and Improvement Center for Advanced Purchasing Studies*, University of Alabama, 1998.

Chapter 4

Organisational and supply chain structures

Learning outcomes

With reference, where applicable, to supply and value chain, this chapter aims to provide an understanding of:

- organisational structure
- new type organisations
- the organisation of the future
- factors in configuration
- lean organisations
- agile organisations and production
- supply and value chain mapping
- types of change
- centralised procurement
- decentralised procurement
- cross-functional procurement.

Key ideas

- Specialisation and outsourcing.
- Age, technical systems, power and the environment as determinants of structure.
- The reasons for and characteristics of new type structures.
- Network structures: basic concepts, classifications, configurations and optimisation.
- Tiering: levels, reasons for tiering, responsibilities of first-tier suppliers and the consequences of tiering.
- Lean organisations and lean thinking, production, structures and the advantages and disadvantages of lean production.
- Agile organisations: the drivers, characteristics and enablers of agile manufacturing and the concepts of postponement and agility.
- Supply chain mapping: forms, purposes, methodology of supply chain mapping and value stream mapping tools.

Introduction

This chapter falls into two broad sections. The first provides a general introduction to organisational structures. The second is concerned with 'new type' structures, such as networks, lean and agile organisations and the implications for supply chains. Procurement organisations are dealt with in Chapter 5. It is very relevant to procurement specialists who need to understand the organisational structures and decision making at their strategic suppliers.

4.1 Organisational structures

Mintzberg[1] has defined organisational structure as:

> The sum total of the ways in which the enterprise divides its labour into distinct tasks and achieves coordination among them.

The primary role of organisational structure and controls are twofold: (1) to coordinate the activities of employees so that they work together most effectively to implement a strategy that increases competitive advantage and (2) to motivate employees and provide them with the incentives to achieve superior efficiency, quality, innovation or customer responsiveness.

Organisational structures do not exist as permanent business entities. Procurement exists in a context of continuous business change. This should be the driver for procurement strategies.

Kotter[2] remarks, the case for structural changes is that: 'An organisation with more delegation, which means a flat hierarchy, is a in far superior position to manoeuvre than one with a big, change-resistant lump in the middle.'

There are varied types of organisational structures, including:

Matrix: the reporting relationships are set up as a grid, or matrix, rather than in the traditional hierarchy. Employees have dual reporting relationships, generally to a functional manager and a product manager.

Project: designed to use teams of specialists from different functional areas in the organisation with a clear role of delivering a one-off project.

Divisional: designed, for example, to deal with a product or handle a geographic territory.

Line: a quite traditional form of structure with direct, vertical relationships between different levels in the organisation.

Committee: not uncommon in the public sector which is an association of people set up to arrive at solutions to common business problems. It is highly participative.

4.1.1 Specialisation

Traditionally, specialisation was the division of organisational activities into functions, occupations, jobs and tasks. By means of vertical integration, enterprises also aimed at self-sufficiency – both in the supply of materials and the in-house manufacture of products.

Stemming from the work of Prahalad and Hamel,[3] however, the present emphasis of specialisation relates to *core competences*, or competitive advantage, that satisfy three criteria:

- potential access to a wide variety of markets
- significant contribution to the perceived benefit of the end product(s)
- ideally, a core competence should be difficult for a competitor to imitate.

Core competences arise from the integration of specialist technologies and the coordination of diverse production skills. They result in core products. Examples of enterprises and their core products are:

- Rolls-Royce aircraft engines
- Samsung shipbuilding
- De Beers diamonds.

Such core products can be stand-alone or used to generate a variety of end products.

Many public and private sector organisations have outsourced care competences. This may be one core competence; information technology (IT) being a case in point. It may be a number of core competencies. In the case of public sector organisations it may include IT, HR, Revenues & Benefits, Care Services and Procurement.

The organisational consequences may include:

- difficult and complex communication channels
- senior management transferred to outsourcer under Transfer of Undertakings (Protection of Employment) Regulations (TUPE) failing to understand HR implications
- uncertainty of who is accountable for contract performance
- sharing/isolation of assets
- setting priorities for service reviews involving cross-over services, e.g. finance.

4.1.2 Coordination

Traditionally, coordination is an aspect of organisational theory related to ensuring that people and resources grouped into discrete functions worked together to accomplish organisational goals. The hierarchy of authority was itself a powerful coordinating influence.

Today, coordination is synonymous with *integration*. Essentially, integration is conflict resolution. On the assumption that separate organisational elements and interests will inevitably conflict over scarce resources, objectives, status and similar factors, there must be integrating mechanisms to ensure unity of effort. Where such integration is not achieved, the result will be waste, conflict and low productivity, or *sub-optimisation*. Integration can be both intra-organisational and inter-organisational.

Intra-organisational integration

Figure 4.1 indicates a continuum of intra-organisational mechanisms to enhance communication and integration between the parts of an organisation, or, in the present context, supply chain elements. A matrix organisational structure is shown in Figure 4.2.

Figure 4.1 A continuum of intra-organisational mechanisms

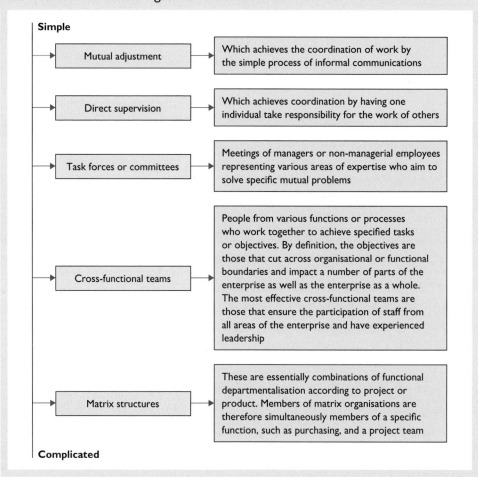

Grinnel and Apple[4] state that matrix structures should be considered only for the following situations:

■ when complicated, low-volume production runs are the principal outputs of an organisation, such as aerospace construction products

■ when a complicated product design calls for both innovation and timely completion.

Matrix structures are generally applicable when the following factors obtain:

■ high uncertainty

■ complicated technology

■ medium/long project duration

■ medium/long internal dependence

■ high differentiation.

Most of the disadvantages of matrix structures derive from the dual or multiple relationships that may lead to conflicts between resources and business managers and confusion

Figure 4.2 A matrix organisational structure

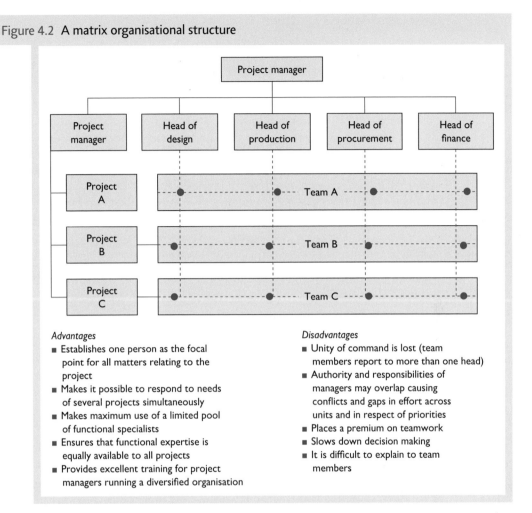

Advantages
- Establishes one person as the focal point for all matters relating to the project
- Makes it possible to respond to needs of several projects simultaneously
- Makes maximum use of a limited pool of functional specialists
- Ensures that functional expertise is equally available to all projects
- Provides excellent training for project managers running a diversified organisation

Disadvantages
- Unity of command is lost (team members report to more than one head)
- Authority and responsibilities of managers may overlap causing conflicts and gaps in effort across units and in respect of priorities
- Places a premium on teamwork
- Slows down decision making
- It is difficult to explain to team members

about where authority lies. More positively, the horizontal communication linkages of matrix organisations encourage integration and teamwork. Horizontal structures and cross-functional management structures are referred to in Chapter 5.

Integration also involves *formalisation*, or the extent to which work behaviour is constrained by rules, regulations, policies and procedures. Formalisation is greatest when the individual discretion given to employees is low. The extent to which an organisation is formalised indicates how top decision makers view their subordinates. Douglas McGregor[5] proposed two contrasting sets of managerial assumptions about the work attitudes and behaviour of their subordinates, which he termed Theory X and Theory Y.

Theory X assumes that the average worker is lazy, dislikes work, will do as little as possible, lacks ambition and seeks to avoid responsibility. Managers therefore maximise their control over worker behaviour.

Theory Y assumes that the work setting determines whether workers consider work to be a source of satisfaction or a chore. Where work is a source of satisfaction, close control of worker behaviour is unnecessary as employees will exercise self-control and be committed to organisational goals.

Inter-organisational structures

No business is an island. Every organisation has relationships as customers, suppliers or as collaborators in innovation with many other organisations. Mechanisms must therefore be developed to resolve possible interorganisational conflicts arising from factors such as loss of control and influence, increased uncertainty, consensus problems and standardisation issues.

By far the most important influence in both intra- and inter-organisational integration is IT. Prior to IT, it was important that organisational structures should, for reasons of coordination or integration, be in physical proximity. With IT, grouping tasks, functions or people in close physical proximity is unnecessary. With e-mail, video conferencing and to a lesser degree fax machines, it is possible to establish and integrate links within and across all organisational boundaries. Software applications such as MRP, MRPII, ERP, ECR and VMI are all approaches to the integration of resources and relationships.

4.1.3 Control

Control is a third aspect of organisational structure. A control system requires two essential elements:

- a power base
- a control mechanism, which may be of one of the following generic types:
  - *Centralisation* – decision making is either carried out by a centralised authority or requires the approval of the centralised authority before it is implemented.
  - *Formalisation* – as stated under the heading 'Intra-organisational integration' in section 4.1.2 above, this relates to regulations, policies, rules and procedures that provide guidelines, objectives or goals.
  - *Output control* – determining objectives or goals that provide the criteria for decision making.
  - *Cultural control* – the shared values and norms that guide decision making. It is often suggested that where culture is strong, strong structures are unnecessary. Cultural control is often exercised via informal structures. Informal organisation covers not only the friendships and animosities of people who work together but also their shared traditions and values that guide their behaviour sometimes to achieve and sometimes to block organisational goals. In practice, the relationship of the informal to the formal organisation determines how effectively the latter will function. No manager can succeed without understanding the informal structures that operate within a particular work setting.

4.1.4 The determinants of structure

What is known as the contingent approach emphasises that there is no one ideal structure. Mintzberg[6] has identified four contingency or 'situational' factors, which are age and size, technical systems, power and the environment.

Age and size

Mintzberg states that the older and larger an organisation, the more standardised will be its behaviour, policies and procedures. Because of these factors, changes are more difficult to implement in older, larger organisations.

Technical systems

Mintzberg suggests that the more a technical system controls the workforce, the more standardised will be the operating system and bureaucratic the organisational structure. Conversely, information and computer technologies may transform a bureaucratic to a flexible structure and lead to changes in the nature of managerial work, job design and working practices.

Power

Power may be defined as the capacity of an individual or group to influence decisions or effect organisational outcomes. Five sources of power are identified by French and Raven[7] under the classifications shown in Figure 4.3.

- *Reward power* is based on individual or group perceptions that another individual or group has the ability to provide varying amounts and types of rewards.
- *Legitimate power* is based on the values held by an individual or the formation of particular values as a result of socialisation. It exists when an individual or group accepts that it is legitimate for another individual or group to influence their actions.
- *Coercive power* is based on individual or group perceptions that another individual or group has the ability to administer penalties.
- *Expert power* is based on individual or group perceptions that another person or group has greater knowledge or expertise than them and is thus worth following.
- *Referent power* is based on the desire of an individual or group to identify with or be like another person or group.

There are significant differences between organisational and personal power. Organisational power is conferred and dependent on the position of the individual or group in the organisational hierarchy. Personal power is inherent and dependent on the personal characteristics of the holder. Personal power is therefore less removable from the holder than organisational power.

The strategic positioning and 'power' of procurement within an organisation stems from the quality of leadership and support team. They have to earn the respect of others in the organisation by offering high quality challenges, innovation, problem solving and solutions to contractual disputes that arise from time to time.

Other research[8] has shown that, in relation to departments or operations, those who are most powerful in an organisation control important resources, have to cope effectively with uncertainty and have scarce expertise. This research implies that the most

Figure 4.3 **The sources of power**

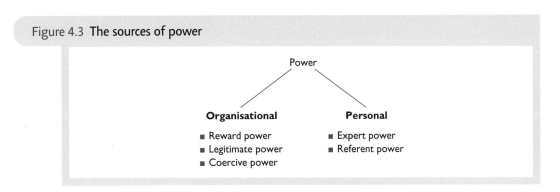

powerful departments or operations are those concerned with uncertainty, such as marketing in highly competitive industries and procurement where materials form a high proportion of the total product or service cost, particularly where the prices of the materials are unstable and where there are extreme vagaries in supply.

The environment

The importance of environmental scanning to the formulation of strategies was discussed in Chapter 2. Environments are both general and specific. Both these aspects must be considered in relation to organisational structures and decision making.

The general environment comprises political, economic, social, technological, environmental and legal conditions (PESTEL) within which all organisations operate at a given time. The specific environment consists of the people, groups and organisations with whom a particular enterprise must interact. These include clients, customers, regulators, resource suppliers, trade unions and numerous others.

Both general and specific environments have specific significance for organisations that operate internationally.

Mintzberg[9] states that environments can range from:

- *stable to dynamic* – in stable environments, more mechanistic structures will apply; the more dynamic the environment, the more organic will be the structure
- *simple to complicated* – the more complicated the environment, the more decentralised the organisational structure, and vice versa
- *integrated to diverse* – the more diversified the organisation's markets, the greater the propensity for it to split into market-based units (these give favourable economies of scale)
- *munificent (liberal and friendly) to hostile* – an extremely hostile environment will drive an organisation to centralise its structure, at least temporarily.

Strategy and structure

Mintzberg's analysis emphasises that different environments lead to different strategies. Different strategies require different structures. Thus, as Chandler[10] concluded after a study of almost 100 large American companies, changes in corporate strategy precede and lead to changes in organisational structure – that is, structure follows strategy. This environment–strategy–structure link is shown in Figure 4.4.

Later writers,[11] however, suggest that Chandler's strategy–structure relationship is too simplistic, that structure may constrain strategy and, once an organisation has been locked into a particular environment–strategy–structure relationship, it may have difficulty pursuing activities outside its normal scope of operations. Often an organisation cannot change strategy until it implements changes in structure.

Figure 4.4 The environment–strategy–structure link

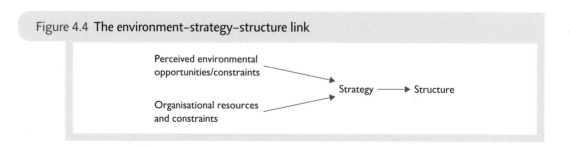

4.1.5 McKinsey's 7S Framework

McKinsey, as quoted by Waterman,[12] also regarded Chandler's strategy–structure model as inadequate and identified seven interrelated factors that organisations wishing to become more customer-orientated need to address. These factors are shown in Figure 4.5.

Figure 4.5 shows that shared values are at the core of the organisation. While formal structure is important, the critical issue is not how activities are divided up but, rather, the ability to focus on those dimensions that are important to organisational development. From a procurement standpoint, these seven dimensions are the following.

■ *Shared values* – the importance of procurement sharing in the corporate culture or 'ways in which things are done around here'. The recognition by the organisation and procurement that procurement is a contributor to the achievement of organisational objectives. Relating all procurement activities to the ethical and environmental policies of the organisation is vital.

■ *Structure* – the breaking down of functional barriers based on specialisation and the integration of procurement into logistics and supply chain processes in a seamless manner.

■ *Skills* – the development of staff knowledge and competences relative to procurement and the sharing of such knowledge and competence with both internal and external suppliers.

■ *Strategy* – in what ways can procurement contribute to the achievement of marketing, alliance, growth, diversification, outsourcing and similar strategies?

■ *Style* – the building of supplier goodwill and cooperation by creating good supplier relationships based on trust, courtesy, information sharing and adherence to ethical principles.

Figure 4.5 McKinsey's 7S model

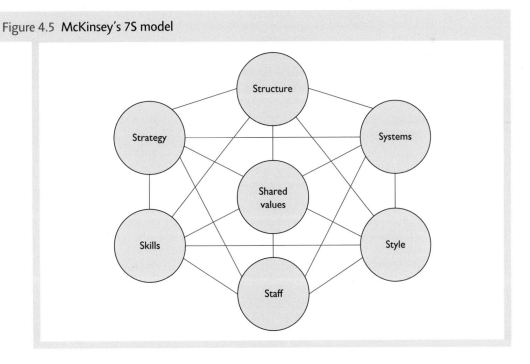

- *Staff* – securing the right mix of procurement and support staff to ensure that procurement contributes to competitive advantages, training and rewarding staff.
- *Systems* – the development of procedures, information flows and the facilitation of e-procurement.

4.2 New type organisations

Traditional bureaucratic structures characterised by vertical 'silos', departmentalisation of functions, rigid hierarchies and 'red tape' have, largely, become dysfunctional because they were too rigid, slow and insufficiently innovative to meet the challenges of international competition, customer procurement initiatives, consumer choice and pressure on input costs.

Quinn[13] identified five factors that have influenced the reform of traditional hierarchical organisations.

1 The pursuit of 'right-sizing' and 'horizontal' organisations, resulting in the reduction of management layers and flat structures.
2 Concurrent actions, including the re-engineering of business processes, followed by organisational redesign and the greater use of multifunctional teams.
3 The need for precision, speed and flexibility in the execution of programmes and strategies.
4 The development of powerful information systems and automated knowledge capture, with the resultant empowerment of employees in the management of business processes.
5 The focus on customer satisfaction and retention by means of enhanced organisational responsiveness.

In procurement, a key factor is the transition from being a purely transactional activity to a key contributor to organisational competitiveness and performance in which the emphasis is on managing the supply chain to meet cost and performance challenges. The above factors are increasingly leading to the adoption of procurement and supply chain networks and the adoption of lean and agile philosophies.

4.3 The organisation of the future

Bersin, McDowell, Rahnema and Durme[14] highlight important factors and considerations in a thought-provoking report.

> HIGH-PERFORMING organizations operate as empowered networks, coordinated through culture, information systems, and talent mobility. Companies are focused on redesigning the organization itself, with nearly half actively studying and developing new models. And many organizations are not only designing but also building this new organization. As networks and ecosystems replace organizational hierarchies, the traditional question 'For whom do you work?' has been replaced by 'With whom do you work?'

As organisations become more digital, they face a growing imperative to redesign themselves to move faster, adapt more quickly, facilitate rapid learning, and embrace the dynamic career demands of their people. This year, leading organisations are moving past the design phase and actively building this new organisation. Still, many business leaders seem to have little confidence they will get the process right.

This concern is warranted. Organisational design and change are complex. Many organisational redesigns fail because they are reduced to an exercise to cut costs. Others face resistance from company leadership. In fact, many consulting firms anecdotally report that up to 70 per cent of reorganisations fall short because of 'creative disobedience' from the executive team.

In the past, most organisations were designed for efficiency and effectiveness, leading to complicated and siloed organisations. The resulting business models, which were based on predictable commercial patterns, are unsuited to an era of unpredictability and disruption. Instead of mere efficiency, successful organisations must be designed for speed, agility, and adaptability to enable them to compete and win in today's global business environment.

Top companies are built around systems that encourage teams and individuals to meet each other, share information transparently, and move from team to team depending on the issue to be addressed. Different networks can have different specialties, such as innovation or getting to market quickly, but the principle is the same.

For a company to stay agile, teams must be formed and disbanded quickly. High-performing companies today may build a 'digital customer experience' group, select individuals for the team, and ask them to design and build a new product or service in a year or two. Afterward, the team disperses as team members move on to new projects. This ability to move between teams without risk is a critical attribute of today's high-performing companies.

Many new tools and techniques offer valuable contributions to building the organisation of the future.

One promising technique is organisational network analysis (ONA), which uses specialised software and methodologies to help companies study 'who is talking to whom.' This type of analysis, which can use patterns in emails, instant messages, physical proximity, and other data, allows leaders to see quickly what networks are in place and identify the connectors and experts.

The above extracts from the report indicate the informed logic and practicality of the Deloitte report. The author strongly recommends the report as an excellent basis for debate and informing business decisions.

4.3.1 Network structures

A network structure is a series of strategic alliances that an organisation forms with suppliers, manufacturers and distributors to produce and market a product. Such structures enable an enterprise to bring resources together on a long-term basis, reduce costs and enhance quality without the high expenditure involved in investing in specialised resources, including research and design, and dedicated technology or the employment of an army of managers and operatives. It follows that:

■ a network, as Ford et al.[15] point out, is 'not a world of individual and isolated transactions. It is the result of complex interactions within and between companies in relationships over time', so, as Ford et al.[16] state elsewhere, 'the time dimension of a relationship requires managers to shift their emphasis away from each discrete purchase or sale towards tracking how things unfold in the relationship over time and changing these when appropriate'

- network structures allow organisations to bring resources (especially expertise), together on a long-term basis to reduce costs, which is why enterprises in Europe and the USA are increasingly turning to global networking as a means of gaining access to low-cost overseas inputs

- networks relate to all aspects of the supply chain, including marketing and distribution, but this book is primarily concerned with networking with suppliers.

4.3.2 Network basics

The typical supply chain network is shown in Figure 4.6.

The nodes represent the business or 'actors', such as suppliers, producers, customers and service providers. The links between the nodes represent relationships. Relationships between actors are like bridges as they give one actor access to the resources and competences of another. Harland[17] points out that some researchers use the term 'network' to describe a network of actors, while others use it to discuss a network of processes or activities. The study of networks can therefore be related to networks of actors (organisations or individuals), activities (or processes) and resources. When discussing networks, it is essential to specify whether or not networks of actors or networks of activities are being considered.

Further aspects of network structure are considered in section 4.4 below.

4.3.3 Network classifications

Typical of numerous classifications of networks are those of Snow et al.,[18] Lamming et al.,[19] Harland et al.[20] and Craven et al.[21]

Internal network firms own most or all of the assets associated with the business and endeavour to capture entrepreneurial and market benefits without engaging in much outsourcing.

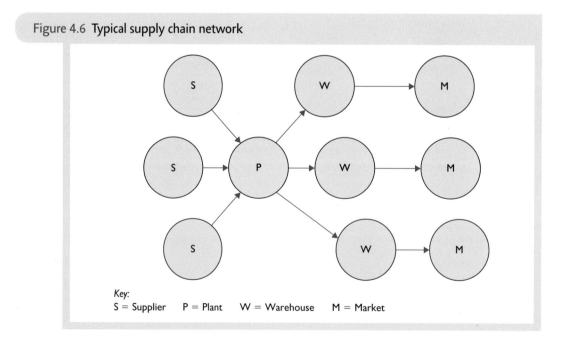

Figure 4.6 **Typical supply chain network**

Key:
S = Supplier   P = Plant   W = Warehouse   M = Market

In *stable networks*, assets are owned by several firms but dedicated to a particular business. As shown, the suppliers nestle round a large core enterprise, either providing supplies or distributing its products.

With *dynamic networks*, there is extensive outsourcing. The lead firm identifies and assembles assets owned wholly or largely by other enterprises on whose core skills it relies. Examples of such core skills cited by Snow *et al.* are manufacturing, such as Motorola, research and development, such as Reebok, or design and assembly, such as Dell Computing. In dynamic organisations, key managers create and assemble resources controlled by outside resources and can therefore be thought of as brokers. Some enterprises rely purely on brokering and are therefore virtual organisations. In virtual organisations an enterprise designs and markets a product but outsources manufacturing to specialist providers and possibly distributors. Some advantages and disadvantages of dynamic networks are shown in Table 4.1.

Lamming *et al.*,[22] building on earlier work by Fisher,[23] suggest two distinctive types of supply networks relating, respectively, to products that are 'innovative-unique' (such as drugs, communications technology and electronics) and 'functional' (such as canned soft drinks, brake cylinders and car window wipers).

Harland *et al.*[24] provide a taxonomy of supplier networks based on two dimensions, which are, first, whether the supply network operates under dynamic or stabilised (routinised) conditions and, second, whether the influence of the focal firm over other supply chain actors, such as customers and suppliers, is high or low.

Craven *et al.*[25] proposed two dimensions for the classification of network organisations: the volatility of environmental changes and the type of relationship between network members, whether it is collaborative or transactional.

Highly volatile situations require that enterprises should have:

■ flexible internal structures capable of rapid adjustment to new environmental conditions
■ flexible external relationships that allow for alteration or termination in a relatively short time period.

Table 4.1 **Some advantages and disadvantages of dynamic networks**

Advantages	Disadvantages
Networks allow organisations to specialise in what they do best and, thus, develop distinctive competences	Network structures have less control over operations. Even slight misunderstandings can result in product misspecifications
Networks can display the technical specialisation of functional structures, the market responsiveness of divisions and the balanced orientation of matrix structures	Network organisations are vulnerable to competition from their manufacturing contractors
Synergy – that is, the whole is greater than the sum of its parts – results from the cooperation of the network partners	If a network partner fails or goes out of business, the entire network can break down. It is difficult to guard innovations developed, designed and manufactured by network partners.
	Dynamic organisations lose their organic advantage when they become legalistic, secretive and too binding on the other partners

Network relationships may range from highly collaborative to largely transactional links. *Transactional linkages* imply discrete exchanges of values where a major issue is price, typified in the economics model of buyer–seller relationships. Transactional links are most likely to occur between parties that do not require collaboration.

Collaborative links may involve:

■ various forms of inter-organisational cooperation and partnering, including the development of formal alliances and joint ventures

■ considerate interactions between organisations to achieve common objectives

■ continuing relationships between the parties that, when they are long-term ones, are likely to involve strategic alliances as a networking method.

4.3.4 Network configuration and optimisation

Configuration

Deciding the configuration of the network – the number, location, capacity and technology of suppliers, manufacturing plants, warehouses and distribution channels – is important for the following reasons:

■ the strategic configuration of the supply chain influences tactical decisions relating to the aggregate quantities and material flows relating to the procurement, processing and distribution of products

■ the supply chain configuration involves the commitment of substantial capital resources, such as plant and machinery, for long time periods

■ factors such as changes in consumer demand and technology and global sourcing lead to changes in network configurations. There is, however, evidence that, configurations, once determined, are difficult to change.

Optimisation

The optimisation of supply chain networks is concerned with decisions relating to what constitutes the ideal number of operating facilities and their locations, as well as the amount of supplies to purchase, the quantity of outputs to manufacturing and the flow of such outputs through the network to minimise total costs.

Network optimisation models (NOM) aim to facilitate optimal materials sourcing, processing, activity and material and product flows throughout the supply chain, taking into account forecasts of future demand. They are a measure of the performance of all the key supply chain operating characteristics and provide indications of risks and returns under a variety of operating environments. A large number of commercial off-the-shelf (COTS) supply chain optimisation software packages are available that focus on both strategic and tactical issues.

Within the FMCG (fast-moving consumer goods) sector, companies such as Walmart, Tesco and Procter & Gamble utilise Collaborative Planning, Forecasting and Replenishment (CPFR[26]), which is a set of business processes that entities in a supply chain can use for collaboration on a number of retailer/manufacturer functions towards overall efficiency in the supply chain.

4.4 Factors in configurations

Network configurations are contingent and will vary widely among organisations. Lambert et al.[27] state that an explicit knowledge and understanding of how the network structure is configured is a key element of supply chain management and identify three primary elements: identification of the supply chain members, structural dimensions and the horizontal position of the focal enterprise.

- *Identification of the supply chain members* – that is, all the organisations with which the focal company interacts directly or indirectly via its suppliers or customers from the point of origin to the point of consumption. These may be divided into primary and supporting network members. The former are those who actually perform operational or managerial activities in the processes leading to the production of a final product. The latter are organisations that provide resources, knowledge, utilities or assets for the primary members of the network, such as those that lease machinery to a contractor or banks that lend money to a retailer.

- *The structural dimensions of the network* – these dimensions are the horizontal and vertical structures and the horizontal position of the focal company within the parameters of the supply chain. The *horizontal structure* is the number of tiers across the supply chain. Supply chains may be short with few tiers or long with many tiers. The *vertical structure* is the number of suppliers or customers represented within each tier. Thus, an enterprise can have a narrow or wide vertical structure with few or many suppliers or customers respectively.

- *Horizontal positioning* – this refers to the positioning of the focal organisation in the supply chain. An enterprise may be located at or near the initial source of the supply, at or near to the ultimate customer or at some intermediate supply chain position.

4.4.1 Tiering

Tiering levels

The automotive industry typically is used to explain Tier 1 and Tier 2 suppliers. Tier 1 suppliers supply parts or systems direct to an Original Equipment Manufacturer (OEM). Tier 2 suppliers manufacture parts that go into automotives, but do not sell directly to OEMs. The term Tier 3 suppliers refer to suppliers of raw, or close-to-raw, materials sent as plastics and metal.

Reasons for tiering

Lamming shows that tiers may form for three reasons:

1 Because the assembler may require first-tier suppliers to integrate diverse technologies not possessed by one organisation.
2 Components required for systems will be very specialised and, thus, made by a small number of (large) firms, in large quantities (such as electronic parts), so it is sensible for first-tier suppliers to buy these from specialist makers.
3 The third level of subcontracted work covers simple, low value-added items required by first-tier and second-tier suppliers, such as presswork, fasteners.

Responsibilities for tiering

First-tier suppliers are direct suppliers, usually making high-cost, complicated assemblies. They are empowered to relay the assembler's standards to second-tier or indirect suppliers and are responsible for large numbers of second-tier suppliers.

The responsibilities of first-tier suppliers as identified by Lamming include:

- research and development, especially relating to technologies that are being applied to the assembler's product for the first time
- management of second-tier and lower-tier suppliers, including integration previously undertaken by the assembly
- true just-in-time (JIT) supply
- customer-dedicated staff who work in association with the design and production departments of the assembler
- warranties and customer claims.

Some consequences of tiering

The key word at all levels of tiering levels is *collaboration* as much of the competitive advantage required for lean production (described below) derives from the ability to deal with sub-contractors as collaborators or partners.

Where tiering is carried out for either the first or second reasons stated above, the relationship between the two suppliers becomes more akin to a strategic joint venture than a procurement link. The product technology resides in both firms, so the first-tier supplier would find it just as difficult to replace the specialist second-tier supplier as vice versa. In this situation, the suppliers may even set up special companies to conduct business as joint ventures.

4.5 Lean organisations

4.5.1 Lean thinking

The core concept of lean thinking is the Japanese term *muda*, exemplified by the practices of Japanese motor manufacturers described by Womack *et al.*[28] in their book *Machines That Changed the World*. *Muda* means 'waste' or any human activity that absorbs resources but creates no value. Examples of *muda* are spoiled production, unnecessary processing steps, the purposeless movement or movements of employees and goods, time wasted in waiting for materials, uneconomic or unnecessary inventories and goods and services that fail to meet customers' requirements. Lean thinking is mean because it does more with less.

Teich and Faddoul[29] made a significant contribution to the understanding of lean thinking, explaining in some detail the approach of Toyota was used in the Healthcare sector. They comment: 'Lean is a multi-factored concept and requires organisations to exert effort along several dimensions simultaneously; some consider a successful implementation either achieving major strategic components of lean, implementing practices to support operational aspects, or providing evidence that the improvements are sustainable in the long term.'

Teich and Faddoul[30] then expound the main reasons for failures in companies to implement a lean culture. These are identified as, lack of senior commitment, lack of team autonomy, lack of organisational communications, organisational inertia and lack of interest in lean. The wasteful activities are shown as:

1 Overproduction – producing something in excess, earlier, or faster than the next process needs it.
2 Inventory – the cost of managing a large supply inventory may not be obvious at first glance; beside consumption follow-up and space required to store, there is a need to follow expiration dates and to constantly ensure that the items in the inventory are not technologically obsolete. It was already shown that the overall cost of smaller and more frequent shipments is lower than a large-volume purchase for which a discount was provided.
3 Motion – a lot of walking waste can arise from poor design of the working area.
4 Transportation – in healthcare this can be evident when moving patients, lab tests, information, etc.
5 Over-processing – there are times when material provided to the customers (patients) mandated by regulations can be confusing. For example, multiple insurance claim forms, including ones that are not bills, can confuse the unexperienced 'novice'.
6 Defects – there are many examples for these defects that can be related to poor labelling of tests, incomplete information in patients' charts or in instructions provided to referrals, etc.
7 Waiting—there is not much need to explain why waiting a few hours in line is a wasteful activity.
8 Under-utilising staff – under-use is not only time-dependent but also involves deeper levels such as not sharing knowledge or not taking advantage of someone's skills and creativity; under-use typically shows in hierarchical structures and not using teams.

Challenges towards lean implementation in healthcare are related to the concepts of value, metrics and evidence. Evidence shows that healthcare in the USA lacks efficiency, is not patient-centered, does not provide timely services, and is not equitable (the last two being related to many patients bring under-insured). Redesigning such a system around values such as patients being 'primary customers' emphasising clinical and services outcomes, using evidence-based tools, and adopting rigorous quality improvement methods may be a phenomenal challenge if it is improved at the macro or even the meso strategic levels.

Lean thinking can be applied in any organisational environment.

4.5.2 Lean production

Some aspects of lean production, such as the attempt to eliminate waste, the purchase of whole assemblies and tiering, have been referred to above. Other aspects of lean production, as identified by Womack *et al.*, include the following.

■ Target costing – for example, a car assembler establishes a target price for the vehicle, then the assembler and suppliers work backwards to ascertain how the car can be made for the price, while allowing a reasonable profit for both the assembler and suppliers. This differs from the traditional approach in which:

$$\text{Sales price} = \text{Cost} + \text{Profit}$$

The lean production approach is:

$$\text{Profit} = \text{Sales price} - \text{Cost}$$

- The use of value engineering, value analysis and learning curves to reduce initial and subsequent cost of suppliers.
- The use of cross-functional teams of highly skilled workers and highly flexible automated machines.
- A JIT pull system in which nothing is moved or produced until the previous process is completed.
- Zero defective parts. When a supplier fails to meet quality or reliability requirements, a cooperative effort is made to ascertain the cause. In the interim, part of the business is transferred to another supplier.
- Cooperation between the assembler and first-tier suppliers effected by supplier associations. They meet to share new findings on better ways to make parts. Some companies also have associations with their second-tier suppliers.
- After negotiations, the assembler and supplier agree on a cost-reduction curve over the four-year life of the product. Any supplier-derived cost savings beyond those agreed go to the supplier.
- Relationships between the assembler and suppliers are based on a 'basic contract' that expresses a long-term commitment to working together for mutual benefit. The contract also lays down rules relating to prices, quality assurance, ordering, delivery, proprietary rights and materials supply.

4.5.3 Lean production structures

Lean production, as Toni and Tonchia[31] point out, leads to a management by process organisation designed to link all the activities in order to achieve the unified objective of customer satisfaction in all its aspects.

The characteristics of a lean operation include:

- an orderly, clean workplace
- utilisation of standardised best practice methods
- plant layout designed to facilitate continuous product flow
- just-in-time processing driven by customer demand
- single piece or small batch continuous workflow
- quick changeovers of machines
- minimal inventories
- short order-to-ship cycle times
- total quality control
- defect prevention built into processes
- rigorous application of preventative maintenance
- team based continuous improvement
- partnerships relations with suppliers.

4.6 Agile organisations and production

Agile production is the latest stage of a development away from the mass production of the 1970s, through the decentralised production of the 1980s and on to the supply chain management and lean production of the 1990s.

4.6.1 Drivers of agility

The main drivers of agility include rapidly changing and unpredictable markets, the rapid rates of technological innovation, customers' requirements for customisation and choice, competitive priorities of responsiveness, shorter lifecycles, concern for the environment and international competitiveness. Goldman et al.[32] state that the four underlying components of agility are:

- delivering value to the customer
- being ready for change
- valuing human knowledge
- forming virtual partnerships.

4.6.2 Agile characteristics

Based on Goldman, Aitken et al.[33] have identified the core characteristics of agile manufacture shown in Table 4.2.

4.6.3 Postponement

Postponement and decoupling are important concepts of agility. By making customised product changes as close as possible to the time of purchase by the end-customer it is possible to provide a wide variety of customised products without incurring high inventory, processing and transportation costs. Suppose the manufacture and assembly of a product requires 40 steps. By proceeding as far as step 30 and then putting the partly completed product into inventory, the final 10 steps have been postponed.

The above is an example of *manufacturing postponement*, the object of which is to maintain flexibility by keeping products in a neutral or uncommitted state for as long as possible. Examples of manufacturing postponement are found in vehicle manufacturers when colours and non-standard components or additions are deferred until the receipt of specific instructions from the customer. In house building, the basic shell may be constructed, but kitchen and bathroom fitting and decorating will not proceed until the requirements of the individual customer have been ascertained.

There is also *geographic*, or *logistics*, *postponement*, which is the exact opposite. The basic notion of geographic postponement according to Bowersox et al.[34] is 'to build and stock a full line inventory at one or two strategic locations'. Forward deployment of inventory is postponed until customers' orders are received. An example is the keeping of critical spares at a service centre to ensure their rapid availability to customers. Once an order for spares is received, it is transmitted electronically to the central service centre, from where the required items are rapidly transported to the customer and replacements manufactured. The outcome is highly reliable customer service with low inventory.

Table 4.2 Comparison of lean and agile production systems

Factor	Lean production	Agile production
Primary purposes	Meeting predictable demand efficiently at the lowest possible cost. Elimination of waste from the supply chain	Rapid response to unpredictable demand to minimise stockouts, forced markdowns and obsolete inventory
Manufacturing focus	Maintenance of a high average utilisation unit	Deployment of excess buffer capability
Inventory strategy	High stock turnover and minimum inventory	Deployment of significant buffer stocks of parts to respond to demand
Lead time focus	Shortened lead time, providing it does not increase cost	Investing aggressively in resources that will reduce lead times
Approach to supplier selection	Selecting for cost and quality	Selecting primarily for speed, flexibility and quality
Supply linkages	Emphasis on long-term supply chain partnerships that are consolidated over time	Emphasis on virtual supply chains where partnerships are reconfigured according to new market opportunities
Performance measurement	Emphasis on world class measures based on such criteria as quality and productivity	Emphasis on customer-facing metrics, such as orders met on time, in full
Work organisation	Emphasis on work standardisation – doing it the same way every time	Emphasis on self-management and ability to respond immediately to new opportunities from all involved in work processes
Work planning and control	Emphasis on the protection of operation's core by a fixed period in the planning cycle to help balance resources, synchronise material movements and reduce waste	Emphasis on the need for immediate interpretation of customer demand and instantaneous response

Van Hoek[35] has identified the following advantages of postponement:

- inventory can be held at a generic level so that there will be fewer stock variants and, therefore, less total inventory
- because inventory is generic, its flexibility is greater – that is, the same components or modules can be embodied on a variety of end products
- forecasting is easier at the generic level than for finished products
- the ability to customise products locally means that a higher level of variety may be offered at a lower cost.

4.6.4 Decoupling

The decoupling point is defined by Christopher[36] as 'the point to which real demand penetrates upstream in a supply chain'. Decoupling is closely associated with postponement and the type of customer demand. Figure 4.7[37] shows how the positioning of the decoupling point changes with different supply chain structures.

The organisations downstream from the decoupling point are organised for agility and the ability to cope with variability in demand volume and high levels of product variety.

Figure 4.7 Family of supply chain structures

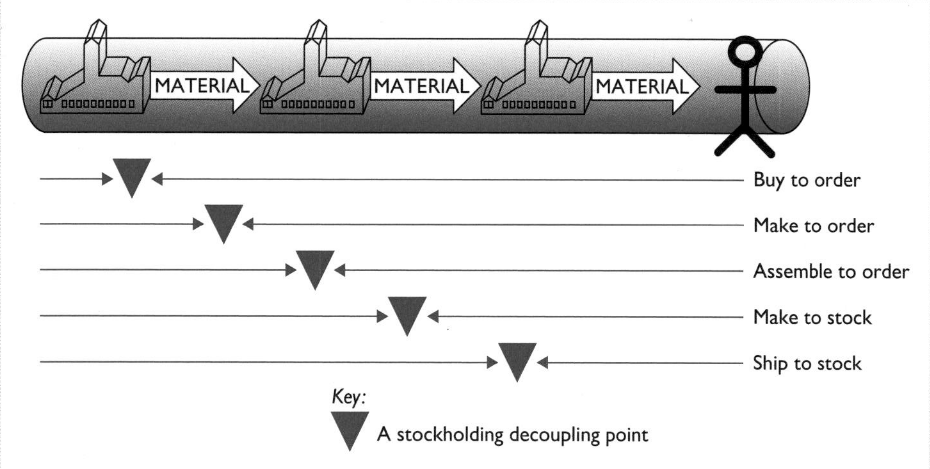

Source: Hoekstra and Romme, 1992

Upstream organisations work to a stable demand with relatively low variety and can therefore focus on lean, low-cost manufacture.

Christopher and Towill[38] point out that, in real-world supply chains, there are actually two decoupling points. The first relates to 'material' and is where strategic inventory is held in as generic a form as possible. Inventory should therefore lie as far downstream in the supply chain and as near to the final marketplace as possible. The second is the 'information' decoupling point. Ideally this should lie as far as possible upstream as, in effect, it is the furthest point to which information on real final demand penetrates.

4.7 Supply and value chain mapping

Introduction

The Supply Chain School[39] have defined a Vision and Definition of Supply Chain Mapping (SCM).

■ *Vision*: supply chain mapping is a consistent approach for identifying, managing and mitigating significant sustainability risks through an agreed mapping process for construction and facilities management (FM).

■ *Definition*: supply chain mapping is the visual representation of the sequence/system and location of activities, resources and organisations involved in providing goods or services to the end customer.

They have also provided a mapped supply chain for a garment product (see Figure 4.8)

A map is a visual representation of some actuality. Maps also enable us to comprehend and communicate information. Maps assist comprehension as a picture is 'worth a thousand words'. Maps also communicate specific and general information. Architects' plans and road maps communicate specific and general information respectively. A supply network diagram is a form of supply chain mapping.

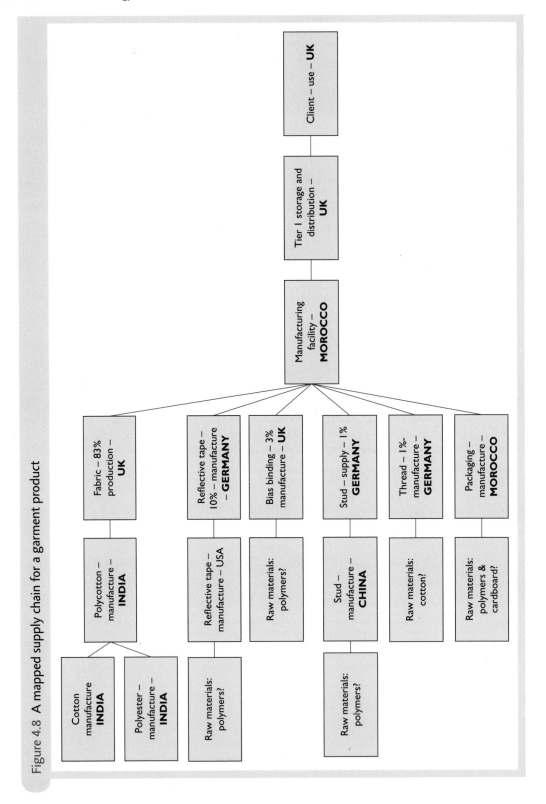

Figure 4.8 A mapped supply chain for a garment product

Table 4.3 **Distinguishing strategic supply chain and process mapping**

Characteristics	Supply chain mapping	Process mapping
Orientation	*External*: focuses on how goods, information and money flow upstream and downstream and through a firm	*Internal* (typically): focuses on a single operation or system with an enterprise
Level of detail	*Low to moderate*: emphasises high-level measures, such as volume, cost or lead time. Gives an overall perspective on how processes work together between enterprises. May exclude non-critical entities	*High*: breaks down a process into activities and steps. Every step includes information to characterise the system being mapped
Purpose	*Strategic*: mapping aims to create a supply chain conforming to a strategy or ensure that the current chain fulfils that strategy adequately	*Tactical*: process map originates from the recognition of a problem area and the need to improve operating efficiency. Goal is to make changes in current operations. Efforts normally limited to one process or function at a time

4.7.1 Forms of mapping

As supply and value chain mapping is undertaken for a specific purpose – normally for supply chain redesign or modification or the elimination or reduction of waste – the number of options for mapping to meet the needs of users is large. Gardner and Cooper[40] distinguish between strategic supply chain mapping and process mapping regarding three characteristics: orientation, level of detail and purpose. These distinctions are set out in Table 4.3.

4.7.2 The purpose of supply chain mapping

Gardner and Cooper[41] state that a well-executed strategic supply chain map can:

> . . . enhance the strategic planning process, case distribution of key information, facilitate supply chain redesign or modification, clarify channel dynamics, provide a common perspective, enhance communications, enable monitoring of supply chain strategy and provide a basis for supply chain analysis . . . Thus a map can be quite helpful in understanding a firm's supply chain, for evaluating the current supply chain and for contemplating realignment of a supply chain.

4.7.3 The Supply chain mapping: an example

A supply chain map is a time-based representation of the processes and activities that are involved as the materials or products move through the chain.

4.7.4 The methodology of mapping

A supply chain map[42] (see Figure 4.9 for an example) may be linked to or built directly from a database or built by hand. Gardner and Cooper state that 'the complexity of mapping is influenced by three supply chain map attributes: geometry, perspective and implementation issues'.

Figure 4.9 A supply chain map

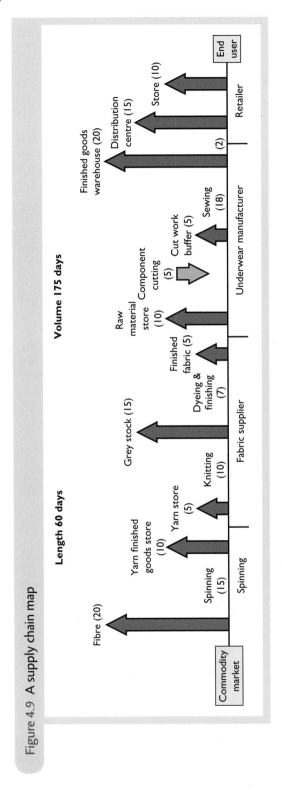

Geometry is concerned with such aspects as:

- the number of sequential business units performing transactions leading to the final consumer
- direction – whether it is supplier-orientated or customer-orientated or both
- length – the number of tiers up and down
- aggregation (width) – the degree of specificity within a tier, which may be high (one box per tier), medium (types of firms at each level identified) or low (some firms are named at each level)
- spatial – is the map geographically representative?

Perspective is concerned with issues relating to:

- the focal point – whether the maps takes a firm-centred or industry-centred view
- scope – whether the breadth of product coverage included in the map is strategic business unit (SBU)-wide or by product category, product or component
- whether or not the map includes key processes beyond logistics
- whether or not the map includes a complete set of key business processes
- whether or not the map includes reverse logistics and other feedback loops.

Implementation issues:

- whether the density of information integrated into the visual map is high or low
- whether or not the map is linked to an existing corporate or supply chain database
- how the completed map shall be made available – paper, electronically or on the Web?

4.7.5 Value stream mapping tools

Hines and Rich[43] distinguish between traditional supply or value chains and value streams. The former includes the complete activities of all the companies involved, while the latter refers only to the specific parts of the firms that actually add value to the product or service under consideration.

Hines and Rich identify seven mapping tools designed to reduce or eliminate seven forms of waste in a manufacturing organisation – overproduction, waiting, transportation, inappropriate processing, unnecessary inventory, unnecessary motion and defects. These take three forms, which are product (not identified by inspection and passed on to customers), service (not directly relating to products but to service, such as late delivery or incorrect documentation) and internal scrap (defects identified during inspection). The seven mapping tools are described in Table 4.4.

It is impractical in this book to give a detailed explanation of the implementation of the seven tools[44] so we will confine ourselves to the following observations.

- The process activity mapping tool provides an example of a typical mapping exercise directed at eliminating or reducing waste.
- The first step is the preparation of a *process map* – a detailed flow chart that indicates every activity involved in making or doing something. It is critical to include all activities – not only those that are obvious.

Once the process map has been developed, a value chart can be constructed that attaches a cost or value to every activity. This cost is obtained after considering factors

Table 4.4 Hines and Rich's seven value stream mapping tools

Mapping tools	Purpose and application
Process activity mapping	Reducing waste by eliminating unnecessary activities, simplifying other activities or changing process sequences
Supply chain response matrix	Reducing lead times and inventory amounts
Production variety funnel	Targeting inventory reduction and changes in the processing of products in companies with varying activity patterns
Quality filter mapping	Identifying, for the purpose of improvement, the location of product and service defects, internal scrap, and other problems, inefficiencies and wasted effort
Demand amplification mapping	Identifying demand changes along the supply chain within varying time buckets to manage or reduce fluctuations in regular, exceptional and promotional demand
Decision point analysis	Particularly applicable for regular, unvarying production of multiple identical items, as in a chemical plant. Involves identifying the point at which products stop being made in accordance with actual demand and start to be made against forecasts alone. Identifying this point indicates whether processes are aligned with push or pull philosophies
Physical structure	Overviewing a particular supply chain from an industry perspective. This information may result in a redesign along the lines indicated for process activity mapping

such as the machine or area used for the activity, distance moved, time taken and number of people employed.

Activities fall into four categories:

1 production or service time (value-added activity)
2 inspection time – performing quality control (non-value-added activity)
3 transfer time – movement of products or components (non-value-added activity)
4 idle time – storage time or time wasting during the production process (non-value-added activity).

The lead time for the process is therefore:

$$\text{Production time} + \text{Non-value-added time}$$

While in theory inspection and transfer time are regarded as non-value-added activities, they cannot, in practice, be completely eliminated.

The final stage involves using the process map and value chart to identify where savings can be made or value added.

4.8 Types of change

The author has identified ten types of external and internal change that affect organisations and which, in some way, will impact on procurement and supply change management. These types of change include external and internal factors as shown in Table 4.5.

Table 4.5 **Types of external and internal changes that affect organisations**

External changes	Internal changes
Political influences	New senior management
Financial market influences	Product rationalisation
Competitor actions	IT systems
Legislation	Organisation restructuring
Mergers & Acquisitions	People relationships
Supply chain costs	Outsourcing
Consumer spending	New product development
Product formulations impacted by health/safety scares	Devolution of procurement
Regulatory bodies	Supplier payment policy
New technology	Product end of life

4.8.1 Perspectives on organisational change

Changes can be considered from three perspectives – structural, cultural and individual.

Structural change

If structure follows strategy, then changes in strategy arising from any of the above drivers will be followed by structural changes. This can be exemplified by technological drivers, such as IT, and administrative or business drivers resulting in the decision to outsource.

IT, with its capability to communicate and share information, has caused traditional hierarchies to be replaced with horizontal structures. The need to physically locate people and units together to ensure coordination and supervision or to choose between centralised or decentralised structures is also increasingly invalidated by IT, with a consequent focus on projects and processes rather than standard procedures and tasks. IT can be substituted for layers of management and a number of managerial tasks. Lucas and Baroudi[45] give examples of how IT can create virtual organisations that do not exist in physical form. Mail-order companies, for example, employ individuals working from home using a special phone connected to an 0800 number to take orders from customers who have their catalogues. Manufacturers can use parts suppliers to substitute for their inventory. The supplier, linked electronically with the manufacturer, can use overnight delivery to ensure that the parts are delivered just-in-time for production. The manufacturer, thus, has a virtual parts inventory that is owned by the supplier until it arrives for production.

Cultural change

Organisational culture is a 'pattern of belief and expectations shared by organisational members'[46] or 'the way things are done around here'.[47]

129

Culture is an important aspect of change as culture might either block or facilitate it and also because changes in organisational strategies usually require changes in organisational structure. Thus, a change from transactional to partnership procurement will require a cultural reorientation on the part of the staff involved so that its suppliers are no longer regarded as adversaries to be kept at arm's length, but, instead, as allies. Developments such as total quality management (TQM) require the acceptance by all employees of a culture of continuous improvement in which people at all organisational levels accept responsibility for identifying quality problems early on. TQM also requires a culture of 'learning together', with guidance and support for the learning process being provided by management. With TQM it is also a management responsibility to develop a culture in which every employee is encouraged and empowered to take ownership of outputs, customer problems and improvement actions. Such changes in cultural outlook will usually require a significant investment in education and training and the use of an internal or external change agent responsible for ensuring that the planned change is properly implemented.

Individual change

People usually respond to change with hostility and apprehension due to numerous factors, including insecurity, lack of information regarding proposed changes, the break-up of work groups, perceived threats to expertise, status or earnings, inconvenience of new working conditions and changes in management and supervisory personnel.

Preparing for change

An evaluation by management of structural, cultural and individual issues is the essential first step in the implementation of change at both organisational and functional levels.

4.8.2 The implementation of change

Kurt Lewin,[48] a behavioural scientist, argues that the process of implementing change involves three basic steps:

1 *unfreezing* – enabling people or organisations to be willing to change
2 *changing* – selection of techniques to implement change
3 *refreezing* – reinforcing and supporting the change so that it becomes a relatively permanent part of organisational processes.

Lewin's view of the change process is shown in Figure 4.10.

Numerous writers have produced step-by-step guides for the implementation of change and the following extension of Lewin's approach by Kotter and Schlesinger[49] is typical. This model suggests an eight-step process for the successful implementation of change – the first four steps being directed at the defrosting of a hardened status quo (or culture), steps five and seven introduce new practices and the last step corresponds to Lewin's 'refreezing', which helps to make them stick. The eight steps are:

1 *establishing a sense of urgency* – recognising the need for the enterprise or a function within the enterprise to change if it is to achieve and retain competitive advantage or cope with crises and opportunities
2 *creating the guiding coalition* – creating and empowering a group to lead change and encouraging the group to work as a team

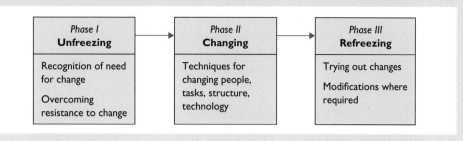

Figure 4.10 Lewin's view of the change process

3 *developing a vision and a strategy* – 'vision' in this context means having a clear sense of what the future requires and the strategies required to turn the vision into reality

4 *communicating the change vision* – using every available communication media to create an awareness of the visions and strategies to employees and others affected and secure their cooperation and involvement

5 *empowering broad-based action* – removing obstacles, changing structures or systems and encouraging new approaches

6 *generating short-term wins* – strategies usually involve some shorter-term goals as the achievement of these goals provides encouragement to sustain people in their efforts to attain longer-term objectives

7 *consolidating gains and producing more change* – reinvigorating the process with new projects, themes and change agents

8 *anchoring new approaches in the culture* – stabilising change at the new level and reinforcing it by means of such supporting mechanisms as policies, structure or norms.

Collins[50] criticises what he terms 'n-step' models of change implementation on three grounds:

■ they assume that organisations act in a rational predictable way, while the reality is that they consist of a diverse range of people with diverse ideas and opinions about the right course of action

■ n-step models assume that change management can be reduced to a number of discrete, sequential steps and that change has an identifiable beginning and end, while the reality is that it is uncertain, unpredictable and contingent and 'we cannot expect the processes and final outcomes of change to map out clearly before us'

■ n-step models fail to recognise that the creative and critical skills required by managers to successfully engender change cannot be captured in 'a few rules or simple recipes for success'.

Collins, therefore, concludes that, rather than offer simplistic n-step accounts, writers should recognise that their models need to incorporate some of the complexities of real life. N-step models are dishonest and paint an inaccurate and oversimplified picture of the change process.

Probably the best approach is to recognise the importance in all change situations of communicating the need for change, consultation with all affected by the change and commitment to the successful implementation of change by all involved. In any event, learning organisations do not suddenly adopt strategic change but, rather, are perpetually seeking it.

4.9 Centralised procurement

The Aberdeen Group Inc.[51] have produced the attributes of organisational models, see Table 4.6. They advocate the centre-led structure, postulating that this provides the best of both worlds. This is an opinion, not a proven fact. There are varied structures and the author has seen them all in practice.

Table 4.6 Attributes of organisation models

	Decentralised	Centre-led	Centralised
Organisation	■ Sourcing decisions and procurement activities executed at the business or local level ■ Spending rarely leveraged across sites or business units ■ Procurement reports to plant or business unit manager	■ Sourcing coordinated across business units ■ Spending leveraged across businesses and regions - especially for strategic categories ■ Procurement reports to senior supply chain or C - level exec	■ Sourcing decisions and procurement activities executed at central command and control centre ■ Spending leveraged centrally ■ Procurement reports to senior supply chain executive
Process	■ Limited or no process standardisation ■ Process efficiency and effectiveness varies greatly by business unit or site ■ Limited sharing of resources or best practices across sites	■ Standardised processes and policies tailored and executed at local level ■ Process compliance, efficiency, and effectiveness consistent across the enterprise ■ Resources and best practices shared across sites	■ Standardised processes and policies executed centrally ■ Process compliance, efficiency, and effectiveness vary by business or site ■ Resources and best practices controlled centrally
Knowledge	■ Skills and category expertise vary by business unit or site ■ Limited visibility into spending, compliance, and performance	■ Skills, category expertise coordinated across businesses and sites ■ Visibility into spending, compliance, and performance at aggregate and local levels	■ Skills and category expertise controlled centrally ■ Visibility into spending compliance, and performance at aggregate level ■ Limited understanding of these factors at local level
Technology	■ Technology decisions and usage vary by business unit or locale	■ Technology decisions and deployment coordinated across sites ■ Technology deployment and usage coordinated across sites	■ Technology decisions and deployment made at corporate level ■ Technology deployment and usage vary based on schedule and budget
Performance	■ Metrics used vary by business unit or locale ■ Cost and performance vary greatly across the enterprise	■ Standard metrics used enterprise-wide, but support for local variances ■ Metrics and incentives shared by procurement, functions and businesses ■ Cost, compliance, and performance consistent across the enterprise	■ Standard metrics used at corporate level ■ Metric compliance varies across the organisation ■ Cost, compliance, and performance vary across the enterprise

Arcelor Mittal[52] the world's leading integrated steel and mining company have a very informative website, including information on Global procurement. The 2017 annual report shows a turnover of $68.7 billion for year ended 31 December 2017. The global procurement team structure is shown in Table 4.7.

The logic and frustrations of centralising procurement are expounded in a UK Committee of Public Accounts[53] report.

> There is a tension between the government's drive to centralise procurement and its commitment to localism. The Cabinet Office has focused its efforts on central government, covering around £45 billion of goods and services in 2011–12. However, this is a small proportion of total procurement spending across the public sector. This is estimated to be around £200 billion when you include the wider public sector, covering bodies such as local authorities, schools, and NHS Trusts. The principles of localism inhibit the Cabinet Office's ability to force public bodies outside of central government control to buy goods and services through central contracts. This is especially important on ICT contracts as the localism agenda could inhibit Government ambitions like achieving a paperless NHS. The Cabinet Office and the Government Procurement Service need to ensure greater use of the central contracts in local bodies by providing robust data to demonstrate the benefits, and by improving their communication with the wider public sector.

> Departments are obliged to use GPS's centrally managed contracts but this is not enforced in practice, and departments are finding excuses not to participate. The Cabinet Office explained that it tried to build a coalition of interests and work with departments, because departments hold the budgets and are therefore ultimately responsible for their own spending decisions. The Ministry of Defence told us that it did not disagree with being obliged to use central contracts, but that there needs to be mutual accountability and responsibility attached to it.

Table 4.7 Global procurement team structure

Local	Regional	Global
One-time purchase (e.g. Capex)		
Infrastructure & sustaining Capex depending on value threshold		High-value equipment (production equipment, greenfield & brownfield projects)
Recurrent spend		
Ind. Services (waste treatment, fire protection, etc.)	Scrap and scrap substitutes	Iron One
Fuel	Rolls	Coal/Coke
	Coating and paints	Ocean freight
	Industrial services (water treatment, slag handling, maintenance)	Ferro alloys and Base metals
	Roads & rail logistics	Refractories
	MRO, consumables, Oils & greases	Energy
	Packaging	IT and professional services
	Inland water freight	Telecom
	Chemicals (glues, detergents . . .)	Travel, fleet management
	Stationery	
	Communications	
	Training	

4.9.1 Economies of scale – centralised procurement

Centralised procurement enables an organisation to leverage its purchasing power to the best effect as:

- forecasts can be prepared of the total quantities of items likely to be required by the whole organisation for a specified period
- such consolidation of quantities can form the basis for negotiating quantity discounts, rebates or learning curve reductions
- suppliers dealing with a centralised procurement department have an incentive to compete for 'preferred supplier status' or the whole or a substantial proportion of the undertaking's requirements
- suppliers may be able to reduce prices by spreading overheads over longer production runs
- the supplier base may be reduced by the award of 'preferred supplier status' to one or two providers
- centralisation permits the employment of procurement professionals in a way that is not possible with diversified procurement and who can become expert in the procurement of special classes of materials or products following market trends and the development of reliable and economic supply sources or of import and export procedures where there is substantial global sourcing.

4.10 Decentralised procurement

A SIGMA[54] report set out the key arguments in support of decentralised procurement as:

- reduced incentives for corruption via large-scale protectionism or favouritism
- a closer matching of goods and services delivered to the detailed requirements of end users
- reduced scope for mistakes affecting large volume purchases that result in unnecessary over-spending
- less bureaucracy because of shorter time frames and fewer forms for both purchasers and suppliers
- greater possibilities for SMEs to compete successfully for contracts
- opportunities for local purchasers to obtain lower prices for locally manufactured goods
- more scope for employees to take individual responsibility and develop a 'service' mentality.

Some of the advantages and disadvantages of decentralised procurement are shown in Table 4.8.

4.11 Cross-functional procurement

4.11.1 Definition

The Institute of Supply Management (USA)[55] states that cross-functional teams are:

> groups of individuals from various organisational functions who are brought together to achieve clear, worthwhile, and compelling goals that could not be reached without a team.

Table 4.8 Advantages and disadvantages of decentralised procurement

Advantages	Disadvantages
Closer to users and better understanding of local needs	Reduced leverage that exists with consolidation of purchases
Response time to divisional or plant needs may be rapid and of higher quality	Focus on local rather than corporate and operational rather than strategic considerations
Possibly closer relationships with suppliers	Procurement will tend to report to a lower organisational level
Local suppliers and consequent lower transportation costs	Limited expertise in requirements and few opportunities for cross-functional collaboration
Where plants are profit centres the view is expressed that if procurement costs are a high percentage of total costs then each profit centre should make its own decisions regarding procurement and suppliers	Possibly lack of standardisation Restricted career opportunities for local procurement staff Cost of procurement relatively high
Geographical, cultural, political, environmental, social, language and currency appropriateness	

Teaming leverages organisational resources while utilising the expertise of team members. Purchasers typically participate in teams dealing with sourcing, commodities, quality, and new product/service development.

4.11.2 Reasons for the formation of cross-functional teams

The involvement of procurement in multi-skilled teams drawn from several functions is attributable to at least six factors:

- the involvement of procurement in strategic procurement decisions
- the concept of the 'supply chain', which emphasises the need to deal with work flow in an integrated way by means of materials management and logistics approaches
- teams may make better use of the vastly increased information availability and ability to communicate effectively provided by IT and ICT
- the development of such approaches as ERP, MRP and JIT, together with single and partnership sourcing and outsourcing
- the recognition that, because of such developments as global procurement, more complicated price and cost analyses, the need to integrate procurement processes with those of manufacturing and the enhanced importance of quality, procurement often needs expert advice and support in decision making
- the recognition, based on research findings, that 'teams out-perform individuals acting alone or in large organisation groupings, especially when performance requires multi-skills judgments and experience.'[56]

4.11.3 The purpose and structure of cross-functional teams

Cross-functional teams may be formed for a wide variety of purposes covering the whole supply chain spectrum. Aspects of procurement for which cross-functional teams have

Part 1 · Introduction and strategy

special relevance include sourcing, global sourcing, outsourcing, new product development, value management and analysis, quality management, capital equipment buying and staff development and training.

Cross-functional teams may be either short-term or long-term in duration. Short-term cross-functional teams are essentially task forces formed for a particular purpose and are disbanded when that purpose has been accomplished. Long-term teams are permanent or semi-permanent. With a project such as nuclear submarine design, development, build and commission, for example, the total cycle to decommissioning could exceed 20 years.

Long-term cross-functional teams will serve full time in a project team as members of a self-contained unit headed by a project manager.

4.11.4 The advantages of cross-functional teams

Parker[57] has listed six important competitive advantages that accrue to organisations that successfully implement cross-functional teams:

1 *speed* – reduction in the time it takes to get things done, especially the product development process
2 *complexity* – improvement in the organisation's ability to solve complicated problems
3 *customer focus* – focusing the organisation's resources on satisfying the customers' needs
4 *creativity* – by bringing together people with a variety of experiences and backgrounds, cross-functional teams increase the creative capacity of the organisation
5 *organisational learning* – members of cross-functional teams are more easily able to develop new technical/job skills, learn more about other disciplines and how to work with people who have different team player styles and cultural backgrounds
6 *a single point of contact* – the promotion of more effective cross-functional teamwork by identifying one place to go for information and decisions about a project or customer.

Another advantage is an increased understanding between functions of each other's problems. Production and quality assurance may develop an enhanced appreciation of the difficulties of dealing with suppliers and procurement develop an awareness of the problems faced by production and design.

Procurement staff can make high-quality contributions to cross-functional teams by effectively dealing with such things as supply chain risk, preparing tailor made contracts, exposing product and services cost drivers, applying high-level negotiation skills and conducting financial due diligence.

4.11.5 Some problems of cross-functional teams

A number of problems have been reported in relation to cross-functional teams. Sobek et al.[58] point out that:

> cross-functional coordination has improved, but at the cost of depth of knowledge within functions, because people are spending less time within their own functions. Organisational learning across products has also dropped as people rapidly rotate through positions. Standardisation across products has suffered because product teams have become autonomous. In organisations that combine functional and project-based structures, engineers are often torn between the orders of their functional bosses on the one hand and the demands of project leaders on the other.

136

Other problems of cross-functional teams include:

- the need for a substantial investment in the training and retraining of team leaders in interpersonal skills and of team members in adopting a cross-functional, rather than a silo, orientation
- cross-functional teams require members to attend numerous meetings
- because of their expertise, some members are required to participate in several teams concurrently with a resultant competition for priorities.

Finally, it should not be forgotten that the basic reason for cross-functional teams is to break down functional silos. This does not mean the abdication of functional responsibilities. Those responsible for product design must retain that responsibility even when working in a product team. While cross-functional sourcing may share responsibility for decision making, procurement is not absolved from the duty of ensuring that the team has full information on potential suppliers and products and services that provide maximum value for money spent.

Discussion questions

4.1 Why, in your opinion, are many local authorities and central government outsourcing services that have traditionally been seen as strategic, for example, revenues and benefits?

4.2 Do you believe that it is inevitable that procurement will be a function that is, increasingly, outsourced?

4.3 Contrast the strengths and weaknesses in a large multinational organisation of 'centralised procurement' and 'devolved procurement'. Assume that in the latter situation there is complete autonomy for each operating division to determine its procurement strategy, even if the same goods and services are purchased in a number of locations.

4.4 What are the hallmarks of effective communication between procurement and stakeholders?

4.5 Why is it important for a procurement or supply chain professional to know whether they are employed by organisations concerned with innovative-unique or functional-type products?

4.6 The three key characteristics of networks have been identified as:
  (a) transactional – what is exchanged between network members
  (b) the nature of links – the strengths and qualitative nature of the network relationships, such as the degree to which members honour their network obligations or agree about the appropriate behaviour in their relationships
  (c) cultural characteristics – how members are linked and the roles played by individuals within the network.
  With reference to suppliers with whom you network, identify examples to illustrate each of the above characteristics.

4.7 What is a lean supply chain and who is accountable for establishing it?

4.8 Taking Lamming's definition of a first-tier supplier, what responsibilities do they have to fully support the buying organisation at all stages of product design through to ultimate disposal?

4.9 If you were conducting a supplier selection on an 'agile' producer, what are the key questions you would ask to satisfy yourself that they are an agile producer?

4.10 What is the purpose of a supply chain map?

4.11 If you were to evaluate the structure of a supplier's procurement operation what would you want to check to convince yourself that they satisfy a rating of 'excellent'?

References

1 Mintzberg, H., *The Structure of Organisations*, Prentice Hall, Upper Saddle River, New Jersey, USA, 1979, p. 2.

2 Kotter, J. P. *Leading Change*. Harvard Business School Press. Boston, MA, USA p. 169.

3 The main ideas about core competences were developed by Prahalad, C. K. and Hamel, G. in a series of articles in the *Harvard Business Review*, Vol. 88, 1990, and in their book *The Core Competence of the Corporation*, Harvard Business Press, Brighton, Massachusetts, USA, 1990.

4 Grinnel, S. and Apple, H. P., 'When two bosses are better than one', *Machine Design*, 9 January, 1975, p. 86.

5 McGregor, D. M., *The Human Side of Enterprise*, McGraw-Hill, New York, USA, 1960.

6 As 1 above, Ch. 15.

7 French, P., Jr. and Raven, B., 'The basis of social power' in Cartwright, D. (ed.), *Studies in Social Power*, Michigan Institute for Social Research, 1959.

8 Hickson, D., *et al.*, 'A strategic contingencies theory of organisational power', *Administrative Science Quarterley*, No. 16, 1971, pp. 216–19.

9 As 1 above.

10 Chandler, A. D., *Strategy and Structure: Chapters in the History of the Industrial Enterprise*, MIT Press, Cambridge, Massachusetts, USA, 1962.

11 For a discussion of this point, see Banter, D. K. and Gogne, T. E., *Designing Effective Organisations*, Sage, Thousand Oaks, California, USA, 1995, Ch. 16.

12 Waterman, R., 'The seven elements of strategic fit', *Journal of Business Strategy*, No. 3, 1982, pp. 68–72.

13 Quinn, J. B., *Intelligent Enterprise*, Free Press, New York, USA, 1992.

14 The organisation of the future: Arriving now. Deloitte Insights. 2017. www.2.deloitte.com

15 Ford, D., Gadde, L-E., Hakansson, H. and Snehota, I., *Managing Business Relationships*, 2nd edn, John Wiley, Hoboken, New Jersey, USA, 2003, p. 18.

16 As 15 above, p. 38.

17 Harland, C. M., 'Supply chain management: relationships, chains and networks', *British Journal of Management*, Vol. 7, March, 1996, Special Issue, pp. 63–80.

18 Snow, C. C., Miles, R. E. and Coleman, H. J., 'Managing 21st century network organisations', *Organisational Dynamics*, 20:3, winter, 1992, pp. 5, 20.

19 Lamming, R., Johnsen, T., Zheng, J. and Harland, C., 'An initial classification of supply networks', *International Journal of Operations and Production Management*, Vol. 20, No. 6, 2000.

20 Harland, C., Lamming, R. C., Zheng, J., and Johnsen, T. E., 'A taxonomy of supply networks', *Journal of Supply Management*, Vol. 37, No. 4, Fall, 2001, pp. 21–7.

21 Craven, D. W., Piercy, N. F. and Shipp, S. H., 'New organisational forms for competing in highly dynamic environments', *British Journal of Management*, Vol. 7, 1996, pp. 203–18.

22 As 19 above.

23 Fisher, M. L., 'What is the right supply chain for your product?', *Harvard Business Review*, March/April, 1997, pp. 105–16.

[24] As 20 above.

[25] As 21 above

[26] CPFR is a registered trademark of the Voluntary Interdustry Commerce Solutions Association.

[27] Lambert, D. H., Cooper, M. C. and Pagh, J. D., 'Supply chain management implementation issues and research opportunities', *International Journal of Logistics Management*, Vol. 9, No. 2, 1998, pp. 1–9.

[28] Womack, J. P., Jones, D. T. and Roos, D., *The Machine that Changed the World*, Maxwell Macmillan, New York, USA, 1990.

[29] Teich, S. T. and Faddoul, F. F. 'Lean management – the journey from Toyota to healthcare', *Rambam Maimonides Medical Journal* April 4 (2), 2013.

[30] As 29 above.

[31] Toni, A. D. and Tonchia, S., 'Lean organisation, management by process and performance measurement', *International Journal of Operations and Production Management*, Vol. 16, No. 2, 1996, pp. 221–36.

[32] Goldman, S. L., Nagel, R. N. and Preiss, K., *Agile Competitors and Virtual Organisations: Strategies for Enriching the Customer*, Van Nostrand Reinhold, New York, 1995.

[33] Aitken, J., Christopher, M. and Towill, D., 'Understanding, implementing and exploiting applications', *Supply Chain Management*, Vol. 5, No. 1, 2002, pp. 206–13.

[34] Bowersox, D. J., Class, D. J. and Cooper, M. B., *Supply Chain Logistics Management*, International edition, 2002, McGraw-Hill, New York, USA, pp. 16–19.

[35] Van Hoek, R., 'Reconfiguring the supply chain to implement postponed manufacturing', *International Journal of Logistics Management*, Vol. 9, No. 1, 1998, pp. 1223–47.

[36] Christopher, M., 'Managing the global supply chain in an uncertain world', India Infoline Business School at: www.Indiainfoline.com/bisc/gscm.html, pp. 1–5.

[37] Hoekstra, S. and Romme, J., *Integral Logistics Structures: Developing Customer-orientated Goods Flow*, McGraw-Hill, 1992, quoted in Naim, M., Naylor, J. and Barlow, J., 'Developing lean and agile supply chains in the UK housebuilding industry', Proceedings IGLC-7, 26–28 July 1999, University of California, pp. 159–68.

[38] Christopher, M. and Towill, D. R., 'Supply chain migration from lean and functional to agile and customised', *Supply Chain Management*, Vol. 5, No. 4, 2000, pp. 206–13.

[39] Supply Chain Mapping Guidance Protocol. Version 1. May 2017. www.supplychainschool.co.uk.

[40] Gardner, J. T. and Cooper, M. C., 'Strategic supply chain mapping approaches', *Journal of Business Logistics*, Vol. 24, No. 2, 2003, pp. 37–64.

[41] As 40 above.

[42] Scott, C. and Nestbrook, R., 'New strategic tools for supply chain management', *International Journal of Physical Distribution & Logistics Management* Vol. 21, No 1, 1991.

[43] Hines, P. and Rich, N., 'The seven value stream mapping tools', *International Journal of Operations and Production Management*, Vol. 17, No. 1, 1997, pp. 37–64.

[44] Interested readers are referred to Hines, P., Lamming, R., Jones, D., Cousins, P. and Rich, N., *Value Stream Mapping*, Part One, Pearson, Harlow, UK, 2000, pp. 13–92.

[45] Lucas, H. C. and Baroudi, J., 'The role of information technology in organisation design', *Journal of Management Information Systems*, Vol. 10, No. 4, Spring, 1994, pp. 9–23.

[46] Hellriegel, D., Slocum, J. W. and Woodman, R. W., *Organisational Behaviour*, West Publishing, USA, 1986, p. 340.

[47] Handy, C., *Understanding Organisations*, 4th edn, Penguin, London, UK, 1993.

48 Lewin, K., *Field Theory in Social Science*, Harper & Row, USA, 1951.

49 Kotter, J. P. and Schlesinger, L. A., 'Choosing strategies for change', *Harvard Business Review*, March–April, 1979, pp. 107–9.

50 Collins, D., *Organisational Change*, Routledge, 1998. The authors are indebted to Harty, C., 'Do n-step guides for change work?' CIPS Knowledge in Action series, for the information contained in this section.

51 Attributes of Organization Models. Source Unknown. Aberdeen Group Inc.

52 https://corporate.arcelormittal.com

53 House of Commons Committee of Public Accounts. Cabinet Office: Improving government procurement and the impact of government's ICT savings initiatives. Sixth Report of Session 2013-14.

54 CCNM/SIGMA/PUMA, *'Centralised and Decentralised Public Procurement'*, 2000, 108, p. 5.

55 Institute of Supply Management (USA), *Glossary of Key Supply Management Terms*, see ISM website: www.ism.ws

56 Torrington, D. and Hall, L., *Personnel Management*, Prentice Hall, Upper Saddle River, New Jersey, USA, 1991, p. 208.

57 Parker, G. M., 'How to succeed as a cross-functional team', Proceedings of 79th Annual International Purchasing Conference of the National Association of Purchasing Managers, 1 May, 1994.

58 Sobek, I. I., Durward, K., Liker, J. K. and Ward, A. C., 'Another look at how Toyota integrates product development', *Harvard Business Review*, Vol. 76.4, July/August, 1998, p. 36.

Chapter 5

Procurement policies, procedures and support tools

Learning outcomes

With reference to procurement and supply management, this chapter aims to provide an understanding of:

- exemplar procurement policy
- procurement procedures
- procurement process failures
- e-commerce, e-business, e-SCM and e-procurement
- the evolution of e-procurement models
- electronic data interchange (EDI)
- e-hubs, exchanges, portals and market places
- e-catalogues
- e-auctions
- reverse auctions
- e-payment
- low-value purchases
- procurement manuals
- procurement playbook

Key ideas

- The need for business-related procurement policies and procedures.
- E-commerce, e-business, e-SCM and e-procurement.
- Electronic data interchange (EDI).
- E-hubs, exchanges and marketplaces.
- E-catalogues and reverse auctions.
- E-payment.
- Procurement manuals and playbooks – business benefits.

Introduction

Procurement Policy

The term policy includes 'all the directives, both explicit and implied, that designate the aims and ends of an organisation and the appropriate means used in their accomplishment. Policy refers to a set of purposes, principles and rules of action that guide an organisation'.[1]

There are four major levels of organisation policy, namely:

Executive policies	■ Sets out executive management's directives
	■ Provides guidance for strategic direction of the organisation
	■ Defines strategic intent of the organisation
Functional policies	■ Provides guidance for functional areas, e.g. procurement
	■ Aligns functional policies with executive policies
	■ Defines specific facets of functional policy
Operating procedures	■ Describes range of functional duties
	■ Describes mandatory steps to complete specific tasks, e.g. Contract Award
	■ Provides supportive detail for each procedure
Rules and regulations	■ Sets constraints on individual behaviour, e.g. hospitality
	■ Establishes minima behaviour for audit purposes
	■ Describes organisational rules that govern professional behaviour

5.1 Exemplar Procurement Policy – The Crossrail Project

The London Crossrail Project began at North Dock in Canary Wharf in May 2009. In 2014 it was the biggest railway construction project in Europe. It consists of 21 km of new twin bore tunnels under central London and ten new world-class stations constructed under the largest city in the European Union. There is a £17.6 billion envelope (some £2.8 billion more than the level of funding announced in 2010).

5.1.1 Crossrail Procurement Policy[2]

The Crossrail Procurement Policy is an 18-page document that comprehensively sets out the salient detail of a robust policy.

5.1.2 Purpose of the Policy

The purpose of this Policy is to ensure that all procurement activities carried out by, or on behalf of CRL (Crossrail Ltd):

■ provide best affordable value in delivering the Crossrail project objectives;

■ are conducted in a fair, objective and transparent manner;

- are compliant with the regulatory framework of all relevant legislation, the CRL governance and audit framework and delegated levels of authority;
- use best practice in the application of ethical standards;
- are aligned with the CRL vision and values; and
- adhere wherever appropriate to Government procurement policies and TFL/GLA Responsible Procurement Policy.

5.1.3 Overarching objectives

In line with TfL's policy, CRL's procurement activities will be guided by the following overarching objectives:

(a) **Deliver Best Affordable Value** – achieve best affordable value in delivering CRL's high-level objectives. Seek opportunities for efficiency and economies of scale across the Programme by working with TfL and industry partners. The achievement of best affordable value also requires that the procurement procedures and contractual arrangements support the delivery of related Government and TfL policies.

(b) **Establish Effective Governance and Control** – conduct procurement activities in a manner that satisfies the requirements of accountability and internal control, fulfils CRL's legal obligations, complies with financial constraints and effectively manages commercial risk.

(c) **Apply Standardised Approaches** – provide and enforce effective, efficient and consistent commercial arrangements for procuring works, products and services of a common nature.

(d) **Build and Maintain Effective Supplier Relationships** – recognise that in order to achieve best affordable value appropriate relationships must be developed and maintained with suppliers and their supply chains.

5.1.4 CRL Key Policy Principles

On the basis of the above key policy documents and supporting publications CRL has developed Key Policy Principles (KPPs) which will be applied to the delivery of the Crossrail procurement requirements. These are set out below in the following main areas:

- General Procurement;
- Supply Chain Management and Engagement;
- Supplier Selection Procedures;
- Contracting Arrangements;
- Risk Allocation;
- Fair Payment Procedures;
- Performance Management.

For illustrative purposes, set out below are extracts from the Procurement Policy document the KPPs for General Procurement and Supply Chain Management and Engagement. The author strongly recommends readers to access the full document to facilitate learning.

General Procurement Key Policy Principles

KPP1 – CRL will adopt a risk-based approach to the development and evaluation of procurement strategies, detailed procurement plans and processes.

Risk-based procedures to evaluate the optimal approach to procurements will be developed based on best practice and guidance issued by HMT and OGC. These will be aimed at ensuring that delivery risks are identified, evaluated, and allocated appropriately to achieve best affordable value in the management of the risks. The procedures will be designed to meet the requirements set out in OGC Gateway guidance notes so that the project passes through OGC and Major Project Review Group project reviews as efficiently as possible and with minimal impact on the programme.

KPP2 – CRL's procurement activities will be carried out on the basis of achieving best affordable value.

The achievement of best affordable value means delivering CRL's high level objectives for the Crossrail Programme within the affordability criteria.

KPP3 – CRL will ensure that it has access to the necessary experienced and competent resources needed to deliver the project successfully.

CRL's approach to procurement and project delivery will be aimed at ensuring the availability of the skilled resources required for the delivery of the Crossrail Programme. Expert delivery partners and specialist advisers will be used as necessary to support CRL. Strong client capability will help establish CRL's reputation as a best practice client which will help to attract the best suppliers and ensure strong competition for its contracts. CRL will undertake reviews of resource pressures in the supply chain and develop plans to address potential shortages.

KPP4 – CRL will ensure that its procurement plans and procedures support delivery of CRL Health, Safety and Environment policies.

CRL's procurement plans and procedures will be aligned with the policies and requirements set out in the CRL publication 'Health, Safety and Environment Standard – Contractors and Industry Partners'.

KPP5 – CRL will implement best practice Responsible Procurement policies and processes based on TfL and GLA approach to responsible procurement.

CRL's procurement plans and procedures will be aligned with the policies and requirements set out in the CRL publication 'Crossrail's Approach to Delivering Responsible Procurement'. In developing its procurement plans CRL will seek to prioritise opportunities to support the Government priority policy areas of apprentices, skills and youth employment, small businesses and low carbon resource efficiency.

KPP6 – CRL will collaborate with Industry Partners and other clients where appropriate to deliver efficiencies and savings through collaborative purchasing initiatives.

In particular CRL will work closely with Network Rail, London Underground, TfL and utilities companies to ensure that procurement plans are coordinated and any opportunities are taken to deliver better value through collaborative working.

Supply Chain Management and Engagement Key Policy Principles

KPP7 – CRL will establish early and regular consultation arrangements with the market to develop well informed and well-prepared suppliers to help achieve strong competition for its full range of contracts.

CRL will undertake early engagement and consultation with the market and suppliers to review options for procurement plans and programmes and to help ensure that suppliers are well prepared for opportunities as they come to the market.

KPP8 – CRL will incorporate Optimised Contractor Involvement principles into its contracting arrangements to involve contractors and suppliers as early as possible prior to construction or manufacture phases.

CRL will aim to achieve the early involvement of the supply chain in a flexible manner which is being referred to as Optimised Contractor Involvement (OCI). This will ensure the involvement of the supply chain in the finalisation of the designs and delivery plans in a way that is best suited to the scope of the works package.

The objective of this approach is to bring the skills and expertise of the supply chain into the development of the final engineering solution to produce better solutions and improved value for money. The earlier involvement of the supply chain in the finalisation of the detailed design is aimed at delivering the following benefits:

- improved buildability of the works;
- identification of better solutions and cost savings through value engineering;
- elimination of unnecessary scope or unnecessarily elaborate specifications;
- improved understanding and management of health and safety issues;
- improved understanding and management of construction risks;
- more time for the planning of resource requirements;
- more time for the contractor to become familiar with the environmental and local community requirements; and
- creation of integrated delivery teams who are incentivised to work together to resolve problems as quickly and efficiently as possible.

KPP9 – CRL will develop and maintain effective collaborative working relationships with the supply chain.

CRL will develop and implement appropriate arrangements with its suppliers to support the successful delivery of the project objectives and individual contracts. Partnering arrangements and integrated and co-located teams will be established where appropriate.

5.1.5 Contracting arrangements

There are relevant and informative KPPs for 'Contracting Arrangements' that can be cross referenced to Chapter 7 of this book. For example, KPP 19 details:

KPP19 – CRL will seek parent company guarantees from the ultimate parent company of all main contractors, and where the contract is with a joint venture, CRL will normally require guarantees from the ultimate parent of each joint venture member.

A parent company guarantee provides protection for the employer through a guarantee that the contract will be properly performed by its subsidiary. If the contractor is in breach of contract then the guarantor must perform in his place or be liable for any resultant loss. The value of the guarantee is only as good as the strength of the parent company and generally therefore, CRL will seek guarantees from the ultimate parent to minimise the risk that voluntary corporate restructuring reduces the net asset value of the guarantor company.

5.2 Procurement procedures

A *procedure* is a system of sequential steps or techniques for getting a task or job done. Procedures are also the formal arrangements by means of which policies linking strategies are implemented. A cluster of reliable procedures, each comprised of a number of operations that, together, provide information enabling staff to execute and managers to control those operations, is called a system.

5.2.1 The sequence and impact of procurement procedures

It is essential that there are procurement procedures to set out how procurement departments make their contribution at key phases of the procurement cycle and explain how stakeholders and others interface with the procedures and decision making. There are, potentially, serious implications when procurement procedures are not complied with.

5.2.2 Salient content of procurement procedures

A procurement procedure will set out:

- how procurement will engage in each facet of the process, including identifying the business need and subsequent specification development
- the need to deal effectively with intellectual property rights
- the process for engaging with the supply market, including soft market testing
- how to avoid creating a monopoly supply scenario
- the need for usage forecasts to be as accurate as possible
- how potential suppliers will be pre-qualified; for example, through the use of pre-qualification questionnaires, interviews and other evidence of competencies.

5.2.3 Notification of authority to purchase

The procurement procedure will set out:

- who and how an appropriate requisition will be initiated or other means to authorise the purchase
- budget approval and appropriate finance code
- issue of bills of material when these are applicable
- the management of emergency needs to purchase and to permit a standard procedure to be bypassed according to defined rules.

5.2.4 Requests for quotations (RFQs) and invitations to tender (ITTs)

The procurement procedure will set out:

- how the value of the purchase will impact on the methodology to be adopted; for example, high value contracts must have a minimum number of quotations/tenders
- the content required when RFQs or ITTs are submitted
- the methodology to be applied to the evaluation of RFQs or ITTs to avoid biased decisions being made
- how and in what circumstances negotiations will take place
- the time lines for decision making
- how authority to purchase shall be signed off at this stage
- how to evaluate risk appropriate to the purchase.

5.2.5 Creating a legally binding contract

The procurement procedure will set out:

- how purchase orders are to be raised and issued
- how one-off contracts are to be negotiated and issued
- the methodology for dealing with order acknowledgements and the implications of accepting the supplier's sales acknowledgement
- what actions to take when a supplier fails to enter into a contract
- how to create and maintain a master contract file.

5.2.6 The contract management phase

The procurement procedure will set out:

- who is accountable for contract management
- the requirement for prompt supply of management information by the supplier
- the involvement of procurement when disputes arise
- acceptance procedures for goods and services
- payment processes
- contract close-out procedure
- feedback of supplier's performance into a vendor rating system.

In summary, procurement procedures are essential but the danger is that they can become mechanistic and stifle business initiatives. Reactive procurement is not the way forward.

5.3 Procurement process failures

Procurement processes can fail due to many actions, or lack of actions. Table 5.1 represents procurement process failures encountered by the author in his consultancy practice.

It is a fact the public procurement processes are more frequently published than are private sector processes. There is considerable learning from published reports. Such is the case with The Garden Bridge Design Procurement.[3]

Table 5.1 Reasons for procurement process failures
Unpublished or ill-explained process
Determination by buyer or other influence to undermine the process
Specification that can only be met by one supplier
Passing confidential information to a preferred bidder
Failing to engage in a credible tendering process
Bias in evaluating tenders
Failure to evaluate all bids in a consistent manner
Engaging in fraudulent practices
False reporting of supplier's capabilities
Having a personal interest (financial) in the supplier
Manipulating timescales for submission of tender and their evaluation
Engaging in selective negotiations
Revealing tender prices to preferred supplier

The report highlights the complexity of influences and actions on the award of a contract for £60,000 to Heatherwick Studio. The executive summary of the report includes the following:

> In February 2013, Transport for London (TfL) invited three companies to tender for the design contract for a 'pedestrian footbridge' from Temple to South Bank. The three organisations which submitted proposals were Marks Barfield, Wilkinson Eyre and Heatherwick Studio. In April, Heatherwick Studio was awarded the contract, valued at £60,000. The contract was to 'secure design advice to help progress ideas for a new footbridge crossing of the River Thames in Central London.'

> The GLA Oversight Committee has held four meetings to shed some light on both the procurement process and the internal audit review. This was not an investigation into the merits or otherwise of a Garden Bridge but instead focused solely on the procurement processes around its design. Our investigation has allowed us to conclude that:

> ■ The Mayor should have been more upfront about the range and nature of contacts between his Office, TfL senior management and Heatherwick Studio.

> ■ TfL did not have a clear idea of the extent of its involvement in the early stages of the project, leading to the decision to run a closed tendering process for the design contract. Senior managers now admit that TfL would have followed a different path if it had had a better understanding of its role earlier in the process.

> ■ There was a series of procedural errors in the procurement process including informal communication between TfL and the selected design firms; questions over how the bids were scored and why it was left to just one individual to score the bids; and the loss of key documents which would have provided a detailed paper trail for the tender evaluation.

> One of the reasons this degree of contact was problematic was that it gave one potential bidder – Heatherwick Studio – access to more information about the Mayor's vision for this project. TfL's Invitation to Tender specified only that it was looking to commission a pedestrian footbridge. In fact, it was clear, as evidenced by TfL Legal Opinion from 8 January 2013, that the Mayor was looking for a Garden Bridge

> TfL Legal had highlighted the level of contact between the Mayor, TfL and Heatherwick Studio as a potential risk to the fairness of the procurement process for the Garden Bridge. On 8 January 2015, it sent a memo to senior management outlining its advice on how the procurement should be managed. In it, it stressed the importance of ensuring a 'level playing field' for all contenders.

> TfL's internal audit review of the design contract procurement uncovered a series of smaller, procedural errors made by management during the process. These included:

> ■ Informal communication between TfL and the selected design firms, which was contrary to TfL's policy on engagement with bidders. These communications included the release of a design brief to all three firms, discussion with Heatherwick Studio on its day rates, and an informal notification of success to Heatherwick ahead of the formal announcement. The review states that 'communications outside of the formal tender process are inconsistent with TfL policy and procedure'.

5.4 E-commerce, e-business, e-SCM and e-procurement

5.4.1 E-commerce

In March 2002 the United States General Accounting Office (GAO)[1] produced a report that sought to clarify e-commerce (in an international context) and e-business. The report observes that there has been:

a general acceptance of transaction-based definitions many of which require an online commitment to sell a good or service for an activity to be categorised as electronic commerce. In a transaction-based definition, electronic commerce is restricted to buying and selling, as distinct from conducting e-business – includes all aspects of online business activity – purchasing, selling, tracking inventory, managing production, handling logistics, and supply communications and support services.

Zwass[5] defined e-commerce as, 'the sharing of business information, maintaining business relationships, and conducting business transactions by means of tele-communications networks. . . . E-commerce includes the sell-buy relationships and transactions between companies, as well as the corporate processes that support the commerce within individual firms.'

Hackbarth and Kettinger[6] set out the E-business development stages as shown in Table 5.2.

5.4.2 E-business

Greenstein and Feinmann[7] offer the following perspective.

The term electronic commerce is restricting, however, and does not fully encompass the true nature of the many types of information exchanges occurring via telecommunication devices. The term electronic business also includes the exchange of information not related to the actual buying and selling of goods. Increasingly businesses are using electronic mechanisms

Table 5.2 E-business development stages

Stages / Indicators	Corporate traditional approach to E-business	Corporate Integration exists but lacks complete foresight	Corporate Transformation has been achieved
E-business Strategy	Corporately there is no initiative or desire to adopt E-business	E-business strategy supports the current strategy of the organisation but should be refreshed	E-business strategy is the corporately delivered strategy of the complete organisation
Organisation Strategy	No corporate awareness *between* e-business strategy and organisation's strategy	E-business strategy is *dependent* on the strategy of the organisation but further clarity is required	E-business strategy *coordinates* all facets of the organisational strategy
Goal	Oriented on selective parts of the organisation	All corporate functions have total commitment	It is demonstrable that all parts of the organisation are involved in E-business
Results	An absence of definitive evidence that an E-business model will operate corporately	■ Business benefits ■ Customer response improved ■ Deprived business credibility ■ Motivation for E-business is enhanced	■ New business attracted ■ Less inventory ■ Customer service levels enhanced ■ Continual improvement achieved
Means	Technological and infrastructure required not understood	Business processes redesigned, tested prior to launch	An integrated corporate approach involving key personnel, technology and key stakeholders
Role of Information	No active vision on this matter	Internal and external information flows designed and monitored	Information used to enhance internal performance and relationships with all strategic customers of the business

to distribute information and provide customer support. These activities are not 'commerce' activities; they are 'business' activities. Thus the term electronic business is broader and may eventually replace the term electronic commerce.

In a Canada Transportation Act review there was a very useful analysis of the barriers to e-Business adoption. This analysis can be summarised as follows:

- cost can prevent any firm from adopting Internet technology more extensively
- many marine and rail industry participants already have electronic data transfer and legacy information systems in place, reducing the commercial benefits of adopting more accessible Internet-based systems
- much of the uncertainty about potential benefits arises from inadequate customer readiness
- lack of action by all participants in the supply chain
- interoperability between logistics providers
- insufficient interoperability also arises from shipper demands for specific formats and methods of communication
- inadequate technical skills and training
- security and protecting commercially sensitive information are also a concern
- organisational culture and traditional practices in both carrier and partner firms are key factors to overcome.

5.4.3 E-SCM

E-supply chain management (e-SCM) is concerned with streamlining and optimising the whole supply chain by means of internal applications, with the aim of ensuring maximum sales growth at the lowest possible cost. This includes setting up an internal online procurement system, joining an industrywide electronic marketplace and implementing e-SCM across the entire value chain.

The concepts of supply chain management and supply chain optimisation were discussed in sections 3.5 and 3.9. Unsurprisingly, the Internet provides present and future benefits to both the management and optimisation of supply chains. Purchasers and suppliers can derive the following benefits from e-SCM.

Procurement benefits include:

- the ability to purchase, both directly and indirectly, materials at a lower cost, primarily due to price transparency and competition, so, while large purchasers can exert powerful leverage to obtain more substantial price reductions and discounts, small purchasers using such systems can obtain more favourable prices as many suppliers are competing for the business of purchasers via the medium of e-marketplace and trading exchanges
- achievements of greater efficiency when purchasing goods and services and ultimately lowering the overall cost of transactions, as business-to-business marketplaces often offer smaller purchasers opportunities to discover lower prices for things that would be prohibitively expensive to discover by human effort alone
- purchasers being able to form strong ties with suppliers, in forecasting, scheduling and planning production data and sharing product data designs to develop supplier collaboration.

Supplier benefits

Supplier benefits tend to fall into two classes, depending on whether the e-SCM program emphasises collaboration or commercial opportunities. The latter includes the enhancement of forecasting ability, resulting in the capacity to meet and exceed customers' demands, achieve the right combination of products and services at the right time and align their production schedules, manufacturing capacity and inventory to customers' buying patterns.

When the emphasis is on collaboration, suppliers can benefit from participating in large, active online marketplaces. If frequented by a critical mass of buyers, such market places can provide a cost-effective way to reach new customers and increase sales.

'A Survey and Implementation of e-Commerce in Supply Chain Management' by Hui-Chun Lee (KSI-Chicago)[8] resulted in the production of the following figure, which is an example of an integration model of e-SCM.

Figure 5.1 An example of an end-to-end integrated model of e-SCM

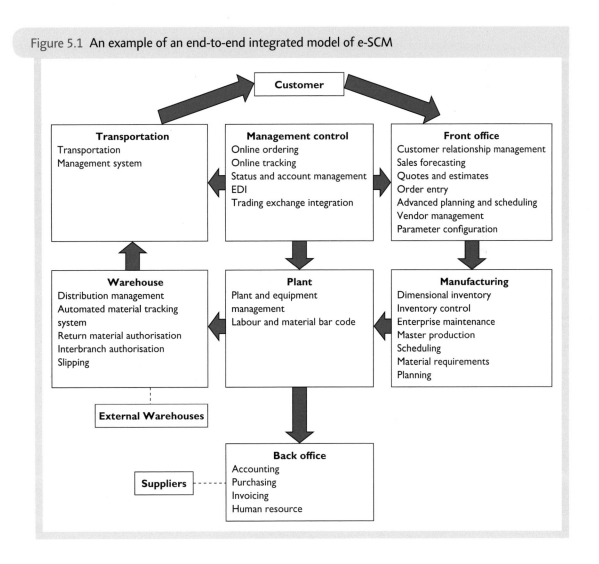

5.4.4 E-procurement

The Chartered Institute of Procurement and Supply (CIPS) definition of e-procurement is:

> E-procurement is using the Internet to operate the transactional aspects of requisitioning, authorising ordering, receiving and payment processes for the required services or products.

The CIPS statement also points out that e-procurement is typically the focus of local business administrators (one of the key goals of e-procurement is to devolve buying to local users) and covers the following areas of the buying process:

- requisition against agreed contract
- authorisation
- order
- receipt
- payment.

The key enabler of all the above is the ability of systems to communicate across organisational boundaries. While the technology for e-commerce provides the basic means, the main benefits derive from the resultant changes in business procedures, processes and perspectives. E-commerce is made possible by the open standard of extensible mark-up language (XML) – a structured computer programming language that allows for the easy identification of data types in multiple formats and can be understood across all standard Internet technologies. Adoption of XML will help organisations to integrate applications seamlessly and exchange information with trading partners.

5.5 The evolution of e-procurement models

Kalakota and Robinson[9] have identified seven basic types of e-procurement trading models. These, together with their key differences, are shown in Table 5.3.

5.6 Electronic data interchange (EDI)

5.6.1 Definition

Electronic data interchange (EDI) may be defined as follows:

> The technique based on agreed standards, which facilitates business transactions in standardised electronic form in an automated manner directly from a computer application in one organisation to an application in another.

A *transaction* in EDI-speak is a term used to describe the electronic transmission of a single document. Each transaction set is usually referred to by a name and number, which are defined by the ASC X12 or EDIFACT standards referred to below. Thus, a purchase order in X12 is number 850. Each line of a transaction is termed a *segment* and piece of information in the line an *element*. In a purchase order, for example, the segment is the name and address of the purchaser or supplier. The segment is broken down into such data elements as organisation name, address line 1, address line 2, address line 3, postcode and country.

Table 5.3 Comparison of various e-procurement models (Kalakota and Robinson[10])

Trading model	Characteristics
EDI networks	■ Handful of trading partners and customers ■ Simple transactional capabilities ■ Batch processing ■ Reactive and costly value-added network (VAN) charges
Business-to-employees (B2E) requisition applications	■ Make buying fast and hassle-free for a company's employees ■ Automated approvals routing and standardisation of requisition procedures ■ Provide supplier management tools for the professional buyer
Corporate procurement portals	■ Provide improved control over the procurement process and let a company's business rules be implemented with more consistency ■ Custom, negotiated prices posted in a multi-supplier catalogue ■ Spending analysis and multi-supplier catalogue management
First-generation trading exchanges: community, catalogue and storefronts	■ Industry content, job postings, and news ■ Storefronts: new sales channel for distributors and manufacturers ■ Product content and catalogue aggregation services
Second-generation trading exchanges: transaction-orientated trading exchanges	■ Automated requisition process and purchase order transactions ■ Supplier, price and product/service availability discovery ■ Catalogue and credit management
Third-generation trading exchanges: collaborative supply chains	■ Enable partners to closely synchronise operations and enable real-time fulfilment ■ Process transparency, resulting in restructuring of demand and the supply chain ■ Substitute information for inventory
Industry consortia: buyer and supplier led	■ The next step in the evolution of corporate procurement portals

5.6.2 Standards

Data elements and codes are described in a directory relating to the message standard used. By the use of trade, national and international standards, organisations can trade electronically. Early message standards were developed by communities of organisations relating to an industry, such as automotive, construction and electronic enterprises, which had an interest in trading together. Thus, automotive manufacturers, including Ford, General Motors, Saab, Renault, Fiat, Austin Rover and Citroën and suppliers Lucas, Perkins, Bosch, GKN, SKF and BCS, set up ODETTE (Organisation for Data Exchange by Tele-Transmission in Europe). ODETTE sets the standards for e-business, engineering data exchange and logistics management that link the 4000 plus businesses in the European motor industry and their global partners.

Although there are still many EDI standards, only two – namely ASC X12 and EDIFACT – are widely used and recognised. ASC X12 standards were created in 1979 by the Accredited Standards Committee of the American National Standards Institute. These standards define the data formats and encoding rules for business transactions, including order placement and transportation. EDIFACT (EDI for Administration, Commerce and Transport) was developed by the United Nations in 1985 for the purpose of providing EDI standards that would support world trade. This international standard has been ratified as ISO 9735. UN/EDIFACT directories are published twice yearly by the United Nations.

5.6.3 How EDI works

How EDI is implemented is shown by Figure 5.2. The sequence is as follows:

1 Company A creates a purchase order using its internal business software.

2 EDI software translates the order.

3 Company A sends the purchase order to company B over a third-party value-added network (VAN) or encrypted in EDIFACT format over the Internet.

4 Company B receives the purchase order document and will translate it from EDI to its proprietary format and, typically, company B will send an acknowledgement to company A.

5.6.4 The advantages of EDI

■ Replacing the paper documents – purchase orders, acknowledgements, invoices and so on – used by buyers and sellers in commercial transactions with standard electronic messages conveyed between computers, often without the need for human intervention.

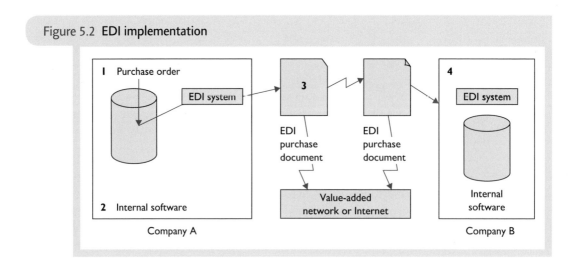

Figure 5.2 **EDI implementation**

EDI at the supermarket

One of the best examples of EDI is EPOS (electronic point-of-sale) at the supermarket. When a product is purchased, the checkout operator scans a barcode on its label, which automatically registers the price on the cash till.

That same signal also triggers a computer process that reorders the item from the manufacturer, sets off a production cycle, and arranges invoicing, payment and transportation of the new order. EDI effectively puts the product back on the shelf with no paperwork and a minimum of human involvement.

- Reduction in lead times as buyers and suppliers work together in a real-time environment. Armstrong and Jackson[11] provide a real-life example of pre-EDI and post-EDI lead times. The latter shows a reduction of eight days for acknowledging the order and five days to deliver it. The total time was therefore reduced from 19 to 11 days.
  - Day 1: Order prepared and authorised electronically, then posted to EDI service.
  - Day 2: Order taken from EDI service by recipient and put straight into order processing system. An acknowledgement is created automatically and sent to the EDI service.
  - Day 3: Manufacturing process begins (seven days). The acknowledgement is received by the originator and processed automatically.
  - Day 9: Manufacturing is completed.
  - Day 11: Delivery complete.

- Reduction in the cost of inventory and release of working capital.
- Promotion of such strategies as JIT as a consequence of the previous two points.
- Better customer service.
- Facilitation of global procurement using international standards, such as EDIFACT, which is compatible with most equipment in most countries. In 1970, SITPRO (Simplifying International Trade Procedures Board) was established in the UK and whose primary objectives are to reduce the costs of trading particularly to business, and to help the UK meet the challenges of globalisation. SITPRO works with the British Standards Institution (BSI) in connection with EDI standards.
- Facilitation of invoice payments by the computer-to-computer transfer of money, which eliminates the need for the preparation and posting of cheques.
- The integration of functions, particularly marketing, procurement, production and finance.
- EDI tends to promote long-term buyer–supplier relationships and increase mutual trust.

5.6.5 Some potential problems in implementing EDI

Killen and Kamauff[12] point out that before adopting EDI an organisation should:

- ensure that exchanging information electronically supports the overall organisational strategy

- consider the cost and ramifications of EDI's standard tools and techniques, including implementation, software maintenance, manpower and participant training and how to promote systems and applications integration
- consider the organisational and process changes involved.

In relation to the second point, Norman[13] states that the more the data is processed and reprocessed, the more room there is to save time and money. Potential EDI users should therefore calculate the cost per transaction. If it is cheaper to fax or manually perform the task, the buyer probably lacks the volume to invest in EDI. Monczka and Carter[14] propose the following indicators of a reasonable opportunity for the application of EDI in the procurement environment:

- a high volume of paperwork transaction documents
- numerous suppliers
- a long internal administration lead time associated with the procurement cycle
- a desire for personnel reductions, new hire avoidance or both
- a need to increase the professionalism of procurement personnel.

5.6.6 EDI limitations

Historically, the two principal limitations of EDI relate to cost and flexibility.

Cost

EDI was, and still is, an expensive option, given that, until recently, organisations sent all EDI transactions over a VAN (value-added network) that had set-up and running costs often on a per thousand characters transmitted basis. The scope of EDI was also intentionally limited to ensure controlled activity within a closed-door environment. The high levels of overheads associated with EDI infrastructure were prohibitive for many small-sized to medium-sized enterprises.

Internet and extranet approaches can, however, enable a small business to link into secure EDI networks at minimal cost. The Internet pricing model of flat monthly rates has forced most of the VAN networks to lower their pricing structures. A new market shift is also underway in which organisations are moving from proprietary technology to extranet solutions. A comparison of EDI and extranet technologies is shown in Table 5.4.

Small businesses using the Internet can compete on a level playing field with large competitors, expand globally and improve their trading partner relationships.

Inflexibility

EDI is a cumbersome, static and inflexible method of transmitting data, most suited to straightforward business transactions, such as the placement of purchase orders for known requirements. It is not suitable for transactions requiring tight coupling and coordination, such as the consideration of several possible purchase alternatives or supply chain optimisation. Unlike human beings, computers are poor at interpreting unstructured data and cannot derive useful information from Web documents that are not predefined and permanent. The standard document language used to create web pages is hypertext mark-up language (HTML). Although HTML is able to display data and focuses on how data look, it cannot describe data. Although HTML can state what items a supplier can offer, it cannot describe them. Traditional EDI approaches do not, therefore, provide the flexibility required in a dynamic Internet environment.

Table 5.4 **Comparison of EDI and extranets**

Characteristics	EDI	Extranets
Infrastructure	Customised software	Packaged solutions that leverage and extend existing Internet technology and intranet investment
Transmission costs	Extensive VANS or leased lines, slow dial-up connections	Inexpensive and fast Internet connections
Access	Proprietary software	Web browsers support EDI protocols as well as many other open standards
Scale	Restricted to only the largest vendors who can support EDI infrastructure	Support real-time buying and selling, allowing for tighter and more proactive planning

5.6.7 EDI and XML

XML (referred to in section 5.4.4 above) is an attempt to meet the problems of cost and inflexibility and the provision of a whole new way of communicating across the Internet and beyond.

The major difference between EDI and XML is that the former is designed to meet business needs and is a *process*. XML is a *language* and its success in any business will always depend on how it is being used by a given application.

As a language, XML provides a basic syntax that can be used to share information between many kinds of computer, different applications and different organisations.

XML can also describe – as distinct from display – data. It can, for example, enable a purchaser to understand in detail what a supplier has to offer. It also ensures that a purchase order accurately describes what the purchaser requires. It therefore provides a direct route between purchaser and supplier; irrespective of the size of either, that was unavailable with EDI.

XML/EDI is an attempt to provide a standard framework for the exchange of different types of data, such as a purchase order, invoice or healthcare claim, so that the information, whether in a transaction, exchanged in an application program interface (API) database portal catalogue or a work flow document or message, can be searched, decoded, processed and displayed consistently and correctly by first implementing EDI questionnaires and extending our vocabulary via online repositories to include our business language, rules and objectives. Thus, by combining XML and EDI, we create a new, powerful approach that is different from XML and EDI.

In addition to EDI and the Internet, there are other ways of transmitting data electronically between two or more organisations. For small businesses, encrypted e-mails are very cost-effective. Orders can be collected securely online and put into existing in-house systems that automatically e-mail suppliers when stock values reach lower limits. Technology is also changing. Although until recently PCs were the Internet access device of choice, preferred substitutes, such as mobile phones and personal digital assistants (PDAs), are outselling PCs several times over.

The National Computing Centre[15] points out that, 'the latest business buzz word is Business Process Integration' (BPI), which is all about the processes that cross the buying and selling organisations – that is, there is greater benefit from automating the interactions than in the transactional aspects of ordering and invoicing.

Business process integration is important because of:

■ an increasing business imperative to increase process efficiency
■ a focus on making core processes more flexible and efficient
■ increasing traceability within a process
■ an increasing requirement to understand how data is passed and by what applications
■ improved recoverability
■ reduced elapsed process delivery time.

5.7 E-hubs, exchanges, portals and marketplaces

Some writers believe that a distinction can be made between these terms.

5.7.1 Hubs

In the context of internal technologies, a hub is a device that connects several networks together. As used in e-businesses, a hub generally means a central repository or private exchange, such as the star network shown in Figure 5.3.

In the network shown in Figure 5.3, the *server* is a control computer that holds databases and programs for many PC workstations or terminals, which are called *clients*. The clients of the information hub may be internal customers or external organisations, such as suppliers.

5.7.2 Exchange

An exchange is a business-to-business (B2B) website where purchasers and suppliers meet to transact business. A distinction may be made between private and public exchanges.

Private exchanges can be either one-to-one (1T1) or one-to-many connections (1TM). The former are direct connections, while the latter connect all the actors through the central Internet hub. Private exchanges are normally specified by a single operation and available by invitation only to the organisation's suppliers and trading partners. Such

Figure 5.3 **A star network**

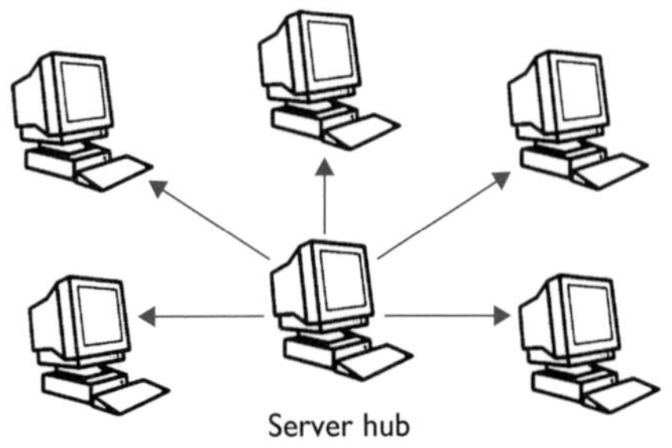

Server hub

private exchanges are frequently used for collaborative business procedures, such as real-time supply chain management and logistics.

Public exchanges – often referred to as *portals* – extend outside the boundaries of the company and involve many-to-many (MTM) interactions. Public exchanges may be run either by a consortium of big players within a specific industry (consortium portals) or by an independent entity starting up its business as an intermediary (independent portals).

Independent portals, such as ChemConnect and VerticaInet, have some advantages relative to consortia and private e-markets. They can act more rapidly as they do not need to mediate among multiple owners as consortium portals do. Because they have comparatively few proprietary interests, they are also seen to be neutral, unlike the consortia and private e-markets. With all public exchanges, organisations pay a fee to become a member and possibly an additional transaction fee.

Both private and public exchanges can be either buy-side or sell-side, although this distinction is more usual with private exchanges. A *buy-side exchange* is built to interact with suppliers. Conversely a *sell-side exchange* is built to interact with customers. These are shown in Figure 5.4.

5.7.3 Marketplace

Like an exchange, a marketplace is a website that enables purchasers to select from many suppliers. With e-marketplaces, the buyer is in control as open marketplaces enable purchasers to evaluate all potential suppliers for a particular product or service and make informed decisions regarding what and where to buy.

E-marketplaces are particularly applicable where:

■ markets are large and the search costs to find suppliers are high because of the large number of potential suppliers

■ product specifications and information are subject to rapid change

■ buyers have difficulty in comparing similar products from different vendors because of an excess of features and characteristics that may not be clearly indicated

■ internal costs of such processes as locating, appraising and evaluating the performance of suppliers are high.

Figure 5.4 **Buy-side and sell-side exchanges**

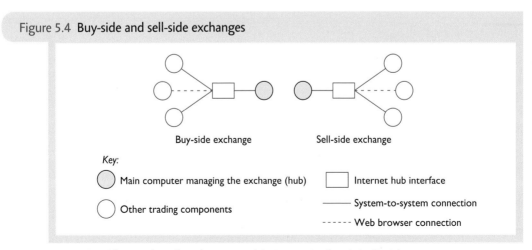

Source: Adapted from Ronchi, Stefano, *The Internet and the Customer Supplier Relationship*, Ashgate, 2003, p. 48.

Figure 5.5 **Hubs, exchanges and marketplaces in context**

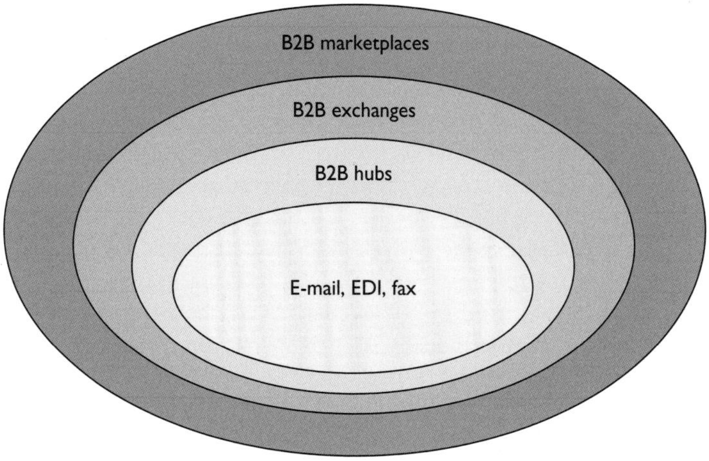

In summary, it may be said that e-marketplaces offer greater functionality than exchanges, which, in turn, offer more functionality than hubs.

Figure 5.5 shows how hubs, exchanges and marketplaces interrelate in context with existing electronic communications, such as EDI, e-mail and fax.

5.8 E-catalogues

The Belgian Federal Public Service set up an e-catalogue platform, implementing one of the modules of the large e-procurement project. The Belgian e-catalogue platform is an autonomous, open, secure, inter-operable and re-configurable platform where public officers and companies can perform multiple tasks relating to their electronic purchase process. The electronic catalogues' format is based on the VBL 2.0 standard.

5.8.1 Definition

At their simplest, B2B marketplaces are just online catalogues. An e-catalogue may be defined as:

> A web page that provides information on products and services offered and sold by a vendor and supports online ordering and payment capabilities.

5.8.2 Advantages of e-catalogues

E-catalogues benefit both purchasers and suppliers in that they:

- facilitate real-time, two-way communication between buyers and sellers
- allow for the development of closer purchaser–supplier relationships due to improved vendor services and by informing purchasers about products of which they might otherwise be unaware

- enable suppliers to respond quickly to market conditions and requirements by adjusting prices and repackaging
- virtually eliminate the time lag between the generation of a requisition by a catalogue user and the issue of the purchase order as:
  - authorisation, where required, can be done online and notified and confirmed by e-mail
  - where users are authorised to generate their own purchases (subject to value and item constraints), the order can be automatically generated without the intervention of the purchasing department
- maverick or 'off-contract' purchasing is reduced because it is simpler and quicker to purchase from contracted suppliers than to go outside the official system.

5.8.3 Types of e-catalogue

Sell-side catalogues

These provide potential purchasers with access to the online catalogues of a particular supplier who provides an online purchasing facility.

Sell-side catalogues provide many benefits to suppliers, including ease of keeping the contents up to date, savings on advertising costs and the costs of processing a sale. The benefits to potential purchasers include 24/7 access to information and ease of ordering.

Sell-side catalogues have, however, several disadvantages, including:

- purchasers having insufficient time to surf all the available supplier websites
- buyers perhaps becoming overly dependent on particular suppliers as training in the use of new software may be required if suppliers are changed
- where the price of a product differs from one purchaser to another, the use of personalised, restricted, prenegotiated catalogues or encrypted catalogues may be necessary.

Buy-side catalogues

These are catalogues created by procurement organisations. Normally, such catalogues are confined to goods covered by prenegotiated prices, specifications and terms and run by a programme that is integrated into the procurement organisation's intranet. An example of the operation of buy-side catalogues is shown in Figure 5.6.

The benefits to purchasers include:

- reduced communication costs
- increased security
- many catalogues can be accessed via the same intranet application.

The compilation and updating of buy-side catalogues does, however, require a large investment in clerical resources that will be uneconomical for all but the largest organisations. Suppliers wishing to be included in the catalogue will also be required to provide their content in a standard format. For suppliers dealing with a large number of purchasers, the workload in terms of providing information in the form required by each online catalogue will be unsustainable.

Figure 5.6 Buy-side catalogue operation

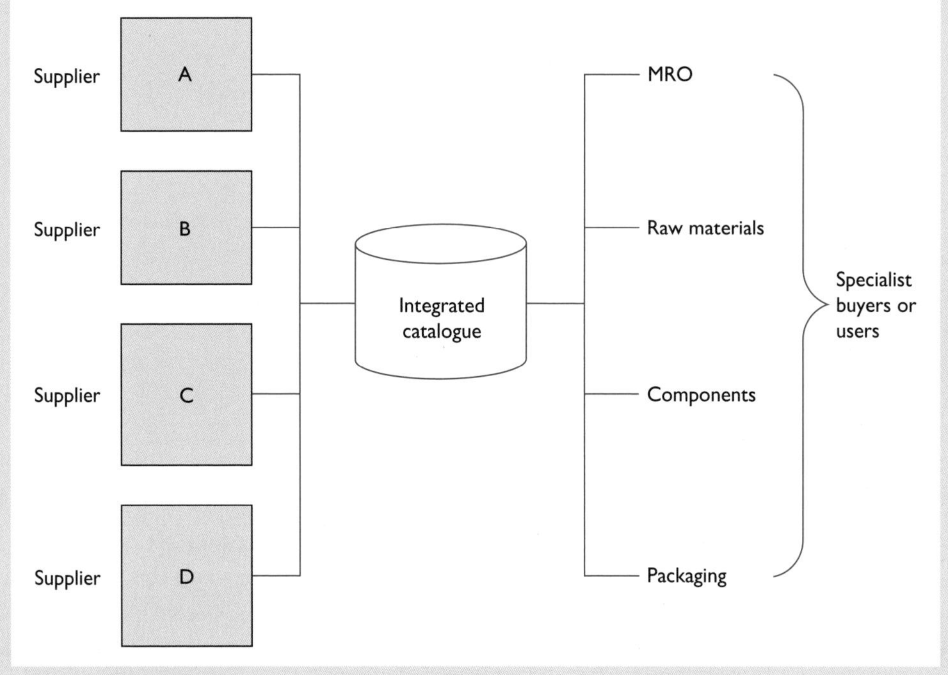

Third-party catalogues

The disadvantages of sell-side and buy-side catalogues can be minimised by outsourcing the process to an electronic marketplace or buying consortium.

■ Standard information for inclusion in the 'market site' or 'master catalogue' is provided by the suppliers. This information is then made available to the in-house catalogues of individual procurement organisations.

■ Product information from suppliers can either reside in the in-house catalogue or be hosted in the master catalogue.

■ The responsibility of managing and updating product and other information rests with the suppliers.

Advantages of this system include that:

■ suppliers have a good incentive to provide information in the specified standard format as the master catalogue will be available to a large number of procurement organisations

■ the in-house procurement catalogues draw product and other information from the master catalogue and purchasers or users can pass electronic orders to suppliers via the market site

■ product information can be divided into two parts – public and encrypted and public information will include a basic product description and specification, often accompanied by an illustration or diagram, while encrypted information will provide details of prices, discounts and similar matters applicable to specific purchasers that cannot be accessed by unauthorised users.

5.9 E-auctions

One step up from e-catalogue is e-auctions. An e-auction may be defined as:[16]

> An electronic auction (eAuction) is a procurement tool that uses web-based software to permit potential suppliers to compete online, in real time, to provide prices for goods/services under auction. E-Auctions are a legally compliant legal process.

Web auctions may follow English, Dutch, Japanese sealed-bid and reverse-bid processes.

- *English bid process* – in this process, bids are successively replaced by higher bids to obtain the highest price for a given item.
- *Dutch bid process* – the English process is unsuitable for selling thousands of items to a number of different buyers. This can, however, be easily and quickly done in a 'Dutch auction', developed in the seventeenth century in Amsterdam for the sale of flowers. In a Dutch auction, the auctioneer starts at a high price and then descends by steps until a bid is received. The successful bidder then decides whether to buy the whole or a portion of the items on offer at that price. The auctioneer increases the offer price for any items remaining in the current lot and then again descends by steps and continues in this manner until either all the items comprising the lot are sold or a reserve price is reached.
- *Japanese bid process* – bidders must accept the opening price, defined by the buyer, in order to be able to participate in the auction. By accepting the opening price, the bidder is agreeing to supply the goods or services for the price defined by the buyer. As bidders agree to prices, the bid price is reduced at pre-defined intervals and bidders are prompted to accept or reject the new price. This continues until there is only one bidder remaining.
- *Sealed-bid process* – this is broadly similar to tendering. A potential purchaser issues a request for bids to be submitted by a prescribed date and time according to a sealed format. At the specified date and time, the purchaser's representatives will evaluate and compare the bids according to a rating grid. The winning bid is the one that achieves the maximum score. Should several bids obtain the same score, the bid offering the best price is the winner.
- Reverse-bid processes – see section 5.10.

Intergraf[16] have observed that among the several e-commerce business forms, e-auctions are a very special one. Reverse auctions (in which supplier companies compete for a job providing increasingly lower prices) are particularly interesting, but can be dangerous for competing companies if transparency, clarity and honesty aren't assured.
The Code of Conduct published by Intergraf in 2005 includes:

> The **promoter** and the **participant buyer** are bounded to guarantee the honesty, transparency and equity of the conditions in which the e-auction is done, namely regarding the relations with the participant supplier and the following topics:

- Supply to all the participant suppliers the same information, according to the same divulgation criteria
- Supply to each participant supplier all the information necessary to present the bid, namely:
  - specify all the technical, packaging and service aspects relevant to each product or service of the buyer's proposal, as well as all the details that can contribute to define the price. The promoter/buyer must, as a consequence, provide each participant supplier a sample of the product or products taken to auction, at least 10 days before the auction takes place. If this sample is not available, an equivalent or similar product must be provided
  - specify whether mixed proposals – which have different products and/or services – are accepted
  - specify the duration of the electronic auction
  - specify the conditions of the contract, namely the ones regarding payment conditions, currency to be used in the business, delivery places, minimum and maximum amount per delivery place, deadline accorded after the issuing of the order, etc.
- Supply all the participant suppliers with a complete list of participant suppliers in the e-auction, at least 24 hours before it starts
- Clear identification of the participant suppliers' pre-selection and selection criteria and of the relative importance of each of these criteria; reasons for not being selected must be communicated to the non-selected.

5.10 Reverse auctions

5.10.1 What is a reverse auction?

In a reverse auction, buying organisations post the item(s) they wish to buy and price they are willing to pay while suppliers compete to offer the best price for the item(s) over a prescribed time period.

For example, a buying organisation is interested in purchasing 1000 castings to a published specification at the lowest possible price. It therefore creates a reverse auction, stating the dimensions, quality, performance and delivery requirements and, often, bid decrements. Suppliers enter the marketplace and bid on the auction. Winners are declared according to the agreed auction rules. Thus, e-auctions may be structured using the lowest price or most economically advantageous tender (MEAT) options.

At the conclusion of the auction, both purchaser and supplier are bound by the sale. If a reserve price is set but not met, the buying organisation decides the winning bid. Suppliers can bid more than once in the prescribed time. Apart from the names of the suppliers and reverse sealed bid auctions, all the bids are available for everyone to see. Most online auction sites use automatic bidding against agents or a 'proxy bidder' that automatically place bids on the suppliers' behalf.

5.10.2 When to use reverse auctions

Most reverse auctions are used for spot buying and eliminate the time-consuming offline process of selecting suppliers, requesting quotations and comparing quotes received. Marketplaces with many suppliers can offer purchasers a compiled list of suppliers. Procurement organisations conducting reverse auctions on their own sites must invite prospective suppliers in advance if they wish such suppliers to participate. Reverse auctions are particularly useful in the following circumstances:

Example 5.1

Reverse auction 1

Bids are solicited for 100 product Xs. The opening bid is £25 per product, with bid decrements of £5:

- supplier A bids £25 each for 100 items
- supplier B bids £20 each for 50 items
- supplier C bids £15 each for 50 items.

The result of the auction is that:

- supplier A is unsuccessful
- supplier B sells 50 items for £20
- supplier C sells 50 items for £15.

There are several variations on the bidding process. In what is known as the reverse English manual system, the buying organisation specifies the opening bid and the supplier bids higher. At the conclusion of the auction, the purchaser selects the winners manually. Each winning bidder sells at the bid price made. The criteria for the winning bid may not be disclosed.

Example 5.2

Reverse auction 2

Bids are solicited for 100 product Xs. The opening bid is £25:

- supplier A bids £18 per item for 100 items
- supplier B bids £20 per item for 100 items
- supplier C bids £20 per item for 100 items.

The result of the auction is that:

- supplier A is unsuccessful
- supplier C sells 100 items for £20, because of closer geographical proximity to the purchaser than supplier B.

- when there is uncertainty as to the size of the market and the willingness of sellers to supply a product
- when purchasing large quantities of an item for which clear specifications are possible
- when selling surplus assets
- for some services, such as car rentals, freight services, travel.

The consensus used to be that the lowest-price reverse auction process should be used only when there is little concern about production specifications or the selected suppliers.

Reverse auctions were not considered appropriate for complicated products or projects requiring collaboration or considerable negotiation. *Buy IT,*[17] however, states that software providers are now expanding their offerings to ensure that online auction tools become an integral part of the broader procurement strategy process, including the creation and management of optimal long-term value partnerships. As the goods or services became more difficult to specify and the relationships between purchasers and suppliers became more integrated, online auctions became less about driving cost out of the supply chain and more of a tool for collaboration.

5.10.3 The reverse auction process

Figure 5.7 indicates the principal steps involved.

5.10.4 Reverse auction guidelines

A useful summary of online auction 'dos and don'ts', which, if followed, all help to ensure a successful auction, is shown in Figure 5.8.

5.10.5 Advantages of reverse auctions

Reverse auctions provide benefits for both buyers and sellers. The benefits for buyers include:

■ savings over and above those obtained from normal negotiations as a result of competition – on average, the auction process drives down supplier process by 11 per cent, with savings ranging from 4 to 40 per cent[18]
■ reductions in acquisition lead times
■ access to a wider range of suppliers
■ a global supply base can be achieved relatively quickly
■ sources of market information are enhanced
■ more efficient administration of requests for quotations (RFQs) and proposals
■ auctions conducted on the Internet generally provide total anonymity so time is not wasted on seeing suppliers' representatives.

The benefits for suppliers include:

■ an opportunity to enter previously closed markets, which is particularly important for smaller companies
■ reduced negotiation timescales
■ provision of a good source of market pricing information
■ clear indications of what must be done to win the business.

5.10.6 Disadvantages of reverse auctions

Some objections to reverse auction include that they:

■ are based on a win–lose approach – the seller is trying to get the most money while the buyer is after the best deal and the goal is to screw your opponent to win either a good deal or a profitable deal at the other person's expense, so the logical progression

Figure 5.7 **The reverse auction process**

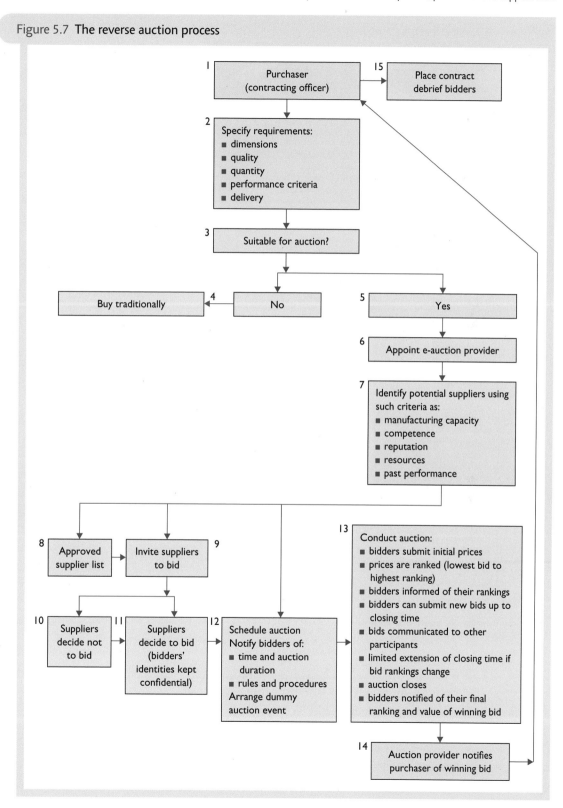

Figure 5.8 Online reverse auction

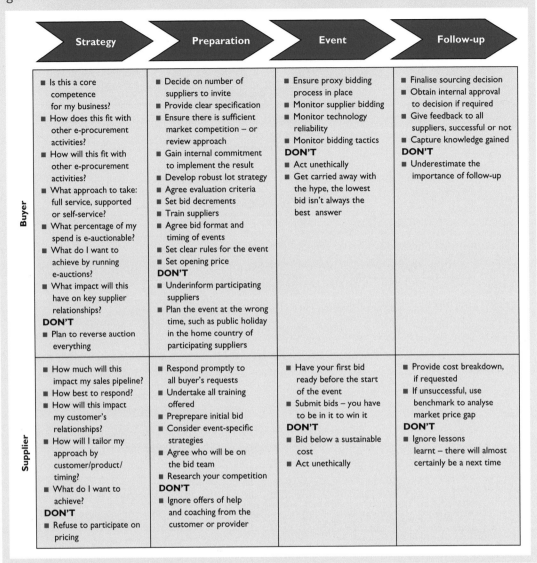

	Strategy	Preparation	Event	Follow-up
Buyer	▪ Is this a core competence for my business? ▪ How does this fit with other e-procurement activities? ▪ How will this fit with other e-procurement activities? ▪ What approach to take: full service, supported or self-service? ▪ What percentage of my spend is e-auctionable? ▪ What do I want to achieve by running e-auctions? ▪ What impact will this have on key supplier relationships? **DON'T** ▪ Plan to reverse auction everything	▪ Decide on number of suppliers to invite ▪ Provide clear specification ▪ Ensure there is sufficient market competition – or review approach ▪ Gain internal commitment to implement the result ▪ Develop robust lot strategy ▪ Agree evaluation criteria ▪ Set bid decrements ▪ Train suppliers ▪ Agree bid format and timing of events ▪ Set clear rules for the event ▪ Set opening price **DON'T** ▪ Underinform participating suppliers ▪ Plan the event at the wrong time, such as public holiday in the home country of participating suppliers	▪ Ensure proxy bidding process in place ▪ Monitor supplier bidding ▪ Monitor technology reliability ▪ Monitor bidding tactics **DON'T** ▪ Act unethically ▪ Get carried away with the hype, the lowest bid isn't always the best answer	▪ Finalise sourcing decision ▪ Obtain internal approval to decision if required ▪ Give feedback to all suppliers, successful or not ▪ Capture knowledge gained **DON'T** ▪ Underestimate the importance of follow-up
Supplier	▪ How much will this impact my sales pipeline? ▪ How best to respond? ▪ How will this impact my customer's relationships? ▪ How will I tailor my approach by customer/product/ timing? ▪ What do I want to achieve? **DON'T** ▪ Refuse to participate on pricing	▪ Respond promptly to all buyer's requests ▪ Undertake all training offered ▪ Preprepare initial bid ▪ Consider event-specific strategies ▪ Agree who will be on the bid team ▪ Research your competition **DON'T** ▪ Ignore offers of help and coaching from the customer or provider	▪ Have your first bid ready before the start of the event ▪ Submit bids – you have to be in it to win it **DON'T** ▪ Bid below a sustainable cost ▪ Act unethically	▪ Provide cost breakdown, if requested ▪ If unsuccessful, use benchmark to analyse market price gap **DON'T** ▪ Ignore lessons learnt – there will almost certainly be a next time

Source: The authors are grateful to David Eaton and the *Buy IT* e-procurement Best Practice Network for permission to use this figure, taken from 'Buy IT Online Auctions', 2001, p. 5.

is always towards cheating and, therefore, such a system cannot be sustained without burdensome watchdogs and regulators

▪ can cause an adverse shift in buyer–seller relationships as the supplier may feel exploited and become less trustful of buyers

▪ can have long-term adverse effects on the economic performance of both suppliers and purchasers as:

- some suppliers may not be able to sustain sharp price reductions in the long term
- suppliers that cannot compete at the lower price levels may be removed, or ask to be removed, from the purchaser's approved supplier list so those purchasers eventually have reduced supplier bases
- in order to ensure that the exact goods and services required are obtained, considerable time may be needed to complete detailed specification sheets.

5.11 E-payment

E-payment may be by a standalone method, as with a purchasing card, or incorporated into software, as with the UK Ministry of Defence's (MoD) purchase to payment (P2P) system. This system enables:

- an electronic order for goods and services to be sent to a trading partner
- an electronic receipt to be held and linked to the order for goods and services
- an electronic invoice to be sent to the MoD
- the order, receipt and invoice to be matched online, generating an electronic message authorising the processing of payment that is sent to the trading partner.

Figure 5.9 provides a useful map of e-payment and invoicing applications and the vendors that provide them, placing the different options according to whether the value of the purchase to which the payment relates is high or low and also the frequency of payments.

Security and auditing are important aspects of e-payments. Security risks include unauthorised access by hackers, illegal acquisition of PINs and data theft. Approaches to security concerns include:

- *encrypted technologies* – the art of encoding information in such a way that only the holder of a secret password can decode and read it
- *certification authorisations* – organisations that clarify and provide proof that a signature is valid.

In any e-payments system, it is vital that each invoice and payment is traceable throughout the system. The audit trail should track every line of data right back to the file where it originated.

5.12 Low-value purchases

There can be a disproportionate amount of time spent by procurement departments processing small value purchases where the administrative expenditure cannot be counterbalanced by any savings. The potential scale of these small value purchases can be illustrated by reference to the Acquisitions Branch of Public Works & Government Services Canada who in 2002 issued 33,000 contracts and 11,000 amendments worth more than $10bn in goods, services and construction. Of those contracts 62 per cent were below $25,000.

Low-cost procedures for the efficient handling of low-value purchases include the following.

Figure 5.9 Solutions landscape for electronic invoicing and payments

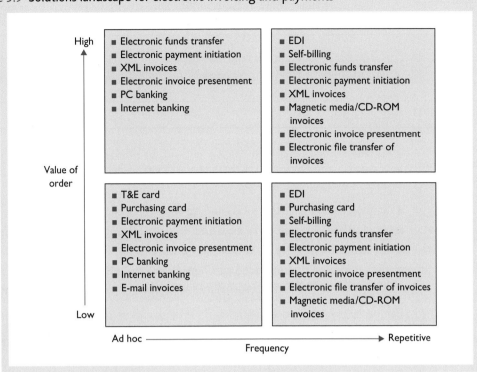

Source: We are grateful to CIPS for permission to reproduce this figure, taken from 'The CIPS e-procurement guidelines: e-invoicing and e-payment'

5.12.1 Delegated order placement to users

This is the placement of orders by users within specified limits and with approved suppliers over the Internet.

5.12.2 Procurement cards

These are similar to credit cards and involve a provider such as an International Bank and usually an issuing bank. When used for low-value purchases, they enable any user, such as a foreman on a building site, to make purchases and provide payments to suppliers. Richardson[19] has listed the following benefits of using procurement cards:

- compliance levels can improve where more orders are going through preferred suppliers, which can lead to better volume discounts
- average transaction and order processing costs can drop dramatically
- implementation costs are 10 to 100 times less than for an ERP or e-procurement system
- suppliers are paid faster, enabling them to invest in their business and improve their services to clients
- greater and improved documentation of data on accounts, suppliers and taxes

- less procurement employee time spent on order paperwork and chasing, allowing more time for strategic and tactical work.

Clearly the issue and use of procurement cards has to be carefully controlled. The cardholder should be held responsible for protecting the procurement card and for all purchases made using a particular procurement card number.

Neither the physical procurement card nor its account number should be shared with or transferred to any other person to use. A procurement card internal review should be held periodically to ensure compliance with controls, appropriateness of purchases, that cards are actually in the possession of the authorised holders and that there is general adherence to specific procurement procedures.

5.12.3 Other methods of dealing with low-value purchases

Other methods of dealing with low-value purchases are listed below.

- *Telephone orders* – requirements are telephoned to the supplier who is provided with an order number. The agreed price is recorded on the order form, but this is not sent to the supplier. The goods are invoiced by the supplier against the order form.

- *Petty cash purchases* – items are obtained directly from local suppliers on presentation of an authorised requisition form and paid for at once from petty cash. The main problem is that of controlling the numbers and sizes of such purchases. This can be done by providing potential users with a petty cash imprest, out of which such payments are made.

- *Standing orders* – all orders for a range of items, such as electrical fittings, fasteners, are placed with one supplier for a period of, say, 12 months. A special discount is often negotiated and quantities may or may not be specified. Required items are called off by users who transmit releases directly from the supplier via a fax, telephone or computer interface. The amount due is summarised by the supplier, either electronically or tabulated as a single invoice, and segregated by users' cost centres for easier coding by the accounts function.

- *Self-billing* – this uses EDI. When the former Rover Group, which traded electronically, received goods from a supplier, it checked that the goods were ordered and then simply paid. The supplier did not need to raise an invoice. Self-billing enables both customer and supplier to make saving.

- *Blank cheque orders* – a system devised in the USA. A cheque form with a specified liability is attached to the order form. On forwarding the goods, the supplier fills in the cheque, which he or she deposits in his or her own bank. The cheque can only be deposited, not cashed, until authorised by the purchaser. The need for invoicing and forwarding of payment is thus avoided.

- *Stockless buying* – this is virtually the same as blanket ordering, but the supplier agrees to maintain stocks of specified items.

5.13 Procurement manuals

5.13.1 What is procurement manual?

Essentially, a procurement manual is a medium for communicating information regarding procurement policies, procedures, instructions and regulations.

- *Policies* may be general or consequential. *General policies* state, in broad terms, the objectives and responsibilities of the procurement function. *Consequential policies* state, in expanded form, how general policies are applied in specific activities and situations, such as the selection of suppliers.
- *Procedures* prescribe the sequence of activities by which policies are implemented, such as the receipt of bought-out goods.
- *Instructions* give detailed knowledge or guidance to those responsible for carrying out the policies or procedures, such as suppliers with whom call-off contracts have been negotiated.
- *Regulations* are detailed rules regarding the conduct of procurement and ancillary staff in the various situations arising in the course of their duties, such as concerning the receipt of gifts from suppliers.

When drafting a procurement manual, it is useful to keep these distinctions clearly in mind.

5.13.2 Advantages of procurement manuals

Advantages claimed for procurement manuals include the following:

- writing it down helps with precision and clarity
- the preparation of the manual provides an opportunity for consultation between procurement and other departments to look critically at existing policies and procedures and, where necessary, change them
- procedures are prescribed in terms of activities undertaken or controlled by purchasing, thus promoting consistency and reducing the need for detailed supervision of routine tasks
- a manual is a useful aid in training and guiding staff
- a manual can help the annual audit
- a manual coordinates policies and procedures and helps to ensure uniformity and continuity of procurement principles and practice, as well as providing a point of reference against which such principles and practice can be evaluated
- a manual may help to enhance the status of procurement by showing that top management attaches importance to the procurement function
- computerisation, which needs detailed and well-documented systems, has given further impetus to the preparation of procurement manuals.

5.13.3 Disadvantages of procurement manuals

Some disadvantages of manuals are that they:

- are costly to prepare
- tend to foster red tape and bureaucracy and stifle initiative
- must be continually updated to show changes in procedures and policy.

5.13.4 Format

Although hard-copy manuals are still produced, the most suitable format is that of an operational database used to process the information needed to perform operational tasks.

This can be available internally via an intranet or externally on the Internet. As the manual is freely accessible, it encourages transparency and can easily be updated.

5.13.5 Contents

A procurement manual may consist of three main sections, dealing respectively with organisation, policy and procedures.

- Organisation
  - Charts showing the place of procurement within the undertaking and how it is organised, both centrally and locally.
  - Possibly job descriptions for all posts within the procurement function, including, where applicable, limitations of remits.
  - Teams relating to procurement and supply chain activities.
  - Administrative information for staff, such as absences, hours of work, travelling expenses and similar matters.

- Policy
  - Statements of policy, setting out the objectives, responsibilities and authority of the procurement function.
  - Statements, which can be expanded, of general principles relating to price, quality and delivery.
  - Terms and conditions of contract and use of Standard Forms of Contract.
  - Ethical relationships with suppliers, especially regarding gifts and entertainment.
  - Environmental policies.
  - Supplier appraisal and selection.
  - Employee purchases.
  - Reports to management.

- Procedures
  - Descriptions, accompanied by flow charts, of procedures relating to requisitioning, ordering, expediting, receiving, inspecting, storing and payment of goods with special reference to procurement.
  - Procedures relating to the rejection and return of goods.
  - Procedures regarding the disposal of scrap and obsolete or surplus items.

5.14 Procurement playbook

'Supplier Manual' has become, in some measure, an outdated concept. The more modern approach is to create a playbook. Russell Investments,[20] through their Director Global Sourcing and Procurement, provide a detailed explanation of how they created the playbook. It mirrors the author's experience creating a playbook for an international financial institution.

At the time Russell Investments' Global Sourcing & Procurement team had 30 associates responsible for $1 billion in spend.

They explain the signs that your sourcing/supplier management organisation needs a playbook:

- Negative feedback from stakeholders
  - Engaging sourcing/supplier management is too complex and confusing
  - Quality depends on who I work with
  - A lot of re-work and delay

- Your team is confused about what they are expected to do
- People try to apply best practices but find conflict or contradiction
- Missing stakeholders: negotiate a good deal and discover nobody is using the product.

In the author's experience these warning signs can be extended to include:

- Internal audit exposes significant non-compliance with policies
- Stakeholders unaware of contractual obligations they create
- Life-cycle costs not taken into account at time of purchase
- Stakeholders circumvent procurement procedures
- Supplier regularly by-pass procurement specialists
- Specifications favour a specific supplier.

5.14.1 Playbook requirements

Russell Investments[21] outline their components of the sourcing playbook:

- Engagement
- Triage (contemplates what is in scope and what is not; what is subject to playbook and what is not)
- Requirements gathering
- Project kick-off
- Conduct sourcing
  - Quick quote
  - eRFP
  - e-auction

- Contracting
- Implementation
- Assigning a supplier tier
- Transition from sourcing to supplier relationship management.

Russell Investments[22] include a thought-provoking checklist for the analysis phase of creating a playbook.

Requirements Checklist – Sample

1   Analysis Phase

Your primary objective is: To understand and to gather as much information. Try to be a detective, to make no assumption, and to challenge all assumptions. You must not figure out the solution (not how you are going to source or construct the event).

1.1 Understand the product or service like an expert
1.1.1 Staple yourself to the product or service, understand how it is being used, how it is made, how we consume it
1.1.2 Challenge the defined scope/specs
1.1.3 Can it be different, what if we don't have any constraints
1.1.4 Make a list of all the assumptions that the business/sourcing are making
1.1.5 Understand all assumptions that may impact competition
1.1.6 Understand the service component (SLAs, delivery requirements, support, helpdesk, lead-time, warranty, disposal etc. . . .)
1.1.7 What happens if the service or product is not delivered (impact to business etc.)?

1.2 History
1.2.1 Is the product or service new?
1.2.2 When was the last time this was sourced?
1.2.3 Are there any performance issues with the service?
1.2.4 Alternatives
    1.2.4.1 Can you identify 2 alternatives ways to get the product or service?

1.3 To understand the supplier base. Think like a supplier
1.3.1 Gather supplier information from Sourcing & LOB
    1.3.1.1 Conduct your own supplier search (Web, associations, union, catalog, competitor to the incumbent, diversity suppliers)
    1.3.1.2 Look for big suppliers, small suppliers, vertically integrated
    1.3.1.3 Make sure you have a good mixture of suppliers
    1.3.1.4 Which suppliers will be hungry / desperate? Will the incumbent defend its position?
    1.3.1.5 Is there any certification or prequalification requirements for suppliers?
    1.3.1.6 Is geography or logistics a factor in supplier choice?

1.4 To understand the baseline:
1.4.1 How much $ spend via AP, AA? If possible over last 2-3 years. Minimum 1 year / 12 months.
1.4.2 How much $ spend via supplier/Sourcing/LOB

Discussion questions

5.1 Describe the four major levels of organisation policy.

5.2 Using the Crossrail Procurement Policy as your reference, find another published Procurement Policy and identify the purpose of this latter policy.

5.3 Identify four Key Policy Principles for General Procurement.

5.4 What is a Procurement Procedure and how does it help the procurement function to fulfil its corporate obligations?

5.5 (a) Prepare a flow chart of a traditional, paper-based procurement system from the receipt of a requisition to the payment of the supplier.
(b) Estimate the time taken and the cost of each stage in the above process.
(c) Prepare a flow chart showing how the same activities would be done under e-procurement.
(d) Estimate the savings in time and cost using e-procurement.

5.6 Why, in many organisations, is e-procurement limited to MRO (maintenance, repair and operating) items?

5.7 E-procurement can rarely be a total success because it depersonalises the process. The absence of personal contact can lead to misunderstandings and weaken relationships. Would you agree with this? Why do you hold your views?

5.8 What are the classic problems of introducing EDI?

5.9 Why is Business Process Integration of strategic importance to an organisation?

5.10 Do you purchase using an e-catalogue? If you do, what are your views on:
(a) how it is kept up to date?
(b) how the range of products compares with what is available in the market?
(c) its advantages over a buyer conducting their own market search?

5.11 Reverse auctions are an increasing facet of procurement. At the end of the process prices are agreed without any face-to-face negotiation. Comment on this in regard to the following:
(a) It is impossible to understand the cost drivers.
(b) The purchase was made on price alone.
(c) The supplier with the lowest price must cut his quality to make a profit.

5.12 XML offers its users many advantages, including:
(a) simplicity
(b) extensibility
(c) interoperability
(d) openness.
Give one example of how XML provides each of the above advantages.

5.13 In what ways do you predict the use of e-procurement will next develop? When you respond please consider:
(a) the international dimension of procurement
(b) the fact that supply chains are becoming extended through many tiers
(c) the need for effective contract management
(d) the potential for fraud with electronic systems.

References

1   Klein, W. C. and Murphy, D. C., *Policies: Concept in Organisational Guidance*. Little-Brown, Boston, USA, 1973, p. 2.

2   Crossrail Procurement Policy Document Number CR/QMS/PROC/POL/1101.

3   London Assembly. GLA Oversight Committee. March 2016 The Garden Bridge Design Procurement.

4   International Electronic Commerce. Definitions and Policy Implications, GAO-02-404.

5   Zwass, V., 'Electronic commerce: structures and issues', *International Journal of Electronic Commerce*, Vol 1. No. 1. Fall 1996, pp. 3–23.

6   Hackbarth, G. and Kettinger, W. J., 'Building an E- business strategy', *Information Systems Management* Vol. 17, 2000, p. 78.

7   Greenstein, M. and Feinmann, T. *Electronic Commerce Security, Risk Management & Control* Irwin McGraw-Hill, Boston, 2000.

8   Hui-Chun Lee, 'A Survey and Implementation of e-Commerce in Supply Chain Management, Knowledge Systems Institute. Chicago. Partial fulfilment of MSc degree.

9   Kalakota, R. and Robinson, M., *E-business 2.0*, 2nd edn, Addison Wesley, Boston, USA, 2001, p. 310.

10 As 8 above.

11 Armstrong, V. and Jackson, D., *Electronic Data Interchange: A Guide to Purchasing and Supply*' CIPS, Stamford, UK, 1991, pp. 15–16.

12 Killen, K. H. and Kamauff, J. W., *Managing Purchasing*, Irwin, 1995, p. 60.

13 Norman, G., 'Is it time for EDI?', Logistics Supplement, *Journal of Purchasing and Supply Management*, June, 1994, p. 20.

14 Monczka, R. M. and Carter, J. R., 'Implementation of electronic data interchange', *Journal of Purchasing and Supply Management*, Summer, 1998, pp. 2–9.

15 National Computing Centre, 'The impact of e-purchasing on supply chain management', *My IT Adviser*, 17 September, 2002.

16 International confederation for printing and allied industries, 'E-Auctions – Code of Conduct', March 2005.

17 *Buy IT*, 'Online auctioning: e-procurement guidelines', issued by Buy IT Best Practice Network, October, 2001, pp. 13–14.

18 Lascelles, D., *Managing the Supply Chain*, Business Intelligence, 2001, p. 44.

19 Richardson, T., 'Guide to purchasing cards', Supplement, *Purchasing and Supply Management*, 2003, p. 7.

20 www.sig.org 'How to create a Playbook for a best-in-class Supplier Lifecycle Program' 2015.

21 Same as 20 above.

22 Same as 21 above.

Part 2

Strategy, tactics and operations 1: Procurement factors

Chapter 6

Supplier relationships and partnering

Learning outcomes

This chapter aims to provide an understanding of:

- relationship procurement and procurement relationships
- the application of power in relationship management
- supplier relationship management – strategic focus
- the contrast between transactional and relationship procurement taking account of contractual requirements
- collaborative business relationships
- SRM model
- models of supplier relationships
- supplier relationship management – a critique
- the termination of relationships
- relationship breakdown on an IT project
- further aspects of relationships.

Key ideas

- Effective procurement planning to create positive relationships.
- Key considerations of transactional and relationship procurement.
- Relationship formation.
- Classification and analysis of supplier relationships.
- Contract governance principles and application.
- The business benefits of supplier relationship models.
- Evaluating mutual benefits from the relationship.
- Factors to consider when terminating relationships.

Introduction

This chapter provides an understanding of procurement–supplier relationships from the perspectives of both theory and practice. A critical scrutiny of the history of such relationships has demonstrated the opportunities for buyer and seller when genuine long-term relationships are established. For these relationships to be achieved it will require an investment of resources, changes in attitudes and the abandonment of adversarial business practice.

6.1 Relationship procurement and procurement relationships

Relationships apply when individuals, organisations and groups within and external to an enterprise interact. Apart from the field of industrial sociology, concerned with the study of group interaction within a workplace environment, the application of the study of business relationships began with the concept of relationship marketing.

Supplier relationship management (SRM)[1] is an approach between two parties to work towards the integration of their organisations, where that integration will bring greater value for money for the customer and enhanced margin for the supplier and will assist in meeting the strategic objectives of both. It is not an agreement to sole source, or outsource to a supplier, rather to integrate aspects of the two organisations for mutual benefit. These benefits must be real and tangible, not just relationship indicators.

The most successful relationships are those where customers and suppliers develop trust and an understanding of their respective requirements and interests, accompanied by a desire for both to learn from and provide assistance to each other. Where such conditions exist, the ultimate outcome should be the creation of established, positive and dependable procurement–supplier relationships.

6.2 The application of power in relationship management

It is inevitable that power will be exercised in relationship management. In 1959 French and Raven[2] identified five bases of power, coercive, reward, legitimate, referent and expert. In 1965 Raven[3] added a sixth, informational power. These bases of power are very relevant to supplier relationship management, as outlined below

Coercive	This is where the threat of price is used to gain compliance from another. Suppliers use the threat of preventing supply unless price increases are agreed immediately.
Reward	This is where a supplier offers or denies rewards to the buyer. An example is promotional support to a retail buyer provided exclusivity is agreed for a range or specific lines.
Legitimate	This power comes from those in elected or selected positions of authority. An example is the insistence by a supplier that the buyer only deals with a nominated person in a senior position.
Referent	This power is rooted in supplier affiliations that are made. It can be positive when common business ideals are shared, such as long-term business.

Expert	This power is based on knowledge, skills and experience. If, for example, the buyer has expert knowledge of a supply market it strengthens his position.
Informational	This is a crucial power for a buyer and others engaged in relationship management. For example, an impeccable understanding on a supplier's performance is very useful at contract reviews.

6.3 Supplier relationship management – strategic focus

During 2018 the author helped a European manufacturer to resource key components, previously manufactured in Europe to be, in future, manufactured in Korea. The resourcing was a tangible leap in procurement strategy for senior management and procurement who had never changed this source of supply in the history of the manufacturer. Extensive strategic supply chain planning took place and ten factors were to determine where focused relationship management was necessary. These are shown in Table 6.1, together with a salient description of each factor.

Factors affecting supply chain collaboration – Ding[4] has produced a very useful table, see Table 6.2, of the factors affecting supply chain collaboration.

Table 6.1 Farrington determinants of supply chain relationship

Determinant	Description
1. RISK	A preparedness by the supplier to accept certain risks and contract accordingly.
2. CONTRACTUAL OBLIGATIONS	A preparedness by the supplier to accept specific obligations and the attendant liabilities.
3. WORLD-WIDE DISTRIBUTION	Acceptance that the supplier had a robust world-wide distribution network.
4. DISTRIBUTOR LOGISTICS	The existence of a proven distributor network and associated logistics.
5. MARKETING SUPPORT	The supplier to create and provide a marketing budget and campaigns to support buying organisations marketing.
6. TECHNOLOGY DEVELOPMENT	Proof that Research & Development is a continuing business activity and evidence of historical product improvements.
7. COST/COMPETITIVENESS	There are other suppliers, so the cost must be competitive and sustainable.
8. BUSINESS GROWTH INCENTIVES	The supplier must reward the buying organisation's business growth with additional marketing cooperation.
9. CULTURE MANAGEMENT	The buying organisation sells product into diverse cultures and requires the expertise of the seller to assist in culture management.
10. CORPORATE RELATIONSHIP	There must be regular high-level reviews of relationships and performance.

Table 6.2 Factors affecting supply chain collaboration

Variables	Definition
Independent variables	
TRUST	A positive belief, attitude, or expectation of one party concerning the likelihood that the action or outcomes of another will be satisfactory. This factor therefore affects positively on supply chain collaboration
POWER	When designing a supply chain and cooperating with other companies, one has to consider the other actor's size, impact, and status. If the other actor is larger in size, has greater impact, and higher status, it will have more power in that relation. With greater power comes the ability to force a weaker actor to make decisions that are merely favourable for the powerful actor. The effect of power in supply chains has in fact been pointed out by several authors
MATURITY	Increased supply chain interaction maturity leads to reduced uncertainty, and improved business performance and is the best route to follow to achieve competitive advantage. The characteristics of process maturity are predictability, capability, control, effectiveness, and efficiency
FREQUENCY	Frequency refers to how often a transaction occurs. More transactions suggests greater routinisation of interaction and is hence, an implication/incitement to form a closer relationship to make sure that transactions run smoothly
DISTANCE	Distance between the partners in the supply chain refer to the geographical distance, the culture distance and the organisational gap between partners through the supply chain
CULTURE	Defined as a shared values and belief that can help to understand organisational functioning and provide behavioural norms. The collective programming of the mind which distinguishes the members of one group or category of people from another. Differences in organisational or social level, could create differences of opinion or conflicts of interest
STRATEGY	Collaborative planning refers to collaborations among trading partners to develop various plans such as production planning and scheduling, new product development, inventory replenishment, and promotions and advertisement. Decision synchronisation refers to the process by which supply chain partners orchestrate decisions in supply chain planning and operations that optimise the supply chain benefits
POLICIES	Governmental intervention in business activities. Local governments exert more direct influences by implementing formal and informal policies related to economic activity
COMMITMENT	Commitment refers to the willingness of trading partners to exert effort on behalf of the relationship and suggests a future orientation in which firms attempt to build a relationship that can be sustained in the face of unanticipated problems (Porter et al., 1974)
Dependent variable	
Collaboration in supply chain of mechanical enterprises in Vietnam	

Source: Summarised by author (2015). *International Journal of Managing Value and Supply Chains (IJMVSC)* Vol. 6, No. 4, December 2015.

Table 6.3 The main differences and contractual requirements of transactional and relationship procurement

Transactional	Relationship	Contractual requirement
Focus on discrete procurement actions and one-off contracts	Focus on supplier retention providing KPIs are satisfied	One-off as opposed to long-term contract with commitments to offtake
Short-term orientation	Long-term orientation	Supplier commitment to continuous improvement and investment in research
Arm's length	Closeness	Creation of joint partnering board, Open Book and sharing of long-term business plans
Simple buyer–seller relationship	Integrated relationship with involvement of stakeholders	Dedication to bringing about teamwork, effective contract review meetings and effective evaluation of issues
Emphasis on price, quality and delivery. No innovation	Sophisticated requirement for innovation, continuous improvement, opportunity for gainshare and visibility of research	Create requirement for demonstrable innovation with defined benefits for both parties
Moderate (or modest) supplier contact	High level of contact, including at senior level in both organisations. Consistent review of performance	Creation of operational and partnering boards, good frequency of review meetings
Little sharing of information; opaqueness	Significant sharing of information	Provision of management information, Open Book on costs and profit, transparency of business plans
Intellectual property not a key consideration	Intellectual property is a key consideration offering additional benefits through exploitation in market as a whole	IP ownership is joint when buyer sharing cost or acting as a BETA site. Licence agreed on agreed financial basis

6.4 The contrast between transactional and relationship procurement, taking account of contractual requirements

Table 6.3[5] has been adapted to include a consideration of contractual requirements to emphasise that, regardless of the relationship, the supplier is agreeing to meet certain contractual obligations.

6.5 Collaborative business relationships

The International Organisation for Standardisation published ISO 44001 in 2017 and this replaces BS11000 – 1:2010. ISO44001 specifies requirements for the effective identification, development and management of collaborative organisations of all sizes. Figure 6.1 illustrates the components of a successful collaborative business relationship.

185

6.5.1 Some of the core concepts of ISO 44001

The core concepts are:

Concept	Comment
Context of the organisation	The range of issues (see below) that can affect, positively or negatively, the way an organisation manages its collaborative relationship responsibilities.
Issues	Issues can be internal or external, positive or negative and include a number of things that either affect or are affected by the organisation.
Interested parties	Much more detail about considering stakeholder needs and expectations, then deciding whether to adopt any of them as compliance obligations.
Leadership	Requirements specific to top management; who are defined as a person or group of people who direct and control an organisation at the highest level.
Risk and opportunities	Refined planning process replaces preventive action. Aspects and impacts now part of risk model.
Communication	There are explicit and more detailed requirements for both internal and external communications.
Nonconformity and corrective action	More detailed evaluation of both the nonconformities themselves and corrective actions required.
Performance evaluation	Covers the measurement of the collaboration management system to identify how operations could be improved or enhanced.

The author is indebted to the Institute of Collaborative Working[6] for the following insight into ISO 44001.

ISO 44001 is not 'a one size fits all' approach and organisations will certainly require tailoring to suit specific and varied situations.

The ISO high level structure of management systems

The original life cycle model as defined by CRAFT was an innovation to change the way organisations looked to develop more integrated relationships. Its core principle was that collaboration frequently failed because it was not fully considered until organisations had largely progressed to contract. Figure 6.2 illustrates the high level structure of management.

The components of a successful collaborative business relationship includes eight components and the author has selected two stages that will be of great interest to procurement and supply chain specialists.

Stage 4 – partner selection

This is an area that can be improved in many organisations. The investment of time and resources will reap later rewards.

It is important to understand the differing dynamics of a collaborative approach and assess the strengths and weaknesses, whatever the route to selection. Where an existing provider is perhaps a single-source option their collaborative capability is frequently

Figure 6.1 **The components of a successful collaborative business relationship**

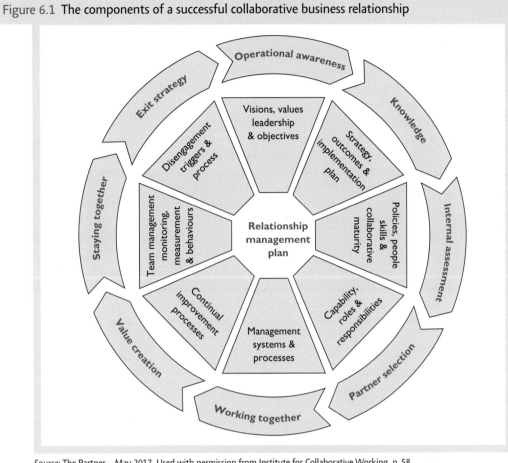

Source: The Partner – May 2017, Used with permission from Institute for Collaborative Working, p. 58

Figure 6.2 **The ISO high-level structure of management**

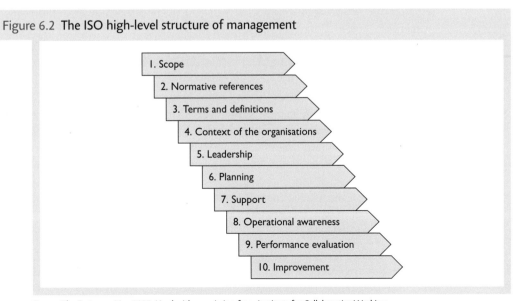

Source: The Partner – May 2017, Used with permission from Institute for Collaborative Working

ignored, as there is no other choice. It is clearly important to ensure that selection maintains the competitive edge that many see only coming from competition and to build confidence in the selection process clearly defining the endgame upfront to avoid confusion later.

- *Nomination of potential collaborative partners.* Whatever the drivers for collaboration, it is important to have a clear perspective on which the potential partner(s) might be. It is unlikely that every potential partner would meet the aspirations and it is sensible to prioritise the business objectives.

- *Partner evaluation and selection.* Assessing a collaborative partner goes beyond compliance to a contract. Organisations may have the attributes to deliver a sound proposition and an established performance record that supports their ability to meet the required performance. However, they may have not progressed in developing an appropriate performance culture that would enable them to fit into the business process of other organisations.

- *Development of engagement and negotiation strategy for collaboration.* The process of negotiation is frequently a significant weakness in the development of collaborative arrangements. The traditional engagement and negotiating models often referred to as win/lose. Negotiations will set a baseline for the relationship and need to be managed in a more structured way around the concepts of win/win. It is important to recognise that trying to force a commercial advantage at this early stage will almost certainly damage the future relationship.

- *Initial engagement with potential partners.* The end game of a sustainable relationship requires consideration as to the steps taken in engaging the market. While this may require a staged approach, each step needs to clearly support the focus for collaboration.

- *Assessment of joint objectives.* Throughout the selection process it is advisable to work with the potential partners to understand their objectives, as well as building a dialogue around common objectives and outcomes. These may not always be the same as yours but should be evaluated for alignment and compatibility.

- *Assessment of joint exit strategy.* In considering the implications of a collaborative engagement the potential partners should jointly evaluate the key aspects of disengagement. Establishing potential triggers and rules of disengagement, possible transition and future development during the partner selection and contracting stage builds confidence between the parties.

- *Selection of preferred partners.* How organisations expect they will be working together will help to define the nature of the contracting relationship and the style of integration and level of interfaces. This will have a significant impact on the development of risk management approaches.

- *Initiation of joint Relationship Management Plan.* Once a collaborative partner has been selected the organisations should incorporate all the principles that have been agreed into a joint Relationship Management Plan and upon which formal arrangements shall be based.

Stage 6 – value creation

This links into contractual requirements for 'continuous improvements'. The procurement profession should, carefully, elaborate on the four bullet points in the ISO 44001 stage 6. For example, the first bullet point 'Establishment of the value creation process' has useful words, including, 'Establishing a joint process that ensures both targeted support and encourages new ideas is very powerful'. What would this mean in practice? It needs a joint technical review team; agreement of intellectual property ownership for joint new developments; active review of field failures and frequency of reviews.

To harness added value means challenging the traditional thinking, creating new value or alternative value propositions beyond those contracted. Innovation is a critical factor in the value creation process. A parallel benefit that comes from introducing a structured approach to value creation is that it supports organisations and teams working together. How organisations choose to encourage innovation depends on a wide variety of factors, but is often managed well by establishing joint cross-functional teams that can be brought together to address specific challenges or ideas.

- *Establishment of the value creation process* While there is great value in a spontaneous approach to innovation, establishing a joint process that ensures both targeted support and encourages new ideas is very powerful. A structured approach will underpin sustainable engagement; it will provide a measure of integration and continual focus on driving greater value from the relationship.

- *Identification of improvement and setting of targets* The key to optimising co-creation is to ensure that identified issues are regularly reviewed and, where necessary, removed if not delivering. This ensures resources are not wasted or diverted from the primary objectives. In a collaborative environment, value creation is about delivering innovative solutions or releasing value that could not be generated by one organisation alone.

- *Utilisation of learning from experience* As organisations begin to work together more closely it is equally important to capture the lessons learned. This is a key aspect of creating value and setting the agenda for innovation.

- *Updating the Joint Relationship Management Plan* The JRMP should be updated to incorporate value creation initiatives which after evaluation and development, as required, are to be incorporated into the operations.

6.6 SRM model

PWC[7] in a research report included a 'Detailed SRM maturity model' that is a very useful tool for procurement and supply chain specialists to review their SRM approach.

6.7 Models of supplier relationships

There are models, including the Farrington hierarchy of procurement/supplier relationships as shown in Figure 6.3. The hierarchy develops from a totally negative scenario to a very positive relationship that delivers mutual benefits to the parties involved.

6.7.1 The Farrington hierarchy of procurement/supplier relationships

The challenge of moving relationships from the first stage in the hierarchy to more positive relationships should not be underestimated. In the author's experience an intransient procurement operation can require 3/6 months for relationship management skills to reach the appropriate level.

Table 6.4 SRM maturity model

	1. No SRM	2. Exploring	3. Established	4. World-Class
Strategy & Governance	■ Focus on 'performance to contract' ■ No alignment between business and procurement ■ No company-wide SRM strategy and objectives ■ No SRM policies and guidelines	■ Focus on TCO reduction ■ Business and procurement have initial discussion on value ■ SRM strategy & objectives formulated but poorly understood ■ SRM guidelines & policies are documented	■ Partial focus on value creation ■ Value mapping as input for SRM strategy ■ SRM strategy & objectives known and fully understood ■ SRM policies and guidelines are communicated and fully understood	■ Full focus on value creation ■ SRM fully aligned with corporate/business strategies ■ SRM strategy and objectives are frequently challenged and updated ■ SRM policies and guidelines are frequently challenged and updated.
Process	■ No specific SRM process in place ■ All suppliers are treated the same ■ Supply base is primarily managed by contracts and growing ■ No defined supplier development/improvement programme	■ Documented SRM process with basic process toolkit ■ Different views on relationships but little differentiation ■ Basic supplier strategies, stable supply base ■ Regular review meetings with suppliers to identify improvement opportunities	■ SRM process known and fully understood and advanced toolkit ■ Supplier segmentation drives supplier differentiation ■ Advanced supplier strategies, supply base is decreasing ■ Multi-functional teams meet to discuss issues & opportunities with suppliers on a regular basis	■ SRM process is frequently challenged and updated ■ Same value drivers are applied during entire supplier lifecycle ■ Partnership strategy jointly developed and managed ■ Proactive supplier development, Supplier is proactive in seeking out improvement opportunities
Structure	■ Procurement not recognised as process owner ■ Divisions, functions and business units run autonomously ■ Unclear roles & responsibilities, no partnerships or alliances	■ Procurement is taking the lead, limited business recognition ■ Business stakeholder involvement has not been formalised ■ Roles & responsibilities are formalised and partially applied for pilot project but on an ad-hoc basis	■ Procurement seen to be owner of process and is involved in the majority of key relationships ■ Executive sponsorship of individual strategic relationships ■ Roles & responsibilities are consistently applied at partnerships and centrally coordinated	■ Procurement seen to be owner of process and facilitator. Fully involved in all key relationships ■ Senior executive sponsorship of individual strategic relationships ■ All partnerships are organised according to standard structure and centrally managed

	1. No SRM	2. Exploring	3. Established	4. World-Class
People	■ Procurement staff low skilled in SRM, focus on technical/functional skills ■ No training in SRM ■ No knowledge management	■ Basic SRM skills are developed, attention for relational/developmental competencies ■ Training requirements known, limited number of SRM courses ■ Internal knowledge management process & system developed	■ Advanced SRM skills are developed, relational/developmental competencies elaborated ■ SRM training curriculum extended ■ External knowledge management initiated	■ Procurement staff have broad skills, focus on technical, relational and developmental competencies ■ Comprehensive range of training programme linked to procurement and business needs ■ Joint knowledge management
Technology	■ ERP is available to support supplier management ■ Supplier integration to share transactional data only ■ No online collaboration and decision-making	■ Basic eProcurement/APS/PLM technology are available/used ■ Contract, performance and planning data are shared ■ Limited online collaboration and decision-making	■ Advanced eProcurement/APS/PLM technology are available/used ■ Contract, performance, planning and engineering data are shared ■ Partially online collaboration and decision-making	■ Full process scope is supported by appropriate technology ■ Operational, tactical and strategic data and information are shared on a real-time basis ■ Full online collaboration and decision-making
Performance management	■ Focus on operational performance measures ■ Buying company measures and assess suppliers ■ Initiatives driven by issues	■ Focus on tactical/strategic performance measures ■ Initial discussions on joint KPIs ■ Basic continuous improvement cycle, manual scorecards	■ Performance measures partially driven by value mapping ■ Joint discussion on KPI setting and targets ■ Joint continuous improvement cycle with basic reward system, semi-automated scorecards	■ Performance management fully driven by value mapping ■ Joint balanced scorecard measures partnership performance ■ System with full sharing of investments, risks and benefits, based on fully automated scorecards
Risk management	■ No visibility on risks ■ Ad-hoc risk management ■ No planning of disruptional events	■ Moderate visibility on main risks ■ Basic risk management process, mainly qualitative ■ Mitigation plans for most severe risks	■ Partner resilience monitoring ■ Full risk management process with quantitative measurement ■ Joint business continuity plans	■ Full and online visibility on joint supply risks ■ Supplier risk segmentation strategy and approaches ■ Joint investments to create flexibility

Figure 6.3 The Farrington hierarchy of procurement/supplier relationships

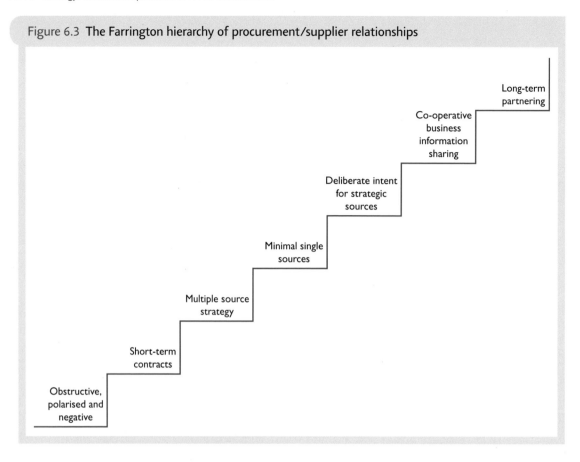

Transaction cost theory (TCT)

Transaction cost theory (TCT), associated with Coase[8] and Williamson,[9] refers to the idea of the cost of providing for some good or service if it was purchased in the market-place rather than from within the firm. Three key concepts are those of transaction costs, asset specificity and asymmetrical information distribution.

Transaction costs comprise:

- search and bargain costs
- bargaining and decision costs
- policing and enforcement costs.

Asset specificity is the relative lack of transferability of assets intended for use in a given transaction to other uses. Williamson identifies six main types of asset specificity:

- site
- physical asset
- human asset
- brand names
- dedicated assets
- temporal.

Asymmetrical information distribution means that the parties to a transaction have uneven access to relevant information. One consequence is that, within contractual relationships, either party may engage in post-contractual opportunism if the chance of switching to more advantageous partnerships arises.

Resource-based theory (RBT)

Resource-based theory emphasises that each firm is characterised by its own unique collection of resources of core competences. Thus, Kay[10] argues that the source of competitive advantage is the creation and exploitation of distinctive capabilities that are difficult to build and maintain, codify and make into recipes, copy and emulate and can't simply be bought off the shelf. Kay identifies three basic types of distinctive capability.

1 *Corporate architecture* – the capacity of the organisation to:
   - create and store organisational knowledge and routines
   - promote more effective cooperation between network members
   - achieve a transparent and easy flow of information
   - adapt rapidly and flexibly.

2 *Innovation* – the capacity to lower costs, improve products or introduce new products ahead of competitors. The successful exploitation of new ideas incorporating new technologies, designs and best practice is difficult and uncertain. Often, innovation can only be achieved by cooperating and collaborating with partners.

3 *Reputation* – the capacity to instil confidence in an organisation's credibility, reliability, responsibility, trustworthiness and, possibly, accountability. Organisations can only achieve a positive reputation over time, but once achieved, their ability to provide quality assurance may enable them to obtain a premium price for products.

From the insights provided by TCT and RBT, Cox derives the following propositions.

■ *Arm's length relationships* are associated with low asset specificity and low supplier competences that can easily be bought off the shelf as there are many potential suppliers.

■ *Internal contracts* – in-house provision – are associated with high asset specificity and core competences:

> The more competences approximate to core competences of high asset specificity, then the greater the likelihood that external relationships may lead to merger or acquisition or, failing that, result in very close, single-sourced negotiated contracts in which both parties have some clear ownership rights in the goods and services produced.[11]

■ *Partnership relationships* apply to assets of medium specificity and ascend in steps according to the distance of the complementary competences provided by external suppliers from the core competences of a particular firm:

> The nearer they [complementary competences] are to the core competences of the firm, the more the firm will have to consider vertical integration through merger and acquisition. The further away from the core competences of the firm the less there is a need for medium asset-specific skills to be vertically integrated.[12]

Cox's classification of contractual relationships

The five steps in the ladder of contractual relationships each represent a higher level of asset specificity and strategic importance to the firm of the specific goods and services. Each step also represents relative degrees of power between the relationship's participants and in the relative ownership of the goods and services emanating from the relationships. Strategic supplier alliances are the final stage before a firm considers a complementary supplier to be so important that vertical integration through merger and acquisition is undertaken.

■ *Adversarial leverage* – up to the mid-1980s, approaching the marketplace on an adversarial basis was the norm. Thus, Porter,[13] writing in 1980, advocates that purchasers should multi-source, negotiate short-term contracts, maintain secrecy regarding costs, sales and product design and make (or receive) no improvement suggestions to (or from) suppliers.

■ *Preferred suppliers* – providers of complementary goods and services of medium asset specificity or strategic importance who have been placed by the purchaser on a restricted list of potential suppliers after a process of vendor rating and accreditation.

■ *Single sourcing* – procurement from a single supplier of medium asset specificity complementary goods or services of relatively high strategic importance. As Cox observes, the aim of single sourcing is to reduce transaction costs and economise, but without the costs associated with vertical integration.

■ *Network sourcing and partnerships* – networks have been considered earlier in section 4.3. According to Cox, network sourcing 'is the idea that it is possible to create a virtual company at all levels of the supply chain by engineering multiple tiered partnerships at each stage, but without moving to vertical integration'. With network sourcing:

 – the prime contracting firm acts as the driver for the reduction of transaction costs within the whole supply and value chain

 – cost reduction is achieved by a partnership between the prime contractor and a first-tier supplier who controls an important medium asset for the prime contractor and also forms similar partnerships with second-tier suppliers (see section 4.4.1)

 – each tiering level of the supply chain is effectively a joint venture in which firms at each stage will inform and educate their respective partners by sharing best practice and 'fit for purpose' techniques

 – such network sourcing relationships will only be possible in mature industries 'where asset specificity has constantly been reduced and multiple and serial subcontracting thereby facilitated. In such supply chain relationships issues of ownership, control and power become increasingly difficult to allocate.'

■ *Strategic supplier alliances* – classically referred to as joint ventures, these are defined by Cox as 'negotiated single-sourced relationships with the supplier of a complementary product or service'. Such relationships form a completely new and independent legal entity, distinct from the firms comprising the alliance. As both parties have some degree of proprietorship (not necessarily 50/50) in the outcome of the relationship, the basis of such relationships is power equivalence and a high degree of complementarity.

6.7.2 The Bensaou model

The Bensaou model is based on a study of eleven Japanese and three US automobile manufacturers. Bensaou[14] suggests a framework for managing a portfolio of investments for the purpose of enabling senior managers to answer two questions.

Q1 Which governance structure or relational design should a firm choose under different external contingencies?

This is a strategic decision because it affects how a firm defines its boundaries and core activities.

Q2 What is the appropriate way to manage each different type of relationship?

This is an organisational question.
Bensaou suggests four buyer relationship profiles:

- market exchange
- captive buyer
- captive supplier
- strategic partnerships.

For each profile, Bensaou identifies distinguishing product, market and supplier characteristics.
Finally, he suggests that the four profiles can be arranged in a matrix to indicate whether the buyer's and the supplier's tangible or intangible investments in the relationship are high or low. Tangible investments, in this context, are buildings, tooling and equipment. Intangible investments are people, time and effort spent in learning supplier–purchaser business practices and procedures and information sharing.
The Bensaou matrix, as adapted, is shown in Figure 6.4.
Bensaou also identified three management variables for each profile, which are:

- information-sharing practices
- characteristics of 'boundary-spanner' jobs
- the social climate within the relationship.

The management practices that high performers in each cell use to match the coordination, information and knowledge exchange requirements presented by the external context are shown in Figures 6.4 and 6.5.
Bensaou concluded the following:

- Many large firms in manufacturing are moving away from traditional vertical integration and towards the external contracting of key activities.
- As interfirm relationships increase, firms cannot manage with one design for all relationships and so need to manage a portfolio of relationships.
- There are two kinds of successful relationship: high requirement–low capabilities and low requirements–high capabilities. There are also two paths to failure: under-designed

Figure 6.4 Supplier's specific investment

High	

Captive buyer

Product characteristics:
- technically complicated
- based on mature, well-understood technology
- little innovation and improvement to the product

Market characteristics:
- stable demand with limited market growth
- concentrated market with few established players
- buyers maintain an internal manufacturing capability

Supplier characteristics:
- large supply houses
- supplier proprietary technology
- few strongly established suppliers
- strong bargaining power
- car manufacturers heavily depend on these suppliers, their technology and skills

Strategic partnership

Product characteristics:
- high level of customisation required
- close to buyer's core competency
- tight mutual adjustments needed in key processes
- technically complicated part or integrated subsystem
- based on new technology
- innovation leaps on technology, product or service
- frequent design changes
- strong engineering expertise required
- large capital investment required

Market characteristics:
- strong demand and high growth market
- very competitive and concentrated market
- frequent changes in competitors due to instability or lack of dominant design
- buyer maintains in-house design and testing capability

Partner characteristics:
- large multiproduct supply houses
- strong supplier proprietary technology
- active in research and innovation (R&D costs)
- strong recognised skills and capabilities in design, engineering and manufacturing

Market exchange

Product characteristics:
- highly standardised products
- mature technology
- little innovation and rare design changes
- technically simple product or well-structured complicated manufacturing process
- little or no customisation to buyer's final product
- low engineering effort and expertise required
- small capital investments required

Market characteristics:
- stable or declining demand
- highly competitive market
- many capable suppliers
- same players over time

Supplier characteristics:
- small 'mom and pop' shops
- no proprietary technology
- low switching costs
- low bargaining power
- strong economic reliance on automotive business

Captive supplier

Product characteristics:
- technically complicated products
- based on new technology (developed by suppliers)
- important and frequent innovations and new functionalities in the product category
- significant engineering effort and expertise required
- heavy capital investments required

Market characteristics:
- high growth market segment
- fierce competition
- few qualified players
- unstable market with shifts between suppliers

Supplier characteristics:
- strong supplier proprietary technology
- suppliers with strong financial capabilities and good R&D skills
- low supplier bargaining power
- heavy supplier dependency on the buyer and economic reliance on the automotive sector in general

Low

Relationship investment   Low   High

Figure 6.5 Management profile for each contextual profile

Captive buyer	**Strategic partnerships**
Information-sharing mechanisms: ■ 'broadband' and important exchange of detailed information on a continuous basis ■ frequent and regular mutual visits Boundary-spanner tasks' characteristics: ■ structured tasks, highly predictable ■ large amount of time spent by buyer's purchasing agents and engineers with supplier Climate and process characteristics: ■ tense climate, lack of mutual trust ■ no early supplier involvement in design ■ strong effort by buyer towards cooperation ■ supplier does not necessarily have a good reputation	Information-sharing mechanisms: ■ 'broadband' frequent and 'rich media' exchange ■ regular mutual visits and practice of guest engineers Boundary-spanner tasks' characteristics: ■ highly ill defined, ill structured ■ non-routine, frequent, unexpected events ■ large amount of time spent with supplier's staff, mostly on coordinating issues Climate and process characteristics: ■ high mutual trust and commitment to relationship ■ strong sense of buyer fairness ■ early supplier involvement in design ■ extensive joint action and cooperation ■ supplier has excellent reputation
Market exchange	**Captive supplier**
Exchange-sharing mechanisms: ■ 'narrowband' and limited information exchange, heavy at time of contract negotiation ■ operational coordination and monitoring along structured routines Boundary-spanner tasks' characteristics: ■ limited time spent directly with suppliers' staff ■ highly routine and structured tasks with little interdependence with supplier's staff Climate and process characteristics: ■ positive social climate ■ no systematic joint effort and cooperation ■ no early supplier involvement in design ■ supplier fairly treated by the buyer ■ supplier has a good reputation and track record	Information-sharing mechanisms: ■ little exchange of information ■ few mutual visits, mostly from supplier to buyer Boundary-spanner tasks' characteristics: ■ limited time allocated by buyer's staff to the supplier ■ mostly complicated, coordinating tasks Climate and process characteristics: ■ high mutual trust, but limited direct joint action and cooperation ■ greater burden put on the supplier

and overdesigned relationships. *Overdesign* takes place when firms invest in building trust as a result of frequent visits and cross-company teams when the market and product context call for simple, impersonal control and information exchange. Such overdesign is both costly and risky, especially in terms of the intangible investments in people, information or knowledge.

■ Building or redesigning relationships according to the Bensaou model therefore involves the following three analytical steps:

1 the strategic selection of relational types to match the external conditions relating to the product, the technology and the market (see Figure 6.4)

2 the identification of an appropriate management profile for each type of relational design

3 matching the design of the relationship, which could be overdesigned or underdesigned, to the desired management profile.

6.8 Supplier relationship management – a critique

The Rand Corporation[15] in 2012 produced a report 'Best Practices in Supplier Relationship Management and their early implementation in the Air Force Material Command.' As always with the Rand Corporation there is impeccable research, analysis and conclusions. The report is highly recommended to our readers.

Six practices are shown as characterising best SRM practices:

1 Manage total business with each supplier (consolidate contracts, tie future business to performance)

2 Measure and shape supplier performance (establish performance measurement system, rank suppliers, set targets, reward performance)

3 Involve key suppliers early in product design (leverage their design capabilities and knowledge of manufacturability and innovation, reduce complexity)

4 Host high-level meetings that promote dialogue with suppliers (demonstrate mutual commitment to the relationship, promote dialogue on expectations and whats to improve, share future plans and technology roadmaps, present awards)

5 Recruit skilled personnel (recruit experienced personnel who have the right qualitative and quantitative skills)

6 Develop personnel so they have a thorough knowledge of suppliers (educate personnel so they know suppliers' processes, costs, capacities and capabilities, and can work with and help suppliers fix processes to meet current needs and continually improve).

Rand expound the view that although price is a consideration for SRM, so are non-price costs, including:

■ internal business cost

■ transportation

■ warehousing

■ inventory carrying costs

■ purchasing administration

■ factory yield

■ damaged field product

■ joint supplier/company/customer life cycle cost

■ production capacity

■ research and development (R&D)

■ specifications

■ expediting.

Rand refer to the Krause and Handfield Supplier Development Model, reproduced in Figure 6.6.

Figure 6.6 Krause and Handfield Supplier Development Model

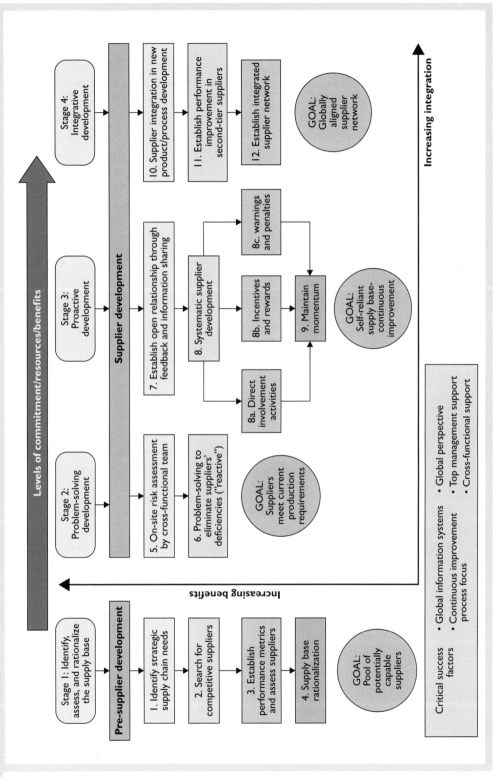

Source: Adapted from Krause and Handfield, 1999. Institute for Supply Management and W.P. Carey School of Business at Arizona State University

6.9 The termination of relationships

No relationship can or should be expected to last forever as organisations operate in a dynamic environment. The ending of a relationship does not necessarily mean failure and there may be positive as well as negative outcomes for one or both of the parties involved.

6.9.1 Reasons for termination

Mitchell[16] describes how it is possible to detect that a relationship is changing:

> A primary tip-off that the nature of the relationship is changing can be seen in requests that are made by you or by the supplier. Are multiple requests necessary before action is taken? Are requests necessary for items or service that used to be offered without asking? Perhaps the request is granted, but the requester feels like he or she is cashing in on his or her last favour with each request . . . When you start to work out issues and compromises and you get the impression that your partner is nickel and dimeing you all the way you know that your alliance is coming to an end.

Mitchell also points out that, although partnering principles and objectives can be well outlined at an organisational level, success is often dependent on individuals:

> All individuals for both organisations must be committed and resistance can begin on either side of the fence. If the problems have roots in the purchasing and supply organisation, at least the purchasing supply manager will be able to take an active part in determining the cause and correcting it. . . If the problem seems to stem from the supplier organisation, the outcome is a bit more unpredictable.

In practice, most partnership break-ups derive from:

- inadequate understanding of what 'partnership' means
- rapidly changing circumstances that cause one or both parties to revise their priorities and concentrate on achieving their own organisational objectives at the expense of the partnership.

Such circumstances, as identified by Southey[17] in the UK and Campbell and Pollard[18] in the USA, include:

- *changes in business direction(s)* – an existing partnership may no longer have value if either the procurement or supplier organisation has shifted its strategic direction
- *product obsolescence* – the product or service provided by the supplier is becoming obsolete without any replacement options
- *the supplier is unable to meet service levels* – certain objectives basic to the partnership can no longer be met
- *short-term attitude* – either partner may consider that the long-term benefits of the partnership have not been realised sufficiently quickly or have been insufficient to warrant a continued commitment to a particular supplier/purchaser
- *economic factors* – a supplier has become 'at risk' financially, with the danger of potential liquidation
- *external economics* – a recession may force suppliers to cut back on product development, training and other resources, such as product engineers, and, consequently, they will be unable to meet the 'continuous improvement' objectives of the partnership

- *mergers and acquisitions* – such ventures can create new business models for either the purchaser or supplier
- *corporate divestiture* – may create a situation where, because parts of the business have been sold, the organisation can no longer provide a product or service
- *instability and inconsistency* – acquisitions or disposals of companies or rapid changes in key personnel or organisational philosophy often adversely affect years of previous relationship building based on trust and stability.

In the last analysis, however, successful partnerships can only be built if trust and cooperation exist between purchaser and supplier.

6.9.2 The process of termination

It is a truism that good contract management is not reactive but aims to anticipate and respond to future contingencies. Every well-written contract should anticipate the possibility of terminating the relationship.

Some writers, however, criticise the inadequacies of legal contracts for governing partnerships, especially in the face of uncertainty and dependence. Sitkin and Roth,[19] for example, describe legalistic remedies as weak, impersonal substitutes for trust. Contractual provisions may also lack flexibility, which might enable terminations to be made more amicably and easily than following the 'letter of the law'. Ouchi,[20] however, points out that formal control mechanisms are more effective in obtaining compliance with specifiable objectives than in obtaining commitment to a general value orientation.

Timing, relationship aspects, legal considerations and succession issues are important aspects of termination.

6.9.3 Timing

Mitchell[21] states that, whenever possible, the timing of the termination should be synchronised with the expiration of the agreement currently in force. Giving too much advance warning to a supplier can lead to deterioration in service. Conversely, termination may not come as a surprise to a supplier that has received regular negative feedback on performance. Decisions may also have to be made on whether the termination should be immediate or gradual. Such decisions may be governed by terms and conditions relating to termination in the current agreement.

6.9.4 Relationship aspects

Terminations may be amicable or hostile. Campbell and Pollard[22] refer to the three Ps that can aid in minimising possible hostility encountered in the termination process:

- positive attitude
- pleasant tone
- professional treatment.

A positive attitude recognises that both organisations will survive apart and that recriminations will help neither. Further, both organisations may need each other in the future. A pleasant tone can be more effective than harsh words. Professional justification for the termination is essential. Termination is not a personal issue. The procurement executive's job is to obtain the best possible value in order that his or her organisation can remain ahead of the competition.

6.9.5 Legal considerations

Among such factors are:

- *the financial consequences of terminating the contract* – in some cases, it may be possible to negotiate a settlement, in others the contract will be specific regarding payments to be made in the event of fault or non-fault termination
- *confidentiality agreements* – where such agreements are part of the contract terms, they must be honoured for the prescribed time
- *intellectual property issues* – drawings, designs prepared during the contract term, computer software and so on
- *capital property issues* – especially in relation to materials or capital equipment located at the supplier's site
- *security issues* – it is necessary to change passwords or security codes shared with the other party to the agreement
- *obtaining clear signed records of any settlement employee rights* – if they were transferred under the Transfer of Undertakings (Protection of Employment) (TUPE) Regulations.

6.9.6 Succession issues

Before deciding to terminate, it will be necessary to ensure that steps have been taken to ensure a continuity of supplies. This will entail:

- discussion with internal customers regarding groups, systems and projects that will be affected by the change of supplier
- reflecting on the lessons learned from the terminated relationship
- conducting market analysis to determine other supplier options
- preparing specifications (possibly revised)
- selection of a new supplier – an important factor will be the potential supplier's reputation for trustworthiness
- negotiation of a relationship agreement.

Finally, as Campbell and Pollard[23] observe:

> As a result of thinking through the options and creating a professional plan for separation, supply managers can disprove the old maxim that 'marriages are made in heaven, but the divorce is the very devil'.

6.10 Relationship breakdown on an IT project

Relationship behaviour is sometimes exposed when a project goes wrong. These projects provide excellent studies for students and practitioners of procurement. The Queensland Health Payroll System project[24] is an example. Extracts from the Report are shown below and give a flavour of the issues. The Report is compelling reading.

The Honourable Richard Chesterman 40 RFD QC was appointed to make full and careful inquiry 'in an open and independent manner, into the implementation of the Queensland Health payroll system with respect to . . . '. The scope of the inquiry included:

a. the adequacy and integrity of the procurement, contract management, project management, governance and implementation process, and

c. the contractual arrangements between the State of Queensland and IBM Australia Ltd and why and to what extent the contract price for the Queensland Health payroll system increased over time.

Some of the salient points in the Report (the references are those in the Report) are:

2.12   IBM was the successful tenderer and on 5 December 2007 it and the State of Queensland executed a contract for the provision of shared services to nominated departments.

2.13   By October 2008 IBM had not achieved any of the contracted performance criteria; but it had been paid about $32M of the contract price of $98M; and it forecast that to complete what it had contracted to undertake would cost the State of Queensland $181M.

2.15   The replacement of the QH payroll system must take a place in the front rank of failures in public administration in this country. It may be the worst.

3.11   . . . many witnesses claimed to have no memory of important events which they observed or in which they took part. Many answers were evasive and some were dishonest . . . Even more remarkable was the fact that some witnesses involved in the delivery of the payroll system proclaimed it a success.

6.10.1 Procurement issues on an IT project

1.1   IBM complained that the three stages of the procurement process . . . were a "working assumption . . . adapted, uncritically . . . , and wrongly." IBM contends that the procurement process only commenced on 16 August 2007 . . . The events preceding 16 August 2007 were described as 'informal', 'casual', and 'loose'.

1.2   The reason for the submission is readily apparent. The Inquiry uncovered several instances of serious misconduct by IBM's employees during the RFP . . .

2.9   . . . The Inquiry into the tender process did reveal serious deficiencies in it and serious dereliction of duty by those charged with the responsibility of spending the State's money effectively.

2.24   . . . Mr. Uhlmann advised that the current rate of expenditure by CorpTech on the program was $15,400 per person per month and that there were at the time 481 persons involved in the project. Mr. Uhlmann thought that if the program ran over time by 12 months the extra cost would be $90M and if it ran over time by 18 months the additional cost would be $135M.

4.9   . . . More curious is the fact that there does not appear to have been any serious analysis of what was the best available 'vendor engagement and solution model'. The only model considered in the RFP was the Prime Contractor one.

4.11   There is evidence of haste and a lack of premeditation in the change to the new model . . . In a well-ordered process, the State's legal right to appoint a Prime Contractor would have been ascertained before it called for tenders for such a contract.

4.12   The RFP took the form on the one brief email from Mr. Burns to the vendors dated 25 July 2007.

4.15   Logica submitted a detailed response although only for the Finance requirements of the SS Initiative. Its estimates cost range for the work it undertook to perform was between

$84.7M and $116.8M. IBM's response was briefer. It estimated its cost of providing the whole of the work required to deliver the Initiative at between $155M and £190M. SAP also responded but did not give a fixed price. It proposed a variety of pricing models for different components of the work. Its overall, indicative, estimate of cost was between $93M and $123M. Accenture, which put in a detailed response, gave an estimate price for the whole of the SS Initiative of $176M.

4.28 Mr. Atzeni, through these interactions with Mr. Cameron, offered considerable assistance in IBM growing its role in the SS Initiative. On at least one occasion, he gave Mr. Cameron information confidential to government. Mr. Cameron said that all of the documents provided by Mr. Atzeni were freely available to any person working on the whole-of-government program and were not required to be treated as confidential. If that were so one wonders why Mr. Cameron asked for them, or why Mr. Atzeni bothered to send them. Mr. Atzeni met with IBM staff very shortly after the RFP was issued to give it information relevant to its bid without which IBM would have been at a disadvantage.

4.33 Mr. Burns discussions and meetings with IBM representatives in contemplation of the RFP tender process were inappropriate. Best practice in procurement requires that all competitors receive the same information. That approach aids transparency as well as promoting effective competition. Effective competition in turn ensures the best chance of obtaining value for money.

5.61 Mr. Lewis, who led the Governance Panel, was an even more unsatisfactory witness. He, too, denied any recollection of the 'rescoring' meeting, though he accepted that his Panel scores changed to prefer IBM. He was evasive with respect to the simplest proposition, such as whether his Panel even read the ITO responses prior to scoring them. He had no explanation for the increase in IBM's score. When confronted with the fact that his Panel had actually decreased Accenture's score, he was equally bereft of explanation. Mr. Lewis, I regret to find, was not candid about his Panel's rescoring and the reasons for it.

5.62 It is, I think, the fact that the pressure Mr. Burns put on the Panel leaders, though effective, was improper and affected the integrity of the procurement process. It is for that reason that Mr. Hood and Mr. Lewis were evasive. They are, I conclude, deeply embarrassed that they permitted themselves to be manipulated and to acquiesce in the distortion of the procurement. The embarrassment is no doubt increased by the magnitude of the subsequent failure of the project for which they recommended IBM.

5.123 The clearest point to emerge from this aspect of the evidence is that there were serious shortcomings in the State's scrutiny and assessment of price during its evaluation of the ITO responses.

6.10.2 Contract and Project Management issues on an IT project

1.8 The story of the Project's conception through to its implementation is one of bad decisions: a failure of State employees in particular properly and diligently to discharge their responsibilities; IBM as a commercially motivated vendor doing little to rectify or make up for the State's shortcomings; the State lacking in discipline in expending very large amounts of taxpayers' funds; and, in general, an almost total reluctance by both parties to face what had become obvious at a relatively early stage of the Project, that the system which the State had commissioned and which IBM was to deliver would be seriously deficient and not operate as any payroll system ought, namely to pay staff on time and to do so accurately.

2.29 Within about six months from its start, problems with the Project's scoping emerged. A dispute arose about how the system was to integrate with the existing (legacy) finance system within QH. IBM claimed it had been delayed in its work. The State decided that further workshops were needed (to be facilitated by IBM) to ascertain what ought to be done and paid IBM $1.88M as a result of the delay which IBM claimed.

It is an extensive Report, probing many facets of relationships and IT project delivery, pricing, contract changes, User Acceptance Testing and other facets. It gives an insight into a project fraught with problems.

6.11 Further aspects of relationships

These include collaboration in innovation and design, the supply base, supplier appraisal, outsourcing, make-or-buy decisions, partnerships and supplier performance and they are dealt with in appropriate sections elsewhere in this book.

Discussion questions

6.1 In what significant ways does a partnering relationship with a supplier differ from the traditional adversarial relationship?

6.2 'The most successful relationships are those where customers and suppliers develop trust and an understanding of their requirements and interests, accompanied by a concern for both learning from and providing assistance to each other.'
(a) Define the words 'trust' and 'understanding'.
(b) Can there be trust without understanding?
(c) What are the characteristics of a 'learning organisation'?

6.3 What impact does assertive negotiation have on supplier relationships?

6.4 To what extent do you consider 'adversarial leverage' to still be prevalent? Can you provide an example of adversarial leverage from your own experience?

6.5 What is the eight-stage framework set out in PAS 11000? How would you evaluate whether your own organisation is positioned to collaborate?

6.6 What information can a supplier include in a tender document to persuade the buyer that future relationships will be positive?

6.7 In your opinion does competitive tendering help or hinder buyer–seller relationships? Why?

6.8 Is the 'traditional' type of contract suitable for a partnering relationship? What impact on relationships would the following have:
(a) including 'damages' for non-performance in the contract?
(b) including a clause for termination at the buyer's convenience?
(c) including a clause requiring continuous improvement in manufacture/service delivery?

6.9 How would you 'sell' to senior management the concept of a single source of supply, for a long-term contract, for a strategically vital manufactured item to your company?

6.10 Do suppliers who own intellectual property rights tend to be more aggressive than suppliers who have no such rights?

6.11 Who should be accountable for supplier relationship management? Is it better handled by procurement or the department who are dependent on the supply of goods/services? Why?

6.12 Giving due consideration to the Bayer model, how effective is your approach to supplier performance evaluation or 'vendor rating' as it is sometimes called?

References

1 Office of Government Commerce. Category Management Toolkit. Office of Government Commerce, London.

2 French, J and Raven, B. H. *The Bases of Social Power Studies in Social Power*, Institute for Social Research 1959.

3 Raven, B.H. *Social Influence and Power in I.D. Current Studies in Social Psychology*. New York. Holt, Rinehart, Winston, 1965.

4 Luss Tien Ding, 'Supply chain collaboration in mechanical enterprises in Vietnam', *International Journal of Managing Value and Supply Chains*, Vol. 6, No. 4, December 2015.

5 The authors gratefully acknowledge permission to quote from the CIPS booklet 'How to manage supplier relationships', written by Dr Kenneth Lysons.

6 www.instituteforcollaborativeworking.com.

7 PWC, Detailed SRM maturity model.

8 Coase, R. H., 'The nature of the firm', *Economica*, No. 4, 1937, pp. 386–405.

9 Williamson, O. E., 'Transaction cost economics: the governing of contractual relations', *Journal of Law and Economics*, Vol. 22, 1979, pp. 232–61.

10 Kay, J., *Foundations of Corporate Success: How Business Strategies Add Value*, Oxford University Press, Oxford, UK, 1995.

11 Cox, A., 'Regional competence and strategic procurement management', *European Journal of Purchasing and Supply Management*, Vol. 2, No. 1, 1996, p. 64.

12 As 11 above, p. 63.

13 Porter, M., *Competitive Strategy*, Free Press, New York, USA, 1980, pp. 106–7.

14 Bensaou, M., 'Portfolio of buyer–supplier relationships', *Sloan Management Review*, Summer, 1999, pp. 35–44.

15 https:www.rand.org.

16 Mitchell, L. K., 'Breaking up is hard to do – how to end a supplier relationship', ISM resource article at: www.ism.ws/ResourceArticles/2000/cpoomitchell.cfm

17 Southey, P., 'Pitfalls to partnering in the UK', PSERG Second International Annual Conference 1993, in Burnett, K. (ed.) *Readings in Partnership Sourcing*, CIPS, Stamford, 1995.

18 Campbell, P. and Pollard, W. M., 'Ending a supplier relationship', *Inside Supply Management*, September, 2002, pp. 33–8.

19 Sitkin, S. B. and Roth, N. L., 'Explaining the limited effectiveness of legalistic "remedies" for trust/distrust', *Organisation Science*, Vol. 4 (3), 1993, pp. 367–92.

20 Ouchi, W. G., 'A conceptual framework for the design of organisational control mechanisms', *Management Science*, Vol. 25 (9), 1979, pp. 833–48.

21 As 16 above.

22 As 18 above.

23 As 18 above.

24 Queensland Health Payroll System. Commission of Inquiry Report July 2013.

Chapter 7

Legal and contractual management

Learning outcomes

This chapter aims to stimulate the professional buyer, particularly those aspiring to senior positions in the procurement profession to understand:

- the procurement specialist and Contract Law
- formation of a contract
- acceptance
- contracts for the Sale of Goods
- contracts for the Supply of Services
- consideration
- capacity to contract
- drafting the detail of contract clauses
- misrepresentation
- the right to terminate a contract
- HOT TOPICS
- standard forms of contract.

Key ideas

- Understanding contractual detail is necessary for procurement specialists.
- Accessing case law is informative and necessary to keep abreast of developments.
- Negotiating contractual detail is sometimes essential and should reduce risks for the organisation.
- Badly worded contracts present unacceptable risks to the parties involved.
- The offer and acceptance actions must be understood and managed.
- Jurisdictional issues are relevant to risk management.
- Contract law is always evolving.
- Procurement have a need to engage in all phases of a contract.

7.1 The procurement specialist and Contract Law

In the modern industrial world, the procurement specialist has a critical role to fulfil in the formation, implementation and execution of contracts. Defining contracts, negotiating contracts, ensuring they are in place in a timely manner, and ensuring the supplier performs the contract in an acceptable manner, are very demanding tasks. While it is relevant to obtain a theoretical knowledge of contract law when qualifying for the Chartered Institute of Procurement & Supply, it is dangerous to believe that this knowledge will be sufficient to continually undertake procurement duties. There is a constant flow of new legislation and development of existing law through case law. The demand for knowledge is exacerbated when purchases are made offshore. This requires knowledge of jurisdictional issues, arising from different legal systems and applicable contract law.

The starting point for many buyers when entering into contracts is their own Contract Terms and Conditions. Often these have been written by in-house, legal services or usurped from another organisation. It is not unusual for buyers not to have been briefed on the detail of the Terms & Conditions or their legal implications. Some buyers acknowledge that the detail of contracts bores them and they lack the motivation to study contract law or to actively embrace its finer points. There are considerable business risks when this attitude prevails. Two key risks are a lack of professional credibility with the in-house legal services team and with suppliers who will rapidly identify those who are inept at negotiating contractual detail.

The majority of buyers want to engage in negotiations. This is admirable, although contractual negotiations require high-level knowledge and skills. It is likely, on high-risk purchases, that the tenders that are received will include non-compliance statements on the buyers' proposed Contract Terms and Conditions. A resolution to these issues will often require the involvement of legal specialists, on both sides, thereby creating complex relationship and communication considerations. The buyer should not be a passive participant in negotiations and should make positive, informed inputs to contract discussions.

This chapter aims to motivate readers to commit to continually acquiring knowledge and skills in the field of contract law. This is an important differentiator between procurement specialists. It should be recognised that the content of the chapter is a 'taste' and that there are specialised books on all facets of contract law. These books range from introductory texts to highly specialised textbooks on a single facet of law, for example intellectual property rights. Caveat Emptor, the law is constantly developing. This requires a commitment to the acquisition of knowledge.

7.2 Formation of a contract

There are five basic requirements that need to be satisfied in order to make a legally binding contract. There must be an agreement between the parties; an intention to be legally bound by the agreement; certainty as to the terms of the agreement; capacity to contract and consideration.

Whether a legally binding contract exists is of constant concern to a buyer, particularly when there is an allegation of non-performance or actuality of non-performance. An offer is a statement by one party (in this explanation, a supplier) of a willingness to enter into a contract on the terms that he has put forward. Legal textbooks, for understandable reasons, go into great detail about the complexity that surrounds an offer. Among the issues for a buyer are:

a did the person/organisation making the offer have the legal capacity to do so and

b are the terms of the offer quite clear; for example, are the terms and conditions of contract clearly set out and communicated.

Contracts can be entered into in a variety of ways, in writing or orally; by letter, fax or e-mail; in writing resulting from simple or complex negotiations; by conduct of the parties; by an exchange of promises. A typical procurement procedure will require the buyer to issue a Purchase Order or to draw up a detailed contract and schedules. Within these requirements are a host of potential difficulties.

The Purchase Order and its attendant detail must be robust. It must set out the Terms & Conditions of the deal, usually printed on the reverse of the Purchase Order. If not, the supplier's attention should point out that the Terms & Conditions are available upon request. A difficulty with 'standard' Terms & Conditions of purchase is that they may fail to deal with all the specifics of the purchase. Some buying organisations attempt to deal with all types of purchases, with only one set of Terms and Conditions. In the opinion of the author, this is a seriously flawed approach. The fact that a Purchase Order was sent to the supplier does not mean there is now a legally binding contract in existence. This will be explained later, in 'Acceptance'.

Lord Wilberforce[1] said: 'It is only the precise analysis of this complex of relations into the classical offer and acceptance, with identifiable consideration, that seems to present difficulty, but this same difficulty exists in many situations of daily life, e.g. sales at auction ... manufacturer's guarantees ... '

Invitations to tender are a common practice in the public and private sector. The invitation to tender is used in many public sector procurement situations for a range of procurement categories, including construction, IT systems, services, consultancy, outsourcing and security. Whether the invitation to tender is an offer to purchase or an invitation to negotiate will depend on the facts and circumstances of the individual case.

The Blackpool and Fylde Aero Club Ltd[2] case provides an insight into legal issues associated with invitations to tender. The council invited tenders, stating, 'The Council do not bind themselves to accept all or any part of any tender. No tender which is received after the last date and time specified shall be admitted for consideration.' The complexity of the case began when the Council refused to consider the tender from the Aero Club on the basis it had been received late. In fact it had not. The Aero Club brought an action for damages against the Council and it was held by the trial judge and by the Court of Appeal that the Council were contractually obliged to consider the Aero Club's tender. Counsel for the Aero Club submitted that an invitation to tender was no more than a proclamation of willingness to receive offers. The invitation to tender in its specific form was an invitation to treat, and no contract of any kind would come into existence unless or until, if ever, the Council chose to accept any tender or other offer.

Pickfords Ltd v Celestica Ltd [2003] EWCA CIV 1741 (19 November 2003)

Lord Justice Dyson said 'this case raises some basic questions in relation to offer and acceptance in the law of formation of contract.' Three documents were relevant to the appeal being heard.

1 A fax from Pickfords dated 13 September 2001 which included 'we estimate 96 vehicle load will be required', and 'therefore we have an estimated budget figure to include all the above at £100k'.

2 On the 27 September 2001 Pickfords sent a proposal document, the last page of which was entitled 'Fixed Price Schedule'. It included a fixed price of £98,760.00.

3 On the 15 October 2001 Celestica (the buyer) sent a fax to Pickfords, referring to Pickfords' fax of the 13 September, including the words 'Not to exceed 100K'.

At the date of the trial Celestica had paid only £33,000 plus VAT. Pickfords argued the figure should have been £98,760.00.

This was a complex hearing; some salient points are:

(i) Pickfords argued that the proposal document revoked the offer in the 13 September fax.

(ii) It was held that Celestica's fax of the 15 October accepted the 13 September offer – not the 27 September offer.

(iii) The reference to 'not to exceed 100K' being salient to the hearing.

Pickford lost the case and were not awarded £98,760.00. The case is very useful in understanding offer and acceptance.

The buyer must be clear whether an offer remains open to acceptance. In general, an offer can be withdrawn by the offeror at any time prior to acceptance. The offer can also lapse after a 'reasonable time' has passed, noting that the time will depend on the nature of the transaction or commodity. The offer can, of course, be rejected by the buyer.

There are some procurement scenarios in which the buyer does not want the offeror to withdraw their offer. This is the case in some public tender situations where there may only be a few bidders and the withdrawal of an offer may jeopardise the procurement by removing important competitive forces. The UK Department of Transport in an Invitation to Tender for the Thames Link, Southern and Great Northern Franchise, included at 4.6 'validity of Bids' the following statement, 'All bids including the terms, Bid price, and any subsequent changes agreed shall be held valid for a period of 275 calendar days from the date of Bid submission. Bidders are required to confirm this in their Form of Tender.' The effect of this is that the offer will lapse at midnight of the 275th calendar day, unless previously accepted. The period of 275 calendar days is a long period, justified by the complexity of the procurement and the decision-making process. It is more usual to see a period of 60–120 calendar days used in invitation to tender documents.

A requirement for bid (or tender) bonds is issued by the buyer to provide an incentive for the bidder not to withdraw their tender prior to completion of the procurement exercise. Danske Bank explain, 'A bid bond (also called a tender bond) is issued to ensure that the exporter submits realistic bids under the tender process and to protect the reporter for any less that might occur if the exporter fails to sign the contract. A bid bond also assures the importer that the exporter will comply with the terms of the contract in the event that the tender is accepted. Bid bonds are usually issued for 2 per cent to 5 per cent of the tender amount.' The word exporter could read 'bidder' and importer could read 'buyer'.

An on demand Bid Bond issued by Danske Bank reads:

Bid bond – on demand

Name and address of beneficiary

Guarantee no.

Amount

Date of Expiry

At the request of (name and address of applicant), we hereby guarantee you irrevocably for the above maximum amount to secure that they fulfil their obligations as tenderer in accordance with their bid covering (description of goods/project).

Your claim(s), if any, duly made and presented to us under the guarantee, will be honoured on your first demand also stating that (name of applicant) have not fulfilled their above tender obligations towards you.

Any demand for payment or request for extension under this guarantee must be made via authenticated SWIFT message through your bank confirming that the signatures on your signed written demand are legally binding upon your company.

Where we have received no such claim by (expiry date) at the latest, we stand released from our liability under this guarantee.

We will reduce the guarantee maximum by any such amount, as we have had to pay in order to meet your claim(s) duly made and presented under the guarantee.

When the guarantee expires, please return this document to us.

7.3 Acceptance

An acceptance is an unqualified expression of assent to the terms proposed by the offeror. There is no rule that acceptance must be made by words. It can be by conduct, noting that buyer's training will include indoctrination of the Carlill[3] case.

Procurement professionals should be on the alert to ensure that acceptance is on the terms stipulated in the purchase order. A purported acceptance which does not accept all the terms and conditions proposed by the offeror (buyer) but which in fact introduces new terms is not an acceptance but a counter-offer. This is then treated as a new offer which is capable of acceptance, rejection or potential further change.

The 'Battle of the Forms', remains a thorn in the side of those dealing with offer and acceptance. The Butler Machine Tool[4] case is often a starting point for consideration of the implications. The then Master of the Rolls, Lord Denning explained that Butler quoted a price for a machine tool of £75,535. On the back of the quotation there were terms and conditions, one of which was a price variation clause. When the machine tool was delivered Butlers claimed an additional sum of £2,892 due under the price variation clause. The buyer's (Ex-Cell-O) rejected the excess charge, relying on their own terms and conditions. Butler's quotation included a general condition: 'All orders are accepted only upon and subject to the terms set out in our quotation and the following conditions. These terms and conditions shall prevail over any terms and conditions in the Buyer's order.' That, however, was not the end of the matter. The buyers replied, placing a purchase order in these words: 'Please supply on terms and conditions as below and overleaf.' On the foot of the buyer's order there was a tear-off slip headed 'acknowledgement worded: Please sign and return to Ex-Cell-O. We accept your order on the terms and conditions stated thereon – and undertake to deliver by – Date – signed.' Butler replied including these words: 'We return herewith duly completed your acknowledgement of order form.' They enclosed the acknowledgement form duly filled in with the delivery date March/April 1970 and signed by the Butler Machine Tool Co.

Lord Denning stated:

> In many of these cases our traditional analysis of offer, counter-offer, rejection, acceptance and so forth is out of date. The better way is to look at all the documents passing between the parties – and glean from them – or from the conduct of the parties – whether they have reached agreement on all material points – even though there may be differences between the terms and conditions printed on the back of them.

The Transformers & Rectifiers Ltd[5] case sheds further light on the courts positioning on the battle of the forms. In this case Mr Justice Edwards-Stuart found that neither party's terms and conditions were incorporated into the two relevant purchase orders. The issue centred on two contracts for the purchase of nitrile gaskets. It was alleged that the gaskets supplied by Needs Ltd were unsuitable for their purpose and not in accordance with the contract. The judge analysed the course of dealing between the parties. There are lessons here for procurement specialists. The parties had stated over an extended period and orders were placed on almost a weekly basis. It was found that the buyer's method of placing orders did not always follow exactly the same pattern: sometimes orders were placed by fax, sometimes as a pdf attachment to an e-mail and, occasionally, by post. At paragraph 7 of the judgement a basic issue is highlighted:

> The top copy of the claimant's purchase orders was printed on white paper. On the reverse, printed in small type and high coloured lettering, were the claimant's terms and conditions. I was shown an example of the top copy of a blank purchase order and it was not obvious on reading it that there was any printing on the reverse. Accordingly a person receiving the document would probably not know that there was any writing on its back unless he or she happened to turn it over or had been specifically referred to its existence.

At paragraph 9 of the judgment it stated,

> However, when the claimant placed an order by either fax or e-mail it did not transmit a copy of the conditions on the reverse of the purchase order. All that was sent was the front page of the purchase order so that the Defendant did not receive a copy of the terms and conditions on the back.

7.3.1 Terms of the Contract

Elliott and Quinn[6] illustrate contractual terms as shown in Figure 7.1:
The procurement specialist should always bear in mind:

– how statements made in negotiation become part of the contract
– statements may be held to be a representation that encouraged one party to make a contract but does not become part of a contract

Figure 7.1 Illustration of Contract terms

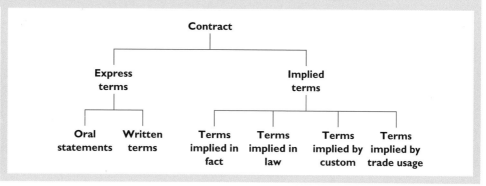

- the more emphatically a statement is made, the more likely the courts will be to regard it as a term
- written terms can be incorporated into a contract in three ways: by signature, by reasonable notice and by a previous course of dealing
- terms implied in fact are terms not laid down in the contract, but which it is assumed both parties would have intended to include if they had thought about it
- terms implied in law are those which the law dictates must be present in certain types of contract – see Smith v Wilson (1832) where under local custom 1000 rabbits meant 1200 rabbits
- terms implied by trade usage can be seen by British Crane Hire Corp Ltd v Ipswich Plant Hire Ltd (1975).

7.4 Contracts for the Sale of Goods

The procurement professional should be aware of the Acts that may impinge on their duties. These are the Trade Descriptions Act 1968, the Unfair Contract Terms Act 1977, the Sale of Goods Act 1979, the Supply of Goods and Services Act 1982 and the Sale and Supply of Goods Act 1994. This section of the chapter is not intended to put any focus on consumer law.

Section 2(1) of the Sale of Goods Act 1979 defines a sale of goods contract as one 'by which the seller transfers or agrees to transfer the property in goods to the buyer for a money consideration, called the price.' The 1979 Act does not cover services. Goods have been held to include packaging surrounding goods.

There is a set of implied terms in all contracts covered by the 1979 Act. These are:

- *Title.* It is implied that the seller has a right to sell the goods and is also able to pass good title to the buyer – Section 12(1).
- *Sale by description.* The Act states that 'where there is a contract for the sale of goods by description, there is an implied condition that the goods will correspond with the description' – Section 13(1).
- *Satisfactory quality.* The Act states that goods are of a satisfactory quality if they 'meet the standard that a reasonable person would regard as satisfactory, taking into account any

description of the goods, the price (if relevant) and all other relevant circumstances' – Section 14(2). Professional buyers should note that the term 'merchantable quality' was succeeded because it was considered too imprecise.

■ *Fitness for purpose.* This is an important provision providing, in summary, that if a buyer tells the seller the goods are required for a particular purpose, and the seller sells them, the goods must be fit for that purpose 'whether or not that is a purpose for which such goods are commonly supplied' – Section 14(3).

■ *Correspondence with sample.* There is an implied condition that the bulk of the goods will correspond with the sample, that the buyer will have a reasonable opportunity of comparing the bulk with the sample, and that the goods will be free from any defect, rendering them unsatisfactory, which would not be apparent on reasonable examination of the sample – Section 15.

7.5 Contract for the Supply of Services

There are implied terms under the Supply of Goods and Services Act 1982. These are:

■ *Care and skill.* The position is 'that the supplier will carry out the service with reasonable care and skill' – Section 13.

■ *Time.* The provision is that 'where the parties do not specify a time by which the job should be finished that the supplier will carry out the service within a reasonable time' – Section 14(1).

■ *Price.* Where the parties have not fixed a price there is an implied term 'that the party contracting with the supplier will pay a reasonable price' – Section 15(1).

■ *Property.* Where a service contract involves the transfer of property to the customer Sections 2–5 of the 1982 Act imply terms as to title, description, satisfactory quality, fitness for purpose and sample, essentially the same as Section 12–15 of the Sale of Goods Act 1979.

7.5.1 The Unfair Contract Terms Act 1977 (UCTA)

The UCTA is only concerned with exclusion clauses. An 'exclusion clause' is not defined in the Act but section 13 indicates that it can include any clause attempting to:

■ restrict or exclude a liability
■ make a liability, or the enforcement of a liability, subject to restrictive or onerous conditions
■ restrict the rights and remedies of an aggrieved party or
■ restrict rules of evidence or procedure.

There are exceptions where the UCTA is not applicable, including employment contracts, contracts relating to interests in land, or contracts regarding intellectual property rights.

The UCTA is very relevant to the professional buyer's role. In the Lloyds Bank case[7] Lord Denning said,

English law gives relief to one who, without independent advice, enters into a contract upon terms which are very unfair or transfers property for a consideration which is grossly inadequate, when his bargaining power is grievously impaired by reason of his own needs or desires, or by his own ignorance or infirmity, coupled with undue influences or pressures brought to bear on him or for the benefit of the other.

The FG Wilson case[8] contains a salutary lesson for professional buyers. The issue was whether a clause contained in FG Wilson's standard terms and conditions satisfied the test of reasonableness under the UCTA. The relevant clause provided 'Buyer shall not apply any set-off to the price of seller's products without prior written agreement by the Seller'. ('The no set-off clause'.) The judge held that the no set-off clause was not particularly unusual or onerous. He also said that the relative size in corporate terms of FG Wilson and Holt was not a significant factor. He went on to say that Holt had been able by a process of commercial negotiation to secure price discounts and extended credit terms and successfully negotiated a resumption of supply on credit notwithstanding a significant overdue debt measured in millions of pounds. No attempt was made to negotiate or object to the no set-off clause.

7.6 Consideration

It is important that the procurement community understand that in English Law, an agreement is not usually binding unless it is supported by consideration (see Figure 7.2).

The classic definition of consideration by Lush J[9] was 'A valuable consideration, in the sense of the law, may consist either in some right, interest, profit, or benefit accruing to the one party, or some forbearance, detriment, loss, or responsibility, given, suffered, or undertaken by the other.'

In respect of buying of goods or services consideration is often expressed as the promise to pay when the goods or services have been satisfactorily provided. Treitel[10] expresses it as follows,

In English law, a promise is not, as a general rule, binding as a contract unless it is either made in a deed or supported by some 'consideration'. The purpose of the requirement of consideration is to put some legal limits on the enforceability of agreements even where they are intended to be legally binding and are not vitiated by some factor such as mistake, misrepresentation, duress or illegality ... the present position therefore is that English law limits the enforceability of agreements (not in deeds) by reference to a complex and multifarious body of rules known as 'the doctrine of consideration.

Figure 7.2 Consideration elements

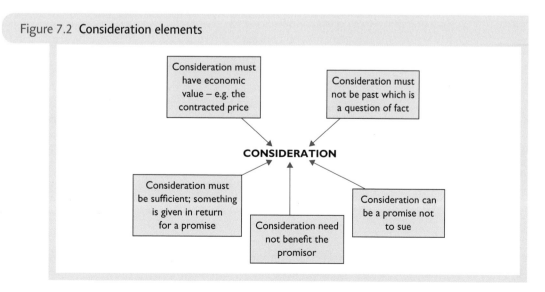

215

7.6.1 Adequacy of consideration

This is of interest to a buyer because a promise has no contractual force unless 'some' value has been given for it. The courts do not ask if adequate value has been given or whether the agreement is harsh or in favour of only one of the parties. Treitel[11] observes that:

> This state of the law sometimes causes dissatisfaction, e.g. when it is alleged that 'excessive' profits have been made out of a government contract or that 'irrationally generous' payments have been made out of public funds or when, in times of scarcity, it is said that 'excessive' prices are charged for goods or services or accommodation.

Expressed in a different way, it can be said there is a commercial onus on the procurement profession to negotiate and agree appropriate prices.

7.7 Capacity to Contract

Minors, the mentally incapacitated and companies have limited contractual capacity. It is the latter upon which buyers need to focus. A company is a legal person which is separate and distinct from its shareholders. If a company acts beyond its objects in its memorandum of association it acts ultra vires, in other words it has acted beyond its capacity. The courts have offered some protection for innocent third parties, significantly through Section 39(1) of the Companies Act 2006. This states, 'The validity of an act done by a company shall not be called into question on the grounds of lack of capacity by reason of anything in the company's constitution.'

There are potential complexities within an organisation as to who is authorised to contract on behalf of the organisation, public or private. Safeguards are often attempted to be put in place, such as forbidding a buyer to place a contract with a value in excess of £x, unless it is authorised by a designated senior person. The difficulty with this approach is that suppliers are probably unaware of this administrative control. The courts will most certainly examine the history of procurement practices within the organisation and will take custom and practice into consideration. In the CRJ Services Ltd[12] case the two businesses had been doing business for a number of years. Lanstar carried on business of environmental waste management and recycling. The case focused on contracts signed by Mr Vaughan who was not an employee of Lanstar and had described himself as a consultant and later as a manager. Mr Vaughan's engagement with Lanstar was terminated. Business events resulted in Lanstar terminating the hire of plant arranged by Mr Vaughan. Lanstar held that Mr Vaughan was 'at no material time given express authority to sign any long term hire agreements on behalf of CSG, as the only individuals who have such authority were the Finance Director and the Managing Director.' The matter had been subjected to adjudication and the adjudicator found that CRJ Services Ltd were entitled to payment for off-hire fee, interest and late payment compensation totalling £165,505.52 together with the adjudicator's fees totalling £8,520 inclusive of VAT. This decision was upheld by Mr Justice Akenhead.

The judgment included:

> There is no evidence that generally or specifically Lanstar told, or made it clear to CRJ that Mr Vaughan's authority was limited to contracts for short hire periods of a few days, a week or a month.

> On the evidence put before this Court, I do not consider, for the reasons given above, that there is any reasonable prospect of it being established that Mr Vaughan did not have appropriate authority to enter into the Hire Contract in question.

Within the judgment there is the inclusion of 'agency' because Mr Vaughan was acting as an agent of Lanstar. It was stated that so far as what was material to the case was three types of agency, namely express, implied or ostensible. Lanstar had paid all invoices raised by CRJ Services, hence it pointed strongly to Mr Vaughan having been given implied authority so far as the outside world was concerned or ostensible or apparent authority from the job and job description to which he was appointed.

An example of a Battle of the Forms was the GHSP Inc. dispute.[13] GHSP Inc. is a Michigan company and a designer and manufacturer of electro-mechanical controls systems for motor vehicles. AB Electronic Ltd is an English company manufacturing automotive and industrial position sensors. Mr Justice Burton said the issues in the case were:

> Did the parties conclude a contract in relation to the supply by the Defendant of Item No 7774106 B (the three track sensors) incorporating as terms either 1.1 the terms of the Claimant's Purchase Order (including the terms included in the Claimant's Supplier's Manual); or 1.2 the Defendant's Terms and Conditions of Sales; or 1.3 some other terms and if so which.

The judgment at paragraphs 10–13 set out the Law. It is an excellent summary for procurement specialists. In the case of Butler Machine Tools Co[14] Lord Denning MR said,

> ... in most cases when there is a 'battle of the forms', there is a contract as soon as the last of the forms is sent and received without objection being taken to it ... The difficulty is to decide which forms, or which part of which form, is a term or condition of the contract. In some cases, the battle is won by the man who fires the last shot ... There are yet other cases where the battle depends on the shots fired on both sides. There is a concluded contract but the forms vary. If ... they are mutually contradictory .... then the conflicting terms may have to be scrapped and replaced by a reasonable implication.

In the event, the Judge concluded that a contract had been made on the terms implied by the Sale of Goods Act 1979. The essence of the dispute was each party's position on liabilities. Unsurprisingly the Defendant wanted a cap on liability whereas the Claimant wanted unlimited liability. The Judge at paragraph 37 of the judgment put the matter into a practical reality:

> The reality seems to me clear. As must be the case very regularly in commercial discussions, both sides buttoned their lips, or fastened their seatbelts, and hoped that there would never be a problem, or that, if a problem arose, it would be a small enough one that, with goodwill, it could be settled 'on a case by case basis.'

7.8 Drafting the detail of contract clauses

There is no avoiding the issue that procurement specialists should have a significant role in drafting, negotiating and finalising the detail of contract clauses. It will, usually, require an active interface with in-house legal services. In the examples that follow the intention of the author is to stimulate an interest in detail and to promote the idea that attention to contractual detail will have positive results for the buying organisation.

7.8.1 Situation 1

This relates to a contract at Fiddlers Ferry Power Station near Warrington.[15] Clause 9 of the contract provided that:

> The parties agree that liquidated or unliquidated damages shall not be applicable to the contract in the event of delays to completion of the works, irrespective of the causes of such delays, and accordingly the purchaser shall not hold the contractor liable for late completion and/or consequential costs arising therefrom.

What do you think this means? Dwell on the actual words for a few minutes. At first sight, you may be convinced that if the contractor is late with delivery, no damages can be claimed by the purchaser. The contract delivery was late and £3.75 million was owed in damages by the purchaser to their customer. It was found that in regard to the contractor, while the provision might apply to a claim based on a delay in overall completion, it did not apply to a claim based on a delay in achieving the individual tie-in (milestone) dates.

Adjudication took place and the Adjudicator's decision was that the contractor, Thermal Energy Construction Ltd should be paid £904,567.60 plus VAT. The purchaser sought to overturn the Adjudicator's decision. His Honour Judge Stephen Davies found that the Adjudicator's decision could not be enforced. This decision left the matter to be resolved, either by mutual agreement or by a trial.

7.8.2 Situation 2

This situation relates to the proper construction of a contract for the design of the process engineering elements of a waste energy plant by Haase Environmental Consulting GmbH.[16] The judgment included a number of contract clauses from which this author is being selective for the purpose of illustrating how contract clauses interlock and why the wording is crucially important.

Clause 5.9.1 said:

> The Consultant accepts full responsibility for designing the Process Technology (including the selection of components for incorporation in the Process Technology) and the Consultant warrants to the Contractor that there has been exercised and will be exercised in the design of the Process Technology all the reasonable skill, care and diligence to be expected of properly qualified and competent design professional experienced in the design of works similar in size, scope nature and complexity to the Process Technology.

Clause 11 of the Appointment was entitled 'Principal Obligations' and at Clause 11.3 required the consultant to design, commission and test the Process Technology: 11.3.1 in accordance with the EPC Output Specifications and Schedule 16 and 11.3.2 in accordance with the EPC Delivery Plan.

It was held that Clause 5.9.1 applied and that the obligation was an appropriate starting point for consideration of other factors. The requirements of Clause 11 (11.3) began with the words 'Subject to the terms of this Appointment . . . ' Hence, the clauses both applied.

7.9 Misrepresentation

Elliott and Quinn[17] explain that a misrepresentation is an untrue statement of fact by one party which has induced the other to enter into the contract. A misrepresentation renders the contract voidable and it may also give a right to damages depending on the type of misrepresentation that has occurred. For a misrepresentation to be actionable, it has to fulfil three requirements: there must be an untrue statement; it must be a statement of fact, not mere opinion; and it must have induced the innocent party to enter the contract.

Section 2(1) of the Misrepresentation Act 1967 provides as follows:

> Where a person has entered into a contact after a misrepresentation has been made to him by another party thereto and as a result thereof he has suffered loss, then, if the person, making the misrepresentation would be liable to damagers in respect thereof had the misrepresentation been made fraudulently, that person shall be so liable notwithstanding that the misrepresentation was not made fraudulently, unless he proves that he had reasonable grounds to believe and did believe up to the time the contract was made the facts represented were true.

Court judgments provide the procurement specialist with a wealth of informed comment, such as Kingspan Environmental & Ors v Borealis A/s & Anov.[18] Mr Justice Christopher Clarke, commented:

> The effect of section 2(1) – see above – is to make a representor who cannot prove reasonable grounds for a false representation liable as if the statement had been fraudulent. In effect the Act imposes an absolute obligation not to state facts which are untrue and which the representor cannot prove he had reasonable grounds to believe. There is no need for the representee to establish that the representor acted negligently.

> A misrepresentation is a false statement of fact, as distinct from a statement of opinion – which is not to be regarded as a statement of fact merely because it turns out to be wrong. In certain circumstances a statement of opinion may be regarded as a statement of fact: chitty at 6-007.

> If a statement has more than one meaning, the question is whether or not it was understood by the representee in the meaning which the court ascribes to it – which is the meaning which would be attributed to it by a reasonable person in the position of the representee – and that having that understanding he relied on it.

We are, here, considering misrepresentation from the point of view of how a procurement specialist may encounter it at the Pre-Qualification and/or tender stages of a procurement (see Table 7.1 for selected examples). We should also recognise that misrepresentation may arise during negotiations. This reinforces the need for procurement to keep an immaculate audit trail of documentation and discussions.

Table 7.1 Selected examples of the potential for misrepresentation by suppliers

Example	Implications
Specialist resources exist.	If these resources do not exist the buyer must expect a delay arising from the suppliers' recruitment needs
Key personnel have appropriate academic qualifications.	CVs have been falsified by claiming academic qualifications that were never awarded. One implication is that the individual neither has the knowledge or intellectual rigour of the specific subject matter
There is no conflict of interest	The legal profession endeavours to ensure they are not conflicted by acting for the two parties to a contract. There may not be the requisite rigour by other professions, such as management consultancy
The company has the relevant experience	Not uncommonly, at the PQQ phase, three references/examples are sought whereby the applicant demonstrates they have relevant experience. It is possible that false claims or exaggerations are made
The company can mobilise resources by a specified date	If mobilisation does not occur by a specified date, a project will suffer delay. On a construction project, site facilities (including accommodation and IT), plant and equipment, storage facilities must be on time
The company has never had a contract terminated for non-performance	If they have had contracts terminated for non-performance and do not declare it there is a risk that they will not perform on their latest contract. The lack of this knowledge could persuade the buyer not to negotiate tougher remedies for non-performance
The specification will outperform those of competitors	The suppliers' claims for their specification performance could damage the buying organisations' reputation by inadequate goods or services being supplied
We have the items in stock	The supplier then claims that they have been sold and replacements will be with them very shortly

7.10 The right to terminate a contract

Treitel[19] explains as a matter of general law, the right to terminate for breach arises in three situations: renunciation (or repudiation), impossibility and substantial failure to perform. A party is guilty of renunciation where, by words or conduct, he evinces a 'clear' and 'absolute' refusal to perform. Impossibility refers to the 'situation where one party has by his 'own act or default' disabled himself from performing. Both renunciation and impossibility may occur at or during the time fixed for performance but, in such cases, the court will assess whether that which one party is refusing to do, or cannot now do, is sufficiently serious to justify termination, i.e. whether it amounts to a substantial failure to perform (or one of the exceptions thereto, e.g. breach of condition). In the case of termination for actual breach, the general requirement is that the party in default must have been guilty of a substantial failure to perform.

The action to terminate a contract should not be taken lightly. There are lessons to be learnt in the Bluewater case.[20] The contractual provision for termination was contained in Clause 30 of the contract and provided as follows:

30.1 Bluewater shall have the right by giving notice to terminate all or any part of the WORK or the CONTRACT at such time or times as BLUEWATER may consider necessary for any or all of the following issues:

(a) To suit the convenience of BLUEWATER

(b) Subject only to clause 30.2 in the event of any default on the part of the CONTRACTOR; or

(c) . . . .

30.2 In the event of a default on the part of the CONTRACTOR and before the issue by BLUEWATER of an order of termination of all or any part of the WORK of the CONTRACT, BLUEWATER shall give notice of default to the CONTRACTOR giving the derails of such default. If the CONTRACTOR upon receipt of such notice does not immediately commence and thereafter continuously proceed with action satisfactory to BLUEWATER to remedy such default BLUEWATER may issue a notice of termination in accordance with the provisions of clause 30.1.

The Hon MR JUSTICE RAMSEY said that it can be seen that where Bluewater seeks to terminate all of the work of the Contract under Clause 30.1 (b) and 30.2 then there were a number of steps to be complied with:

1 Bluewater must give notice of default to Mercon giving 'details of such default' ('Notice of Default')
2 Upon receipt of the notice Mercon must 'immediately commence and thereafter continuously proceed with action . . . . to remedy such default';
3 That action to remedy the default must be 'satisfactory to BLUEWATER'; and
4 If MERCON does not take such action, Bluewater 'may issue a notice of termination' under clause 30.1(b) for default on the part of Mercon ('Notice of Termination').

There was an issue between the parties as to the standard to be applied under clause 30.2 to determine whether or not action taken by Mercon is satisfactory. The phrase used is 'action satisfactory to BLUEWATER'. Bluewater submitted that this is a matter which depends on the subjective view taken by Bluewater as to whether that action is satisfactory and that there is no objective reasonableness that need be imported. It submits that it is not for the courts retrospectively to superimpose its own view on what Bluewater may or may not have found to its satisfaction. Mercon submitted that the action satisfactory to Bluewater had to be objectively reasonable so that it was not a question of the subjective satisfaction of Bluewater.

The judge found that Bluewater was entitled to and did terminate the Contract under Clause 30. The judgment is extensive, including claims and counterclaims, and is very informative for procurement specialists.

7.10.1 Contract termination for convenience

There is an increasing provision in contracts for a right of 'termination for convenience'. Basically, this means that the contractor has not done anything wrong and is not in breach of contract. Nevertheless, the buying organisation finds it to its advantage to terminate the contract. The simplest set of circumstances is when another contractor offers a much better deal. In public sector procurement, Central Government may decide that the public sector will, no longer, provide a specific service, thereby leaving little option but to terminate the contract 'for convenience'.

There isn't extensive case law on 'termination for convenience' although TSG Building Services PLC v South Anglia Housing Ltd [2013] EWHC 1151 (TCC) sheds an important light on the subject. TSG and South Anglia entered into a contract for the provision by TSG of a gas servicing and associated works programme relating to South Anglia's housing stock. At clause 13.1, it was agreed that the term of the contract was to be 'an initial period of four years extendable at the Client's sole option to a further period of one year.' At clause 13.3 it said:

> If stated in the Term Partnering Agreement that this clause 13.3 applies, the Client may terminate the appointment of all other Partnering Team members, and any other Partnering Team member stated in the Term Partnering Agreement may terminate its own appointment, if any time during the Term or as otherwise stated by the period(s) of notice to all other Partnering Team members stated in the Term Partnering Agreement.

In this case, Mr Justice Akenhead said that there was no real suggestion in the evidence that over the next 13 months TSG performed their work badly or incompetently. South Anglia terminated the contract and TSG claimed £900,682.94. They did so under four heads of claim; under recovery of overheads and profit, under recovery of contract set-up and termination costs.

Mr Justice Akenhead at para 51 of the judgment said:

> I do not consider that there was an implied term of good faith in the Contract. The parties had gone as far as they wanted in expressing terms in clause 1.1 about how they were to work together in a spirit of 'trust fairness and mutual cooperation' and to act reasonably … or restrict what the parties had expressly agreed in clause 13.3, which was in effect that either of them for no good or bad reason could terminate at any time before the term of four years was completed. That is the risk that each voluntarily undertook when it entered into the contract, even though, doubtless, initially each may have thought, hoped and assumed that the contract would run its full term.

It was found that TSG had no entitlement (whether as damages for breach of contract, or as a sum due under the contract) to receive monies and/or compensation in respect of overheads and profit which it would have recovered over the balance of the Term of the Contract following termination had the Contract not been terminated.

7.11 HOT TOPICS

7.11.1 HOT TOPIC – Breach of Contract

A definition of breach of contract is, 'committed when a party without lawful excuse fails or refuses to perform what is due from him under the contract, or performs defectively or incapacitates himself from performing.' Breach of contract is of serious concern to the buyer who usually has no choice but to get involved in dealing with the consequences of the breach. The actions may include consideration of rectification plans and actions, claiming damages, invoking 'step-in rights' or terminating the contract.

McKendrick[21] explains that in all cases the failure to provide the promised performance must be 'without lawful excuse'. Thus where the contract has been frustrated there is no liability for breach of contract because both parties have been provided with a 'lawful excuse' for their non-performance. Although the breach can take the form of words (such as an express refusal to perform the terms of the contract), it need not do so and can be evidenced by the conduct of one party in disabling himself from performing his obligations under the contract or by performing defectively.

McKendrick[22] further explains that the question whether or not a particular contract has been breached depends upon the precise construction of the terms of the contract. It is for the party alleging the existence of the breach of contract to prove that a breach has occurred. A breach of contract does not automatically bring a contract to an end. Rather, a breach of contract gives various options to the party who is not in breach (the innocent party). Three principal consequences of a breach of contract can be identified. The first is that the innocent party is entitled to receive damages in respect of the loss which he has suffered as a result of the breach. The second is that the party in breach may be unable to sue to enforce the innocent party's obligations under the contract. The third consequence is that the breach may entitle the innocent party to terminate further performance of the contract.

Elliott and Quinn[23] say that 'a contract is said to be breached when one party performs defectively, differently from the agreement, or not at all (actual breach) or indicates in advance that they will not be performing as agreed (anticipatory breach). The terms of a contract can be divided into conditions, warranties and innominate terms. Breach of a condition allows the innocent party to terminate the contract; breaches of warranty do not justify termination, although they may give rise to an award of damages. Where the relevant term is classified by the courts as innominate, it will be one which can be breached in both serious and trivial ways, and whether the innocent party is entitled to terminate or not will depend on how serious the results of the breach are.

Elliott and Quinn[24] show the effect of breach in Figure 7.3.

7.11.2 HOT TOPIC – Public Sector Tender Evaluation

It should be of great concern to public sector procurement specialists that there are frequent challenges from private sector organisations to contract award decisions made by the public sector. Some of the disputes are not resolved amicably and reach the courts. Such an example is, Woods Building Services v Milton Keynes Council.[25] This case is founded on the tender evaluation process and scoring of specific questions. Woods claimed that the tender evaluation process was unfair. Mr Justice Coulson at paragraph 5 observed that 'the award criteria must be formulated, on the contract documents or

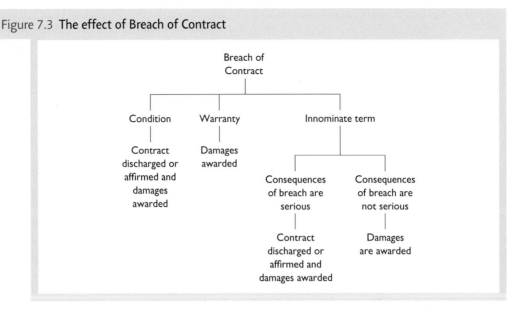

Figure 7.3 **The effect of Breach of Contract**

the contract notice, in such a way as to allow all reasonably well-informed and diligent tenderers to interpret them in the same way.'

The scoring system was on a scale 0–10. There was a definition for 0–2–4–6–8–10. To illustrate the difficulties and consequences of scoring we will examine what emerged in the case with regard to question 2.1. It asked: 'Provide a method statement (of two A4 pages maximum) setting out your proposals to meet the requirements of the service information.' This was an important question because it was worth 50 per cent of all the marks available for five questions. EAS (to whom the Council wanted to award the contract) score the maximum of 10 Marks. Woods argued that EAS should have scored zero because EAS wholly failed to deal with the reinstatement works in their Method Statement. The undisputed evidence was that the reinstatement element of the work would be worth approximately 40 per cent of the total contract value of £8 million.

Mr Justice Coulson observed that there was a raft of other matters which were not within the EAS Method Statement. There were no proposals in relation to IT, or quality assurance, or progress reports, or protecting the premises during the works. Mr Justice Coulson decided that there had been a manifest error and that a zero score should have been applied to the EAS answer to question 2.1. He said a score of 10 was incapable of rational explanation.

In summary, Mr Justice Coulson also adjusted other scores awarded to EAS, by reducing six scores to answers. He also increased two scores awarded to Woods. He concluded that Woods outscored EAS so that there would have been a different result. The outcome was that the judge would listen to counsel's submissions as to what relief should be granted to Woods.

7.11.3 HOT TOPIC – Retention of Title

In 1976 there was a watershed case, Aluminium Industrie Vaasen BV v Romalpa Aluminium Ltd [1976] 1 WLR 676. In essence, the decision of the Court of Appeal was such that the seller retained property in the goods until the purchaser paid for the goods. Not only that, the seller could trace the proceeds of sub-sales which had been entered into by the buyer, where the goods the subject matter of the sub-sales included goods supplied by the sellers to the buyers. The retention of title clause can be found in the judgment, noting it began with the ominous words, 'The ownership of the material to be delivered by A.I.V. will only be transferred to purchaser when he has met all that is owing to A.I.V., no matter on what grounds.'

McMeel and Ramel[26] provide a comprehensive analysis of retention of title issues/problems including:

a issues as to incorporation of clauses;

b issues as to the construction of clauses, and the related process of characterising such terms;

c issues as to which claims an administrator of company should allow, including claims to the goods supplied, including where the goods have been altered, mixed or manufactured into another form, and claims to proceeds of sub-sales;

d issues as to impact of such clauses on third parties, in particular sub-purchasers; and

e practical issues, including officer-holder liability and procedural matters.

McMeel and Ramel[27] explain that the choice of retention clauses is between 'simple' clauses (title reserved until particular consignment of goods paid for) and the 'all moneys' type (where property to all goods supplied is retained until all debts owed to seller are discharged). Virtually all the modern cases deal with the latter type, which has generally been successful where claims to the (unaltered) goods themselves are advanced. There are three principal 'bolt-on' sub-clauses:

a a tracing clause which lays claim to resale proceeds:

b a 'mixing' or 'aggregation' clause which lays claim to the mixed or manufactured product to which the goods supplied have been added;

c a 'following' or 'extended' clauses, which purports to extend the claim to the goods (or their product') in third party (sub-buyer) hands. These 'bolt-on' clauses have achieved only limited success in English law.

7.11.4 HOT TOPIC – Contract definitions

In a well-drafted contract there will be a list of definitions. These are of great relevance to a buyer, particularly when there are potential disputes over the meaning of words in the contract. Not unnaturally, very precise meanings have to be attached to a word. In many contracts there is a reference to 'day'. The convention is that a capitalised word, e.g. 'Day', should have a definition. The author has encountered disputes over:

– What is the working day? Is it, for example, 8am–6pm?

– Does day include Saturdays and Sundays?

– Does the working day include, or exclude, travelling time?

– What are the implications if the supplier's services are required outside the specified and agreed hours?

– What is the charge rate for overtime?

– How will the supplier account for hours worked?

An example of a definition is 'Change of Ownership' to deal with situations where a company who were awarded a contract, subsequently goes into the ownership of another party. A contract clause will spell out the consequences and the definition will set out what a 'Change of Ownership' means:

(a) any sale, transfer or disposal of any legal, beneficial or equitable interest in any or all of the shares in the Service Provider and/or its holding company and/or the Guarantor (including the control over exercise of voting rights conferring on those shares, control over the right to appoint or remove directors or the rights to dividends);

and/or

(b) any other arrangements that have or which result in the same effect as paragraph (a) above.

Another example of a definition is 'Direct Losses' to deal with situations where a contractor may require recompense under the contract. There will be a clause setting out the circumstances when Direct Losses can be claimed and the definition sets out what Direct Losses means:

all damage, losses, indebtedness, claims, actions, cash, expenses (including the cost of legal or professional services, legal costs being an agent/client, client (paying basis), proceedings, demands and charges whether arising under statute, contract or at common law but to avoid doubt, excluding Indirect Losses.

7.11.5 HOT TOPIC – Letters of Intent

Buyers are sometimes pressurised to issue a letter of intent to a supplier. In some buying organisations, Legal Services have a policy to prevent letters of intent being issued. The author agrees with this stance. The legal status of a letter of intent is uncertain. It depends on the wording whether a contract is created. In Cunningham v Collett and Farmer [2006] EWHC 1771 (TCC), Judge Coulson explained that a letter of intent 'properly so called' which

expresses an intention on the part of party A to enter into a contract in the future with party B, but creates no liability in regard to that future contract. It is expressly designed to have no binding effect whatsoever.' The second type of letter of intent is a letter which gives rise to limited rights and liabilities.

He also said,

It is usual for such documents to limit the employer's liability for the works to be carried out pursuant to the letter of intent. Commonly this is done, either by limiting the amount of money that the contractor can spend pursuant to the letter, or by reference to the particular elements of work that the contractor is permitted to carry out.

In Diamond Build Ltd v Clapham Park Homes Ltd [2008] EWHC 1439 (TCC) there is considerable detail (too much to include here) about how letters of intent impact on relationships and operate in practice. Clapham Park Homes (CPH) wished to have refurbishment and regeneration work carried out to a number of houses and flats. Diamond Build (DB) submitted a tender in the sum of £2,489,302. At paragraph 7 of the judgment, the full details of the letter of intent are included. The details are:

We confirm that it is our intention to enter into a contract with you on the basis of a JCT Intermediate Form of Contract, 2005 Edition with further amendments as specified in the Specification upon which your tender of 2nd April 2007 was based on.

Clapham Park Homes Ltd wish that you now commit the appropriate resources to permit you to take possession by no later than 28 calendar days from the date of this letter and to regularly and diligently proceed with the refurbishment works to achieve an overall completion with 36 working weeks from the date of possession.

The Contract Sum will be £2,489,302.00 as set out in your tender.

Should it not be possible for us to execute a formal Contract with you in place of this letter, we undertake to reimburse your reasonable costs up to and including the date on which you are notified that the Contract will not proceed provided that the Supervising Officer is satisfied that those costs are appropriate and that, in any event, total costs will not exceed the sum of £250,000 ...

Clapham Park Homes Ltd do not undertake to reimburse any anticipated profits for the works as a whole, nor actual costs or actual or theoretically incurred general or specific overheads arising after the date of notification that no further work is to be carried out.

You are to comply with the Construction (Design and Management) Regulations 2007 ('the CDM Regulations') and be the 'Principal Contractor' for the Project as defined in the CDM Regulations and fulfil in relation to the Project all the obligations of the Principal Contractor as set out in the CDM Regulations ...

You are also to effect all insurances stipulated in the Form of Contract and Specification referred to above and relevant to the work undertaken pursuant to this letter.

It is hereby confirmed that the undertakings given in this letter will be wholly extinguished upon the execution of the formal Contract.

Please confirm receipt of this letter and indicate acceptance of its terms by signing and returning the enclosed copy where shown.

Work on the project continued and DB incurred costs in excess of £250,000. On the 16 November 2007 CPH told DB that 'no further work is to be carried out under that letter (the letter of intent)'. The judge found that the letter of intent gave rise to a simple form of contract. DB sought to receive all their expenditure. DB argued that the cap (£250,000) produced an unfair position for DB because it was foreseeable that the cap would be reached within a relatively short time. The judge rejected this argument for a number of reasons, including that it was always open to DB to commit itself to its subcontractors and suppliers in a similar way to that predicated by the Letter of Intent. DB's claim was dismissed by the court.

This case illustrates how, in this instance, the court dealt with a letter of intent. It illustrates to procurement specialists the implications of inserting a financial cap into a letter of intent.

7.11.6 HOT TOPIC – Limit of Liability Cap

This facet of business risk must be comprehensively dealt with in a contract. It is therefore necessary that procurement specialists are very knowledgeable in this area. Suppliers will, for understandable reasons, seek to limit their liability under a contract and it is prudent for them to do so. Equally, it is prudent for the buyer to ensure his organisation is not exposed to unacceptable losses arising from a supplier failing to meet their contractual obligations. The liability cap establishes the maximum amount which can be claimed from a supplier in the event of a deficiency in their services. In the case of Trustees of Ampleforth Abbey Trust v Turner & Townsend Project Management Ltd [2012] EWHC 2137 (TCC), Turner & Townsend were appointed on their standard terms of engagement. These included a limit of liability clause:

Liability for any negligent failure by us (TTPM) to carry out our duties under these Terms shall be limited to such liability as is covered by our Professional Indemnity Insurance Policy terms, and in no event shall our liability exceed the fees paid to us (£111,321 in this case) or £1m whichever is the less.

It is pertinent to note that the Terms required TTPM to have a policy of professional indemnity insurance with a limit of indemnity of £10 million.

TTPM were project managers on three construction projects for the Trust. The works were completed significantly later than envisaged. In this case the Trust claimed against TTPM damages for professional negligence, in the amount of £750,000. His Honour Judge Keyser QC held that TTPM was in breach of a duty to exercise reasonable care and skill in that they failed to exercise sufficient focus on the matters holding up execution of the contract or to exert sufficient pressure on Kier (the contractor) to finalise the contract. Judge Keyser held that TTPM was not entitled to rely on the limitation clause and assessed the quantum of damages as £226,667. It was found that:

> The central factor that leads me to that decision (that the limitation clause was not unreasonable) is that the contract imposed on TTPM an obligation to take out professional indemnity insurance to a level of £10 million. The cost of such insurance would, as a matter of commercial reality, be passed on to the Trust within the fees payable. Yet the limitation clause would result in a limit of liability equal to the fees paid to TTPM, which is £111,321 (together with whatever might be awarded on the counterclaim). In the absence of any explanation as to why in this case TTPM should have stipulated insurance cover of £10 million despite a limitation of liability to less than £200,000, I consider it unreasonable that the contract purported to limit liability in that manner.

7.11.7 HOT TOPIC – Force Majeure

Procurement specialists must exercise great care in determining the precise wording of a Force Majeure clause. This clause entitles a party to suspend or terminate the contract on the occurrence of an event which is beyond the control of the parties and which prevents, impedes, or delays the performance of the contract. The procurement specialist must ensure that:

1 there is a definition of force majeure events; and
2 the operative clause that sets out the effect on the parties' rights and obligations if the force majeure event occurs.

The detail is often a matter for negotiation because of the allocation of risk. Suppliers generally seek a non-exhaustive list of events or circumstances that would qualify as force majeure including 'acts of God, earthquake, fire, flood or other natural disasters, acts of war, riot, insurrection, rebellion, sabotage, or acts of terrorism, shortage of materials and/or labour, IT systems failures, strikes, lockouts or any other cause beyond the seller's reasonable control.' All of these 'events' are worrying for the buyer who must probe the seller's business continuity plans should an alleged force majeure situation(s) arise. For example, if there is a fire at the supplier's premises:

■ How quickly will he be able to continue his business?
■ How long is the buyer prepared to tolerate non-performance before the contract is terminated?
■ How long after the force majeure situation is ended will the supplier be 100 per cent effective?

In the case of Tandrin Aviation Holdings Ltd v Aero Toy Store LLC & Anor [2010] EWHC 40 (Comm), there was an issue with the Force Majeure clause. The contract concerned the sale by Tandrin to ATS of a new Bombardier executive jet aircraft. The Force Majeure clause read:

> Neither party shall be liable to the other as a result of any failure of, or delay in the performance of, its obligations hereunder, for the period that such failure or delay is due to: Acts of God or the public enemy; war, insurrection or riots; fires; governmental actions; strikes or labour disputes; inability to obtain aircraft materials, accessories, equipment or parts from vendors; or any other cause beyond seller's reasonable control. Upon the occurrences of any such event, the time required for performance by such party of its obligations arising under this Agreement, shall be extended by a period equal to the duration of such event.

It is a complex case (as they often are) in that ATS refused to accept delivery of the Aircraft because the alleged 'unanticipated, unforeseeable and cataclysmic downward spiral of the world's financial market' triggered the force majeure clause in the Agreement. Mr Justice Hamblen dissected the force majeure clause wording, including: 'whether a force majeure clause in a contract is triggered depends on the proper construction of the wording of that clause', and the phrase 'any other cause beyond the seller's reasonable control' should be read in the context of the entire clause.' Mr Justice Hamblen refused to allow ATS to claim force majeure because the wording referred only to the 'Seller's reasonable control' and did not include the Buyer's reasonable control.

7.11.8 HOT TOPIC – Key Personnel

Key personnel are a vital feature of many contracts. At the tender stage, suppliers are keen to emphasise that some key people are central to performance of the contract. On many projects, including outsourcing, there will be key personnel named in the tender. This warrants a clause in the contract. A real-life example is the Bluewater case.[28] Clause 9 of Section 2 of the Contract related to Contractor Personnel. Clause 9.3 provided: 'The KEY PERSONNEL shall be provided by [MERCON] and shall not be replaced without the prior approval of BLUEWATER. Any replacement shall work with the person to be replaced for a reasonable handover period.'

Clause 3 of Section 9 of the contract provided as follows:

> KEY PERSONNEL [Mercon] shall provide the KEY PERSONNEL as listed in Attachment 9B and as indicated on the Organisation chart within Attachment 9C. KEY PERSONNEL shall be engaged in the WORK on a full-time basis, unless otherwise agreed with BLUEWA-TER. KEY PERSONNEL shall not be replaced without the prior approval of BLUEWATER. [MERCON] shall pay the liquidated damages specified in Attachment 9B for each replacement, unless otherwise agreed with BLUEWATER.'

There were seven contractor's key personnel listed, including:

Name	Position	Liquidated damage in case of replacement
A.C. van den Brule	Project Manager	€ 50,000
Mr J Liet	Construction Manager	€ 49,000
J. Marijunnissen	Transport & Logistics Manager	€ 30,000

In English law at the time of this case liquidated damages must be a genuine pre-estimate of less. Mercon accepted that it did not strictly operate the procedures for Key Personnel and did not seek Bluewater's prior approval for the replacement of some Key Personnel.

The judge found that Bluewater were entitled to liquidated damages in the sum of €150,000. The sums calculated for liquidated damages were not a penalty. The judge stated that 'I do not consider that in the context of this project the sums of €20,000 to €50,000 can be described as being inconsiderable in terms of being extravagant or exorbitant.'

7.11.9 HOT TOPIC – Liquidated Damages

It is probably inevitable that a buyer, at some stage in their career, will encounter a liquidated damages scenario. This is a remedy intended to compensate an aggrieved party to a contract where there has been a delay in meeting a contracted date(s) and where the cause can be laid at the door of the supplier. The contract must make provision for liquidated damages. In the case of Alfred McAlpine Capital Projects Ltd v Tilebox Ltd[29] the contract provided that McAlpine should pay liquidated and ascertained damages 'at the rate of £45,000 per week or part thereof.' The contract sum was £11,573,076. The building works were completed 2.5 years later than the due date. Tilebox claimed £5.4 million as liquidated and ascertained damages. Unsurprisingly, McAlpine claimed that the liquidated damages provision was a penalty clause and therefore invalid. Lord Dunedin in Dunlop Pneumatic Tyre Company v New Garage and Motor Company Ltd [1915] AC 79 said,

> Though the parties to a contract who use the word 'penalty' or 'liquidated damages' may prima facie be supposed to mean what they say, yet the expression used is not conclusive. The Court must find out whether the payment stipulated is in truth penalty or liquidated damages. This doctrine may be said to be found passim in nearly every case.

It was also said that, 'The exercise of a penalty is the payment of money stipulated as in terrorem of the offending party; the essence of liquidated damages is a genuine covenanted pre-estimate of damages.'

Keeping abreast of changes in law that impact on procurement is essential. In 2015 a UK Supreme Court ruling in the case of Cavendish Square Holdings BV and Total EI Makdessi became a landmark decision in relation to commercial contracts between sophisticated parties. Prior to this ruling the pre-determined level of liquidated claims had to be a genuine pre-estimate of the employer's (a term used in construction contracts) likely loss should a specified breach of contract occur. If it was deemed a penalty clause it would not be recoverable as a matter of English common law. It was the case that if the amount of liquidated damages bore absolutely no resemblance to the loss, was extravagant and unconscionable, and was intended to deter a breach of contract, the court would likely construe it as an unenforceable penalty.

In 2015 the UK Supreme Court held that the doctrine of penalties should not be abolished. They held that the correct approach in commercial cases was to have regard to the nature and extent of the innocent party's interest in the performance of a contractual obligation. The Supreme Court explained that a penalty clause whose purpose was to punish the contract breaker was likely to be an unenforceable penalty clause. However, the Supreme Court said that a clause that is intended to deter a breach of contract is less likely to be a penalty clause, even if it does not represent a genuine pre-estimate of loss. This is a ground-breaking finding that impacts directly on procurement decisions and negotiations on Damages clauses.

7.12 Standard Forms of Contract

There are a plethora of Standard Forms of Contract available to the procurement community. The following are examples only and not intended to be a comprehensive listing. Great care must be taken when selecting a Standard Form of Contract, with advice from specialists in their field of expertise and legal specialists. An advantage of Standard Forms of Contract is that they are recognised by many suppliers as an excellent basis for a contracting relationship.

Joint Contracts Tribunal[30]

Design & Build Contract 2016

Intermediate Building Contract 2016

Intermediate Building Contract with Contractor's Design 2016

Minor Works Building Contract 2016

Minor Works Building Contract with Contractor's Design 2016

Standard Building Contract with Quantities 2016

Standard Building Contract with Approximate Quantities 2016

Standard Building Contract without Quantities 2016

Prime Cost Building Contract 2016

Construction Management Trade Contract 2016

Short Form of Sub-Contract 2016

Repair & Maintenance Contract 2016

New Engineering Contract (NEC4)[31]

Design Build and Operate Contract

Dispute Resolution Service Contract

Engineering and Construction Contract

Engineering and Construction Contract (ECC) Option A: Priced contract with activity schedule

ECC Option B: Priced contract with bill of quantities

ECC Option C: Target contract with activity schedule

ECC Option D: Target contract with bill of quantities

ECC Option E: Cost reimbursable contract

ECC Option F: Management contract

Engineering and Construction Short Contract

Engineering and Construction Short Subcontract

Engineering and Construction Subcontract

Framework Contract

Professional Services Contract

Professional Services Short Contract

Professional Services Subcontract

Supply Contract

Supply Short Contract

Term Service Contract

Term Service Short Contract

The Project Partnering Suite of Contract[32]

PPC 2000 (Amended 2013) – Standard Form of Contract for Project Partnering

TPC 2005 (Amended 2008) – Standard Form of Contract for Term Partnering

SPC 2000 (Amended 2008) – Standard Form of Specialist Contract for Project Partnering

PPC International – Standard Form of Contact for Project Partnering

SPC 2000 Short Form (Issued 2010) – Standard Form of Specialist Contract for Project Partnering

SPC International – Standard Form of Contract for Project Partnering

STPC 2005 (Issued 2010) – Standard Form of Specialist Contract for Term Partnering

FIDIC – International Federation of Consulting Engineers[33]

The Red Book: Conditions of Contract for Construction for Building and Engineering Works Designed by the Employer

The Yellow Book: Conditions of Contract for Plant and Design-Build

The Silver Book: Conditions of Contract for EPC/Turnkey Projects

The Green Book: Conditions of Short Form of Contract

RIBA – Royal Institute of British Architects[34]

Concise Building Contract 2018

Domestic Building Contract 2018

Concise Professional Services Contract 2018: Architectural Services

Domestic Professional Services Contract 2018: Architectural Services

Principal Designer Professional Services Contract 2018

Standard Professional Services Contract 2018: Architectural Services

Sub-consultant Professional Services Contract 2018

IET – Institute of Engineering and Technology[35]

Model Forms of Contract for the design, supply and installation of electrical, electronic and mechanical plant. MF1. (Rev 6)

Discussion questions

7.1 A procurement specialist cannot be effective unless they have an excellent knowledge of Contract Law. Do you agree?

7.2 What are the implied terms of the Sale of Goods Act 1979?

7.3 In what respects is the Unfair Contract Terms Act 1977 relevant to the work of a procurement specialist?

7.4 Define the word 'Consideration' in English Law. Why is it important in a practical business sense?

7.5 Discuss the concept of 'Capacity to Contract' using the CRJ Services Ltd case as your basis for discussion.

7.6 Why do you believe the 'Battle of the Forms' is a recurring problem in business?

7.7 What are the dangers presented by a potential supplier's misrepresentation? What due diligence can procurement conduct to lessen the opportunity for a contract to be placed when misrepresentation took place?

7.8 Explain the difference between 'Liquidated Damages' and 'Penalties'.

7.9 Why are Standard Forms of Contract helpful to a procurement specialist?

7.10 Does your organisation have 'Standard Terms & Conditions' for the procurement of Goods & Services? If so, have you been trained to understand their detail?

References

[1] New Zealand Shipping Co Ltd v AM Satterthwaite & Co Ltd (The Eurymedon) [1975] AC 154.

[2] Blackpool and Fylde Aero Club Ltd v Blackpool Borough Council [1990] W&R 1195. Court of Appeal.

[3] Carlill v Carbolic Smoke Ball Co [1893] 1 QB 256.

[4] Butler Machine Co Ltd v Ex-Cello Corporation (England) Ltd [1979] 1 WLR 401.

[5] Transformers & Rectifiers Ltd v Needs Ltd [2015] EWHC 2689 (TCC).

[6] Elliot, C. and Quinn, F., *Elliott and Quinn Contract Law*, Pearson, Harlow, UK, 2019.

[7] Lloyds Bank Ltd v Bundy [1975] QB.326. CA.

[8] FG Wilson (Engineering) Ltd v John Holt & Company (Liverpool) Ltd [2012] EWHC 2477 (Comm)

[9] Curries v Misa [1875] LR10 Ex153,162

[10] Peel. E., *Treitel The Law of Contract*. Sweet and Maxwell, London, UK, 2007.

[11] Same as 10 above.

[12] CRJ Services Ltd v Lanstar Ltd (Ha CSG Lanstar) [2011] EWHC 972 (TCC).

[13] GHSP Inc v AB Electronic Ltd [2010] EWHC 1828 (Comm).

[14] Butler Machine Tools Co Ltd v Ex-Cell-O Corpn (England) Ltd, [1979] 1 WLR 401.

[15] Thermal Energy Construction Ltd v AE & E Lantjes UK Ltd [2009] EWHC 408 (TCC).

[16] MW High Tech Projects UK Ltd v Haase Environmental Consulting GmbH [2015] 152 (TCC).

[17] Elliot, C. and Quinn, F., *Elliott and Quinn Contract Law*, Pearson, Harlow, UK, 2013.

[18] Kingspan Environmental & Ors v Borealis A/s & Anor [2012] EWHC 1147 (Comm).

[19] Peel. E., *Treitel The Law of Contract*. Sweet and Maxwell, London, UK, 2015.

[20] Bluewater Energy Services BV v Mercon Steel Structures BV & Ors [2014] EWHC 2132

[21] McKendrick, E., *Contract Law*, Palgrave Macmillan, New York, 2009, p. 310.

[22] Same as 21 above.

[23] Elliot, C. and Quinn, F., *Elliott and Quinn Contract Law*, Pearson, Harlow, UK, 2015, p. 326.

[24] Same as reference 23.

[25] Wood Building Services v Milton Keynes Council [2015] EWHC 2011 (TCC) Case No HT-2015-000058

[26] Professor Gerald McMeel and Stefan Ramel. *Retention of Title – A thorn in the side?* Guildhall Chambers, June 2009.

[27] Same as 26 above.

[28] Bluewater Energy Services BV v Mercan Steel Structures BV & Ors [2014] EWHC 2132.

[29] Alfred McAlpine Capital Projects Ltd v Tilebox Ltd [2005] EWHC 281 (TCC) 25 February 2005.

[30] The Joint Contracts Tribunal, 28 Ely Place, London, EC1N 6TD.

[31] NEC, One Great George Street, London, SW1P 3AA.

[32] Association of Consultant Architects, 60 Gobutin Road, Bromley, BR2 9LR.

[33] FIDIC, World Trade Center 11, Geneva Airport, Box 311, 29 route de Pres-Bass CH 1215, Geneva.

[34] RIBA, 66 Portland Place, London, W1B 1AD.

[35] IET The Institution of Engineering and Technology, Michael Faraday House, Six Hills Way, Stevenage, SG1 2AY, UK.

Chapter 8

Quality management, service and product innovation

Learning outcomes

With reference to procurement and supply chain management this chapter aims to provide an understanding of:

- what is quality?
- quality systems
- total quality management
- specifications
- alternatives to individual specifications
- standardisation
- variety reduction
- quality assurance and quality control
- tests for quality control and reliability
- the cost of quality
- value management, engineering and analysis.

Key ideas

- Definitions and dimensions of world class quality standards and quality management.
- Considerations of quality management when entering into contracts.
- The principles of total quality management (TQM).
- Specifications from a procurement perspective.
- Variety reduction and ensuring sustainable savings.
- Varied approaches to creating specifications.
- Standardisation with special reference to BS EN ISO specifications.
- Standardisation from a procurement perspective.
- Public sector procurement implications of specifying goods and services.
- Inspection, statistical quality control, quality loss function, robust design, quality function deployment (QFD) and failure mode and effects analysis (FMEA) as tools for quality control and reliability.
- Costs of quality conformance and non-conformance.

8.1 What is quality?

8.1.1 Definitions

There are numerous definitions of quality. ISO 8402 (replaced in December 2000 by ISO 9000 and updated in September 2005) defined the fundamental terms relating to quality concepts, stating that quality is:

> The composite of all the characteristics, including performance, of an item, product or service, that bears on its ability to satisfy stated or implied needs. In a contractual environment, needs are specified, whereas, in other environments, implied needs should be identified and defined. In many instances, needs can change with time; this implies periodic revision of requirements for quality. Needs are usually translated into characteristics with specified criteria. Quality is sometimes referred to as 'fitness for use', 'customer satisfaction', or 'conformance to the requirements'.

In this definition there is the implication of an ability to identify what quality aspects can be measured or controlled or constitute an acceptable quality level (AQL). Needs which are defined relate to the value of the product or service to the customer, including economic value as well as safety, reliability, maintainability and other relevant features.

Crosby[1] defines quality as 'conformity to requirements not goodness.' He also stresses that the definition of quality can never make any sense unless it is based on what the customer wants, that is, a product is a quality product only when it conforms to the customer's requirements.

Juran[2] defines quality as 'fitness for use'. This definition implies quality of design, quality of conformance, availability and adequate field services. There is, however, no universal definition of quality. Garvin, for example, has identified five approaches to defining quality[3] and eight dimensions of quality.[4] The five approaches are as follows:

- The *transcendent approach* – quality is absolute and universally recognisable. The concept is loosely related to a comparison of product attributes and characteristics.
- The *product-based approach* – quality is a precise and measurable variable. In this approach, differences in quality reflect differences in the quantity of some product characteristics.
- The *use-based approach* – quality is defined in terms of fitness for use or how well the product fulfils its intended functions.
- The *manufacturing-based approach* – quality is 'conformance to specifications' – that is, targets and tolerances determined by product designers.
- The *value-based approach* – quality is defined in terms of costs and prices. Here, a quality product is one that provides performance at an acceptable price or conformance at an acceptable cost.

These alternative definitions of quality often overlap and may conflict. Perspectives of quality may also change as a product moves from the design to the marketing stage. For these reasons, it is essential to consider each of the above perspectives when framing an overall quality philosophy.

Garvin's eight dimensions of quality are:

1 *performance* – the product's operating characteristics
2 *reliability* – the probability of a product surviving for a specified period of time under stated conditions of use
3 *serviceability* – the speed, accessibility and ease of repairing the item or having it repaired
4 *conformance* – measures the projected use available from the product over its intended operating cycle before it deteriorates
5 *durability* – measures the projected use available from the product over its intended operating cycle before it deteriorates
6 *features* – 'the bells and whistles' or secondary characteristics that supplement the product's basic functioning
7 *aesthetics* – personal judgements about how a product looks, feels, sounds, tastes or smells
8 *perceived quality* – closely identified with the reputation of the producer and, like aesthetics, it is a personal evaluation.

While the relative importance attached to any of the above characteristics will depend on the particular item, the most important factors in commercial or industrial procurement decisions will probably be performance, reliability, conformance, availability and serviceability.

8.1.2 Reliability

As shown above, reliability is an attribute of quality. It is, however, so important that the terms 'quality and reliability' are often used together. Reliability has been defined as:[5]

> A measure of the ability of a product to function successfully when required, for the period required, under specified conditions.

Reliability is usually expressed in terms of mathematical probability, ranging from 0 per cent (complete unreliability) to 100 per cent (or complete reliability).

Failure mode and effect analysis (FMEA), performed to evaluate the effect on the overall design of a failure in any one of the identifiable failure modes of the design components and to evaluate how critically the failure will affect the design of performance, is referred to in section 8.9.7 below.

8.2 Quality systems

8.2.1 What is a quality system?

A *quality system* is defined as:[6]

> The organisational structure, responsibilities, procedures, processes and resources for implementing quality management.

A quality system typically applies to, and interacts with, all activities pertinent to the quality of a product or service. As shown in Figure 8.1[7] it involves all phases, from the initial identification to final satisfaction of requirements and end-of-life customer expectations.

Figure 8.1 **The quality loop visualisation**

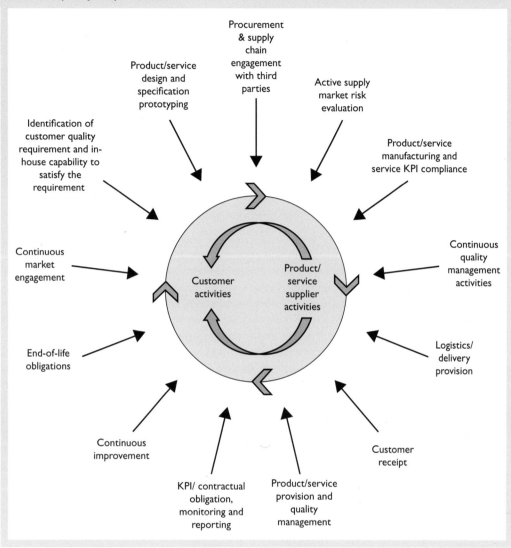

All organisations have a quality management system. This may, however, be informal and insufficiently documented. The advantages of a properly documented system, such as that required by BS EN ISO 9001:2015, are that it:

- ensures all aspects of quality are controlled
- ensures consistent, efficient work practices
- indicates best practice
- provides objective evidence for determining and correcting the causes of poor quality
- increases customer confidence
- gives competitive advantage
- focuses attention on the management of risks.

8.3 Total quality management

8.3.1 Definitions

Total quality management (TQM) has been defined as:[8]

> A way of managing an organisation so that every job, every process, is carried out right, first time and every time.

This means that each stage of manufacture or service is 'total' – that is, 100 per cent correct before it proceeds. An alternative definition is:[9]

> An integrative management concept of continually improving the quality of delivered goods and services through the participation of all levels and functions of the organisation.

8.3.2 TQM principles

TQM is based on three important principles.

1 *A focus on product improvement from the customer's viewpoint* – the key ideas in this principle are product improvement and customer product improvement. Juran[10] emphasised the importance of achieving annual improvements in quality and reductions in quality-related costs. Any improvements that take an organisation to levels of quality performance that they have previously not achieved is termed a 'breakthrough'. Breakthroughs are focused on improving or eliminating chronic losses or, in Deming's[11] terminology, 'common causes of variation'. All breakthroughs follow a common sequence of discovery, organisation, diagnosis, corrective action and control. The term 'customer' in this context is associated with the concept of 'quality chains', which emphasises the linkages between suppliers and customers. Quality chains are both internal and external. Thus, internally, procurement is a customer of design and supplier production. Staff within a function or activity, are also suppliers and customers. Like all chains, the quality chain is no stronger than its weakest link. Without strong supplier–customer links, both internally and externally, TQM is doomed to failure. Quality chains are one way in which to outmode the functional conflict and power tactics referred to elsewhere in this book. The first step in implementing an internal quality chain approach is for each activity to determine answers to the following questions relating to customers and suppliers.[12]

   ■ Customers
     – Who are my internal customers?
     – What are their true requirements?
     – How do, or can, I find out what their requirements are?
     – How can I measure my ability to meet their requirements?
     – Do I have the necessary capability to meet their requirements? (If not, then what must change to improve the capability?)
     – Do I continually meet their requirements? (If not, then what prevents this from happening when the capability exists?)
     – How do I monitor changes in their requirements?

   ■ Suppliers
     – Who are my internal suppliers?
     – What are my true requirements?

- How do I communicate my requirements?
- Do my suppliers have the capability to measure and meet the requirements?
- How do I inform them of changes in the requirements?

The second step, based on answers to questions such as the above, is to determine the level of service that a function such as procurement will provide. Cannon[13] has identified four factors affecting decisions about service types and levels:

- what the customer wants
- what the function can provide
- close collaboration to solve disagreements
- redefining both type and level of service at regular intervals.

It is also important to determine the technical expertise of procurement as 'it is this expertise which enables the function to add value to the procurement activity beyond that which the internal customer can perform without the function's assistance'. The questions posed earlier in this section can also be reframed by substituting the word 'external' for 'internal' so that external quality chains can be considered from both supplier and customer angles, too. In the capacity of customers, procurement organisations expect suppliers to compete in terms of quality, delivery and price. Zaire[14] states that the best approach to managing suppliers is based on JIT, which, from its inception, has the objective of obtaining and sustaining superior performance. The other important aspect of external customer supplier value chains refers to the management of customer processes as the purpose of TQM is customer enlightenment and long-term partnerships.

2 *A recognition that personnel at all levels share responsibility for product quality* – the Japanese concept of *kaizen*, or ongoing improvement, affects everyone in an organisation, at all levels. It is therefore based on team rather than individual performance. Thus, while top management provides leadership, continuous improvement is also understood and implemented at shop floor level. Some consequences of this principle include:

- provision of leadership from the top
- creation of a 'quality culture' dedicated to continuous improvement
- teamwork – that is, quality improvement teams and quality circles
- adequate resource allocation
- quality training of employees
- measurement and use of statistical concepts
- quality feedback
- employee recognition.

Zaire[15] states:

> Once a culture of common beliefs, principles, objectives and concerns has been established, people will manage their own tasks and will take voluntary responsibility to improve processes they own.

3 *Recognition of the importance of implementing a system to provide information to managers about quality processes that enable them to plan, control and evaluate performance.*

8.3.3 The benefits of TQM

TQM is a *philosophy* about quality that involves everyone in the organisation. It follows that the success of TQM depends on a genuine commitment to quality by every organisational member. Some benefits claimed for TQM include:

- improved customer satisfaction
- enhanced quality of goods and services
- reduced waste and inventory with consequential reduced costs
- improved productivity
- reduced product development time
- increased flexibility in meeting market demands
- reduced work-in-progress
- improved customer service and delivery times
- better utilisation of human resources.

8.3.4 Criticisms of TQM

TQM is not without its critics. Some objections include:

- that overly zealous advocates of TQM may focus attention on quality even though other priorities may be important, such as changes in the market – exemplified by the manager who said:

  > Before we invested in TQM, we churned out poorly made products that customers didn't want. We now churn out well-made products that customers don't want.

- that it creates a cumbersome bureaucracy of working parties, committees and documentation relating to quality
- that it delegates the determination of quality to quality experts because TQM is a complicated entity beyond the comprehension of the average employee
- that some workers and unions regard TQM as management-by-stress and a way of de-unionising workplaces.

8.4 Specifications

8.4.1 Why specifications are important in procurement decision making?

Procurement should have an active involvement in ensuring that specifications are adequately included in a contract. The key reasons are:

- specifications determine who in the supply market has the capability to tender for the work
- ensuring that the contract includes the detail of evaluating quality performance and the consequences of a supplier failing to meet the output requirements
- ensuring that bidders adequately explain HOW they will meet the performance specifications and the quality control measures to evaluate performance
- the need for continuous improvement and how it will be achieved.

8.4.2 Definitions

Specifications must be distinguished from standards and codes of practice. A *specification* has been defined as:

- A statement of the attributes of a product or service.[16]
- A statement of requirements.[17]
- A statement of needs to be satisfied by the procurement of external resources.[18]

A *standard* is a specification intended for recurrent use.

Standards differ from specifications in that, while every standard is a specification, not every specification is a standard. The guiding principle of standardisation, considered later in this chapter, is the elimination of unnecessary variety.

Codes of practice are less specific than formal standards and provide guidance on the best accepted practice in relation to engineering and construction and for operations such as installation, maintenance and service provision.

8.4.3 The purpose of specifications

Both specifications and standards aim to:

- *indicate fitness for purpose or use* – fitness for purpose or use was the definition of quality given by Joseph Juran, who also stated that quality is linked to product satisfaction and dissatisfaction, with satisfaction relating to superior performance or features and dissatisfaction to deficiencies or defects in a product or service
- *communicate* the requirements of a user or purchaser to the supplier
- *compare* what is actually supplied with the requirements in terms of purpose, quality and performance stated in the specification
- *provide evidence*, in the event of a dispute, of what the purchaser required and what the supplier agreed to provide.

8.4.4 Types of specification

As shown in Figure 8.2, specifications can broadly be divided into two types.

Several of the elements listed in Figure 8.2 may, of course, be combined in one specification. Thus, a specification for a component (a thing) may also state how it shall be made (a process) and how it shall be tested (a procedure). The specification may also state what the component is intended to do (function) and what a product or service should achieve under given conditions (performance).

8.4.5 The ISO 10000 portfolio of quality management standards

The astute buyer will have a working knowledge of the ISO 10000 portfolio of quality management standards, namely:

ISO 10001	Customer satisfaction – Guidelines for codes of conduct for organisations
ISO 10002	Customer satisfaction – Guidelines for complaints handling in organisations handling complaints
ISO 10003	Customer satisfaction – Guidelines for dispute resolution external to organisations

Figure 8.2 **Types of specification**

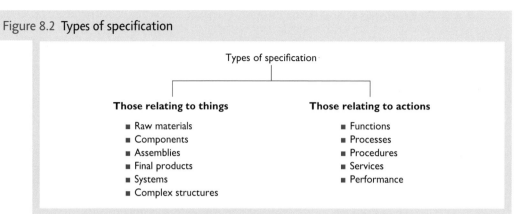

ISO 10004	Customer satisfaction – Guidelines for monitoring and measuring.
ISO 10005	Guidelines for quality plans
ISO 10006	Guidelines for quality management in projects
ISO 10007	Guidelines for configuration management
ISO 10008	Customer satisfaction – Guidelines for business-to-consumer electronic commerce transactions
ISO 10012	Measurement Management Systems – Requirements for measurement processes and measuring equipment.
ISO/TR 10013	Guidelines for quality management system documentation
ISO 10014	Guidelines for realising financial and economic benefits
ISO 10015	Guidelines for training
ISO/TR 10017	Guidance on statistical techniques for ISO9001
ISO 10018	Quality Management – Guidelines on people involvement and competence
ISO 10019	Guidelines for the selection of quality management system consultants and use of their services
ISO 19011	Guidelines for auditing management systems.

8.4.6 The BS7373 Specification Guides

The British Standards Institute publish the following:[19]

BS 7373-2:2001	Product Specifications, Guide to identifying criteria for a product specification and to declaring product conformity.
BS 7373-3:2005	Guide to identifying criteria for specifying a service offering.

8.4.7 Some principles of specification writing

Purdy[20] has identified four principles that should be observed by all specification writers. These and other principles are as follows:

- *If something is not specified it is unlikely to be provided* – the corollary is that all requirements should be stated in the specification before awarding the contract. Suppliers will normally charge for requirements subsequently added as 'extras'.

- *Every requirement increases the price* – all specifications should therefore be subjected to rigorous value analysis (considered later in this chapter).

- *The shorter the specification, the less time it takes to prepare it* – the expenditure in staff time devoted to the preparation of a specification can be high. This can be significantly lower when the length of a specification and the time taken in its preparation is reduced.

- *The specification is equally binding on both the purchaser and the vendor* – omissions, incorrect information or imprecision in a specification can be cited by the vendor in any dispute with the purchaser. A rule of evidence is that words are construed against the party who wrote them. Where there is uncertainty about the meaning of a specification, the court will generally interpret it in the vendor's favour.

- *Specifications should, so far as possible, be presented in performance terms rather than as a detailed design* – this is particularly applicable to items about which the purchaser has little expert knowledge. According to section 14(3) of the Sale of Goods Act 1979 as amended by the Supply and Sale of Goods Act 1994, where the seller sells goods in the course of a business and the buyer expressly, or by implication, makes known to the seller any particular purpose for which the goods are being bought, there is an implied 'term' that the goods supplied under the contract are of satisfactory quality. For the purpose of the Supply and Sales of Goods Act 1994 (SSGA), goods are of satisfactory quality if 'they meet the standard that a reasonable person would regard as satisfactory, taking account of any description of the goods, the price (if relevant) and all other relevant circumstances'.

- *Specifications should, whenever possible, be 'open', not closed* – closed specifications are referred to in section 8.5.3 below. Open specifications are written so that the stated requirements can be met by more than one supplier. By making the requirements sufficiently flexible to be met by several suppliers, competition is encouraged and prices reduced.

- Specifications must not conflict with national or international standards or health, safety or environmental laws and regulations – national and international specifications should be incorporated into individual specifications and identified by their numbers and titles.

8.5 Alternatives to individual specifications

8.5.1 Existing specifications

It should only be necessary to write a specification for non-standard requirements. For most standard industrial and consumer products it is usually sufficient to use:

- manufacturers' standards, as stated in catalogues or other promotional literature
- national or international standards.

All products or services will require materials, components or other elements for which existing standards will be available. An essential first step for designers or specification writers is to ascertain what relevant standards already exist. Searching for such standards is facilitated by consulting reference publications, especially the British Standards Catalogue (available in most large libraries), or databases. Especially useful are the services provided by Technical Indexes Ltd (www.iberkshire.co.uk), who offers comprehensive, reliable, full-text databases of manufacturers' technical catalogues, national and international standards and legislative material, delivered online via the Internet on an annual subscription basis. Technical Indexes' Ltd information services cover more than 90 per cent of the world's most commonly used standards, including:

- British Standards Online – a complete collection of over 35,000 British Standards
- Worldwide standards on the Internet
- UK and US Defence standards
- US Government Specifications Service.

8.5.2 Adapting existing specifications

This is often the most economical approach for construction projects or computer systems where architects or suppliers may be able to amend existing specifications to meet a new application.

8.5.3 Alternative methods of specifying

These include the use of brand or trade names and specifying by means of samples.

The use of a brand or trade names

England[21] lists the following circumstances in which descriptions by brand may be not only desirable but necessary, such as when:

- the manufacturing process is secret or covered by a patent
- the vendor's manufacturing process calls for a high degree of 'workmanship' or 'skill' that cannot be defined exactly in a specification
- only small quantities are bought so that the preparation of specifications by the buyer is impracticable
- testing by the buyer is impracticable
- the item is a component so effectively advertised as to create a preference or even a demand for its incorporation into the finished product on the part of the ultimate purchaser
- there is a strong preference for the branded item on the part of the design staff.

The main disadvantages of specifying branded items are as follows.

- The cost of a branded item may be higher than that of an unbranded substitute.
- The naming of a brand effectively results in what Haslam[22] refers to as a 'closed specification', which can take the form of naming a particular brand and the manufacturer or supplier not permitting the use of alternatives. Closed specifications are most applicable when the need for duplication of an existing product is important or it is desirable

to maintain a low spares range. Such specifications inhibit competition but also cut out fringe suppliers that may be unable to meet the quality requirements.

Specification by sample

The sample can be provided either by the buyer or seller and is a useful method of specification in relation to products such as printing or materials such as cloth. When orders are placed and products specified by reference to a sample previously submitted by a supplier, it is important that the sample on which the contract is based should be:

- identified
- labelled
- the signed and labelled samples retained by both purchaser and supplier.

Under section 5 of the Supply of Goods and Services Act 1982 (SGSA) and section 15 of the Sale and Supply of Goods Act 1994 (SSGA) there is an implied 'term' (later defined as a 'condition') that where goods are sold by sample:

- the bulk must correspond to the sample in quality
- the buyer must have a reasonable opportunity to compare the bulk with the sample
- the goods must be free from any defect making 'their quality unsatisfactory' (not unmerchantable), which a reasonable examination of the sample would not reveal.

Performance specification

A performance specification states requirements in terms of the required results and the criteria for verifying compliance, without specifically stating how the results are to be achieved. A performance specification describes the functional requirements for an item, its capabilities, the environment in which it must operate, and any interface, interoperability, or compatibility requirements. It does not present a preconceived solution to a requirement.

Some basic questions to ask when developing performance requirements are:[23]

- Which requirements are minimum or threshold requirements?
- What is each threshold? The best way to gain this understanding is to be sure that the user is involved in developing the requirement.
- What constraints apply? All constraints governing operation or use must be addressed, such as natural and induced environments, interfaces with other systems or equipment, and operator and maintainer limits.
- Is the requirement necessary?
- Is the requirement achievable?
- Is the requirement verifiable?
- How will we verify the requirement?
- What type of testing will need to be performed?

The Performance Specification Guide SD – 15[24] provides a very useful performance versus detail specification comparison. Part of this is reproduced below and all our readers will find the whole comparison of great professional interest.

Performance versus detail specification comparison

Specification requirements	Performance specification	Detail specification
Section 1 – Scope	Same for both	
Section 2 – Applicable Documents	Performance specifications usually have fewer references. They refer to test method standards; interface drawings, standards, and specifications; and other performance specifications. However, sometimes a performance specification can have a greater number of references, especially, if there are numerous test method standards to verify that performance requirements have been met. In general, performance specifications should not reference detail specifications, except when necessary to ensure interfaces, interoperability, or compatibility with other systems, equipment, components, or operating environments.	Detailed specifications usually cite a greater number of references than a performance specification since they require the use of materials and part and component specifications; manufacturing process documents; and other detail specifications as references
Section 3 – Requirements	The biggest differences between performance and detail specifications are in Section 3.	
1. General	States what is required, but not how to do it. Should not limit a contractor to specific materials, processes, parts, etc., but can prohibit certain materials, processes, or parts when Government has quality, reliability, environmental or safety concerns.	Includes 'how to' and specific design requirements. Should include as many performance requirements as possible, but they must not conflict with detail requirements.
2. Material	Leaves specifics to contractor, but may require some materiel characteristic; e.g., corrosion resistance. May also prohibit the use of certain materials, hazardous or toxic substances, or environmentally damaging substances.	May require specific material, usually in accordance with a specification or standard.
3. Performance	States what the item or system shall do in terms of capacity, function or operation. Upper and lower performance characteristics are stated as requirements, not as goals or best efforts.	Detail specifications often have performance requirements. This can be risky, however, if other detail design requirements create a situation where it is not possible to meet the performance requirement.
4. Design	Does not apply 'how to' design but should include requirement for design verification. Design verification is an integral element of performance specifications that the material; and parts meet all performance requirements.	Includes 'how to' and specific design requirements. Often specifies exact parts and components. Routinely states requirements in accordance with specific drawings.
5. Physical Characteristics	Gives specifics only to the extent necessary for interface, interoperability, environment in which item must operate, overall weight and envelope dimensions, or human factors.	Details weight, size, dimensions, etc. for item and component parts. Design-specific detail often exceeds what is needed for interface, etc.

Specification requirements	Performance specification	Detail specification
6. Interface Interoperability, and Compatibility Requirements	Similar for both detailed and performance specifications. Form and fit requirements are acceptable to ensure interoperability, interchangeability and compatibility.	
7. Processes	Usually does not specify processes, but if it does, the requirement is stated as the desired outcome from a process, requires the contractor's normal commercial processes, or 9s provided as guidance.	Often specifies the exact processes and procedures to follow – temperature, time, and other conditions – to achieve a result; for example, tempering, annealing, machining and finishing, painting, welding, and soldering procedures
8. Parts	Does not require specific parts.	States which fasteners, electronic piece parts, cables, sheet stock, etc. will be used.
9. Construction, Fabrication, and Assembly	Usually does not specify construction, fabrication, and assembly requirements.	Describes the steps involved or references procedures which must be followed; also describes how individual components are assembled.
10. Operating Characteristics	Omits, except very general descriptions in some cases.	Specifies in detail how the item shall work.
11. Workmanship	Very few requirements	Specifies steps or procedures in some cases.
12. Reliability	States reliability in quantitative terms. Must also define the conditions under which the requirements must be met. Minimum values should be stated for each requirement, e.g., mean time between failure, mean time between replacement, etc.	Often achieves reliability by requiring a known reliable design.
13. Maintainability	Specifies quantitative maintainability requirements such as mean and maximum downtime, mean and maximum repair time, mean time between maintenance actions, the ratio of maintenance hours to hours of operation, limits on the number of people and level of skill required for maintenance actions, or maintenance cost per hour of operation. Additionally, existing Government and commercial diagnostic equipment used in conjunction with the item must be identified. Compatibility between the item and the diagnostic equipment must be specified.	Specifies how preventive maintainability requirements shall be met; e.g., specific lubrication procedures to follow in addition to those stated under Performance. Also, often specifies exact designs to accomplish maintenance efforts.
14. Environmental Requirements	Both performance and detail specifications can have requirements for humidity, temperature, shock, vibration, and other environmental operating requirements to obtain evidence of failure or mechanical damage.	

8.5.4 Public sector buyers – technical specifications

The Public Contracts Regulations 2015 at Regulation 42 sets out the implications for contracting authorities when dealing with technical specifications.

Paragraph (4) of Regulation 42 explains the characteristics required of a material, product or supply, which may include:

a) levels of environmental and climate performance, design for all requirements (including accessibility for disabled persons) and conformity assessment, performance, safety or dimensions, including the procedures concerning quality assurance, terminology, symbols, testing and test methods, packaging, marketing and labelling, user instructions and production processes and methods at any stage of the life cycle of the works:

b) rules relating to design and costing, the test, inspection and acceptance conditions for works and methods or techniques of construction and all other technical conditions which the contracting authority is in a position to prescribe, under general or specific regulations, in relation to the finished works and to the materials or parts which they involve.

Paragraph (10) stresses: 'Technical specifications shall afford equal access of economic operators to the procurement procedure and shall not have the effect of creating unjustified obstacles to the opening up of public procurement to competition.'

8.6 Standardisation

Standards are documents that stipulate or recommend minimum levels of performance and quality of goods and services and optional conditions for operations in a given environment. Standards may be distinguished according to their subject matter, purpose and range of applications.

8.6.1 Subject matter

This may relate to an area of economic activity, such as engineering, and items used in that field, such as fasteners. Each item may be further subdivided into suitable subjects for standards. Thus, 'fasteners' may lead to standards for screw threads, bolts and nuts, washers and so on.

8.6.2 Purpose

Standards may relate to one or more aspects of product quality. These include:

■ *dimensions* thus encouraging interchangeability and variety reduction – for example, BS EN ISO 6433:1995 is a British Standard that lays down technical drawing principles and conventions widely accepted in the UK and will be easily understood worldwide.

■ *performance requirements* for a given purpose, such as PD 5500:2009, which covers the specification for unfired fusion welded pressure vessels necessary for a design to meet statutory requirements and those of manufacturers and users of safe performance.

■ *environmental requirements* relating to such matters as pollution, waste disposal on land, noise and environmental nuisance – for example, environmental performance objectives and targets are covered by BS EN ISO 14001:2004.

In addition to the above, standards may also cover codes of practice, methods of testing and glossaries. Codes of practice, as stated earlier, give guidance on the best accepted practices in relation to engineering and construction techniques and for operations such as installation, maintenance and provision of services. Methods of testing are required for measuring the values of product characteristics and behaviour standards. Glossaries help to ensure unambiguous technical communication by providing standard definitions of the terms, conventions, units and symbols used in science and industry.

8.6.3 Range of application

This relates to the domain in which a particular standard is applicable. There are several kinds of standards and it is also the case that different standards and specifications can often be used in conjunction.

- *Individual standards* – these are laid down by the individual user.
- *Company standards* – these are prepared and agreed by various functions to guide design, procurement, manufacturing and marketing operations. Ashton[25] has drawn attention to the importance of keeping registers or databases of bought-out parts and company standards that can be referred to by codes listed in a codes register as a means of variety reduction and obviating variations in tolerances, finishes, performance and quality.
- *Association or trade standards* – these are prepared by a group of related interests in a given industry, trade or profession, such as the Society of Motor Manufacturers and Traders.
- *National standards* – British Standard specifications of particular importance are BS 4778-3.1:1991 Quality vocabulary, BS 6143-1:1992 Guide to the economics of quality, BS 7850-1:1992 Total quality management and BS EN ISO 9000:2005 Quality management systems.
- *International standards* – the two principal organisations producing worldwide standards are the International Electrotechnical Commission (IEC) and the International Organisation for Standardisation (ISO). The former, established in 1906, concentrates on standards relating to the electrical and electronic fields. The latter, founded in 1947, is concerned with non-electrical standards. Both organisations are located in Geneva. In Western Europe, progress is being made in the development of standards that will be acceptable as both European and international standards. This work is being done via the European Committee for Standardisation (CEN), formed by Western European standards organisations. The demarcation of European standardisation mirrors the international arrangement, with CEN covering non-electrical aspects and the European Committee for Electrotechnical Standardisation (CENELEC) and the European Telecommunications Standards Institute (ETSI) being responsible for the others.

8.6.4 BS EN ISO 9000

Although TQM preceded the ISO 9000 series as a method by which organisations could increase their reputation for quality and profitability, compliance with ISO standards and ISO certification is widely regarded as providing the framework and essential first step to TQM.

The CEN (European Committee for Standardisation) and CENELEC (European Committee for Electrotechnical Standardisation) were created in the late 1960s – the former to 'promote technical harmonisation in Europe in conjunction with worldwide bodies and its partners in Europe'.

The ISO (International Organisation for Standardisation) was founded in 1946 as the existence of non-harmonised standards for similar technologies can constitute technical barriers to international trade. BS EN ISO 9000:2005, as the worldwide derivative of BSI's BS 5750 Quality Management System, launched in 1979, appeared in 1987. ISO standards, now adopted by over 140 countries, are revised every five years.

The current BS EN ISO 9000:2005 series, published in September 2005, provides the principles that are put into practice by the BSI system for the Registration of Firms' Assessed Capability. To be registered, an organisation is required to have a documented quality system that complies with the appropriate parts of BS EN ISO 9000 and a quality assessment schedule (QAS) that defines in precise terms the scope and special requirements relating to a specific group of products, processes or service. QASs are developed by the BSI in cooperation with a particular industry after consultation with procurement and associated interests.

When an undertaking seeking registration has satisfactory documentation procedures, the BSI arranges for an assessment visit by a team of at least two experienced assessors, one of whom is normally from the BSI inspectorate. Afterwards, a report confirming any discrepancies raised and the outcome of the assessment is sent to the undertaking seeking registration. The initial assessment is followed by regular unannounced audit visits at the discretion of the BSI to ensure standards are maintained.

As shown by Figure 8.3, the main documents relating to the system are a vocabulary and separate standards.

Although the revised 9001:2015 and 9004:2009 are standalone standards, they constitute a 'consistent pair' aimed at facilitating a more user-friendly introduction of quality management systems into an organisation.

8.6.5 ISO 9001:2015

The current version of ISO 9001 was released in September 2015. Organisations who were certified to the ISO 9001:2008 standard have a three-year transition to the 2015 standard. The changes introduced are intended to ensure that ISO 9001 continues to adapt to changing environments in which organisations operate. A welcome change for procurement professionals is an emphasis on risk-based thinking.

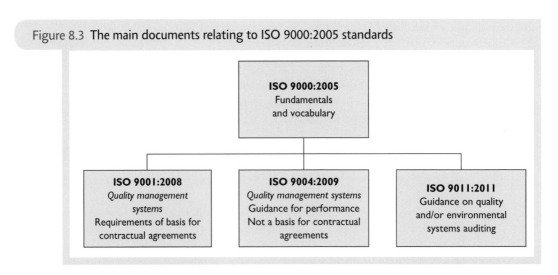

Figure 8.3 The main documents relating to ISO 9000:2005 standards

There are six clauses in ISO 9001:2015 which require an organisation to consider risk:

- Clause 4 – determine the risks which can affect its ability to meet these objectives
- Clause 5 – top management are required to commit to ensuring Clause 4 is followed
- Clause 6 – take action to address risks and advance opportunities
- Clause 8 – implement processes which identify and address risk in its operations
- Clause 9 – monitor, measure, analyse and evaluate the risks and opportunities
- Clause 10 – improve by responding to changes in risk.

There are seven quality management principles:

1 Customer focus
2 Leadership
3 Engagement of people
4 Process approach
5 Improvement
6 Evidence based decision making
7 Relationship management

8.6.6 Procurement and standardisation

Procurement staff should be aware of the major trade, national and international standards applicable to their industry and the items bought. They should also appreciate the advantages that standardisation offers to the buying organisation:

- clear specifications and the removal of any uncertainty as to what is required on the part of both buyer and supplier
- standardisation helps to achieve reliability and reduce costs
- saving of time and money by eliminating the need to prepare company specifications and reducing the need for explanatory letters, telephone calls and so on
- the saving of design time may also reduce the time for production of the finished product
- accurate comparison of quotations as all prospective suppliers are quoting for the same thing
- less dependence on specialist suppliers and greater scope for negotiation
- reduction in error and conflict, thus increasing supplier goodwill
- facilitation of international sourcing by reference to ISO standards
- saving in inventory and cost as a result of variety reduction (see Chapter 10) – by coordinating the efforts of procurement, design and production, a company reduced 30 different paints to 15, 120 different cutting fluids to 10, 50 different tools steel to 6, and 12 different aluminium casting alloys to 3. Standardisation and coding of items also discovered 36 different terms in use for a simple washer
- reduced investment in spares for capital equipment
- reduced cost of material handling when standardisation is used

- elimination of the need to purchase costly brand names
- irregular purchases of non-standard equipment supplies are revealed.

8.6.7 Independent quality assurance and certification

Independent quality assurance and certification is of great benefit to the user, purchaser and manufacturer. The BSI, via its Kite mark, Safety Mark, Registered Firms and Registered Stockist Schemes, put into practice the principles of BS EN ISO 9000, setting out procedures by which a product's safety and a suppliers' quality management systems can be independently assessed.

About 30 third-party certification bodies are members of the Association of British Certification Bodies (ABCB). Some are set up by trade associations, such as the Manchester Chamber of Commerce Testing House for the Cotton Trade, Bradford Chamber of Commerce for the Wool Trade, the Shirley Institute, Manchester, and the London Textile Trading House. Certification bodies assessed by the National Accreditation Council for Certification Bodies (NACCB) are entitled to use the NACCB National Quality 'Tick'.

8.7 Variety reduction

Variety reduction can make substantial savings in inventory by standardising and rationalising the range of materials, parts and consumables kept in stock. Variety reduction can be proactive or reactive.

Proactive variety reduction can be achieved by using, so far as possible, standardised components and sub-assemblies to make end products that are dissimilar in appearance and performance so that a variety of final products use only a few basic components. Proactive approaches to variety reduction can also apply when considering capital purchases. By ensuring compatibility with existing machinery, the range of spares carried to insure against breakdowns can be substantially reduced.

Reactive variety reduction can be undertaken periodically by a special project team comprised of all interested parties who examine a range of stock items to determine:

- the intended use for each item of stock
- how many stock items serve the same purpose
- the extent to which items having the same purpose can be given a standard description
- what range of sizes is essential
- how frequently each item in the range is used
- which items can be eliminated
- to what extent sizes, dimensions, quality and other characteristics of an item can be standardised
- which items of stock are now obsolete and unlikely to be required in the future.

The advantages of variety reduction include:

- reduction of holding costs for stock
- release of money tied up in stock

- easier specifications when ordering
- narrower range of inventory
- a reduced supplier base.

8.8 Quality assurance and quality control

8.8.1 Quality assurance

Quality assurance is defined as:[26]

> All those planned and systematic activities implemented within the quality systems and demonstrated as needed to provide adequate confidence that an entity will fulfil requirements for quality.

Quality assurance is concerned with defect prevention. Therefore, it can involve a number of approaches, including:

- quality systems, including BS EN ISO 9000:2015
- new design control, aimed at getting it right first time
- design of manufacturing processes aimed at eliminating defects at source
- incoming materials control – most organisations now require that their suppliers provide proof, such as BS EN ISO 9000:2015 accreditation certification, that their processes are under statistical control
- supplier appraisal, to ensure that only suppliers able to meet quality requirements are approved – this is especially important with JIT procurement.

8.8.2 Quality control

Quality control (QC) is defined as:[27]

> The operational techniques and activities that are used to fulfil requirements for quality. Quality control is concerned with defect detection and correction and relates to such activities as determining where, how and at what intervals inspection should take place, the collection and analysis of data relating to defects and determining what corrective action should be taken.

As defects are detected after they have been made, Schonberger[28] has referred to QC as 'the death certificate' approach.

8.9 Tests for quality control and reliability

It is impracticable in this book to attempt even an outline of quality assurance, control and liability techniques. So, in this section, brief mention is made of inspection, statistical quality control and six sigma, quality loss function, robust design, quality function deployment (QFD) and failure mode and effects analysis (FMEA).

8.9.1 Inspection

Although inspection is a non-value-adding activity, some form of inspection, either at source or on delivery, is often unavoidable. The four main inspection activities are shown in Figure 8.4.

Figure 8.4 **The four main inspection activities**

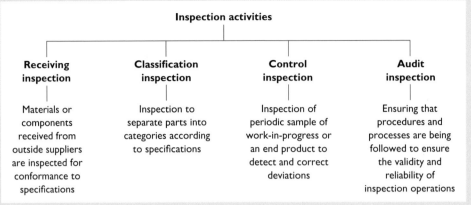

Important aspects of inspection are as follows:

- *How much to inspect and how often* – only rarely is a 100 per cent inspection required, and the greater the frequency of inspections, the greater the cost. In general, operations with a high human input necessitate more inspection than mechanical operations, which tend to be more reliable. The usual basis of inspection is an agreed sample, such as 5 per cent. The size of the sample will be determined by which statistical quality control method is to be used. Often the checking of dimensions or measurements can be done automatically by the use of go/no-go gauges.

- *Where to inspect* – most operations have numerous possible inspection points. Generally, inspection should take place:
  - when material is received from suppliers, although the tendency is for responsibility for quality to be placed with the supplier
  - before dispatch, as repairing or replacing products after delivery is more costly than at the factory and there is also damage to customer goodwill
  - before a costly operation
  - before parts are joined irreversibly to other parts
  - before a covering process, as painting or plating can often mask defects.

8.9.2 Statistical quality control

The basis of statistical quality control is sampling. A sample is a subset of a population or an entire set of objects or observations that have something in common. If a factory produces 1000 items of component X in one day, the population or 'universe' of component X for that day is 1000.

There are three main reasons for using sampling rather than 100 per cent inspection:

- sampling saves time
- sampling saves money
- sampling provides a basis for control.

From the quality standpoint, sampling can take one of two forms:

■ *Acceptance sampling* tests the quality of a batch of products by taking a sample from each batch and testing to see whether the whole batch should be accepted or rejected. Acceptance sampling can be applied when bought-out items are received from suppliers or as a final inspection of goods produced before they are dispatched to customers.

■ *Process control* is a more proactive approach, aimed at ensuring that parts and components meet specifications during the production process, not after a batch has already been manufactured.

The concepts of the arithmetic mean and standard deviation (referred to in the next section) provide the basis for the book *Economic Control of Manufactured Products*, published in 1931 by Dr Walter Shewart of the Bell Telephone Company. This book is the foundation of modern statistical process control (SPC) and provides the basis for the philosophy of total quality management by means of sampling.

Shewart also developed the statistical process control chart to provide a visual indication of quality variations.

If, for example, the ideal length of a steel spindle is 6 cm and there is a tolerance of 0.005 cm, then components of 5.995 cm or 6.005 cm will be acceptable.

As sample batches of the spindle are taken, the average value of each batch is calculated and logged on the chart, as shown in Figure 8.5.

So long as the results are within the upper and lower limits, there is no need for action. However, if a value falls outside these limits – as with samples 4 and 8 – the reason(s) must be investigated and rectified. It is possible, for example, that the machine settings for these batches needed resetting or adjusting.

Figure 8.5 Statistical process control chart

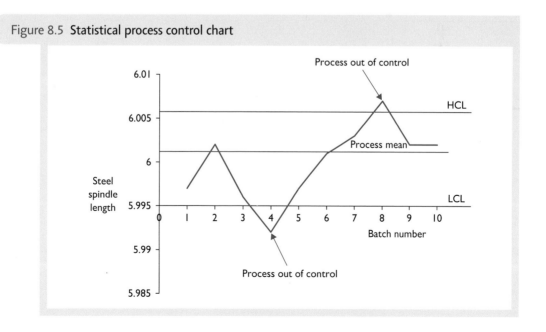

8.9.3 Six Sigma

The concept of the arithmetic mean, standard deviation and normal curve are the basis of Six Sigma. The business management strategy Six Sigma was originated at Motorola in the early 1980s and is an approach for improving customer satisfaction, by reducing and eliminating product defects. It aims to achieve virtually defect-free processes and products.

A normal distribution curve is shown in Figure 8.6.

The arithmetic mean (x) is obtained by dividing the sum of two or more quantities by the number of items. For example, the arithmetic mean of 5, 10 and 12 is $27/3 = 9$.

The standard deviation measures the extent to which sample scores are spread around the mean or average. For example, suppose that the scores from a series of inspections are normally distributed with a mean of 80 and a standard deviation of 8. Then the scores that are within one standard deviation of the mean are between $80 + 8 = 72$ and $80 - 8 = 88$. One standard deviation from the mean in either direction accounts for somewhere around 68 per cent of all items in the distribution. Two standard deviations from the mean accounts for roughly 95 per cent and three standard deviations for 99 per cent of the distribution spread. The term 'Sigma' is a Greek alphabet letter 'σ', used to describe variability. In Six Sigma the common measurement is defects per million operations (DPMO). Six Sigma – or six standard deviations from the mean – therefore indicates a target of 3.4 defects per million opportunities (or 99.99966 accuracy), which is as close as anyone is likely to get to perfection.

Achieving a Six Sigma level of quality output means reducing process variation by means of a technique called define, measure, analyse, improve and control (DMAIC), which uses a variety of statistical tools, including process maps, Pareto charts, control

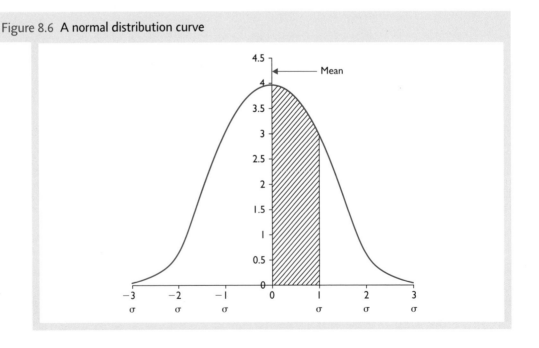

Figure 8.6 **A normal distribution curve**

charts, cause and effect diagrams and process capability ratio, most of which are beyond the scope of this book. Suffice to say that, as a result of the application of DMAIC, organisations identify and eliminate special cause variations from their processes until Six Sigma quality output is achieved.

8.9.4 Quality loss function (QLF)

This, together with the concept of robust design referred to in section 8.9.5, below, developed from work undertaken by Dr Genichi Taguchi while working for the Japanese telecommunications company NTT in the 1950s and 1960s.

Taguchi's approach is based on the economic implications of poor quality. He defines quality as:[29]

> The quality of a product is the minimum loss imparted by the product to society from the time the product is shipped.

The loss to society includes costs arising from the failure of the product to:

- meet customers' expectations
- achieve desired performance characteristics
- meet safety and environmental standards.

QLF is based on the principle that 'quality should be measured by the deviation from a specific target value rather than by conformance to preset tolerance limits'. Thus, the greater the deviation from a given target, the greater will be customers' dissatisfaction and the larger the loss concept.

The QLF approach is shown in Figure 8.7. The aim is to keep the product as near to the target as possible.

Figure 8.7 Taguchi's loss function

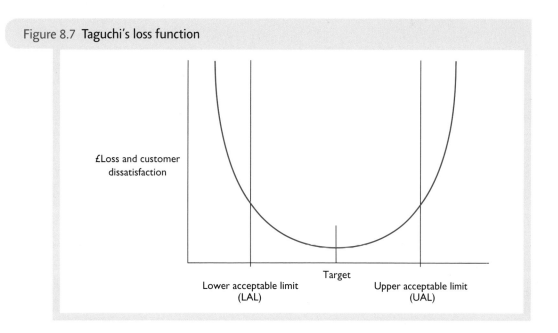

£Loss and customer dissatisfaction

Target

Lower acceptable limit (LAL)

Upper acceptable limit (UAL)

This loss function can be approximately calculated by using the formula:

$$L(x) = R(x + T)^2$$

where:

    L = the loss in monetary terms
    x = any value of the quality characteristics
    T = the target value
    R = some constant

Example 8.1

Example of use of the loss function

Assume a quality characteristic has a specification of 0.500 ± 0.020. Further, assume that, on the basis of company records, it has been found that if the quality characteristic exceeds the target of 0.020 on either side, there is a probability that the product will fail during the warranty period and the cost of rectifying it will be £100.

    Then:

$$£100 = R(0.020)^2$$

$$R = \frac{100}{(0.020)^2} = \frac{100}{0.0004} = 250,000$$

Therefore, the loss function is:

$$L(x) = £250,000(x - T)^2$$

Thus, if the deviation is only 0.005, the estimated loss will be:

$$L(0.005) = £250,000(0.005)^2 = £6.25$$

For a batch of 50 products, the cost would be 50 × 6.25 = £312.50

    The loss function approach has been criticised on the grounds that the practicalities of determining the constant R with any degree of accuracy are formidable.

    The Taguchi loss function can be applied to any non-conformance cost, such as complaint handling, inspection and testing, rework of defective parts, scrap and warranty repairs. All such costs arise from not doing the work right first time. By improving quality, such costs can be reduced. Thus, the cost of quality is a misnomer as quality can actually produce a profit.

8.9.5 Robust design

Some products are designed for use only within a narrow application range. Others will perform well in a much wider range of conditions. The latter have robust design. Think of a pair of bedroom slippers. These are clearly unsuitable for walking in mud or snow. Conversely, a pair of Wellington boots is exactly what is required. The Wellington boots are more robust than the slippers.

A product or service may be defined as 'robust' when it is insensitive to the effects of source of variability, even though the sources themselves have not been eliminated. The more designers can build robustness into a product, the better it should last, resulting in a higher level of customer satisfaction.

Similarly, environmental factors can have a negative effect on production processes. Furnaces used in the production of food, ceramics and steel products may not heat uniformly. One approach to the problem might be to develop a superior oven. Another is to design a system that moves the product during operation to achieve uniform heating.

Taguchi's approach involves determining the target specifications of limits for the product or design process and reducing variability due to manufacturing and environmental factors. As shown in Figure 8.8, Taguchi distinguishes between controllable and non-controllable factors, or 'noise'.

'Noise' factors are primarily responsible for causing the performance of a product to deviate from its target value. Hence, by means of analytical methods or carefully planned experiments, parameter design seeks to identify settings of the control factors that make the product more robust – that is, less sensitive to variations in the noise factors. Taguchi states that many designers consider only system and tolerance factors. He maintains, however, that without parameter design it is almost impossible to produce a high-quality product.

Taguchi's concepts of QLF and design have been criticised mainly on the grounds that the constant R in the QLF equation is difficult to determine with any degree of accuracy

Figure 8.8 Taguchi's concept of controllable and non-controllable factors

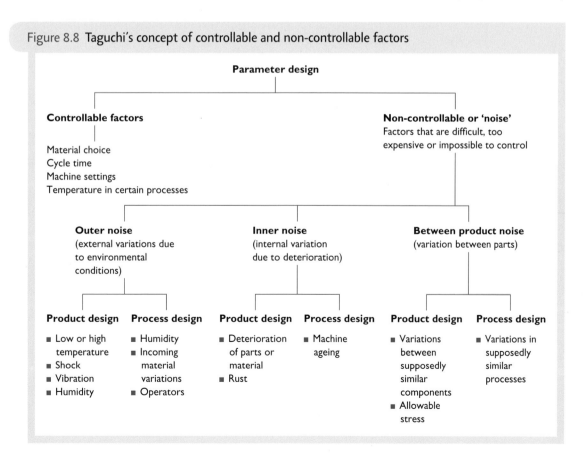

and that the large number of possible parameters in robust design make it impossible to investigate all such combinations. Nevertheless, his methods are used by many world class organisations.

8.9.6 Quality function deployment (QFD)

QFD is a translation of the Japanese *Kanji* characters *Hin Shitsu Ki Ten Kai*, which can be broadly translated as meaning, 'how we do understand the quality that our customers expect and make it happen in a dynamic way?'

QFD has been defined as:

> A structured approach to defining customers' needs or requirements and translating them into specific plans to meet those needs.

The term used to describe stated or unstated customer requirements is the 'voice of the customer'.

Information on customers' requirements is obtained in a multiplicity of ways, including market research, direct discussion, focus groups, customer specifications, observation, warranty data and field reports.

QFD ensures that customers' requirements are met by means of a tool called the 'house of quality' – an outline of which is shown in Figure 8.9. Using this tool, producers are able to reconcile customers' needs with design and manufacturing constraints.

The house of quality or product planning is, however, only the first of a four-stage process – the other three sequential phases being product design, product planning and process control. These four phases are shown in Figure 8.10.

Figure 8.9 **House of quality**

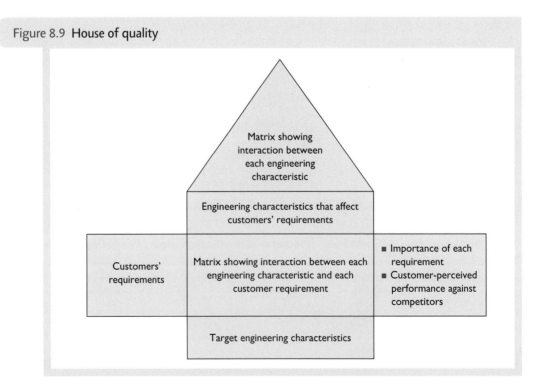

Figure 8.10 The four phases in QFD

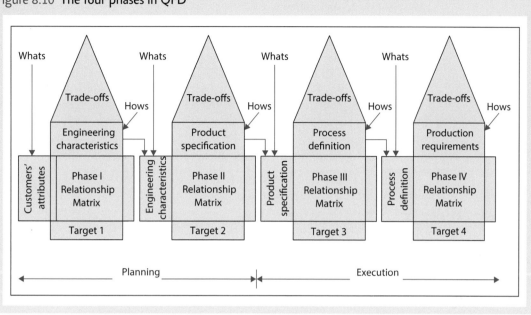

The QFD process involves the following steps:

1 Details of customers' requirements, or 'attributes', are obtained from sources such as those referred to earlier and listed under 'Customers' requirements' in the house of quality.

2 The relative importance assigned to each attribute is expressed on a scale of 1–5 or in percentage terms and entered under 'Importance of each requirement' in the house of quality.

3 For products that are intended to beat the competition, it is essential to know how they compare with those of competitors. A comparison of the rankings of each attribute will be made under 'Customer-perceived performance against competitors'.

4 Customers' attributes are translated into key engineering characteristics. Thus, for a car, the customers' attribute of 'fast start' would be translated into a 'specified' acceleration from 0 to 60 mph and entered into 'Engineering characteristics that affect customers' requirements'.

5 The strength of the relationship between customers' requirements and the technical requirements can be explored and expressed as 'very strong', 'strong' or 'weak' and entered into the 'Matrix showing interaction between each engineering characteristic and each customer requirement'. Blank rows or columns indicate no relationship or technical requirements as no customer requirement exists. It is also now possible to compare the performance of the product against customers' requirements and those of competitors and to set targets for improved design or performance. These are entered under 'Target engineering characteristics'.

6 The 'roof' of the house matrix encourages creativity by considering potential trade-offs between engineering and customer characteristics, such as performance and cost. This may lead to some changes in the target outcomes. While some organisations go no further than the first house of quality concerned with customers' requirements, others continue the process through the further stages of product specification, process definition and production requirements shown in Figure 8.10.

■ The *production specification house* is concerned with the detailed characteristics of subsystems and components and the determination of target values for such aspects as fit, function and appearance.

■ The *process definition house* is where components characteristics are related to key process operations. This stage represents the transition from planning to execution. If a product component parameter is critical and is created or affected during the process, it becomes a control point. This tells us what to monitor and inspect and becomes the basis for a quality control plan for the achievement of customer satisfaction.

■ The *production requirements house* relates the control points to specific requirements for quality control and includes the specification of control methods and what sample sizes are required to achieve the appropriate quality level.

Thus, as shown in Figure 8.10, the target technical levels of 'hows?' of one stage are used to generate the 'whats?' of the succeeding stage.

The main benefits of QFD are that:

■ the design of products and services is focused on customers' requirements and driven by objective customers' needs rather than by technology

■ it benchmarks the performance of an organisation's products against those of competitors

■ it reduces the overall length of the design code

■ it substantially reduces the number of post-release design changes by ensuring that focused effort is put into the planning stage or stages

■ it promotes teamwork and breaks down barriers between the marketing, design and production functions.

8.9.7 Failure mode and effects analysis (FMEA)

What is FMEA?

FMEA, which originated in the USA aerospace industry, is an important reliability engineering technique that has the following main objectives:

■ to identify all the ways in which failure can occur

■ to estimate the effect and seriousness of the failure

■ to recommend corrective design actions.

FMEA has been defined as:[30]

> A systematic approach that applies a tabular method to aid the thought process used by engineers to identify potential failure modes and their effects.

As a tool embedded within six sigma methodology, FMEA can help identify and eliminate concerns early in the development of a product or process. It is a systematic way to prospectively identify possible ways in which failure can occur.

Types of FMEA

It can take three forms:[31]

1 *Systems FMEA* is used to analyse systems and subsystems in the early concept and design stages. System function is the design or purpose(s) of the system and is derived

from customers' wants. It can also include safety requirements, government regulations and constraints.

2 *Design FMEA* is used to analyse products before they are released to production.

3 *Process FMEA* is used to analyse products before they are released to the customer.

The preparation of an FMEA

The Ford Motor Company, which was the first of the UK motor manufacturers to request suppliers to use FMEA in its advance quality planning, recommends a team approach led by the responsible system, product or manufacturing/assembly engineer, who is expected to involve representatives from all affected activities. Team members may be drawn from design, manufacturing, assembly, quality, reliability, service, procurement, testing, supplier and other subject experts as appropriate. The team leader is also responsible for keeping the FMEA updated.

For proprietary designs, the preparation and updating of FMEAs is the responsibility of the suppliers.

With a design FMEA, for example, the team is initially concerned with identifying how a part may fail to meet its intended function and the seriousness of the effect of a potential failure, which is rated on a ten-point scale, as shown in Table 8.1.

Starting with the failure modes with the highest severity ratings, the design FMEA team then ascertains the possible causes of failure, based on two assumptions:

- that the part is manufactured/assembled within engineering specifications
- that the part design may include a deficiency that may cause an unacceptable variation in the manufacturing or assembling process.

The team then proceeds to ascertain:

- the probability of failures that could occur over the life of the part – see Table 8.2; design evaluation techniques that can be used to detect the identified failure causes – see Table 8.3
- what design actions are recommended to reduce the severity, occurrence and detection ratings.

The completed design FMEA for a lighting switch subsystem is shown in Table 8.1. The technique is further described in BS EN ISO 9000.

Advantages of the FMEA approach

These include:

- improved quality, reliability and safety of products and processes
- increased customer satisfaction
- early identification, rectification and elimination of potential causes of failure
- ranking of product or process deficiencies
- documentation and tracking of actions to reduce failure risk
- minimisation of late product or process changes and associated cost
- it is a catalyst for teamwork and the cross-functional exchange of ideas and knowledge.

Table 8.1 Severity rating table for design FMEA

Effect	Rating	Criteria
No effect	1	No effect
Very slight effect	2	Very slight effect on vehicle's performance. Customer not annoyed. Non-vital fault noticed sometimes
Slight effect	3	Slight effect on vehicle's performance. Customer slightly annoyed. Non-vital fault noticed most of the time
Minor effect	4	Minor effect on vehicle's performance. Fault does not require repair. Customer will notice minor effect on vehicle's or system's performance. Non-vital fault always noted
Moderate effect	5	Moderate effect on vehicle's performance. Customer experiences some dissatisfaction. Fault on non-vital part requires repair
Significant effect	6	Vehicle's performance degraded, but operable and safe. Customer experiences discomfort. Non-vital part inoperable
Major effect	7	Vehicle's performance severely affected, but drivable and safe. Customer dissatisfied. Subsystems inoperable
Extreme effect	8	Vehicle inoperable but safe. Customer very dissatisfied. System inoperable
Serious effect	9	Potentially hazardous effect. Able to stop vehicle without mishap – gradual failure. Compliance with government regulation in jeopardy
Hazardous effect	10	Hazardous effect. Safety related – sudden failure. Non-compliance with government regulation

Note: Severity rating corresponds to the seriousness of the effect(s) of a potential failure mode. Severity applies only to the effect of a failure mode.

Table 8.2 Probability of failure rating table

Probability of failure	Failure probability	Ranking
Very high: failure is almost inevitable	> 1 in 2	10
	1 in 3	9
High: repeated failures	1 in 8	8
	1 in 20	7
Moderate: occasional failures	1 in 80	6
	1 in 400	5
	1 in 2000	4
Low: relatively few failures	1 in 15,000	3
	1 in 150,000	2
Remote: failure is unlikely	< 1 in 1,500,000	1

Table 8.3 **Design evaluation – detecting causes of failure**

Detection	Likelihood of detection by design control	Ranking
Absolute uncertainty	Design control cannot detect potential cause/mechanical and subsequent failure mode	
Very remote	Very remote chance the design control will detect potential cause/mechanism and subsequent failure mode	
Remote	Remote chance the design control will detect potential cause/mechanism and subsequent failure mode	
Very low	Very low chance the design control will detect potential cause/mechanism and subsequent failure mode	
Low	Low chance the design control will detect potential cause/mechanism and subsequent failure mode	
Moderate	Moderate chance the design control will detect potential cause/mechanism and subsequent failure mode	
Moderately high	Moderately high chance the design control will detect potential cause/mechanism and subsequent failure mode	
High	High chance the design control will detect potential cause/mechanism and subsequent failure mode	
Very high	Very high chance the design control will detect potential cause/mechanism and subsequent failure mode	
Almost certain	Design control will detect potential cause/mechanism and subsequent failure mode	

Some disadvantages of the FMEA approach

The disadvantages include:

- the required detail makes the process time consuming
- the process relies on recruiting the appropriate participants
- FMEA assumes the causes of problems are all single event in nature
- requires open and trusting behaviour, not defensiveness of vested interests
- requires follow-up sessions otherwise the process will not be effective
- it is difficult to examine human error and this facet is sometimes not scrutinised.

8.10 The cost of quality

8.10.1 The complexity of evaluating the costs of quality

The cost of quality may be defined as 'the expenditure incurred in defect prevention and appraisal of activities plus losses due to the internal and external failure'.

Table 8.4 shows the cost of quality associated with four areas of quality management.

Table 8.4 The costs of quality

Cost of conformance

Prevention costs	Appraisal costs
Costs of any action taken to investigate, prevent or reduce defects and failures, including: ■ quality engineering (or quality management, department or planning) ■ quality control/engineering, including design/specification review and reliability engineering ■ process control/engineering ■ design and development of quality measurement and control equipment ■ quality planning by other functions ■ calibration and maintenance of production equipment used to evaluate quality ■ maintenance and calibration of test and inspection equipment ■ supplier assurance, including supplier surveys, audits and ratings, identifying new sources of supply, design evaluation and testing of alternative products, purchase order review before placement ■ quality training ■ administration, audit and improvement	Cost of assessing the quality achieved: ■ laboratory acceptance testing ■ inspection tests, including goods inward ■ product quality audits ■ set-up for inspection and test ■ inspection and test material ■ product quality audit ■ review of test and inspection data ■ field (on-site) performance testing ■ internal testing and release ■ evaluation of field stock and spare parts ■ data processing inspection and test reports

Costs of non-conformance

Internal failure	External failure
Costs arising within the manufacturing organisation before transfer of ownerships to the customer: ■ scrap ■ rework and repair ■ troubleshooting or defect/failure analysis ■ reinspect, retest ■ scrap and rework, fault of vendor, downtime ■ modification permits and concessions ■ downgrading – losses for quality reasons resulting from a lower selling price	After transfer of ownership to the customer: ■ complaints ■ product or customer service, product liability ■ products rejected and returned, recall reject ■ returned materials for repair ■ warranty costs and costs associated with replacement

---

8.11 Value management, engineering and analysis

The terms value management (VM), value engineering (VE) and value analysis (VA) are often regarded as synonymous. Each term may, however, be distinguished from the others.

8.11.1 Value management (VM)

VM is defined by BS EN 12973:2000 as:

> A style of management, particularly dedicated to mobilise people, develop skills and promote synergies and innovation with the aim of maximising the overall performance of an organisation.

As indicated by this definition, VM is a style of management aimed at instilling a culture of best value throughout an organisation. 'Best value' implies that a product or service will meet customers' needs and expectations at a competitive price. VM applies at both the corporate and operational levels of an organisation. At the corporate level it emphasises the importance of a value-orientated culture aimed at achieving value for customers and stakeholders. At the operational level it seeks to implement a value culture by the use of appropriate methods and tools.

The Society of American Value Engineers (SAVE), formed in 1959, became the prototype for similar institutions in other countries. In the UK, the Institute of Value Management was formed in 1966, while, in 1991, the European Committee for Standardisation (CEN) sponsored the Federation of National Associations to produce BS EN 12973: Value Management, published in 2000.

8.11.2 Value engineering (VE)

Value engineering is an organised effort directed at analysing the functions of systems, equipment, facilities, services and supplies for the purpose of achieving the essential functions at the lowest lifecycle cost consistent with required performance, reliability, quality and safety.

Value engineering emphasises the importance of applying this discipline as early as possible in the design process. VE follows a structured thought process to evaluate options, namely the:

- gathering of relevant information
- consideration of what is being achieved now, if it is an existing product or service?
- measurement of all facets of performance, e.g. mean time between failures (MTBF)
- consideration of how alternative designs and performance will be measured?
- analysis of functions
- consideration of what must be done as opposed to 'nice to haves'
- consideration of the actual cost?
- generation of ideas through structured open challenge
- consideration of alternatives?
- evaluation and ranking of ideas for further action
- ideas which appear to offer the greatest potential
- development and expansion of these ideas
- consideration of the impacts and cost?
- consideration of the performance?
- presentation of ideas and agreement of action plan.

The Institute of Defence Analysis, 'VE Handbook'[32] gives a number of examples where VE has delivered outstanding results. These include:

SSQ-110A Sonobuoys

SSQ-110A sonobuoys are an active acoustic system that provides significant improvement over existing active sonobuoys and ameliorates the loss of long-range, passive acoustic detection capability. Current aging stockpiles of these sonobuoys were experiencing significant reliability problems. This, in turn affected crew confidence in the system, as well as operational effectiveness during tactical employment on station. Interrupting the search progression to replace failed sonobuoys resulted in a net reduction in system effectiveness. VE was used to develop a rework and inspection strategy that included new O-ring seals, a new 9-volt battery, and new seawater batteries. The arrival of refurbishment units helped personnel to accept active prosecution as a viable tactic and enabled quality training to be conducted. Cost savings and avoidances are estimated to be $40.7 million over 6 years.

There is an increasing use of value engineering change proposals (VECPs) which are used to incentivise the contractor to propose contract modifications which reduce cost without reducing product or process performance. Brian Farrington Ltd[33] has used VECPs in outsourcing contracts for the provision of back-office services, property and construction. These contracts include a 'Gainshare' provision whereby the contractor retains an agreed percentage of the savings achieved.

8.11.3 Value analysis

Value analysis (VA) was developed by the General Electric Company in the USA at the end of the Second World War. One of the pioneers of this approach to cost reduction was Lawrence D. Miles, whose book *Techniques of Value Analysis and Engineering* (McGraw-Hill, 1972) is still the classic on the subject.

The term 'value engineering' (VE) was adopted by the US Navy Bureau of Ships for a programme of cost reduction at the design stage, the aim of which was to achieve economies without affecting the needed performance, reliability, quality and maintainability. Miles has described value analysis as:

> A philosophy implemented by the use of a specific set of techniques, a body of knowledge, and a group of learned skills. It is an organised, creative approach which has for its purpose the efficient identification of unnecessary cost, i.e. cost which provides neither quality nor use, nor life, nor appearance, nor customer features.

VA results in the orderly utilisation of alternative materials, newer processes and the abilities of specialist suppliers. It focuses engineering, manufacturing and procurement attention on one objective: equivalent performance at lower cost. Having this focus, it provides step-by-step procedures for accomplishing its objective efficiently and with assurance. An organised and creative approach, it uses a functional and economic design process that aims to increase the value of a VA subject.[34]

The key words for an understanding of VA are 'function' and 'value'. The function of anything is that which it is designed to do, and should normally be capable of being expressed in two words – a verb and noun. Thus, the function of a pen is to 'make marks'. 'Value' is variously defined. The most important distinction is between use value – that is, that which enables an item to fulfil its stated function – and esteem value – factors that increase the desirability of an item. The function of a gold-plated pencil and a ballpoint pen, costing £70.00 and 50p respectively, is, in both cases, to 'make marks'. The difference of £69.50 between the price of the former over the latter represents esteem value.

8.11.4 Implementing VA

The necessary implementation of VA depends on choosing the right people and the right projects.

The right people

VA may be carried out by the following:

- a team of representatives from such departments as cost accounting, design, marketing, manufacturing, procurement, quality control research and work study
- a specialist VA engineer, where the company's turnover warrants such an appointment, who will often have the responsibility of coordinating a VA team, so such a person should have:

  - experience of design and manufacturing related to the product(s)
  - understanding of a wide range of materials, their potentials and limitations
  - a clear concept of the meaning and importance of 'value'
  - creative imagination and a flair for innovation
  - knowledge of specialist manufacturers and the assistance that they can provide
  - a capacity to work with others and a knowledge of how to motivate, control and coordinate.

Just-in-time approaches emphasises the importance of consultation with suppliers and their co-option to VA teams.

The right project

In selecting possible projects, the VA team or engineer should consider the following:

- what project shows the greatest potential for savings – the greater the total cost, the larger the potential savings, so, for example, consider two hypothetical projects, A and B:

	A	B
Present cost each	10p	100p
Possible savings (10%)	1p	10p
Annual usage	100,000	1000
Projected annual savings	£1000	£100

Component A offers the greatest potential return for the application of VA.

- what products have a high total cost in relation to the functions performed – that is, whether or not it is possible to substitute a cheaper alternative
- what suggestions for projects emanate from design, production staff and suppliers
- are there any drawings or designs that have been unchanged in the last five years?

- manufacturing equipment installed more than, say, five years ago that may now be obsolete
- any inspection and test requirements that have not been changed in the last five years?
- single-source orders where the original order was placed more than, say, two years ago that may offer possibilities for savings.

Here are some typical areas warranting VA investigation:

- Product performance – what does it do?
- Product reliability – reducing or eliminating product failure or breakdown.
- Product maintenance – reducing costs of routine maintenance, such as cleaning, lubrication and so on and emergency repairs and replacement.
- Product adaptability – adding an extra function or expanding the original use.
- Product packaging – improving the saleability of or protection given to the product.
- Product safety – eliminating possible hazards, such as sharp edges, inflammability.
- Product styling – specifying lighter, stronger or more flexible materials or simplifying instructions.
- Product distribution – making it easier to distribute by, for example, reducing its weight or finding better transportation options.
- Product security – making the product less liable to theft or vandalism by using better locks, imprinting the customer's name on easily moveable equipment and so on.

8.11.5 Value analysis procedure

The job plan for a VA project involves the following six stages:

1 *Project selection – see the list above.*
2 *Information stage*
   - Obtain all essential information relating to the item under consideration – cost of materials and components, machining and assembly times, methods and costs, quality requirements, inspection procedures and so on.
   - Define the functions of the product, especially in relation to the cost of providing them.
3 *Speculation or creative stage* – have a brainstorming session in which as many alternative ideas as possible are put forward for achieving the desired function, reducing costs or improving the product. Some questions that may promote suggestions at this stage include the following.
   - What *additional* or *alternative* uses can we suggest for the item?
   - How can the item be *adapted* – what other ideas does the item suggest?
   - Can the item be *modified*, especially with regard to changes in form, shape, material, colour, motion, sound or odour?
   - Can the item be *augmented* – made stronger, taller, longer, thicker or otherwise developed to provide an extra value and so on?

- Can the item be *reduced* – made stronger, smaller, more condensed, lighter or unnecessary features omitted?
- Can the item be *substituted* – would other materials, components, ingredients, processes, manufacturing methods, packaging and so on improve it?
- Can we *rearrange* the item – change its layout or design, alter the sequence of operations, interchange components?
- Can the item or aspects of the item be *reversed* – reversing its roles or functions or positions, turning it upside-down or front to back?
- What aspects of the product can be *combined* – its functions, purposes, units, other parts and so on?

4 *Investigation stage* – select the best ideas produced at the speculation stage and evaluate their feasibility. When VA is organised on a team basis, each specialist will approach the project from his or her own standpoint and report back.

5 *Proposal stage* – recommendations will be presented to that level of management able to authorise the suggested changes. The proposals will state:

- what changes or modifications are being suggested
- statements relating to the cost of making the suggested changes, the projected savings, the period(s) over which the savings are likely to accrue.

6 *Implementation stage* – when approved by the responsible executive, the agreed recommendations will be progressed through the normal production, procurement or other procedures.

8.11.6 VA checklists

The following checklist, which every material, component or operation must pass, was prepared by the General Electric Company:

- Does its use contribute value?
- Is its cost proportionate to its usefulness?
- Does it need all its features?
- Is there anything better for the intended use?
- Can a usable part be made by a lower-cost method?
- Can a standard product be found that will be usable?
- Is it made on the proper tooling, considering the quantities used?
- Are the specified tolerances and finishes really necessary?
- Do materials, reasonable labour, overheads and profit total its cost?
- Can another dependable supplier provide it for less?
- Is anyone buying it for less?

As stated earlier, whenever appropriate, suppliers should be invited to participate in a VA exercise. Miller[35] has prepared the checklist given in Figure 8.11. It can accompany requests for quotations or be used in supplier discussions relating to the design of a new product.

Figure 8.11 Miller's checklist

Question	Brief description of suggestion	Estimated savings of suggestion
1 What standard item do you have that can be satisfactorily substituted for this part? 2 What design changes do you suggest that will lower the cost of this item? 3 What part of this item can be more economically produced (considering tooling and so on) by casting, forging, extruding, machining or any other process? 4 What material can you suggest as a substitute? 5 What changes in tolerances would result in lower manufacturing costs? 6 What finish requirements can be eliminated or relaxed? 7 What test or qualification requirements appear unnecessary? 8 What suggestions do you have to save weight, simplify the part or reduce its cost? 9 What specifications, tests or quality requirements are too stringent?		
Will you attend a meeting to discuss your ideas if requested? Do you have a formal value analysis programme? If not, would you like help in setting one up? Company: Address: Signature: Title: Date:		

8.11.7 VA and functional analysis (FA)

As stated in section 8.11.3, the function of anything is 'that which it is designed to do'. Value can be defined as:

$$\frac{\text{Performance capability}}{\text{Cost}} \quad \text{or} \quad \frac{\text{Function}}{\text{Cost}}$$

Functional analysis (FA) involves identifying the primary and secondary functions of an item and decomposing them into the sub-functions at an ever-increasing level of detail. The application of FA, particularly at the information and creative stages, can indicate ways of reducing cost either by eliminating or modifying output functions. Conversely, a designer may seek to enhance value by adding new functions to an output. The latter can only be achieved when the target profit exceeds the cost of providing the additional functions. An extension of function analysis is cost function analysis, which identifies the cost of alternative ways of providing a given function.

8.11.8 Cost function analysis

This involves the following steps, which we shall illustrate by reference to a ballpoint pen, the existing components of which are shown in Figure 8.12.

Figure 8.12 **Using the components of a ballpoint pen as an example of cost function analysis**

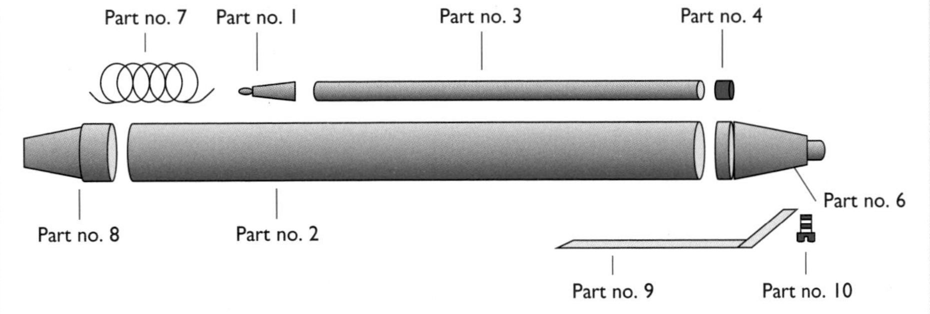

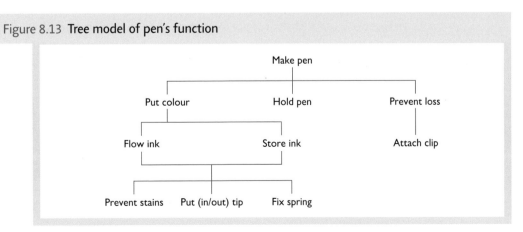

Step 1: Identify the primary and secondary functions of the item

Primary functions are those that the output must achieve. Thus, the primary function of a ballpoint pen is 'to make a mark'.

Secondary functions are support functions. These may be a necessary part of the function but do not themselves perform the primary function. Thus, to 'make a mark', secondary functions such as 'put colour' and 'hold pen' are required.

As stated earlier, the function should be capable of being expressed by two words – a verb and a noun – and, wherever possible, should have measurable parameters, such as 'prevent rust', 'reduce noise'.

Step 2: Arrange the functions in a tree model

Define the primary functions first and decompose them to lower-level functions. Thus, for the ballpoint pen, the resultant tree might be like that shown in Figure 8.13.

Step 3: Undertake a cost function analysis

A cost function analysis involves breaking down each function into components or general areas and allocating a target or estimated cost to each. A component or area may contribute more than one function. It is important to know how much each component or area contributes to each function. Thus, the initial design for the ballpoint pen could include details of the parts and costs set out in a matrix, as shown in Table 8.5.

Figure 8.13 **Tree model of pen's function**

Table 8.5 **A cost function analysis of the parts of a ballpoint pen**

Part numbers	Names of parts	Functions		Cost (£)
		Transitive verb	Noun	
1	Tip	Flow	Ink	0.50
2	Barrel	Hold	Pen	0.70
3	Cartridge	Store	Ink	0.23
4	Top	Store	Ink	0.15
5	Ink	Put	Colour	0.10
6	Cap	Pull in/out	Tip	0.01
7	Spring	Pull in/out	Tip	0.09
8	Stopper	Fix	Spring	0.10
9	Clip	Prevent	Loss	0.10
10	Screw	Attach	Clip	0.02
				2.00

From such a matrix, it is possible to account for the total cost of each part by adding them together horizontally and the cost of each function by totalling them vertically. The total cost of each function is usually expressed as a percentage of the total cost of the activity. It is at this stage that the VA team will use its judgment to decide whether the cost of each function is high, reasonable or low – that is, whether or not it represents good value.

It should be noted that, of itself, cost function analysis does not provide savings or solutions. The purpose of such analysis is to:

■ provide the VA team with an in-depth understanding of the VA project by identifying the purpose of each element of cost

■ indicate what functions provide poor value or where, because of the high cost of a function relative to the total cost of the activity, there is a potential for reducing cost or increasing value.

Assume that, as a result of the cost function analysis, the ballpoint pen is redesigned, using the components shown in Figure 8.14. Also, assume that, by negotiating with suppliers and dealing with new suppliers, the price for Part no. 1 has been reduced, but the cost of Part no. 2 has slightly increased as it now incorporates former Part no. 6.

Figure 8.14 **The components of the ballpoint pen after redesigning**

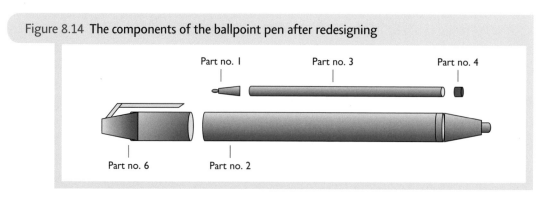

Part no. 1   Part no. 3   Part no. 4

Part no. 6   Part no. 2

Table 8.6 Revised cost function analysis of the parts of the redesigned ballpoint pen

Part numbers	Names of parts	Functions		Cost (£)
		Transitive verb	Noun	
1	Tip	Flow	Ink	0.40
2	Barrel	Hold	Pen	0.80
3	Cartridge	Store	Ink	0.23
4	Top	Store	Ink	0.15
5	Ink	Put	Colour	0.10
6	Cap	Pull in/out	Tip	0.01
				1.69

The new cost function matrix is as shown in Table 8.6.

- The above approach is particularly useful when the aim is to produce an item to a target cost. The aim in the above example might have been to produce a ballpoint pen at a target cost of below £1.75 (the component prices given in the example are for example only and bear no relation to reality).

- In general, the more components required to make an item, the greater the complexity. The greater the complexity, the greater the cost. Product(s) should therefore be designed with as few components as possible.

- Wherever possible, standard components should be used. Non-standard components increase costs and reduce flexibility. Standard components can be obtained from many suppliers, with short lead times at low cost and in smaller quantities.

8.11.9 Two simple examples of VA

Example of VA

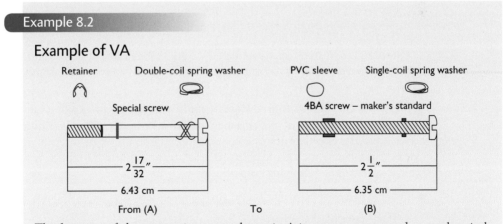

The function of the connecting screw shown in A is to secure parts and carry electrical current, the retainer holding the two items loosely together as a subassembly when the screw is released from a third point.

In B, a maker's standard screw is now in use, the retainer being replaced by a small PVC sleeve. A single-coil spring washer takes the place of the double-coil one. Total saving = 76 per cent.

Example 8.3

Another example of VA

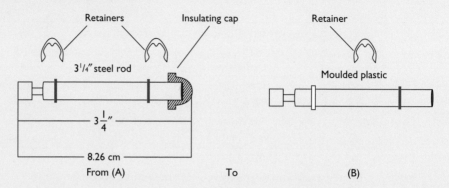

A push rod moving a contact operates against springs under digital pressure. It had been a machined steel rod with two retainers (for the springs) and an insulating cap because, on occasions, direct digital contact would be made (A).

It was decided to mould the rod in plastic, complete with a flange to replace one retainer. The insulating cap is no longer necessary because the rod itself is now an insulator. The cost of the new mould was recovered in less than four months and a total saving made of 60 per cent.

8.11.10 Value and procurement

Two quotations from Miles,[36] himself a procurement agent, indicate the close relationship between VE, VA, VM and procurement:

> Close and extensive relationships must exist between procurement and value analysis.

> Effective value analysis greatly improves the grade and degree of procurement work and efficient execution of certain procurement activities greatly improve the degree and amount of value analysis accomplishments.

VA and VE can enhance procurement performance by creating a value culture that permeates every aspect of procurement activity. Procurement, as a boundary-spanning activity, has the opportunity to increase value as a result of its internal interactions and external involvements. As members of a VA team, representatives of procurement can, inter alia, make the following contributions:

■ Provide essential information on such matters as:

  – the capabilities of existing or potential suppliers
  – availability of substitutes for existing outputs
  – quality issues
  – prices and costs of suggested alternatives

- delivery times
- legal, economic, ethical and environmental issues
- make-or-buy decisions.

■ Provide a procurement perspective to contrast with the perspectives of design and production representatives on the value project team.

■ Establish buyer–supplier relationships. Procurement can work closely with suppliers to reduce costs, improve quality and shorten lead times. It can also be a link between the value team and suppliers so that the latter can also be a source of innovation and creativity. Hartley[37] suggests that collaborative arrangements between purchasers and suppliers, such as partnerships, co-development, co-ownership and supplier associations can provide such benefits as:

- access to the supplier's knowledge
- greater understanding by the supplier of the customer's needs
- greater trust
- suppliers learning about VA
- increased supplier motivation.

By active and aggressive participation in VA, procurement professionals will not only enhance their individual reputations but also the status of procurement throughout their organisation and, often, with suppliers.

Discussion questions

8.1 Can you identify the role of procurement in managing quality throughout the complete cycle of events from specification through to end-of-life of a product?

8.2 What is the difference between an output specification and a prescriptive specification? Which one would you believe a supplier would prefer and why?

8.3 Take two similar products, such as two washing machines or two vacuum cleaners and compare them to Garvin's eight dimensions of quality. On the basis of your comparison, recommend which of the two you consider gives the best value for money.

8.4 An important aspect of *kaizen* is the creation of a quality culture. One definition of 'culture' is:

'The system of shared values, beliefs and habits within an organisation, that interacts with the formal structure to produce behavioural norms.'
(a) How would you go about creating a quality culture?
(b) How might a quality culture sometimes clash with marketing and production cultures?

8.5 With what 'quality guru' do you associate the following?
(a) quality loss function
(b) *poka-yoke*
(c) 'It is always cheaper to do the job right first time.'
(d) 'Quality is fitness for purpose.'
(e) robust design.

8.6 What are the different quality considerations when you purchase a service as opposed to a manufactured good?

8.7 What are Purdy's four principles that should be observed by all specification writers?

8.8 Standards include five areas of application. What are they?

8.9 If you are purchasing an off-the-shelf software product, how do you know what quality standard has been applied in its production?

8.10 When buyers negotiate a price the supplier is certain to reduce the quality! Do you agree?

8.11 An international airline may purchase meals from suppliers in many different countries. The suppliers will purchase the ingredients from many suppliers. How is it possible to manage quality in such a complex business situation?

8.12 A manufacturer of high-performance, high-quality automotives has recently had new vehicles catching fire when being driven. The manufacturer has decided to recall all 250 cars that have been sold. What are the implications if:
(a) the fault is due to a manufacturing problem in their own factory?
(b) the fault is due to a part supplied by a strategic supplier?

8.13 How would you define FMEA? What are the main objectives of FMEA?

8.14 What is a definition of value management? What contribution does procurement make to the overall performance of an organisation?

8.15 The US DoD has applied value engineering to a wide range of purchases. How would you approach applying value engineering to the following procurement categories:
(a) learning and development?
(b) construction work?
(c) facilities management?
(d) hire of vehicles?

8.16 If a company providing your organisation with a range of back-office services did not have ISO 9001:2015 accreditation, what arguments would you use to persuade them to obtain the accreditation?

8.17 Quality of services and products is an essential contractual requirement. What do your terms and conditions of contract say about quality?

8.18 If you were asked to lead a quality inspection of a strategic supplier how would you approach each of the following:
(a) those who should be part of the inspection team?
(b) the role of procurement?
(c) the evidence that you would require to prove compliance with all the specification requirements?
(d) the benefits of 'spot' inspections?

8.19 What exactly does the term 'cost of quality' mean? Can you give ten examples of the cost of quality?

References

[1] Crosby, P. B., *Quality is Free*, Mentor Books, Dublin, 1980, p. 15.

[2] Juran, J. M., *Quality Control Handbook*, 3rd edn, McGraw-Hill, New York, 1974, section 2, p. 27.

[3] Garvin, D. A., 'What does product quality really mean?', *Sloan Management Review*, Fall, 1984, pp. 25–38.

[4] Garvin, D. A., 'Competing in eight dimensions of quality', *Harvard Business Review*, November/December, No. 6, 1987, p. 101.

[5] Logothetis, N., *Managing Total Quality*, Prentice Hall, Upper Saddle River, New Jersey, USA, 1991, pp. 216–17.

[6] As 3 above.

[7] Farrington, B., *The Quality Loop Visualisation*, 2019.

[8] DTI, *Total Quality Management and Effective Leadership*, London, UK, 1991, p. 8.

[9] Evans, J. R., *Applied Production and Operations Management*, Southwestern Publishing, Tennessee, USA, 4th edn, 1993, p. 837.

[10] See Table 8.1.

[11] See Table 8.1.

[12] As 3 above, p. 10.

[13] Cannon, S., 'Supplying the service to the internal customer', *Purchasing and Supply Management*, April, 1995, pp. 32–5.

[14] Zaire, M., *Total Quality Management for Engineers*, Woodhead Publishing, Cambridge, UK, 1991, p. 193.

[15] As 14 above, p. 216.

[16] BSI, *British Standards Specification* (BS) 7373.

[17] Purdy, D. C., *A Guide to Writing Successful Engineering Specifications*, McGraw-Hill, New York, 1991.

[18] The Office of Government Commerce, 'Specification writing', *CUP Guidance Note 30*, CUP, Cambridge, 1991.

[19] British Standards Institute, 21 December, 2005, ISBN 0580474372.

[20] As 17 above.

[21] England, W. B., *Modern Procurement*, 5th edn, Irwin, Homewood, Illinois, 1970, p. 306.

[22] Haslam, J. M., 'Writing engineering specifications', E. and F. N. Spon, Andover, UK, 1988, p. 31.

[23] www.navair.navy.mil Performance Specification Guide SD – 15.

[24] Same as 23 above.

[25] Ashton, T. C., 'National and International Standards', in Lock, D. (ed.) *Gower Handbook of Quality Management*, Gower, Hants, UK, 2nd edn, 1994, pp. 144–5.

[26] BS EN ISO 8402 1995, section 3.5, pp. 25–6.

[27] BS EN ISO 8402 1995, section 3.4, p. 25.

[28] Schonberger, R. J., *Building a Chain of Customers*, Free Press, New York, USA, 1992.

[29] Taguchi, G., *Introduction to Quality Engineering*, Asian Productivity Organisation, 1986, p. 1.

30 Ford Motor Co. Ltd, *Failure Mode and Effects Analysis Handbook*, Ford Motor Co. Ltd Dearborn, MI, 1992, p. 22.

31 As 29 above, pp. 24–5.

32 www.dtic.mil.

33 See website www.Brian Farrington.com.

34 BSI 'PD6663:2000 Guidelines to BS EN 12973 Value Management', BSI, 2000, p. 26.

35 Miller, J., 'The evolution of value analysis', NAPM, *Insights*, 1 December, 1993, pp. 13–14. Original source of this checklist was George Fridholm Associates.

36 Miles, D., *Techniques of Value and Value Engineering*, 3rd edn, McGraw-Hill, New York, 1989, p. 243.

37 Hartley, J. L., 'Collaborative value analysis: experiences from the automotive industry', *Journal of Supply Management*, Fall, 2000, pp. 27–36.

Chapter 9

Matching supply with demand

Learning outcomes

With reference to procurement and supply management, this chapter aims to provide an understanding of:

- inventory, logistics and supply chain management
- reasons for keeping inventory
- inventory classifications
- scope and aims of inventory management
- some tools of inventory management
- the economics of inventory
- inventory performance measures
- safety stocks and service levels
- the right quantity
- the nature of demand
- forecasting demand
- 'push' and 'pull' inventories
- independent demand
- dependent demand
- just-in-time (JIT)
- materials and requirements planning (MRP)
- manufacturing resource planning (MRPII)
- enterprise resource planning (ERP)
- supply chain management systems
- distribution requirements planning (DRP)
- vendor-managed inventory (VMI)
- procurement and inventory.

Key ideas

- Inventory classifications.
- ABC analysis.
- Barcoding and radio frequency identification (RFID) technology.
- Acquisition, holding and stockout costs.
- Reordering of stock.
- Safety stocks.
- Approaches to forecasting.
- Economic order quantities (EOQs) and periodic systems.
- Just-in-time (JIT) systems and their objectives.
- JIT II.
- MRP, MRP II, ERP, DRP and VMI systems.

9.1 Inventory, logistics and supply chain management

The Institute of Logistics and Transport[1] defines inventory as:

A term used to describe:

- all the goods and materials held by an organisation for sale or use
- a list of items held in stock.

An alternative definition is:[2]

Materials in a supply chain or in a segment of a supply chain, expressed in quantities, locations and/or values (synonym stock).

As shown in Figure 3.2, inventory and its management are related both to materials management (MM) and physical distribution management (PDM). MM and PDM together constitute logistics management, or the process of managing both the movement and storage of goods and materials from their source to the point of ultimate consumption. As logistics is an aspect of the wider subject of supply chain management (SCM), it follows that inventory is a key business consideration in the attempt to achieve supply chain optimisation. As indicated in section 3.5, control of inventory is also an important element in demand management, which constitutes one of the eight supply chain processes identified by the International Centre for Competitive Excellence. In this chapter, inventory and demand management are considered primarily from the standpoints of materials management and production.

In an NAO Report HC 190 Session 2012–13 'Managing the defence inventory' it is stated that:

Inventory management is a recognised professional skill. The object of inventory management is to minimise the risk of having insufficient stock while also minimising the cost of holding stock, and reducing the amount of money tied up in stock holdings.

Figure 9.1 Pharmacy inventory management process within a hospital setting

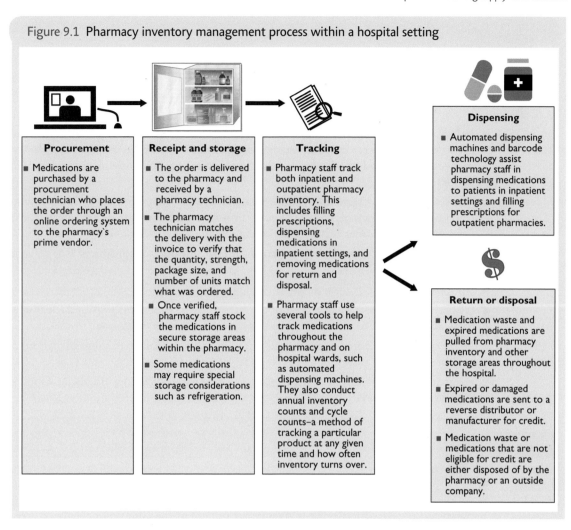

Procurement

■ Medications are purchased by a procurement technician who places the order through an online ordering system to the pharmacy's prime vendor.

Receipt and storage

■ The order is delivered to the pharmacy and received by a pharmacy technician.

■ The pharmacy technician matches the delivery with the invoice to verify that the quantity, strength, package size, and number of units match what was ordered.

■ Once verified, pharmacy staff stock the medications in secure storage areas within the pharmacy.

■ Some medications may require special storage considerations such as refrigeration.

Tracking

■ Pharmacy staff track both inpatient and outpatient pharmacy inventory. This includes filling prescriptions, dispensing medications in inpatient settings, and removing medications for return and disposal.

■ Pharmacy staff use several tools to help track medications throughout the pharmacy and on hospital wards, such as automated dispensing machines. They also conduct annual inventory counts and cycle counts–a method of tracking a particular product at any given time and how often inventory turns over.

Dispensing

■ Automated dispensing machines and barcode technology assist pharmacy staff in dispensing medications to patients in inpatient settings and filling prescriptions for outpatient pharmacies.

Return or disposal

■ Medication waste and expired medications are pulled from pharmacy inventory and other storage areas throughout the hospital.

■ Expired or damaged medications are sent to a reverse distributor or manufacturer for credit.

■ Medication waste or medications that are not eligible for credit are either disposed of by the pharmacy or an outside company.

It is unfortunate that many public and private sector organisations still fail to recognise the role, influence and impact of inventory management.

For large organisations inventory management is a complex matter. An excellent reference report can be found in the USA GAO September 2018 report.[3] Their figure (see Figure 9.1) outlines the pharmacy inventory management process. The report's findings included:

■ the Department of Veteran Affairs' (VA's) oversight of Department of Veterans Affairs Medical Centre's (VAMC's) pharmacy inventory management is limited as VA lacks a comprehensive inventory management system or a focal point for a system-wide oversight

■ in May 2018, VA signed a contract for a new electronic health records system. VA officials expect implementation of this system to take up to 10 years.

9.2 Reasons for keeping inventory

Notwithstanding such developments as just-in-time (JIT), discussed later in this chapter, computer-based production methods and the aims of lean production, there are a number of reasons why most organisations keep inventory. These include wanting to:

■ reduce the risk of supplier failure or uncertainty – safety and buffer stocks are held to provide some protection against such contingencies as strikes, transport breakdowns due to floods or other adverse weather conditions, crop failures, wars and similar factors

■ protect against lead time uncertainties, such as where supplier's replenishment and lead times are not known with certainty – in such cases an investment in safety stocks is necessary if customer service is to be maintained at acceptable levels

■ meet unexpected demands, or, demands for customisation of products as with agile production

■ smooth seasonal or cyclical demand

■ take advantage of lots or purchase quantities in excess of what is required for immediate consumption to take advantage of price and quantity discounts

■ hedge against anticipated shortage and price increases, especially in times of high inflation or as a deliberate policy of speculation

■ ensure rapid replenishment of items in constant demand, such as maintenance supplies and office stationery.

9.3 Inventory classifications

The term 'supplies' has been defined as:[4]

> All the materials, goods and services used in the enterprise regardless of whether they are purchased outside, transferred from another branch of the company or manufactured in-house.

The classification of supplies for inventory purposes will vary according to the particular organisation/business. In a manufacturing enterprise, for example, inventory might be classified as:

■ raw materials – steel, timber, chemicals and so on in an unprocessed state awaiting conversion into a product

■ components and sub-assemblies – ball bearings, gearboxes, and so on that are to be incorporated into an end product

■ consumables – all supplies in an undertaking classified as indirect and that do not form part of a saleable product and that may be sub classified into production (such as detergents), maintenance (such as lubricating oil), office (such as stationery), welfare (such as first-aid supplies) and so on – all of which are often referred to as maintenance, repair and operating (MRO) items

■ finished goods – products manufactured for resale that are ready for dispatch.

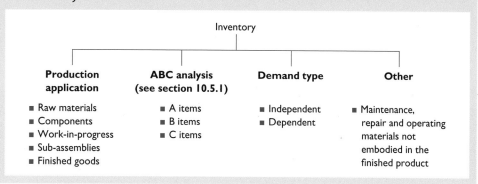

Figure 9.2 Inventory classifications

Following supply chain usage, inventory may also be classified into:

■ primary inventory – raw materials, components and sub-assemblies, work-in-progress (WIP) and finished goods

■ support inventories – MRO consumables of various categories.

A third classification is shown in Figure 9.2.

9.4 Scope and aims of inventory management

9.4.1 The scope of inventory management

Inventory management covers a wide variety of activities. These activities will vary from organisation to organisation. The scope of inventory management will also be influenced according to whether it is primarily concerned with MM or PDM or centralised or decentralised. There is clearly a significant difference in the complexity of managing inventory based at a single location and that where inventory is located at possibly hundreds of distribution centres. Globalisation is another factor that increases the complexity of inventory management. Irrespective of such considerations, however, inventory management is likely to comprise such activities as:

■ demand management – ensuring that required operational and maintenance supplies are available in the right quantities and at the right time

■ forecasting future demand requirements

■ managing items with difficult supply and demand patterns related to seasonal demand, changes in end use applications or meeting demands for the customisation of products

■ reviewing safety stock levels and controlling minimum and maximum amounts of inventory in terms of both quantity and value

■ implementing lean inventory policies, such as JIT contracts to minimise investment in inventory

■ liaising with procurement to ensure that supplies are replenished in accordance with corporate and procurement policies

- developing cost-effective systems and procedures relating to the ordering, procurement and budgeting of supplies
- controlling the receipt, inspection (where necessary), recording, location and issue of supplies to users
- ensuring the safety and security of supplies and the avoidance of loss as a result of deterioration, theft, waste and obsolescence
- coordination of inventory to ensure that supplies can be rapidly located
- variety reduction and standardisation of inventory
- preparation and interpretation of reports on stock levels, stock usage and surplus stock
- liaison with auditors regarding all aspects of inventory
- appropriate disposal of scrap, surplus and obsolete items.

9.4.2 The aims of inventory management

The four main aims of inventory management are to:

- provide both internal and external customers with the required service levels in terms of quantity and order rate fill
- ascertain present and future requirements for all types of inventory to avoid overstocking while avoiding 'bottlenecks' in production
- keep costs to a minimum by variety reduction, economical lot sizes and analysis of costs incurred in obtaining and carrying inventories
- provide upstream and downstream inventory visibility in the supply chain.

9.5 Some tools of inventory management

ABC analysis, barcoding, radio frequency identification (RFID) and inventory software are four important tools of inventory management.

9.5.1 ABC analysis

A household will buy many different items in the course of a year. The weekly shopping will include a number of basic food items, such as bread, milk, vegetables and so on. These basic food items may account for the bulk of the annual expenditure in shops. Because these items are so important in the household budget, it is worth taking care to choose a shop that gives good value. Information about the prices charged elsewhere can be obtained from advertisements and visits to other retail outlets. In ABC analysis these items are known as Class A items. They merit close day-to-day control because of their budgetary importance.

Other items, such as replacement rubber washers for water taps, may be needed occasionally. A packet of washers costs between 30 and 50 pence. Spending hours comparing the prices of these at different suppliers does not make economic sense. The possible saving is, at most, a few pence and a year or more may elapse before another packet is needed. Items like these that account for only a small proportion of spending, are known as Class C items.

Class B is the set of items that is intermediate between Class A and Class C. They should be regularly reviewed but are not as closely controlled as Class A items.

The Italian statistician Vilfredo Pareto (1848–1923) discovered a common statistical effect. About 20 per cent of the population own 80 per cent of the nation's wealth. About 20 per cent of employees cause 80 per cent of problems. About 20 per cent of items account for 80 per cent of a firm's expenditure. The two terms 'Pareto analysis' and 'ABC analysis' are used interchangeably.

Table 9.1 summarises the main points of ABC analysis. In the table, the term 'usage' means the value in money terms of the stock items consumed.

The following example illustrates how items may be divided into classes A, B or C.

Table 9.1 ABC analysis

	Percentage of items	Percentage value of annual usage	
Class A items	About 20%	About 80%	Close day-to-day control
Class B items	About 30%	About 15%	Regular review
Class C items	About 50%	About 5%	Infrequent review

Example 9.1

ABC analysis

A procurement department surveyed the ten most commonly used components last year.

Item number	101	102	103	104	105	106	107	108	109	110
Unit cost (pence)	5	11	15	8	7	16	20	4	9	12
Annual demand	48,000	2000	300	800	4800	1200	18,000	300	5000	500

Step 1

Calculate the annual usage in £s and the usage of each item as a percentage of the total cost.

Item number	Unit cost (pence)	Annual demand	Usage (£) $\frac{\text{Demand} \times \text{Cost}}{100}$	Usage as % of total $\frac{\text{Usage} \times 100}{\text{Total}}$
101	5	48,000	2400	32.5%
102	11	2000	220	3.0%
103	15	300	45	0.6%
104	8	800	64	0.9%
105	7	4800	336	4.5%
106	16	1200	192	2.6%
107	20	18,000	3600	48.8%
108	4	300	12	0.2%
109	9	5000	450	6.1%
110	12	500	60	0.8%
Total usage			7379	

Step 2

Sort the items by usage as a percentage of the total. Calculate the cumulative percentage and classify the items (see Table 9.2).

Table 9.2 **Calculations for step 2**

Item number	Cumulative % of items (*)	Unit cost (pence)	Annual demand	Usage (£)	% of total	Cumulative % of total	Classification
107	10	20	18,000	3600	48.8	48.8	A
101	20	5	48,000	2400	32.5	81.3	A
109	30	9	5000	450	6.1	87.4	B
105	40	7	4800	336	4.5	91.9	B
102	50	11	2000	220	3.0	94.9	B
106	60	16	1200	192	2.6	97.5	B
104	70	8	800	64	0.9	98.4	C
110	80	12	500	60	0.8	99.2	C
103	90	15	300	45	0.6	99.8	C
108	100	4	300	12	0.2	100.0	C

*Column 2 – There are 10 items, so each item accounts for 10/100 = 10% of usage

Step 3

Report your findings (see Table 9.3).

Table 9.3 **Results of calculations for step 3**

Items	Item number	Percentage of items	Percentage usage	Action
A	107, 101	20	81.3	Close control
B	109, 105, 102, 106	40	16.2	Regular review
C	104, 110, 103, 108	40	2.5	Infrequent review

Step 4

Illustrate your report with a diagram if required. The diagram is a percentage ogive and is called a Pareto diagram. This is done by plotting the cumulative percentage usage against the cumulative percentage of items. The data needed have been extracted to create Table 9.4.

Table 9.4 **Data for Pareto diagram for step 4**

Item number	107	101	109	105	102	106	104	110	103	108
Cumulative % items	10	20	30	40	50	60	70	80	90	100
Cumulative % usage	48.8	81.3	87.4	91.9	94.9	97.5	98.4	99.2	99.8	100
Classification	A	A	B	B	B	B	C	C	C	C

In practice, there may be hundreds of items in inventory and use. Computer software can easily determine the percentage of annual usage for each item and sort the items into A, B or C categories.

9.5.2 Barcoding

Invented in the 1950s, barcodes accelerate the flow of products and information throughout business. The most familiar example of the use of barcodes is electronic point of sale (EPOS), which is when retail sales are recorded by scanning product barcodes at checkout tills. An EPOS system verifies, checks and charges transactions, provides instant sales reports, monitors and changes prices and sends intra-store and inter-store messages and data.

Some production applications for barcoding include:

- counting raw materials and finished goods inventories
- automatic sorting of cartons and bins on conveyor belts and palletisers
- lot tracking
- production reporting
- automatic warehouse applications, including receiving, put away, picking and shipping
- identification of production bottlenecks
- package tracking
- access control
- tool cribs and spare parts issue.

Barcoding provides the following benefits:

- *Faster data entry* – barcode scanners can record data five to seven times as fast as a skilled typist.
- *Greater accuracy* – keyboard data entry creates an average of one error in 300 keystrokes, but barcode entry has an error rate of about 1 in 3 million.
- *Reduced labour costs* – as a result of time saved and increased productivity.
- *Elimination of costly overstocking or understocking* and the increased efficiency of JIT inventory systems.
- *Better decision making* – barcode systems can easily capture information that would be difficult to collect in other ways, which helps managers to make fully informed decisions.
- *Faster access to information.*
- *The ability to automate warehousing.*
- *Greater responsiveness to customers and suppliers.*

9.5.3 Radio frequency identification (RFID)

An RFID tag contains a silicon chip that carries an identification number and an antenna able to transmit the number to a reading device. This means improved inventory management and replenishment practices, which, in turn, results in a reduction of interrupted production or lost sales due to items being out of stock.

The reduction in the cost of silicon chips to a point where they can be used to track high-volume, low-cost stores and individual items rather than an aggregate SKU (stock keeping unit) is revolutionary in its implications for inventory control and intelligence.

The following advantages and limitations of RFID technology are listed by GS1 UK.[5]

Advantages

- *Line of sight* – tags can be read without being visible to the scanner. They can be read as long as they pass through the field emitted by the reader. This reduces manual handling and, therefore, cost.

- *Range* – tags can be read over a very long range – many hundreds of metres in the case of specialised tags. RFID devices used in mass logistics applications need a range of at least 1 metre and up to 4 or 5 metres.

- *Bulk read* – many tags can be read in a short space of time – a typical read rate is hundreds of tags per second.

- *Selectivity* – data can be inserted into the tags so that they are only read if the value requested from the reader is the same as the value embedded within the tag. This allows the reader to read only pallets or only outer cases.

- *Durability* – barcodes can be ripped, soiled and performance is impaired if they become wet. These are not issues that affect RFID tags.

- *Read/write* – data incorporated within the tags can be updated to accommodate simple changes in status – such as 'paid for' or 'not paid for' retail electronic article surveillance tags – or more complicated information, such as a car's warranty and service history.

Limitations

- *Cost* – RFID tags will always be more expensive than barcodes. The cost is offset by the extra business benefits that RFID technology can provide. It is envisaged that the cost of tags will drop dramatically as production volumes are increased.

- *Moisture* – depending on the frequency used, radio waves may be absorbed by moisture in the product or the environment.

- *Metal* – radio waves are distorted by metal. This means that tags might be unable to be read if there is metal within packaging or the environment (warehouse automation).

- *Electrical interference* – electronic noise, such as fluorescent lights or electric motors, may produce interference with radio frequency communications.

- *Accuracy* – it can be difficult to identify and read specific tags separately from all the others that are within the range of the reader. For example, when attempting to read a tag identifying a pallet, the reader may also read the tags on all the cases on the pallet as well.

- *Overcompensation* – additional data stored within the tag will provide functionality. However, this will increase both the cost of the tag and the time required to read it.

- *Security* – the ability to write information into tags is one of the main benefits of RFID technology. The mechanism required, however, needs to be secure to ensure that rogue parties are unable to write false information into the tag.

9.5.4 Software

Numerous software programs are available, providing complete inventory and stock management systems. Such software can provide such facilities as maintaining supplier and customer databases, create picking lists and receipts, provide instantaneous stock balances and automatic reordering, barcode reading, support grouping of inventory items, remove barriers between suppliers and customers, enhance profitability and implement such approaches as JIT, MRO, ERP, DRP and VMI, described later in this chapter.

9.6 The economics of inventory

The economics of inventory management and stock control are determined by an analysis of the costs incurred in obtaining and carrying inventories under the following headings.

9.6.1 Acquisition costs

Many of the costs incurred in placing an order are incurred irrespective of the order size, so, for example, the cost of an order will be the same irrespective of whether 1 or 1000 tonnes are ordered. Ordering costs include:

■ preliminary costs – preparing the requisition, vendor selection, administering the procurement process
■ placement costs – order preparation, stationery, postage
■ post-placement costs – progressing, receipt of goods, materials, handling, inspection, certification and payment of invoices.

In practice, it is difficult to obtain more than an approximate idea of ordering costs as these vary according to:

■ the complexity of the order and the seniority of staff involved
■ whether order preparation is manual or computerised
■ whether or not repeat orders cost less than initial orders.

Sometimes the total cost of a procurement department or function over a given period is divided by the number of purchase orders placed in that time. This gives a completely false figure as the average cost per order reduces as the number of orders placed increases, which may be indicative of inefficiency rather than the converse.

9.6.2 Holding costs

There are two types of holding costs:

■ *cost proportional to the value of the inventory* such as:
  – financial costs, such as interest on capital tied up in inventory, which may be bank rate or, more realistically, the target return on capital required by the enterprise
  – cost of insurance
  – losses in value due to deterioration, obsolescence and pilfering.
■ *cost proportional to the physical characteristics of inventory* such as:
  – storage costs – storage space, stores' space charges, light, heat and power
  – labour costs, relating to handling and inspection
  – clerical costs, relating to stores' records and documentation.

9.6.3 Cost of stockouts

The costs of stockouts – the costs of being out of inventory – include:

- loss of production output
- costs of idle time and of fixed overheads spread over a reduced level of output
- costs of any action taken to deal with the stockout, such as buying from another stockist at an enhanced price, switching production, obtaining substitute materials
- loss of customer goodwill due to the inability to supply or late delivery.

Often the costs of stockouts are hidden in overhead costs. Where the costs of individual stockouts are computed, these should be expressed in annual figures to ensure compatibility with acquisition and holding costs. Costs of stockouts are difficult to estimate or incorporate into inventory models.

9.7 Inventory performance measures

A number of key performance indicators (KPIs) have been devised to measure the extent to which an undertaking has the right quantity of inventory in the right place at the right time. Some of the most useful performance indicators are the following.

- *Lead times* – the length of time taken to obtain or supply a requirement from the time a need is ascertained to the time the need is satisfied.
- *Service levels* – the actual service level attained in a given period, which can be ascertained from the formula:

$$\frac{\text{Number of times the item is provided on demand}}{\text{Number of times the item has been demanded}}$$

Service levels are closely related to safety stocks, as shown later.

- *Rate of stock turn* – this indicates the number of times that a stock item has been sold and replaced in a given period and is calculated by the formula:

$$\frac{\text{Sales or issues}}{\text{Average inventory (at selling price)}}$$

What is considered a good stock turn varies by product and industry. Turnover of supermarket breakfast foods is 20–25 times that of pet foods. For car showrooms, a stock turn of six means that, on average, the stock of a particular car changes every two months.

- *Stockouts in a given period* – this can be expressed as a percentage of the total stock population during a given period.
- *Stock cover* – this is the opposite of stock turn and indicates the number of days the current stock of a stock keeping unit (SKU) will last if sales or usage continues at the anticipated rate. As an historic figure, it can be calculated by dividing the rate of stock turn into the yearly number of working days or 365 to give the average days' cover. For a simple SKU it can be calculated as:

$$\text{Days' stock coverage} = \frac{\text{Current quantity in stock}}{\text{Anticipated future daily rate of usage or sales}}$$

The ratio can be used to evaluate the effect of longer lead times or the danger of imminent stockouts.

9.8 Safety stocks and service levels

Safety stock is needed to cover shortages due to the agreed lead time being exceeded or the actual demand being greater than that anticipated.

Figure 9.3 shows that the service levels and safety stock are related. Thus, by increasing the investment on inventory, service levels can be increased.

For single items, an extra investment in inventory (higher levels of safety stock) will always increase customer service levels. Conversely, higher service levels imply larger quantities of safety stocks and an increased investment in inventory.

It is not possible to achieve 100 per cent service levels for the total inventory. High levels of safety stocks for all items would be uneconomical and the costs would be prohibitive.

JIT implies a low level of or zero inventory. This is achieved by removing uncertainty regarding supply. Safety stock is a cost-adding factor and so should, as far as possible, be eliminated.

If the uncertainty regarding supply cannot be eliminated, safety stocks are required.

In practice, the items that have high stockout costs can be identified by ABC analysis and, for such items, an acceptable risk of stockout should be determined.

Statistical theory provides methods for ensuring that the chances of a stockout do not exceed an acceptable risk level.

The probability that demand exceeds a particular distribution during a given lead time can be found from the normal distribution (see Figure 9.4).

Tables of this distribution, such as Table 9.5, are found in statistics textbooks.

■ For each SKU, find the data on which the order was placed and the date of delivery. From stores' records, calculate the demand between these dates.

Figure 9.3 Service level to inventory trade-off curve

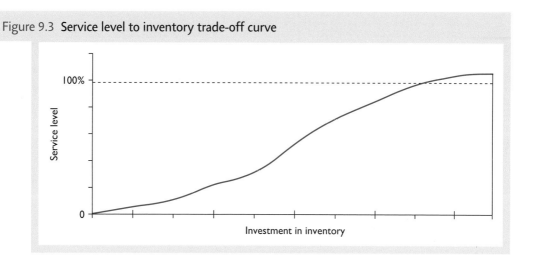

Figure 9.4 **The normal distribution curve**

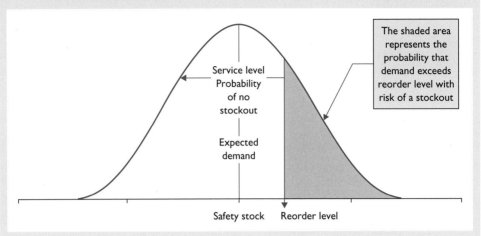

- Find the mean or arithmetic average demand during the lead time:

$$\text{Mean(x)} = \frac{\text{Sum of the demands}}{\text{Number of lead times}} = \frac{\sum x}{n}$$

- Calculate the standard deviation (s or σ) of demand from the formulae:

$$\sigma = \sqrt{\frac{\sum (x - \bar{x})^2}{n - 1}} \quad \text{or} \quad \sigma \sqrt{\frac{\sum x^2 - \frac{(\sum x)^2}{n}}{n - 1}}$$

or by using the statistical functions on your calculator or spreadsheet. In simple terms, calculating the standard deviation involves the following steps:

1 Determine the mean (average (x)) of the set of numbers:

$$1,2,3,4,5 = \frac{15}{5} = x = 3$$

2 Determine the difference between each number and the mean:

$$(1) = -2, (2) = -1, (3) = 0, (4) = +1, (5) = +2$$

3 Square each difference:

$$+4 \quad +1 \quad 0 \quad +1 \quad +4 \quad = \quad 10$$

4 Calculate the square root of $10/(n-1) = \sqrt{(10/4)} = \sqrt{2.5}$

$$\text{Standard deviation } (\sigma) = 1.58$$

The reorder level required and stockout probability can then be found from Table 9.5.

Table 9.5 Probabilities table

Reorder levels in standard deviations above the mean	Service level %	Probability of a stockout %
1.00	84.13	15.87
1.05	85.31	14.69
1.10	86.43	13.57
1.15	87.49	12.51
1.20	88.49	11.51
1.25	89.44	10.56
1.30	90.32	9.68
1.35	91.15	8.85
1.40	91.92	8.08
1.45	92.65	7.35
1.50	93.32	6.68
1.55	93.94	6.06
1.60	94.52	5.48
1.65	95.05	4.95
1.70	95.54	4.46
1.75	95.99	4.01
1.80	96.41	3.59
1.85	96.78	3.22
1.90	97.13	2.87
1.95	97.44	2.56
2.00	97.72	2.28
2.05	97.98	2.02
2.10	98.21	1.79
2.15	98.42	1.58
2.20	98.61	1.39
2.25	98.78	1.22
2.30	98.93	1.07
2.35	99.06	0.94
2.40	99.18	0.82
2.45	99.29	0.71
2.50	99.38	0.62
2.55	99.46	0.54
2.60	99.53	0.47
2.65	99.60	0.40
2.70	99.65	0.35
2.75	99.70	0.30
2.80	99.74	0.26
2.85	99.78	0.22
2.90	99.81	0.19
2.95	99.84	0.16
3.00	99.87	0.13

Example 9.2

Calculating the required reorder level

The average (mean) demand is 10. A 99 per cent service level is required – that is, the probability of stockout is 1 per cent or less. Assume an average reorder level of 140.

Table 9.5 shows that, for a service level of 99.1 per cent, the reorder level should be 2.35 standard deviations above the mean.

Thus, the reorder level is $140 + (2.35 \times 10) = 163.5$ or 164.

9.9 The right quantity

In manufacturing or assembly-type organisations, the most important factors that determine the right quantity are as follows:

- The demand for the final product into which the bought-out materials and components are incorporated.
- The inventory policy of the undertaking.
- Whether job, batch, assembly or process production methods are applicable.
- Whether demand for the item is independent or dependent (see section 9.10 below).
- The service level – that is, the incidence of availability required. The service level required for an item may be set at 100 per cent for items where a stockout would result in great expense due to production delays or, as with some hospital supplies, where lack of supplies may endanger life. For less crucial supplies, the service level might be fixed at a lower level, such as 95 per cent. The actual service level attained in a given period can be computed by the formula:

$$\frac{\text{Number of times the item is provided on demand in period}}{\text{Number of times an item has been demanded in period}}$$

- Market conditions, such as financial, political and other considerations that determine whether or not requirements shall be purchased on a 'hand-to-mouth' or 'forward' basis.
- Factors determining economic order quantities (see section 9.13.2 below). In individual undertakings, the quantity of an item to be purchased over a period may be ordered or notified to purchasing in several ways, as shown in Table 9.6.

9.10 The nature of demand

When forecasting the future requirements for supplies, we have to distinguish between independent demand and dependent demand.

The main points of difference are set out in Table 9.7.

As shown in Figure 9.5, the distinction between dependent and independent demand is fundamental to inventory management.

Table 9.6 Procurement and quantities

Type of purchase	Indicators of quantities
Materials or components required for a specific order or application, such as steel sections not normally stocked	■ Material specifications or bill of material for the job or contract
Standard items kept in stock for regular production, whether job, batch or continuous flow	■ Materials budgets derived from production budgets based on sales/ output target for a specified period ■ One-off material specifications or bills of materials showing quantities of each item needed to make one unit of finished product. These are then multiplied by the number of products to be manufactured ■ Material requisitions raised by storekeeping or stock control ■ Computerised reports provided at specified intervals – daily, weekly – relating to part usage, stocks on hand, on order and committed. With some programs, reordering can be carried out automatically
Consumable materials used in production, plant, maintenance or office administration, such as oil, paint, stationery and packing materials	■ Requisitions from stores or stock control or computerised inventory reports as above. These may be ordered directly by users against previously negotiated contracts or procurement consortia arrangements
Spares – these may be kept to maintain production machinery or bought-out components for resale to customers who have bought the product in which the component is incorporated	■ Requisitions from sales department ■ Computerised inventory reports as above

Table 9.7 The main differences between independent and dependent demand

Independent demand	Dependent demand
Independent demand items are finished goods or other end items	Dependent demand items are typically sub-assemblies or components used during the production of a finished or end product
Demand for independent items cannot be precisely forecast	Demand is derived from the number of units to be produced – for example, demand for 1000 cars will give rise to a derived demand for 5000 car wheels

Figure 9.5 Demand situation

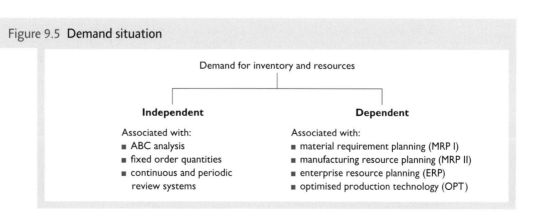

9.11 Forecasting demand

9.11.1 What is forecasting?

Forecasting, which may be defined as the prediction of future outcomes, is the basis of all planning and decision making. We listen to the weather forecasts, for example, before planning a picnic. Similarly, the decision to enlarge a factory will be based on a forecast of increased demand for the product manufactured.

Forecasts, however, are rarely spot on, simply because they are always based on assumptions that may be wrong or affected by unforeseen events, such as war, economic and social factors and even the weather. All forecasts, therefore, are subject to uncertainty. This uncertainty will be enhanced as the time horizon of the forecast increases.

9.11.2 Forecasting issues

Forecasting involves asking six basic questions.

1 *What is the purpose of the forecast?* The answer to this question determines the accuracy required and expenditure on the resources necessary to obtain the required information.
2 *What is the time horizon?* All forecasts must have a time limit. Forecasts may be classified as being for the long, medium or short term.
   – Long-term forecasts – with time horizons exceeding two years – usually apply to strategic planning and carry the greatest uncertainty.
   – Medium-term forecasts – with time horizons of between three months and two years – apply to both strategic and tactical planning and carry less uncertainty than long-term forecasts.
   – Short-term forecasts – with time horizons of less than three months – apply to tactical planning and are likely to achieve a high level of accuracy.

   The above times are, however, arbitrary and depend on circumstances. Thus, long, medium and short term may equally be one year, between three months and one year and three months respectively.
3 *What forecasting technique(s) is/are most appropriate?* See Figure 9.6.
4 *On what data must the forecast be based and how shall it be analysed?* This depends on the purpose of the forecast, the accuracy required and the resources available for forecasting.
5 *In what form shall the completed forecast be presented?* This will normally be in some form of report stating the purpose of the forecast, what assumptions have been made, the forecasting techniques used and the forecasts or conclusions reached.
6 *How accurate is the forecast?* All forecasts should be monitored to ascertain the degree of accuracy achieved. Where actual events are substantially different from those predicted, the forecast, assumptions, techniques and validity of the data must be examined and, where necessary, the original forecast revised.

9.11.3 Forecasting techniques

As shown in Figure 9.6, forecasting techniques or approaches fall into two broad categories.

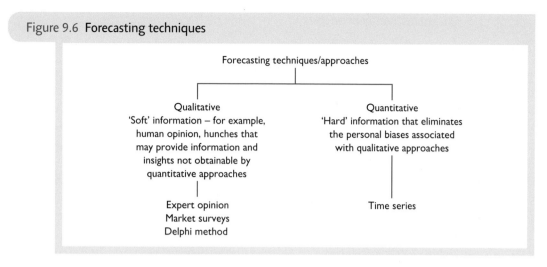

Figure 9.6 **Forecasting techniques**

9.11.4 Qualitative approaches

- *Expert systems* – gathering judgments or opinions from people with special knowledge or experience. Such people may be executives, external consultants or sales or production personnel who have first-hand experience of what customers require or operating problems encountered. The value of their opinions, however, depends on the knowledge and experience of those giving them. Experts are sometimes wrong.

- *Test marketing* – this is frequently used as a forecasting technique in connection with new products to ascertain the percentage of customers likely to adopt the product. It may also be used to work out why sales are declining or what aspects of competing products appeal to buyers. It can also be used to see how a product will sell under actual conditions and the success of advertising and sales promotion campaigns. It has been estimated that only about a third of products tested in this way are finally put into production. An extension of test marketing is the market survey, which uses published data and survey techniques to find out what the total market is for all products serving a similar purpose, such as family cars, and the percentage of the market likely to be achieved by an individual manufacturer.

- *Delphi method* – named after the ancient Greek religious site where the gods were believed to communicate answers to humans' questions about the future, this technique involves the following four steps.

  1 Estimates or forecasts are solicited from knowledgeable people within a company or industry about the matter under consideration. The names of the people approached are not known to each other.

  2 Statistical averages of the forecasts are computed. If there is a high level of agreement about the forecasts, the procedure ends there.

  3 If, as often happens, there is considerable divergence between the forecasts, the group averages are presented to the individuals who made the original forecasts, asking them why their forecasts differ from the average or group consensus and asking for new estimates.

  4 Steps 2 and 3 are repeated until agreement is reached.

The Delphi method is particularly useful where there is a lack of historical information on which to base a more objective forecast and predict changes in technology.

9.11.5 Quantitative approaches

A *time series* is a set of observations measured at successive times over successive periods. Time series forecasting methods make the assumption that past patterns in data can be used to forecast future data points. Time series demand consists of the following five components:

1 *average* – the mean of the observations over time
2 *trend* – a gradual increase or decrease in the average over time – a trend pattern exists when there is a long-term pattern of growth (upwards trend) or decline (downwards trend) in sales
3 *seasonal influence* – a predictable short-term cycling behaviour due to the time of day, week, month or season, so, for example, sales of swimming costumes are greater in the summer than the winter
4 *cyclical movement* – unpredictable long-term cyclical behaviour due to business or product/service lifecycles. Sales of dishwashers, refrigerators and similar household appliances reflect a fairly constant cyclical pattern
5 *random error* – the remaining variation that cannot be explained by the other four components, such as when sales fluctuate in an erratic manner and reflect inconsistency.

The most frequently used methods of calculating time series are moving averages and exponentially weighted averages.

9.11.6 Moving averages

A *moving average* is an artificially constructed time series in which each annual (or monthly, daily and so on) figure is replaced by the average or mean of itself and values corresponding to a number of preceding and succeeding periods.

At each step, one term of the original series is dropped and another introduced. The averages, as calculated for each period, will then be plotted on a graph. There is no precise rule about the number of periods to use when calculating a moving average. The most suitable, obtained by trial and error, is that which best smooths out fluctuations. A useful guide is to assess the number of periods between consecutive peaks and troughs and use this.

Example 9.3

Moving averages

The usage of a stock item for six successive periods was 90, 84, 100, 108, 116 and 127. If a five-period moving average is required, the first term will be:

$$\frac{90 + 84 + 100 + 108 + 116}{5} = 99.6$$

The average for the second term is:

$$\frac{84 + 100 + 108 + 116 + 127}{5} = 107$$

9.11.7 Exponentially weighted average method (EWAM)

The moving average method has been largely discarded for inventory applications as it has a number of disadvantages:

- it requires a large number of separate calculations
- a true forecast cannot be made until the required number of time periods have elapsed
- all data are equally weighted, but, in practice, the older the demand data, the less relevant it becomes in forecasting future requirements
- the sensitivity of a moving average is inversely proportional to the number of data values included in the average.

These difficulties are overcome by using a series of weights with decreasing values that converge at infinity to produce a total sum of one. Such a series, known as an *exponential series*, takes the form:

$$a + a(1 - a) + a(1 - a)2 + a(1 - a)3 \ldots = 1$$

where a is a constant between 0 and 1.

In practice, the values of 0.1 and 0.2 are most frequently used. Where a small value such as 0.1 is chosen as the constant, the response, based on the average of a considerable number of past periods, will be slow and gradual. A high value – $a = 0.5$ – will result in 'nervous' estimates responding quickly to actual changes. With exponential smoothing, all that is necessary is to adjust the previous forecast by a fraction of the difference between the old forecast and the actual demand for the previous period, that is, the new average forecast is:

$$a(\text{actual demand}) + (1 - a) \quad (\text{previous average forcecast})$$

Example 9.4

Exponentially weighted average

The actual demand for a stock item during the month of January was 300 against a forecast of 280. Assuming a weighting of 0.2, what will be the average demand forecast for February?

Solution

$$0.2(300) + (1 - 0.2)(280) = 60 + 224$$

Forecast for February = 284. By subtracting the average computed for the previous month from that calculated for the current month, we obtain the trend of demand.

9.11.8 The bullwhip effect

All forecasting depends on the reliability of the information on which the forecast is based. The so-called 'bullwhip effect' is the uncertainty caused by information flowing upstream and downstream in the supply chain. In particular, forecasts of demand become less reliable as they move up the supply chain from users or retailers to wholesalers, to manufacturers, to suppliers. Conversely, the forecast demand variability, though present, lessens as the point of forecast moves downstream.

The most common drivers of demand distortion are:

- unforecasted sales promotions, which have a ripple effect throughout the supply chain
- sales incentive plans when extended to, say, three months often result in sales distortion
- lack of customer confidence in the ability of suppliers to deliver orders on time, leading to over ordering
- cancellation of orders, often resulting from previous over ordering
- freight incentives, such as transportation discounts for volume orders, that may cause customers to accumulate orders and then order in bulk.

The results of the bullwhip effect are:

- excessive inventory quantities
- poor customer service
- cash flow problems
- stockouts
- high material costs, overtime expenses and transport costs.

Example 9.5

Impact of supply disruption due to the bullwhip effect

Customer demand forecast is 40 units.

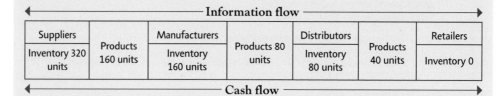

	Information flow						
Suppliers	Products 160 units	Manufacturers	Products 80 units	Distributors	Products 40 units	Retailers	
Inventory 320 units		Inventory 160 units		Inventory 80 units		Inventory 0	
	Cash flow						

The distributor anticipates a shortage and decides to keep a buffer stock of twice the demand forecast.

To accommodate anticipated demand fluctuations, manufacturers also increase their inventories by twice that required.

The suppliers, at the head of the supply chain, receive the harshest impact of the bullwhip effect. The result is a general lack of coordination throughout the supply chain.

In a worst-case scenario, working capital reduces, costs increase, customer service is unsatisfactory, lead times lengthen, production needs to be rescheduled and sales are lost.

The fundamental approach to resolving the bullwhip problem is to ensure transparency and information sharing throughout the supply chain. Many of the problems can be avoided by relying less on forecasting and more on direct demand data. Supply chain systems that provide open communication and reliable demand data avoid situations in which small demand fluctuations become high variability swings at the production stage.

9.12 'Push' and 'pull' inventories

'Push' and 'pull' inventories derive from push and pull strategies.

A *push strategy* is when products are manufactured in anticipation of demand and production is based on long-term forecasts and, therefore, uncertain. Push-based supply chains are associated with high inventory levels and high manufacturing and transportation costs, due to the need to respond quickly to demand changes.

A *pull strategy* is when products are manufactured to specific orders rather than forecasts. Thus, demand is certain and inventory is low or non-existent. Because information about customer demand is quickly transmitted to the various supply chain participants, the bullwhip effect is avoided.

Push–pull strategies are those in which some (usually the first stages) of the supply chain are operated on a push basis and the remaining stages on a pull basis. The interface between the push-based and pull-based stages is known as the push–pull boundary and occurs at a place somewhere along the supply chain timeline. Postponement, which was mentioned earlier in section 4.6.3, aims to cater for customisation requirements by keeping products in a neutral or uncommitted state for as long as possible and this is a good example of a push–pull strategy. The concept of push–pull is shown in Figure 9.7.

The inventory control systems associated with each of the three above strategies are shown in Figure 9.8.

Figure 9.7 The push–pull concept

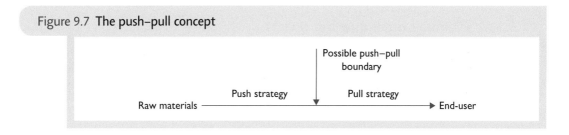

Figure 9.8 Inventory control system associated with different push and pull strategies

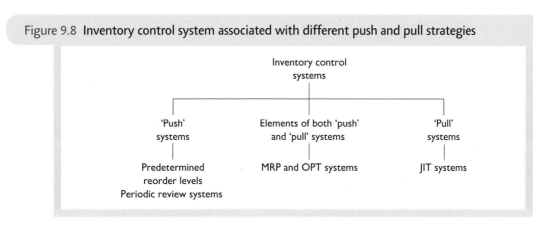

9.13 Independent demand

The nature of independent demand was discussed in section 9.10 above. Independent demand is related to 'push' systems as (see Figures 9.5 and 9.8) both are concerned with fixed order quantities and periodic review systems.

9.13.1 Fixed order quantities

With fixed order quantities, inventory is replenished with a predetermined quantity of stock every time the inventory falls to a specific order level. The reorder level is the quantity to be used during the lead replenishment time plus a reserve. This level can be calculated by using the formula:

$$\text{Maximum usage} \times \text{Maximum lead time}$$

Thus, if the lead time is 25 to 30 days and the maximum usage in the lead time is 200 units, then the reorder level will be:

$$200 \times 30 = 6000 \text{ units}$$

Reorder levels may be indicated by:

- simple manual methods, such as the two-bin system, which is that the stock of a particular item is kept in two bins and when the first bin is empty, a supply is reordered
- computerised systems, which trigger replacements when inventory has fallen to the specified reorder point – such systems usually use barcoding to record withdrawals from stock.

The fixed quantity is, however, usually based on an economic order quantity (EOQ).

9.13.2 Economic order quantity (EOQ)

The EOQ is the optimal ordering quantity for an item of stock that minimises cost.

To calculate the EOQ, a mathematical model of reality must be constructed. All mathematical models make assumptions that simplify reality. The model is only valid when the assumptions are true or nearly true, so, when an assumption is modified or deleted, a new model must be constructed.

The basic (or simple) EOQ model makes the following assumptions:

- demand is uniform – that is, certain, constant and continuous over time
- the lead time is constant and certain
- there is no limit on order size, due either to stores capacity or other constraints
- the cost of placing an order is independent of the size of the order – the delivery charge is also independent of the quantity ordered
- the cost of holding a unit of stock does not depend on the quantity in stock
- all prices are constant and certain – there are no bulk purchase discounts
- exactly the same quantity is ordered each time that a purchase is made.

The two basic types of inventory costs are:

1 acquisition (see section 9.6.1)
2 holding (see section 9.6.2).

There are several ways in which to calculate EOQs, but the basic formula is:

$$EOQ = \sqrt{\frac{2DS}{CI}}$$

where:

EOQ = economic order quantity
C = cost of the item
I = annual carrying cost interest rate
D = annual anticipated demand
S = order cost per order

Example 9.6

Worked example of the basic EOQ formula

Assume the following figures:

- annual demand = 1500 units
- unit cost per item = £10
- cost per order = £50
- carrying cost interest rate = 20 per cent.

Then:

$$EOQ = \sqrt{\frac{2 \times 1500 \times £50}{10 \times 0.20}} = \sqrt{\frac{150,000}{2}} = \sqrt{75,000} = 274$$

In practice, the EOQ would be increased to 300 items ordered five times yearly.

It should be recognised, however, that the EOQ may be misleading for the following reasons:

- annual demand is a forecast, so it is unlikely to be an exact figure
- order costs are assumed to be constant, but these may change due to use or the introduction of e-purchasing
- the interest rate is assumed to be constant, but, in practice, interest rates frequently change
- cost per item is likely to change in the course of a year, so we have to decide whether to use average cost, replacement cost, actual cost or anticipated future cost in the equation.

Many of the criticisms of EOQs derive from inaccurate data inputs, such as exaggerated carrying and order costs. Many ERP packages also have built-in programs that calculate EOQs automatically. Often, these built-in programs need modification to deal with changes in usages and products.

Sometimes EOQs are regarded as being in conflict with JIT approaches, but EOQs can be used to determine what items fit into the JIT model and what level of JIT is economically advantageous to the particular organisation.

While EOQs are not applicable to every inventory situation, they should be considered for repetitive procurement situations and MRO items.

9.13.3 Periodic review system

As the name implies, in this system an item's inventory position is reviewed periodically rather than at a fixed order point. The periods or intervals at which stock levels are reviewed will depend on the importance of the stock item and the costs of holding that item. A variable quantity will be ordered at each review to bring the stock level back to maximum – hence, the system is sometimes called the 'topping-up' system.

Maximum stock can be determined by adding one review period to the lead time, multiplying the sum by the average rate of usage and adding any safety stock. This can be expressed as:

$$M = W(T + L) + S$$

where:

M = predetermined stock level

W = average rate of stock usage

T = review period

L = lead time

S = safety stock

Safety stock may be calculated in a similar manner to that indicated for the fixed order point system.

Example 9.7

Periodic review system

Assume that:

- average rate of usage is 120 items per day
- review period is 4 weeks – say, 20 days
- lead time is 25 to 30 days
- safety stock is 900 items

$$M = 120\,(20 + 30) + 900 = 6900 \text{ items}$$

If, at the first review period, the stock was 4000 items, an order would be placed for 2900 items – that is, 6900 maximum stock minus actual stock at the review date.

9.13.4 Advantages and disadvantages of fixed order point and periodic review systems

Fixed order point

Advantages:

- on average, levels of stock are lower than with the periodic review system
- EOQs are applicable
- enhanced responsiveness to demand fluctuations

- replenishment orders are automatically generated at the appropriate time by comparing actual stock levels with reorder levels
- appropriate for widely differing inventory categories.

Disadvantages:

- the reordering system may become overloaded if many items of inventory reach their reorder levels simultaneously
- random reordering pattern, due to items coming up for replenishment at different times.

Periodic review

Advantages:

- greater chance of elimination of obsolete items due to periodic review of stock
- the procurement load may be spread more evenly, with possible economies in placing of orders
- large quantity discounts may be negotiated when a range of stock items is ordered from the same supplier at the same time
- production economies, due to more efficient production planning and lower set-up costs, may result from orders always being in the same sequence.

Disadvantages:

- on average, larger stocks are required than with fixed order point systems as reorder quantities must provide for the period between reviews as well as between lead times
- reorder quantities are not based on EOQs
- if the usage rate changes shortly after a review period, a stockout may occur before the next review date
- difficulties in determining appropriate review period, unless demands are reasonably consistent.

9.13.5 Choice of systems

- A fixed order point system is more appropriate if a stock item is used regularly and does not conform to the conditions for periodic review systems.
- A periodic review system is most likely to be appropriate if orders are placed with and delivered from suppliers at regular intervals, such as daily, monthly, or a number of different items are ordered from and delivered by the same supplier at the same time.

9.14 Dependent demand

Dependent demand is associated with pull systems and push–pull systems, discussed in section 9.12 above, and relates to just-in-time (JIT), materials and requirements planning (MRP), distribution requirements planning (DRP), enterprise resource planning (ERP) and vendor-managed inventory (VMI).

9.15 Just-in-time (JIT)

9.15.1 What is JIT?

The following comprehensive definition of JIT is provided by the American Production and Inventory Control Society:[6]

> A philosophy of manufacturing based on planned elimination of all waste and continuous improvement of productivity. It encompasses the successful execution of all manufacturing activities required to produce a final product from design engineering to delivery and including all stages of conversion from raw material onward. The primary elements include having only the required inventory when needed; to improve quality to zero defects; to reduce lead time by reducing set-up times, queue lengths and lot sizes; to incrementally revise the operations themselves; and to accomplish these things at minimum cost.

In short, JIT production is:

> Making what the customer needs, when it is needed and in the quantity needed using the minimum resources of people, materials and machinery.

From the above definitions, it can be seen that JIT is more than delivering an item where and when required and at the right time. JIT is both a production scheduling and inventory control technique and an aspect of total quality management (TQM). As a production control technique, it is concerned with adding value and eliminating waste by ensuring that any resources needed for a production operation – whether raw material, finished product or anything in between – are produced and available precisely when needed. This emphasis on waste elimination means that JIT is an essential element in lean production, discussed in section 4.5.2. As a philosophy that aims at zero defects or never allowing defective units from the preceding process to flow into and disrupt a subsequent process, it is an aspect of TQM.

A useful distinction may be made between its two forms:

- *BIG-JIT* or lean production focusing on all sources of waste, as outlined in the first of the above definitions
- *Little-JIT* focusing more narrowly on scheduling goods, inventories and providing resources where needed.

It is with 'little-JIT' that the present section is primarily concerned.

9.15.2 The background of JIT

JIT is generally agreed to have been developed by Talichi Ohno, a vice-president of the Japanese Toyota motor company in the 1960s. It should be noted, however, that Henry Ford practised mass production with a JIT approach in 1921. By 1924, the production cycle of the Model T – from processing the core material to the final product – was only four days.

9.15.3 The objectives of JIT

These have been concisely summarised as:

- *zero defects* – all products will more than meet the quality expectations of the customer

- *zero set-up time* – no set-up time results in shorter production time, shorter production cycles and smaller inventories
- *zero inventories* – inventories, including work-in-progress, finished goods and sub-assemblies, will be reduced to zero – this is the opposite of the traditional manufacturing philosophy of maintaining buffer stocks as a precaution against unreliable suppliers or fluctuating demand
- *zero handling* – the elimination, so far as possible, of all non-value-adding activities
- *zero lead time* – in some markets, this is impossible, but the aim is to increase flexibility by using small batches of components or assemblies
- *lot size of one* – this makes it possible to adapt quickly when demand is changing so if, for example, the lot size is 200 and demand is changing, either the supplier or customer ends up with a quantity of inventory that will either never or only very slowly reduce.

The requirements for successful JIT:

- uniform master production schedules
- 'pull' production systems
- good customer–supplier relationships
- short distance between customer and supplier
- reliable delivery
- consistent quality with zero defects
- standardisation of components and methods
- material flow system.

9.15.4 JIT and kanban systems

The *kanban* system is an essential aspect of JIT. In Japanese, the word *kanban* means 'ticket' or 'signal' and in JIT refers to an information system in which instructions relating to the type and quantity of items to be withdrawn from the preceding manufacturing process are conveyed by a card that is attached to a storage and transport container. The card identifies the part number and contained capacity. The two principal types of *kanban* are:

- *production kanban, or P kanban* signals the need to produce more parts
- *conveyance kanban, or C kanban* signals the need to deliver more parts to the next work centre.

The operation of a two-card *kanban* system within a work cell is shown in Figure 9.9. The rules for operating a two-card *kanban* system are therefore:

- each container must have a *kanban* card
- parts are only 'pulled' – that is, the user centre must go for them
- no parts can be obtained without a conveyance *kanban*
- all containers hold standard quantities and only standard quantities can be used
- no extra production is permitted – production can only start with a production *kanban*.

Figure 9.9 A two-card *kanban* system – the flow within a cell

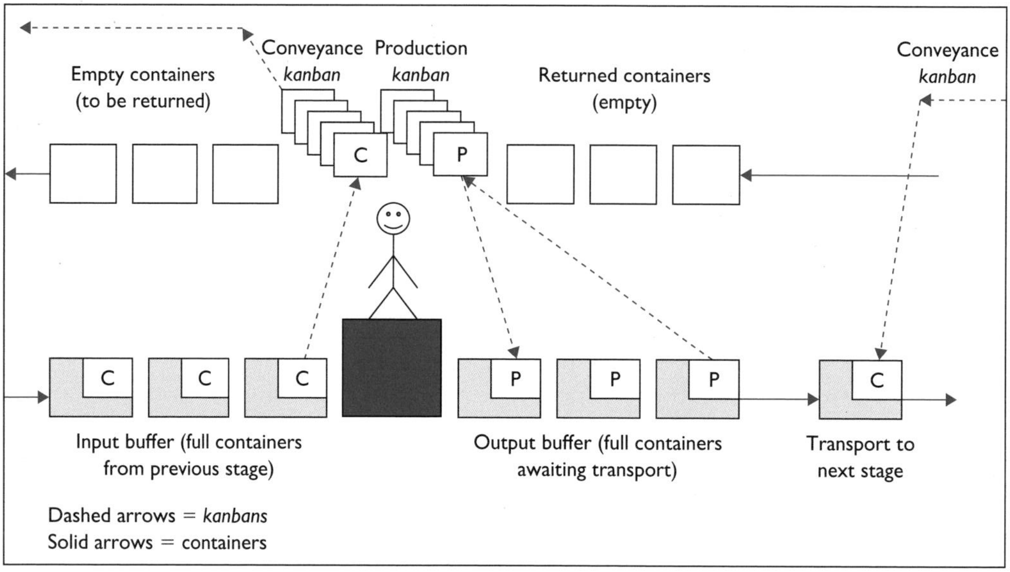

It follows that the amount of work-in-progress inventory is equal to the number of *kanban* cards issued multiplied by the capacity of the container used. The *initial* number of *kanban* cards required is calculated by the formula:

$$\text{Number of K cards} = \frac{D(T_w + T_p)(1 + a)}{C}$$

where:

D = average daily production rate, as indicated by the master production schedule

T_w = waiting time of *kanban* cards in decimal fractions of a day

T_p = the processing time per part in fractions of a day

C = the capacity of a standard container

a = a policy variable determined by the efficiency of the work centre using the part

Thus, if:

$$D = 100 \text{ parts/day}, T_w = 0.25, T_p = 0.15, C = 10 \text{ and } a = 1$$

then the number of *kanban* cards will be:

$$\frac{100(0.25 + 0.15)(1 + 1)}{10} = 8$$

The dual card system described above is reportedly used by Toyota for car production. A more common approach is a one-card system, which signals requirements from the preceding work centre, as shown in Figure 9.10.

Figure 9.10 One-card system signalling requirements from previous work centre

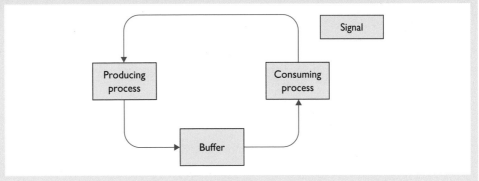

In Figure 9.10, a signal is sent back from the consuming work centre to the supplying work centre (or supplier). This is a signal:

■ to send some more (a transfer batch), via a buffer stock

■ to produce some more (a process batch), at the supplying work centre.

9.15.5 Benefits of JIT

The potential benefits of JIT to an organisation and its procurement function in particular, have been summarised by Schonberger and Ansari[7] as follows:

■ *part costs* – low scrap costs, low inventory carrying costs

■ *quality* – fast detection and correction of unsatisfactory quality and, ultimately, higher quality of purchased parts

■ *design* – fast response to engineering change requirements

■ *administrative efficiency* – fewer suppliers, minimal expediting and order release work, simplified communications and receiving activities

■ *productivity* – reduced rework, reduced inspection, reduced parts-related delays

■ *capital requirements* – reduced inventories of purchased parts, raw materials, work-in-progress and finished goods.

9.15.6 Possible disadvantages of JIT

Some organisations have experienced problems with JIT for the following reasons:

■ faulty forecasting of demand and inability of suppliers to move quickly to changes in demand

■ JIT requires the provision of the necessary systems and methods of communication between purchasers and suppliers, ranging from vehicle telephones to EDI, so problems will arise if there is inadequate communication both internally – from production to procurement – and externally – from procurement to suppliers – and vice versa

■ organisations with, ideally, no safety stocks are highly vulnerable to supply failures

■ purely stockless buying is a fallacy – lack of low-cost C class items can halt a production line as easily as a failure in the delivery of high-priced A class items

■ the advantages of buying in bulk at lower prices may outweigh the savings negotiated for JIT contracts as suppliers may increase their prices to cover costs of delivery, paperwork and storage required for JIT

■ JIT is not generally suitable for bought-out items that have short lifecycles and are subject to rapid design changes

■ JIT is more suitable for flow than batch production and may require a change from batch to flow methods, with consequent changes in the systems required to support the new methods

■ even for manufacturers that mass-produce items, a substantial percentage of components are made by number, if not value, in batches, as well as a small number of high-value components, on dedicated flow lines

■ apart from suppliers, JIT requires the total involvement of people from all disciplines and the breaking down of traditional barriers between functions within an organisation, which may involve a substantial investment in organisational development training

■ Rhys et al.[8] have drawn attention to Japanese transport factors arising from some suppliers relocating at greater distances from purchasers (although these are normally still nearer to users than in Europe), road congestion and lighter vehicles – that is, for every one vehicle required in Europe, two or three are required in Japan, so JIT in Japan is now 'neither lean nor green'.

Further, Hayes and Pisano[9] suggest that the problems of implementing JIT derive from the fact that:

> most companies focus on the *mechanics* of JIT and TQM rather than on their *substance*, the skills and capabilities that enable a factory to excel and make it possible for improvement programmes to achieve their desired results. The consequence of this outlook is that managers have tended to view such programmes as solutions to specific problems rather than as stepping stones in an intended direction.

Hayes and Pisano also warn that, if an organisation lacks the skills, such as low set-up times and defect rates, that make JIT work, the adoption of the approach is likely to be costly. Adopting the system, will, however, provide strong incentives to develop such skills and induce an ethic of continuous improvement. Over time, a true JIT system may emerge.

9.15.7 JIT and procurement

Apart from the general commitment to JIT mentioned above, two things essential to the successful implementation of JIT are that:

■ all parts must arrive where they are needed, when they are needed and in the exact quantity needed

■ all parts arriving must be usable.

Where these requirements are not achieved, JIT may easily become 'just-too-late'.

In achieving these requirements, procurement has the responsibilities summarised below.

■ *Liaison with the design function* – the emphasis should be on *performance* rather than *design* specifications. Looser specifications enable suppliers to be more cost-effective by being more innovative with regard to the quality and function aspects of supplies. In JIT purchasing, value analysis is an integral part of the system and should include suppliers.

■ *Liaison with suppliers* to ensure that they understand thoroughly the importance of consistently maintaining lead times and a high level of quality.

■ *Investigation of the potential of suppliers* within reasonable proximity of the purchaser to increase certainty of delivery and reduction of lead time.

■ *Establishing strong, long-term relationships with suppliers* in a mutual effort to reduce costs and share savings. This will be achieved by the purchaser's efforts to meet the supplier's expectations regarding:

  - continuity of custom

  - a fair price and profit margin

  - agreed adjustments to price when necessary

  - accurate forecasts of demand

  - firm and reasonably stable specifications

  - minimising order changes

  - smoothly timed order releases

  - involvement in design specifications

  - prompt payment.

■ *Establishment of an effective supplier certification programme* which ensures that quality specifications are met before components leave the supplier so that receiving inspections are eliminated.

■ *Evaluation of supplier performance* and the solving of difficulties as an exercise in cooperation.

9.15.8 JIT II

This is a registered trademark of the Bose Corporation and is a customer–supplier partnerships concept practised by a number of companies and their suppliers. In a JIT II relationship, a supplier's representative – referred to as an 'in-plant representative' – functions as a member of the customer's procurement department while being paid by the supplier. The representative issues purchase orders to his/her own company on behalf of the customer. The representative is also involved in such activities as design, production planning and value analysis.

It is claimed that this arrangement provides benefits to both the customer and the supplier.

From the customer's perspective, benefits include that because:

■ the supplier's representatives are full-time employees of their customer's, they have ready access to information that can be used to reduce lead times and inventories and lead time reductions due to JIT II partnerships are generally greater than those achieved with conventional JIT

■ communications are improved because the representatives have a real-time awareness of the supplier's needs

■ transportation costs are lower as a result of organisations partnering transportation companies to deliver incoming items

■ the supplier is involved in concurrent design and value analysis so that it works with the customer from the inception of the design

- material costs are reduced by large orders with consequent discounts and lower transportation costs
- administrative costs are lower as there is a reduction in paperwork and the customer's procurement staff are released for other duties.

From the supplier's perspective, benefits include that:

- once a JIT II partnership has been agreed, an 'evergreen' contract is awarded, which has no end date and no requoting or tendering is required, and the resultant security enables the supplier to direct financial resources to managing the customer's account rather than seeking or renegotiating business.

JIT II is clearly not without risks and not always appropriate. There are various factors to be considered:

- the volume of business must be sufficient to assign a representative exclusively to one customer and, unless this is achieved, the JIT II approach may not be effective, so it is only an option for a customer able to place a very substantial volume of business with one supplier
- a supplier may be reluctant to share costs or processes with a customer and, conversely, a customer may be reluctant to divulge information about new designs or processes to a supplier
- a customer may be reluctant to award a long-term contract because of the fear that the supplier's performance might deteriorate.

Pragman[10] states that the JIT II concept has expanded from merely purchasing materials to include logistics, engineering and services. It does, however, demand a strategic alliance between partners based on trust.

9.16 Materials and requirements planning (MRP)

MRP, developed in the 1960s, is a technique that assists in the detailed planning of production and has the following characteristics:

- it is geared specifically to assembly operations
- it is a dependent demand technique
- it is a computer-based information system.

The aim is to make available either purchased or company manufacturing assemblies just before they are required by the next stage of production or for delivery. MRP enables items/batches to be tracked throughout the entire manufacturing process and assists procurement and control departments to move the right supplies at the right time to manufacturing or distribution points.

9.16.1 MRP and JIT

MRP has many similarities to JIT. Some comparisons are shown in Table 9.8.

JIT and MRP should not, however, be thought of as opposing systems. In many organisations, the two systems are successfully combined. For example, it is important that a strong MRP II (see section 9.17) planning environment will facilitate JIT execution. Ideally the two systems are not alternative but complementary.

Table 9.8 Comparison of MRP and JIT

Operating system characteristics	MRP	JIT
System	'Push' system	'Pull' system
Focus	Bottlenecks	'Quality'
Rates of output	Variable production plan	Level schedule
Work authorisation	Master production schedule	*Kanban*
Inventory status	Inventory no problem, but the less the better	Reducing inventory to zero
Administrative personnel	Increased	Fewer
Forms of control	Management reports	Shop floor, visual
Capacity adjustment	Capital requirements planning (deferred)	Visual, immediate (demand surge)
Scheduling	MRP says 'which job next'	*Kanban* says 'make it now'

9.16.2 MRP terminology

MRP has its own terminology, as follows:

- a *bill of materials*, or BOM, contains information on all the materials, components and sub-assemblies required to produce each end item
- an *end item*, or master scheduled item, is the final product sold to the customer and the inventory for end items, from the accounting standpoint, will either be work-in-progress or finished goods
- a *parent* is an item manufactured from one or more component items
- a *component* is one item that goes through one or more operations to be transformed into a parent
- an *intermediate item* is one that has at least one parent and one component – classified as work-in-progress
- a *sub-assembly*, as it is 'put together', rather than other means of transformation, is a special case of intermediate item
- a *purchased item* is one that has no components because it comes from a supplier but has one or more parents, so, for accounting purposes, inventory or purchased items, is regarded as raw materials
- *part commodity* is the extent to which a component (part) has one or more parents – a concept related to standardisation – so a standard ball bearing may have numerous parents
- *usage quantity*, which is the number of units of a component required to make one unit of its parent
- a *bucket* is a time period to which MRP relates, for example, one week.

9.16.3 The essential elements of an MRP system

These are shown in Figure 9.11.

Figure 9.11 **Essential elements of an MRP system**

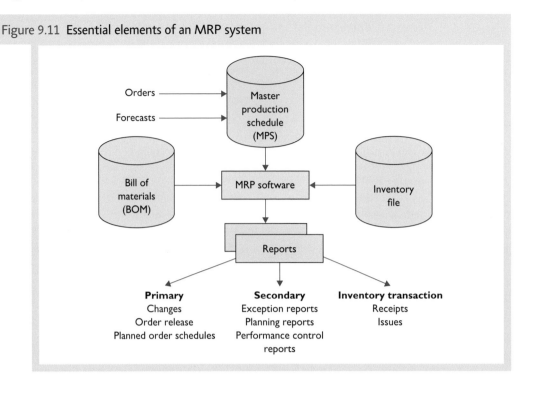

9.16.4 MRP inputs and outputs

The process starts at the top level with a master production schedule (MPS). The information in the MPS comes from a number of sources, including orders actually received and forecasts of demand, usually produced using the forecasting techniques described earlier. Two key MPS activities are the determination of planning horizons for the end product and the size of time buckets.

■ *The master production schedule(s) (MPS)* uses the inputs from marketing and sales to forecast demand for quantities of the final product over a planned time horizon subdivided into periods known as time buckets (see Figure 9.12). These buckets are not necessarily of equal duration. Without the MPS(s), MRP cannot generate requirements for any item.

Figure 9.12 **Master production schedule**

Week	1	2	3	4	5	6	Time horizon
Product X	30		14		10	8	Time buckets
Product Y		38	13	30	13	13	

■ *The bill of materials file (BOM)*, also known as the product structure, lists all the items that comprise each assembly and sub-assembly that make up the final product or end item. Each BOM is given a level code according to the following logic:

  – Level 0: the final product or end item not used as a component of any other product
  – Level 1: direct component of a level 0 item
  – Level 2: direct component of a level 1 item
  – Level *n*: direct component of a level ($n - 1$) item.

Assume the demand for product X is 30 units. Each unit of X requires three units of A and two of B. Each A requires one C, one D and three Es. Each B requires one E and one F. Each F requires three Gs and two Cs. Thus, the demand for A, B, C, D, E, F and G is completely dependent on the demand for X. From the above information, we can construct a BOM or product structure for the related inventory requirements, as in Figure 9.13.

■ *The inventory file* is the record of individual items of inventory and their status. The file is kept current by the online posting of inventory events, such as the receipt and issue of items of inventory or their return to store.

■ *The MRP package* uses the information provided by the MPS, BOM and inventory files to:

  – explode or cascade the end product into its various assemblies, sub-assemblies or components at various levels, so the number of units of each item needed to produce 30 units of product X would be:

Part A = 3 × no. of Xs	3 × 30	= 90
Part B = 2 × no. of Xs	2 × 30	= 60
Part C = 1 × no. of As + 2 × no. of Fs	(1 × 90) + (2 × 60) = 210
Part D = 1 × no. of As	1 × 90	= 90
Part E = 3 × no. of As + 1 × no. of Bs	(3 × 90) + (1 × 60) = 330
Part F = 1 × no. of Bs	1 × 60	= 60
Part G = 3 × no. of Fs	3 × 60	= 180

Figure 9.13 **Product structure for X**

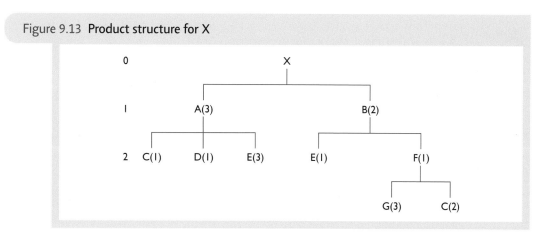

So, to produce 30 units of X, we shall need 90 units of A, 60 units of B, 210 units of C, 90 units of D, 330 units of E, 60 units of F and 180 units of G

– offset for lead time – lead times for each item must be fed into the system, then, subtracting them from the date of the net requirement so as to position the planned order release date in advance of the timing of the net requirement it covers is called *offsetting the lead time*

– net out on-hand and on-order balances using the equation:

$$\underset{}{\text{Net requirements}} = \underbrace{\underset{}{\text{Gross requirements}}}_{\text{Total requirements}} \underbrace{- \underset{}{\text{Inventory on hand}} + \underset{}{\text{Units on order}}}_{\text{Available inventory}}$$

In an MRP system, net requirement quantities are always related to some date or period – that is, they are time phased (as shown by Figure 9.12). The primary outputs of the MRP system are:

■ order release instructions for the placement of planned – that is, future – production or procurement orders

■ rescheduling instructions notifying the need to advance or postpone open orders to adjust inventory coverage to net requirements

■ expediting instructions that relate to overdue orders

■ cancellation or suspension instructions relating to open orders.

MRP systems also have the capacity to produce much secondary data, such as reports relating to exceptions or deviations from normal planning and performance.

9.16.5 Applications of MRP

While having elements in common to all inventory situations, MRP is most applicable where:

■ the demand for items is dependent

■ the demand is discontinuous – 'lumpy' and non-uniform

■ in job, batch and assembly or flow production, or where all three manufacturing methods are used.

9.17 Manufacturing resource planning (MRP II)

9.17.1 Definition

MRP II may be defined as:

> The extension of computerised MRP to link together such functions as production planning and control, engineering, procurement, marketing, financial/cost accounting and human resource management into an integrated decision support system.

In MRP II, the production process is still driven by a master production schedule, but additional inputs are received from production control, procurement and engineering. The computerised system also collects data to support financial or cost accounting, marketing and human resource management.

9.17.2 The advantages of MRP II

An overview of MRP II is provided by Figure 9.14.

- It coordinates the efforts of production, engineering, procurement, marketing and human resources to achieving a common strategy or business plan.

- Managers are able to analyse the 'What if . . .' implications of their decisions, such as what if the sales forecasts of marketing cannot be met by the available production capacity? What would be the financial implications of outsourcing?

- Better utilisation of marketing, finance and human resources in addition to physical plant and equipment.

- Changes can be easily factored into the system as they arise, such as rush orders.

- Cost of resources used or considered for use can be converted into money values, thus facilitating budgeting and budgetary control.

- Coordination of production with procurement, marketing and human resources in such ways as timing of supplies deliveries, using sales forecasts to determine master budgets and planning recruitment or run-down of personnel.

9.18 Enterprise resource planning (ERP)

9.18.1 What is ERP?

ERP is the latest and possibly the most significant development of MRP and MRP II. While MRP allowed manufacturers to track supplies, work-in-progress and the output of finished goods to meet sales orders, ERP is applicable to all organisations and allows managers from all functions or departments to have a consolidated view of what is or is not taking place throughout the enterprise. Most ERP systems are designed around a number of modules, each of which can be standalone or combined with others.

- *Finance* – this module tracks financial information, such as accounts receivable and payable, payroll and other financial and management accounting information throughout the enterprise.

- *Logistics* – this module is often broken down further into submodules covering inventory and warehouse management and transportation.

- *Manufacturing* – this module tracks the flow of orders or products, including MRP and the progress and coordination of manufacturing.

- *Supplier management* – this module tracks the procurement process, from requisitioning to the payment of suppliers, and monitors delivery of supplies and supplier performance.

- *Human resources* – this module covers many human resource management activities, including planning, training and job allocation.

ERP can be defined as:

> A business management system that, supported by multimodule application software, integrates all the departments or functions of an enterprise.

Initially, ERP systems were enterprise-centric. The development of the Internet and e-business has, however, made the sharing of accurate real-time information across the

Figure 9.14 An overview of an MRP II system

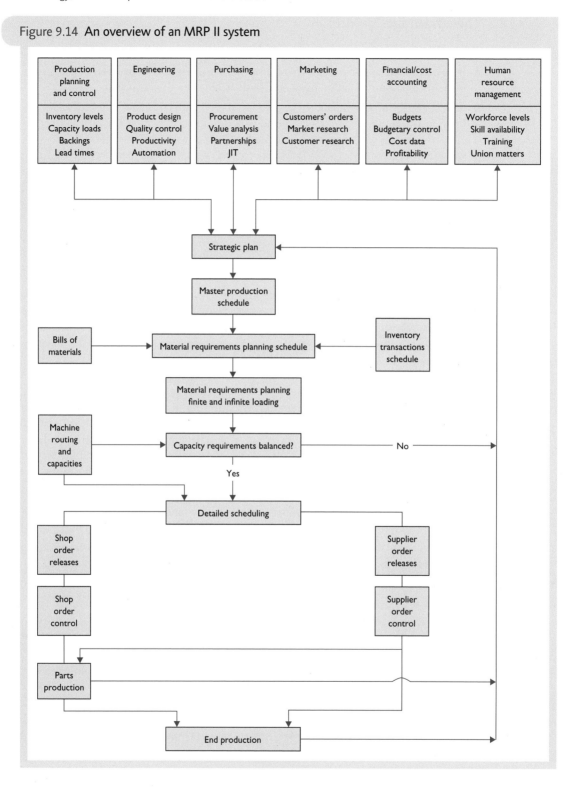

whole supply chain essential to business success. Gartner – the consultancy that coined the term ERP – now uses ERP II to refer to systems that facilitate collaborative commerce, or c-commerce, in which a key requirement is the sharing of information outside the enterprise. Some differences between ERP and ERP II are shown in Table 9.9.

9.18.2 The advantages of ERP

These can be summarised as:

- *faster inventory turnover* – manufacturers and distributors may increase inventory turns tenfold and reduce inventory costs by 10 to 40 per cent
- *improved customer service* – in many cases, an ERP system can increase fill rates to 80 or 90 per cent by providing the right product in the right place at the right time, thus increasing customer satisfaction
- *better inventory accuracy, fewer audits* – an ERP system can increase inventory accuracy to more than 90 per cent while reducing the need for physical inventory audits
- *reduced set-up times* – ERP can reduce set-up time by 25 to 80 per cent by grouping similar production jobs together, ensuring coordination of people, tools and machinery, together with the efficient use of equipment and minimising downtime by virtue of efficient maintenance
- *higher-quality work* – ERP software, with a strong manufacturing component, proactively pinpoints quality issues, providing the information required to increase production efficiency and reduce or eliminate rework
- *timely revenue collection and improved cash flow* – ERP gives manufacturers the power to proactively examine accounts receivable before problems occur instead of just reacting, which improves cash flow.

Table 9.9 **Differences between ERP and ERP II**

Factor	ERP	ERP II
Role	Concerned with optimising within an enterprise	Concerned with optimising across the whole supply chain by collaborating with business partners
Domain	Focused on manufacturing and distribution	Crosses all sectors and segments of business, including service industries, government and asset-based industries, such as mining
Function	General applications	Designed to meet the needs of specific industries, thereby providing steep functionality for users
Process	Internally focused	Externally focused, especially on connecting trading partners, irrespective of location
Architecture	Monolithic and closed	Web-based and open to integrating and interoperating with other systems. Built around modules or components that allow users to choose the functionality they require
Data	Information on ERP systems is generated and consumed within the enterprise	Information available across the whole supply chain to authorised participants

9.18.3 The disadvantages of ERP

- *ERP implementation is difficult* – this is because implementation involves a fundamental change from a functional to a process approach to business
- *ERP systems are expensive* – this is especially so when the customisation of standard modules to accommodate different business processes is involved – it has been estimated that some 50 per cent of ERP implementations fail to deliver the anticipated benefits and the cost is often prohibitive for small enterprises
- *cost of training employees to use ERP systems can be high*
- *there may be a number of unintended consequences* such as employee stress and a resistance to change and sharing information that was closely guarded by departments or functions
- *ERP systems tend to focus on operational decisions* and have relatively weak analytical capabilities (this topic is briefly dealt with below).

9.19 Supply chain management systems

While ERP systems can provide a great deal of planning capability, the various material, capacity and demand constraints are all considered separately in relative isolation from each other. Further, ERP systems have many tasks to fulfil. Analytical supply chain management systems, however, can consider all relevant factors simultaneously and perform real-time adjustments in the relevant constraints. Thus, while getting decisions or information from an overloaded ERP system can take hours, a separate SCM system may provide the required answers in minutes. SCM systems such as Technologies and Manugistics usually span all the supply chain stages and have the analytical capabilities to produce planning solutions and strategic-level conditions. Analytical systems do, however, rely on legacy systems or ERP systems to provide the information on which the analysis is based. Because of this, there is currently a rapid convergence of ERP and SCM software.

9.20 Distribution requirements planning (DRP)

9.20.1 What is DRP?

Distribution requirements planning (DRP) is an inventory control and scheduling technique that applies MRP principles to distribution inventories. It may also be regarded as a method of handling stock replenishment in a multi-echelon environment. Applied to distribution, the term 'multi-echelon' means that, instead of independent control of the same item at different distribution points using EOQ formulae, the dependent demand at a higher echelon (such as a central warehouse) is derived from the requirements of lower echelons (such as regional warehouses). DRP is useful for both manufacturing organisations, such as car manufacturers that sell their cars via several distribution points, such as regional and local distributors, and purely merchandising organisations, such as supermarkets (see Figure 9.14).

All levels in a DRP multi-echelon structure are dependent, except for the level that serves the customer, which are the retailers in Figure 9.15.

Figure 9.15 A supermarket multi-echelon distribution system

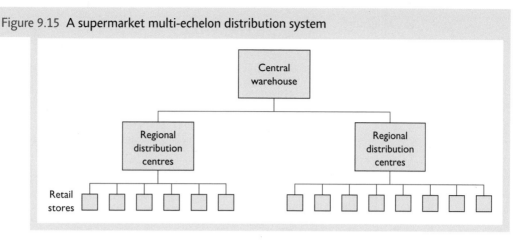

9.20.2 DRP and MRP

DRP has been described as the mirror image of MRP. Some of the contrasts between the two approaches are set out in Table 9.10.

MRP and DRP approaches have, however, many common aspects:

- as planning systems, neither uses a fixed or periodic review approach
- both are computerised systems
- just as MRP has been expanded into MRP II, so DRP has been expanded into DRP II
- DRP utilises record formats and processing logic consistent with MRP.

The last point is the most important of all as it provides the basis for integrating the database throughout the whole supply chain, from procurement through to distribution. Thus, both MRP and DRP contribute to a logistics system, as shown in Figure 9.16.

Thus as Vollman et al.[11] observe:

> Distribution requirements planning serves a central role in coordinating the flow of goods inside the factory with the system modules that place the goods in the hands of the customers. It provides the basis for integrating the manufacturing planning and control (MRP) system from the firm to the field.

Table 9.10 Comparison of MRP and DRP

MRP	DRP
■ The bill of materials applies time-phased logic to components and sub-assemblies to products in the MOM (management of materials) network ■ An 'explosion' process from a master production schedule to the detailed scheduling of component replenishments ■ Goods in course of manufacture	■ The bill of distribution (the network) uses time-phased order point logic to determine network replenishment requirements ■ An 'implosion' process from the lowest levels of the network to the central distribution centre ■ Finished goods

Figure 9.16 Distribution requirements planning and logistics

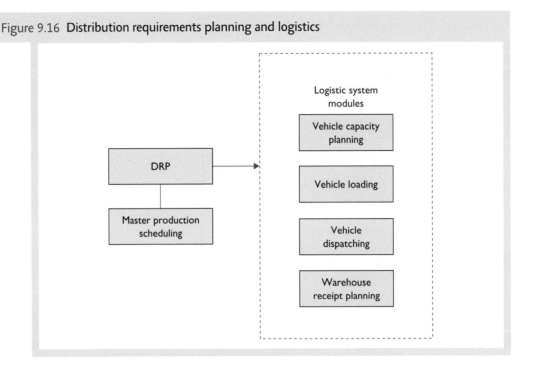

9.21 Vendor-managed inventory (VMI)

Vendor-managed inventory (VMI) is a JIT technique in which inventory replacement decisions are centralised with upstream manufacturers or distributors. Acronyms for VMI include:

■ continuous replenishment programs (CRP)

■ supplier-assisted inventory management (SAIM)

■ supplier-assisted inventory replenishment (SAIR)

■ efficient consumer response (ECR).

VMI may also be considered to be an extension of distribution requirements planning (DRP).

9.21.1 The aim of VMI

This is to enable manufacturers or distributors to eliminate the need for customers to reorder, reduce or exclude inventory and obviate stockouts. With VMI, customers no longer 'pull' inventory from suppliers. Rather, inventory is automatically 'pushed' to customers as suppliers check customers' inventories and respond to previously agreed stock levels. VMI is particularly applicable to retail distribution. VMI can also relieve the customer of much of the expense of ordering and stocking low-value MRO items.

Figure 9.17 A simple VMI model

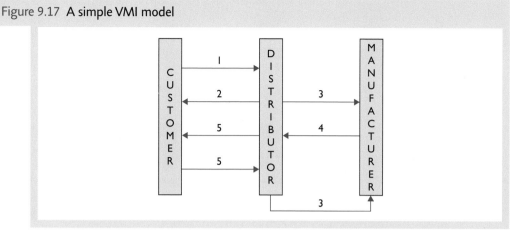

Source: Adapted from Vollman, T. E., Berry, W. L. and Whybark, C. D., *Manufacturing Control Systems*, 2nd edition, Irwin, 1988, p. 788

9.21.2 Implementing VMI

A simple model of VMI is shown in Figure 9.17.

This model is based on the assumption that the customer has entered into a collaborative or partnership agreement with a distributor, under which the latter agrees to stock a specified range of items and satisfy specified service levels. In return, the customer undertakes to buy the specified items solely from the distributor and no longer keeps the items in stock. There must, therefore, be a high level of trust between the customer and the distributor.

The various steps in Figure 9.17 may be explained as follows:

Step 1 The customer sends information on items sold to the distributor. This information may be collected by barcoding and scanning technology and transmitted to the distributor by EDI or the Internet.

Step 2 The distributor processes the information and forwards an acknowledgement to the customer, giving details of the quantities and descriptions of the products to be delivered, delivery date and destination, and releases the goods.

Step 3 The distributor collects details of all the customer's orders, which are consolidated and sent daily to the manufacturers via EDI or the Internet.

Step 4 The manufacturer replenishes the distributor's stock.

Step 5 The distributor invoices the customer, who remits payment. Very large customers may transmit their requirements directly to the manufacturer, from whom they receive direct deliveries.

Normally, VMI implementation involves four stages:

1 *Preparation* – in addition to initial negotiations between a customer and the supplier and setting up project teams with clearly defined roles and responsibilities, this stage involves collaborative planning, forecasting and replenishment (CPFR), the aim of

which is to minimise inventories and focus on value-added process activities. By focusing on the flow of supply to consumers without the complication of inventory, the project's participants can often discover previously undetected hidden bottle-necks in the flow that can be eliminated.

2 *Pre-implementation* – this is an extension of CPFR involving the determination of fore-cast quantities, safety stocks, lead time, service levels and key performance indicators and ownership issues.

3 *Implementation*

4 *Refinement* – improvements that may be made in the light of experience, including the resolution of technical difficulties encountered subsequent to implementation.

9.21.3 Advantages of VMI

VMI is advantageous to both suppliers and customers. For suppliers, the advantages include:

- *demand smoothing* – VMI information improves forecasts of customers' requirements, thereby enabling manufacturers to plan production to meet customer demand
- *long-term customer relationships* due to the high cost to the customer of switching to an alternative supplier
- *enhanced operational flexibility* enabling production times and quantities to be adjusted to suit the supplier.

For customers, the advantages include:

- *reduced administrative costs* due to the elimination of the need to monitor inventory levels, paper to computer entries and reduced reordering costs
- *enhanced working capital* due to reduced inventory levels and obsolescence and enhanced stock turn with improved cash flow
- *reduced lead times* with enhanced sales and a reduction of list sales due to stockouts.

9.21.4 Disadvantages of VMI

These also apply to both suppliers and customers. Disadvantages for suppliers include:

- *transfers of customer costs to the supplier* – these include those relating to administration and the cost of carrying increased inventory to meet customer demand
- *reduced working capital* due to the enhanced inventory and administration costs stated above.

Disadvantages for customers include:

- *increased risk* resulting from dependence on the manufacturer or distributor
- *disclosure of potentially sensitive information to the supplier* – the possession of such infor-mation will put the supplier in a strong position when a contract is renegotiated
- *customers may be better positioned than suppliers to make replenishment decisions* – Chopra and Meindl[12] point out that:

    One drawback to VMI arises because retailers often sell products from competing manufacturers that are substitutes in the customer's mind. For example, a customer may substitute detergent manufactured by Proctor & Gamble with detergent manufactured by Lever Brothers. If the retailer has a VMI agreement with both manufacturers, each will ignore the impact of substitution when making its inventory decisions. As a result, inventories at the retailer will be higher than optimal.

9.22 Procurement and inventory

Inventories are essential for business, financial and reputational reasons. The development of systems such as MRP, MRP II, ERP and VMI has meant that procurement as a supply chain activity has possibly less involvement, especially with dependent demand items. In many organisations, an inventory management function will be responsible for many of the activities outlined in this chapter. It is important, however, that procurement professionals should have a sound grasp of inventory management, for at least the following four reasons.

1   Inventory in many undertakings – for example, the construction industry – is an important asset. In some small companies, inventory may be the most important asset.

2   Inefficient inventory management will increase costs and reduce profitability. Too much working capital tied up in inventory can cause problems of cash flow, result in expensive borrowing and prevent desirable expenditure in other directions. There are also the ever-present risks of theft, deterioration and obsolescence. Conversely, holding inventory can, in a time of rising prices, be a source of windfall profits.

3   Holding inventory can enhance flexibility and provide competitive advantage, due to the ability to respond rapidly to customers' requirements, as with agile production. What inventory policy to pursue is therefore an important strategic business decision.

4   Efficient and effective inventory management can only be achieved with the cooperation of efficient and effective suppliers. The selection of such suppliers and negotiation of all aspects of contracts relating to inventory are activities in which procurement professionals should expect to play a leading role. The importance of sourcing is discussed in the next chapter.

Discussion questions

9.1   Can you explain the role of procurement in managing inventory in a business? Having explained the role, can you explain the differences between this role in:
1   a large government department with multiple locations?
2   an international airlines availability of spare parts in distant airports served by the airline?
3   a volume production automotive manufacturer?

9.2   Calculate the rate of stock turn using the following information:

Turnover at *selling* price	= £125,000
Mark-up	= 25%
Opening stock at *selling* price	= £160,000
Closing stock at *selling* price	= £70,000

9.3 Calculate the rate of stock turn using the following information:

Turnover at *cost* price	= £100,000
Opening stock at *cost* price	= £48,000
Closing stock at *cost* price	= £56,000

9.4 Do you agree with the concept of a supplier having consignment stock at the buyer's premises and the buyer only paying when the stock is used? Why would a supplier agree to this?

9.5 The Bluebird Transport company manufactures a range of travel homes. The Production Director has suggested that any inventory valued at less than £5 an item should be made available as open access on the shop floor. No requisitions will be required to access the inventory. What are the procurement implications?

9.6 What information does an operations manager require to make effective use of dependent demand inventory models?

9.7 The Horsk Shipping Company has reviewed the inventory held at their strategic warehouses in Cape Town, Southampton and New York. They have found that the cost of carrying slow moving stock, e.g., engines, parts, steel-plate and furnishings, is 30 per cent of the value. What percentage would you predict might be allocated to each of the following constituents?
   (a) cost of money, that is, interest on capital tied up in stock
   (b) rates/rental charges
   (c) warehouse expenses
   (d) physical handling
   (e) clerical and stores control
   (f) obsolescence
   (g) deterioration and pilferage.

9.8 Procurement should not be accountable for the amount of inventory held in business. They do not forecast, determine order quantities or the time for delivery. Do you agree? Why?

9.9 The major disadvantages of bar-coding are uniformity and cost. Discuss this statement.

9.10 As RFID systems make use of the electromagnetic system, they are relatively easy to jam using energy at the right frequency. What might the implication be for:
   (a) customers at a supermarket checkout?
   (b) hospitals or military applications of RFID?

9.11 If a company categorises its inventory into three classifications according to their usage value, calculate the usage values of the following items and classify them along Pareto lines into A, B and C items.

Item no.	Annual quantity used	Unit value
1	75	£80.00
2	150,000	£0.90
3	500	£3.00
4	18,000	£0.20
5	3,000	£0.30
6	20,000	£0.10
7	10,000	£0.04

9.12 What are the business implications of the effect of information delays up and down the supply chain? What might be the consequence for inventory and profitability of such information delays?

9.13 There are six basic questions associated with forecasting, what are they?

9.14 What are the advantages of Enterprise Resource Planning (ERP)?

9.15 Each winter your local council requires a supply of salt to treat the roads. What are the considerations the council must take into account to effectively manage the inventory of salt?

9.16 If it were to be suggested that your organisation should outsource the stores function what advantages and disadvantages could you identify?

References

1 Institute of Logistics and Transport, *Glossary of Inventory and Materials Management Definitions*, 1998.

2 Institute of Logistics and Transport, *How to Manage Inventory Effectively*, Added Value Publication Ltd, Altrincham, UK, 2003, p. 94.

3 GAO-18-658 'VA Pharmacy Inventory Management', United States Government Accountability Office, 2018.

4 Compton, H. K. and Jessop, D., *Dictionary of Purchasing and Supply Management*, Pitman, London, UK, 1989, p. 135.

5 See GS1 UK's website at: www.e-centre.org.uk.

6 The Association for Operation Management (APICS), Chicago, Illinois. Founded in 1957 as the American Production and Inventory Control Society.

7 Schonberger, R. J. and Ansari, A., 'Just-in-time purchasing can improve quality', *Journal of Purchasing and Materials Management*, Spring, 1984.

8 Rhys, D. G., McNash, K. and Nieuwenhuis, P., 'Japan hits the limits of just-in-time EIU', *Japanese Motor Business*, December, 1992, pp. 81–9.

9 Hayes, R. H. and Pisano, G. P., 'Beyond world class: the new manufacturing strategy', *Harvard Business Review*, January–February, 1994, p. 75.

10 Pragman, C. H., 'JIT II: a purchasing concept for reducing lead times in time-based competition', *Business Horizons*, July–August, 1996, pp. 54–8.

11 Vollman, T. E., Berry, W. L. and Whybark, C. D., *Manufacturing Control Systems*, 2nd edn, Irwin, 1988, p. 788.

12 Chopra, S. and Meindl, P., *Supply Chain Management*, Prentice Hall, Upper Saddle River, New Jersey, USA, 2001, p. 247.

Chapter 10

Sourcing and the management of suppliers

Learning outcomes

This chapter aims to provide an understanding of:

- what is sourcing?
- the strategic sourcing process
- Sourcing information
- analysis of market conditions
- directives
- e-sourcing
- supplier evaluation
- supplier approval
- evaluating supplier performance
- policy issues in sourcing
- the supplier base
- outsourcing
- make vs buy
- partnering
- intellectual property rights (IPRs)
- procurement management of IPRs
- procurement support for in-house marketing
- intra-company trading
- procurement consortia
- sustainability
- sourcing decisions
- factors in deciding where to buy.

Key ideas

- Sourcing information.
- Analysis of market conditions.
- The main aspects of supplier appraisal.
- The purpose, scope and methods of evaluating supplier performance.
- The supplier base and selecting competent suppliers.
- Make vs buy decisions.
- Outsourcing and insourcing actions.
- Subcontracting.
- Partnering.
- Reciprocity.
- Intra-company trading, local suppliers and small or large suppliers.
- Procurement consortia.
- Factors determining where to buy.
- Buying centres, teams and networks.
- Straight rebuy, modified rebuy and new buy procurement situations.

10.1 What is sourcing?

The USA, GSA (General Services Administration) define strategic sourcing as 'a structured process which optimises the government's supply base while reducing Total Cost of Ownership (TCO) and improving mission delivery. Strategic sourcing solutions are based on a robust analysis of spending patterns, the clear definition of business needs and requirements, and the alignment of government needs with supply market capabilities and commercial best practices.'

10.1.1 Tactical sourcing

Tactical and operational sourcing is concerned with low-level procurement decisions that may relate to low-risk, non-critical items and services. Tactical sourcing is also concerned with short-term adaptive decisions as to how and from where specific requirements are to be met. For example, there may be a strategic sourcing strategy to obtain contract staff from one source who have a five-year call-off contract. In a short-term emergency, caused by flooding or other force majeure situations, it could be necessary to use other suppliers to obtain the immediate skills that are required.

10.1.2 Strategic sourcing

A sourcing strategy is a process, not an isolated decision.[1] It continuously

- balances internal and external activities, services and know-how
- aligns business strategy, business processes and 'product' requirements
- balances the results that must be achieved and the future options available.

Figure 10.1 **Stages in the sourcing strategy maturity cycle**

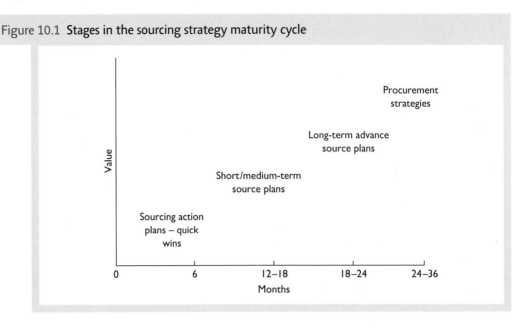

Strategic sourcing is the structured and collaborative process of critically analysing an organisation's spending patterns to better leverage its purchasing power, reduce costs, and improve overall performance. The level of sourcing maturity ranges from development of short-term tactical plans to long-term sourcing strategies. Figure 10.1 shows the stages in the maturity profile.

Strategic sourcing is concerned with top-level, longer-term decisions relating to high-profit, high supply risk strategic items and low-profit, high supply risk bottleneck products and services. It is also concerned with the formulation of long-term procurement policies, the supplier base, partnership sourcing, reciprocal and intra-company trading, globalisation and countertrade, and the procurement of capital equipment and ethical issues.

The status and importance of procurement has required a transition from thinking of procurement as a purely tactical activity to seeing it as a strategic activity. In transactional sourcing, procurement is viewed as a function concerned with the placement of orders. In strategic sourcing, procurement is viewed as a knowledge-based activity concerned with the total cost of ownership rather than the price paid per item with optional mix of relationships to provide competitive advantage.

10.2 The strategic sourcing process

Strategic sourcing is a complicated process involving a number of interrelated tasks. The process cannot be managed solely by procurement. Depending on the organisation it may, for example, involve design, finance, manufacturing/service delivery, quality management, environmental and health and safety.

The author has designed a seven-phase strategic sourcing process as shown in Table 10.1.

Table 10.1 Seven-phase strategic sourcing process

Phases	Key elements
Phase 1. Review of current status and business Planning	■ Critical appraisal of current status ■ Long-term expenditure profile ■ Vendor risk profiling ■ Stakeholder engagement ■ Contracting strategy ■ Drivers for sourcing strategy
Phase 2. Facets of strategic sourcing process plan.	■ Accountabilities for delivery of plans ■ Timescales ■ Engagement with supply chain ■ Identify supply market differentiators ■ Determine communication protocol
Phase 3. Research, data acquisition and business Analysis	■ Structure of the supply market ■ On-shore and off-shore capacity ■ Stability of the supply market ■ Competitive forces in play ■ Major procurement players
Phase 4. Conclusions reached from Phase 3	■ Hypothetical sourcing strategy ■ Business risk profiling ■ Impact on cost and profit ■ Contracting model ■ Engagement to implement strategy ■ Negotiation strategy
Phase 5. Supplier selection, mobilisation and relationship management	■ Pre-qualification modelling ■ Conduct due diligence ■ Contract & risk management ■ Key personnel reliance ■ Finalise strategy ■ Business sign-off
Phase 6. Implementation	■ Commit specialist resources ■ Ensure category management planning ■ Institute quality management ■ Review key performance indicators ■ Re-evaluate operational risks ■ Inform senior management
Phase 7. Report and measure performance and deliver continuous improvement	■ Exert robust contract management ■ Monitor contract deliverables compliance ■ Agree corrective actions for non-performance ■ Test quality of relationship management ■ Monitor new technologies ■ Monitor continuous improvements

10.3 Sourcing information

Sourcing information can be analysed in the areas shown in Figure 10.2. Each area is discussed below.

Figure 10.2 Areas of sourcing information

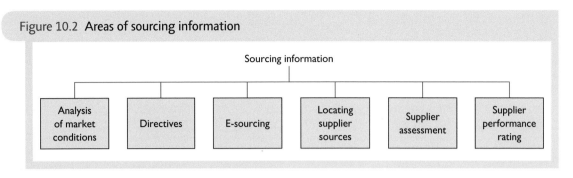

10.4 Analysis of market conditions

10.4.1 What is a market?

The term 'market' can mean:

- a place where goods and services are bought and sold – for example, the European Union is a market created by agreement between the participating countries to reduce barriers to the internal movement of labour and capital
- large groups of buyers and sellers of wide classes of goods, such as the consumer goods market, the equipment market and so on
- demand and supply of a single class of community, such as the steel market, the cotton market
- the general economic conditions relating to the supply of goods and services applying at a particular time – of special importance to procurement is the distinction between a buyer's and a seller's market.

10.4.2 Value chain structures

Mocenco[2] points out that, globally, the airline industry value chain comprises all phases directly or indirectly involved in meeting customer requirements. This network of production usually involves many actions with different functions (manufacturers, suppliers, transporters, warehouses, retailers, etc.).

There are also several categories of suppliers participating in the development of aircraft, classified in many levels:

- The Original Equipment Manufacturers (OEMs) – these are the companies that assemble large aircraft components and provide final products to customers. Their work involves: design, development and manufacturing or complete assembling of the aircraft as well as their testing (transport planes, fighter jets, helicopters, etc.). The main OEMs on the aviation industry global market are: Airbus – Europe and Boeing – USA, followed by Bombardier – Canada, Embraer – Brazil and United Aircraft Corporation of Russia.
- First-tier suppliers – they are the direct OEM suppliers. First-tier suppliers manufacture/assemble major sections, aircraft systems (including engines, avionics, aircraft interior, landing gear, etc.). First-tier suppliers are companies like Alenia in Italy, Dasa in Germany and Casa in Spain. Prime contractors are also the engine manufacturers such as Rolls Royce, Pratt & Whitney and General Electric.

- Second level suppliers – usually are the key suppliers of the tier I (first tier suppliers). These are commonly small and medium-sized companies. A second-tier supplier delivers complex manufacturing products obtained from their own production or a variety of other external providers, for example Sonaca Montreal, Areola

- Third level suppliers – perform special components and specific processes, e.g. raw materials, electronic components, etc.

This explanation demonstrates the importance of understanding the value chain and also highlights how buying organisations must evolve their relationships with the supply chain. In recent years the aerospace industry has been based on an extensive process of outsourcing. More complex work packages are being awarded, with subsequent changes and emphasis on risk management. It may be argued that the outsourcing means that the aircraft manufacturers become increasingly dependent on the performance of their subcontractors and suppliers.

10.4.3 What sources of information relating to market conditions are available?

Information relating to market conditions may be obtained from the following sources:

- primary data – field research that can use one or more approaches, such as observation, analysis of internal records, such as sales trends and order book levels, visits to suppliers, questionnaires

- secondary data – statistics and reports issued by external information, many of which are on databases

- international sources – a survey of information sources is provided by globalEDGE™ created by the Center for International Business Education and Research for Michigan State University, which is a knowledge portal that connects business professionals worldwide to a wealth of information, insights and learning resources on global business activities, while a further useful site is Business Information on the Internet, provided by the Federation of International Trade Associations based in Reston, Virginia and New York.

- UK government sources – full details of publications can be obtained from The Stationery Office. The most important sources include:

  - Abstracts of Statistics, published annually and monthly
  - Economic Trends
  - Census of Production
  - Department of Employment Gazette
  - Department for Business, Enterprise & Regulations Reform reports/publications
  - Bank of England Reports

- US government sources

  - STAT-USA – The Department of Commerce's site for economic and business data: retail sales, wholesale trade, business conditions, CPI, gross domestic product, etc. Includes the full and up-to-date National Trade Databank. The office ceased operations on 30 September 2010, but they have created a STAT-USA/ Internet Transition web page with links to the data sources.

  - The NTDB (National Trade Data Bank) – provides access to Country Commercial Guides, Market Research reports, Best Market reports. The NTDB also provides

US import and export statistics, as well as over 75 other reports and programmes. This service was provided by STAT-USA (please see comments above).

- Foreign trade statistics – Census Bureau.
- Business Gateway at FirstGov – easy access to government services for US businesses. Includes e-services, buying and selling to the government, statistics, laws and regulations, international trade services, publications.
- Export.gov – online trade resources with links to many federally produced market research products.
- Small Business Administration – links to a multitude of federal, state and local government websites useful to the small businessperson – start-up help, financing, business opportunities and more.
- US Business Advisor – over 100,000 businesses trade and labour web pages from government sites.
- EDGAR – filings for all US public companies are available from US Securities and Exchange Commission. Included are annual (10K), quarterly (10Q) reports, annual reports to shareholders and other material for a comprehensive overview of the financial condition of companies.

■ non-government sources – these include:

- Economist Intelligence Unit
- Chambers of Commerce
- professional associations – of particular importance to procurement staff is *Supply Management*, the journal of the Chartered Institute of Procurement and Supply (CIPS), and both the CIPS and the USA Institute of Supply Management have online databases.

■ the press in the UK – such as *The Economist*, *Financial Times* and the 'quality' daily and Sunday newspapers

■ economic forecasts – such as the Confederation of British Industries' (CBI) 'Economic Situation Report' and Oxford Economic Forecasting's range of publications, including *UK Economic Prospects*, *World Economic Prospects*, *UK Industrial Prospects* and *European Economic Prospects*.

10.5 Directives

A 'directive' is a general instruction. Typical directives relating to procurement and sourcing include those issued by the EU, central and local government offices and companies. An EU Directive is a form of legislation that is 'directed' at the Member States. It will set out the objective or policy which needs to be attained. The Member States must then pass the relevant domestic legislation to give effect to the terms of the Directive within a time frame set in the directive, usually two years.

10.5.1 EU Public Procurement Directives

A package of three Public Procurement Directives set out the EU legal framework for procurement by public authorities and utilities: the Public Contracts Directive 2014, The Concessions Contracts Directive 2014 and the Utilities Directive 2014.

The above Directives have been transposed into UK law by the following Regulations:

- The Public Contract Regulations 2015
- The Utilities Contracts Regulations 2016

The Remedies Directive, introduced in 2009, sets out the principal means of enforcement for a breach of the Regulations. The Remedies Directive is included in the Public Contracts Regulations 2015 at Chapter 6.

The principal means of enforcement for a breach of the Regulations are:

- actions by suppliers against individual contracting authorities in the High Court; and
- action by the EU Commission against Member States in the Court of Justice of the European Union (CJEU).

The remedies available for a breach of the Regulations include:

- contract making suspended by challenge to award decision
- suspension of the procedure
- order the setting aside of the decision or action concerned
- order the contracting authority to amend any document
- award damages to an economic operator which has sufficient loss or damage as a result of the breach.

10.5.2 Criticisms of public sector procurement practices

There are widespread criticisms of central and local government procurement practices including:

- The procurement process is unduly bureaucratic and time consuming for bidders
- Contract awards are biased to large organisations
- Small Medium Enterprises (SMEs) are unlikely to win contracts
- The Pre-Qualification process is harsh and repetitive across public sector organisations
- Procurement processes are manipulated at tender evaluation phase
- Incumbent service providers are likely to be favoured
- Contract awards are made without a transparent process being followed
- Contracts are extended without proper contract provision for doing so
- Timescales for tender responses are inadequate
- Contract liabilities required are unreasonable.

There is empathy to some criticisms as evidenced by the Lord Young report.[3] There is an attempt to make access to public sector contracts easier for SMEs; however, the 2015 regulations do not mandate breaking procurement into Lots. The European Single Procurement Document (ESPD) self-declaration form is a significant help to SMEs. However, a major benefit for SMEs is the fact that Contracting Authorities are only allowed to ask for suppliers who have a turnover that is twice the value of the contract they are applying for.

10.5.3 Company directives

Company directives may be issued by the top management of an organisation, instructing that, for reasons of strategy or in pursuance of agreements, particular supplies must be obtained from a specific source. An example would be directives relating to intra-company or reciprocal trading.

10.6 E-sourcing

E-procurement, along with e-marketplaces, e-catalogues and e-auctions, was discussed in Chapter 5. E-sourcing is defined by the CIPS[4] as:

> using the Internet to make decisions and form strategies regarding how and where services or products are obtained.

Although both e-procurement and e-sourcing are integral to the procurement cycle, the two terms are distinguished. E-procurement is usually concerned with non-core goods and services. These can, however, cover far more than routine MRO items or office supplies. As Waller[5] has stated:

> For telecommunications companies, network switches are indirect goods. For oil refineries, large condensers, costing millions of dollars are indirect goods. For companies that operate petrol stations, forecourts signs and fascias are indirect goods.

E-sourcing allows research, design and procurement personnel to find parts, components and sub-assemblies for prototypes and subsequent production models.

10.7 Supplier evaluation

10.7.1 When to evaluate suppliers

A requirement for supplier evaluation will arise when a prospective supplier applies to be placed on the buyer's approved list, responds to the buyer's request to pre-qualify for a forthcoming procurement process or where the buyer decides to conduct soft market testing and associated due diligence. The purpose is to assure the buying organisation that the prospective supplier can, reliably, meet the quality, operational, technical, financial and commercial requirements.

Supplier evaluation can be a time-consuming and costly activity, for the following reasons:

- designing an effective pre-qualification questionnaire
- designing the evaluation scoring and weightings model
- creating and briefing an evaluation team that represents a cross-section of specialities
- analysing and reporting on the responses submitted
- making reference site visits
- taking up references
- undertaking due diligence to ascertain, for example, if the supplier is litigious by nature.

The situations when evaluation is essential include:

- one-off purchases where the buyer has no established strategic source of supply
- where potential suppliers do not hold BS EN ISO 9000:2015 or other accreditations
- purchase of outsourced services such as IT and Asset Management
- purchase of construction, capital equipment and ICT systems
- considering the use of SMEs and Third Sector organisations
- when establishing procurement consortia agreements
- when re-tendering Framework Agreements
- when engaged in global sourcing
- when 'local content' purchases are required as part of, for example, an off-shore defence or infrastructure contract
- when major sub-contractors will be used by the prime contractor
- when long-term product support is required
- when a current strategic supplier is encountering adverse trading conditions and/or is experiencing severe financial problems.

10.7.2 What should be assessed?

Supplier evaluation is situational. What to evaluate is related to the requirements of the particular purchaser. All evaluations should, however, evaluate potential suppliers from at least ten perspectives:

- finance
- insurance
- productive capacity and facilities/service support capability
- quality
- health and safety
- environmental management
- existing contracts held and performance thereof
- organisational structure and key personnel – resources
- sub-contracting – proposed actions
- procurement capability and supply chain management.

This information is gathered, typically, by issuing a Pre-Qualification Questionnaire that is tailored to the specific requirements.

10.7.3 Finance

A robust financial appraisal should reduce, but will not eliminate, the risk of awarding a contract to a supplier whose financial viability will change over time. It does, however, provide information enabling considered decisions to be made. It may, for example, lead to a decision to require an 'on-demand' performance bond. There are some checks that must be considered:

- the last three years' turnover, split between UK and off-shore business
- the profitability and the relationship between gross and net profit over the last three years
- any losses in any period being examined and reasons for such losses; for example, write-offs against unsatisfactory contract performance
- the value of capital assets and return on capital assets
- the scale of borrowings and the ratio of debts to assets
- the possibility of takeover or merger affecting ability to supply
- the scale of pension fund deficits.

These enquiries are advisable for small and medium-sized enterprises (SMEs) in relation to one-off or annual contracts in excess of, say, £15,000 bearing in mind that their finances may not be entirely robust. Ideally, procurement specialists will have the ability, with colleagues in finance to undertake robust financial appraisals and to resolve any queries that arise.

The use of financial information, in procurement decision making, is not an exact science. In April 2018, the shares in Interserve fell 13 per cent in one day. The company employs 80,000 people worldwide and pre-tax losses had widened to £244m from £91.1m a year earlier. It was claimed that there was 'margin pressure' on contracts for the British Government and a £217m loss on a contract to build waste-to-energy plants. Revenue had remained stable at about £3.2 bn while its debt nearly doubled from £274m to £502.6m. It is interesting to reflect on the potential or actual risks of awarding a contract to Interserve when in possession of this information.

In the USA, 'FORM 10K' is an annual report submitted by US companies to the Securities and Exchange Commission, pursuant to Section 13 or 15(d) of the Securities Exchange Act of 1934. There is also the 'FORM 10Q', a quarterly report. The information contained in these documents exceeds, greatly, that typically found in UK companies' annual reports. There is vital company and market intelligence of value to procurement decisions. Examples of information contained are details of companies' major markets, products, business risks, outstanding legal writs and their nature, divisional financial results, investments and competition. These reports can be obtained free of charge from the companies themselves and many are available on the Internet.

Credit reports may also be obtained from bankers or credit references and credit reports provided by such agencies as Dun and Bradstreet. Important information provided by Dun and Bradstreet's supplier evaluation reports include:

- sales – gives a picture of the firm's financial size in terms of sales/revenue volume
- financial profile – evaluates how the enterprise is doing financially compared with its industry and, to understand the profitability and solvency of a supplier, five key financial ratios are calculated that provide industry benchmarks against a peer group of suppliers
- supplier risk score – an evaluation of the risk involved in dealing with a supplier that presents an at-a-glance 1–9 rating based on financial and public records and operational information, with 1 being the lowest and 9 the highest risk (this predictive score helps procurement to understand the general financial status of a supplier and benchmark it against others).

In addition, it is recommended that basic checks should be made on a UK company's title and its registered number at Companies House to see whether the company is dormant or trading and whether it is owned by another company or supported by a venture capital organisation.

10.7.4 Financial ratios

It has been argued, for years, that buyers should know all about financial ratios. The author is indebted to Steven Leon[6] for the motivation to recreate this section of my book. He explains that ratios tell a story about how a company is performing and that decisions must be made regarding the number of and which performance ratios to use.

He explains that financial ratios calculated from financial statements primarily fall into the following categories:

1 Liquidity
2 Profitability
3 Valuation
4 Asset management
5 Debt management

Liquidity ratios

These ratios are used to identify whether or not a company can meet its short-term obligations.

$$\textbf{Current ratio} = \text{Current assets/Current liabilities}$$

A current ratio of 1.0 indicates that the company can exactly meet its short-term obligations; whereas a ratio less than 1.0 means that a company cannot meet these obligations.

$$\textbf{Quick ratio} = (\text{Current assets} - \text{Inventories})/\text{Current liabilities}$$

This is sometimes called the acid test ratio, except that inventories are removed from the calculation.

$$\textbf{Operating cash flow ratio} = \text{Operating cash flow/Current liabilities}$$

This provides information to determine a firm's solvency through a cash flow point of view. This ratio shows whether or not a firm is generating enough cash from its operations to pay current debts.

Profitability ratios

Profitability ratios are used to measure management's effectiveness in generating returns on sales and return on stockholder financing.

Leon explains that many people use the terms profit, earnings, and income interchangeably, hence the multitude of terms is challenging.

Buyers should note that:

$$\text{COGS} = \text{Cost of Goods Sold}$$

$$\text{Revenues} - \text{COGS} = \text{Gross Profit}$$

$$\text{Gross Profit} - \text{Operating expenses} = \text{Operating Profit (EBIT)}$$

$$\text{Operating Profit (EBIT)} - \text{Interest} - \text{Income Taxes} = \text{Net Profit}$$

$$\textbf{Operating profit margin ratio} = \text{Operating profit (EBIT)/Sales Revenue}$$

$$\textbf{Gross profit margin} = (\text{Sales revenue} - \text{COGS})/\text{Sales revenue}$$
$$= \text{Gross profit/Sales revenue}$$

$$\textbf{Return of total assets (ROA)} = \text{Net income available to}$$
$$\text{common stockholders/Total assets}$$

Valuation ratios

Our readers are encouraged to read the Leon explanation of these ratios. The market value of a firm is a reflection of what investors think of the company's past performance and future outlook. This perception is portrayed through valuation ratios.

Asset management

These ratios are of direct interest to procurement and supply chain specialists.

$$\textbf{Inventory turnover} = \text{COGS/Inventory}$$

$$\textbf{Days in inventory} = 365 \text{ days/Inventory turnover ratio}$$

$$\textbf{Accounts receivable turnover} = \text{Net credit sales/Net accounts receivable.}$$
* There are also other ratios relating to Asset management.

Debt management ratios

These are also known as leverage ratios and show the extent to which a company is financed with debt.

$$\textbf{Debt ratio} = \text{Total liabilities/Total assets}$$

This shows how much of the company's funds come from sources other than equity.

$$\textbf{Debt-to-equity ratio} = \text{Debt-to-assets/(1 - Debt-to-assets).}$$

Investopedia[7] succinctly provide warning signs of a company in trouble. These are:

- dwindling cash or mounting losses
- interest payments in question
- switching auditors or going concern basis
- dividend cut
- top management defections
- big insider or institutional sales
- selling flagship products, equipment or property
- big perk cuts.

In the case of substantial contracts, the procurement organisation should question whether or not the supplier is likely to become overly dependent on them.

10.7.5 Insurance

Typically, a buyer will establish:

1 the types of insurance the prospective supplier holds and
2 the cover value of each insurance (establishing if the cover value is 'per claim' or 'in the aggregate').

The types of insurance that the buying organisation may require include:

- Public liability insurance covers any award of damages given to a member of the public because of an injury or damage to their property.

- Employer's liability insurance enables businesses to meet the costs of damages and legal fees for employees who are injured or made ill at work through the fault of the employer.

- Product liability insurance covers the fact that products must be fit for purpose. The supplier is legally responsible for any damage or injury that a product he supplies may cause.

- Professional indemnity insurance protects a business against claims for loss or damage by a client or a third party if the company/consultant have made mistakes or are found to have been negligent in some or all of the services that have been provided.

- Directors' and officers' liability insurance, to cover the cost of compensation claims made against directors and officers for alleged wrongful acts, including breach of duty, neglect and wrongful trading.

10.7.6 Productive capacity and facilities/services support capability

'Capacity' has been defined as:[8]

> The limiting capability of a productive unit to produce items within a stated time period normally expressed in terms of output units per unit of time.

Capacity is an elusive concept because it must be related to the extent that a facility is used – that is, it may be the policy to utilise production capacity five days weekly, one shift daily or produce a maximum of 2000 units monthly. Plant capacity can normally be increased by working overtime or adding new facilities. Contracts for services will, in large measure, require the capacity of people providing the services. This capacity must be sufficient to cope with maximum demand for the services, some of which may be required outside normal working hours.

In appraising supplier capacity, attention should be given to the following considerations:

- the maximum productive capacity in a specified working period
- the extent to which capacity is currently over-committed or under-committed – for example, a full order book may raise doubts about the supplier's capacity to take on further work
- how existing capacity might be expanded to meet future increased demand
- the percentage of available capacity utilised by existing major customers
- what percentage of capacity would be utilised if the potential supplier were awarded the business of the purchaser
- what systems are used for capacity planning?

An appraisal of production facilities depends on the purpose of it. Appraisal of machinery, for example, depends on what is to be produced. In general, attention should be given to answering the following kinds of questions.

- Has the supplier the full range of machinery needed to make the required product?
- How would any shortage of machinery be overcome?

- Are machines modern and well maintained? (Machine breakdowns will affect delivery.)
- Is the plant layout satisfactory?
- Is there evidence of good housekeeping?
- Has the supplier adopted such approaches as computer-aided design (CAD), computer-aided manufacture (CAM) or flexible manufacturing systems (FMS)?

10.7.7 Quality

For suppliers not included on the BSI's Register of Firms of Assessed Quality, appraisal may require satisfactory answers to such questions as the following:

- Has the supplier met the criteria for other BSI schemes, such as the Kite mark, Safety Mark and scheme for registered stockists?
- Has the supplier met the quality approval criteria of other organisations, such as the Ford Quality Awards, the Ministry of Defence, British Gas or others?
- To what extent does the supplier know about and implement the concept of total quality management?
- What procedures are in place for the inspection and testing of purchased materials?
- What relevant test and inspection process does the supplier use?
- What statistical controls are applied regarding quality?
- Does quality control cover an evaluation of quality?
- Can the supplier guarantee that the purchaser can safely eliminate the need for all incoming inspection? (This is especially important for JIT deliveries.)

10.7.8 Health and Safety

It is necessary to establish:

- the supplier's written Health and Safety policy
- the supplier's Health and Safety auditing arrangements
- details of Health and Safety Executive Improvement or Prohibition Notices or Prosecutions
- first aid and welfare provision
- name and title of director responsible for Health and Safety
- details of any safety organisations you belong to, e.g., ROSPA, IOSH, etc.
- how the company communicates its Health and Safety policy and procedures to employees
- examples of the risk assessment process applied in previous contracts of a similar nature.

10.7.9 Environmental management

ISO 14001:2015 provides guidelines on environmental policies and, where applicable, suppliers should be required to have an environmental policy and procedures for the implementation of such a policy. A large number of EU directives have also been issued relating to air, water, chemicals, packaging and waste.

There is a comprehensive Environmental Management System Questionnaire published by NSAI[9] (National Standard Authority of Ireland).

Procurement may consider asking:

- Has responsibility for environmental management been allocated to a particular person?
- Are materials obtained from sustainable sources – such as timber – where in the UK there are labelling schemes such as those run by the Forest Stewardship Council.
- What is the lifecycle cost of the suppliers' product?
- What facilities does the supplier have for waste minimisation, disposal and recycling?
- What energy savings, if any, do the supplier's products provide?
- What arrangements are in place for the control of dangerous substances and nuisance?

10.7.10 Supplier's performance against key performance indicators on current contracts

A key feature of the buyer's due diligence is to understand the supplier's existing contract commitments and performance against the contractual obligations. It is unlikely that suppliers will divulge sensitive information but that should not discourage the buyer seeking to:

- identify the supplier's key customers
- establish past and present contractual dispute information that is in the public domain
- understand the extent of the supplier's bid pipeline
- establish the extent of claims settled in respect of contractual non-performance
- identify data sources that hold historical media outputs
- identify the key performance indicators (KPIs) specifically relevant to the buyer's contract.

10.7.11 Organisational structure and key personnel

It is advisable to establish:

- the organisational structure of the company providing the goods or services
- the wider corporate structure and reporting accountabilities
- where procurement/supply chain fits into the structure
- the key personnel who will be accountable for delivering the contract and their operational base
- if the supplier is a multinational, who does the CEO (UK) report to?

10.7.12 Sub-contracting – proposed actions

The nature and extent of the supplier's sub-contracting can have a great impact on contract performance; hence it is advisable to ascertain:

- Will sub-contracting take place?
- What is the extent and nature of sub-contracting – value and specific goods/services?
- What due diligence is carried out on sub-contractors and how are they appointed?

- What specific contract terms and conditions are used?
- Will the buying organisation's contract key clauses be flowed down to sub-contractors, e.g. right of audit, insurance, liability and reporting?

10.7.13 Procurement supply chain management capabilities

It is very surprising that these facets are rarely the subject of pre-qualification questionnaires (PQQs) – they should be!

As a minimum, the following questions should be answered:

- Is there a well-established procurement function?
- Who is the head of the function and who do they report to?
- How is the function organised, e.g. category management?
- How will they manage costs throughout the supply cycle?
- Who is accountable for supply chain performance?
- What are the perceived procurement risks?
- How will these risks be mitigated?
- What accountability do they have for achieving continuous improvement?

10.7.14 Obtaining information for supplier evaluation

This may be done by means of a tailored questionnaire, supplemented where appropriate by soft market testing and visits to the potential suppliers.

10.7.15 Appraisal questionnaires

The topics in sections 10.7.3 to 10.7.14 above can easily be adapted to include in a questionnaire. Some general principles relating to questionnaires should be remembered:

- Keep the appraisal questionnaire as short as is reasonably possible.
- Explain how the responses will be evaluated, particularly the scoring and weighting mechanism.
- Ask only what is necessary and obtain only information that will be used.
- Divide the various sections of the questionnaire into 'fields', each relating to a particular area of investigation, as in sections 10.7.3 to 10.7.14 above.
- Consider whether or not respondents will understand the wording of questions – are you using technical or cultural-specific words or abbreviations, for example.
- Ask only one question at a time.
- Start with factual and then go on to opinion-based questions.
- Ensure that the questionnaire is signed, dated and the title of the respondent is indicated.

10.7.16 Supplier visits

Supplier visits should always be undertaken by a cross-functional team that includes a senior member of procurement and specialists on quality and production engineering (or such disciplines as are relevant). Each member of the team is able to evaluate the supplier from a specialist viewpoint. This ensures shared responsibility for the decision to approve or reject a supplier. The purposes of a supplier visit include:

- confirmation of information accuracy provided by the supplier in response to the questionnaire
- an in-depth discussion of the products and services offered by the potential supplier and ways in which the supplier can contribute to the requirements of the buying organisation
- sight of manufacturing/service provision facilities and related quality management and I.T. Systems
- understanding what mobilisation actions will have to be taken prior to the supplier performing his obligations under the contract.

Prior to the visit, a checklist of matters to be reviewed should be prepared. This ensures that no important questions are overlooked, and it provides a permanent record of the visit and reasons for the decisions reached. On supplier visits, important sources of information will include observation and informal conversations. Particular attention should be given to the following areas.

- Personal attitudes – an observant visitor can sense the attitudes of the supplier's employees towards their work. This provides an indication of the likely quality of their output and service dependability. The state of morale will be evident from:
  - an atmosphere of harmony or dissatisfaction among the production workers
  - the degree of interest in customer service on the part of supervisory staff
  - the degree of energy displayed and the interest in getting things done
  - the use of manpower – whether economical, with everyone usually busy, or extravagant and costly, with excess people doing little or nothing.

- Adequacy and care of production equipment – close observation of the equipment in a manufacturing location will indicate whether it is:
  - modern or antiquated
  - accurately maintained or obviously in a state of disrepair
  - well cared for by operators or dirty and neglected
  - of proper size or type to produce the buyer's requirements
  - of sufficient capacity to produce the quantities desired.

- The presence or absence of ingenious self-developed mechanical devices for performing unusual operations will be indicative of the plant's manufacturing and engineering expertise.

- Technological know-how of supervisory personnel – conversations with senior supervisors, shop superintendents and others will indicate their technical knowledge and ability to control and improve the operations of processes under their supervision.

- Means of controlling quality – observation of the inspection methods will indicate their adequacy to ensure the specified quality of the product. Attention should be given to:
  - whether or not materials are chemically analysed and physically checked
  - frequency of inspection during the production cycle

    – employment of such techniques as statistical quality control

    – availability of statistical quality control.

■ Housekeeping – a plant that is orderly and clean in its general appearance indicates careful planning and control by management. Such a plant inspires confidence that its products will be made with the same care and pride as to their quality. The dangers of breakdown, fire or other disasters will also be minimised, with a consequent increased assurance of continuity of supply.

■ Competence of technical staff – conversations with design, research or laboratory staff indicate their knowledge of the latest materials, tools and processes relating to their products and anticipated developments in their industry.

■ Competence of management – all of the areas are, in essence, a reflection of management and, highlight its business qualities. Particularly in the case of a new supplier, an accurate appraisal of executive personnel is of paramount importance.

10.8 Supplier approval

Supplier approval is the recognition, following a process of appraisal, that a particular supplier can meet the standards and requirements of the specific procurement whether that be a specific 'item' or a category of expenditure.

There are three important aspects of approved supplier lists:

1 the current emphasis is on having a small supplier base and so additions to an approved list must be carefully controlled

2 the supplier's application to be placed on an approved list should be considered fairly and, as far as possible with the minimum of bureaucracy

3 directives such as those of the EU have reservations about whether or not approved lists invalidate the EU principles of transparency, equality of treatment, proportionality and mutual recognition. In this context, Framework Agreements represent an approved list.

Approval should be decided by a cross-functional team that may give various levels of approval, such as A for unconditional, B for conditional subject to the potential supplier meeting prescribed conditions or C for unsuitable for approval.

Airbus[10] on 1 November 2018 published the Airbus Approval Suppliers List. It contained 171 pages and included the Product Group for which an approved supplier had prequalified.

Approved suppliers may also be graded into such categories as:[11]

1 *partnership* – a one-to-one relationship with a supplier in which a corporate single-source agreement will be in place

2 *preferred* – there is an agreed number of suppliers for one product or service with a corporate agreement

3 *approved suppliers* – suppliers have been assessed as satisfactory suppliers for one or more products or services

4 *confirmed suppliers* – those that have been specifically requested by a user, such as design or production, and accepted by procurement – the acceptance process being:

    (a) no preferred, partnership or approved supplier is on the procurement database for an identical requirement

    (b) there will not be a continuing demand on the supplier

5 *one-off supplier* – suppliers in this category are accepted on the following conditions:

(a) no preferred, partnership or approved supplier is on the procurement database for identical goods or services

(b) procurement card payment is not appropriate or possible

(c) supplier will be closed after the transaction is complete.

In general, approval in the first instance should be for one year. Suppliers that consistently meet or exceed the prescribed performance standards over a period of, say, three years may be upgraded from 'approved' to 'preferred'. Conversely, suppliers that fail to meet performance standards should be removed from the database of approved suppliers.

10.9 Evaluating supplier performance

10.9.1 Why evaluate supplier performance?

There are many business reasons why the evaluation of supplier performance is necessary and important.

- Evaluation and its feedback can significantly improve supplier performance. Emptoris[12] states that, properly done, supplier performance management can provide answers to questions such as the following:
  - Who are our highest-quality suppliers?
  - What sets them apart from the other suppliers?
  - How can relationships with the best suppliers be enhanced?
  - How can supplier performance be incorporated into total cost analysis?
  - How can buyers ensure that suppliers live up to what was promised?
  - How should feedback to suppliers be shared based on experience with the supplier?
  - How can underperforming suppliers' problems be tracked and fixed?
- Evaluation assists decision making whether a supplier is retained or removed from an approved list.
- Evaluation assists in deciding with which suppliers a specific purchase order/contract should be placed.
- Evaluation provides suppliers with an incentive for continuous improvement and prevents performance 'slippage'.
- Evaluation can assist in decisions regarding how to distribute the spend for an item among several suppliers to better manage risk.

10.9.2 What to evaluate?

Traditionally, the KPIs for the evaluation of supplier performance have been price, quality and delivery. While these are still basic to supplier evaluation, such developments as JIT, lean manufacturing, integrated supply chains and e-procurement have made a more comprehensive evaluation of supplier relationships an important consideration.

Such relationships, as Kozak and Cohen[13] point out, include such qualitative factors as intercompany communication and high levels of trust, which are not easy to assess other than subjectively. Apart from subjectivity, qualitative evaluations are often subject to 'halo effects' – the tendency to bias scoring in favour of a particular supplier due to irrelevant considerations, such as the friendly approach of its sales representatives. There is, however, an element of subjectivity in all evaluation systems.

The number of KPIs that may be used is almost limitless. A USA survey by Simpson et al.[14] reported 142 evaluation items, which they arranged under 19 categories of criteria, the first 10 of which are shown in Table 10.2.

The researchers concluded that, on the basis of these criteria, suppliers should concentrate on quality issues first – especially the ability to meet customers' order requirements – followed by continuous improvement and innovation efforts. Importantly, while not completely ignoring pricing issues, suppliers may want to place less emphasis on price when attempting to secure and retain customers.

10.9.3 Quantitative approaches to supplier evaluation

The aim of quantitative ratings is to provide a sounder basis for evaluation than subjective ratings. There are a number of considerations, including:

■ determining what can be quantified – there are the obvious candidates, including, deliveries on time, quality defects (perhaps graded according to severity and impact on the buyer's business), response times for resolving queries, fault correction times (IT software support), resolution of disputes and timely delivery of IT consumables

■ the cost and ability to collect the relevant data on which ratings are based, recognising that there are now software programmes to facilitate this – depending on the nature of the buyer's business the ratings can be provided at specified intervals

■ ratings are no more accurate than the assumptions on which they are based

■ a recognition that the supplier's performance can be adversely affected by the buyer's or third-party actions.

Table 10.2 Supplier evaluation factors considered by relative frequency of mention and importance (Simpson et al.[15]) – first ten factors only

Evaluation criteria	Number of items by category	Percentage mentioning	Relative importance rating
Quality and process control	566	24.9	1
Continuous improvement	210	9.2	2
Facility environment	188	8.2	2
Customer relationship	187	8.2	2
Delivery	185	8.1	2
Inventory and warehousing	158	7.0	2
Ordering	132	5.8	2
Financial conditions	126	5.5	2
Certifications	81	3.6	3
Price	81	3.6	3

10.9.4 Service level agreements

A service level agreement is 'a formal, negotiated document that defines (or attempts to define) in quantitative (and perhaps qualitative) terms the service being offered to a Customer'.[16] Confusion must be avoided whether the quantitative definitions constitute thresholds for an acceptable service, targets to which the supplier should aspire or expectations that the supplier should strive to exceed. Typically, a service level agreement will cover service hours, service availability, customer support levels, throughputs and responsiveness, restrictions, functionality and the service levels to be provided in a contingency.

10.9.5 The seven Cs of effective supplier evaluation

Many of the aspects of supplier appraisal are neatly summarised by Carter[17] as the 'seven Cs of supplier evaluation':

1 *Competency* of the supplier to undertake the tasks required
2 *Capacity* of the supplier to meet the purchaser's total needs
3 *Commitment* of the supplier to the customer in terms of quality, cost driving and service
4 *Control systems* in relation to inventory, costs, budgets, people and information
5 *Cash resources and financial stability* ensuring that the selected supplier is financially sound and is able to continue in business into the foreseeable future
6 *Cost* commensurate with quality and service
7 *Consistency* – the ability of the supplier to deliver consistently and, where possible, improve levels of quality and service.

10.9.6 Evaluation of supplier performance – a case study

Fredriksson and Gadde[18] have published a 'Competitive Paper' which reviews the literature on supplier evaluation, presents a case study illustrating the evaluation of the performance of a car manufacturer's suppliers and a discussion on the findings and implications of the case study.

Table 10.3 shows the Volvo perspective when evaluating a module supplier and its performance. It shows the use of a number of different evaluation dimensions, criteria, scope, time horizons and methods. Consequently, people with different expertise in several departments are involved in the evaluation of the supplier's performance.

Table 10.3 Volvo evaluation model

Dimensions, criteria and scopes	Frequency (time horizon)	Method (quant = quantitative qual = qualitative)	People involved (department)
Module quality performance			
■ Function, geometry, looks and noise module features at and after the line	1 time/minute	Formal, quant. and qual.	Assembly operators (Assembly) QA engineers (Assembly) SQA engineers (Logistics)
■ Quality processes and structures	When quality	Semi-formal, quant.	SQA engineer (Logistics)
– inside module supplier	defects occur	and qual.	Assembly managers (Assembly)
– on its supply side	1–2 times/2 years	Formal	SQA engineer (Logistics)
– in interaction with Volvo	(future oriented)		Procurement engineer (Procurement)

Table 10.3 *Continued*

Dimensions, criteria and scopes	Frequency (time horizon)	Method (quant = quantitative qual = qualitative)	People involved (department)
■ **Delivery precision performance**			
■ Module carrier on time at loading dock	1–2 times/hour	Formal, quant.	Delivery controller (Logistics)
■ Modules in right box in carrier at line	1 time/minute	Formal, quant.	Assembly operator (Assembly)
■ No. of restrictions in Volvo's plans	On occurrence	Formal, quant.	Delivery controller (Logistics)
■ Logistics processes and structure	When delivery	Semi-formal, quant.	Delivery controller (Logistics)
– inside module supplier	deviations occur	and qual.	Delivery controller (Logistics)
– on its supply side	1–2 times/2 years	Formal, quant. and	Logistics engineer (Procurement)
– in interaction with Volvo	(future oriented)	qual.	
■ **Cost performance**			
■ Module price	>1 time/year	Formal, quant.	Purchaser (Procurement)
■ Processes and structures	(future oriented)		Supplier park manager
– inside module supplier and its suppliers			(Procurement)
– in interaction with Volvo			
– contribution to supplier park			
■ Logistics costs	Varying, but about	Formal, quant. and	Logistics engineer (Logistics)
– processes and structures in relation to the total logistics system	1–2 times/year (future oriented)	qual.	
Overall performance			
■ Quality	■ Management	>1 time/2–4 years	Semi-formal, quantitative
■ Delivery	■ Supply	(future oriented)	
■ Cost	management		
	■ Environment		

10.10 Policy issues in sourcing

There are numerous aspects of sourcing policy and strategy, but ten of the main ones considered in this chapter are shown in Figure 10.3.

Figure 10.3 **Aspects of sourcing policy and strategy**

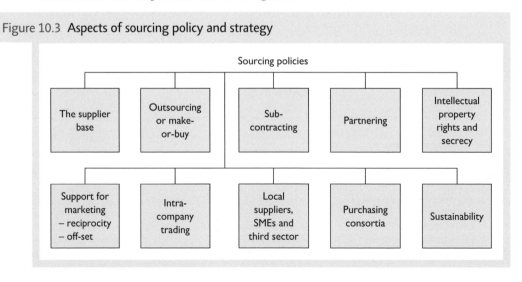

10.11 The supplier base

10.11.1 What is the supplier base?

The supplier base relates to the number, range, location and characteristics of the vendors that supply the purchaser.

Supplier bases may be described as broad, lean, narrow, single-sourced, local, national, international, diversified or specialised. They can relate to a 'family' or related products and suppliers or the totality of vendors with whom a purchaser does business.

Factors influencing the supply base of an enterprise include:

- the range of purchases including goods and services
- the core competencies of the buying organisation
- investment requirements in product/service long-term capacity
- supply chain risks
- inventory investment
- ability to respond to emergencies and changing market conditions
- short-term procurement actions or long-term partnering
- miscellaneous factors such as the social responsibilities to local industry or support of SMEs and third sector
- customer preference
- offset requirements stipulated in buying organisation's contract with third party.

10.11.2 Supplier base optimisation

Supplier base optimisation or rationalisation is concerned with determining a strategy that will identify the optimum number of suppliers required to fulfil the requirements to supply all procurement categories.

In some organisations there are too many suppliers who are awarded business in an ad hoc manner. The need for rationalisation includes:

- focusing purchases on a limited number of competent and cost-effective suppliers
- requirement to control cost and procurement processes
- generate confidence for suppliers to make long-term investments
- encourage innovation and continuous improvement
- enhance the availability of meaningful management information
- optimise risks in the supply chain.

There are a number of approaches that can be adopted to achieve supplier base optimisation, including:

- electing for a single or dual source of supply
- an approved or preferred supplier list
- outsourcing a range of services thereby eliminating individual suppliers to the services
- redesign of products to reduce reliance on those owning previous IPRs
- aggregating purchases with other buyers to make quantity feasible to larger suppliers.

10.11.3 Possible risks of a reduced supplier base

These include:

- complacency among suppliers resulting in repetitive actions cutting out innovation
- reduced competition in the supply market
- exit of marginal supplier reducing available capacity
- threats to supply arising from force majeure events
- lack of knowledge of supply market developments and market intelligence
- Inflexibility in contractual obligations.

10.12 Outsourcing

10.12.1 Outsourcing definition

Oxford Economics[19] defined outsourcing as, 'The supply of services governed by an ongoing or time-specific agreement involving a degree of delegation of management responsibility, where that service would more typically be provided, or would in the past (UK 1950s–2000s) have been more typically provided, by an in-house team of the customer themselves.'

10.12.2 Outsourcing – a critique

Outsourcing has a chequered history. There have been successes and failures. The greater visibility of the public sector has ensured that outsourcing 'disasters' are well publicised. The UK Committee of Public Accounts[20] published a very informative report. Their summary is shown below:

> NHS England's outsourcing of primary care support services to Capita Business Services Ltd (Capita) was a shambles. Its short-sighted rush to slash by a third the £90 million it cost to provide these services was heedless of the impact it would have on the 39,000 GPs, dentists, opticians and pharmacists affected. Capita recognises that the service it provided was not good enough. Its failures have not only been disruptive to thousands of GPs, dentists, opticians and pharmacists, but potentially have also put patients at risk of serious harm. We acknowledge that Capita has now apologised for its mistakes and will hold it to its commitment to improve services over the remaining life of the contract.

Neither NHS England nor Capita understood the service that was being outsourced, and both misjudged the scale and nature of the risks. They ignored many of the basic rules of contracting, and, once problems emerged, did not do enough to stop the issues from getting worse. Rather than focusing on improving the service, NHS England and Capita have spent too long disputing basic elements of the contract and are still in disagreement over future payments. It is clear that NHS England ignored the many lessons this Committee has constantly highlighted about how to outsource effectively and benefit both users and taxpayers.

We replicate some detail from the report to highlight outsourcing matters that typically can be transferred as learning to other outsourcing decisions.

- NHS England focused on maximising financial savings quickly, at the expenses of service quality.

- NHS England paid only lip service to engagement with doctors, dentists, opticians and pharmacist on service changes.
- Performance indicators did not cover all the services that Capita was required to deliver and were not agreed from the start of the contract.
- There was poor data on the volume, cost and performance of services and not enough was known about how local services were working and in particular what was working well, which could have informed the transformation.
- Stakeholders also raised concerns about: missed and inaccurate payments to practitioners; backlogs of half a million patient registration letters; market entry delays for pharmacists; failures to deliver NHS stationery and medical supplies; and poor service from the customer support centre.
- The office closures resulted in the loss of local expertise and meant Capita did not have the resources needed to deliver the services required. NHS did not have the contractual mechanisms to stop Capita going ahead with its plans.
- However, some two and a half years into the contract, basic elements of the contract between NHS England and Capita are still not agreed.

The National Audit Office[21] has also published a report on the Capita contract.

10.12.3 Services that are outsourced

The range of services that can be outsourced is almost limitless. Those listed below represent some of the possibilities:

- IT and data-related services
- catering (food services management)
- combined facilities management
- property services/maintenance/cleaning
- property portfolio/real estate management
- security services
- warehousing/storage
- employment placement/agency activities
- call centre operations/customer care
- other office/administrative support services
- business consultancy/advisory services
- technical/engineering/scientific services
- waste management
- educational services
- health-related services
- residential care and social work
- procurement
- legal services
- travel.

10.12.4 Outsourcing procurement

Organisations may consider outsourcing procurement in the following circumstances:

- where procurement is a peripheral rather than a core activity. The characteristics of peripheral work, as identified by Atkinson and Meager,[22] are that it has:

  - low or generalised skill requirements
  - internally focused responsibilities
  - well-defined or limited tasks
  - jobs that are easily separated from other work
  - no supply restrictions.

- These are also the characteristics of low-level operational procurement. Beauchamp[23] also identified the following items as suitable for outsourcing consideration:

  - purchase orders, one-off and repeat needs
  - locally and nationally procured needs (international sourcing and procurement may be rather specialised for outsourcing)
  - low-value or low-value/large order acquisitions
  - brand name requirements
  - call-offs against internally approved agreements
  - set-up of commodity-based or service-based contracts
  - obtaining goods for batch or volume manufacturing
  - stocking and providing for private-sector or public-sector needs
  - computerised procurement or software-based manufacturing procurement
  - all administration and paperwork associated with procurement needs
  - supply of stores staff at varying levels of skill
  - multidimensional and multidepartmental sourcing.

- Where the supply base is small and based on proven cooperation and there are no supply restrictions, the following may be outsourced:

  - well-defined or limited tasks
  - jobs that are easily separated from other work
  - jobs that have no supply restrictions.

- The above characteristics also apply to low-level operational procurement.
- Where there is a small supplier base providing non-strategic, non-critical, low-cost/low-risk items. In such cases, procurement may be outsourced to:

  - specialist procurement and supplies organisations
  - buying consortia.

- Such organisations provide the advantage of:

  - bulk procurement, giving them a strong negotiating position over a wide range of products.

10.12.5 Drivers of outsourcing

Beulen et al.[24] suggest that there are five main drivers for outsourcing:

1 *Quality* – actual capacity is temporarily insufficient to comply with demand. The quality motive can be subdivided into three aspects: increased quality demands, shortage of qualified personnel, outsourcing as a transition period.

2 *Cost* – outsourcing is a possible solution to increasing costs and is compatible with a cost leadership strategy. By controlling and decreasing costs, a company can increase its competitive position.

3 *Finance* – a company has a limited investment budget. The funds must be used for investments in core business activities, which are long-term decisions.

4 *Core business* – a core business is a primary activity that enables an organisation to generate revenues. To concentrate on core business activities is a strategic decision. All subsequent activities are mainly supportive and should be outsourced.

5 *Cooperation* – cooperation between companies can lead to conflict. In order to avoid such conflict, those activities that are produced by both organisations should be subject to total outsourcing.

A further factor is that of human resource management. The internal culture and attitude of employees may result in strong trade union and internal opposition to the introduction of necessary changes in work processes and restructuring. Such changes may also require the acquisition of new employee skills. Outsourcing may avoid conflicts and provide expertise and experience within a matter of days to fill gaps for which recruitment and training would take some time.

Monczka[25] observes that, historically, outsourcing decisions have been limited to decisions about a particular outsource instead of the more holistic approach of asking 'Looking at the entire supply chain, who would be doing what?'

10.12.6 Types of outsourcing

In relation to IT, Lacity and Hirscheim[26] provide taxonomy of outsourcing options categorised as body shop, project management and total outsourcing.

■ *Body shop outsourcing* is a situation where management uses outsourcing as a means of meeting short-term requirements, such as a shortage of in-house skills to meet a temporary demand.

■ *Project management outsourcing* is employed for all or part of a particular project, such as developing a new IT project, training in new skills, management consultancy.

■ *Total outsourcing* is where the outsourcing supplier is given full responsibility for a selected area, such as catering, security.

10.12.7 Benefits of outsourcing

There is a range of benefits from outsourcing. These benefits depend on the nature of the outsourcing and may include:

■ obtaining immediate investment which is recovered over the long term

■ accessing an ICT infrastructure that is 'state-of-the-art'

- reduced costs in excess of 10 per cent on historical service costs
- reduced staffing levels achieved through efficiency and use of systems
- freeing senior management time to concentrate on core business
- higher levels of service performance generating greater customer satisfaction
- agreed supplier commitments to achieve higher performance levels
- accessing proven technical and commercial world-class practice.

10.12.8 Problems of outsourcing

Outsourcing is not, however, without its problems. It can be up to two years before an organisation begins to benefit from any savings and in some cases the whole process is cost neutral.

Perkins[27] reports that an informal survey of his clients showed that:

> By the end of the first year, more than 50 per cent of the companies that have outsourced major IT functions are unhappy with their outsourcers . . . By the end of the second year 70 per cent are unhappy.

Other surveys relating to aspects of outsourcing have shown that between 30 and 50 per cent of executives are disappointed with the results of outsourcing. Problems reported include:

- overdependence on suppliers
- cost escalation
- lack of supplier flexibility
- lack of management skills to control suppliers
- unrealistic expectations of outsourcing providers due to over-promising at the negotiations stage.

Reilly and Tamkin[28] mention that a principal objection to outsourcing is the possible loss of competitive advantage, particularly in the loss of skills and expertise of staff, insufficient internal investment and the passing of knowledge and expertise to the supplier, which may be able to seize the initiative.

Lacity and Hirscheim[29] also point out that outsourcing does not seem to work well in the following areas:

- where a specific or unique knowledge of the business is required
- where all services are customised
- where the employee culture is too fragmented or hostile for the organisation to come back together.

Problems reported in relation to outsourced suppliers include:

- high staff turnover
- poor project management skills
- lack of commitment to the client or industry
- shallow expertise
- insufficient documentation

- lack of control over larger suppliers
- poor staff training
- complacency over time
- divergent interests of the customer and provider
- cultural mismatches between customer and provider organisations.

10.12.9 Handling an outsourcing project

The practice will differ between the public and private sectors. In the former case there is the probability that the value of the project, typically a ten-year period, will exceed the threshold for advertising under EU Procurement Directives. Outsourcing and the creation of a Public–Private Partnership (PPP) can take, in the public sector, up to 18 months from start to contract signature. The cost of such an exercise must not be under-estimated. Costs in excess of £500K are not unusual when outsourcing back-office services.

The following steps will need to be considered, some taking place simultaneously.

1 Set up a project steering group to:
   - decide the scope of services to be outsourced
   - consider soft market testing
   - determine the strategic reasons for outsourcing
   - record the desired outcomes including cost reduction
   - evaluate potential risks
   - commence an effective staff consultation and communication protocol
   - determine what external support will be required, e.g. procurement and legal.
2 Issue a comprehensive pre-qualification questionnaire (PQQ) for completion by interested parties.
3 Commence preparation of:
   - service specifications
   - cost model and affordability envelope
   - invitation to tender documentation (may be referred to in the public sector as 'invitation to participate in a competitive dialogue')
   - the terms and conditions of contract and outline of schedules to the contract.
4 Evaluate responses to the PQQ:
   - using pre-determined evaluation criteria and weightings
   - having respondents make a presentation on key facets
   - creating a short-list of potential suppliers.
5 Continue with essential actions, including:
   - identifying contracts for novation
   - prepare licence to occupy building or lease agreement
   - risk register and mitigation strategies
   - maintain the project plan.

6 Issue invitation to tender.

7 Evaluate responses to the tender

- use pre-determined evaluation criteria and weightings

- seek clarification on all matters of uncertainty.

8 Short-list the preferred supplier and appoint reserve bidder in case the negotiations break down.

9 Engage in post-tender negotiations (or clarification and fine tuning using the competitive dialogue) and finalise contract terms and schedules. This may include:

- finalising staff transfer arrangements including pensions

- applying damages for contractual non-performance

- confirming investment

- finalising the mobilisation and transformation phases

- novation of contracts

- partnering and operational boards terms of reference

- provision of performance bond or parent company guarantee

- transfer of assets

- rights of termination.

10 Make recommendations to award contract or not to proceed if the deal is wrong.

11 Award contract.

12 Commence contract management activity.

13 Conduct lessons learned from the project.

10.12.10 Mitigation and managing outsourcing risks

The Central Bank of Ireland ('Central Bank')[30] recommends that the Board of Directors and senior management of firms consider the following questions as they assess their outsourcing oversight:

- **Monitoring:** Does the firm have appropriate KPIs and monitoring tools that are properly aligned to the outsourced activity and embedded in the risk framework?

- **Reporting:** Is the reporting on the performance of the outsourcing provider, including Board reporting, sufficiently detailed and does the frequency of reporting correspond to the criticality of the outsourced activity?

- **Appraisal:** Is the Board satisfied that the initial due diligence analysis on the outsourcing provider was suitably rigorous and that on going appraisals are equally thorough?

- **Business Continuity:** Does the firm have documented succession or remedial action plans in the case of disruption or termination of service and are these subject to robust testing on an ongoing basis?

- **Outsourcing Policy:** Does the firm's outsourcing policy take into account the entire life cycle of outsourcing?

These are very pertinent questions, the answers to which are not known to some Boards of Directors and senior managers.

10.13 Make vs buy

10.13.1 Types of make-or-buy decisions

Probert[31] identifies three levels of make-or-buy decisions.

Strategic make-or-buy decisions

Strategic make-or-buy decisions (see Figure 10.4) determine the shape and capability of the organisation's manufacturing operation by influencing:

- what products to make
- what investment to make in machines and labour to make the products
- ability to develop new products and processes as the knowledge and skills gained by manufacturing in-house may be critical for future applications
- the selection of suppliers as they may need to be involved in design and production processes.

Conversely, inappropriate allocation of work to suppliers may damage an enterprise by developing a new competitor or damaging product quality or performance, profit potential, risk and flexibility.

Strategic decisions also provide the framework for shorter-term tactical and component decisions.

Tactical make-or-buy decisions

These deal with the issue of a temporary imbalance of manufacturing capacity:

- changes in demand may make it impossible to make everything in-house, even though this is the preferred option
- conversely, a fall in demand may cause the enterprise to bring in-house work that was previously bought-out, if this can be done without damaging supplier relationships and without defaulting on a contract.

Figure 10.4 Decision processes for make or buy

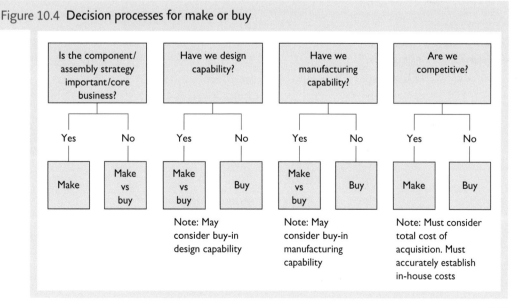

In such situations, managers require criteria for choosing between the available options. Such criteria may be quantitative, qualitative or both.

Component make-or-buy decisions

Component make-or-buy decisions are made, ideally, at the design stage and relate to whether a particular component of the product should be made in-house or bought-in.

10.13.2 Make-or-buy decision tree

A sample make-or-buy decisions tree (see Figure 10.5) is reproduced courtesy of AT Kearney Inc.[32]

The following case study[33] on make-or-buy decisions is extremely informative. It demonstrates the detailed cost analysis that is required in these circumstances.

This case study is based on a detailed study conducted at a medium size valve manufacturing company, located at Chakan in Pune district (Maharashtra) in the

Figure 10.5 A sample make-or-buy decision tree

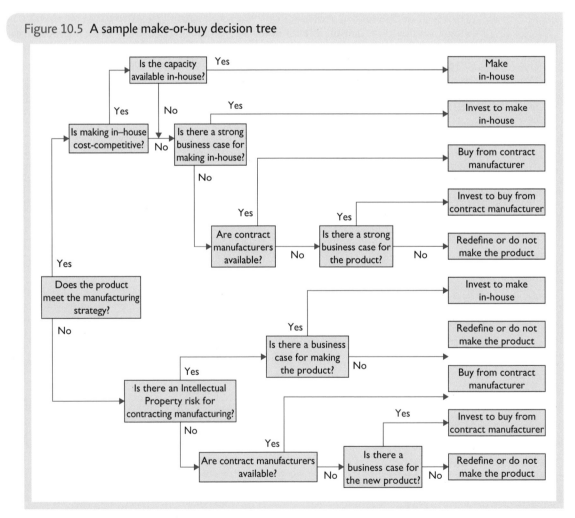

Source from: Make Vs Buy Revisited - AT Kearney Inc.

area of make-or-buy decisions. The study was conducted, with an object to evaluate and justify whether an adaptor part of 1a 6'#150 tunion plate valve actuator is to be make or outsource based on total cost approach. Tables 10.4a–10.4c show the

Table 10.4a Data for operation and time for a part

Part name	Operation	Machine	Cycle time	Setup time	Batch Qty	Total time
	Turning	CNC Turning DX 200	33.5	60	100	34.1
	Drilling	VMC 1000	40	80	100	40.8
Adaptor	Milling	HMC500	44	40	100	44.4
	Boring	HBM-China	20	120	100	21.2

Table 10.4b Data for operation and time for a part

	VMC1000	HMC500	CNC Turning DX 200	HBM – China
Machine basic cost	3,000,000	5,700,000	1,552,200	9,000,000
Area required sq. ft	400	500	150	700
Interest rate in %	16	16	16	16
Depreciation rate in %	10.3	10.3	10.3	10.3
Machine life	10 years	10 years	10 years	10 years
Rent in Rs. per sq. foot	16	16	16	16
Tooling cost (Avg)	12	60	18	60
Consumable (Avg)	4	4	4	4
Rent/hr.	13	16	5	22
Energy charge/hr.	40	25	25	100
Depreciation/hr.	48	91	25	112
Interest/hr.	80	152	41	240
Maintenance/hr.	10	10	10	10
Total	207	358	129	549
Overhead contribution of M/c cost to total cost of all M/c	6%	12%	3%	19%
Overheads in Rs/hr.	11	22	6	34

Table 10.4c Data for operation and time for a part

Overhead structure		For in-house manufacturing	
Position	No of position	Salary monthly (Rs)	Total salary (Rs)
Manager	1	40,000	40,000
Shop in-charge	1	22,000	22,000
Supervisor	2	17,000	34,000
Helper	3	6000	18,000
		TOTAL	96,000

operation performed, machine used, cycle time, setup time, batch quantity, total time for machining an adaptor part. In a company there are a total of nine different machines to machine the different parts of valve. The machines are used for a machining adaptor and other details are given in the tables for cost analysis. Operators rate monthly $[(\text{Rs.}900/26\,(\text{days}))/7\,(\text{hrs.})) = \text{Rs.}49/\text{hr.}]$

A similar cost analysis calculation has been done for collecting data from vendor as given in Table 10.5 below.

Table 10.5 Cost comparison between in-house manufacturing and from outside

Cost element	Make in-house	Outsource
Raw material cost	1242.00	1242.00
Labour cost (Total time × Rs/hr./pc)	115.00	89.00
Tooling cost (on machine)	82.00	92.00
Overheads		
i) Indirect labour (Σ(time on each m/c × overhead rate)	39.00	23.00
ii) Depreciation of M/c used (Σ(time on each m/c × depreciation rate)	154.00	170.00
iii) Interest (Σ(time on each m/c × interest rate/hr.)	275.00	294.00
iv) Cost of space used by m/c (Σ(time on each m/c × rent/hr.)	43.00	50.00
Variable overheads		
i) Consumables	9.00	6.00
ii) Electric charges (Σ(time on each m/c × Energy Charge/hr.)	92.00	118.00
iii) Maintenance	23.00	26.00
Purchase cost (Admin OH + Selling OH + Profit)		217.00
TOTAL	2063.00	2327.00

The part taken for case study was outsourced at Rs.2327/Pc. When the detailed in-house cost analysis was carried out it can be seen from Table 10.5 the cost of manufacturing in-house is less than outside hence the industry should go for in-house manufacturing.

10.13.3 Considerations in make-or-buy decisions

Apart from those mentioned above, a number of other quantitative and qualitative factors must be considered in deciding whether to make or buy.

Quantitative factors in favour of *making* include:

- chance to use up idle capacity and resources
- potential lead time reduction
- possibility of scrap utilisation
- greater procurement power with larger orders of a particular material
- large overhead recovery base
- exchange rate risks
- cost of work is known in advance.

Quantitative factors in favour of *buying* include:

- quantities required are too small for economic production
- avoidance of costs of specialist machinery or labour
- reduction in inventory.

Qualitative factors in favour of *making* include:

- ability to manage resources
- commercial and contractual advantages
- worries are eliminated regarding such matters as the stability and continuing viability of suppliers or possible repercussions of changes in supplier ownership
- maintaining secrecy and protecting competitive edge.

Qualitative factors in favour of *buying* include:

- spread of financial risk between purchaser and vendor
- ability to control quality when purchased from outside
- availability of supplier's specialist expertise, machinery and/or patents
- buying, in effect, augments the manufacturing capacity of the purchaser.

10.14 Sub-contracting

10.14.1 What is sub-contracting?

Sub-contracting may be distinguished from outsourcing in that the latter involves the total restructuring of an enterprise around core competences and relationships with the outsourcing provider. Whatever the degree of outsourcing, enterprises must retain certain core capabilities. Outsourcing is a strategic long-term decision. Sub-contracting is a tactical, short-term approach.

10.14.2 Reasons for sub-contracting

The buyer encounters problems that call for sub-contracting in two main areas:

- where the buyer's organisation is the employer or client entrusting work to a main contractor who, in turn, sub-contracts part of the work, which is the case with most construction contracts
- where the buyer's organisation is the main contractor and sub-contracts work for such reasons as:

    - overloading of machinery or labour
    - to ensure completion of work on time
    - lack of specialist machinery or specialist know-how
    - to avoid acquiring long-term capacity when future demand is uncertain
    - subcontracting is cheaper than manufacturing internally.

10.14.3 Organisation for sub-contracting

- When sub-contracting is a regular and significant part of the activity of an undertaking, it may be desirable to set up a special sub-contracting section within or external to the procurement department.
- Arrangements must be made for adequate liaison between all departments connected with sub-contracting – design, production control, construction and site staff, inspection, finance and so on.
- Friction over who should negotiate with the selected suppliers sometimes develops between procurement and design or technical departments. This can be avoided by a proper demarcation of authority and responsibility, procurement having a power of commercial veto, design and technical departments a technical veto.

10.14.4 Selection of sub-contractors

It may be necessary to check whether or not external approval of the selected sub-contractor is necessary, as in government contracts or where a specific sub-contractor has been specified by the client. Some construction contracts may provide that sub-contractors must not be selected on the basis of Dutch auctions.

10.14.5 Liaison with sub-contractors

Matters to be considered include the following:

- planning, to ensure that the sub-contractor can complete by the required date – techniques such as programme, evaluation and review techniques (PERT) are of assistance in this review
- ensuring that the sub-contractor is supplied with the most recent versions of all necessary documentation, including drawings, standards and planning instructions
- arranging with the sub-contractor for the supply, by the main contractor, of materials, tooling, specialist equipment and so on and the basis on which this shall be charged
- control of equipment and materials in the possession of sub-contractors

- arrangements for accountability at stocktaking of free issued materials in the possession of the sub-contractor
- arrangements for visits to the premises of the sub-contractor by progress and inspection staff employed by the main contractor
- arrangements for transportation, especially where items produced by the sub-contractor require special protection, such as components with a highly finished surface
- payment for any ancillary work to be performed by the sub-contractor, such as the painting on of part numbers.

10.14.6 Legal considerations

These will depend on the circumstances of the specific contract. All major contracts for sub-contracting should be vetted and approved by the legal department of the main contractor. Where the buyer's organisation is entrusting work to a main contractor, it is useful to remember the following generic principles.

Unless the contract has been placed on the basis – express or implied – that the work will be wholly performed by the main contractor, the client will have no authority to prevent the sub-contracting of part of the work (this will not apply to contracts for personal service). If, therefore, the client wishes to specify particular sub-contractors or to limit the right of the main contractor to sub-contract, these matters must be negotiated when the contract is agreed. With construction and defence contracts, tenderers are often required to state what parts of the work will be sub-contracted. In particular, it is useful to include contract clauses stating that it is the duty of the main contractor to use best endeavours in the selection of sub-contractors and that responsibility for the performance of these sub-contractors shall exclusively lie with the main contractor.

10.15 Partnering

10.15.1 Partnering and outsourcing

Humbert and Passarelli[34] point out that, at its highest level, outsourcing can take the form of an alliance akin to a partnership (but not a strict legal partnership) or joint venture. Not all outsourcing agreements, however, are partnerships. Humbert and Passarelli state that 'the terms "partnering" or "strategic alliance" should not be used to describe an outsourcing agreement unless the contract is structured to reflect a true relationship of strategic alliance'. The characteristics of such an alliance include close working relationships built on trust, communication and mutual dependency 'where both parties have a vested interest in reducing costs and achieving a favourable business outcome'. Where these conditions obtain, the provider's 'reward' is based on results or attaining objectives rather than being compensated.

When comparing partnering and outsourcing, it is therefore important to distinguish between:

- *different levels of outsourcing*: at the lower levels it will be purely transactional – only at the higher, strategic levels is outsourcing likely to merge into partnering
- *customer–supplier relationships and partnering*: in the former, the emphasis is primarily on cost minimisation, while with the latter the emphasis is additionally on value enhancement and the achievement of joint venture objectives

■ *the contractual differences between outsourcing and partnering*: with the former, the contract relates to clearly specified inputs and these are cost-based over a defined period of time, for which the supplier receives an agreed reward, whereas, as the CIPS[35] points out, because partnerships are based on trust, in theory no form of contractual documentation should be necessary, but it is still desirable that the parties should agree to a set of general guidelines to regulate the partnership, such as the 12 key areas identified by Partnering Sourcing Ltd:[36]

■ general statement of principle

■ scope – what the partnership encompasses

■ costs

■ customer service levels

■ business forecasts

■ technological development strategies

■ continuous improvement policy

■ annual performance objectives

■ mutual assistance to resolve any problems that may arise

■ open book cost structures

■ minimising material costs

■ joint decisions on capital investment projects.

(Two important omissions from the above list are those relating to intellectual property rights and ownership of patents.)

10.15.2 What is partnering?

The need for a broad approach to the concept of partnering is also recognised by Partnership Sourcing Ltd, which defines partnering as:

> A commitment to both customers and suppliers, regardless of size, to a long-term relationship based on clear, mutually agreed objectives to strive for world class capability.

There may, however, be degrees of partnership. Lambert et al.,[37] for example, distinguish between:

■ *type I partnerships* involving organisations that recognise each other as partners and, on a limited basis, coordinate activities and planning – such partnerships generally have a short-term focus and involve only a few areas within each organisation

■ *type II partnerships* involving organisations that have progressed beyond coordination to integration of activities – such partnerships have a longer-term view of the partnership and involve multiple areas within both firms

■ *type III partnerships* involving organisations sharing a significant level of operational and strategic integration – in particular, each partner can make changes to the other's systems without getting approval and such partnerships are of long-term duration with no end in sight, each party viewing the other as an extension of its own firm.

As Knemeyer et al.[38] state:

> The three types of partnership reflect increased strength, long-term orientation and level of involvement between parties . . . No particular type of partnership is better or worse than

Table 10.6 Comparison of traditional and partnering supplier relationships

Traditional	Partnership
Emphasises competitiveness and self-interest on the part of both purchaser and supplier	Emphasises cooperation and a community of interest between purchaser and supplier
Emphasis on 'unit price' with lowest price usually the most important buyer consideration	Emphasis on total acquisition costs (TAC), including indirect and hidden costs, such as production hold-ups and loss of customer goodwill due to late delivery of materials and components. Lowest price is never the sole buyer consideration
Emphasis is on short-term business relationships	Emphasis on long-term business relationships with involvement of supplier at the earliest possible stage to discuss how the buyer's requirements can be met
Emphasis on quality checks, with inspection of incoming supplies	Emphasis on quality assurance based on total quality management and zero defects
Emphasis on multiple sourcing	Emphasis on single sourcing, although it is not, of necessity, confined to single sourcing. It will, however, reduce the supplier base
Emphasis on uncertainty regarding supplier performance and integrity	Emphasis on mutual trust between purchaser and supplier

any other. The key is to try to obtain the type of relationship that is most appropriate given the business situation.

Partnering marks a shift from traditional pressures exerted by larger customers on small and medium-sized suppliers in which the latter were regarded as subordinates. Partnering aims to transform short-term adversarial customer–supplier relationships focused on the use of procurement power to secure lower prices and improved delivery into long-term cooperation based on mutual trust in which quality, innovation and shared values complement price competitiveness.

Some comparisons between traditional and partnering relationships are shown in Table 10.6.

10.15.3 The drivers of partnership sourcing

Some of the main drivers for partnerships have been summarised by Southey[39] as:

- drive for lowest acquisition cost:
  - not only price, but all 'cost in use' elements, such as the benefits or exposure derived from actual product quality, delivery performance and the administration burden.
- reduction in supplier base:
  - need to reduce the supplier base to a number that can be managed effectively.

- shortening of product lifecycles:
  - need for faster response times
  - need for suppliers to be right first time
  - need for supplier involvement from day 1.
- concentration on core business:
  - where most value can be added
  - where distinctive competences exist
  - avoiding unnecessary capital expenditure.
- competitive pressures towards 'lean' supply:
  - competition creating fewer, more technologically sophisticated suppliers that have to collaborate more closely with their customers
  - earlier involvement of predetermined suppliers for development of each individual component
  - pressure on inventory, forcing closer matching customer–supplier output levels and systems
  - need to optimise all linkages in the supply chain network (both internal and external).
- adoption of 'best practices', creating dependence:
  - reduced system slack from TQM, JIT and EDI, creating greater dependence on suppliers
  - more dependency requiring forging of stronger supplier relationships
  - more dependency requiring closer integration of people, plans and systems, both internally and externally.

Southey states that customers enter into partnership sourcing arrangements because of their business-driven need to maximise competitive advantage. They see the benefits of partnering as being that it provides:

- a win–win scenario
- supply chain security
- close working relationships (arms around vs arm's length)
- a route to joint technological development
- the ability to extend total continuous improvement (TCI) culture to critical suppliers
- improved profit contribution (or reduced profit exposure).

10.15.4 What types of relationships are suitable for partnering?

Partnership Sourcing Ltd[40] has identified seven types of relationships that may be suitable for partnership:

- *high spend* – 'the vital few'
- *high risk* – items and services that are vital irrespective of their monetary value

- *high hassle* – vital supplies that are technically complicated to arrange and take a lot of time, effort and resources to manage
- *new services* – new products or services that may involve possible partners
- *technically complicated* – involving technically advanced or innovative supplies where the cost of switching would be prohibitive
- *fast-changing* – areas where knowing future technology or trends or legislation is critical
- *restricted markets* – markets that have few reliable or competent suppliers where closer links with existing or new suppliers might improve supply security.

10.15.5 Advantages of partnering

These are set out in Example 10.1 and Table 10.7.

10.15.6 Implementing partnership sourcing

1 *Identify purchased items potentially suitable for partnership sourcing* such as:

- high-spend items and suppliers – Pareto analysis may show that a small number of suppliers account for a high proportion of total spend
- critical items where the cost of supplier failure would be high

---

Example 10.1

Benefits of partnering

A survey conducted by Partnership Sourcing Ltd in 1995 reported the following benefits (percentages are of those undertakings responding to the survey):

reduced cost	75.5 per cent
reduced inventory	72.9 per cent
increased quality	70.3 per cent
enhanced security of supply	69.4 per cent
reduced product development times	58.4 per cent

Partnership Sourcing Ltd[41] mentions the following important issues:

- ascertain your most important supplies by spend and criticality or customers by turnover and profit
- whether the potential partner is much bigger or much smaller than the enterprise, initiating the partnership is relatively important – small undertakings are more responsive and flexible; larger ones may have better systems
- a potential partner may already have some experience of building partnership relationships and such a company is worth targeting
- that potential partners recognise that:
  - the business of the enterprise seeking to initiate the partnership is important to them
  - there is scope for improvement in the product or service received – in short, that partnering offers potential rewards.

Table 10.7 **Advantages of partnering**

To the purchaser	To the supplier
Procurement advantage resulting from quality assurance, reduced supplier base, assured supplies due to long-term agreements, ability to plan long-term improvement, rather than negotiating for short-term advantage, delivery on time (JIT), improved quality	*Marketing advantage* resulting from stability due to long-term agreements, larger share of orders placed, ability to plan ahead and invest, ability to work with key customers on products and/or services, scope to increase sales without increasing procurement overheads
Lower costs resulting from cooperative cost-reduction programmes, such as EDI, supplier's participation in new designs, lower inventory due to better production availability, improved logistics, reduced handling, reduced number of outstanding orders	*Lower costs* resulting from cooperative cost-reduction programmes, participation in customer's design, lower inventory due to better customer planning, improved logistics, simplification or elimination of processes, payment on time
Strategic advantage resulting from access to supplier's technology, a supplier who invests, shared problem-solving and management	*Strategic advantage* resulting from access to customer's technology, a customer that recognises the need to invest, shared problem-solving and management

- complicated items involving technical and innovative supplies where the cost of switching sources would be prohibitive
- 'new buy' items where supplier involvement in design and production methods is desirable from the outset.

2 *Sell the philosophy of partnership sourcing* to:

- top management – demonstrating how partnership sourcing can improve quality, service and total costs throughout the organisation
- other functions likely to be involved, such as accounting (will need to make prompt payments), design (will need to involve suppliers from the outset), production (will need to schedule supply requirements and changes)
- stress the advantages in section 10.15.5 above.

3 *Define standards that potential suppliers will be required to meet*; these will include:

- a commitment to TQM
- ISO 9000 certification or equivalent
- existing implementation of or willingness to implement appropriate techniques, such as JIT, EDI and so on
- in-house design capability
- ability to supply locally or worldwide as required
- consistent performance standards regarding quality and delivery
- willingness to innovate
- willingness to change, flexibility in management and workforce attitudes.

Partnership Sourcing Ltd[42] state:

> Remember that people are key. It is people who build trust and make relationships work. Are the people right? Is the chemistry right?
>
> Partnership is two-way: if one of your customers was evaluating your business on the same criteria that you are using on suppliers, would you qualify? If not, perhaps you should think again about your minimum entry standards.

4 *Select one or a few suppliers as potential suppliers* – do not attempt to launch too many partnerships at once as a by-product of partnering is that a customer will be giving more attention to fewer suppliers, focusing available time where it will most benefit some issues.

5 *Sell the idea of partnering to the selected suppliers* – stress the advantages in section 10.15.5 above.

6 *If a commitment to partnership sourcing is achieved, determine on the basis of joint consultation what both parties want from the partnership* and:

- decide common objectives, such as:
  - reduction in total costs
  - adoption of TQM
  - zero defects
  - on-time payment
  - JIT or on-time deliveries
  - joint research and development
  - implementation of EDI
  - reduction or elimination of stocks
- agree performance criteria for measuring progress towards objectives, such as:
  - failure in production or with end-users
  - service response time
  - on-time deliveries
  - stock value
  - lead time and stability
  - service levels
- agree administrative procedures:
  - set up a steering group to review progress and ensure development
  - set up problem-solving teams to tackle particular issues
  - arrange regular meetings at all levels with senior management steering the process
- formalise the partnership, which should be on the basis of:
  - a simple agreement
  - a simplified legal contract.

7 *Review and audit the pilot project* by:

- reviewing against objectives
- quantifying the gains to the business as a whole
- reporting back to senior management on what has been achieved.

8 *Extend the existing partnership* by:

- extending existing agreements
- committing to longer agreements
- getting involved in joint strategic planning.

9 *Develop new partners for the future.*

10.15.7 Effective partnering

In the Crown publication, *Effective partnering*,[43] an overview for customers and suppliers, there is a useful checklist for an SRO to consider whether a partnering arrangement would be a good way of meeting the business need.

- What kind of relationship does the business need suggest? Would partnering be appropriate? If so, then why? Is our organisation ready to work with a provider on a partnering basis?
- Do we have the leadership, skills and capability to make it work? What is our track record in building partnering relationships (if any)?
- Could existing relationships, ours or those of other organisations, act as models or exemplars for what we are planning?
- Can we define success in building this relationship, and then set targets, milestones and measures that will enable us to assess how successful we have been in creating it?
- Assuming the relationship can be created successfully; will users and stakeholders 'sign up' to it and add momentum to its development?
- What kind of provider could manage the risks we envisage allocating them? Realistically, would a provider be willing to take them on and can we give them sufficient control so that they can manage them?
- How do we think the provider community would view a partnering approach to meet this requirement?

The advice continues that the unique features of partnering are integrated into the business case.

- Do we still think that partnering is the right way forward for this project? If so, does the business case for the project include the explicit requirement for a partnering arrangement, and justify the approach in terms of business need?
- Are partnering aspects genuinely integral to the business case, or do they appear to be 'bolted on'? Has successful partnering, or a good working relationship, been identified as a critical success factor? If not, why not?
- Does the business case take account of the additional investment (in relationship management etc.) that a partnering arrangement will require, compared to traditional procurement?
- Does the business case take account of any changes in approach or behaviour that your organisation will need to make in order for partnering to work?
- What are the views of the likely providers on partnering and the key features they see as critical to success?
- Are outline plans in place for how risks should be allocated between the partners?

Figure 10.6 Essential features of partnering

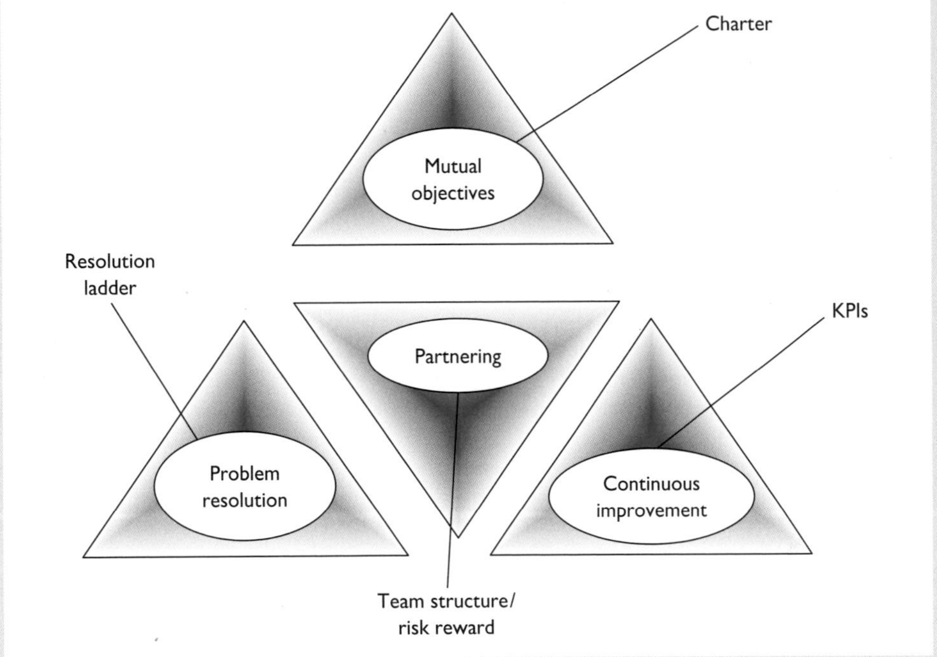

- Do risk plans take account of potential partners' likely attitudes to taking on risk? Is this based on actual discussion with the market, lessons from other projects, or assumption?
- Are management structures ready to open communication flows, both formal and informal, with the partner when the time comes?
- Does this project have the clear top-level commitment necessary to underpin a successful partnership-based approach?

The Centre for Construction Innovation[44] showed the essential features of partnering as illustrated in Figure 10.6.

10.15.8 Problems of partnering sourcing

- *Termination of relationships* – the aim should be to part amicably, preferably over a period of time according to an agreed separation plan.
- *Business shares* – the possibility of the customer being over dependent on the supplier. These issues need to be explored in joint consultation.
- *Confidentiality* – where prospective partners are also suppliers to competitors.
- *Complacency* – avoidance requires the regular review of competitiveness in regular meetings of a multifunctional buying team.
- *Attitudes* – traditionally adversarial buyers and salespeople will require retraining to adjust to the new philosophy and environment.

- *Contractual* – where, for reasons of falling sales, recession and so on, forecasts have to be modified.
- *Legislative* – the CIPS[45] points out that it is less easy to establish partnership relationships in the public sector due to government and EU procurement directive rules. In general, partnership relationships in the public sector should not exceed three to five years, after which retendering should be required, although some partnering deals are 10 to 15 years in duration with an option to extend for a further period of time.

Other problems are that the sharing of information may create a competitor or potential competition and difficulties associated with sharing future profits and the possible foreclosure of other alliance opportunities.

Ramsay[46] rightly observes that:

> As a sourcing strategy, partnerships may be generally applicable to only a small number of very large companies. For the rest, although it may be useful with a minority of purchases and a very small selection of suppliers, it is a high-risk strategy that one might argue ought to be approached with extreme caution. In Kraljic's terms [see section 2.13.11] the act of moving the sourcing of a bought-out item from competitive pressure to a single-sourced partnership increases both supply risk and profit impact. Thus partnerships tend to push all affected purchases towards the strategic quadrant. Strategic purchases offer large rewards if managed successfully, but demand the allocation of large amounts of management attention and threaten heavy penalties if sourcing arrangements fail.

10.15.9 Why partnerships fail

Research by Ellram[47] covering 80 'pairs' of US buying firms and their chosen suppliers used 19 factors identified by previous studies as contributing to partnership failure. These factors, in the order of their ranking of importance by buyers, were:

1 poor communication
2 lack of top management support
3 lack of trust
4 lack of total quality commitment by supplier
5 poor up-front planning
6 lack of distinctive supplier value-added benefit
7 lack of strategic direction to the relationship
8 lack of shared goals
9 ineffective mechanism for cost revision
10 lack of benefit/risk sharing
11 agreement not supportive of a partnering philosophy
12 lack of partner firm's top management support
13 changes in the market
14 too many suppliers for customers to deal with effectively
15 corporate culture differences
16 top management differences
17 lack of central coordination of procurement
18 low status of customer's procurement function
19 distance barriers.

Table 10.8 Top factors contributing to partnerships that have not worked out or have been resolved

Factor	Buyer ranking	Supplier ranking
Poor communication	1	1
Lack of top management support	2	10
Lack of trust	3	4
Lack of total quality commitment by supplier	4	18
Poor up-front planning	5	5
Lack of strategic direction for the relationship	7	3
Lack of shared goals	8	2

As shown in Table 10.8, five of the top seven factors were common to both buying and supplying organisations.

There were also strong differences. Suppliers ranked central coordination of the buyer's procurement function as 12 compared with a ranking of 17 by buyers. Similarly, the low status of the customer's procurement function, lack of strategic direction and lack of shared goals were ranked significantly higher by suppliers than buyers.

The above findings broadly agree with earlier research, although Ellram's sample regarded corporate culture and top management differences as relatively unimportant.

10.15.10 Insourcing

In the first instance, outsourcing is an emotive subject. In the public sector there are, at times, hostile Trade Union and political objections. Given the extent of outsourcing over the years, it is no surprise to find strategic decisions being made to insource services. A healthy, reasoned analysis of outsourced/insourcing decisions is informative. The Reason Foundation[48] commented on a report[49] produced by the City of Austin, Texas. The comments included:

> 'Opponents of the privatisation of municipal services often try to frighten policy makers away from using competitive contracting by claiming that costs will rise because the private sector seeks a profit.'

> 'The report found that transitioning to in-house provision of the services encompassed by the 37 analysed contracts would require an additional $169 million over a five-year period and 687.5 full-time equivalent positions.'

> 'And when you factor in the unsustainable costs of public employee benefits like defined-benefit pensions and retiree healthcare, there can be some major benefits to injecting some tension into the system via public/private competition.'

The detailed City of Austin report, subject 'Recommendations on Resolution No 20120405-054, can be accessed on the internet. There is the detail by Contract, grouped by Major Service Category. These findings and analysis are very informative for procurement specialists. One analysis Ref FR-2/FR-3 is in respect of vehicle car wash and interior cleaning services. Over a 5-year period it was estimated that insourcing would cost an additional $13,332,850. The services include police vehicles which must be completed within 90 minutes of the arrival of a police vehicle. The City Startup costs were estimated at $7,000,000.

Apse[50] in a 2009 report asserted that they had identified four core reasons why services have been returned in-house. These core reasons were:

1 Poor performance against key local and national targets and low levels of service user satisfaction.
2 Drive for quality and value for money – service reviews, performance indicators and benchmarking have enabled local authorities to prove an in-house team can provide better value for money.
3 Strategic governance and local policy drive – services have also been insourced as a result of factors such as local political support and the need for a more strategic, holistic approach to public service provision as part of an integrated service delivery model.
4 The workforce – services insourced as result of unmotivated workforce contributing to poor performance.

10.16 Intellectual property rights

10.16.1 What is Intellectual Property?

Intellectual Property (IP) refers to the proportion of creations of the mind, which have both a moral and a commercial value. IP law typically grants the author of an intellectual creation exclusive rights for exploiting and benefitting from their creation.

10.16.2 Patents

Only inventions can be patented. An invention is a new, inventive and industrially applicable technical solution to a given technical problem. A patent is the legal document that describes the invention and grants a property right to the inventor(s) or their successor(s). In general, the protection of a patent is limited to 20 years, depending on the country.

10.16.3 Copyright and neighbouring rights

Copyright laws deal with the rights of intellectual creation. They are also concerned with different methods of communication, such as print, sound, television and films.

Copyright protects all creations of the human mind whatever their form or merit and regardless of the audience they are destined for. Neighbouring rights were created for those categories of people who are not technically authors, namely, performing artists, producers of phonograms, and those involved in radio and television broadcasting. In most countries, a work is protected during the author's lifetime and after their death their heirs inherit the copyright. In general, the rights last for approximately 70 years after the death of the author before falling into the public domain.

10.16.4 Industrial designs

An industrial design may be three-dimensional based on the shape or surface of the object, or two-dimensional based on the object's patterns, lines or colours. Legally, 'industrial design' is the title granted by an official authority, generally the Patent Office, to protect the aesthetic or ornamental aspect of an object. In general, the period of protection granted is from 10–25 years.

10.16.5 Trade marks

At the time of writing the 10th edition of this book, in the United Kingdom, the current law is the Trade Marks Act 1994. On the 14 January 2019 the 1994 Act was amended and includes the Trade Mark Regulations 2018 (SI 2018/825). In the 1994 Act 'trade mark' means any sign which is capable

(a) of being represented in the register in a manner which enables the registrar and other competent authorities and the public to determine the clear and precise subject matter of the protection afforded to the proprietor, and
(b) of distinguishing goods or services of one undertaking from those of others undertakings.

A trade mark may, in particular, consist of words (including personal names), designs, letters, numbers, colours, sounds or the shape of goods or their packaging.

Protection of a registered trademark is maintained providing that the mark is in use and the registration is renewed by payment of renewal fees in the case of some old marks, after seven years, and in the case of newly registered marks, every ten years.

10.17 Procurement management of IPRs

Procurement must take the lead in managing all facets of IPRs. This may involve:

- getting confidentiality agreements signed with potential suppliers and existing suppliers
- determining, with legal support, which facet of IPRs apply to the specific purchase
- drawing up contractual clauses to deal with IPR issues
- negotiating license fees
- arranging for Escrow
- ensuring no 'reverse engineering' or 'copy action' occur.

10.18 Procurement support for in-house marketing

10.18.1 Reciprocity

What is reciprocity?

Reciprocity – often referred to as 'selling through the order book' – is a policy of giving preference to suppliers that are also customers of the buying organisation.

Reciprocity is influenced by two main factors:

- *the economic climate* – pressures for reciprocity increase in times of recession when sales may attempt to put pressure on their suppliers to buy their products

- *the type of product* – reciprocal dealing is greater when both supplier and buyer are producers of standard, highly competitive products – it does not arise where a purchaser has no alternative but to buy from a given supplier.

Reciprocity policies

The responsibility of procurement professionals is to make procurement decisions on such considerations as price, quality, delivery and service, so reciprocity may be expressly excluded by specific procurement policy statements, such as:

> In no circumstances will the XYZ Co. Ltd use a buying decision as a means of inappropriately enhancing a sales opportunity. Reciprocal trading practices are prohibited.

A more liberal approach is that reciprocity may offer advantages to both parties as:

- supplier and buyer may benefit from the exchange of orders
- supplier and buyer may obtain a greater understanding of mutual problems, thus increasing goodwill
- more direct communication between suppliers and buyers may eliminate or reduce the need for intermediaries and the cost of marketing or procurement operations.

10.18.2 Offset agreements

Offset agreements[51] are commitments by an exporter to a reciprocal purchase obligation. The reciprocal purchase is generally related to the exported product. The defence industry defines an offset as an industrial compensation practice required as a condition of purchase, in either government-to-government or commercial sales of defence articles or defence services as specified by the International Traffic in Arms Regulations (ITAR). Offsets are often comprised of component purchases, technology transfers, investments, training and research programs, and counter purchases. International trade, especially involving military equipment, advanced technology or high value contracts, frequently requires an offset agreement. An exporter's incorporation of offsets into export trade agreements is an integral aspect of the global competitive landscape. Exporters have benefited in procuring contract awards from the early performance of offset arrangements. Exporters may receive extra credits for conducting a specific offset transaction, such as a technology transfer, or a joint-venture.

Type of offsets

- **Direct offsets:** Contractual arrangements that involve defence articles and services referenced in the sales agreement for military exports.
- **Indirect offsets:** Contractual arrangements that involve goods and services unrelated to the exports referenced in the sales agreement.
- **Co-production:** Overseas production based upon a government-to-government agreement that permits a foreign government(s) or producer(s) to acquire the technical information to manufacture all or part of a US origin defence article. Co-production includes government-to-government licensed production, but it excludes licensed production based upon arrangements with US manufacturers.
- **Licensed production:** Overseas production of a US origin defense article based upon the transfer of technical information under the direct arrangements between a US manufacturer and a foreign government or producer.

- **Subcontractor production:** Overseas production of a part or component of a US origin defence article. The subcontract does not necessarily involve licence of technical information and is usually a direct arrangement between the US manufacturer and a foreign producer.

- **Overseas investment:** Investment arising from the offset agreement, taking the form of capital invested to establish or expand a subsidiary, or joint venture, in the foreign country.

- **Technology transfer:** Transfer of technology that occurs as a result of an offset agreement and that may take the form of research and development conducted abroad, technical assistance provided to the subsidiary, or other arrangements between the US manufacturer and a foreign entity.

Transparency International (TI) is an excellent informative report[52] dealing with offset in the defence sector. They say: 'Defence offsets are arrangements in which the purchasing government of the reporting country obliges the supplying company of the exporting country to reinvest some proportion of the contract in the importing country'.

TI assert that defence and security is one of the most corruption-prone sectors, after the construction and the oil and gas sectors. During the period 1993–2008, the average value of offset agreements entered by US defence companies – embedded in what is arguably the largest defence industrial base – with 45 different countries amounted to approximately 71 per cent.

TI also assert that offsets are under much less scrutiny during their negotiation than the main arms deal. Worse, in many countries, there is almost no due diligence on potential improper beneficiaries from the offsets, no monitoring of performance on offset contracts, no audits of what was delivered compared to the pledges, and no publication of the offset results, benefits or performance at all.

The author fully supports the TI recommendation that 'Procurement directors should ensure that the effects team is properly constituted with competent and experienced personnel bound by a robust code of conduct'.

Saudi Arabia's Al-Yamamah contracts with the UK included offsets to develop in-country a Tate & Lyle sugar processing complex, a Glaxo pharmaceutical plant, and commercial computer training facilities. Malaysia's offsets programmes have seen the development of its higher education sector through investments in universities, while Oman has directed investments towards air traffic control colleges and commercial training, and Kuwait has used offsets to develop small and medium enterprise (SMEs) in the civilian sector.

In all the above respects, procurement can make a significant contribution to the marketing activities of an organisation.

10.19 Intra-company trading

Intra-company trading applies to large enterprises and conglomerates where the possibility arises of buying certain materials from a member of the group. This policy may be justified on the grounds that it ensures the utilisation and profitability of the supplying undertaking and the profitability of the group as whole. It may also be resorted to in times of recession to help supplying subsidiaries cover their fixed costs.

Policy statements should give general and specific guidance to the procurement function regarding the basis on which intra-company trading should be conducted. General guidance may be expressed in a policy statement such as the following:

> Company policy is to support internal suppliers to the fullest extent and to develop product and service quality to the same high standards as those available in the external market.

Specific guidance may direct buyers to:

- purchase specified items exclusively from group members regardless of price
- obtain quotations from group members that are evaluated against those from external suppliers with the order being placed with the most competitive source, whether internal or external.

Difficulties can arise where intra-company trading involves import or export considerations.

10.20 Procurement consortia

10.20.1 Definition and scope

Procurement consortia may be defined as:

> A collaborative arrangement under which two or more organisations combine their requirements for a specified range of goods and services to gain price, design, supply availability and assurance benefits resulting from greater volumes of purchases.

In public procurement, for example, several separate authorities may establish a central procurement organisation to provide three basic supply services to its constituent members, namely delivery from stores, direct procurement of non-stock items for users in constituent authorities and the negotiation of call-off or 'standing offer' contracts. Such an organisation is usually self-financed by virtue of the mark-up on the items supplied from store and volume rebates received from suppliers that have agreements with the consortium.

Procurement consortia exist in a wide range of industries and cover for-profit and non-profit organisations, including universities and libraries.

Welsh Procurement Consortium

This consortium has been in existence since 1974 and in 2008 its membership increased to include the sixteen Unitary Authorities in South, Mid and West Wales and from January 2014 the Consortium also includes the three Unitary Authorities in North East Wales. There is also an 'Associate' membership scheme. There are a wide range of contracts in place including, Public Analyst Services, Spot Hire of Specialist Vehicles, Hiring Canteen Equipment and Street Lighting Products.

10.20.2 Advantages of procurement consortia

- The use of a consortium allows the constituent members to benefit from the economics of larger-scale procurement than they could undertake individually.
- Members can utilise the relevant professional procurement skills of the consortium staff who can develop wide-ranging product expertise.

- Saving of time in searching for and ordering standard items.
- Bulk procurement enables the consortium to have strong buying leverage for a wide range of supplies.
- Costs are clearly identified.

10.20.3 Disadvantages of consortia

- A consortium cannot insist on the compliance of individual members, which may treat the consortium as only one of a number of suppliers. This may secure nominal price savings, but is unlikely to affect the administrative costs of appraising the consortium against alternative sources. It also weakens the strength of the consortium.
- When using a consortium, it may be more difficult to agree standard specifications than when dealing with one company.
- Significant areas of spend are not covered by what consortia can provide.
- Some forms of consortia may be prohibited under EU provisions. Thus, Article 85(1) of the EEC Treaty provides that:

  . . . all agreements, decisions and concerted practices (hereafter referred to as agreements) which have as their object or effect the prevention, restriction or distortion of competition within the common market are prohibited as incompatible with the common market . . . this applies, however, only if such agreements affect trade between Member States.

- In general, however, the Commission 'welcomes cooperation among small-sized and medium-sized enterprises where such cooperation enables them to work more efficiently and increase their productivity and competitiveness in a larger market'.[53]

10.21 Sustainability

A definition was put forward in 1987 by the World Commission on Environment and Development. It stated that: 'Sustainable development meets the needs of the present without compromising the ability of future generations to meet their own needs.' BS8903:2010 'Principles and Framework for Procuring Sustainability' requires initiatives from procurement to ensure their supply chain embraces all the sustainability requirements.

The term sustainable procurement encompasses all issues where procurement is seen as having a role in delivering economic, social and environmental policy objectives. Procurement should consider sustainability at all stages of the procurement cycle but the specifications are vital. An idea of the scope is illustrated by the following categories:

- personal computers   (energy saving)
- laser printers   (energy saving)
- copying paper   (recycled content)
- wood products   (either recycled or from legally harvested trees)
- cars   (carbon emissions)
- lighting systems   (energy savings)
- paints and varnishes   (volatile organic compounds)
- soil products   (organic ingredients)

- textiles (specific requirements for cotton fibres, wool fibres and synthetic polyamide and polyester)
- detergents (biodegradability)
- glazing (U-value)

Caterpillar are one of many organisations to publish sustainability reports. In 2017 they commented that 'our power systems use fuels from diverse sources such as gas from landfills, livestock operations, wastewater treatment operations, mine methane, flare gas, syngas and biofuels.'

10.22 Sourcing decisions

Sourcing decisions involve a consideration of:

- factors influencing organisational buying decisions
- buying centres or teams
- buying situations
- factors in deciding where to buy.

10.22.1 Factors in deciding where to buy

Webster and Wind[54] classify factors influencing industrial buying decisions into four main groups, as shown in Table 10.9.

10.22.2 Buying centres, teams and networks

A buying centre is essentially a cross-functional team, the characteristics of which were discussed in section 4.5. Essentially the buying centre is the buying decision-making unit of an organisation and is defined by Webster and Wind[55] as:

all those individuals and groups who participate in the purchasing decision process and who share some common goals and the risks arising from the decision.

Normally a buying centre is a temporary, often informal, group that can change in composition according to the nature of the purchase decision.

Table 10.9 Factors in industrial buying decisions

Environmental	Organisational	Interpersonal	Individual
These are normally outside the buyer's control and include: - level of demand - economic outlook - interest rates - technological change - political factors - government regulations - competitive development	Buying decisions are affected by the organisation's system of reward, authority, status and communication, including organisational: - objectives - policies - procedures - structures	Involving the interaction of several people of different status, authority, empathy and persuasiveness who comprise the buying centre	Buying decisions are related to how individual participants in the buying process form their preferences for products and suppliers, involving the person's age, professional identification, personality and attitude towards the risks involved in their buying behaviour

Buying centres may also be more permanent groups responsible for the sourcing, selection, monitoring and evaluation of suppliers in relation to a specified range of items, such as food, drink, capital equipment and outsourced products and services. Such groups are often referred to as *procurement teams* and may also be responsible for framing procurement policies and procedures. All teams should have a designated chairperson and clearly defined terms of reference and authority.

The composition of the buying centre or team can be analysed as follows:

- By individual participants or job holders, such as the managing director, chief procurement officer, engineer or accountant.
- By organisational units, such as departments or even individual organisations, as when a group of hospitals decide to standardise equipment.
- The buying centre or team is comprised of all members of the organisation (varying from three to twelve) who play any of the following five roles in the procurement decision process:
  - *users* who will use the product or service and often initiate the purchase and specify what is bought
  - *influencers* such as technical staff who may directly or indirectly influence the buying decision in such ways as defining specifications or providing information on which alternatives may be evaluated
  - *buyers* who have formal authority to select suppliers and arrange terms of purchase – they may also help to determine specifications, but their main role is to select vendors and negotiate within purchase constraints
  - *deciders* who have either formal or informal authority to select the ultimate suppliers (in routine procurement of standard items, the deciders are often the buyers, but in more complicated procurement, the deciders are often other officers of the organisation)
  - *gatekeepers* who control the flow of information to others, such as buyers, and may prevent salespeople from seeing users or deciders.

10.22.3 The buying network

The buying centre concept, developed in 1972, has proved remarkably durable and provided the basis for later models of organisational buying behaviour.[56] The Webster and Wind model, however, makes no reference to such aspects as the linkages between procurement and corporate strategies and procurement decisions aimed at enhancing the competitive advantage of buying, such as the decision to source abroad.

Business practice has also changed since 1972 and process-driven management styles and philosophies such as partnering and the impact of IT have changed the way in which buyers and sellers interact.

Such considerations led Bristor and Ryan[57] to suggest that the concept of the buying centre as a group no longer captures the nature of buying behaviour and should be replaced by that of the buying network, which they define as:

> The set of individuals involved in a purchase process, over a specified time frame, and the set of one or more relations that link (or fail to link) each dyad [a dyad is a pair of units treated as one].

Networks have been discussed in section 4.3, but it is useful to mention here two dimensions of networks highlighted by Bristor and Ryan – structure and relationships.

Structure relates to organisational aspects. Thus, the boundaries of a buying centre are those of the organisation. With buying networks, the issue arises as to whether or not it is appropriate to include buying network members from outside the organisation, such as customers or consultants. The nodes of buying centres can also represent roles rather than named individuals.

Relationship aspects of buying networks include communications and influence. IT not only makes information widely available to network members, but developments such as teleconferencing mean that they are no longer required to be in physical proximity.

10.23 Factors in deciding where to buy

Assuming that the decision is made that a product should be bought out rather than made in, many factors determine where the order is placed and by whom the decision is made. Such considerations include:

10.23.1 General considerations

- How shall the item be categorised – capital investment, manufacturing material or parts, operating, supply or MRO item?
- Where does the item fit into the procurement portfolio – leverage, strategic, non-critical or bottleneck (see section 2.13.11)?
- What are our current and projected levels of business for the item?
- Is the item a one-off or a continuing requirement?
- Is the item unique to us or in general use?
- Is the item a straight rebuy, modified rebuy or new task?
- If it is a straight or modified rebuy, from what source was it obtained?
- Is/was the present/previous supplier satisfactory from the standpoints of price, quality and delivery?
- With regard to the value of the order to be placed, is the cost of searching for an alternative supply source justified?
- Which internal customers may wish to be consulted on the sourcing of the item?
- Within what timescale is the item required?

10.23.2 Strategic considerations

- What supply source will offer the greatest competitive advantage from the standpoints of:
  - price
  - differentiation of product
  - security of supplies and reliability of delivery
  - quality
  - added value in terms of specialisation, production facilities, packaging, transportation, after-sales services and so on?

- Is the source one with whom we would like to:
  - single source?
  - share a proportion of our requirements for the required item?
  - build up a long-term partnership relationship?
  - discuss the possibilities of supplier development?
  - Outsource?
  - subcontract?
- Does the supply source offer any possibilities for:
  - joint product development?
  - reciprocity or countertrade?
- What would be our relationship profile with that supply source – market exchange, captive buyer, captive supplier or strategic partnership (see Figure 6.6)?
- What relationships does the supplier have with our competitors?
- Is it desirable that at least part of our requirements should be sourced locally for political, social responsibility or logistical reasons?
- What risk factors attach to the purchase? Is the product high profit impact/high supply risk, low profit impact/high supply risk, high profit impact/low supply risk, low profit impact/low supply risk?

10.23.3 Product factors

- Can the product or components and assemblies be outsourced?
- What critical factors influence the choice of suppliers? Chisnall[58] reports a research finding that seven critical factors were found to influence buyers in the British valve and pump industry in the choice of their suppliers of raw materials: delivery reliability, technical advice; test facilities, replacement guarantee, prompt quotation, ease of contact and willingness to supply range. These attributes helped to reduce the risk element to procurement decisions.
- What special tooling is required? Is such tooling the property of the existing supplier or the vendor?
- To what extent are learning curves applicable to the product? Are these allowed for in the present and future prices?
- Is the product 'special' or 'standardised'?
- In what lot sizes is the product manufactured?
- What is the estimated product lifecycle cost?

10.23.4 Supplier factors

Such factors are those normally covered by supplier appraisal and vendor-rating exercises.

10.23.5 Personal factors

Personal factors relate to psychological and behavioural aspects of those involved in making organisational buying decisions. All procurement professionals should constantly keep in mind the exhortation of the Greek philosopher Diogenes: 'Know thyself.'

Knowledge of our strengths, weaknesses, prejudices, motivations and values will often prevent us from making procurement or other decisions on irrational grounds or as a member of a team being pressurised by 'group-think' influences. Among the many personal factors that may influence decisions relating to where to buy and who to buy from are:

■ cultural factors – the way in which we have been taught to do business
■ the information available to us
■ professionalism, including ethical values and training
■ experience of suppliers and their products
■ ability to apply lateral thinking to procurement problems.

Procurement professionals should also develop the capacity to understand the preferences of users for a particular product and the motivations of suppliers.

Discussion questions

10.1 If you were involved in pre-qualifying a strategic supplier for the manufacture of high-quality components for use in an aircraft engine what would be the six most important questions you want answering about the supplier's procurement department?

10.2 You purchase tyres for a range of cars, vans and lorries. For many years these have been sole sourced with a tyre manufacturer. You have been asked to challenge the procurement strategy. What sources would you use to find other possible sources of supply who would be invited to tender?

10.3 Situation analysis is concerned with taking stock of where an organisation or activity within an organisation has been recently, where it is now and where it is likely to end up using present policies, plans and procedures. As the executive in charge of the procurement of management services, including temporary labour, facilities management, consultancy and security you are asked to effect economies without prejudicing the final service quality. How might an analysis of market conditions help you make constructive recommendations?

10.4 One of your major competitors has just appointed an Administrator. They have severe cash flow problems and many of their contracts have been running at a loss. Your Sales Director has told you that your company has been offered two of your competitor's contracts, providing your organisation accept the work at the current contract prices and terms that the failed company had. He has asked for your opinion on a possible course of action, prior to him talking to the two potential clients. The value of the work being offered is £10 million. This would represent 24 per cent of your current turnover. What would be your opinion and what would it be founded upon?

10.5 You are accountable for procuring all waste management services for a large Council. A trade fair is to be held shortly in Munich and you have asked to attend. Your request has been refused by the Managing Director who says that he is cutting down on 'jollies'. What can you say to persuade him that there are significant benefits in attending?

10.6 The cost of monitoring and evaluating the performance of suppliers can be high.
   ■ What arguments would you use to justify the expenditure on evaluating performance?
   ■ What steps might you take to minimise such expenditure?
   ■ What are the benefits to suppliers in you evaluating their performance?

10.7 Trade unions are opposed to outsourcing of public services and yet there are demonstrable service improvements and quantifiable savings. In your opinion, is outsourcing a sound business strategy?

10.8 What are the different insurances that a supplier must have if you are purchasing goods or services from them? What are the business consequences if they do not have the insurances?

10.9 Explain the typical quantitative and qualitative measures of a supplier's performance

10.10 It is common sense that if you aggregate purchases and shrink the supply base you should make dramatic savings. If this is true, then there is an inevitability that large companies will get the lions' share of work and small companies will lose out. What is an effective procurement strategy to deal with aggregation?

10.11 You have appointed a new supplier for the provision of specialised marketing services. They have advised you that because of staffing difficulties they are sub-contracting your work to one of their 'partners'. How would you deal with this situation?

10.12 You urgently need a sub-contractor to machine your free issue material. This is high-value, special steel. Your Production Director has asked you four questions:
1 What will the contract say about scrap management?
2 How will the issue and transportation of the free issue take place?
3 How will the capacity you require be guaranteed?
4 What happens if you cannot guarantee actual requirements other than on 24-hour notice?

10.13 Partnering often has a requirement for 'open book'. You are negotiating with a supplier who accepts the principle of open book but wants to know what you will use the information for. He has given you an example. He has planned a profit of 12.5 per cent. What happens if the open book shows that through his efficiencies he makes 16.9 per cent? What would you tell him about the specific and the wider principle?

10.14 What advantages do procurement consortia offer?

10.15 You have had external consultants auditing your organisation's energy costs. They say that you could save 45 per cent by switching suppliers. This would mean a saving of £2.45 million in the next three years. The consultants then say that they will reveal the source of lower energy costs when you agree to give the consultants 50 per cent of the savings. What would be your response and why?

10.16 Within the public sector there is the 'competitive dialogue' procedure. Conduct some research and explain whether you think there are any principles that could be usefully applied in the private sector.

10.17 Your company requires the external provision of 7000 hours of specialised design services associated with a military contract that your company has. You have invited tenders. One of the potential suppliers has offered a co-located design team who would work alongside your designers. The supplier's designers would use your IT systems and conform to your quality standards, working hours and practices. It is known by the procurement team that your designers are paid 16 per cent less than the co-located designers are paid. What are the arguments for and against the co-location?

10.18 What are the advantages of having category management specialists in a procurement department?

References

1 Technology Partners International, Inc.: www.technologypartners.ca.

2 Daniela Mocenco, 'Supply Chain Features of the Aerospace Industry: particular case Airbus and Boeing', *Scientific Bulletin – Economic Science*, Vol. 14, Issue 2, 2015.

3 Growing your Business. Lord Young. May 2013 VRN BIS/13/729.

4 CIPS Knowledge Works, *e-sourcing*: www.cips.org.

5 Waller, A., quoted by Lascelles, D., in his *Managing the E-supply Chain*, Business Intelligence, 2001, p. 19.

6 Leon, Steven. M, *Financial Intelligence for Supply Chain Managers*, Pearson Education Inc., Harlow, UK, 2016.

7 www.investopedia.com.

8 Buffa, E. S. and Kakesh, K. S., *Modern Production Operations Management*, 5th edn, John Wiley, Hoboken, USA, 1987, p. 548.

9 NSAI. Environmental Management System Questionnaire applicable to I.S.EN ISO14001:2015 www.nsai.ie

10 www.airbus.com

11 These categories are used in the supplier management policy document of the University of Nottingham.

12 Emptoris Supplier Performance Module at: www.emptoris.com/solutions/supplier_performance_management_module.asp

13 Kozak, R. A. and Cohen, D. H., 'Distributor–supplier partnering relationships: a case in trust', *Journal of Business Research*, Vol. 30, 1997, pp. 33–8.

14 Simpson, P. M., Siguaw, J. A. and White, S. C., 'Measuring the performance of suppliers: an analysis of evaluation processes', *Journal of Supply Management*, February, 2002.

15 As 15 above.

16 ITIL www.knowledgetransfer.net/dictionary/ITIL/en/Service_Level_Agreement.

17 Carter, R., 'The seven Cs of effective supplier evaluation', *Purchasing and Supply Chain Management*, April, 1995, pp. 44–5.

18 Fredriksson, P. and Gadde, L. E., *Evaluation of Supplier Performance – The Case of Volvo Car Corporation and its Module Supplier*, Chalmers University of Technology Sweden, 2005.

19 Oxford Economics Final Report April 2011 The Size of the UK outsourcing market – across the private and public sectors.

20 House of Commons Committee of Public Accounts, Supporting Primary Care Services, NHS England's Contract with Capita, Fifty-Seventh Report of Sessions 2017-19, Published 25 July 2018.

21 National Audit Office, NHS England's management of the primary care support services contract with Capita, Report HC632, Session 2017-2019, Published 17 May 2018.

22 Atkinson, J. and Meager, N., 'New forms of work organisation', IMS Report 121, 1986.

23 Beauchamp, M., 'Outsourcing everything else? Why not purchasing?', *Purchasing and Supply Management*, July, 1994, pp. 16–19.

24 Beulen, E. J. J., Ribbers, P. M. A. and Roos, J., *Outsourcing van IT-dienstverlening: een-make or buy beslissing*, Kluwer, 1994. Quoted by Fill, C. and Visser, E., *The Outsourcing Dilemma: Management Decision 2000*, Vol. 38.1, MCB University Press, Bingley, UK, pp. 43–50.

25 Quoted in Duffy, R. J., 'The outsourcing decision', *Inside Supply Management*, April, 2000, p. 38.

26 Lacity, M. C. and Hirscheim, R., *Information Systems Outsourcing*, John Linley, 1995.

27 Perkins, B., *Computer World*, 22 November, 2003.

28 Reilly, P. and Tamkin, P., *Outsourcing: A Flexibility Option for the Future*, Institute of Employment Studies, London, UK, 1996, pp. 32–3.

29 As 27 above.

30 Central Bank of Ireland The Investment Firms and Fund Servicers Thematic Review Team report www.centralbank.ie.

31 Probert, D. R., '*Make or Buy: Your Route to Improved Manufacturing Performance*', DTI, London, 1995.

32 Monahan S, Van den Bossche, P. and Tomayo. F., *Make Vs Buy Revisited*. AT Kearney Inc., Chicago, Illinois, USA, 2010.

33 Katikar, R. S. and Pawar, M. S. 'Cost analysis for make-or-buy decisions for manufacturing', *International Research Journal of Commerce, Business and Social Science* Vol. 1, No. 9, 2012, pp. 151–156.

34 Humbert, X. P. and Passarelli, C. P. M., 'Outsourcing: avoiding the hazards and pitfalls', Paper presented at the NAPM International Conference, 4–7 May, 1997.

35 CIPS, 'Partnership Sourcing': www.cips.org.

36 Partnership Sourcing Ltd, *Making Partnerships Happen*: www.psicbi.com.

37 Lambert, D. M., Emmelhaing, M. A. and Gardner, J. T., 'Developing and implementing supply chain partnerships', *International Journal of Logistics Management*, Vol. 7, No. 2, 1996, pp. 1–17.

38 Knemeyer, A. M., Corsi, T. M. and Murphy, P. R., 'Logistics outsourcing relationships: customer perspectives', *Journal of Business Logistics*, Vol. 24, No. 1, 2003, pp. 77–101.

39 Southey, P., 'Pitfalls to partnering in the UK', PSERG Second International Conference, April, 2003, in Burnett, K. (ed.), 'Readings in partnership sourcing', CIPS, Stamford, UK (undated).

40 PSL, *Creating Service Partnerships*, Partnership Sourcing Ltd, 1993, p. 7.

41 As 41 above.

42 As 41 above.

43 *Effective partnering*, Crown Copyright, 2003, an overview for customers and suppliers to check.

44 The Centre for Construction Innovation: an Enterprise Centre within the School of the Built Environment at the University of Salford.

45 As 37 above, pp. 5–6.

46 Ramsay, J., 'The case against purchasing partnerships', *International Journal of Purchasing and Materials Management*, Fall, 1996, pp. 13–24.

47 Ellram, L. M., 'Partnering pitfalls and success factors', *International Journal of Purchasing and Materials Management*, Spring, 1995, pp. 36–44.

48 The Reason Foundation. 5737 Mesmer Ave. Los Angeles. California.

49 City of Austin, 'Report on Insourcing Select Service Contracts' 1 October 2012.

50 Association for Public Service Excellence 'Insourcing: A guide to bringing local authority services back in-house', www.apse.org.uk.

51 Trade Offsets, http://offset.wikidot.com.

52 www.treansparency.org, 'Defence Offsets – Addressing the risks of corruption & raising transparency. ', *Transparency International*, Published April 2010.

53 *E.C. Journal*, 84–28.8, 1968.

54 Webster, F. E. and Wind, Y. J., *Organisational Buying Behaviour*, Prentice Hall, Upper Saddle River, New Jersey, USA, 1972, pp. 33–7.

55 As 55 above.

56 A useful summary of research in the 25 years prior to 1996 is provided by Johnston, W. J. and Lewin, J. E., 'Organisational buying behaviour: towards an integrative framework', *Journal of Business Research*, Vol. 35, No. 1, 1996.

57 Bristor, J. M. and Ryan, M. S., 'The buying centre is dead, long live the buying centre', *Advances in Consumable Research*, Vol. 4, 1987, pp. 255–8.

58 Chisnall, P. M., *Strategic Industrial Marketing*, 2nd edn, Prentice Hall, Upper Saddle River, New Jersey, USA, 1989, pp. 82–3.

Chapter 11

Purchase price management and long-term cost-in-use

Learning outcomes

With reference, where applicable, to procurement and supply chain management, this chapter aims to provide an understanding of:

- what is price?
- strategic pricing – an introduction
- the buyer's role in managing purchase prices
- supplier pricing decisions
- the supplier's choice of pricing strategy
- tender pricing
- price and cost analysis
- competition legislation
- collusive tendering
- price variation formulae.

Key ideas

- The business consequences of procurement's ability to control purchase prices.
- The nature and variety of supplier's pricing decisions.
- Firm contract price agreements.
- Cost breakdowns and the potential for challenge.
- Price analysis for the purposes of comparison and negotiation.
- Price variation formulae management.
- The logic for checking price adjustment constituent elements.
- Techniques for obtaining best value for money.

11.1 What is price?

Price can be defined as:

> A component of an exchange or transaction that takes place between two parties and refers to what must be given up by the buyer in order to obtain something offered by the seller.

In effect, price has a different focus for the two parties. The buyer sees price as what is given up to obtain the benefits of goods or services. The seller sees price as generating income and, if correctly applied, in determining profit. While pricing is a key focus for companies examining profitability, pricing decisions are also vital for not-for-profit organisations, such as charities, educational institutions, third-sector bodies and Local Authority Trading Companies.

11.2 Strategic pricing – an introduction

Inevitably, procurement will, in part, be judged on their ability to manage purchase prices using varied approaches including tendering and negotiation. However, the logical starting point must be the supplier's decisions. Nagle, Hogan and Zale[1] observe that 'the economic forces that determine profitability change whenever technology, regulation, market information, consumer preferences, or relative costs change'. They further state that 'few managers, even those in, marketing, have received practical training in how to make strategic pricing decisions'. Ominously, they then say that, 'most companies still make pricing decisions in reaction to change rather than in anticipation of it.'

Assuming an organisation has a pricing strategy; it is worthwhile considering how the strategy will be implemented. There are, of course, different considerations depending on the organisation's products/services. If the organisation is selling the same products on a repetitive basis, that is quite different than one that designs and manufacturers capital equipment. Nagle, Hogan and Zale observe:

> implementing pricing strategy is difficult because it requires input and coordination across so many different functional areas: marketing, sales, capacity management, and finance. Successful pricing strategy implementation is built on these pillars: an effective organisation, timely and accurate information, and appropriately motivated management.

There is a flaw in the above logic. Procurement for whatever reason does not warrant inclusion in the functional areas that provide inputs. Why? In the author's experience there are organisations where procurement is an inclusive member of the pricing decision forum. An example is the pharmaceutical manufacturing sector where procurement must plan the pricing of feedstock, manufacturing and packaging production lines, packaging, storage and distribution. These cost drivers, successfully managed, are central to profitability. This positive example contrasts sharply with a shipbuilding organisation, where the key input costs were determined by the estimating department. The author was retained to challenge input costs on such equipment as radar, navigation engines, propulsion and safety hardware. No negotiations had taken place because the estimators held the view that when the supplier owned intellectual property rights, no negotiation was possible. The consequence, if this position had been maintained, could have been the loss of a prestige contract. However, if procurement is to be a pillar of decision making, the function must have expert pricing knowledge and be skilled negotiators.

11.3 The buyer's role in managing purchase prices

The whole task of managing purchase prices is both an emotional matter and a professional challenge. Traditional procurement theory placed equal weighting on the need to obtain the right quality, right quantity, right delivery, right place and right price. It would, of course, be incorrect to assert that price should be the dominant factor in the sourcing decision. However, price can be seen as a function of the other 'right' characteristics. In other words, the seller will determine a price only when the other factors are known. In the final analysis, the procurement department is accountable for the organisation's expenditure. There cannot be a more responsible task.

The 1970s was a period when pricing decisions were extensively researched and, uniquely, at PhD level.[2] Some of the observations and insights remain challenging. Leighton[3] asserted that, 'Price may be looked at in another way, that is, as the outcome of a power or bargaining relationship.' England and Leenders[4] put forward the view that, 'The determination of price to be paid is one of the major decisions to be made by a purchasing agent. Indeed, the ability to get a good price is sometimes held to be the prime test of a good buyer.' Winkler[5] expressed a somewhat extreme view: 'Inertia is a great weakness of British Buying and some suppliers enjoy enormous profit margins because their customers do not want to take the risk of upsetting the settled routine of things, or to investigate alternate sources of supply.' Ammer[6] stressed a rounded view of the role of procurement,

> In most cases the supplier does not have the last word on prices. Able buyers can exert tremendous leverage if they really understand how prices are set and don't hesitate to use their skills. In doing so, they are doing a service not only to their own company but also to the supplier and to the economy as a whole.

The buyer's involvement in pricing decisions at the new buy, straight rebuy and modified rebuy phases of the procurement cycle is shown in Figures 11.1, 11.2 and 11.3.

11.3.1 The buyer's actions pre-tender

As with everything, procurement actions are dependent upon what is being purchased and whether it has been purchased previously. The analysis that follows is generic in scope and some selectivity will be necessary when applying the logic to specific scenarios (see also Table 11.1).

Differentiating cost analysis and cost estimating

The US Government Accountability Office (GAO) explain:

Cost analysis, used to develop cost estimates for such things as hardware systems, automated information systems, civil projects, manpower and training, can be defined as

- the effort to develop, analyze, and document cost estimates with analytical approaches and techniques
- the process of analyzing, interpreting, and estimating the incremental and total resources required to support past, present, and future systems – an integral step in selecting alternatives; and
- a tool for evaluating resource requirements at key milestones and decision points in the acquisition process.

Figure 11.1 **New buy phase – purchase price management factors**

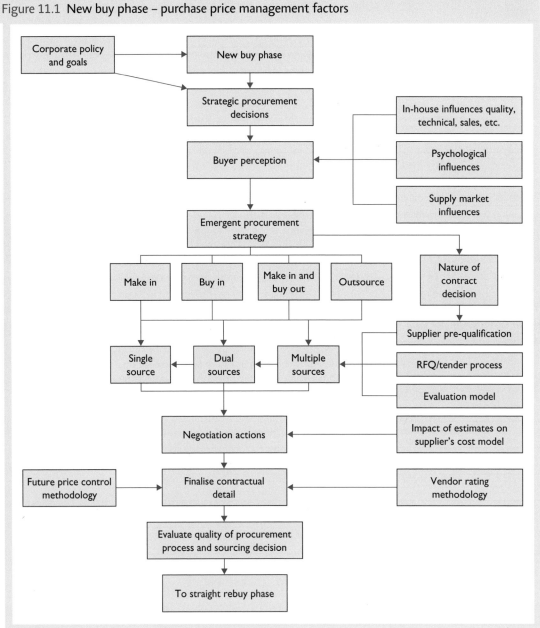

Cost estimating involves collecting and analyzing historical data and applying quantitative models, techniques, tools, and databases to predict a program's future cost. More simply, cost estimating combines science and art to predict the future cost of something based on known historical data that are adjusted to reflect new materials, technology, software languages, and development teams.

Figure 11.2 **Straight rebuy phase – purchase price management factors**

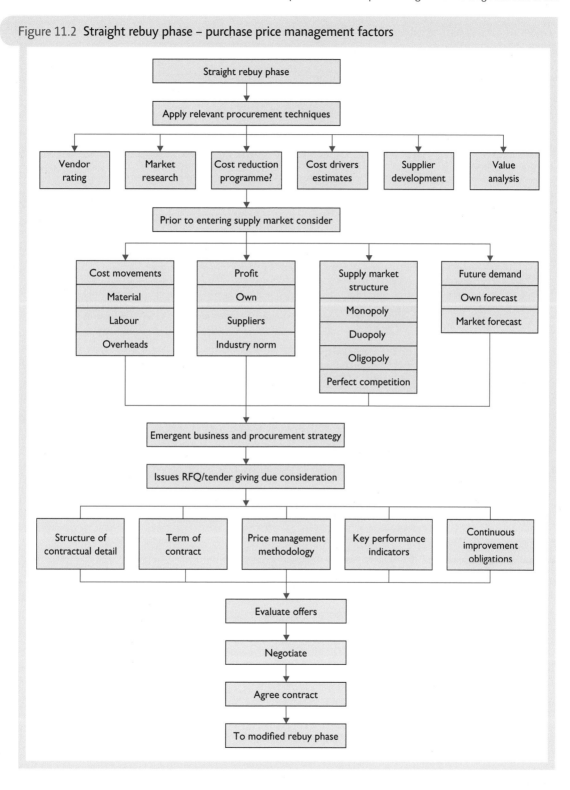

Figure 11.3 Modified rebuy phase – purchase price management factors

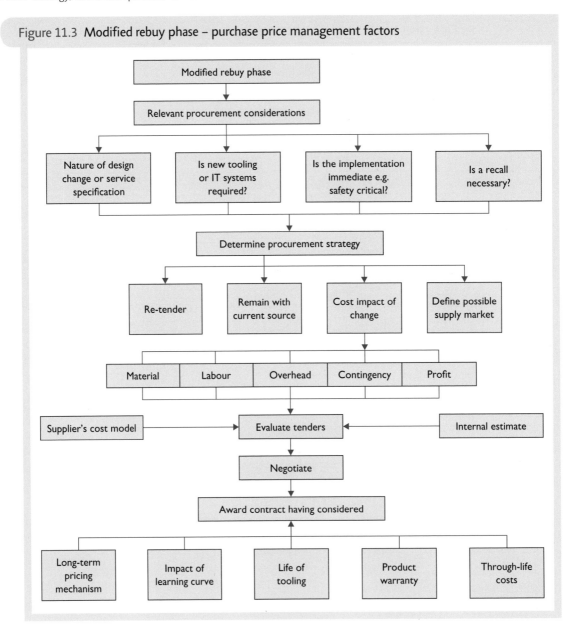

Because cost estimating is complex, sophisticated cost analysts should combine concepts from such disciplines as accounting, budgeting, computer science, economics, engineering, mathematics, and statistics and should even employ concepts from marketing and public affairs. And because cost estimating requires such a wide range of disciplines, it is important that the cost analyst either be familiar with these disciplines or have access to an expert in these fields.[7]

Cost estimating

Cost estimating is widely used to determine potential selling prices, recognising that some buyer's will have a propensity to negotiate and may have access to their in-house estimate to guide them. Tuns[8] points out that cost estimation is very critical and important in

Table 11.1 Pre-tender considerations

Soft market testing	This consists of making contact with existing suppliers in the marketplace and inviting their comments on relevant technical and commercial matters, including price. It may be possible to obtain a 'rough order of magnitude' price to assist with budgetary planning
Estimating – conventional	There is within some engineering, automotive and aerospace organisations an ability to calculate 'should costs' to assist the budgetary process and to give the buyer a target cost and negotiation leverage. Estimating is not a precise science, hence a need to be flexible when using estimates in price negotiations
Estimating – parametrics	This is an estimating technique that uses a statistical relationship between historical data and other variables (for example, square footage in construction, lines of code in software development) to calculate an estimate for activity parameters, such as scope, cost, budget and duration
Access to a benchmarking club	It is not uncommon for a number of local authorities to form a benchmarking club where they exchange price and service performance information
Contribute to a benchmarking service	There are many subscription-based price and performance services. For example, construction costs, telecommunications, pulp and paper, outsourced services and IT are readily available. It is vital, if using these services, to ensure that 'like-with-like' is being compared
Networking within the procurement profession	Members of the procurement profession are often reluctant to exchange price information. Ethical and confidentiality are influences but when organisations are non-competing there is less of an issue

all types of manufacturing processes. Cost estimation is a critically important business function in all industries.

There are four kinds of cost estimation methodologies used throughout the forging industry:

- subjective estimation
- estimation by analogy (comparative estimation)
- parametric estimation (statistical estimation)
- bottom-up estimation (synthetic estimation).

The items that make up a forging cost can be grouped as:

1 material cost
2 forging equipment cost
3 tooling cost
4 labour cost
5 overhead cost
6 billet heating cost
7 secondary operations cost (cleaning, heat treatment, inspection, etc.)
8 quality control cost
9 packaging and transportation cost.

These are elaborated upon in Figure 11.4.

Figure 11.4 Forging work breakdown structure (WBS)

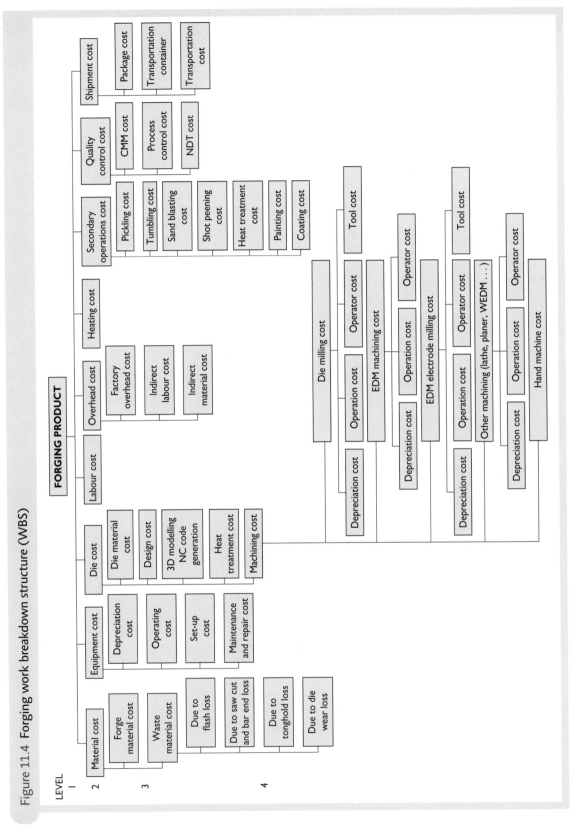

Table 11.2 **Tender stage considerations**

Lump sum prices	This is an unsophisticated approach to determining prices. The limit of information is a total lump sum price from each tenderer. If we assume that five tendered prices have been received: £111,865 £151,490 £154,076 £199,831 £245,641 there are many issues arising, including: 1 Why is there a 119 per cent difference between the lowest and highest prices? 2 Has the lowest priced bidder made a mistake or plans to cut the quality? 3 Is the lowest bidder desperate for work? 4 Is the highest bidder too busy and doesn't want the work?
Elemental cost breakdown	This is where the buyer asks each tenderer to breakdown the tendered price into its key elements, namely, labour, materials, overheads and profit. This methodology does give comparable data not available with a lump sum price
Detailed cost model	In this situation every facet of the tendered price is 'broken down' to give the buyer the classic 'open book' scenario. Refer to Figure 11.5 for an approach to obtaining detailed costs
Reverse auctions	At the tender stage the buyer has comparable price information and then subjects it to a reverse auction where one or more of the tendered prices will reduce, but not against cost disclosure

At the tender stage there are a number of pricing considerations as outlined in Table 11.2.

There is a great deal of skill involved in designing a cost model, where proposed costs are very specific to the goods or service to be supplied. It is possible to purchase cost estimating software such as DeccaPro.[9] Figure 11.5 is adapted from Deccan Systems schematic on using design and task variables to model costs.

When the priced tender has been received, the buyer has a key role in determining the credibility of the price. The key considerations are shown in Table 11.3.

Pricing considerations continue to be relevant after the contract has been awarded. The key considerations affecting most buyers are shown in Table 11.4.

11.3.2 Parametric estimating

Procurement should be aware of any cost estimating techniques that will assist in the setting of in-house budgets and in the evaluation of tendered prices. Parametric estimating is an ideal consideration for project and IT procurement. The International Society of Parametric Analysts[10] have published the Parametric Estimating Handbook, Fourth Edition – April 2008. The following content is informed by the Handbook and is in summary form.

Parametric estimating can be defined as 'a technique that develops cost estimates based upon the examination and validation of the relationships which exist between a project's technical, programmatic and cost characteristics as well as the resources consumed during its development, manufacture, maintenance, and/or modification.'

Figure 11.5 Designing a cost model

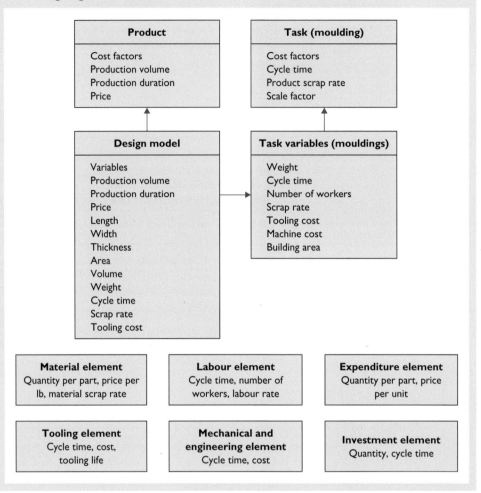

Table 11.3 Post-tender stage considerations

Interrogate costs	When a detailed cost breakdown has been obtained, the buyer should lead the activity to interrogate all costs and overhead recovery and declared profit. This activity will require the support of technical and finance colleagues. The comparison between different tenderers' cost opinions can be very revealing
Clarification	Where there are discrepancies between tendered prices and between the in-house estimated price it is the buyer's task to seek clarification. This may reveal that the supplier cannot purchase materials competitively; labour costs are too high, long-term cost-in-use is too high and so on
Negotiation	The negotiation of price is a valid activity, providing the highest ethical standards apply. That means not conducting Dutch auctions or revealing one tenderers' prices to another tenderer. Within the public sector, buyers must ensure they do not breach EU Regulations or Standing Orders

Table 11.4 Post-contract award stage considerations

Indexation	In many long-term contracts and projects the tendered price is subject to indexation, meaning the price could decrease and increase. Contracts may refer to VOP (variation of price), CPA (contract price adjustment) or PVF (price variation formula). They all mean the same. In each case there will be a formula included in the contract, either from a trade body or devised by the buying organisation
Claims for extras	There are occasions in the life of a contract when the buying organisation will change some parameters, such as specification, delivery times and product support requirements. This will probably trigger a claim for extra payment. The detailed basis of the claim must be exposed and, when appropriate, negotiated to a level that is acceptable to the buying organisation
Contract change notices (CCN)	There is a provision in some contracts for a contract change notice (CCN) to be issued when a formal change to a contract is proposed. There will be a defined process to consider price and other impacts of the change, such as extending delivery date(s)
Cost in the event of termination	There is a possibility that a contract will be terminated prior to its defined end date. Termination is a regular source of disputes, many of which finish up in the courts. The contract should include a right for the buyer to terminate in the event of default and, in some cases, for 'convenience'. It is almost inevitable that some 'costs' will have been incurred by the supplier for which recompense will be required. There is a legal onus on the supplier to mitigate their losses
Continuous improvement obligations	A requirement for continuous improvement is not an unreasonable demand, particularly on long-term contracts for the supply of goods or services. It recognises that the supplier, with the buyer's support, should be able to reduce costs. The classic approach of value analysis and process improvements can help to reduce prices. In some service contracts there is a requirement to reduce annual costs by, say, 3 per cent. If a higher figure is obtained there can be a profit-sharing arrangement
Apply benchmarking clause	Some contracts have an annual benchmarking requirement where, for example, prices are checked against a basket of comparable products. If the basket shows lower costs the supplier has the option of matching them, or the buyer can purchase the items elsewhere. This approach can, for example, be applied to IT supplies
Active cost reduction programme	In well-managed procurement departments there will be an active cost reduction programme and each buyer will be given a specific target. Achieving cost reduction will require varied initiatives. In a manufacturing environment, cost reduction is vital to maintaining market position and profitability. Engagement with the supply chain is essential if unnecessary cost is to be driven out
Resisting price increase requests	Price increases will erode competitiveness and profit in a manufacturing environment. In the public sector they will threaten the ability to provide the same level and quality of services. The skill of procurement to resist price increase requests is an acid test of competence. The skill of evaluating the reasoning behind the proposed price increase is a professional requisite

It is asserted that cost estimating has a very ancient history. It is even Biblical; Luke 14:28.29 discusses the importance of '. . . [He should] sitteth down first, and counteth the cost, [to see] whether he have sufficient to finish it.'

Parametric tools and techniques have much more versatility than other estimating approaches. There are numerous reasons for this. Here are a few:

■ Better estimates are provided, often in a matter of minutes
■ There exists a high-quality link between the technical and cost proposals
■ The data is well understood through the calibration and validation activities

- It is much easier to estimate conceptual designs
- Early costing cannot be done effectively any other way
- No bill of material (BOM) is required
- It is much easier to handle scope, technical and performance changes.

11.3.2.1 Project activities that cause material differences in cost

In Table 11.5 is an extract from the NASA Cost Estimating Handbook[11] showing the strengths, weaknesses and applications of Parametric Cost Estimating Methodology.

Some project activities have shown by experience to cause material differences in cost; they also frequently occur. This includes:

- *Timing*
  Timing of historical values versus future costs is of importance for at least one main reason: variations in the value of currencies, also called inflation or deflation.

- *Labour versus material*
  In common parlance the difference between labour and material is clear. But it is not always clear in the world of accounting, which is the source of data used to build cost estimating relationships (CER).

- *Recurring versus non-recurring*
  Costs relating to initial development of a product are frequently referred to as non-recurring costs on the grounds that they will only occur once. Costs related to production of a product are referred to as recurring costs on the grounds that they will recur every time the product is built.

- *Production quantity and rate*
  While quantity is the main driver of total production cost, the well-known learning effect can also have a considerable impact.

- *Team skills*
  The modern trend is for competitive project organisations to engage in some form of continuous improvement, thereby becoming more cost effective in their work. Team self-improvement is the common purpose.

Table 11.5 **Strengths, weaknesses and applications of parametric cost estimating methodology**

Strengths	Weaknesses	Applications
Once developed, CERs are an excellent tool to answer many 'what if' questions rapidly	Often difficult for others to understand the statistics associated with the CERs	- Design-to-cost trade studies - Cross-checking
Statistically sound predictors that provide information about the estimator's confidence of their predictive ability.	Must fully describe and document the selection of raw data, adjustments to data, development of equations, statistical findings, and conclusions for validation and acceptance	- Architectural studies - Long-range planning - Sensitivity analysis - Data-driven risk analysis - Software development
Eliminates reliance on opinion through the use of actual observations	Collecting appropriate data and generating statistically correct CERs is typically difficult, time consuming, and expensive	
Defensibility rests on logical correlation, thorough and disciplined research, defensible data, and scientific method	Loses predictive ability/credibility outside its relevant data range	

- *Team tools*
  'Tools' can include everything from buildings to production machines to computers and software. As tools improve, cost effectiveness increases.

- *Volatility*
  The most effective project environment is one in which project requirements, labour force, and infrastructure is stable.

- *Accounting changes*
  There are mandated changes from the Government, internal decisions to change cost accumulation procedures, adjustments to account for new ways of doing business, and mergers and acquisitions.

- *Special constraints*
  Various kinds of special constraints can seriously affect cost. Among them are: overly short or long project schedules; staff shortages; ill-advised attempts to reduce costs; high levels of project secrecy.

11.3.3 Procurement cost reduction

There is a continuing need for procurement to manage a cost reduction programme. There should be an agreed, and well-defined, programme for the procurement department and for each buyer. Table 11.6 sets out a range of possibilities for cost reduction attention.

Table 11.6 Possibilities for cost reduction attention

1 Challenge existing contracts for price competitiveness	■ Select long-term contracts ■ Benchmark in market ■ Establish the cost drivers
2 Challenge design/specification	■ Use concurrent engineering ■ Implement 'design for lean' ■ Use value analysis methodology
3 Negotiate reduction in overhead charges	■ Adopt electronic procurement systems ■ Reduce levels of inventory ■ Build to order
4 Adopt standardisation	■ Reduce varieties ■ Use one supplier's range ■ Design out duplicate ranges
5 Challenge supply chain costs	■ Incoterms ■ Packaging ■ Mode of transport
6 Consider outsourcing	■ Select non-core services ■ Market test ■ Set sights high
7 Better use of working capital	■ Payment terms ■ No advance payments ■ Reduce inventory
8 Eradicate uncompetitive suppliers	■ Issue RFQs ■ Negotiation with new suppliers ■ Terminate ineffective contracts

11.4 Supplier pricing decisions

The supplier's pricing decision will be made in a number of scenarios, including:

- selling a range of standard products either through published price lists or 'ad hoc' pricing decisions
- one-off project requirement that has no directly comparable precedence
- launching a new product or service
- selling a product or service to meet an 'emergency' situation, e.g. a technical solution to the failure of a safety critical piece of equipment
- a strategic decision to stop selling a range of products at the end of their design life.

There will be many general considerations to take into account, including:

- the ability to achieve an appropriate profit
- the nature of demand and supply, and current market forces
- existing capacity to provide the goods/services
- available inventory
- the buyer's location and status, e.g. are they are a well-established customer or a 'one-off' buyer
- required levels of investment, if any
- demands made on key personnel
- risk presented by the contractual terms and conditions
- any special environmental and health and safety requirements
- extent of sub-contracting and supply chain
- requirement for performance bonds/parent company guarantees
- product support requirements
- special insurances demanded
- intellectual property ownership
- urgency of requirement.

11.5 The supplier's choice of pricing strategy

A supplier has many options when deciding how to price goods or services. When the buyer receives a price from the supplier, it is difficult to know what approach has been taken, hence the need to probe tendered prices. Outlined below are some pricing strategies that may be used by a supplier.

11.5.1 Skimming pricing

This strategy involves charging a relatively high price for a period of time particularly where a new, innovative, or much improved product is launched on the market. The product may be protected by a patent as is often the case with pharmaceutical products. The protection will come to an end and competitors will then be attracted, hence dramatic reductions in price occur. For prestige goods and services, price skimming can be successful because the buyer is more concerned with prestige than price. First-class air travel and designer-label clothing are examples of skimming pricing.

11.5.2 Penetration pricing

In this instance, the price charged for products and services is set artificially low in order to:

(a) gain entry into a customer who is held to be of long-term strategic importance and/or
(b) gain market share.

It will be evident that such 'low' prices cannot be sustained in the longer term. When a buyer is faced with a tendered price that is, say, 40 per cent lower than the next ranked price there is the danger that the low price is linked to a perception of poor quality. So how does the supplier give such a low price? One way is to seek only to recover the net cost of materials and labour and to either not apply overhead recovery or to apply marginal overheads and not generate any profit.

11.5.3 Full cost pricing

The supplier, in this case, includes every cost that is believed to be attracted to the purchase. All material costs will be recovered, plus an allowance for scrap. All labour costs will be recovered at rates charged for each grade of labour, including management time. All overheads deemed to apply will be applied to labour and materials in a manner determined by Finance and may include corporate overheads imposed on the specific business operation. It is probable that a contingency provision will be included, as may be 'agent's fees', 'negotiation allowance', finance/cash/low risk provision and so on. It is believed that about 80 per cent of all supplier pricing decisions are made on the basis of full costs.

11.5.4 Buyer-related pricing

A deliberate strategy is for the supplier to offer a price that, in some way, directly relates to the 'buyer's' competence. The supplier will form a view on competence by the manner in which the purchase is approached. The disclosure of a budget is not a sign of competence. Neither are the following comments:

'Please do the best you can.'

'We are not asking anyone else to quote.'

'No doubt your prices have increased since we last purchased.'

'Can you supply us immediately and sort out the price later?'

11.5.5 Promotional pricing

This is common in the retail field with BOGOF (Buy One Get One Free), buy two and get 50 per cent discount on the second product, and seasonal offers. They are not uncommon in industry when suppliers seek to dispose of slow-moving inventory, dispose of products at the end of their life and in situations where the manufacturer is promoting a specific product for a limited period.

11.5.6 Prestige pricing

This is not dissimilar to skimming pricing and is used by suppliers who can capture part of a market and who want a 'prestige' service. The international airlines with first class travel at fares that can be six times 'economy' travel is one example, as are Savile Row suits, top-range motor vehicles and top-end wines.

The skill for buyers is to understand the basis of prices offered. This requires diligence in probing and understanding costs and, on occasions, the application of high-level negotiation skills.

11.5.7 Diversionary pricing

Some have argued that this is a practice used by deceptive service firms, suggesting that it is somehow illegal. The fact is that it is a legitimate business practice where a low price is stated for one or more services (emphasised in promotion) to give an illusion that all prices are low. An example is an ice cream manufacturer who offers freezers at a very low purchase price but only on condition their products can be stored in them.

11.5.8 Target pricing

This is where the buyer provides a target price to suppliers. The context in which this is done should be understood before a supplier responds. The target price could be the outcome of a genuine cost estimate when the buying organisation has very good knowledge of the product or service. In this situation the target price has some credibility. However, the unethical buyer may 'make up' a target price and pressurise suppliers to meet it, even if they cannot make a profit.

11.6 Tender pricing

Getting the inside story on tender pricing is notoriously difficult. The following insight is taken (extracts only) from a legal case involving the National Health Service in the United Kingdom.[12] It was a complex case. SRCL were one of five commercial operators that had been appointed by the NHSE under a tender process for a Framework Agreement. That appointment merely entitled each provider to enter into 'mini-competitions' for Call Off contracts for services. The legal case was in regard to such a mini-competition for 'Wave 6' services for Cumbria and the North East of England.

A reverse auction was held, following which SRCL Ltd were unsuccessful. SRCL Ltd submitted only one bid of £479,999. The successful bidder was HES at £310,000. The next lowest bidder was Smartsharp at £313,000. SRCL Ltd then made a complaint that the winning bid was an abnormally low tender.

During the case hearing it emerged (para 44) that the national average gross profit margin being achieved by SRCL across the UK from NHSE was 49%. The judge observed 'These levels of gross profit appear very high.' 'In money terms, gross profit to SRCL out of these revenues paid by NHSE was £2.24 million. The cost of the service to SRCL was £2.096 million. This hardly looks like value for money for NHSE . . . '

The judge (paras 91 and 95) commented on tendering and commercial judgements. 'To deal with these complexities (of the nature of the services) by a sweeping "minimum overhead and profit percentage of X%" is simply wrong.' The judge also said,

> If each tenderer for a project was to bid on the same basis, treating the same commercial risks in the same way, and allocating the same absolute minimum percentage of overhead and profit, then all tenders would end up (more or less) the same in financial value. Part of the business skill of any business manager involved in tendering . . . . is to use their commercial judgement in knowing what the commercial risks are, and correctly accommodating those risks (or pricing for them) in the tender price.

Our public sector readers will have more than a passing interest in the implications of TUPE on the pricing of tenders. At para 97 the judge said:

> what SRCL produced was, in my judgement, obviously misleading, and deliberately so. This was done by SRCL both to disrupt the auction process and also to put off other potential bidders from bidding. It overstated the number of employees who may transfer to the winning bidder under TUPE.

11.7 Price and cost analysis

Price analysis is designed to show that the proposed price is reasonable when compared with current or recent prices for the same or similar goods or services, adjusted where necessary to reflect changes in market conditions, economic conditions, quantities, or/ and terms and conditions under contracts that resulted for adequate price competition achieved through a RFQ (request for quotation) or tendering process.

Cost analysis is the review and evaluation of the separate cost elements, overhead recovery and profit in the tendered price (including cost or pricing data or information other than cost or pricing data) and the application of professional judgment to determine how appropriate the proposed costs are to setting the purchase price, assuming reasonable economy and efficiency.

11.7.1 Considerations when requesting prices from suppliers

There are many considerations when requesting prices from suppliers, including:

- the value of the contract
- if detailed cost information is provided, who has the competence to evaluate it?
- do we have the ability to prepare the cost model template?
- what benchmarking information do we have?
- what layers of labour costs do we want, e.g. by labour grades and time?
- how do we want overheads (fixed, variable and corporate) to be shown?
- how will we evaluate profit returns, taking into account investment?
- how do we propose to evaluate costs associated with risk?
- recognition that a proposed price may not be related to cost
- dealing with discounts and/or rebates
- the use to which the data will be put, e.g. negotiation
- the need to respect the supplier's confidentiality.

11.7.2 Price analysis

When tendered prices are being compared there are various bases on which a comparison can be made. These include:

- a simple comparison of proposed prices once it is ascertained that 'all things are equal', including compliance with the specification and contract terms and conditions
- the use of parametric estimating methods where key metrics are available
- comparison with competitive published price lists
- the use of comparable market prices through third-party consultants, e.g. energy pricing
- comparison with in-house generated 'should cost' estimates
- comparison with the output of value engineering/value analysis studies
- liaising with buyers in a wider procurement community, e.g. government buying operations in different departments.

11.7.3 Cost analysis

This is a far more demanding activity than price analysis because it requires the buying organisation to have the resources and expertise to analyse all costs, and to effectively challenge areas where it is believed the costs are inappropriate. The following facets of the price will need to be analysed, questioned and resolved:

- What constitutes material costs based ideally on a bill of materials and costed for base metals, materials, scrap allowance and bought-in sub-assemblies? Differences in these costs may be accounted for by good/bad procurement, efficiencies/inefficiencies in managing waste and so on.
- What constitutes labour costs, accounted for by the hourly cost of labour at various grades including operatives, supervision, management and any director involvement? There are significant differences between labour rates in, for example, UK, USA, India, Morocco, Vietnam and Israel.
- How are overheads being recovered? There are fixed and variable overheads to be considered and, depending on the suppliers' organisation structure, the possibility of corporate overheads used, for example, to recover corporate IT legal and financial services provision.
- It is probable that the supplier will apply a contingency factor, often a percentage of material, labour and overheads. The provision for contingency includes the potential of 'unexpected' factors arising such as labour disputes, unexpected surges in raw material prices, poor cost estimating and difficulties meeting the specification.
- The inclusion of costs to comply with the demands of the contract, such as:
  - provision for liquidated damages
  - provision of a performance bond or parent company guarantee
  - excessive inspection demands and testing procedures
  - attendance at contract review meetings.
- The declared profit that can be based on varied approaches, including:

- the recovery of investment such as research and development
- excessive profit return when skimming pricing used
- demands made by 'corporate' to justify bidding for the contract
- the need to generate financial reserves.

Tables 11.7 and 11.8 show examples of cost breakdowns, included to illustrate the depth of detail that can be pursued.

11.7.4 The buyer's control of purchase price

There should be a continuous review of the effectiveness of a buyer's control of purchase prices. This should include independent audits, taking into consideration, as a minimum:

- the award of contracts that are not subjected to tenders
- price increases allowed without scrutiny
- no scrutiny of cost drivers
- an absence of negotiation
- an absence of benchmarking data
- contract terms extended without tendering
- contract 'extras' allowed without challenge
- poor contract change procedures
- no consideration of reverse auctions
- single tendering permitted
- no control over price variation formulae
- no control over purchase prices linked to currency movement.

11.7.5 Cost breakdowns

Buyers engaged in high volume purchases are advised to get cost breakdowns from potential and existing suppliers. Experience has shown that some suppliers will provide the information but others will not. The following example has its origins in fact although

Table 11.7 Extract from services cost model

Employee costs	ICT costs
Salaries	Hardware
Overtime	Software
Pensions	Depreciation
National Insurance	Support
Supplementary benefits	Internal recharging
Car allowance	Other (name)
Public transport	
Training	
Recruitment	
Temporary employees	
Other (name)	

Table 11.8 Capital cost breakdown – base case – 65,000 tpd mill

Area	US$M
Process Plant	
Excavation & Backfill	2.7
Primary Crushing	9.3
Coarse Ore Reclaim	10.6
Concentrate Electrical	12.4
Grinding	81.9
Flotation	24.9
Concentrate Pumping and Concentrate Pipeline	55.7
Concentrate Dewatering	17.7
Reagent Handling	1.3
Concentrate Loadout	3.7
Plantsite Utilities, Comms	2.4
PLC & Software	0.5
Total Process Plant Cost	**223.1**
Infrastructure	
Shop & Warehouse	2.2
Truck Shop	9.0
Administrative Building	3.8
Plant access Roads, Tunnels & Bridges	97.2
Power supply	42.3
Water Supply	6.8
Water Rock/Tailing Storage/Water Diversion	72.5
Water Management	46.1
Camp	12.6
Airstrip	3.0
Other Buildings	1.9
Plant Mobile Equipment	3.2
Total Infrastructure Cost	**300.6**
Mine	
Haul Roads (includes Plant Site Roads)	4.7
Prestripping	78.8
Mine Equipment	133.7
Mine Dewatering	7.5
Mine Electrical	2.9
Magazine	0.2
Fuel Storage, Disposing and Magazine	1.3
Total Mine Cost	**229.1**
Total Project Direct Cost	**752.8**
Indirect Costs	
EPCM	65.3
Construction Indirects	81.4
Commissioning, Start-up, & Vendor Reps	1.7
Spares	12.3
First Fill	4.0
Freight	17.6
Owners Costs	22.5
Total Project Indirect Costs	**204.8**
Contingency	**144.1**
Total Project Costs	**1101.7**

the cost data has been modified to respect confidentiality. The example emanates from the food industry.

Cost breakdown

All costs are in respect of 1 tonne of finished product produced

Ingredients	£307.82
Labour	£120.00
Wear	£35.00
Energy	£30.00
Overheads	£78.11
Delivery	£32.61
Packaging	£41.00
Mark-up	£103.13
TOTAL	**£747.67** = **Selling Price**

The astute buyer will now further interrogate the information provided. If ingredients are further explained by the supplier it will reveal that:

Ingredients

There are six as shown in Table 11.9.

Is the buyer in a position to challenge the ingredient costs? To do so would require research to answer the following questions.

(i) What are the competing uses for the first four ingredients that account for 95.6 per cent of the ingredient costs?

(ii) Has the supplier included any wastage allowance in his calculations?

(iii) How does the supplier purchase the ingredients? Is it a long-term contract or spot purchase?

(iv) For what length of time are the ingredients costs fixed?

(v) Who has the capability to check the formulation costs and ingredient allowances?

Our readers can apply similar logic to question other costs and mark-up.

Table 11.9 Ingredient costs

	Kg	Tonne price	Formulation cost
Ingredient 1	438.13	£160.00	£70.10
Ingredient 2	375.54	£262.00	£98.39
Ingredient 3	212.80	£350.00	£74.48
Ingredient 4	125.18	£440.00	£51.32
Ingredient 5	12.52	£72.00	£0.90
Ingredient 6	25.04	£504.00	£12.62
TOTAL	**1189.00**		**£307.82**

11.7.6 Managing a key cost driver

In some sales prices there is a key cost driver, for example, a precious metal (Gold) used in electronics manufacture. International airliners have to deal with fluctuating aviation fuel prices on a continuing basis. JT Murphy[13] has written a very informative paper on fuel provisions for dredging projects. He explains that fuel can easily represent 30 per cent of dredging cost. He sheds light on the upfront owner costs, such as surveys, design, specifications, advertisement, coordination, evaluation, award and administration. A typical large dredge can easily accommodate 750,000 litres of marine diesel and use 20,000 litres per day. Typical contract documents require the potential dredging contractor to fill in the following (worked example):

$$p = b + cq$$

where
p = total dredging cost per cubic metre (cubic yard)

b = contractor provided dredging price per cubic metre (cubic yard)

c = owner provided price of fuel per litre (gallon)

q = contractor provided fuel requirement litres (gallons) per cubic metre (cubic yard)

b = \$7.85

c = \$0.85

q = 2.50

p = \$7.85 + \$0.85/litre $\times$ 2.50 litres/cubic metre

p = \$9.98 cubic metre

The management of the fuel pricing requires astute procurement strategic considerations, including definitive commitment, long-term supplier agreement, hedging or take the risks associated with supply market fluctuations.

11.8 Competition legislation

11.8.1 Introduction

On 18 March 2010, The National Audit Office published its report[14] 'Review of the UK's Competition Landscape'. At paragraph 2 it points out that the UK's competition regime is largely the result of the Competition Act 1998 and the Enterprise Act 2016. There is other legislation which impacts on the UK competition regime, such as the Communications Act 2003, Communications Legislation Amendment Act (No1) 2004 and the underpinning EU framework.

11.8.2 UK anti-competition agencies

Within the UK and Europe there are extensive measures in place, seeking to control anti-competition practices. On 15 March 2012 the UK Government's Department for Business, Innovation and Skills announced proposals for strengthening competition in the UK by merging the Office of Fair Trading and the Competition Commission to create a new single Competition and Markets Authority (CMA). The formation of CMA was enacted in Part 3 of the Enterprise and Regulatory Reform Act 2013 which received royal assent on 25 April 2013.

In situations where competition could be unfair or consumer choice may be affected, the CMA is responsible for:

- investing mergers
- conducting market studies
- investigating possible breaches of prohibitions against anti-competitive agreements under the Competition Act 1998
- bringing criminal proceedings against individuals who commit cartels offences
- enforcing consumer protection legislation, particularly the Unfair Terms in Consumer Contract Directive and Regulations
- encouraging regulators to use their competition powers
- considering regulatory reference and appeals.

The bodies are outlined below:

- The Competition Appeal Tribunal (CAT) is a specialist judicial body with cross-disciplinary expertise in Law, Economics, Business and Accountancy whose function is to hear and decide cases involving competition or economic regulatory issues. The CAT was created by Section 12 and Schedule 2 to the Enterprise Act 2002 which came into force on 1 April 2003. Judgments can be found on the CAT website: www.catribunal.org.uk
- There are a number of industry authorities, namely:
  - Civil Aviation Authority for airports and air traffic services
  - Monitor, for health services in England
  - Utility Regulator, for gas, electricity, water and sewerage in Northern Ireland
  - Ofcom, for television, radio, telephone, postal and internet services
  - Ofgem, for gas, electricity in England, Wales and Scotland
  - Ofwat, for water and sewage services in England and Wales
  - Office of Rail Regulation, for railways in England, Wales and Scotland.
- For the European Commission there is the Directorate-General for Competition. The European Commission, together with the national competition authorities, directly enforces EU competition rules, Articles 101-109 of the Treaty on the functioning of the EU (TFEU), to make EU markets work better, by ensuring that all companies compete equally and fairly on their merits. This benefits consumers, businesses and the European economy as a whole.

11.8.3 The Competition Act 1998

The Competition Act 1998 prohibited both anti-competition agreements and the abuse of a dominant position.

An 'agreement' is an undertaking or contract between companies or associated companies, whether in writing or otherwise. Examples of such agreements include:

- agreeing to fix procurement or selling prices or other trading conditions
- agreeing to limit or control production, markets or technical developments of investment

- agreeing to share markets or supply sources

- agreeing to apply different trading conditions to equivalent transactions, thereby placing some parties at a competitive advantage.

An agreement is, however, considered to be unlikely to have an appreciable effect where the combined market share of the parties involved does not exceed 25 per cent. This said, agreements to fix prices, impose minimum resale prices or share markets may be regarded as having an appreciable effect even when the parties' combined market share is below 25 per cent.

Whether or not a company is in a 'dominant position' will be decided by the OFT according to the company's market share. In general, a company is unlikely to be regarded as dominant if it has a market share of less than 40 per cent, although a lower market share may be considered dominant if the market structure enables it to act independently of its competitors.

Ways in which a dominant company may abuse its position include:

- imposing unfair procurement or selling prices

- limiting production, markets or technical development to the prejudice of customers

- applying different trading conditions to equivalent transactions and thereby placing certain parties at a competitive advantage

- attaching unrelated supplementary conditions to a contract.

11.9 Collusive tendering

Collusive tendering is a pernicious and criminal practice. A definition is 'when companies making tenders secretly share information or make arrangements among themselves in order to control the result.' There is extensive reference material emanating from authorities, such as the Office of Fair Trading Decisions CA98/03/2013 'Collusive tendering in the Supply and Installation of certain access control and alarm systems to retirement properties' (Case CE/9248-10), 6 December 2013. Selected findings are shown below:

> 1.6 ... The infringements comprised of three separate bilateral collusive tendering arrangements between Cirrus and each of O'Rourke, Owens and Jackson with a total of 65 tenders, with an aggregate value of approximately £1.4million being the subject of collection.

> 3.38 In order for a concerted practice to be regarded as having an anti- competitive object, it is sufficient that it has the potential to have a negative impact on competition.

> 4.6 An essential feature of any tender process (whether open of selective) is that the prospective suppliers should compete with each other and prepare and submit bids adequately.

Procurement should have an active role in seeking to determine whether collusive tendering has or is likely to have occurred. In the above case the procurement authority was PMSL who sought at least, two bids. One was always from CCSL part of the PMSL corporate group and the other from a contractor nominated by CCSL.

At 5.31 a CCSL internal document exposed the collusive relationship: 'Hello, I have updated the process but think it's best if we keep this one "in house" as the bits in red are what we do behind the scenes and not an official part of the process (tee hee).'

11.10 Price variation formulae

Traditionally, whenever, price variation formulae have been discussed, reference has been made to the formula developed by the British Electrotechnical and Allied Manufacturers Association (BEAMA). Variations in the cost of materials and labour are calculated in accordance with the following formula:

$$P_1 = P_0\left(0.05 + 0.475\left(\frac{M_1}{M_0}\right) + 0.475\left(\frac{L_1}{L_0}\right)\right)$$

where:

P_1 = final contract price

P_0 = contract price at date of tender

M_1 = average of producer price index figures for materials and fuel purchased for basic electrical equipment as provided by the Office for National Statistics, commencing with the index last provided before the two-fifths point of the contract period and ending with the index last provided before the four-fifths point of the contract period

M_0 = producer price index figure of materials and fuel purchased for basic electrical equipment last provided by the Office for National Statistics before the date of tender

L_1 = average of the BEAMA labour cost index figures for electrical engineering published for the last two-thirds of the contract period

L_0 = BEAMA labour cost index figure for electrical engineering published for the month in which the tender date falls.

It is essential that a professional buyer has a good working knowledge of the way in which price variation formulae are constructed and applied. The complexity will depend on the nature of the actual purchase.

The Indian Electrical and Electronics Manufacturers Association (IEEMA) have devised a PVF for a copper wound transformer. This is reproduced below.

The price quoted/confirmed is based on the input cost of raw materials/components and labour cost as on the date of quotation and the same is deemed to be related to prices of raw materials and all India average consumer price index number for industrial workers as specified in the price variation clause given below. In case of any variation in these prices and index numbers, the price payable shall be subject to adjustment, up or down in accordance with the following formula:

$$P = \left(13 + 23\frac{c}{c_0} + 27\frac{ES}{ES_0} + 9\frac{IS}{IS_0} + \frac{IM}{IM_0}11\frac{TB}{TB_0} + 12\right)$$

where:

P = Price payable as adjusted in accordance with the above formula

P_0 = Price quoted/confirmed

C_0 = Average LME settlement price of copper wire bars

This price is as applicable for the month, *two* months prior to the date of tendering

ES_0 = C&F price of CRGO Electrical Steel Sheets

This price is as applicable on the first working day of the month *one* month prior to the date of tendering.

IS_0 = Wholesale price index number for iron and steel (base 1993–94 = 100)

This index number is as applicable for the week ending first Saturday of the month *three* months prior to the date of tendering.

IM_0 = Price of insulation materials

This price is as applicable on the first working day of the month, *one* month prior to the date of tendering.

TB_0 = Price of transformer oil base stock

This price is as applicable on the first working day of the month, *two* months prior to the date of tendering.

W_0 = All India average consumer price index number for industrial workers, as published by the Labour Bureau, Ministry of Labour, Government of India (base 1982 = 100)

C = Average LME settlement price of copper wire bars

This price is as applicable for the month, *two* months prior to the date of delivery.

ES = C&F price of CRGO electrical steel sheet

This price is as applicable on the first working day for the month, *one* month prior to the date of delivery.

IS = Wholesale price index number for iron and steel (base: 1993–94 = 100)

This index number is as applicable for the week ending first Saturday of the month, *three* months prior to the date of delivery.

IM = Price of insulating material

This price is as applicable on the first working day of the month, *one* month prior to the date of delivery.

TB = Price of transformer oil base stock

This price is as applicable on the first working day of the month, *two* months prior to the date of delivery.

W = All India average consumer price index number for industrial workers, as published by the Labour Bureau, Ministry of Labour, Government of India (base 1982 = 100)

This index number is as applicable on the first working day of the month, *three* months prior to the date of delivery.

Another price adjustment formula, this time one applied in the South African engineering sector is reproduced below.

In accordance with Clause 49(2), the value of each certificate issued in terms of Clause 52(1) shall be increased or decreased by the amount obtained by multiplying 'Ac', defined in Clause 2 of this Schedule, by the Contract Price Adjustment Factor, rounded off to the fourth decimal place, determined according to the formula:

$$CPAF = (1 - X)\left[\frac{aLt}{L_0} + \frac{bPt}{P_0} + \frac{cMt}{M_0} + \frac{dFt}{P_0} - 1\right]$$

in which the symbols have the following meaning:

'X' is the proportion of 'Ac' which is not subject to adjustment unless otherwise stated in the Appendix; this proportion shall be 0.15.

'a', 'b', 'c', and 'd' are the coefficients determined by the engineer and specified in the Appendix, and which are deemed, irrespective of the actual constituents of the work, to represent the proportionate value of labour, plant, materials (other than 'special materials' specified, in terms of Clause 49(3), in the Appendix) and fuel respectively. The arithmetical sum of 'a', 'b', 'c' and 'd' shall be unity.

'L' is the 'Labour Index' and shall be the actual wage rate index for all workers in the civil engineering industry of the Central Statistical Service.

'P' is the 'Plant Index' and shall be the 'Civil Engineering Plant Index' as published in the Statistical News Release (PO 142.2) of the Central Statistical Service.

'M' is the 'Materials Index' and shall be the 'Price Index of Civil Engineering Materials', as published in the Statistical News Release (PO 142.20) of the Central Statistical Service.

'F' is the 'Fuel Index' and shall be the weighted average of the fuel indices for 'Diesel, before deduction of refund' and 'Diesel, after deduction of refund', as published in the Statistical News Release (PO 142.20) of the Central Statistical Service for the 'Coast' or 'Witwatersrand'. The weighting ratio and the use of the 'Coast' and 'Witwatersrand' indices shall be as specified by the engineer in the Appendix unless otherwise specified by the engineer in the Appendix, the weighting ratio shall be 1 to 1.

The suffix 'o' denotes the basic indices applicable to the base month, which shall be the month prior to the month in which the closing date for the tender falls.

The suffix 't' denotes the current indices applicable to the month in which the last day of the period falls to which the relevant payment certificate relates.

If any index relevant to any particular certificate is not known at the time when the certificate is prepared, the engineer shall estimate the value of such an index. Any correction which may be necessary when the correct indices become known shall be made by the engineer in subsequent payment certificates.

Discussion questions

11.1 What are the consequences of procurement failing to effectively manage purchase prices?

11.2 How would you define price:
   (a) from the buyer's viewpoint?
   (b) from the supplier's viewpoint?

11.3 At the pre-tender phase of procurement, how may the following activities aid the control of purchase prices:
   (a) engaging in soft market testing?
   (b) using parametric estimating?
   (c) networking within the procurement profession?
   (d) contributing to a benchmarking service?

11.4 If a supplier provides a detailed cost breakdown, what roles can be played in evaluating it, by each of the following:

(a) the buyer?

(b) the accountant?

(c) the technical specialist in the goods/service?

(d) the estimator?

11.5 You have been asked to purchase a hot air balloon. Your sales director has obtained a single quotation from a well-known manufacturer. The price is quoted as £35,500 and the following information has been provided:

	£
Envelope	15,000
Envelope scoop	1000
Padded covers × 4	500
Inflator fan	2500
Tether line	400
Shadow double burner	5500
Basket	4500
Fuel cylinders × 4	4500
Instruments	1000
Cushion floor	100
Other equipment	500
Artwork	AT COST

What specific actions would you consider taking in regard to:

(a) inviting other quotations?

(b) challenging the cost breakdown?

(c) asking where the overhead recovery and profit is hidden?

(d) taking a negotiating stance to get the price reduced?

11.6 If you received a price increase request from a strategic supplier of goods, for which there is competition, and the request was for an increase of 4.5 per cent due to 'abnormal trading conditions, raw material increases, energy prices and overheads', what would be your next actions?

11.7 What are the six most significant considerations that a supplier will take into account when making a price decision?

11.8 Buyers are only driven by price. How would you counter this proposition?

11.9 You have been asked to draft a guidance procedure for inclusion in a Procurement Manual. The topic is 'Conducting cost analysis on tendered prices'. What headings would you include and what, specifically, would you say about profit?

11.10 What are the salient aims and facets of the UK competition regime?

11.11 Describe how a price variation formula is typically constructed and explain why such formulae are used.

11.12 What types of pricing agreements would you recommend the procurement specialist to adopt for the following situations?

(a) The provision of specialist consultancy services for a period of six months to support the purchase of a new IT system.

(b) The manufacture of a new component for incorporation in a new product that will be launched in six months' time.

(c) The building of a new school where the contract requires the contractor to supply all the furnishings and equipment.

(d) The retention of a professional institute to provide three years training services where the content and quantity is currently unknown.

(e) A one-year contract for the supply of external catering services, including the provision of food.

11.13 'It is a myth to believe that any buyer controls prices. The initiative is always with the supplier.' Discuss.

References

1 Nagle, T. T., Hogan, J. E. and Zale, J. *The Strategy and Tactics of Pricing. A Guide to Growing More Profitably*, Pearson Education Limited, Harlow, UK, 5th edn, 2014, p. 1.

2 Farrington, B., 'Industrial Purchasing Price Management', PhD, University of Brunel (Henley College), 1978.

3 Leighton, D. S. R., *International Marketing*, McGraw Hill, New York, USA.

4 Leenders, M. R., Fearson, H. E. and England, W. B. *Purchasing & Materials Management*, R D Irwin Inc., Homewood, Illinois, USA, 1980.

5 Winkler, J., *Winkler on Marketing Planning*, Wiley & Sons, Hoboken, USA, 1973.

6 Ammer, D. S., *Materials Management*, RD Irwin, 1968.

7 GAO Cost Estimating and Assessment Guide.' March 2009. GAO-09-3SP.

8 Tuns, M., 'Computerised cost estimation for forging industry', a thesis submitted to the Graduate School of Natural and Applied Sciences of the Middle East Technical University, September 2003.

9 Deccan Systems Inc., Ohio, USA: www.deccansystems.com.

10 International Cost estimating and Analysis Association 8221 Old Courthouse Road, Suite 106 Vienna, VA 22182.

11 NASA Cost Estimating Handbook Version 4.0. February 2015. NASA CEHv4.0.

12 SRCL Ltd V The National Health Service Commissioning Board (NHS) [2018] EWHC 1985 (TCC) (27July 2018).

13 Fuel Provisions for Dredging Projects. Proceedings WEDA XXXII Technical Conference & TAMU 43 Dredging Seminar J.T. Murphy Project Manager. US Army Corps of Engineers.

14 National Audit Office, 'Review of the UK's Competition Landscape', published 18 March, 2010.

Part 3

Public sector procurement and sustainable procurement

Chapter 12

Public sector procurement

Learning outcomes

This chapter aims to provide an understanding of:

- understanding the context of public procurement
- procurement – an integral element of the commissioning cycle
- the complexity and nature of public sector procurement
- Public Accounts Committee
- Procurement of goods and services
- EU procurement thresholds
- OJEU minimum timescales
- public procurement procedures
- pre-qualification to supply a public sector organisation
- tender evaluation
- the legal context of challenges to public sector contract award
- public sector risk
- public sector procurement fraud
- Aviation Department fraud – USA
- Mighty River Power Ltd fraud – New Zealand
- the Fat Leonard case fraud – USA
- public sector projects – procurement learning.

Key ideas

- The impact of public procurement on the economy.
- Complexities of public procurement.
- Choice of procurement procedures.
- Dealing with the regulatory environment.
- Positive evaluation of tenders.
- Risk management.
- Fraudulent activities in public procurement.
- Procurement and public sector projects.

Introduction

Public procurement has a compelling influence on national economies. The following extract from an EU publication[1] adequately explains why.

> Public procurement is a key aspect of public investment: it stimulates economic development in Europe and represents an important element for boosting the Single Market. Public procurement matters – it represents around 19 per cent of the EU's GDP and is part of our everyday life. Public administrations purchase goods and services for their citizens: this must be done in the most efficient way. Public procurement also offers opportunities to enterprises thereby fostering private investment and contributing to growth and jobs on the ground. Finally, public procurement plays an important role in channelling European Structural and Investment Funds.

> It is estimated that around 48 per cent of the European Structural and investment Funds is spent through public procurement. Projects in the Member States co-financed by the EU funds must be in line with the applicable public procurement rules which ensure value for money and fair competition in the market. Transparency and integrity in the relevant procedures is also essential for maintaining citizens' trust in government.

> For all the reasons above, the correct and coherent implementation of public procurement rules results in benefits in terms of efficiency and effectiveness for everybody – for public administrations at national and regional level, for enterprises and for citizens. It helps us all make the most out of public investment and guarantee the maximum benefits from the EU funds. Yet, data show that a significant part of the overall total of errors in the spending of EU funds is due to an incorrect application of the EU rules on public procurement.

12.1 Understanding the context of public procurement

There is a very informative report 'Public Procurement in Wales'[2] which sets out what effective procurement involves:

- having adequate numbers of appropriate qualified staff and appropriate organisational structures and policies to manage and govern procurement activity
- a well-planned process for deciding what the public body needs, including deciding how the public body should provide services and looking at alternative ways of delivering services
- sourcing strategies and collaborative procurement – having a good idea of how the public body can best meet its needs
- effective contract and supplier management and
- effective and reliable processes and ICT systems to support procurement.

They also observe:

> Para 22 'Public bodies face challenges in balancing potentially competing procurement priorities and in responding to new legislation and policy and are responding in different ways.'

The report sets out at page 19 the legislative and policy framework for public procurement in Wales.

There is a Welsh Public Procurement Policy based upon the following principles:

- strategic
- professionally resourced

Figure 12.1 The legislative and policy framework for Public Procurement in Wales

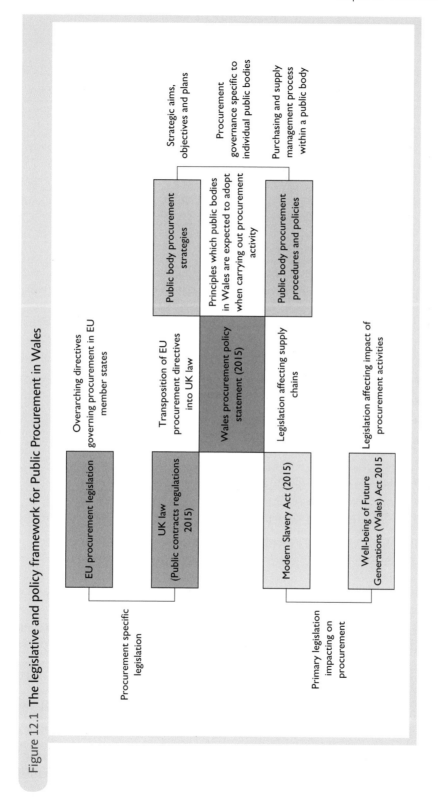

Figure 12.2 Procurement spend by category in Wales 2015/16

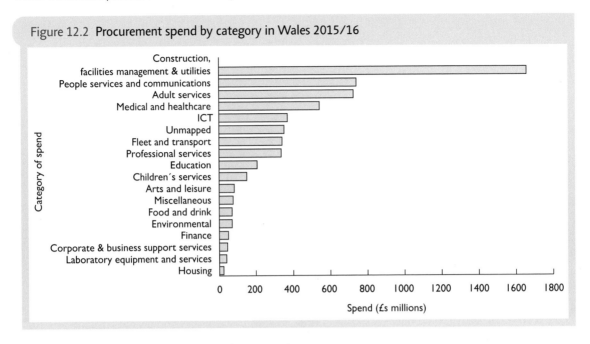

- value for money in terms of economic, social and environmental impact
- community benefits
- open accessible competition
- simplified standard processes
- collaboration
- supplier engagement and innovation
- support achievement of the seven well-being goals for Wales
- measurement and impact.

The Welsh profile of expenditure in 2015/16 is shown in Figure 12.2.

12.2 Procurement – an integral element of the commissioning cycle

Procurement does not operate in a vacuum. It is part of the commissioning cycle. The Institute of Public Care[3] publish a 'Commissioning Cycle' (see Figure 12.3).

They define commissioning as 'the process of identifying needs within the population and developing policy directions, service models and the market, to meet those needs in the most appropriate and cost-effective way.'

They define procurement as 'the process of acquiring goods, works or services from (usually) external providers or suppliers and managing these through to the end of the contract.'

They define contracting as 'the process of negotiating and agreeing the terms of a contract, e.g. for services, and on-going management of the contract including payment and monitoring.'

Figure 12.3 Commissioning cycle – The Institute of Public Care

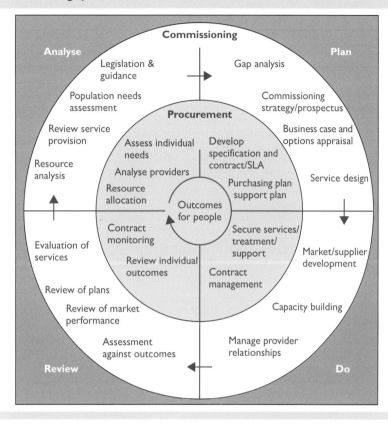

12.3 The complexity and nature of public sector expenditure

Table 12.1 is indicative of the complexity and nature of public sector expenditure. In respect of the countries in the EU it is possible to check on a daily basis what business opportunities exist with http://ted.europa.eu. It is interesting to reflect that while many

Table 12.1 Complexities and nature of public expenditure

Project	Goods	Services	Works
New railway infrastructure	Inorganic & organic chemicals	Education & training	Gas distribution
New hospitals/schools	Adhesive tape	Social work	Clinic construction
Nuclear submarines	Orthopaedic supplies	Financial & Insurance	Construction work for
New military hardware	Civil engineering machinery	Refuse recycling	leisure, sports, culture,
Water supply	Firefighting vehicles	School catering	lodging and restaurants
Transport infrastructure	Bulldozers	Air transport	Multi-dwelling
IT systems	Ships and boats	Business Services, law,	buildings
New prisons	Pharmaceutical products	marketing, consulting	Canal construction
Sewage treatment	Medical breathing devices	Public relations	Swimming pool
Military transport helicopters		Pipeline design	construction
Surveillance and security systems & devices			Sports hall construction

public sector organisations have category management specialists, there are constant challenges for procurement to have the relevant expertise to effectively manage the procurement processes across the range of expenditure.

The author accessed in March 2019 contract opportunities for Ireland. A random sample of four procurements showed:

1 the supply, delivery, installation, commissioning and support of Instrument Runway Visual Range (IRVR) Systems for the Irish Aviation Authority (IAA) – estimated value 2,500,000.00 EUR

2 provision of archaeological consultancy services in advance of the construction of the NS Ballaghadereen to Scrahmoge Road Project – estimated value 12,700,000.00 EUR

3 to use the models developed by EirGrid and functionality contained in the current WSAT tool or to develop a new software application – estimated value 3,650,000.00 EUR

4 design, build and construction of a 22 m passenger ferry for tourism – estimated value 850,000.00 EUR.

12.4 Public Accounts Committee

In the UK The Committee of Public Accounts is appointed by the House of Commons to examine: 'the accounts showing the appropriation of the sums granted to Parliament to meet the public expenditure and of such other accounts laid before Parliament as the Committee may think fit' (Standing Order No. 148).

The Committee scrutinises the value for money – the economy, efficiency and effectiveness – of public spending and generally holds the government and its civil servants to account for the delivery of public services. The Committee has spread its work to also examine public bodies and private companies providing public services.

Procurement is a focus of the Committee and a relevant Briefing Paper[4] is available. Some salient points include:

- procurement accounts for about a third of public spending in the UK
- value for money is defined as 'securing the best mix of quality and effectiveness for the least outlay over the period of use of the goods or services bought. It is not about minimising upfront prices.'
- in 2016/17 the UK public sector spent an estimated £255 billion with external suppliers. Of this, £118 billion was procurement by central government and £70 billion by local government.

The Committee observes that contracts can and do, go wrong in various ways. The Committee pointed out in 2014[5]:

> The public's trust in outsourcing has been undermined recently by the poor performance of G4S in supplying security guards for the Olympics, Capita's failure to deliver court transportation services, issues with Atos's work capability assessments, misreporting of out of hours GP services by Serco, and most recently, the astonishing news that G4S and Serco had overcharged for years on electronic tagging contracts.

12.5 Procurement of goods and services

At Figure 12.4 is a decision flow chart produced by Lichfield Council.[6] The financial amounts shown were correct at the time of drafting this chapter.

Figure 12.4 Decision flow chart for the procurement of goods and services

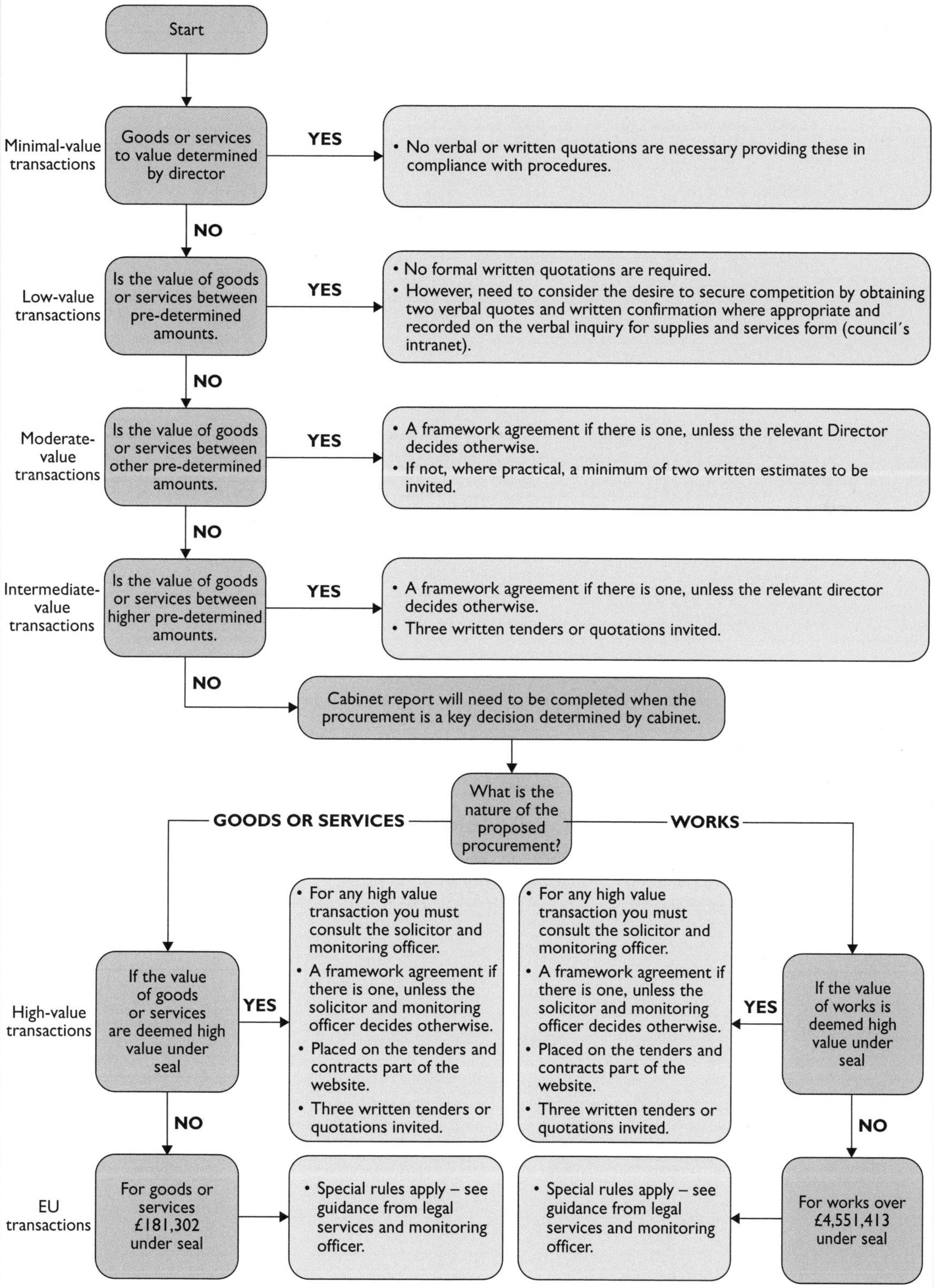

Start

Minimal-value transactions
Goods or services to value determined by director — **YES** → No verbal or written quotations are necessary providing these in compliance with procedures.

NO

Low-value transactions
Is the value of goods or services between pre-determined amounts. — **YES** →
- No formal written quotations are required.
- However, need to consider the desire to secure competition by obtaining two verbal quotes and written confirmation where appropriate and recorded on the verbal inquiry for supplies and services form (council's intranet).

NO

Moderate-value transactions
Is the value of goods or services between other pre-determined amounts. — **YES** →
- A framework agreement if there is one, unless the relevant Director decides otherwise.
- If not, where practical, a minimum of two written estimates to be invited.

NO

Intermediate-value transactions
Is the value of goods or services between higher pre-determined amounts. — **YES** →
- A framework agreement if there is one, unless the relevant director decides otherwise.
- Three written tenders or quotations invited.

NO

Cabinet report will need to be completed when the procurement is a key decision determined by cabinet.

What is the nature of the proposed procurement?

← GOODS OR SERVICES | **WORKS →**

High-value transactions

If the value of goods or services are deemed high value under seal — **YES** →
- For any high value transaction you must consult the solicitor and monitoring officer.
- A framework agreement if there is one, unless the solicitor and monitoring officer decides otherwise.
- Placed on the tenders and contracts part of the website.
- Three written tenders or quotations invited.

YES ← If the value of works is deemed high value under seal
- For any high value transaction you must consult the solicitor and monitoring officer.
- A framework agreement if there is one, unless the solicitor and monitoring officer decides otherwise.
- Placed on the tenders and contracts part of the website.
- Three written tenders or quotations invited.

NO | **NO**

EU transactions

For goods or services £181,302 under seal →
- Special rules apply – see guidance from legal services and monitoring officer.

- Special rules apply – see guidance from legal services and monitoring officer.
← For works over £4,551,413 under seal

431

Table 12.2 Thresholds for 2018/2019

	Supply, services (1) and design contracts	Works contracts (2)	Social and other specific services (3)
Central government (4)	£118,133 €144,000	£4,551,413 €5,548,000	£615,278 €750,000
Other contracting authorities	£181,302 €221,000	£4,551,413 €5,548,000	£615,278 €750,000
Small lots	£65,630 €80,000	£820,370 €1,000,000	N/A

12.6 EU financial thresholds

When procuring goods or services over the financial threshold a public authority must do so under the Public Contracts Regulations 2015 in England, Wales and Northern Ireland. The 2018/2019 thresholds are shown in Table 12.2 (noting the thresholds are addressed every two years). Any requirements over the thresholds must be advertised in the *Official Journal of the European Journal* (*OJEU*), rather than just advertising it nationally. The calculation of the estimated value of procurement shall be based on the total amount payable, net of VAT, as estimated by the contracting authority, including any form of option and any renewals of the contracts as explicitly set out in the procurement documents.

12.7 OJEU minimum timescale

The complexities of public procurement when an *OJEU* advertisement is involved can be seen in Table 12.3. The general rules are set out at Regulation 47 of the Public Contracts Regulations 2015.

Table 12.3 Minimum timescales for procurement regulations 2018

Procedure	Selection stage[1]	Tender stage	If electronic ITT accepted[2]	Tender following PIN[3]	Tender by arrangement[4]	Urgency[5]
Open	N/A	35 days	30 days	15 days	N/A	15 days
Restricted	30 days	30 days	25 days	10 days	Minimum 10 days	15 days / 10 days
Competitive with negotiation	30 days	30 days	25 days	10 days	Minimum 10 days	15 days / 10 days
Competitive dialogue	30 days	N/A	N/A	N/A	N/A	N/A
Innovation partnership	30 days	N/A	N/A	N/A	N/A	N/A

The Public Contracts Regulations 2015 set out specific procedures which may be used for contracting and the subsequent minimum timescales that may be applied. Table 12.3 details these timelines including the additional time reduction benefits that can be applied when using electronic means in the procurement process.

Notes

1. Where a Prior Information Notice has been used as a Call for Competition in the Restricted Procedure and the Competitive Procedure with Negotiation, the 30-day timescale commences from when the invitation to confirm interest is sent.

2. Where the Contracting Authority accepts that tenders may be submitted by electronic means, the time limit for receipt of tenders may be reduced by 5 days.

3. Where a Prior Information Notice was sent for publication between 35 days and 12 months before the contract notice was sent.

4. In the Restricted Procedure and Competitive Procedure with Negotiation, the Contracting Authority may set the time limit for receipt of tenders by mutual agreement with all candidates. Evidence of any such agreement must be retained for audit purposes. In the absence of such an agreement, the time limit must be at least 10 days.

5. In matters of urgency, duly substantiated by the Contracting Authority (and evidence retained for audit), the time limit for tenders shall be no less than 15 days in the Open Procedure. In the Restricted Procedure and Competitive Procedure with Negotiation, the timescale for the selection stage shall be no less than 15 days and for the tender stage, shall be no less than 10 days.

12.8 Public procurement procedures

There follows a brief description of the five procedures (more detail can be found in The Public Contracts Regulations 2015).

12.8.1 Open procedure: Regulation 27 PCR 2015

The timescales for the open procedure are given in Table 12.3. This is a process where all providers interested in the contract and who have responded to an advertisement can submit tenders. All such tenders must be considered without any prior selection process. It is advisable to only use the open procedure when competition is limited to a few candidates. See Table 12.4 for the advantages and disadvantages of the open procedure.

12.8.2 Restricted procedure: Regulation 28 PCR 2015

The timescale for the restricted procedure is given in Table 12.3. This is a two-stage process where only those providers who have been invited may submit tenders. The Directive sets a minimum of five candidates. The contracting authority may impose a limit on the maximum number for a given procedure. See Table 12.5 for the advantages and disadvantages of the restricted procedure.

Table 12.4 Advantages and disadvantages of the open procedure

	Advantages	Disadvantages
Open procedure	■ Highly competitive due to the unlimited number of tenders ■ All documentation from tenderers received at the same time for evaluation, i.e. time saving ■ Both selection criteria and award criteria indicated in advance in the contract notice ■ The speed of the procedure ■ complaints seeking remedies are less likely since the actions and decisions of the contracting authority are related only to 'one process' procedure ■ Easier to defend the decision as straight forward focus on the award	■ The process can seem to take a long time as all compliant tenders must be examined by the contracting authority. This can delay the awarding procedure. ■ Resource intensive for the contracting authority and the tenderers ■ Unknown number of tenders to be received making work load planning difficult

Table 12.5 Advantages and disadvantages of the restricted procedure

	Advantages	Disadvantages
Restricted procedure	■ Limited number of tenders to evaluate and therefore less resource intensive for the evaluation panel ■ Possibility to restrict participation only to market operators with high level of specialisation (in the case of complex contracts for which preparing a tender involves significant costs, limiting the number of tenderers through pre-qualification can make the tender more attractive as the chance to win the tender is higher for pre-qualified tenderers than in an open procedure)	■ Less competition due to the limited number of tenderers ■ More possibilities for complaints seeking remedies since the actions and decisions of the Contracting Authority are related to a two-process procedure ■ More difficult, high requirements to transparency

Table 12.6 Advantages and disadvantages of the competitive procedure

	Advantages	Disadvantages
Competitive procedure	■ Enables Contracting Authority to closely examine and negotiate key facets of the tenders ■ Those tendering know the intended process ■ Ability to apply complex negotiation skills ■ Buyer can set the agenda and control the timescale ■ Best & Final offers can be requested.	■ The potential for challenge ■ Maintaining a robust audit trail ■ Negotiators for Contracting Authority may disclose unwittingly confidential data from one bidder to another ■ Bidder may have more advanced negotiation skills than Contracting Authority ■ Minimum requirements must be met and not, unwittingly, changed during negotiations

12.8.3 Competitive procedure with negotiation: Regulation 29.PCR 2015

The timescale for the competitive is shown in Table 12.3. This is, potentially, a complex process as set out in Regulation 29. This procedure, by comparison with the open and restricted procedures, is not in extensive use. See Table 12.6 for the advantages and disadvantages of the competitive procedure with negotiation.

Table 12.7 Advantages and disadvantages of competitive dialogue procedure

	Advantages	Disadvantages
Competitive dialogue	■ If the process is managed professionally it engenders goodwill and problem solving ■ Alternative solutions can be actively considered ■ Relationship building is achieved ■ Bidders realise it is a genuine competitive process.	■ One or both parties have serious misgivings about the process ■ An imbalance of skills between the parties ■ Bidders have superior technical knowledge ■ The Contracting Authority requires a surfeit of external advisers ■ Comparison of options is very challenging

12.8.4 Competitive dialogue: Regulation 30. PCR 2015

The timescale for the competitive dialogue procedure is shown in Table 12.3. This procedure is ideal for complex procurements, particularly where the end solution cannot be specified or where the end solution generates potential difficulties in evaluating alternative, initial offers.

12.8.5 Innovative Partnership: Regulation 31.PCR 2015

The timescale for the innovative partnership is given in Table 12.3. This is a completely new procurement procedure introduced by the PCR 2015. The Public Sector Blog[7] explained the innovative partnership as follows:

> The reason for the introduction of innovation partnership is linked to the *Europe 2020 strategy*. Recital 47 of Directive 2014/24/EU specifically refers to the strategy and indicates the need for innovation to address 'major societal challenges'. It acknowledges existing procurement models but says that the new directive should facilitate innovation. Recital 49 therefore refers to a 'specific procurement procedure . . . (to) allow contracting authorities to establish a long-term innovation partnership for the development and subsequent purchase of a new, innovative product, service or works provided that such innovative product or service or innovative works can be delivered to agreed performance levels and costs, without the need for a separate procurement procedure for the purchase'.
>
> Regulations 31 (10) and (11) indicate that the innovation partnership shall be structured in 'successive stages'; with 'intermediate targets' and remuneration in instalments. Such a partnership therefore opens up the possibility to enter into an agreement in the form of an incremental contractual arrangement using two distinct stages – the first being the 'R&D' or design stage to develop the solution; followed by the service contract that delivers the solution. The ability to incorporate both a research and a commercial phase in a single procurement may have been the driver for the introduction of this process though, being a common law jurisdiction, our contracts already allow for this flexibility. The procedure may also feature the termination of the partnership after each phase (*regulation 31(12)*).

Our readers are advised to read an EU 'Commission Notice' document.[8]

12.9 Pre-qualification to supply a public sector organisation

12.9.1 Introduction

In public procurement there is the 'Restricted Procedure' under EU Regulations. It requires potential suppliers to engage in the procurement process by, initially, completing a Pre-Qualification Questionnaire (PQQ). A case in point was a PQQ in respect of

Table 12.8 **Durham Tees Valley Airport scoring matrix**

Score	Classification	Definition
0	Unacceptable	No response, or totally unacceptable and does not meet the requirement in any way.
1	Inadequate	Does not meet the Airport's expectations in some significant areas. Considerable reservations of the Applicant's ability, understanding, experience, skills, resources, or quality measures.
2	Weak	A response that does not fully meet requirements. Response may be minimal with little or no detail or evidence given to support and demonstrate sufficiency or compliance.
3	Satisfactory	Response meets requirements and evidence is given to support the answers, but may be brief.
4	Good	Requirements are met and evidence is provided to support the answers demonstrating sufficiency, compliance and significant experience.
5	Excellent	Requirements exceeded and are robustly and clearly evidenced. Response goes above and beyond requirements and demonstrate additional value for the Airport, without additional cost.

the supply of a Primary Surveillance Radar (PSR) in support of approach operations at Durham Tees Valley Airport, England. The procurement was conducted in accordance with the Utilities Contracts Regulations 2016.

The purpose of the PQQ was to allow the Airport to identify a shortlist of suitably qualified and experienced applicants, in particular those who demonstrated capability to offer a proven solution.

12.9.2 Evaluation scoring matrix

When PQQ questions are being evaluated there must be a scoring matrix. Table 12.8 shows the Airport PQQ scoring matrix.

12.9.3 PQQ questions – weighting

In the Airport PQQ were two 'sections' and thirteen questions.

– Financial status & insurance	– 10 per cent of the marks
– Professional standing	– 10 per cent of the marks
– Solution capability	– 35 per cent of the marks (7 questions)
– Solution implementation and support	– 10 per cent of the marks (3 questions)
– Solution viability and delivery	– 35 per cent of the marks (2 questions)

One of the skills required in developing a PQQ is the ability to ask the 'right' questions. Question 9 in the PQQ read:

Please explain how your company will be able to provide a full PSR solution (including tower, UPS, other necessary equipment and spares), support the integration with other ATM systems, provide necessary safety assurance documentation, and prepare and deliver training for all users. If your company cannot provide all of these, please provide an explanation of how these needs will be met. Please cross-reference your response with that for question 12 if your services/options will influence the price (or vice versa). Please provide supporting evidence in the Reference Annex (see below). This response should be limited to 2 sides of A4.

Readers will note the complexity of the question and the fact that only two sides of A4 are permitted to answer the question. It may be argued that the page restriction is a disadvantage to bidders.

12.10 Tender evaluation

12.10.1 Introduction

Bidders who respond to an Invitation to Tender (ITT) will have invested time and resources to formulate their reply. It is incumbent upon the public sector to evaluate all tenders in an equitable manner and in accordance with the evaluation mechanism stated in the ITT. The purpose of the tender evaluation is to identify the tender offering the ideal solution.

12.10.2 Key points for the ITT

It is essential that the ITT includes (as an absolute minimum) the following:

- all relevant information on how the evaluation will be carried out, the evaluation criteria and weightings
- whether alternative proposals will be considered and, if so, on what basis
- compliance with the EU Contract Notice, e.g. Most Economically Advantageous Tender (MEAT)
- whether there are PASS/FAIL criteria and, if so, the basis upon which a PASS or FAIL will be determined
- whether there are successive rounds in the process as permitted in the Negotiation Procedure and Competitive Dialogue procedures
- how non-compliant tenders will be dealt with.

12.10.3 The Tender Evaluation Panel

- The Tender Evaluation Panel must be constructed to typically consist of a cross-functional group, including specialist advisors (if any required).
- It may include, for example, procurement, finance, operational, legal, health & safety and environmental specialists.
- Each member of the panel must have a clearly defined role and be fully briefed on the evaluation process prior to conducting the evaluation.
- The panel members must not have any conflicts of interest.
- Each member of the panel must conduct their initial evaluation and scoring quite independently of other panel members
- A rigorous audit trail must be kept of the evaluation process, including tender scoring moderation meetings.

See Figure 12.5 for a process chart of the Tender Evaluation Process.

Figure 12.5 Tender evaluation process

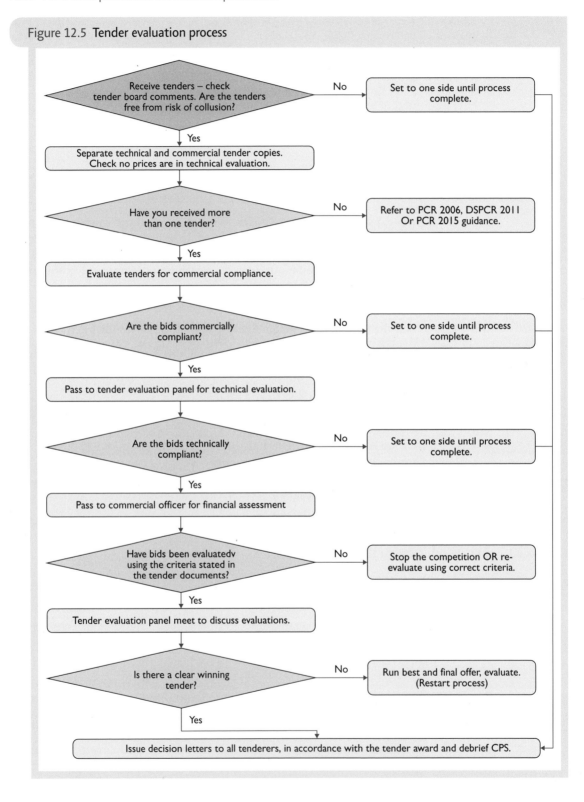

12.11 The legal context of challenges to public sector contract award

12.11.1 Introduction

There is a plethora of legal judgments in the UK courts, relating to challenges to public sector contract awards. The judgments provide a rich source of information and guidance of evaluation panels. The author has been selective in his choice of judgments due to space restrictions in this book.

12.11.2 Salient points of legal challenges

The case of Woods Building Services v Milton Keynes Council[9] provides relevant comment of some salient points of legal challenges to contract award. It outlines the law on transparency in the following terms (the paragraph numbers are those from the case):

Para 5.   In this case, the duty of transparency focused on the award criteria. It is trite law that 'the award criteria must be formulated, in the contract documents or the contract notice, in such a way as to allow all reasonably well-informed and diligent tenderers to interpret them in the same way': see **SIAC Construction Ltd v County Council of the County of Mayo** [2001] ECR1-7725, at paragraph 41.

Para 6.   The award criteria must be drawn up 'in a clear, precise and unequivocal manner in the notice or contract documents so that first, all reasonably informed tenderers exercising care can understand their exact significance and interpret them in the same way and, secondly, the contracting authority is able to ascertain whether the tenders submitted satisfy that criteria applying to the relevant contract': see **Commission v The Netherlands** [2013] All ER(EC) 804 at paragraph 109.

Para 7.   The true meaning and effect of the published award criteria is a matter of law for the court: see **Clinton (t/a Aureal Training Services) v Department of Employment and Learning and Another** [2012] NICA 48 at paragraph 33. A failure to comply with the criteria is a breach of the duty of transparency: see **Easycoach Ltd v Department for Regional Development** [2012] NIQB10.

Para 8.   Unlike other allegations commonly made during procurement disputes, such as whether or not a manifest error has been made in the evaluation, a breach of the transparency obligation does not allow for any 'margin of appreciation': see paragraph 36 of the judgment of Morgan J in **Lion Apparel Systems v Firebuy Ltd** [2007] EWHC 2179 (Ch).

This emphasises the relevance and importance of determining the award criteria. The references to other cases, is a source of research for public sector buyers and stakeholders engaged in determining such criteria.

The tender document in the Woods Building Services case set out the evaluation at the ratio of 60 per cent for cost and 40 per cent for quality. The scoring criteria were expressly stated as follows in Table 12.9.

Para 31. In fact, at all three stages, the notes on the spreadsheets were extremely brief. They amounted either to a brief conclusion (rather than a statement of reasons) or a paraphrase of the scoring criteria. Thus, by way of example, for an answer where Woods scored 6, the evaluators noted that the response was generally of a good standard with no significant weaknesses, issues or omissions. That was simply a repetition of the scoring criteria. There was no explanation as to why Woods had achieved that score, much less anything to indicate why it had not received a score of 8 or 10. Similarly, for some of the EAS scores that received 10, the notes simply said 'the panel were of the opinion that the response provided was to a very high standard, robust and will add

Table 12.9 **Scoring criteria**

Number of points	Definition
0	Response does not meet requirements and/or is unacceptable. Insufficient information to demonstrate Tenderer's ability to deliver the services.
2	Response partially meets requirements but contains material weaknesses, issues or omissions and/or inconsistencies which raise serious concerns.
4	Response meets requirements to a minimum acceptable standard, however contains some weaknesses, issues or omissions which raise minor concerns.
6	Response generally of a good standard. No significant weaknesses, issues or omissions.
8	Response meets requirements to a high standard. Comprehensive, robust and well justified showing full understanding of requirements.
10	Response meets requirements to a very high standard with clear and credible added value and/or innovation.

           value to the contract'. This was another paraphrase of the scoring criteria. It offered no reasons for the score awarded.

Para 32.   This lack of detailed explanation can be seen in the letter to Woods of 5 February 2015 which informed them that their tender had been unsuccessful. It identified the marks given to them for each question, the marks given to EAS for each question, and then set out the short notes from the spreadsheet to which I have already referred. There was no other explanation because there were no other contemporaneous notes on which such an explanation could be based.

There is a significant learning opportunity by reading Mr Justice Coulson's critical analysis of scoring specific questions.

Question 2.1 asked: 'provide a method statement (of two A4 pages maximum) setting out your proposal to meet the requirements of the service information'. EAS (who were to be awarded the contract) received a score of 10. Woods argued the score should have been zero because EAS wholly failed to deal with the reinstatement works. Mr Justice Coulson observed that it was the only question that required the tenderers to produce a document that would then have contractual status and effect. At para 50 of the judgment it was found that apart from the reinstatement elements of the work there were no proposals in relation to IT, or quality assurance, or progress reports, or protecting the premises during the works.

At para 147 of the judgment is Mr Justice Coulson's rescoring of the two bids. It is a remarkable revelation. EAS who were to be awarded the contract had their score reduced by 40 marks to now score 64, while Woods' score was increased by 6 marks to now score 94.

12.11.3 The importance of evaluation panels.

In the case of Resource (NI) v Northern Ireland Courts & Tribunals [2011] NIQB 121 18.11.11 at para 35 there was a very important statement about evaluation panels, namely, 'meetings of contract procurement evaluation panels are something considerably greater than merely formal events. They are solemn exercises of critical importance to economic operators and the public and must be designed, constructed and

Table 12.10 Bid rescoring by Mr Justice Coulson

Section / Question	EAS score	Woods score
6.1 / Q 2.1	0 (Reduced from 10)	8 (Unchanged)
6.2 / Q 2.2	0 (Reduced from 6)	6 (Unchanged)
6.3 / Q 2.3	8 (Unchanged)	8 (Increased from 6)
6.4 / Q 2.4	8 (Unchanged)	8 (Unchanged)
6.5 / Q 2.5	10 (Unchanged)	10 (Increased from 6)
6.6 / Q 3.1	8 (Unchanged)	8 (Unchanged)
6.7 / Q 3.2	8 (Unchanged)	8 (Unchanged)
6.8 / Q 3.3	0 (Reduced from 8)	8 (Unchanged)
6.9 / Q 3.4	6 (Reduced from 10)	6 (Unchanged)
6.10 / Q 4.1	6 (Reduced from 8)	6 (Unchanged)
6.11 / Q 4.2	0 (Reduced from 10)	8 (Unchanged)
6.12 / Q 5.1	8 (Unchanged)	8 (Unchanged)
TOTALS	64 (A reduction of 40)	94 (An increase of 6)

transacted in such a manner to ensure that full effect is given to the overarching procurement rules and principles.'

The judge also said,

> I had the opportunity to assess these two witnesses during relatively lengthy periods and, further, to address various questions to them. I observe, first of all, that they provided accounts of the crucial Evaluation Panel meeting which were notably different. This inspired little judicial confidence in either version.

12.11.4 Scores not awarded lawfully and manifest error in the evaluation

In the case of Energy Solutions EU Limited v Nuclear Decommissioning Authority [2016] EWHC 1988 (TCC), a number of very serious points arose in regard to the tender evaluation. The High Court held that the Nuclear Decommissioning Authority (NDA) 'manipulated' and 'fudged' its tender process for a nuclear clean up contract worth in excess of £4 billion.

Some salient points from an extensive judgment are:

■ The Judge criticised the NDA for the manner it ran the procurement process in that it was concerned about a legal challenge from the outset and so some of its governance arrangements for the process, although well planned out, were aimed at defending a procurement challenge rather than running a process to comply with the principles of transparency, equal treatment and non-discrimination.

- The fact that no notes on the dialogue stages were kept (noting the dialogue stage extended over months).
- Although there was a data room with documents for the bidders to refer to during the procurement process, the evaluators themselves had not read/could not remember the documents within the data room.
- Some individual evaluators' scores were changed following the moderation/consensus meeting and once they had been closed down in the procurement portal with no notes explaining the reasons for the changed scores, the decision as to whether the winning bidder should actually have been disqualified was made in an unrecorded conversation so no one could explain how the decision had been taken.

12.11.5 Technical evaluation of tenders

The split of technical/pricing can vary from tender to tender. Sixty per cent technical and 40 per cent price is an example. It may be noted that the author is aware of a tender that was 10 per cent technical and 90 per cent price.

In the following worked example, quality was weighted at 40 per cent. The scoring marking scheme was in the range 0–5. A score of 0 was an 'Unacceptable Response'. A score of 5 was an 'Excellent response'. All potential scores were defined and published in the I.T.T. In respect of a specific question if, for example, the weighting is 20 per cent and the maximum mark is 5 and the mark received is 3, the weighted score would be 12 ($3/5 \times 20 = 12$). All the weighted scores for quality would be added together to give the total quality score.

The scoring of price can be achieved using the following mechanism, and for the purpose of this example, price is weighted at 40 per cent. We will assume that three compliant bids have been received and the prices are:

Tender A	£2,345,811
Tender B	£2,867,000
Tender C	£2,048,333

The formula would be:

$$\text{Pricing Score} = \text{Total Available Marks} \times \left[\frac{\text{Lowest Price Compliant Tender}}{\text{Tender Price}} \right]$$

Tender A calculation

$$40 \times \left[\frac{£2048333}{£2345811} \right] = 40 \times 0.873 = 34.92$$

Tender B calculation

$$40 \times \left[\frac{£2048333}{£2867000} \right] = 40 \times 0.714 = 28.58$$

Tender C calculation

$$40 \times \left[\frac{£2048333}{£2048333} \right] = 40 \times 1.000 = 40$$

12.12 Public sector risk

In Australia, the Public Governance, Performance and Accountability Act 2013 places a duty on Accountable Authorities of Commonwealth entities to establish and maintain appropriate systems of risk oversight and management for the entity.

This logic is transferable to all public sector entities in all countries. There is, typically a Corporate Risk Register, populated at the highest level in the entity. The effective management of risks assists to:

- set and achieve strategic objectives
- comply with legal and policy obligations
- improve decision making
- allocate and utilise resources
- understand the mitigation strategies to manage the risks
- identify dependence in third parties, e.g. suppliers
- understands the financial/service implications if the risks materialise
- understand where accountability for risk management rests.

An indication of enterprise level risks, is referenced by the Australian Department of Health.[10]

Department of Health

The Department of Health (Health) is a large entity, with around 5037 staff at 30 June 2016. Health had a total budget of approximately $54.3 billion in 2015–16.

Health is responsible for achieving the Australian Government's health priorities through evidence based policy, program administration, research, regulatory activities and partnerships with other government entities, consumers and stakeholders.

The department has identified the following enterprise level risks:

- The department's regulatory policies and practices are not able to adequately protect the health and safety of the community and/or, reduce excessive regulatory burden on business, healthcare professionals and consumers [Regulatory risk].
- Inadequate assessment and management of the health and wellbeing of our people and in particular departmental inspectors, investigators and laboratory staff, resulting in diminished productivity, disengagement or injury [People risk].
- Failure to recognise and respond to inappropriate influence or corruption of a public official leading to loss of confidence in the department and diversion of resources from intended purposes [Fraud risk].
- The department's health system strategy and implementation (short, medium and long term) is insufficient to mitigate the growth in outlays [Policy risk].
- Inadequate capability and tools to collect and utilise data sets and health system information to optimise health, ageing and sport policy outcomes [Policy risk].
- Co-ordination and integration of policy and programs across the department and external partners are insufficient, leading to poor outcomes for the community and/or an adverse budgetary effect [Delivery risk].
- Failure to learn through measuring and evaluating policies, programs and service outcomes [Delivery risk].

Figure 12.6 Elements of the Commonwealth Risk Management Policy

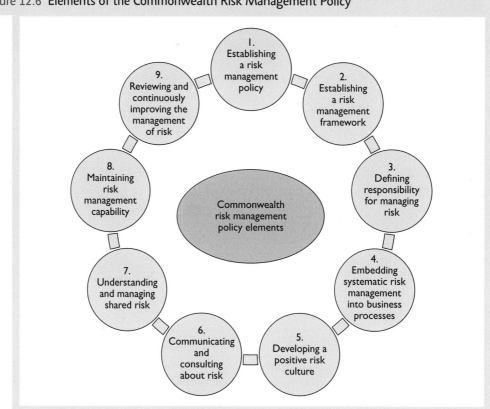

- Failure to ensure resources are allocated to the highest priorities of the Minister and the Department in a responsive and adaptive way [Governance risk]
- Failure to promptly recognise the impact of poor data management, IT capacity and lack of skilled staff on the delivery of health and ageing services [Delivery risk].
- Failure to recognise or respond promptly, proactively and effectively to an interruption of delivery of Commonwealth funded health and ageing services to the community [Delivery risk].
- Governance arrangements don't support the provision of timely, accurate and robust advice [Governance risk].
- Poor IT stability and security leads to ineffective and inefficient Health administration or unauthorised access to personal data [Information risk].

The elements of the Commonwealth Risk Management Policy are shown in Figure 12.6.[11]

12.13 Public sector procurement fraud

Chapter 17 provides a detailed insight into procurement fraud. The public sector is not immune from such fraud. The author has researched this on an international basis. The reader will find the examples breath-taking and will reflect on the lack of governance that undoubtedly contributed to the problem.

12.13.1 Fraud and corruption in procurement in WA Health[12]

This situation involved a facilities development manager at a major public hospital. He was responsible for procurement in a number of different site-specific and WA Health capital works projects, including refurbishments and building renovations. It was reported that he corruptly benefited to the amount of $490,267.50 over a six year period.

The report noted:

- there were no written contracts between WA Health and each consultant and contractor

- Wickramasinghe (the facilities development manager) 'W' did not allow any extra invoices for variations to be submitted by contractors in excess of their initial quotation

- 'W' carried out most of the design documentation, saving on the cost of architects

- WA Health procurement processes were not followed

- 'W' engaged in 'circular tendering', continually using the same consultants and contractors on different capital works projects.

A conclusion in the report was that 'W's' conduct went undetected for six years because of **poor supervision and financial controls** (our emphasis). 'W' was sentenced to 4 years' imprisonment.

12.14 Aviation Department Fraud – United States

There are occasions when the scale of a procurement fraud is beyond belief. In a United States fraud[13] it was alleged that during the course of a conspiracy, the co-conspirators defrauded the Miami-Dade County Aviation Department of approximately $5,250,000. The United States Attorney's office, Southern District of Florida[14] said 'Corruption by those who hold the public's trust corrodes the practice of fair business dealings.' The defendant Ivan Valdes was in charge of the preparation and administration of the annual operating budget for facilities and terminal maintenance, oversight for terminal maintenance building shops, and the day-to-day operations for facilities and terminal maintenance, including lighting for the Miami International Airport.

As set forth in the charging documents, Bustillo was the exclusive area representative in South Florida for the sale of certain LED light fixtures. In or about 2010, Ivan Valdes told Barroso that he would request that the Miami-Dade County Aviation Department purchase the light fixtures represented by Bustillo, if he was paid a share of the proceeds. Valdes and Barroso agreed and during the period of 2010 through and including 2015, the Miami-Dade County Aviation Department issued approximately twenty requests for Invitations to Quote for the purchase of millions of dollars of LED light fixtures. Bustillo provided a quote to each of the vendors interested in competing for the Invitation to Quote. Global Electrical & Lighting Supplies, Inc., owned by Rolando Perez, submitted bids and was awarded the contracts for each and every Invitation to Quote issued. Perez and Bustillo had a secret agreement wherein Perez would be the only vendor who knew the actual price that Bustillo had agreed upon with the lighting manufacturer for the light fixtures and that a fake mounting accessory was included in the Invitations to Quote. Knowing the additional profit that was to be received from each of the contracts, Bustillo and Perez were able to win the Invitation to Quote by keeping Perez' bid price low. In order to help ensure that Perez was awarded each of the contracts, Ivan Valdes paid thousands of dollars in cash to Ygnacio Valdez, whose duties in the procurement section in the Miami-Dade County Aviation Department, included collecting and tallying the bids and declaring the lowest responsive bidder on the Invitations to Quote.

On two occasions, Ivan Valdes instructed Barroso to direct Perez to bid on an Invitation to Quote for light fixtures, but he further instructed that the light fixtures should not be ordered from the lighting manufacturer. Instead, on one occasion the conspirators used light fixtures already in stock at the Miami-Dade County Aviation Department to satisfy the purchase. On the other occasion, no light fixtures were ever provided, not even from those already in stock. Perez bid and won the contracts and he and his co-conspirators were paid approximately $500,000 for light fixtures that were never provided to Miami-Dade County Aviation Department.

In effect the Airport paid $8.8 million for LED lights that were worth about $3.5 million. Valdes received a prison sentence of 7 years and was ordered to pay £5.4 million in restitution. It was reported that Valdes regularly collected grocery bags full of kickback money in an airport parking lot.

12.15 Mighty River Power Ltd Fraud – New Zealand

Mighty River Power Ltd[15] is an electricity retailer and generator, which operates the Waikato Hydro System. Paul Kenneth Rose (Rose) was employed as an Electrical Engineer and part of his role was to identify what equipment was required to be ordered, or services to be provided for the operation of the plant.

Rose had two businesses, Penrose Electrical Services Ltd and Aero Automation Ltd. He did not report this conflict of interest. The judgment stated that Rose was convicted on a total of 174 payments to his own companies. These payments totalled approximately $2.2 m.

At paragraph 45 of the judgement, the judge stated

Although I cannot determine the precise figure by which yon personally benefitted from Aero Automation's profits, it is nevertheless clear from this evidence that you shared, in a substantial way, in the ill-gotten gains from your offending. . . . The motivation for your offending, Mr Rose, was greed.

Rose was sentenced to imprisonment of three years, two months.

12.16 The Fat Leonard Case[16] USA

The indictment in this case runs to 79 pages. There were nine defendants. Astonishingly, the defendants included a Captain in the US Navy and a Colonel in the US Marine Corps. Charged elsewhere was a Commander in the US Navy. The defendants all held 'Secret' or 'Top Secret' clearances. The contractor involved was Glenn Defence Marine Asia (GDMA), headquartered in Singapore. Leonard Glenn Francis, a citizen of Malaysia was the owner, President and CEO of GDMA. GDMA's main business involved 'Ship husbanding', involving such services as tugboats, fenders, port authority fees, food, fuel, water and trash removal. The indictment stated that Francis and others would directly and indirectly, corruptly give, offer, and promise things of value to the defendants, collectively and individually, including meals, entertainment, travel and hotel expenses, gifts, cash and the services of prostitutes. It was alleged that the defendant provided Francis with classified US Navy ship schedules and internal proprietary US Navy information.

It was reported that at 1 February 2018,[17] 20 of 29 defendants charged had pleaded guilty. It was reported at 1 December 2017[18] that US Navy Commander Pitts was sentenced to 18 months in prison and fines of $22,500. It was estimated the fraud and bribery scheme cost the government about $35 million.

12.17 Public sector projects – procurement learning

Informed reports on public sector projects provide learning opportunities for procurement specialists. The ANAO report[19] on a $52 million project is comprehensive and worthy of serious study. We are providing selective comments to highlight some important learning points. The report refers to the BIS project. The findings include:

- While management of the BIS procurement process was largely effective, the subsequent administration of the BIS project was deficient in almost every significant respect. None of the project's milestones or deliverables were met.

- However, two critical requirements were overlooked in the requirements gathering phase and the approach to negotiating and entering into the contract did not effectively support achievement of outcomes. This was a result of the contract not explaining the milestones and performance requirements in a manner that was readily understood and applied.

- ACIC did not effectively manage the BIS project with its approach characterised by: poor risk management; not following at any point the mandated process in the contract for assessing progress against milestones and linking their achievement to payment; reporting arrangements not driving action; non adherence to a detailed implementation plan; and inadequate financial management, including being unable to definitively advise how much they had spent on the project.

- Risk registers established for the project were not used effectively.

- External reviews in June and November 2017 identified the absence of a robust governance structure

- Contract management was not effective

- ACIC agreed to pay more than $12 million in additional work. Documentation showed that some of this work may have been unnecessary and other work may have already been covered by the contract.

- Financial management of the BIS project was poor

- ACIC made a 'goodwill' payment of $2.9 million to NEC which was not linked to the achievement of any contract milestone. ACIC was not able to provide details of how the quantum of this payment was calculated.

12.18 Conclusion

This chapter has focused on public procurement topics that are central to understanding the compelling reasons for expert procurement professionals to lead the procurement process. The regulatory environment is inescapable, as is public accountability. The fact that public procurement 'dictats' are well publicised is indicative of this accountability. The 'disasters' should not divert attention or energies away from the enormous public benefits that are continually delivered by public sector contracts and positive performance.

Discussion questions

12.1   What are the most important roles for public procurement specialists?

12.2   The costs of procured goods and services are very important to public sector buyers. Whilst this is true what other factors are also important?

12.3   Does the public sector regulatory regime impact positively or negatively on procurement goals?

12.4   Explain procurement within the context of the commissioning cycle.

12.5   Identify five public sector procurement categories that demonstrate the procurement complexities that exist.

12.6   What is the purpose of EU financial thresholds?

12.7   Explain the advantages of the EU 'Restricted Procedures'.

12.8   Why is supplier pre-qualification necessary? Illustrate your answer with three examples.

12.9   Explain the role of a tender evaluation panel. Is there a role on such a panel for a procurement specialist? If so, what role(s) can be undertaken?

12.10   Give three examples of legal challenges to public sector contract awards.

12.11   Why, do you believe, there are extreme examples of public sector procurement fraud?

12.12   What role does the National Audit Office investigations play in improving the standard of public sector procurement?

12.13   What learning from public sector procurement fraud investigation reports can be transferred to the private sector?

12.12   Why are negotiation skills of great importance to a public sector procurement specialist?

References

1. 'Public procurement guidance for practitioners' European Commission 2014. http://ec.europa.eu.

2. Public Procurement in Wales. Auditor General for Wales – Archwilydd Cyffredinol Cymmr October 2017.

3. https://ipc.brookes.ac.uk.

4. House of Commons Library. Briefing Paper Number 6029, 19 September 2018 'Public Procurement and Contracts'.

5. Public Accounts Committee, Contracting out public services to the private sector. February 2014.

6. www.lichfield.gov.uk.

7. Public Sector Blog. 22.04.15. publicsectorblog.practicallaw.com.

8. 'Guidance on Innovation Procurement' 15.5.2018 https://ec.europe.eu.

9. Woods Building Services v Milton Keynes Council [2015] EWHC 2011 (TCC).

10. ANAO Report No 6 2017-18 'The Management of Risk by Public Sector Entities'.

11. Australian Government, Department of Finance.

12 'Corruption and Crime Commission – New Zealand' Report on Fraud and Corruption in Procurement in WA Health: Dealing with the Risks. 12 June 2014.

13 United States District Court. Southern District of Florida. United States of America V Ivan Valdes. Case No 18 U.S.C. ε 666 (a)(1)(A).

14 Press Release, 23 September 2016. Department of Justice U.S. Attorney's Office. Southern District of Florida.

15 High Court of New Zealand Decisions. The Queen v Paul Kenneth Rose and Jane Clare Rose. R v Rose [2016] NZHC 1109 (25 May 2016).

16 United States District Court Southern District of California, Case No 17CR0623JLS, January 2016, Grand Jury.

17 CNN 'Politics'.

18 CBS 'News'.

19 The Australian Criminal Intelligence Commission's Administration of the Biometric Identification Services Project, Auditor-General Report No 24 2018-19, Performance Audit.

Chapter 13

Sustainability and socially responsible procurement

Learning outcomes

This chapter provides an understanding of:

- what is sustainability procurement?
- sustainable procurement strategy
- sustainability as an objective in corporate strategy
- sustainable procurement policy
- sustainable procurement guide
- supply chain compliance
- what is social value?
- ISO 14001:2015 Environmental management systems
- BS ISO 20400:2017 Sustainable Procurement
- ISO 14031:2015 Environmental Management
- environmental impact of computers
- addressing environmental issues during the procurement process
- pre-qualification questionnaire – sustainability implications
- new models for sustainable procurement
- environmental technical specifications
- sustainability achievements in public procurement
- contractual implications of environmental and related considerations
- sustainability challenges for procurement
- multinational enterprises
- the Kyoto Protocol.

Key ideas

- Sustainability and socially responsible procurement.
- How procurement can positively impact on improving sustainability.
- Developing a sustainable procurement strategy.

- The need for sustainable procurement policies.
- The content of social value performance.
- Using pre-qualification tools to identify sustainability achievements.
- The impact of technical specifications.
- Long-term impact of sustainability strategies.

13.1 What is sustainability procurement?

The following statement is provided by the NHS:[1]

> Sustainable procurement provides a framework for using economic power in ways that benefit society, the economy and the environment (thus serving the aims of sustainable development). It is about looking beyond short-term costs to make more decisions based on whole-life costs, including social and environmental implications. It offers the opportunity to encourage manufacturers, suppliers and contractors to develop environmentally and socially preferable goods and services (often through collaboration) at competitive prices – thus making longer-term cost savings, sending clear signals to the market, and contributing to wider government agendas. It can also be about social aspects such as using purchasing power to work with small and medium-sized enterprises (SMEs) and to work towards regeneration and employment objectives.

Sustainable procurement is basically good procurement practice and is the process by which organisations buy supplies or services through taking account of:

- **Best value for money** – price, quality, availability, functionality, running costs and other positive benefits such as development of markets and innovative products with additional environmental benefits
- **Environmental aspects** – improving the effects on the environment of a product or service over its whole life cycle, from 'cradle to grave' (raw materials, manufacture, distribution and packaging, use and end-of-life disposal)
- **Social aspects** – support for local communities, regeneration, poverty eradication, international equity in the distribution of resources, fair and legal labour conditions, fairly traded and with respect for basic human rights.

Green Public Procurement (GPP) is defined by the European Commission[2] as

> a process whereby public authorities seek to procure goods, services and works with a reduced environmental impact throughout their life-cycle when compared to goods, services and works with the same primary function that would otherwise be provided.

13.2 Sustainable Procurement Strategy

The British Broadcasting Corporation (BBC), in a somewhat dated 'Sustainable Procurement Strategy'[3] include detail that will help procurement staff when they initiate a sustainable procurement strategy, or receive an existing strategy.

They, rightly, point out that the principles of sustainable procurement are not just about buying 'green', they are instead based on a balance of social, economic and environment considerations. These are:

Environmental	Seeking to minimise any negative environmental impacts of goods and services purchased, across their life cycle from raw material extraction to end of life and supporting the principles set out in the BBC's Environmental Action Plan.
Social	Managing and monitoring supply chains to ensure that fair contract prices and terms are applied and that ethical, human rights and employment standards, as expressed in the International Labour Organisation (ILO)'s Fundamental Conventions,[4] are met.
Economic	The economic principle relates not only to obtaining value for money from our contracts, across the whole life of the product or service, but also ensuring as far as is possible under relevant procurement law, that local businesses, particularly Small and Medium sized Enterprises (SMEs) can benefit from our procurement processes in being able to supply the BBC where it is feasible for them to do so.

The BBC strategy is centred on eight objectives:

1 Carry out an audit of existing sustainability procurement provision within contracts
2 Carry out a sustainability risk assessment of all procurement categories, to use this to prioritise sustainable procurement strategies and to apply it to current and forthcoming contracts
3 Communicate to our suppliers that we procure sustainably and analyse any current supplier sustainability initiatives
4 Develop a whole life costing model to enable tenders to be evaluated on this basis
5 Develop sustainable procurement criteria and embed them into relevant tendering exercises
6 Ensure all procurement professionals understand the importance of sustainable procurement and are sufficiently trained in this area
7 Provide direction and guidance to divisions on sustainable procurement
8 Develop external networks to ensure best practice.

For each of the objectives, there is an explanation of the 'Purpose', 'How' and 'Outcomes'. To illustrate the benefits of studying the BBC approach we are including below, Objectives 1 and 2.

Objective 1	**To carry out an audit of existing sustainable procurement provision within contracts**
Purpose	To provide a clear picture of the nature and extent of clauses that currently exist in specifications, contract terms & conditions, and KPIs. This will provide a baseline for drafting future KPIs and for measuring progress.
How	Undertake an audit of the current contracts in respect of any existing sustainable procurement criteria, conditions and monitoring criteria. Information relating to each contract will be obtained via the contract management tool in Delphi (one of a suite of e-procurement tools used by Procurement).
Outcomes	A clear indication of the sustainable procurement performance measures within existing contracts and a process for monitoring them, subjected to external audit validation.

Objective 2	To carry out a risk assessment exercise on current and forthcoming contracts
Purpose	To identify and evaluate sustainability implications in current and forthcoming contracts to enable sustainability criteria and targets to be developed and implemented to address key risk areas.
How	A standard matrix will be used to map and evaluate the environmental, social and economic risk of the contract. This matrix will follow the Prioritisation Methodology mapping developed by the Sustainable Procurement Task Force and detailed in the Sustainable Procurement National Action Plan.
Outcomes	Analysis will provide intelligence on areas for immediate attention i.e. quick wins and assist with planning to address those contracts where it is possible to achieve long-term sustainability gains. Prioritised list of contracts that could have a sustainable procurement approach applied to them from the identification of need, through the tender exercise and to the contract terms and management.

13.3 Sustainability as an objective in corporate strategy

The United States Environmental Protection Agency (EPA)[5] observes that a growing number of companies are treating 'sustainability' as an important objective in their strategy and operations to increase growth and global competitiveness.

There are a number of reasons why companies are pursuing sustainability:

■ increase operational efficiency by reducing costs and waste

■ respond to or reach new customers and increase competitive advantage

■ protect and strengthen brand and reputation and build public trust

■ build long-term business viability and success

■ respond to regulatory constraints and opportunities.

13.4 Sustainable Procurement Policy

Willmott Dixon Holdings Ltd[6] have produced a comprehensive 'Sustainable Procurement Policy Statement', namely:

Sustainable Procurement Policy Statement

The Willmott Dixon family of companies is one of the UK's largest privately-owned construction, housing and property groups. In creating and maintaining the built environment we select and use a large volume of resources. The choices we make have a significant impact on people, organisations and the wider environment.

We have developed a Sustainable Procurement Policy outlining how we and our supply chain will influence procurement choices of **goods, works** and **services** to; increase value for money; reduce consumption of primary resources; mitigate impacts on the environment; and deliver a healthier built environment.

By operating in line with this policy we will play our part in reducing risks, safeguarding natural resources, delivering value to our Clients, improving resource efficiency, traceability and transparency, as well as leaving a positive legacy on biodiversity and safeguarding natural capital. Our approach to sustainable procurement is in line with the principles contained within BS8903. This standard was created to help pursue best procurement practice.

Our Sustainable Procurement Policy's aims and objectives are to:

- Use fewer resources and less energy through continuous improvement and the use of innovative solutions.
- Procure all timber and timber products from legal and sustainable sources, and procure other construction materials with a preference for recognised responsible sourcing schemes.
- Specify and procure materials and products that strike a responsible balance between social, economic and environmental factors and generate benefits to society and the economy.
- Use resource-efficient products and give due consideration to end-of-life uses.
- Promote, specify and source materials which can be reused, and consider future deconstruction and recovery of resources to embrace the circular economy to leave a sustainable legacy across the built environment.
- Where possible procure locally, providing opportunities for small and medium sized enterprises (SMEs), collaborate with the voluntary sector and increase the use of social enterprises to support local employment, diversity and training.
- Ensure that fair contract prices and terms are applied and respected, and that ethical, human rights and labour standards are met, in line with our Modern Slavery Policy and the United Nations Global Compact principles.
- Source goods, works and services that embody our environmental policy, health & safety policy and support the delivery of our Sustainable Development Strategy.
- Enhance the health and wellbeing of the people and communities we work with by promoting materials and products that improve indoor environmental quality.

13.5 Sustainable Procurement Guide

The Thales Group publish a very informative and enlightening 'Sustainable Procurement Guide'.[7] It has 'suppliers need to consider' checklist for key areas of sustainable performance. These are reproduced below with due acknowledgement to the Thales Group.

EMISSIONS/ENERGY

SUPPLIERS NEED TO CONSIDER:

- To support Thales UK's objective to reduce energy and improve energy efficiency, thereby reducing CO_2 emissions in line with our obligation to the Energy Saving Opportunity Scheme (ESOS/ISO 50001)
- All suppliers of goods, works or services that use gas, electricity or fuel arising in Thales' operations (on site) are able to demonstrate targeted energy and emissions reduction
- All suppliers of goods, works and services that consume gas, electricity or fuel are able to demonstrate good energy management practice and compliance with local legislation as a minimum, i.e. does the supplier have certification to ISO 50001
- Thales UK expects all modes of transport supporting our supply chain to be compliant with relevant local air quality standards
- Reduce energy from buildings, processes, projects and products
- Reduce cost by identifying efficiencies

WASTE

SUPPLIERS NEED TO CONSIDER:

- To support Thales UK's objective to reduce waste to landfill, minimise creation of packaging waste material, promote energy recovery, re-use and increase recycling rate
- All suppliers of goods, works or services that cause waste arising in Thales' operations (on site) are able to demonstrate targeted waste reductions
- All packaging to comply with Packaging Regulations (when applicable) e.g. Valpak Compliance Scheme
- All suppliers of goods, works and services that create (their own) waste are able to demonstrate good waste management practice and compliance with local legislation as a minimum
- Purchases of goods that will be disposed of by Thales and its customers at end of life will reduce waste potential to a minimum and consider how this disposal will be done without causing waste to landfill
- The whole life cost of packaging: this includes the cost of the skip on site, the cost of recycling material, the cost of landfill tax
- What packaging is being used?
- Is the packaging overly heavy/over-sized?
- Can it be designed to be minimal?
- Can any of the packaging be removed, reduced or reused/recycled?
- What is the percentage recycled content?
- What is the percentage raw material that is from a sustainable source?
- Can the packaging be returned?

WATER

SUPPLIERS NEED TO CONSIDER:

- Support Thales UK's objective to reduce water consumption and improve water efficiency
- Be able to demonstrate targeted water reduction consumption
- Be able to demonstrate good water management practice and compliance with local legislation as a minimum

RESOURCE STEWARDSHIP

SUPPLIERS NEED TO CONSIDER:

- To minimise use of natural resources and harm to the natural environment
- Consideration shall be given to the use of secondary materials (re-used and recycled) where they offer equal or greater value for money
- All timber and related products including pallets shall be supplied from FSC or PEFC certified sources where possible
- Raw materials include: timber, rubber, alloys and metals

ECONOMIC SUSTAINABILITY

SUPPLIERS NEED TO CONSIDER:

- To contribute positively to the economic sustainability of their communities
- To not knowingly award contracts that undermine the economic viability of our suppliers
- To pay suppliers in accordance with the contract conditions
- Where appropriate, to seek competitive local supply and labour

- To encourage innovation in the supply chain, particularly where economic, social and environmental benefits can be demonstrated
- To encourage fair trade/fair price
- To consider social issues in procurement that and act in a way that may be considered to 'distort competition' or discriminate against

TRADE COMPLIANCE

SUPPLIERS NEED TO CONSIDER:

- Export control regulations
- The diversity of our customer base, combined with the vast range of suppliers around the world, make Trade Compliance a key area for both supplier and procurement awareness
- Understanding the types of controls applicable to the products we purchase/sell, whether developed in-house, or purchased from a third party, is essential to ensure compliance with various Export Control regimes around the world, not least the UK, EU and USA
- Every country in the world will have specific Export Control restrictions related to products developed in their area. In addition, each country will also have sanctions and embargoes, both local and worldwide, that have to be adhered to
- It is the suppliers responsibility to ensure Thales are made aware of any specific controls that will restrict where the product can be marketed/sold to
- Suppliers should also ensure that any required Export approvals are in place, and include all parties relevant to the transaction

BIODIVERSITY

SUPPLIERS NEED TO CONSIDER:

- All living organisms and your natural surroundings
- All suppliers of goods, works or services in Thales' operations (on site) do not have a negative/detrimental impact on local Thales biodiversity
- All suppliers of goods, works and services, do not have a negative/detrimental impact on biodiversity both locally and during transportation

13.6 Supply chain compliance

The Thales Group also includes in their Sustainable Procurement Guide the following facets of supply chain compliance.

It is the supplier(s) responsibility to comply with all relevant statutes, statutory rules, orders, directives, regulations and standards in force at the time of delivery. Where the supplier suspects a concern regarding the product(s), please inform your local Thales Buyer immediately.

KEY AREAS TO BE AWARE OF:

- REACh

  European Regulation (No: EC/1907/2006) www.echa.europa.eu Thales suppliers shall perform the required due diligence to ensure that the products supplied are REACh compliant and provide the necessary information to allow Thales to confirm its own compliance in line with Article 33 of the REACh Regulations. Suppliers shall also regularly update Thales in relation to any changes to their products any changes to the information that is available in relation to their products and any changes to the information that is available in relation to the substances used in their products. All information shall be provided at the cost of the supplier.

- Conflict

  Minerals US State Dept. Law (Dodd-Frank Act) Thales suppliers are expected to perform the required due diligence to ensure responsibly (non-conflict) sourced materials/minerals. These minerals include tantalum (columbite-tantalite also known as coltan and its derivatives), tin (cassiterite and its derivatives), tungsten (wolframite and its derivatives) and gold.

- Modern Slavery Act (UK)/Human Trafficking

  Thales suppliers shall perform the required due diligence to comply with the requirements of the Modern Slavery Act 2015 to ensure that their supply chains are free of human trafficking and shall provide written confirmation to Thales that they have done so. Thales has the right to audit your due diligence procedures to confirm the steps you have taken to comply with the Modern Slavery Act 2015.

- WEEE

  Waste Electrical and Electronic Equipment www.environment-agency.gov.uk/weee

- RoHS

  Restrictions on Hazardous Substances www.rohs.gov.uk

- Counterfeit Avoidance

  DEF-STAN 05-135 www.dstan.mod.uk

- Rare Earth Metals

  www.iupac.org/rare-earth-metals A set of 17 chemical elements in the periodic table that were defined by the International Union of Pure and Applied Chemistry (IUPAC).

- Cyber Security

  DEF-STAN 05-138. Cyber risk profiles set out the cyber protection measures required at each level of cyber risk. A contract assessed as carrying a cyber risk of 'Low' will only need to comply with the measures set out in the 'Low' profile. This does not preclude you from doing more, and Thales would encourage you to do so, but this will not be a contractual requirement. www.gov.uk/government/publications/defence-cyber-protection-partnership-cyber-risk-profiles/overview-dcpp-and-cyber-security-controls

The above list is currently most important to Thales UK, but not limited to.

13.7 What is Social Value?

The Public Services (Social Value) Act 2012 has resulted in Local Authorities and other public bodies having a legal obligation to consider the social good that could come from the procurement of services, before they embark upon it.

Social Value is defined as:

A process whereby organisations meet their needs for goods, services, works and utilities in a way that achieves value for money on a whole life basis in terms of generating benefits not only to the organisation, but also to society and economy, whilst minimising damage to the environment.

The 2012 Act refers to economic, social and environmental outcomes as the three pillars of sustainable procurement.

It may be noted that the public sector Equality Duty is defined by the Equality Act 2010. Milton Keynes Council[8] have produced a Social Value toolkit. They include excellent examples of Social Values deliverables including:

- new local employees recruited
- upskilling the supply chain

- mock interview events in local schools
- enterprise events
- financial sponsorship of local community days
- a *Dragon's Den* competition in a local school
- toy/clothing donations to disadvantaged children
- in-house grant scheme providing access to items like laptops
- upskilling local volunteers through staff training.

13.8 ISO 14001:2015 Environmental management systems

This standard replaced ISO 14001:2004. Its salient points include:

- Accredited certification to ISO 14001 is not a requirement
- The key improvements to the 2004 standard are deemed to be:
  - Environmental management to be more prominent within the organisation's strategic direction
  - A greater commitment from leadership
  - The implementation of proactive initiatives to protect the environment from harm and degradation, such as sustainable resource use and climate change mitigation
  - A focus on life-cycle thinking to ensure consideration of environmental aspects from development to end-of-life
  - The addition of a stakeholder-focused communication strategy.
- Users of the standard have reported that ISO 14001 helps:
  - Demonstrate compliance with current and future **statutory and regulatory requirements**
  - Increase leadership involvement and **engagement of employees**
  - Improve company reputation and the **confidence of stakeholders** through strategic communication
  - Achieve **strategic business aims** by incorporating environmental issues into business management
  - Provide a **competitive and financial advantage** through improved efficiencies and reduced costs
  - Encourage better **environmental performance of suppliers** by integrating them into the organisation's business systems.

13.9 BS ISO 20400:2017 Sustainable Procurement

This standard superseded BS 8903:2010. The standards include a very important statement, namely:

Procurement is a powerful instrument for organisations wishing to behave in a responsible way and contribute to sustainable development and to the achievement of the United Nations

Sustainable Development Goals. By integrating sustainability in procurement policies and practices, including supply chains, organisations can manage risks (including opportunities) for sustainable environmental, social and economic development.

Figure 13.1 shows a schematic view of the content of ISO 20400.[9]

Figure 13.1 Schematic view of the content of ISO 20400

1. Scope	2. Normative references	3. Terms and definitions

	Description	Mainly intended for
4. Understanding the fundamentals 4.1 Concept of sustainable procurement 4.2 Principles of sustainable procurement 4.3 Core subjects of sustainable procurement 4.4 Drivers for sustainable procurement 4.5 Key considerations for sustainable procurement	Provides an overview of sustainable procurement Describes the scope and principles of sustainable procurement Examines why organizations should undertake sustainable procurement	**All**
5. Integrating sustainability into the organization's procurement policy and strategy 5.1 Committing to sustainable procurement 5.2 Clarifying accountability 5.3 Aligning procurement with organizational objectives and goals 5.4 Understanding procurement practices and supply chains 5.5 Managing implementation	Provides guidance about how sustainable considerations should be integrated at a strategic level within the procurement function to ensure that the intention, direction and priorities are documented and understood by all parties involved in sustainable procurement A key deliverable is the sustainable procurement strategy	**Top management**
6. Organizing the procurement function towards sustainability 6.1 Governing procurement 6.2 Enabling people 6.3 Identifying and engaging stakeholders 6.4 Setting sustainable procurement priorities 6.5 Measuring and improving performance 6.6 Establishing a grievance mechanism	Describes the organizational conditions and management techniques needed in order to successfully implement and continually improve sustainable procurement	**Procurement management**
7. Integrating sustainability info the procurement process 7.1 Building on the existing process 7.2 Planning 7.3 Integrating sustainability requirements into the specifications 7.4 Selecting suppliers 7.5 Managing the contract 7.6 Reiviewing and learning from the contract	Describes how sustainability considerations should be integrated into existing procurement processes A key deliverable is a sourcing strategy that includes sustainability	**Individuals responsible for the actual procurement**

Annexes

13.10 ISO 14031:2015 Environmental Management – Environmental performance evaluation: guidelines

ISO 14031 sets out a process called environmental performance evaluation (EPE) which enables organisations to measure, evaluate and communicate their environmental performance using key performance indicators (KPIs), based on reliable and verifiable information.

Environmental performance evaluation (EPE) is a management process that uses KPIs to compare an organisation's past and present environmental performance with its environmental objectives and targets. The information generated by EPE can help an organisation to do the following:

- identify its environmental aspects and determine which aspects it will treat as significant
- set objectives and targets for improving environmental performance and assess performance against these objectives and targets
- identify opportunities for better management of its environmental aspects
- review and improve efficiency and effectiveness
- identify strategic opportunities
- evaluate compliance or risk of non-compliance with legal requirements and other requirements to which the organisation subscribes related to its environmental aspects
- report and communicate environmental performance internally and externally.

The UK National Audit Office has produced an informative table showing the environmental impacts of high-spend procurement categories (see Table 13.1). It will assist procurement to understand the environmental impacts on expenditure that, typically, accounts for considerable expenditure.

Table 13.1 Environmental impacts of high-spend procurement categories (Source National Audit Office)

	Climate change	Resource depletion	Adverse impacts on air, earth, water and ecosystems
Energy	Greenhouse gas emissions from the burning of fossil fuels to generate heat or electricity	Depletion of fossil fuel resources	Acidification of oceans via absorption of carbon dioxide, leading to impact on marine ecosystems
ICT	Energy consumption during manufacture, use and disposal	Extraction and use of finite raw materials such as copper, for the manufacturing of products	Disposal of hazardous materials including heavy metals
Office supplies and services	Energy consumption during manufacture, use and disposal	Extraction and use of finite raw materials such as copper, for the manufacturing of products	Contamination of water bodies by chemicals used in the paper bleaching process Hazardous chemicals used in the production of plastics Use of heat metals and solvents
Vehicle fleets	Emissions of carbon dioxide	Consumption of fossil fuels	Air emissions such as particulate matter and nitrogen oxide. Lead and acid contamination in the disposal of batteries

Figure 13.2 Whole-life costing and environmental impact for a computer

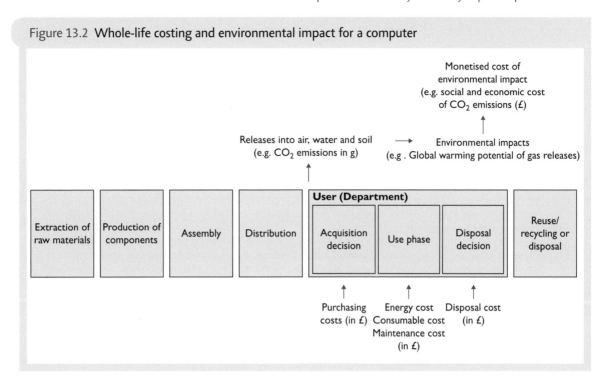

13.11 Environmental impact of computers

Figure 13.2[10] is an excellent example of whole-life costing and environmental impact for a computer.

13.12 Addressing environmental issues during the procurement process

Procurement is in a strong position to influence how environmental issues can be addressed during the procurement process. See Table 13.2 below for comment.

Table 13.2 Environmental issues and the procurement process

Business case.
This is the stage at which there is most scope for considering environmental and sustainability impacts. A key step is considering the need to procure. Through effective demand management the need to procure may be avoided. Alternatively, the need can be defined in such a way as to minimise resources consumed. For example, if the need is for staff to meet, video-conferencing facilities could be procured instead of vehicles.

Specification.
Environmental considerations should be included where they are relevant to the subject matter of the contract. They include what the product consists of (e.g. cleaning services using products with low chemical content), how it performs its function (e.g. energy efficient light bulbs), and its suitability for responsible disposal (e.g. easily recyclable parts). Certain production processes can also be specified (e.g. electricity from renewable sources, timber from sustainably-managed forests). OGC recommends specifying the environmental outcomes that are desired, and giving tenderers the flexibility to offer different ways of achieving or exceeding these outcomes, offering the possibility of market innovation. It is at this point that the Quick Wins should be referred to.

↓

Selection.
At this stage, the procurer should ask tenderers for relevant evidence of technical capability to deliver the environmental specifications.

↓

Award.
All public contracts should be awarded on the basis of value for money on a whole-life cost basis, not lowest up-front price. They should be evaluated from the point of view of the procurer; wider costs or benefits to society should have already been considered and built in to the specification.

↓

Contract and supplier management.
Contract conditions should be used to ensure suppliers provide appropriate information on their performance against environmental/sustainability requirements. Outside of formal conditions, there are often opportunities to work with suppliers and their own supply chain on a voluntary basis to raise awareness of environmental and sustainability objectives.

The source is the UK Office of Government Commerce as cited by the UK National Audit Office.

An illustration of the environmental impacts on four procurement categories is shown in Table 13.3.[11]

Table 13.3 Addressing environmental issues during the procurement process

	Climate change	Resource depletion	Adverse impacts on air, earth, water and ecosystems
Energy	Greenhouse gas emissions from the burning of fossil fuels to generate heat or electricity.	Depletion of fossil fuel resources.	Acidification of oceans via absorption of carbon dioxide, leading to impacts on marine ecosystems.
ICT	Energy consumption during manufacture, use and disposal.	Extraction and use of finite raw materials such as copper, for the manufacturing of products.	Disposal of hazardous materials including heavy metals.
Office supplies and service	Energy consumption during manufacture, use and disposal.	Extraction and use of finite raw materials for the manufacturing of products.	Contamination of water bodies by chemicals used in the paper bleaching process. Hazardous chemicals used in the production of plastics. Use of heavy metals and solvents in pens and glues
Vehicle fleets	Emissions of carbon dioxide	Consumption of fossil fuels.	Air emissions, such as particulate matter and nitrogen oxide. Lead and acid contamination in the disposal of batteries.

13.13 Pre-qualification questionnaire – sustainability implications

It is important that at the pre-qualification stage of a procurement process a supplier's impacts on the environment or sustainability are probed. Brighton & Hove City Council[12] have produced areas of a supplier's operation that may have positive or negative impacts. These are reproduced in Table 13.4.

The drafting on appropriate questions is a skill. Our readers requiring more information are advised that there is excellent guidance provided by the Supply Chain Sustainability School.[13] We have reproduced at Table 13.5 below example questions on materials.

Table 13.4 **Impacts of suppliers operations**

Environmental impacts	Social impacts	Economic impacts
Use of energy	Labour standards	Return on investment
Use and disposal of water	Health and safety	Local economy
Production & disposal of waste	Civil liberties	Market capacity
Land contamination	Social justice	Shareholders value
Emissions to air	Local community	Innovation
Transport	Minority rights	Direct and indirect economic impacts
Site related noise, odours, traffic	Cultural issues	Market presence
Packaging	Accessibility	Economic performance
Product life cycle	Equity	Risk
Abnormal operations: shutdowns	Heritage	Fair trade
Emergencies: fire, spillage, flood	Religious sensitivities	Profit sharing
Planning new developments		Living wages
Suppliers: Environmental policies		

Table 13.5 **Example questions on materials**

SCSS issue area	Question	Basic answer	Good answer (as Basic, plus)	Excellent answer (as Good, plus)
Materials	Please outline your experience in considering resource efficiency and procuring secondary or recycled materials.	Demonstrates an understanding of the issue but has limited experience of delivery.	Provides evidence of past projects either: ■ Reducing the amount of materials used (e.g. through techniques such as (but not limited to) BIM or lifecycle analysis); or ■ Using materials with a high proportion of recycled content (including evidence of percentages achieved) or reused/upcycled/reclaimed products. Please include evidence of how this has delivered benefits for the end client.	Have extensive experience of resource efficiency and the use of secondary materials for projects/services of multiple sizes and complexity. This is supported by evidence and for a wide range of products; and can demonstrate a business case. **OR** Applies circular economy principles and has evidenced the business case.

SCSS issue area	Question	Basic answer	Good answer (as Basic, plus)	Excellent answer (as Good, plus)
	Please advise of your experience in procuring materials from ethical/ responsible sources.	Provides high level statement but limited evidence of delivery.	Provides evidence of past projects, including percentages of responsible content achieved. This could include reference (but not limited) to: ■ FSC or PEFC products or equivalent chain of custody certification ■ Certification to BES6001 or other recognised ethical/ responsible sourcing initiative ■ Fairtrade or equivalent chain of custody certifications in Facilities management.	Has extensive experience of responsible/ ethical sourcing of materials for projects and services of multiple sizes and complexity. This is supported by evidence and for a wide range of products; and can demonstrate a business case.

13.14 New models for sustainable procurement

BSR[14] published a thought-provoking Working Paper in February 2018. Among their observations are

■ As a relatively young discipline, sustainable supply chain management is evolving, and new methods of sustainable procurement are emerging. While the first two decades of the sustainable procurement field focused on codes of conduct, supplier compliance, and auditing, procurement professionals in the vanguard today are looking to do much more with their procurement efforts.

■ Governments have established new regulatory frameworks to mandate greater transparency throughout the supply chain. California, the UK, and France have taken significant steps towards transparency by maintaining disclosure of labour practices and supply chain due diligence for companies meeting certain criteria.

■ At a strategic level; there is often a core concern that transparency will make companies more vulnerable to criticism. This is reasonable, particularly in instances where legal violations are concerned.

■ Companies that have experiences in successful engagement on sustainability topics cite key benefits, including competitive differentiation, enhanced supply chain efficiencies, improved ability to meet stakeholders and regulatory expectations, creation of positive pressure on an industry or region, and improved performance in meeting public commitment, such as emission goals.

The Working Paper includes best practice examples, including:

– Walmart's Project Gigaton that is aimed at supporting the company's goal of preventing the release of 1 Gigaton of emissions in its global supply chain by 2030.

– The BSR HER project relates to the concept of supporting women, especially at the factory and farm level in supply chains. The HER respect programme addresses sexual harassment and violence against women.

- Work is taking place to encourage suppliers to shift from cash payments of workers' wages to digital payment systems. It is held that for women workers this shift can be profound, for example, giving them more influence over household spending.
- Starbucks are credited with initiating the first US Corporate Sustainability Bond. This will enhance its sustainability programs around coffee supply management through Eligible Sustainability Projects.

13.15 Environmental technical specifications

The author is indebted to the European Commission for permission to include some detail from their 'Buying Green' handbook.[15] While the handbook is aimed at the public sector there is content that will materially assist private sector procurement specialists and stakeholders. The following points are worthy of note:

- Technical specifications need to relate to characteristics of the particular work, supply or service being purchased – and not to the general capacities or qualities of the operator. It is also important that they be clear, understandable by all operators in the same way.
- Technical specifications may be formulated by reference to European, international or national standards and/or in terms of performance or functionality.
- Standards have a major role in influencing the design of products and processes, and many standards include environmental characteristics such as material use, durability or consumption of energy or water.
- A performance - based approach (to specifications) usually allows more scope for innovation and in some cases will challenge the market into developing new technical solutions.
- As a contracting authority, you have the right to insist that the product you are purchasing be made from a specific material, or contain a certain percentage of recycled or reused content. You can also set requirements regarding the restriction of hazardous substances in a product.
- Whether you draw upon technical standards, labels, the EU or national GPP criteria when developing your specification, special attention should be paid to how you will verify tenderers' claims to supply.

13.16 Sustainability achievements in public procurement

The following examples are taken from the *Buying Green Handbook*[16] and in addition to the achievements provide relevant reference material for procurement specialists.

1 PIANOo, the Dutch Public Procurement Expertise Centre works for and with a network of around 3500 public procurement professionals. It provides tools and resources including a private discussion platform, access to learning tools and best practices and implementation coaching.
2 The City of Barcelona reviewed and developed new rules governing the inclusion of sustainability criteria in public contracts. Integrating green requirements is now compulsory for all contracting bodies tendering for vehicles, electricity, food and catering services, construction, timber and a range of other high priority procurement categories.

3 The City of Stockholm in 2011 led a joint procurement of 296 organisations for electric vehicles. The partners undertook a joint contribution to vehicle specifications, including criteria for CO_2 emissions and LCC. The first purchase in 2012 resulted in 34 tonnes CO_2 saved, a 95 per cent reduction compared with equivalent petrol vehicles.

4 The Procurement Agency of the Federal Ministry of the Interior, Germany published a tender for 50,000 thin client computer systems to the value of EUR 15m. The five-year energy savings were calculated to be 58,750,000 KWh of electricity, equivalent to 29.000 tonnes of CO_2.

5 The City of Luxembourg in 2013 carried out an open tender for the provision of cleaning products and services. Analysis found that only 15 per cent of previously used products were free of harmful substances. The technical specifications for the new tender included a list of substances banned from products.

13.17 European Directive on clean energy-efficient vehicles

It is sound professional practice for procurement professionals to keep abreast of legal/regulatory developments that will impact on their future roles. An important case in point is the European Council of the European Union who, on the 18 February 2019[17] (when this chapter of the book was being drafted) issued a 'proposal for a Directive of the European Parliament and of the Council amending Directive 2009/33/EC on the promotion of clean and energy-efficient vehicles.'

It is noted at para 5b that:

> while the Union is one of the leading regions for research and high-value eco-innovation, the Asia-Pacific Region is hosting the largest producers of battery-electric bulbs and batteries. Similarly, global market developments in battery electrics vehicles are driven by markets in China and the United States.

It is noted in para 6 that:

> Taking into account that governments' expenditure on goods, works and services represented around 16% of GDP, as of 2018, public authorities, through their procurement policy, can establish and support markets for innovative goods and services.

In essence the scope of the Directive by including practices such as lease, rental and hire-purchase of vehicles, as well as contracts for certain services ensures that all relevant procurement practices are covered. The services to be covered such as public road transport services, special purpose road transport passenger services, non-scheduled passenger transport, as well as (our emphasis) specific mail and parcel services and refuse collection services will be a major element in the contract.

At para 11a the proposal includes:

> In order to avoid imposing disproportionate burdens on public authorities and operators, Members States should be able to exempt from the requirements of this Directive the public procurement of certain vehicles with specific characteristics linked to their operational requirements. These include armoured vehicles, ambulances, hearses, wheelchair accessible MI vehicles, mobile cranes, vehicles designed and contracted for use principally on construction sites or in quarries, port or airport facilities as well as vehicles specifically designed and constructed or adapted for use by the armed forces, civil protection, fire services and forces responsible for maintaining public order. Such adaptations may relate to the installation of

specialised communications equipment or emergency lights. The requirements of this Directive should not apply to vehicles that are designed and constructed specifically to perform work and are not suitable for carrying passengers or for transporting goods. These include vehicles for road maintenance such as snow plows.

These are significant potential exemptions and offer Member States an opportunity to exclude these vehicles.

13.18 Contractual Implications of environmental and related considerations

Good intentions is NOT a contractual obligation. A procurement specialist liaising closely with stakeholders and legal services must ensure that a contract includes appropriate and relevant obligations. What follows is not legal advice and must not be interpreted as such.

The Department for International Development (DFID) have, at clause 47 'Environmental Requirements'.

47. ENVIRONMENTAL REQUIREMENTS

47.1 The Supplier shall provide the Services and any goods & equipment required under the Contract in accordance with applicable national and international laws, including those of the country or countries in which the Services or goods & equipment are to be provided, and DFID's environmental operations policy, which is to conserve energy, water and other resources, reduce waste, phase out the use of ozone depleting substances and minimise the release of greenhouse gases, volatile organic compounds and other substances damaging to health and the environment.

47.2 The UK Government is committed to promoting a low carbon, high growth, global economy. The Supplier shall work with DFID and the populations that are potentially affected by its operations under the Contract regarding any environmental issues that could affect the sustainable development provisions of the International Development Act (2002), comply with special conditions as stipulated in the Terms of Reference and carry out any reasonable additional request to ensure the protection of the environment, society and the economy throughout the contract period.

47.3 The Supplier shall ensure it has the requisite expertise and controls to identify and mitigate all factors that may affect compliance with the conditions outlined in Clauses 47.1 and 47.2 as a result of its own operations or those of Sub-contractors working on its behalf.

47.4 The Supplier shall promptly notify DFID of any changes in potential material adverse effects from its operations under the Contract and of the occurrence of any incident or accident related to the Project that has or is likely to have a significant adverse effect on the environment.

47.5 Nothing in Clauses 47.1 to 47.3 shall relieve the obligations of the Supplier to comply with its statutory duties and Good Industry Practice.

Engie[18] includes in its 'Clause on Ethics and Social and Environmental Responsibility' at (1) and (2), the following:

1   The supplier acknowledges that it has read and agrees to adhere to the commitments adopted by the Group on ethics and social and environmental responsibility, as set out in its reference documents and in its Vigilance Plan (for suppliers with an established commercial relationship, as defined under French law). The Group's commitments can be found on its website (www.engie.com).

2 In this respect, the supplier represents and warrants to Engie that it complies with the international and national laws applicable to the contract (including any amendments made to those laws during the term of this contract) and that it complied with those laws during the six-year period immediately preceding the signing of the contract, relating to:

(i) human rights and individual fundamental freedoms, in particular the prohibition of (a) child labour and any other form of forced or compulsory labour; (b) any type of discrimination within supplier's company – or supplier's group of companies as the case may be - or in its dealings with its suppliers or subcontractors;

(ii) embargoes, arms and drug trafficking and terrorism;

(iii) trade, import and export licences and customs requirements;

(iv) the health and safety of employees and third parties;

(v) employment, immigration and the ban on using undeclared workers;

(vi) environmental protection;

(vii) white-collar crime, mainly corruption and bribery, fraud, influence peddling (or the equivalent offence under the national law applicable to this contract), obtaining by fraud, theft, misuse of company property, counterfeiting, forgery and use of falsified documents, and any related offences;

(viii) anti-money laundering measures;

(ix) competition law.

In summary, the contractual obligations should ensure that suppliers commit to obligations such as those above and to satisfying KPIs for environmental and CSR responsibilities.

13.19 Sustainability challenges for procurement

There is a plethora of future sustainability challenges for procurement. The challenges include

1 having probing and assertive PQQ questions in the procurement process and conducting appropriate due diligence on the responses.

2 keeping abreast of laws, regulations and guidance emanating from a variety of national and international bodies.

3 understanding sustainability issues and risks that exist in the supply chain and designing policies and strategies to manage the issues and risks.

4 working with a wide range of stakeholders to develop KPIs for inclusion in contracts

5 seeking to ensure that long-term contracts include an obligation for suppliers/ contractors to improve their sustainability performance in accordance with minimum standards of improvement.

6 implement life-cycle costing techniques and specifically examining product disposal/ recycling implications.

7 fully understand, influencing and monitoring global cultural differences that affect, for example, the use and abuse of child labour.

8 putting in place effective contract management that are capable of monitoring sustainability performance across a supply chain, including sub-contractor's sustainability performance

9 making an effective contribution to their own corporate sustainability performance

10 taking pro-active actions with trade bodies to ensure sustainability performance is an active agenda topic.

13.20 Multinational enterprises

The International Labour Organisation (ILO)[19] has its roots in the 1919 Treaty of Versailles. The MNE Declaration is the only ILO instrument that provides direct guidance to enterprises (multinational and national) on social policy and inclusive, responsible and sustainable workplace practices.

The ILO published AIM and Scope is set out as follows:

1 Multinational enterprises play an important part in the economies of most countries and in international economic relations. This is of increasing interest to governments as well as to employers and workers and their respective organisations. Through international direct investment, trade and other means, such enterprises can bring substantial benefits to home and host countries by contributing to the more efficient utilisation of capital, technology and labour. Within the framework of sustainable development policies established by governments, they can also make an important contribution to the promotion of economic and social welfare; to the improvement of living standards and the satisfaction of basic needs; to the creation of employment opportunities, both directly and indirectly; and to the enjoyment of human rights, including freedom of association, throughout the world. On the other hand, the advances made by multinational enterprises in organising their operations beyond the national framework may lead to abuse of concentrations of economic power and to conflicts with national policy objectives and with the interest of the workers. In addition, the complexity of multinational enterprises and the difficulty of clearly perceiving their diverse structures, operations and policies sometimes give rise to concern either in the home or in the host countries, or in both.

2 The aim of this Declaration is to encourage the positive contribution which multinational enterprises can make to economic and social progress and the realisation of decent work for all; and to minimise and resolve the difficulties to which their various operations may give rise.

3 This aim will be furthered by appropriate laws and policies, measures and actions adopted by the governments, including in the fields of labour administration and public labour inspection, and by cooperation among the governments and the employers' and workers' organisations of all countries.

4 The principles of this Declaration are intended to guide governments, employers' and workers' organisations of home and host countries and multinational enterprises in taking measures and actions and adopting social policies, including those based on the principles laid down in the Constitution and the relevant Conventions and Recommendations of the ILO, to further social progress and decent work.

13.21 The Kyoto protocol

This is the first international agreement on climate change, under United Nations Framework Convention on Climate Change (UNFCCC).[20] The Kyoto treaty was adopted in Kyoto city in Japan on 11 December 1997. It took more than 7 years to come into force. It entered into force on 16 February 2005. At June 2016, 192 countries are party to the Kyoto protocol.

The first commitment period was 2008–2012.

The second commitment period was 2013–2020.

It is significant that four countries: Canada, Japan, New Zealand and Russia that were part of the first commitment period opted out of the new commitments. The United States of America, the biggest polluter of GHG emissions, refused to become part of Kyoto protocol.

The emissions of six greenhouse gases were targeted to reduce: carbon dioxide (CO_2); methane (CH_4); nitrous oxide (N_2O); hydrofluorocarbons (HFCs); perfluorocarbons (PFCs); and sulfur hexafluoride (SF6).

The UK has two binding targets for UK emissions reduction:

- An 80 per cent cut by 2050, which was made law in the Climate Change Act 2008
- Pin 'interim target' of a 34 per cent cut by 2020 which was made legally binding in the April 2009 budget.

13.22 Conclusion

Procurement has a strategic, policy making and operational role in managing sustainability and all facets of socially responsible procurement.

The long-term implications for the environment are critical to future generations. This must be the driver to make continuous improvement in sustainability performance.

Discussion questions

13.1 Explain how sustainable procurement can benefit society and the environment.

13.2 What are some of the key roles for procurement when managing sustainability actions by suppliers?

13.3 Can you identify three life-cycle considerations when procuring goods?

13.4 If an audit was carried out of existing sustainability procurement provision within contracts, what would you expect the audit to include?

13.5 What impact do specifications have on sustainability performance?

13.6 In your opinion do retailers take sufficient measures to effectively manage the whole life cost of packaging? What are the key reasons for your answer?

13.7 What is the legal requirement on local authorities and other public bodies to consider the social good when procuring services?

13.8 Can you identify six social value deliverables?

13.9 How can environmental issues be addressed during the procurement process?

13.10 What are some sustainability challenges for procurement?

13.11 Can procurement play a positive role in achieving positive outcomes on climate change? What are the key reasons for your answer?

References

1 *Making the Case for Sustainable Procurement: The NHS as a Good Corporate Citizen.* www.bre. co.uk.

2 *Buying Green! A Handbook as Green Public Procurement*, 3rd edition. European Commission, Brussels, Belgium, 2016.

3 Sustainable Procurement Strategy, The Difference – sustainability starts here. downloads.bbc. co.uk, June 2011.

4 ILO Fundamental conventions Ref: http://www.ilo.org/global/standards/introduction-to-international-labour-standards/conventions-and-recommendations/lang--en/index.htm.

5 https://epa.gov.

6 https://www.willmotdixon.co.uk.

7 Thalesgroup.com/uk, Sustainable Procurement Guide.

8 'A Social Value toolkit for Milton Keynes Council', Version 1.0 April 2015 https://www. milton-keynes.gov.uk.

9 http://gpp.golocal-ukraine.com/wp-content/uploads/ISO_20400_2017E-Character_PDF_ document.pdf

10 https://www.nao.org.uk.

11 https://www.nao.org.uk 'Addressing the environmental impacts of government procurement', 29 April 2009

12 https://www.brighton-hove.gov.uk 'Suppliers Guide to completing the Pre-Qualification Questionnaire (PQQ)'.

13 'Recommended pre-qualification questions', Performance Measurement Special Interest Group (May 2016) https://www.supplychainschool.co.uk.

14 www.bsr.org., 'New Models for Sustainable Procurement', February 2018.

15 *Buying Green! A Handbook on Green Public Procurement*, 3rd edition. European Commission, Brussels, Belgium, 2016.

16 Same as 15 above.

17 Council of the European Union, Brussels 18 February 2019. Analysis of the final compromise text with a view to agreement.

18 www.engie.com.

19 International Labour Organisation, *Tripartite Declaration of Principles concerning Multinational Enterprises and Social Policy (MNE Declaration)*, 5th edition. International Labour Organisation, Geneva, Switzerland, 2017.

20 https://unfccc.int/process/the-kyoto-protocol.

Part 4

Strategy, tactics and operations 2: Operation and strategic performance

Chapter 14

Project procurement and risk management

Learning outcomes

This chapter aims to provide an understanding of:

- the project lifecycle
- the project procurement strategy
- role of procurement
- PRINCE 2®
- project management issues
- project risk management
- corporate benefits of world-class project management
- project risk register
- project audit
- procurement management

Key ideas

- Special demands and challenges of a project for procurement.
- Skills and knowledge requirements of procurement.
- Identifying and managing risks in the supply chain.
- Project initiation documents and their impact on project outcomes.
- Contracting options.
- PRINCE2®.
- Project risk registers and management of procurement risks.
- Tailoring contractual detail to specific project needs.
- Through-life considerations and their effective management.
- Price and risk impacts on project outcomes.

Introduction

The main purpose of this chapter is to understand what constitutes a project, how procurement fulfils its professional input to a project and undertakes the risk management process, with an emphasis on procurement and supply chain risks.

Meredith and Mantel[1] define a project as 'A specific, finite task to be accomplished' combined with seven factors common to projects: importance, performance, finite due date, interdependencies (between departments and competing projects), uniqueness, resources and conflict.

One-off projects are likely to be a rare occurrence in some organisations, whereas in others there will be many projects. Each project offers procurement an opportunity to make a significant business contribution to the success of the project (see Table 14.1). This contribution may include a combination of knowledge and high-level skills.[2]

The scope of one-off projects is infinitely variable, as Table 14.2 indicates. The projects are included to provide reference points for learning about project failures and challenges.

Table 14.1 The business contribution of procurement to project success

Contribution to the project business case

Research into the supply chain

Input into the project cost drivers

Input into the project risk register

Managing timelines for the procurement process

Managing pre-qualification and tender processes

Contribution to pre-qualification and tender processes

Development of contract terms and conditions

Analysis of bidders' project cost models

Conducting supply chain due diligence

Negotiation of project costs; contract terms, through-life costs, etc.

Agreeing supply chain mobilisation actions and costs

Liaison with in-house stakeholders

Putting in place effective monitoring of contractors and sub-contractors

Ensuring the necessary contractor insurances and Performance Bonds are in place

Table 14.2 The scope and nature of project failures and challenges

'Creating a marine spatial plan for the Hauraki Gulf'
New Zealand Controller & Auditor General. Report 5 Dec. 2018

'Progress with preparations for High Speed 2'
National Audit Office (UK). HC 235. Session 2016–17. 28 June 2016

'Procurement Processes and Management of Probity by the Moorebank Intermodal Company'
Australian National Audit Office (ANAO). Report No 9 2018–2019. 11 Oct. 2018

'Naval Construction Programs – Mobilisation'
Australian National Audit Office (ANAO). Report 39 2017–18. 14 May 2018

'Performance Audit Report on Road Works'
National Audit Office. The United Republic of Tanzania. March 2010

'Investigation into the Department for Transport's decision to cancel three rail electrification projects'
National Audit Office (UK). HC 835. Session 2017–19. 29 Mar 2018

14.1 The project lifecycle

While all projects will follow a lifecycle, the lifecycle will vary from project to project.

The procurement contribution is capable of adding considerable value at each phase of the lifecycle. The illustrative lifecycle shown in Figure 14.2 has been adapted for the Metrolink[3] Project Management Manuel – Volume 1: PM Desk book.

14.1.1 What is a project?

Vaidyanathan[4] explains a project in the following way.

> A project is a unique activity. A project has a beginning and a definite end. A project expends resources. A project has constraints and requirements that may include scope, budget, schedule, resources, performance factors, and creation of value to stakeholders. A project has a goal and objectives. A project has to add value or beget some kind of benefit.

The Association for Project Management[5] defines projects as 'unique, transient endeavours undertaken to achieve a desired outcome.'

PRINCE2® defines a project as 'A temporary organisation that is created for the purpose of delivering one or more business products according to an agreed Business Case.'

Projects include low value–low-risk one-off projects, in which procurement has a role to play. These projects are important to the organisation that initiates the project. The author is of the view that informed learning is to be found in high-value-high risk projects, largely because they attract more publicity from a number of sources. These include public audit bodies, including the UK National Audit Office, the Australian National

Figure 14.1 The project lifecycle

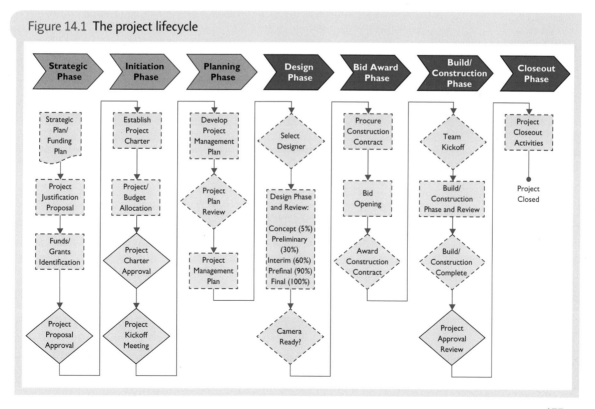

Figure 14.2 Example of illustrative lifecycle

Strategic phase
- Prepare a strategic and funding plan. Procurement has a key role supporting funding estimates, recognising that external purchases may account for >60% of the total project cost.
- Project justification proposal. This is sometimes referred to as the Business Case. The procurement contribution will include risk modelling of supply chain issues.
- Identification of funding source and implications.
- Project proposal approval. This provides the authority to mobilise the in-house and external sources to drive the project forward.

Initiation phase
- Establish the Project Charter.
- Allocate the budget. It may be noted here that many projects include a contingency provision. Procurement has a vital role to manage the supply chain costs, noting potential implications of foreign currency movements, inaccuracies in contractor's tendered sums and through life cost implications.
- Approval of the Project Charter.
- Project kick off meeting. The exclusion of procurement at this phase is an error and exposes the project to risk and delays. Procurement should be an integral member of the project team.

Planning phase
- Develop the Project Management Plan.
- Review the Project Management Plan.
- Finalise the Project Management Plan.
- There are four key steps in a basic planning process, namely (1) break down the project work scope into a set of components tasks (2) arrange the tasks into a network sequence that makes most sense at this point – and create a network diagram (3) estimate the duration of each task (4) identify the critical path, and calculate the planned duration of the project and other useful management information.

Design phase
- Not all projects will have a design phase as is usual in construction, engineering, shipbuilding and IT systems provision.
- Select a designer. This is a key decision point in a project and must involve procurement. For example, the appointment of a 'design practice' to design specialised equipment for a wind farm requires a tendering competition to ascertain skills capability, cost, timescale, contractual accountability and liabilities, ownership of ensuing intellectual property and so on. The management of the tendering competition should be the domain of procurement.
- Identify the design phase and payment schedule. The design phase may be –Concept-Preliminary –Interim – Pre-Final and Final. Procurement must capture this detail in the contract.

Contractor pre-qualification and bid award phase
- The appointment of a contractor is a serious business decision. Typically, a pre-qualification and tendering process will be required. At bid award, the full contract detail will, ideally, be finalised. It is not unusual on complex projects for 'Letters of Intent' to be issued, to authorise the contractor to commence work. There are legal implications of such as those explained in Chapter 7. The award of a contract creates obligations and potential liabilities for the contractor and the buying organisation.

Build/Construction Phase
- Clearly, this project phase is specific to build/construction activities. There is a wealth of activities during this phase, many of which require expert procurement support and active involvement. The activities requiring procurement support at least, include, project review meetings, handling changes to specifications, resolving disputes, monitoring procurement budgets, claiming damages for contractors' non-performance, ensuring appropriate insurances are in place and negotiating claims for extras.

Closeout Phase
- There is a high probability that if the closeout phase is mishandled, the contractor may be motivated to submit a claim. The tasks that require completing, and in which there is a role for procurement, include final settlement of project contracts, acceptance of contract deliverables, collection of contract documents and records (such as built drawings, operation and maintenance manuals, and warranties, etc.). The final payment will be authorised, giving due consideration to payment retentions. Any bonds warranting release must be dealt with.

Audit Office and the United States Government Accountability Office. Some private sector project disputes receive publicity but these are not usually accompanied by pertinent data. Some of this can be found in legal court judgments, accessed through the British and Irish Legal Information Institute (BAILII). This gives access to judgments in many jurisdictions, including, USA, Canada, Germany, Italy, New Zealand, Asia and South Africa.

Projects fall into different categories as illustrated below. This is not a comprehensive listing. It is included to indicate the scope of projects.

Information Systems	– computer-related hardware and software projects
Healthcare	– new hospitals and local health centres
New product development	– new automotive model projects
Construction	– highways, bridges, rail network improvements projects
Defence	– fighting vehicles, fighter aircraft projects
Space exploration	– launch vehicles, spacecraft projects
Shipbuilding	– new cruise liner projects.

Inevitably, there are project failures. The author's research has identified the presence of one or more of the following as major contributing factors to the failures.

- contractor incompetence
- procurement's failure to conduct due diligence on short-listed tenderers
- lack of relevant experience in project teams
- lack of definition in scope of work
- no clarity in decision making
- absence of communication protocol
- badly drafted contracts
- negotiations dominated by contractor
- contract changes inadequately managed
- procurement having a passive role
- lack of visibility of total project costs
- key milestones neither identified nor managed
- internal politics divert attention from project deliverables
- project management deficiencies
- failure to promptly deal with project disputes
- lack of courage to recognise a failing project
- project risks not identified
- absence of project risk mitigation strategies
- fraudulent activity
- lack of flexibility when dealing with project challenges.

14.1.2 Project Initiation Document

Prince® explains that there are three primary uses of the Project Initiation Document (PID), namely to:

- ensure that the project has a sound basis before asking the Project Board to make any major commitment to the project
- act as a base document against which the Project Board and Project Manager can assess progress, issues and ongoing viability questions
- provide a single source of reference about the project so that people joining the 'temporary organisation' can easily find out what the project is about, and how it is being managed.

479

The PID is a living product in that it should always reflect the current status, plans and controls of the project. Its component products will need to be updated and re-baselined, as necessary, at the end of each stage, to reflect the current status of its constituent parts.

The version of the PID that was used to gain authorisation for the project is preserved as the basis against which performance will later be assessed when closing the project.

The Project Initiation Document should cover the following topics:

- project definition
- project approach
- business case
- project management team structure
- role descriptions
- quality management strategy
- configuration management strategy
- risk management strategy
- communication management strategy
- project plan
- project controls
- tailoring of PRINCE2.

The PID is derived from the Project Brief and discussions with user, business and supplier stakeholders for input on methods, standards and controls.

The PID could be a single document; an index for a collection of documents; a document; with cross references to a number of other documents; a collection of information in a project management tool.

14.2 The project procurement strategy

14.2.1 Procurement strategy

The author is indebted to the New Zealand Government Procurement[6] for permission to use extracts from their 'Planning Construction Procurement – A guide to developing your procurement strategy.' The guide abounds with practical, robust guidance that is of great assistance to those engaging in any facet of a project, including procurement.

14.2.2 Components of a good procurement strategy

- Statement of objectives
- Summary and analysis of:
  - project objectives
  - requirements
  - characteristics
  - risks
- Review of client and market capabilities

- An analysis of delivery model options and identification of a recommended delivery model
- Analysis of potential procurement methods and identification of a recommended method
- A project plan showing timing and sequence
- Agency contract management requirements
- Opportunities for bundling or unbundling work and contracts, for example:
  - bundling projects of a similar nature to increases economy of scale, or
  - splitting contracts where speed is a high priority, such as enabling, groundworks and main contract
- Opportunities for use of collaborative methods including ICT based project techniques.

Note: The level of detail for each can be tailored as appropriate for the scale and complexity of the project. Procurement strategies for projects that are low risk and low value may not require all of these elements.

Key success factors when developing an effective procurement strategy

- Fully understand the project characteristics including key drivers, constraints and risks
- Assess client and market, capabilities and capacity
- Evaluate potential delivery models and approach to market for suitability
- Involve key stakeholders and experts early in the planning and development process
- Challenge assumptions in order to better achieve desired outcomes
- Use practical analytical techniques to support the decision-making process

A robust, documented procurement strategy, based on facts and analysis, is an important part of planning successful delivery of a major capital project. One of the key objectives of a procurement strategy is to assess a range of delivery options and identify a recommended delivery model. By assessing a range of options, agencies can maximise opportunities for achieving value for money and optimal project outcomes.

A procurement strategy presents the findings of this assessment based on the individual project's characteristics, risks and circumstances.

A procurement strategy is developed during the planning phases of the procurement lifecycle. It focuses very much on assessing options to select an approach to market that is appropriate for the particular project. The procurement plan follows on from the procurement strategy document, by providing the methodology and approach, process and project management structure for sourcing and managing suppliers (for which there may be multiple transactions, depending on the procurement strategy chosen).

14.2.3 Project requirements

Table 14.3 can be used to identify project requirements.

14.2.4 Project constraints

Table 14.4 can be used to identify project constraints.

Table 14.3 Project requirements

Requirement	Factors to consider
Programme and phasing	■ What are the desired key milestone dates? ■ What is the target date that the facility should be operational?
Service	■ What are the future operational requirements? ■ What are the future maintenance requirements? ■ Would this be suitable for delivery by the private sector?
Design criteria	■ Is a whole life cycle solution required? ■ What functionality is to be delivered by the project? ■ What are the required quality standards? ■ What are the drivers for design? E.g. new technology ■ Is an attractive architectural statement required, reflecting the facility's status in the community? ■ Is there sufficient space to meet the client's immediate and possible future space requirements? ■ Is the site potential being maximised?
Cost certainty	■ Has the budget for the project been finalised? ■ Would the final cost of the project be expected to vary from the budget cost?
Other objectives	■ Are there objectives around aspects of sustainability? ■ Are there objectives around iwi engagement?

Risks

Identify the project risks, including all major risks and opportunities outlined in the projects 'Risk Management Plan'. The following topics may be useful checklist:

- site issues
- permits
- design
- materials
- constructability
- client risk culture
- market maturity
- market capability
- political opportunities and risks
- stakeholder management.

14.2.5 Determine preferred delivery model

Purpose

To undertake an assessment of the range of delivery models against the project characteristics to determine and recommend a preferred option.

Selection of an appropriate delivery model is one of the most important decisions to be made during the construction procurement process. An inappropriate delivery model can increase project risk and negatively impact value for money, quality and timing. Undertaking a delivery model options analysis aims to reduce the risk. It is therefore essential that a robust analysis is undertaken to ensure that the right model is chosen.

Table 14.4 Project constraints

Constraint	Factors to consider
Site status	■ Where is the location? ■ What are possible future developments on or around the site? ■ What is the land ownership? ■ What are the geotechnical conditions? ■ Does the site need remediation due to contamination? ■ Are there demolition and disposal needs? ■ Are there environmental considerations? ■ Are there cultural heritage considerations?
Site condition	■ What type of site? ■ How will contractors price for any risks associated with the site conditions? ■ Have extensive reviews of the site been undertaken as part of the design development process? ■ Is the client willing to retain full control of the design and accept the risk of potential unknown risks?
Planning	■ Is the design sympathetic to the needs of the planning authority and local stakeholders?
Risk allocation	■ Is the client risk averse? ■ What degree of risk is the client prepared to accept?
Degree of client involvement	■ What degree of involvement would the client like to have?
Flexibility for change during design and construction	■ Is cost certainty required? ■ How early in the project will cost certainty need to be fixed? ■ Do the design and construction processes need to be flexible, to allow incorporation of future changes, e.g. development in technology?
Market interest	■ Will the procurement method solicit a good response from contractors?
Design and construction complexity	■ Is the project pushing the boundaries of technology? ■ Is the project technologically complex in terms of services? ■ Does it need specialised or customer-built plant or equipment?
Opportunities	■ Are there opportunities to bundle or unbundle the project with to maximise value for example where the project is part of a wider programme?
Other constraints	■ Are there other constraints specific to this project e.g. the remote location of site?

There are many types (and hybrids) of delivery model to choose from:

- traditional (conventional client led design)
- design and build
- package based
- direct managed
- alliance
- Public Private Partnership (PPP)
- early contractor involvement
- panel of suppliers.

14.3 Role of procurement

The role of a Manager – Procurement can be gleaned from reference to a Manchester Airport Relief Road project.[7]

14.3.1 Manager – procurement

This example is taken from an actual project brief.

The Procurement Manager is a key role which will need significant and wide experience in the procurement of similar engineering projects to be performed effectively.

Knowledge and experience of the current UK procurement regulations is an essential skill.

Equally important, however, is a broad and detailed understanding of the different procurement options that might be relevant to this particular project, their benefits and in particular as the project manager, the outputs required for a successful procurement.

The Procurement Manager must have sufficient experience to be able to look well ahead of programme and advise the Project Manager well in advance when key information is required for input to the selected procurement process. It will be essential as part of the procurement process for a project of this scale and nature that the promoters are perceived by the market place to have credibility. One of the most important aspects in demonstrating this is a well-planned and managed procurement process. Once the bidders are engaged in procurement they will expect it to be an efficient process providing clear instruction according to a clear published programme. Failure to do this may undermine the credibility of both the promoters and the project.

The Procurement Manager must therefore be skilled in forward planning, communicating with the Project Manager well in advance as to the clear requirements to feed into the procurement process.

One key function of the Procurement Manager must be to ensure that due process is followed, that the process is above scrutiny and to put in place all necessary processes to ensure that the procurement is objective in every sense.

The Project Board and Project Director must have sufficient confidence in the Procurement Manager that an efficient and effective procedurally correct process will be implemented.

14.4 PRINCE 2®

14.4.1 Introduction

PRINCE is an acronym for Project In Controlled Environments. It is a UK Government-sponsored approach intended to improve the quality of UK Project Management. PRINCE 2 was launched in 1996 and intended to provide guidance on all types of projects. A signification update[8] was published in June 2009.

14.4.2 The detail

The PRINCE 2 reference book has ten sections:

- Introduction
- Principles

- Introduction to themes
- Themes (7)
- Introduction to processes
- Processes (7)
- Tailoring PRINCE 2
- Appendices (5)
- Further information
- Glossary and index

The seven themes are:

- Business case
- Organisation
- Quality
- Plans
- Risk
- Change
- Progress

The seven processes are:

- Starting up a Project
- Directing a Project
- Initiating a Project
- Controlling a Project
- Managing Product Delivery
- Managing a Stage Boundaries
- Closing a Project

14.4.3 PRINCE 2 perceived deficiencies

ESI International Inc.[9] observes that there are several key project management areas that are not covered by the PRINCE 2 approach. PRINCE 2 holds the view that, despite the importance of those topics, they are specialist areas of knowledge and are covered elsewhere and can be managed using the method as an overall framework. The areas referred to above are:

1 PRINCE 2 Planning process has a structured approach which takes you through sound planning steps, however, when identifying dependencies it proposes a list of activities accompanied by dependencies is produced. A network diagram is illustrated within PRINCE 2; however, carrying out the calculations is not part of any current or proposed PRINCE 2 examination.
2 Estimating techniques are covered, but with a single paragraph explanation of each given technique.
3 Scheduling within PRINCE 2 does not give guidance of how to improve the schedule if overall timescales are unacceptable.
4 Costing and cost control are handled lightly within PRINCE 2.
5 Quality is a major topic but PRINCE 2 does not include techniques such as benefit/cost analysis, benchmarking, flowcharting techniques such as Ishikawa or cause and effect diagrams, design of experiments, and cost of quality.

6 PRINCE 2 gives no guidance in regard to teamwork and communications, progress or escalating concerns.

7 Staff acquisition, performance appraisal and health and safety regulations are not mentioned in PRINCE 2.

8 While PRINCE 2 covers communications, it goes little further than listing headings in the Communication Management Strategy product outline and providing a six-step approach to stakeholder engagement.

9 EDI International Inc. further observe that 'perhaps the largest single section of project management which is not covered in the PRINCE 2 approach is Project Procurement Management' (author's emphasis).

14.5 Project management issues

The Auditor General of Nova Scotia published a report[10] that provided a valuable insight in project failings. The project was the restoration of Bluenose II. The original Bluenose was launched as a Grand Banks fishing and racing schooner in 1921 in Lunenburg, Nova Scotia. It was built by the Smith and Rhuland Shipyard. Bluenose struck a reef off Isle aux Vache, Haiti on 28 January 1946. Bluenose II was launched in 1963. There is a lot of learning in the Audit Report; some extracts are shown below:

- The government as a whole . . . . did not adequately plan the Bluenose II restoration project. This started with leaving responsibility for the project with a Department having little experience managing construction projects.
- The Department did not prepare clearly defined goals or requirements for the project.
- A comprehensive list of risks was not completed and little was done to prepare mitigation plans or assess the potential impact of identified risks.
- The Department did not ensure a realistic and complete project budget was prepared; instead the preliminary cost estimate was used as a final budget. This estimate was prepared without using a robust process and as such was not an adequate first estimate or a final project budget.
- When the main project contractors, project manager, designer, the builder were selected, the Department did not have sufficient details to know what would be required.
- At that point in time, it was unclear what was to be built, resulting in weak contract terms.
- The contracts (for project manager and the designer did not include penalty clauses and were routinely extended throughout the life of the project.
- We also noted the project manager did not attend all required meetings and the Department did not always obtain required monthly status reports. Further, no comprehensive project schedule was prepared.
- As a result of the lack of planning and overall weak management by the Department a number of issues arose during construction.
- We found poor planning and project management by the Department contributed to the project being over budget and delivered years late.
- There was a single risk analysis meeting but no risk management process existed.
- The risk management approach should be an ongoing effort, with regular meetings to monitor the risks identified in planning and consider if any new areas of concern have arisen.
- The project cost estimates at the time the builder's contract was signed in July 2010 already showed an overage of £600,000.
- Those responsible for evaluating the tenders had limited experience with shipbuilding.

- There were two key areas of deficiency in the contracts; a lack of clarity in some of the terms; and specific terms or requirements were missing that we expected to find.

- The build contract did not include penalties for failing to meet the construction deadlines. The Department attempted to include a clause in the contract to address penalties and late fees, but the builder was unwilling to sign the contract so the clause was removed.

These extracts show the learning that can be acquired from a study of audit reports. All procurement staff who are, or will be, involved in project procurement should make a commitment to their continuous learning.

14.6 Project risk management

14.6.1 Introduction

Risk management is defined by the Association for Project Management (APM)[11] as

> a process that allows individual risk events and overall risk to be understood and managed proactively, optimising success by minimising threats and maximising opportunities.

The APM explain that all projects, programmes and portfolios are inherently risky because they are unique, constrained, based on assumptions, performed by people and subject to external influences. Risks can affect the achievement of objectives either positively or negatively. Risk includes both opportunities and threats, and both should be managed through the risk management process.

An MAB/MIAC report[12] states, unequivocally,

> The need to manage risk systematically applies to all organisations and to all functions and activities within an organisation and should be recognised as of fundamental importance by all managers and staff in the APS (Australian Public Service).

In the ADCNET audit report[13] it said that in addressing risk management of the ADCNET project the audit criteria had regard to better practice, which would include:

- a project risk assessment undertaken to identify, assess, prioritise and agree actions required to manage high (particularly business critical) risk issues

- a project risk assessment undertaken to identify, assess, prioritise and agree actions required to manage high (particularly business critical) risk issues

- risk reporting processes which ensure that risk issues are raised at the appropriate levels and forums

- high-level risks being monitored throughout the project lifecycle and the project risk assessment updated to address changing project circumstances and risk profiles and

- appropriate project acceptance criteria clearly defined and deliverables assessed against them.

Appropriate project processes to achieve these risk management outcomes include:

- a formal risk assessment at the commencement of the project and updated at key milestones

- a risk management strategy defined and agreed with the project steering committee

- appropriate risk management activities planned to address key identified risks and be appropriately executed

- regular review of project risks to address project changes and to ensure issues are identified at the earliest possible time and

- close monitoring of risk management activities by the project steering committee.

The findings included the point that there was no evidence of the Risk Management Team meeting prior to February 1992 or after April 1993. It also included the comment that DFAT <u>did not produce a detailed project risk assessment report until 15 months after the project commenced</u> – author's emphasis.

14.7 Corporate benefits of world-class project procurement

Please refer to Figure 14.3 for further information.

Figure 14.3 **Corporate benefits of world-class project procurement risk management**

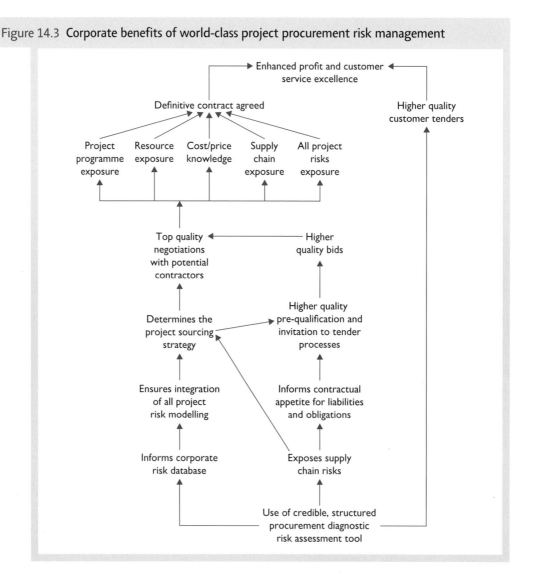

14.8 Project risk register

A risk register can be defined as,

> A risk register is a log of identified risks along with its owners, risk scores, RPNs (Risk Priority Number), risk responses, triggers, residual and secondary risks and contingency plans for cost and schedule.

The risk register should be initiated at the outset of the project and procurement should be a prime contributor.

14.9 Project audit

The Association for Project Management (APM)[14] uses the term 'project' to mean 'a unique, transient endeavour undertaken to achieve planned objectives.'

Auditing is defined by the Chartered Institute of Internal Auditors[15] as:

> an independent, objective assurance and consulting activity designed to add value and improve an organisations operation. It helps an organisation accomplish its objectives by bringing a systematic, disciplined approach to evaluate and improve the effectiveness of risk management, control and governance processes.

National Audit Office

In the UK the National Audit Office (NAO) scrutinises public spending for Parliament to help the government in its drive to improve public services, nationally and locally. This is achieved by auditing the financial statements of all central government departments, agencies and other public bodies and reporting the results to Parliament. Other work comprises value-for- money studies, local audit, investigations, support to Parliament and international activities. More detail can be found on the NAO website.[16]

Procurement specialists have access to NAO reports that include interpretation, analysis, findings and recommendations. An example is the report on The Nuclear Decommissioning Authority's (NDA) Magnox contract.[17]

The key findings included:

- The NDA ran a competitive procurement exercise for decommissioning services at 12 nuclear sites, resulting in the award of a 14-year contract for up to £6.2 billion.
- In July 2016, the High Court found that the NDA had wrongly decided the outcome of the procurement process; the NDA agreed to settle claims in March 2017.

The NDA's fundamental failures in the Magnox contract procurement raise serious questions about its understanding of procurement regulations; its ability to manage large complex procurements; and why the errors detected by the High Court judgment were not identified earlier. In light of these issues, the Department must consider whether its governance and oversight arrangements surrounding the NDA are sufficiently clear and effective in providing the scrutiny and assurance it requires to meet the standards expected in managing public money.

British Army Recruitment Partnering Project: Introduction

A report issued by the UK National Audit Office[18] highlights many issues managing a project. As with all NAO there is a plethora of detail, all informative. Space in this book prevents the whole detail being included. Some salient learning points are outlined below. The background to the project was that the Army needed to ensure a constant flow of new recruits to replace those who leave or retire from service. In 2012, the Army sought to reform its approach to recruitment by entering into a partnering agreement with Capita Business Services Ltd (Capita). It was a 10 year, £495 million contract with Capita to secure its expertise in recruiting and marketing. The key findings of the NAO report were (underlined below):

1 Capita has missed the British Army's (the Army's) annual targets for recruiting new soldiers and officers every year since 2013. The total shortfall each year has ranged from 21% to 45% of the Army's requirement.

2 The recruiting environment is challenging.

3 The Army aimed to recruit the quantity and quality of soldiers it needed each year, while reducing its costs.

4 Neither the Army nor Capita tested the fundamental changes to the recruiting approach prior to its introduction.

   In 2012 a National Recruiting Centre was established and the number of local recruitment offices was reduced from 131 to 68. The Army and Capita did not test whether this approach was appropriate to a military context before introducing it.

5 The online recruitment system was launched 52 months later than originally planned due to delays caused first by the Ministry of Defence and then Capita.

   The MOD failed to meet its contractual obligations to provide an IT infrastructure to host Capita's recruitment software. The Army spent £113 million developing the new system and running the legacy system longer than expected.

6 Capita under-estimated the complexity of the Armed Forces requirements.

   The level of customisation was not recognised and as a result, Capita could not use an 'off-the shelf' commercial solution.

7 Capita encountered significant problems when it launched the online recruitment system, which reduced the number of recruits.

   Applicants had difficulty using the online system. The Army estimated that this resulted in 13,000 fewer applicants between November 2017 and March 2018, compared with the same period in the preceding year and could lead to 1,300 fewer enlistments.

8 The Army does not have full ownership of the online system but will have rights to use and modify the system after the Capita contract ends in 2022.

   The online system is hosted on Capita's IT infrastructure. The Army is negotiating with Capita to secure full access to the source code and has begun to explore whether it can modify the system.

9 In November 2016, the Army and Capita revised their approach to engaging with applicants and enhanced the support available at local offices.

   One salient point here is that the Army will pay Capita an additional £33 million up to 2022 to establish this approach.

10 After an initial fall in 2014–15, the Army has not reduced the time it takes to complete the recruitment process.

   In the first six months of 2018–19, half of regular soldier applicants took up to 321 days to complete the recruitment process.

11 In April 2018, the Army and Capita launched a new project to reduce recruitment times and improve conversion rates.

12 The Army has penalised Capita for missing its recruitment targets, but this has not improved recruitment performance.

Between August 2015 and September 2018, Capita did not meet its performance targets for the number of recruits in 37 out of 38 months. The Army deducted service credits of £26 million.

13 In April 2017, the Army agreed to lower Capita's performance targets and reset the service credit deductions.

Capita proposed a number of amendments to the contract. Targets were reduced which in 2017–18 represented a 20% reduction on the Army's requirements. An improvement plan was implemented but, as of September 2018, Capita was still missing the new recruitment targets.

14 The Army's management of the Programme has limited its ability to refine the recruitment process.

The Army included 10,000 specifications in the Capita contract.

15 In June 2018, the Army and Capita launched the Army Manning Campaign, which is supported by a revised governance structure.

16 The Army and Capita have made significant changes to their overall approach to recruitment, but these have not yet resulted in the Army's requirements for new regular soldiers being met.

17 The Army is forecasting that expenditure will remain within the approved budget, despite the cost of the Capita contract rising by 37% to £677 million.

The Army has used the £199 million contingency that was included in its original budget.

18 The Department (MOD) will not achieve the planned financial savings.

The forecast for planned savings was £267 million by 2022.

The above is merely a synopsis of a lengthy NAO report. There is a great deal of learning for procurement learners and practitioners. The two organisations do not lack resources or knowledge to manage a project of this complexity. They failed, as have many others. Some extracts from actual project audits now follow.

Office of Inspector General.

US Department of Energy. Audit Report DOE-OIG-18-17 February 2018.

- We found that Fossil Energy had not effectively implemented ongoing invoice review controls it put in place to manage the risks associated with this complex project.

- Fossil energy approved approximately $16.9 million in subcontractor costs supported by invoices which did not include details regarding the nature of services provided or hours worked.

- Fossil Energy approved almost $10.8 million in labour and fringe benefit charges for Summit employees without adequate supporting documentation . . . . This was of concern since about 65%, or approximately $7million was charged for seven executives who held positions for multiple entities affiliated with Summit.

- Fossil Energy approved over $8.2 million in subcontractor costs without support demonstrating the actual amount of payments made.

■ We identified over $650,000 in consultancy charges for items such as a spa service, alcohol, first-class travel, limousines services, receipts in foreign currency, and business meals that were prohibited or not fully substantiated.

Auditor of the State of California

California High-Speed Rail Authority. Report 2018-108 November 2018

This project was conceived as the nation's first bullet train. In 2008 major funding of $9.95 billion was authorised.

■ In 2018 the Authority's business plan showed construction overruns and other cost increases, which raised the overall system cost estimate to $77.3 billion.

■ The contract changes have also resulted in significant time delays. The projects expected completion date has been pushed back from 2018 to 2022.

■ The Authority relies on contracted construction oversight firms to evaluate potential change orders' merits and provide independent estimates of how much they should cost. The Authority executed changes for amounts that were greater than the oversight firm recommended. The Construction contractor for Project 1 requested more than $21 million for unanticipated bridge construction. The oversight firm estimated a cost of only $7.4 million. The Authority ultimately authorised a change order for $18.6 million.

■ Weaknesses in the Authority's contract management structure have contributed to its reliance on contractors for important functions – such as contract oversight – that state employees should perform.

■ For the nine contracts we reviewed CMSU's roster of contract managers shows that five contracts had two or three different contract managers in the past year alone.

National Audit Office

The failure of the FiReControl project. Report HC1272 Session 2010-2012 1 July 2011.

This project aimed to improve the resilience, efficiency and technology of the Fire & Rescue Service by replacing 46 local control rooms with a network of nine purpose built regional control centres.

■ The original project estimate was £120m. The total project spend to end March 2011 was £250m. There was a failure to deliver the project and a minimum of £469m was wasted.

■ The Department underestimated the complexity of designing a system to meet the needs of Fire & Rescue Services and then failed to provide effective management.

■ FiReControl was based on unrealistic estimates of project costs and expected local savings.

■ The project lacked consistent leadership and direction, and was characterised by a high turn-over of staff and over-reliance on poorly managed consultants.

■ Until 2009, the Department did not take a sufficient grip to sort out early problems with delivery by the contractor for the IT system. A lack of openness and an adversarial stance between both parties towards problem solving led to the slow resolution of issues.

NASA office of Inspector General

NASA's Management of the Space Launch System Stages Contract. Report No 1G-19-001 October 10, 2018.

NASA contracted with The Boeing Company in 2012 to build two SLS Core Stages – that is, the first stage of the rocket consisting of the fuel tanks and supporting infrastructure – and later on Exploration Upper Stage a new and more powerful second stage. The report included:

At its current rate, we project Boeing will expend at least $8.9 billion through 2021— double the amount initially planned— while delivery of the first Core Stage has slipped

2 1/2 years from June 2017 to December 2019 and may slip further. Between June 2014 and August 2018, Boeing spent over $600 million more than planned on developing Core Stages 1 and 2, and NASA officials have confirmed that in FY 2018 alone Boeing expended $226 million more than planned. Cost increases and schedule delays of Core Stage development can be traced largely to management, technical, and infrastructure issues driven by Boeing's poor performance. For example, Boeing officials have consistently underestimated the scope of the work to be performed and thus the size and skills of the workforce required. In addition, development of command and control hardware and software necessary for Core Stage testing is 2 years behind schedule, while equipment-related mishaps and an extreme weather event contributed to cost and schedule delays. Individually, each of these issues may have caused only minor cost and schedule problems, but taken as a whole they have resulted in a 2 1/2-year slip to the SLS Core Stage delivery schedule and approximately $4 billion in cost increases for development of the first two Core Stages. Furthermore, Boeing's cost and schedule challenges are likely to worsen given that the SLS has yet to undergo its 'Green Run Test' – a major milestone that integrates and tests the Core Stage components.

Based on Boeing's current expenditure rate, NASA will need to increase the contract value by approximately $800 million to complete the first Core Stage for delivery to the Kennedy Space Center in December 2019. If the EM-1 launch takes place in June 2020, more than $400 million–for a total of $1.2 billion–would need to be added to the contract. This amount would only ensure delivery of Core Stage 1 and would not include the billions more required to complete work on Core Stage 2 and the EUS. Consequently, in light of the Project's development delays, we have concluded NASA will be unable to meet its EM-1 launch window currently scheduled between December 2019 and June 2020.

We found that several poor contract management practices by NASA contributed to the SLS Program's cost and schedule overruns. First, contrary to current federal guidance, NASA lacks visibility into the Boeing Stages contract costs because all three of the company's key activities–development of Core Stages 1 and 2 and the EUS–are co-mingled into the same contract line item number, making it difficult for the Agency to track expenditures. As a result, NASA is unable to determine the cost of a single Core Stage, which will affect the Agency's ability to determine pricing for future Core Stages. Second, we found flaws in NASA's evaluation of Boeing's performance, resulting in NASA inflating the contractor's scores and leading to overly generous award fees. Specifically, in the six evaluation periods since 2012 in which NASA provided ratings, Agency officials deemed Boeing's performance 'excellent' in three and 'very good' in three other periods, resulting in payment of $323 million or 90 per cent of the available award and incentive fees. Considering the SLS Program's cost overages and schedule delays, we question nearly $64 million of the award fees already provided to Boeing. Third, contracting officers approved contract modifications and issued task orders to several contracts without proper authority, exposing NASA to $321.7 million in unauthorised commitments, most of which will require follow-up contract ratification. Finally, as NASA and Boeing struggle with completing the first two SLS Core Stages, the Agency's plans are on hold for acquiring additional Core Stages. Given that NASA officials estimate needing 52 months of lead time from issuing a contract to delivery, the earliest a third Core Stage can be produced is 2023, jeopardizing planned launch dates for future missions that require the rocket, including EM-2 and potentially a science mission to Europa, one of Jupiter's moons, in 2022. To its credit, the SLS Program has taken positive steps to address management and procurement issues related to the Boeing Stages contract, including making key leadership changes; requesting reviews of Boeing's management, financial, and estimating systems; adding routine, in-depth performance reviews; and changing the procurement process to improve internal controls. However, the impact of these actions on improving Boeing's future contract performance is uncertain.

14.10 Procurement management

The questions to be addressed should include:[19]

- Is there a procurement strategy and detailed plan? Is it regularly reviewed?
- Are procurement decisions subject to Gateway reviews?
- Is there an approved process for project procurement to ensure financial and project delivery prudence?
- When the main contractor and sub-contractors are appointed has adequate due diligence taken place?
- Was procurement actively engaged in determining the specification and scope of work?
- How does procurement fit into the project organisational structure?
- Did the procurement process include pre-qualification and tender phases?
- Was the pre-qualification and tender evaluation process fully documented and compliant with pre-agreed evaluation criteria and weightings?
- How does the project manage project-relevant information being supplied to sub-contractors?
- How did we agree the contractual requirements and ensure these were included in the final negotiated contract?
- Was a procurement risk log maintained throughout the project?
- Does the project consist of a process to ensure that all contract requirements, due dates, and records are met?
- How have we ensured that all the necessary project insurances and bonds are in place?
- Are all contract changes accounted for, documented, costed and impact on project milestones reported?
- Have we claimed damages for any contractor non-compliance with contract obligations?

14.10.1 Project contracts

Chapter 7 provides the detail of Legal and Contractual issues that face the procurement profession. Projects require very careful thought, prior to selecting the type of contract to use. Procurement should be a major influence on this decision, giving careful consideration to:

- The technical content of the project
- The project risks and who is best placed to manage them
- The extent of supply market competition
- Design complexities
- Project overall timescale and milestones
- The project budget and contingency provision
- The extent to which the contractor will sub-contract
- The project experience of the buying organisation
- The extent to which partnering will be applied to the project.

Essentially, there are six types of projects:

- Fixed-price contracts
- Fixed-price incentive free contracts
- Cost-plus fixed fee contracts
- Cost-plus percentage fee contracts
- Cost-plus incentive fee contracts
- Guaranteed maximum-shared savings contracts.

These contract types do not present a simple choice, and regardless of the choice the project world is littered with contractual disputes – see Chapter 7 for notable examples. Each of the six types is now explained in such a way as to inform procurement where their influence can be applied.

14.10.2 Fixed-price contracts

From a procurement point of view this type of contract is an attraction because, unless there are changes to the scope of the project, the price is known. This is too simplistic a view. The contractor who bids for projects requiring a fixed-price has tough decisions to make, giving consideration to such matters as:

- The accuracy and reliability of the project scope
- The inherent risks within the project and the impact on the contractor's insurances
- The pricing of long lead time items and the risk of any future price increases
- The impact of milestones and project completion times on resource costs and possible sub-contracting
- How to deal with contingency provision in a competitive situation
- The extent to which the buying organisation will negotiate price
- The contractual provision for contract change and how contract price changes will be managed
- The profit that can be realised from the project
- The reliability of in-house estimates for labour, materials, manufacturing, quality management, testing, installation, acceptance and warranty provision.

Fixed-price incentive fee contracts

These are used primarily in government contracting. The author is indebted to Robert Antonio[20] for prompting and providing most of the detail below. These contracts have a provision for adjusting the total profit after the completion of the project that has been agreed to in advance by both client and contractor. A structure could be:

Structure	Description
Target Cost	$76,000,000
Target Profit	$9,700,000
Target Price	$85,700,000

Structure	Description
Ceiling Price	133 percent of Target Cost at $101,000,000
Share Ratio	95/5 between $64,600,000 and $87,400,000 90/10 between $64,600,000 and from $87,400,000 to Point of Total Assumption
Point of total assumption	$92,366,660

The mechanics of this type of contract include:

■ Target cost: The initially negotiated figure for estimated contract costs and the point at which profit pivots

■ Target profit: The initially negotiated profit at the target cost

■ Target price: Target cost plus the target profit

■ Ceiling price: Stated as a percentage of the target cost. This is the maximum price the government expects to pay. Once this amount is reached, the contractor pays all remaining costs for the original work

■ Shared ratio: The government/contractor sharing ratio for cost savings or cost over-runs that will increase or decrease the actual profit. The government percentage is listed first and the terms used are 'government share' and 'contractor share'. For example, on an 80/20 share ratio, the government share is 80 per cent and the contractor share is 20 per cent.

■ Point of Total Assumption. The point where cost increases that exceed the target cost are no longer shared by the government according to the share ratio. At this point, the contractor's profit is reduced one dollar for every additional dollar of cost. The PTA is calculated with the following.

$$\text{PTA} = (\text{Ceiling Price} - \text{Target Price})/\text{Government Share} + \text{Target Cost}$$

Given the above explanation a procurement specialist will have to consider:

– Upon what basis will the target cost be agreed? Will it be a requirement for full cost disclosure, parametric price modelling and informed negotiation?

– Upon what basis will target profit be agreed? This should take into account the risk profiling and who the risks are ascribed to.

– How to base the share ratio. The more the government demands the more likely it is that the contractor will devise ways to counteract the demand.

14.10.3 Cost-plus fixed fee contracts

From a procurement view this is a potentially high risk strategy. The concept is simple. A 'cost' is agreed and the contractor receives a fixed fee on top of the 'cost'. The 'cost' may be estimated, in which case it may be argued that the contractor has an incentive to adopt a pricing strategy by which the estimated costs are the highest possible. The definition of a cost-plus fixed fee contract is 'A cost reimbursable contract that provides for payment to the contractor of a negotiated fee that is fixed at the inception of the contract'. The fixed fee does not vary with actual cost.

This type of contract can be used for the performance of research or preliminary exploration or study, and the level of effort required is unknown.

The procurement specialist must give active consideration to the three main components of the cost-plus contract.

(i)   Direct costs – labour, materials, supplies, equipment and professional consultants being contracted by the contractor

(ii) Overhead costs – these are usually recovered as a percentage of labour and can include office rent, insurances, communication and IT expenses and design equipment

(iii) Fee (Profit) – equivocally, the contractor may be motivated by what they can get away with.

14.10.4 Cost-plus percentage fee contracts

In this type of contract, the contractor is paid all his costs, plus a pre-determined percentage fee (profit). All the pricing, risk is with the client (buying organisation). The Federal Transit Administration,[21] in a Q and A response, clarify what is a cost-plus percentage fee contract.

Q. Is the contract outlined below a cost-plus percentage of cost contract, even if the modifications show a target cost, base fee and maximum available award fee?

- Cost-plus award fee contract. 8 per cent base. 7 per cent award fee.

- Contract ceiling $508 million. Contract grows due to scope changes over a six-month period to almost $1 billion

- Agency continues to pay the award and base fee on the increased cost at the original percentage rates

- First 20 of original contract modifications do not restrict or provide either a target amount for the base or award fee. Contract modifications thereafter contained an identified scope of work and target cost, base fee, and maximum available award fee. These fees, of course, were calculated using the predetermined rates.

A. It is not uncommon to negotiate a profit or fee on changes or added scope using the negotiated percentage in the original contract. This is not the recommended approach but it is not prohibited. The additional fee should be based on such matters as the degree of risk in the added work, the amount of investment, the percentage of work subcontracted, etc. The award fee cannot be a percentage of cost.

However, it is important to distinguish between using ('negotiating') projected/estimated costs vs actual costs in arriving at the profit or fee dollars. If the agency is using the Contractor's projected/estimated (proposed) costs as the basis to negotiate fee, then this is not a CPPC situation. If, however, the agency uses actual costs (i.e. after the costs are incurred) as the basis to establish fee, then we would have a 'de facto' illegal CPPC situation (this principle has been established by the GAO on Federal contracts). We would also note that it would not be legal to establish terms in a contract that promised to pay the Contractor for actual costs incurred plus a predetermined rate of profit on those costs. This too would be a CPPC contract. The fee payable must always be expressed and fixed in the contract in $ terms, not % terms so that if the Contractor overruns the estimated costs in completing the statement of work, there must be no additional fee paid on those cost overruns $. The fee to be paid for completion the scope of work must be fixed and payable regardless of how much it actually costs the Contractor to finish the work.

If the agency is treating all cost growth as fee bearing $ they should document the file to explain that the Contractor in fact completed the scope of work originally established, so that it is clear that the additional estimated costs, and fee negotiated, are associated with 'new' or 'changed' work as defined in the contract modifications.

(Reviewed October 2010)

14.10.5 Cost-plus incentive fee contracts

In this type of contract the client (Buying organisation) pays for all allowable costs plus a predetermined fee plus an incentive bonus. This approach is not for the faint hearted. The first issue is what is meant by 'allowable costs'? How does the buyer determine

(i) what these are? and

(ii) how they shall be monitored?

The predetermined fee is a matter for risk handling and negotiation. The incentive bonus is aimed at the contractor reducing the expected cost of the project. If the expected cost of a project is £2,000,000 with a fee of £150,000 and the sharing ratio is 80/20 and the final price is £1,800,000; the contractor will get paid the final price, the fee of £150,000 and an incentive of 25% of the £200,000 savings, i.e. £40,000.

14.10.6 Guaranteed maximum-shared savings contracts

In this type of contract there is a ceiling price. The contractor is paid the actual costs incurred up to the guaranteed maximum. Savings below this amount are shared between client and contractor in accordance with a pre-determined percentage split. The contractor assumes the responsibility for any cost overruns beyond the maximum.

The Sub-committee T1 of the International Bar Association[22] undertook to compile a library of standard conditions of contract for construction in various jurisdictions across the globe and we are indebted for their permission to use their output. There is a health warning for anyone considering adopting a specific type of contract. Seek legal advice!

The Contracts

(i) need negotiating and

(ii) they change from time to time

1 Federation Internationale des Ingénieurs – Conseils (FIDIC)[23]

The FIDIC Suite of Contracts includes:

1 Conditions of Contract for Construction – The Red Book

2 Conditions of Contract for Plant and Design Build – The Yellow Book

3 Conditions of Contract for EPC/Turnkey Projects – The Silver Book

4 Conditions of Contract for Design – Build and Turnkey – The Orange Book

5 Short Form of Contract – The Green Book

6 Conditions of Contract for Design, Build and Operate Projects

7 Form of Contract for Dredging and Reclamation Works – The Blue Book

8 A form of agreement for engagement of consultants – The White Book

9 A form of agreement for Subcontractors

10 A joint venture agreement form.

2 Institute of Civil Engineers (ICE)[24]

The ICE Conditions of Contract are no longer published. ICE recommends the use of the NEC Suite of Contracts. NEC introduced its fourth edition, NEC4, in 2017.

3 The New Engineering Contract (the NEC)[25]

The NEC4 June 2017 edition complete family of contracts includes:

– Dispute Resolution & Service Contract
– Supply Contract
– Design, Build & Operate Contract
– Engineering & Construction Contract
– Engineering & Construction Sub Contract
– Framework Contract
– Professional Services Contract
– Term Services Contract
– Alliance Contract

4 Institute of Engineering and Technology[26]

The Institute of Engineering and Technology issue a range of model forms of general conditions of contract.

MF/1 Revision 6	Model Form of Contract for the design, supply and installation of electrical, electronic and mechanical plant
MF/2 Revision 1	Supply of Electrical, Electronics or Mechanical Plant home or overseas contracts
MF/3 Revision 1	Supply of Electrical and Mechanical Goods without Erection – home contracts
MF/4	Provision of consultancy services by Engineering Consultants – home or overseas contracts

5 Institute of Chemical Engineers (IChemE)[27]

There are currently two suites of contracts available, one suitable for the UK market and another for international use. The Suites of contracts include:

IChemE (Green) Form of Contract – Reimbursable Contracts – 4th ed. 2013

IChemE (Brown) Form of Contracts – Subcontract for Civil Engineering Works – 3rd ed. 2013

IChemE (Grey) Form of Contract – Adjudication Rules 4th ed. 2016

IChemE (Orange) Minor Works 3rd ed. 2018

IChemE (Pink) Form of Contract – Arbitration Rules – 4th ed. 2005

IChemE (Red) Form of Contract – Lump Sum Contracts – 5th ed. 2013

IChemE (White) Rules for Expert Determination – 5th ed. 2016

IChemE (Yellow) Sub Contracts 4th ed. 2013

IChemE (Green) Reimbursable 4th ed. 2013

IChemE (Burgundy) Target Cost 2nd ed. 2013

IChemE (Silver) Professional Services Agreement 1st ed. 2017

6 The Joint Contracts Tribunal (JCT)[28]

The JCT have an extensive suite of 2016 contracts available, too extensive to replicate here.

7 The Association of Consultant Architects (ACA)[29]

The ACA have a suite of Partnering Contracts including:

1 PPC 2000(Amended 2013) – ACA Standard Form of Contract for Project Partnering

2 TPC 2005(Amended 2008) – ACA Standard Form of Contracts for Terms Partnering

3 SPC 2000 (Amended 2008) – ACA Standard Form of Specialist Contract for Project Partnering

4 SPC 2000 Short Form (Issued 2010) – ACA Standard Form of Specialist Contract for Project Partnering

5 STPC 2005 (Issued 2010) – ACA Standard Form of Specialist Contract for Term Partnering.

8 International Chamber of Commerce (ICC)[30]

The ICC has a series of Model contracts, including:

2018 ICC Model Contract – Joint Venture

2017 ICC Model Contract – International Consulting Services

2016 ICC Model Contract on Distributorship

2016 ICC Model Contract – Consortium Agreement

2016 ICC Model Confidentiality Agreement

9 Liaison Group of the European Mechanical, Electrical, Electronic and Metalworking Industries (ORGALIME)[31]

ORGALIME issued a new standard contract – the ORGALIME Turnkey Contract for Industrial Works – its most comprehensive contract publication to date. ORGALIME's premise was that purchasers and contractors in the engineering sector, who had used existing models, had not found them as suitable for industrial works as for civil engineering contracts.

Discussion questions

14.1 Define a 'Project' and explain how procurement contributes to the success of a Project.

14.2 In what respects is project procurement different to the procurement of goods and services that are regular demand?

14.3 Explain a project lifecycle, ideally using an example from within your organisation or one that you have researched on the internet.

14.4 Many procurement specialists lack technical qualifications. This means they have only a minimal impact on project procurement. Do you agree or disagree? Why?

14.5 When suppliers are pre-qualifying to receive an Invitation to Tender for a high value – high risk project, what six areas of capability would you expect to probe as a procurement specialist?

14.6 What should a Project Initiation Document include and why is it important?

14.7 Discuss the advantages and disadvantages of adopting 'PRINCE 2®' as the basis for project management.

14.8 Discuss six commercial risks that may apply to a project and explain how these risks can be mitigated.

14.9 Do you believe that most projects will have their scope changed during the lifetime of the project? If you have answered 'YES' what is the role of procurement to manage the consequences of project change?

14.10 Do you believe it is astute business practice to incentivise a supplier to complete a project before the planned completion date? Why do you have this belief?

14.11 Using one of the project audit reports outlined in this chapter, explain the significant benefits accruing from such audits.

14.12 Would a project benefit from having full time procurement specialists on the project? Explain why you have this belief.

References

[1] Meredith, J. R. and Mantel, S. J. *Project Management: A Managerial Approach*, 6th edition. John Wiley & Sons, Hoboken, USA, 2006.

[2] Project procurement business contribution to project success. Research Report Brian Farrington Ltd. www.brianfarrington.com.

[3] Metrolink – Governed by the Southern California Regional Rail Authority (SCRRA).

[4] Vaidyanathan, L. *Project Management, Process. Technology and Practice*. Pearson International Edition. Pearson, Harlow, UK, 2013.

[5] Association for Project Management, Princes Risborough Bucks, UK.

[6] www.procurement.govt.nz.

[7] 61007_2.17_002 SEMMS Management Plan Rev 4.0, Oct 2012.

[8] Managing Successful Projects with PRINCE 2. Registered trademark of the Cabinet Office.

[9] www.esi-intl.co.uk.

[10] Bluenose II Restoration Project. Jan 2015.

[11] Association for Project Management http://www.org.uk.

[12] Guidelines for Managing Risk in the Australian Public Service MAB/MIAC No.22 1996.

[13] The Australian Diplomatic Communications Network – Project Management, anao.gov.au.

[14] Association for Project Management, *A Guide to Project Auditing*. Association for Project Management, Berkshire, UK, 2018.

15 https://www.iia.org.uk.

16 www.nao.org.uk/about-us/our work.

17 Report by the Comptroller and Auditor General. HC 408. Session 2017–2019 11October 2017.

18 Investigation into the British Army Recruiting Partnering Project HC 1781. Session 2017–2019 14 December 2018.

19 Adapted from Vaidyanathan, C. *Project Management. Process, Technology and Practice*. Pearson International Edition. Pearson, Harlow, UK, 2013.

20 The Fixed-Price Incentive Firm Target Contract: Not as firm as the same suggests. Robert Antonio. November 2003. www.wifcon.com.

21 US Department of Transportation. 'Cost Plus Percentage of Cost Contracts', http://www.fta. dot.gov/13057_6115.html.

22 http://ibanet.org.

23 http://www.I.fidic.org/resources/contracts.

24 http://www.ice.org.uk/knowledge/downloads_law_asp.

25 http://www.newengineeringcontract.com.

26 https.//www2.theiet.org/resources/books.

27 http://www.icheme.org.

28 www.jctltd.co.uk.

29 http://www.acarchitects.co.uk.

30 http://www.iccwbo.org/law/contract.

31 http://www.orgalime.org/sitemap.htm.

Chapter 15

Global sourcing

Learning outcomes

This chapter aims to provide an understanding of:

- terminology
- motives for buying offshore
- sources of information for offshore suppliers
- overcoming challenges when sourcing offshore
- Incoterms
- Customs and Excise
- freight agents
- methods of payment
- Countertrade (CT)
- the true cost of offshore buying
- global sourcing – Boeing case study
- buying capital equipment offshore
- factors in successful offshore buying.

Key ideas

- Motives for and benefits of global sourcing.
- Information sources for procurement specialists.
- Cultural, political, ethical, quality, exchange risk and legal considerations.
- The definitions of Incoterms 2010.
- Complexities of Customs and Excise requirements.
- Factors in determining freight costs
- Freight agents and freight forwarders roles.
- Logistics and supply chain impacts on corporate performance
- Open accounts, bills for collection and letters of credit.
- Countertrade.
- Ascertaining the true cost of global sourcing.
- Factors in successful global sourcing decisions.

15.1 Terminology

Birou and Fawcett[1] distinguish between international sourcing, multinational sourcing, foreign sourcing and strategic global sourcing. They define the first three terms as:

> buying outside the firm's country of manufacture in such a way that does not coordinate requirements among worldwide business units of a single firm.

Strategic global sourcing is defined as:

> the coordination and integration of procurement requirements across worldwide business units, looking at common items, processes, technologies and suppliers.

Trent and Monczka[2] also differentiate between international and global sourcing. International procurement is:

> a commercial transaction between a buyer and a seller located in different countries.

Global sourcing involves:

> positively integrating and coordinating common items and materials, processes, designs, technologies and suppliers across worldwide purchasing, engineering and operating locations.

Among other important findings, Trent and Monczka conclude that firms engaging in global sourcing are likely to have competitors and be larger than those engaging in international procurement and that 'one can easily conclude that international procurement is best described as a functional activity while global sourcing represents a strategic direction and organisational process'.

These views are supported by Rexta and Miyamoto[3] who suggest that, in general, smaller firms are restricted in their capacity to search for and secure overseas suppliers by their lack of managerial knowledge and capital resources so that 'any supplier found among a small pool of qualified overseas suppliers is a potential candidate so long as it can meet their procurement requirements'. Moreover, the small quantities they are purchasing make the business of smaller firms less attractive to first-class overseas suppliers. In contrast, 'a depth of resource capacity allows large firms to aggressively pursue the full potential of international sourcing by capitalising on the world's best suppliers'.

Regarded from a strategic perspective, global sourcing is more complicated than international procurement. There are, however, aspects where the two approaches converge and international procurement is strategic as well as tactical. Smaller firms also engage in the development and early involvement of their overseas suppliers. Because of such convergence, Trent and Monczka use the generic term 'worldwide sourcing' to describe international procurement and global sourcing. The phrase 'buying offshore', used in this chapter, while also generic, is probably more closely equated with 'international procurement'.

15.2 Motives for buying offshore

There are many motives for buying offshore, not all driven by the buying organisation's initiatives and self-interests. Table 15.1 shows the drivers for buying offshore, identified and experienced by Brian Farrington Limited[4] – a specialist procurement and supply chain consultancy company.

Table 15.1 The drivers for buying offshore

Business drivers	Reasoning
Requirement for offsets	The business requirement where an offshore customer demands the procurement of local content. Offsets may include technology transfer, training and licensed production
Official Journal of the European Union (OJEU) advertisements	The public sector place OJEU advertisements and these sometimes attract offshore tenders. If such a tender is the 'best deal' then the contract will be placed with an offshore supplier
Pressure to reduce costs	There are good examples in IT and retail where advantage is taken of low-cost economies, e.g. the outsourcing of call centres to India and the production of clothing in Sri Lanka
Manufacturing flexibility	Where there are capacity restrictions on UK-based manufacturing organisations, contracts can be placed offshore to guarantee additional capacity. An example is a railway rolling stock manufacturing company contracting supplies from Poland
Access to specialist skills	The UK has deskilled in some fields, e.g. engineering design and, on occasions, will need to access relatively new skills, e.g. offshore wind farms and satellite technology
Market penetration	The desire to enter a new market can be greatly facilitated by procuring goods and services in the target market. An example is contracting for a local supply of components to create employment and overcome restrictive quotas
Domestic non-availability for raw materials	There are some essential raw materials that are not available in the UK, e.g. reserves of commodities such as copper, zinc and gold. This leaves no choice but to purchase offshore

The above are strategic reasons to purchase offshore and others will arise from time to time. The author advised Radical Sportscars Ltd[5] on a global procurement of tyres for their range of highly specialised racing cars, sold to a global clientele. The procurement actively considered leaving a European manufacturer and contracting with a South Korean tyre manufacturer, Hankook.[6]

The procurement and business considerations included the following:

– Hankook's technical and sector reputation
– Hankook's investment in research and development
– Hankook's global distributor reach
– evaluation of supply chain risks and their management
– delivered prices on a global basis
– contract Terms & Conditions with appropriate obligations & liabilities
– Hankook's safety reputation
– Hankook's product range
– Hankook's cultural knowledge and exposure
– Hankook's marketing portfolio

    – product lead times

    – Hankook's corporate commitment

    – the systematic gathering of world-wide sales data and provision of reports

    – both parties' long-term commitment to relationship management

    – Hankook's marketing contribution to radical marketing.

A contract was awarded to Hankook for the global supply of tyres.

15.3 Sources of information for offshore suppliers

A well-organised and structured research programme is required to identify potential offshore suppliers. Clearly, there is a risk to be managed if contracts are placed with suppliers who cannot maintain a high-quality supply. There are many information sources including:

- foreign embassies and high commissions
- import brokers
- trade journals
- directories, such as *Kompass, Thompson, Jaegar* and *Waldman*
- trade fairs and exhibitions
- the World Bank
- the *Official Journal of the European Union*
- shipping and forwarding agents
- Specialist enquiry agents, such as Dun & Bradstreet
- procurement consultants
- trading company websites
- professional and trade organisations
- the Internet.

15.4 Overcoming challenges when sourcing offshore

There are challenges when sourcing offshore because the professional degree of difficulty is a lot higher than when purchasing in the home market. Some key considerations are shown in Table 15.2.

Table 15.2 Key considerations when sourcing offshore

Descriptor	Considerations
1 Buyer's experience	Requires the ability to research sources of supply, conduct vendor appraisal, negotiate and put in place a contract that effectively deals with the risks
2 Currency fluctuations	Requires expert advice from finance/banking specialists to optimise the risk derived from currency fluctuation during the life of the contract

Descriptor	Considerations
3 Supplier evaluation	There is a need to develop and apply a tailored RFI document to probe logistics, product support, contract terms, supply chain, finances and quality management
4 Culture and language	Expert knowledge of cultural differences and how to deal with language barriers will be needed to prevent misunderstandings and breakdowns in communication
5 Political stability	From time to time there are serious political instabilities and uncertainties that impact on trade. Examples are Thailand, Zimbabwe, Egypt, Libya and Cuba
6 Logistics support	The ability to move goods around the world in a timely manner is vital, as is the certainty of shipping, use of special containers and availability of emergency stocks
7 Duty and Customs regulations	This is an ever-changing scene and requires expert support either from in-house specialists or freight forwarders. Delays in customs clearance can lead to contract failures
8 Contractual risk	The basis of legal jurisdiction, dispute resolution, currency, quality standards and inspection rights are classic areas requiring the attention of procurement
9 Contract management	Either the buying organisation or a third party will have to undertake contract management, otherwise there is the risk of non-compliance with the contractual obligations
10 International quality standards	The buyer will need to identify the international quality standards that must apply to a specific purchase, recognising that some standards will exceed British Standards specifications

15.4.1 Cultural factors

The active involvement in international trade requires an in-depth understanding of the cultures with which procurement and firms interact.

> Firms that rely on their familiar home culture to compete in a new market can jeopardise their international success. Indeed, virtually all facets of an international firm's business – including contract negotiations, production operations, marketing decisions and human resource management policies – may be affected by cultural variations.[7]

Culture is the collection of values, beliefs, behaviours, customs and attitudes that distinguish one society from another. The elements of culture[8] are:

- language
- communication
- religion
- values and attitudes
- social structure.

Language

When a buyer engages with another culture it would be wise to remember there are more than 3000 different languages. In India there are 16 official languages and approximately 3000 dialects are spoken within its boundaries. The dominance of English puts many

English speakers at a disadvantage when negotiating on foreign turf. In some instances, translators are used but words of caution are advisable. Translators must be sensitive to subtleties in the connotations of words and focus on translating ideas, not the words themselves. The words 'Yes' and 'No' are not straightforward in any international context. The Japanese often use 'Yes' to mean 'Yes, I understand what is being said.' Directly uttering 'No' is considered impolite or inhospitable in Japan, as well as in China, India and the Middle East.

Communication

The ability of a buyer to communicate their organisation's requirements can be a challenge. The complexities of the specification, pricing model, request for information, the tender evaluation model, instructions to tenderers and contractual requirements make it possible that communication has the potential for misinterpretation and misunderstandings. Verbal communication requires clarity of expression although, of course, there are nuances of nonverbal communication. Ferraro[9] identifies the forms of nonverbal communication:

- dress: fashionable, flashy or conservative
- hand gestures
- facial expressions: smiles, frowns, nods, eye contact (or lack of it)
- hair styles
- greetings: bows, hugs, kisses and hand shakes
- perfumes and colognes
- physical contact: hand holding, pats on the back
- posture: formal or relaxed
- time: arrive promptly, early or late?
- waiting your turn: queue up or not?
- walking: fast, slow; in group or single file; position of leader within group.

Sadly, the skill of communication is not a focus in the learning and developing of procurement specialists. Launching unskilled people into the international arena is unlikely to deliver significant benefits, nor is it likely to create partnering relationships.

Religion

According to *The Economist*,[10] 77 per cent of the World's population adheres to one of four religions: Christianity (31.5 per cent), including Roman Catholics, Protestants and Eastern Orthodox; Islam (23.2 per cent); Hinduism (15.0 per cent); and Buddhism (7.1 per cent). Religion may permeate business relationships, thus requiring the utmost sensitivity when negotiating contracts. It is good advice to consider religious standpoints prior to entering a specific market. It is also good advice not to pointedly introduce religious discussions until there is absolute confidence in the likely response and the person's reaction.

Social structure

This is directly linked to a person's status. The procurement specialist will ignore this factor at their peril. In Japan, a person's status depends on the status of the group to which he or she belongs. In India, status is affected by one's caste. In the United States, hardworking entrepreneurs are honoured. The British social structure is often driven by the quality of education and the individuals' network. There is then, the illogicality of 'knocking' the successful entrepreneurs, driven by envy, jealously or resentment?

15.4.2 Foreign exchange risks

This is the risk that a purchaser of an offshore product will be required to pay more (or less) than expected as a result of fluctuations in the exchange rates between the purchaser's currency and that of the supplier's currency in which payment may be made.

Assume that a UK company buys an item of capital equipment costing $100,000 at a 'spot' price of $2 to the pound, payable in six months' time meaning £50,000. If, at the time of payment, the pound has strengthened against the dollar, so that the exchange rate is $2.5 to the pound, the number of pounds required will be lower – in fact, £44,445. Conversely, if the pound has weakened against the dollar so that the exchange rate is $1.75 to the pound, the number of pounds required to buy $100,000 will be greater – in fact, £57,142. The risk of a rise in price due to an adverse exchange rate is termed *transaction exposure*.

Companies buying offshore can minimise foreign exchange risk in several ways, including the following:

- *Arranging to buy in the currency of the buyer* – this effectively transfers the risk of fluctuations in exchange rates to the supplier. This may not, however, be the best policy. Scott[8] suggests that, when negotiating international deals, purchasers should:

  - research exchange rates for one or two years previously to benchmark the range of fluctuations in the respective currencies
  - price goods in the currency of the supplier if it is anticipated that the purchaser's currency will strengthen further
  - price goods in the currency of the purchaser if it is anticipated that the purchaser's currency will weaken
  - when agreeing to price adjustment clauses, ensure that currency fluctuations are kept separate from cost increases.

- *Reduce the uncertainty by hedging with forward contracts* for a period of no longer than six months. If a purchaser knows that a supplier must be paid a fixed amount in foreign currency in, say, six months, the purchaser can arrange a six-month forward contract with the bank under which the bank will provide a fixed amount of the foreign currency at the end of that time.

- *Buy currency options* – such contracts give the purchaser the right (but not the obligation) to buy or sell foreign currency at a specified price within a specified time period. Under forward contracts, options allow the purchaser to benefit from favourable fluctuations in exchange rates.

- *Buy the offshore currency at the spot price on the day on which the offshore purchase is made* – this uses up capital, but interest may be earned on the currency held and the exchange rate is known from the outset.

- *Negotiate currency adjustment clauses* – these may include clauses specifying that:

  - payments may be in a currency other than that of the purchaser or supplier, such as sterling, US dollars, Swiss francs

- 'this contract is subject to an exchange rate of X, plus or minus Y per cent. If the exchange rate exceeds these parameters then the contract price shall be renegotiated'
- 'the contract shall be subject to an exchange rate fluctuation equal to the average of the exchange rate at the time of signing the contract and that at the date of the delivery'.

Developments such as that of the single European currency may help to simplify currency prices and exchange rates in an international context.

15.4.3 Legal considerations

Contracting with an offshore supplier requires diligent attention to detail regarding the terms and conditions of contract. The detail will include:

- whose legal jurisdiction shall apply? For example, in the USA there is State Law and the Uniform Commercial Code (UCC)
- what are the arrangements for dispute resolution, arbitration or mediation?
- the different types of insurance required to cover off the risks of a transaction including Incoterms® (see section 15.5)
- the scope of *force majeure* provisions, recognising the potential for Force Majeure across the whole supply chain, including shipment
- rights of inspection through in-house quality management or by a third party
- the certainty of price, taking into account currency movements, price change mechanism and impact of commodity price changes, e.g. copper, zinc and gold
- specifications, including units of measurement, national standards and terminology
- documentation, such as bills of lading, certificates of origin and customs entry forms
- redress of complaints – that is, the return to the supplier of goods rejected or damaged in transit – and, as the recovery of damages is awarded to the buyer by the courts or arbitration, it is useful to ascertain what assets, if any, the supplier has in the buyer's country so these can be restrained by the courts in payment of damages due
- avoidance of translation errors when converting an overseas contract into own language
- rights of cancellation and termination
- prevention of use of child labour e.g. India
- rights of supplier to sub-contract or assign
- provision of performance bond/parent company guarantee.

The United Nations Convention on Contracts for the International Sale of Goods 1980 ('CISG') and the process by which it was created, by the United Nations Commission on International Trade Law (UNCITRAL) established a benchmark for the unification of commercial law in the post-war era. The CISG is an important document, since it establishes a comprehensive code of legal rules governing the formation of contracts for the international sale of goods, the obligations of the buyer and seller, remedies for breach of contract and other aspects of the contract. Readers may also wish to note that there is a 'United Nations Convention on the Use of Electronic Communication in International Contracts'.

The CISG has been adopted by eighty-five states (as of May 2016) but there has not been ratification by the United Kingdom. A number of reasons have been given for the UK lack of ratification, including the vagueness of some of the conventions' provision, such as Article 7 on statutory interpretation and good faith.

The Principles of European Contract Law (PECL) represent a ground-breaking project on the road to a common European Private Law. The principles were compiled by the Commission on European Contract Law ('Lendo-Commission') in the early 1980s and comprise three parts. Parts I and II dedicate themselves to the formation of contracts, validity, performance and remedies for non-performance. Part III focuses upon general contract law questions, prescription, set-off, plurality of debtors, illegality, unconscionability, conditions and capitalisation interest.

The International Chamber of Commerce (ICC) International Court of Arbitration is the world's leading institution for resolving international commercial and business disputes. In 2017, 810 new cases were filed, of which North American parties made up 9.5 per cent. The following standard clause is recommended, subject to adjustment to fit national law and the special needs of the deal:

> All disputes arising out of or in connection with the present contract shall be finally settled under the Rules of Arbitration of the International Chamber of Commerce by one or more arbitrators appointed in accordance with the said Rules.

The Arbitration Rules were amended in 2017. The Mediation Rules are in force from 2014.

15.5 Incoterms®

15.5.1 What are Incoterms®?

Incoterms® refer to the set of international rules for the interpretation of the chief terms used in foreign trade contracts first published by the International Chamber of Trade in 1936 (now International Chamber of Commerce (ICC)) and amended in 1953, 1967, 1976, 1980, 1990, 2000 and 2010.

The reason Incoterms® are periodically revised is to ensure that they represent current practice. The ICC are in the process (at the time of revising this 10th edition of the book) of drafting new Incoterms 2020.

Although the use of Incoterms is optional, they can materially reduce difficulties encountered by importers and exporters.

15.5.2 Knowledge of Incoterms®

Prior to deciding which Incoterm to include in a contract it is essential that all the implications are known. Corporate Compliance Insights[11] judiciously comment,

> Incoterms® rules bring predictability to international commercial contracts by defining the responsibilities of the buyer and seller with respect to the packing, transportation and insurance of goods as they are transferred from the seller to the buyer. Incoterms® rules can be invaluable for shifting costs and liability associated with exporting, importing and shipping and for avoiding disputes down the road – but only if companies understand how to use them properly. While many businesses employ Incoterms® rules in their commercial contracts, **these Contracts are often negotiated by individuals who don't really understand what the Incoterms® rule means and don't know how to use them effectively.** (the author's emphasis)

Corporate Compliance Insights give an example of EXW (Ex Works), a commonly used Incoterm. They explain that if the producer contracts to sell to the buyer 1000 widgets 'EXW (Guangzhou factory) on January 1, 2013,' the Producer's obligation is to put the 1000 widgets at the buyer's disposal at the producer's factory in Guangzhou on 1 January. The price quoted for the goods applies only at the factory and all charges for shipping and insurance, including even the loading of the goods at the producer's factory, are the responsibility of the buyer. Title to the goods, and consequently, the risk of loss and damage, pass to the buyer once the goods have been made available to the buyer (or its agent) at the Guangzhou factory.

The author advised a retail organisation that purchased clothing from a producer in Portugal, EXW. These 20-foot sea containers were loaded one afternoon, thereby 'making them available to the buyer.' Overnight a disastrous fire at the producer's factory destroyed the contents of the containers. The consequence was that the goods were then at the buyer's risk, for which, in this instance, they were uninsured. There was a complete financial loss and a failure to meet market demand, resulting in reputation damage.

15.5.3 Format of Incoterms

The Incoterms[®12] rules explain a set of three-letter trade terms reflecting business-to-business practice in contracts for the sale of goods. The Incoterms rules describe mainly the tasks, costs and risks involved in the delivery of goods from sellers to buyers.

15.5.4 How to use the Incoterms® 2010 rules

a) If you want the Incoterms® 2010 rules to apply to your contract, you should make this clear in the contract, through such words as "[the chosen Incoterms rule including the named place, followed by] Incoterms® 2010

b) The chosen Incoterm rule needs to be appropriate to the goods, to the means of their transport, and above all to whether the parties intend to put additional obligations, for example, the obligation to organise carriage or insurance on the seller or on the buyer

c) The chosen Incoterms rule can work only if the parties name a place or port and will work best if the parties specify the place or port as precisely as possible.

A good example of such precision would be:

'FCA 38 Cours Albertler, Paris, France', Incoterm 2010.

15.5.5 Main features of the Incoterms® 2010 rules

The number of Incoterms rules was reduced from 13 to 11. This was achieved by substituting two new rules that may be used irrespective of the agreed mode of transport – DAT, Delivered at Terminal, and DAP, Delivered at Place – for the Incoterms 2000 rules DAF, DES, DEQ and DDU.

15.5.6 Classes of Incoterms®

The 11 Incoterms® 2010 rules are presented in two distinct classes. **Table 15.3 shows the Incoterms rules for any mode of transport, while Table 15.4 shows the Incoterms rules for sea and inland waterway transport.**

Table 15.3 Incoterms: Rules for any mode of transport

EXW Ex Works	'Ex Works' means that the seller delivers when it places the goods at the disposal of the buyer at the seller's premises or at another named place (i.e., works factory, warehouse, etc.). The seller does not need to load the goods on any collecting vehicle, nor does it need to clear the goods for export, where such clearance is applicable
FCA Free Carrier	'Free Carrier' means that the seller delivers the goods to the carrier or another person nominated by the buyer at the seller's premises or another named place. The parties are well advised to specify as clearly as possible the point within the named place of delivery, as the risk passes to the buyer at that point
CPT Carriage Paid To	'Carriage Paid To' means that the seller delivers the goods to the carrier or another person nominated by the seller at an agreed place (if any such place is agreed between parties) and that the seller must contract for and pay the costs of carriage necessary to bring the goods to the named place of destination
CIP Carriage and Insurance Paid To	'Carriage and Insurance Paid To' means that the seller delivers the goods to the carrier or another person nominated by the seller at an agreed place (if any such place is agreed between parties) and that the seller must contract for and pay the costs of carriage necessary to bring the goods to the named place of destination. The seller also contracts for insurance cover against the buyer's risk of loss of or damage to the goods during the carriage. The buyer should note that under CIP the seller is required to obtain insurance only on minimum cover. Should the buyer wish to have more insurance protection, it will need either to agree as much expressly with the seller or to make its own extra insurance arrangements
DAT Delivered at Terminal	'Delivered at Terminal' means that the seller delivers when the goods, once unloaded from the arriving means of transport, are placed at the disposal of the buyer at a named terminal at the named port or place of destination. 'Terminal' includes a place, whether covered or not, such as a quay, warehouse, container yard or road, rail or air cargo terminal. The seller bears all risks involved in bringing the goods to and unloading them at the terminal at the named port or place of destination
DAP Delivered at Place	'Delivered at Place' means that the seller delivers when the goods are placed at the disposal of the buyer on the arriving means of transport ready for unloading at the named place of destination. The seller bears all risks involved in bringing the goods to the named place
DDP Delivered Duty Paid	'Delivery Duty Paid' means that the seller delivers the goods when the goods are placed at the disposal of the buyer, cleared for import on the arriving means of transport ready for unloading at the named place of destination. The seller bears all the costs and risks involved in bringing the goods to the place of destination and has an obligation to clear the goods not only for export but also for import, to pay any duty for both export and import and to carry out all customs formalities

Table 15.4 Incoterms: Rules for sea and inland waterway transport

FAS Free Alongside Ship	'Free Alongside Ship' means that the seller delivers when the goods are placed alongside the vessel (e.g., on a quay or a barge) nominated by the buyer at the named port of shipment. The risk of loss of or damage to the goods passes when the goods are alongside the ship, and the buyer bears all costs from that moment onwards
FOB Free on Board	'Free on Board' means that the seller delivers the goods on board the vessel nominated by the buyer at the named port of shipment or procures the goods already so delivered. The risk of loss of or damage to the goods passes when the goods are on board the vessel, and the buyer bears all costs from that moment onwards
CFR Cost and Freight	'Cost and Freight' means that the seller delivers the goods on board the vessel or procures the goods already so delivered. The risk of loss of or damage to the goods passes when the goods are on board the vessel. The seller must contract for and pay the costs and freight necessary to bring the goods to the named port of destination
CIF Cost, Insurance and Freight	'Cost, Insurance and Freight' means that the seller delivers the goods on board the vessel or procures the goods already so delivered. The risk of loss of or damage to the goods passes when the goods are on board the vessel. The seller must contract for and pay the costs and freight necessary to bring the goods to the named port of destination
	The seller also contracts for insurance cover against the buyer's risk of loss of or damage to the goods during the carriage. The buyer should note that under CIF the seller is required to obtain insurance only on minimum cover. Should the buyer wish to have more insurance protection, it will need either to agree as much expressly with the seller or to make its own extra insurance arrangements.

For a full and complete description of all Incoterms® 2010 it will be necessary to purchase the ICC rules for the use of domestic and international trade terms.[13]

15.6 Customs and Excise

All goods new or used, imported into the EU from outside the EU are subject to customs duty (import duty or import tax) and value added tax (VAT) according to their value and import tax classification. All goods imported into the UK from outside the EU must be declared to HM Revenue and Customs and, in most cases, this includes goods bought via the internet. The importer is legally liable for import duty and VAT.

There is a UK Integrated Tariff, available online from Her Majesty's Revenue & Customs, as a subscription service. The Tariff is used to confirm commodity codes, find duty rates and compliance requirements for each type of 'good' commodity. The Tariff is split into three volumes: Volume 1 contains background and business-oriented information for importers and exporters about policy in specific areas. Volume 2 contains 16,600 goods descriptions with their Commodity Codes and special measures which can be applied. Volume 3 is essential for importers and exporters. It contains a box-by-box guide for both manual and electronic C88 import and export declaration forms and a complete set of Customs Procedure Codes (CPCs). The CPCs identify the customs and/or excise regimes which goods are being entered into and removed from (where this applies).

The rate of import duty varies according to the type of goods imported and the country of origin. Normally, import duty is based on a percentage of the value of the goods, plus the transport and insurance costs to the country of destination and may also include such costs as tools, dies, moulds, design work, royalties and licence fees. VAT, which varies across EU member states, is then added. The process is exemplified by the following illustration:

	£	£
Value of goods, say	100.00	
Shipping and insurance costs to the UK, say	15.00	
Total value for import duty	115.00	
Import duty payable at, say, 5 per cent	5.75	5.75
	120.75	
VAT on £120.75 at 20%	24.15	24.15
	144.90	29.90

From the above example, it can be seen that, in most cases, VAT will be the largest tax to pay on importation. The total tax payable is £29.90 on the original price of these goods.

In addition, a customs clearance fee will be charged by the courier, carrier, freight forwarder or import agent (including the Royal Mail or Parcel Force) for clearing the product through customs. There can be further charges for storage if the goods are held up in customs or due to late payment.

Further details of customs charges can be obtained from the websites of HM Revenue and Customs and the UK Department for Business, Innovation and Skills. Member states of the EU hold commodity codes in a database called the TARIC, or Tariff Intégré Communautaire. The UK Tariff is published once a year with ten monthly updates using data from the TARIC and is supplemented by UK specific data on VAT, licensing, restrictions and excise duties.

15.7 Transport systems, costs and considerations

15.7.1 Road transport

The road system has developed a long way from the first asphalt road in Babylon by 625BC. China had at the end of 2018 a national highway system of 142,500 km. The road and distribution system in all countries raises vital considerations of emissions, noise, safety, congestion, economy and weight of vehicles going across National boundaries.

There is very limited potential to achieve economies of scale, largely because of impositions by Governments. Road transport does have advantages over other modes, including:

- market entry is relatively low cost
- capital costs of vehicles and distribution points are relatively low
- point-to-point delivery times can be effectively managed
- flexibility of route choice gives flexibility when bad weather or accidents occur

- market dominance for short-medium distance journeys
- road users do not bear the full operating costs, e.g. they do not pay for road building and maintenance, despite road taxes and tolls.

15.7.2 Rail transport

The characteristics of rail transport must take account of economic and territorial control. Many rail networks are monopolies or oligopolies. In North America there are seven major railroads and over 500 shortline and regional railroads.

Key considerations of rail transportation include:

- there is effective use of space for the rail lines but distribution points (terminals) require vast space
- freight trains have severe gradient restrictions, e.g. approximately 10 metres per kilometre
- the design of freight wagons is quite flexible, such as hopper wagons for fertilisers and triple hopper wagons for coal
- the standard gauge of 1.435 metres is in wide use
- initial capital costs are very high with some rail companies investing close to 50 per cent of operating revenues in capital and maintenance costs
- the potential for more intermodal transport, for example, using COFC (containers on flat cars)
- emergence and development of high-speed rail networks
- the complexities of tracking shipments.

15.7.3 Pipelines

Under most circumstances, buyer's rarely have occasion to consider pipelines as a transportation mode. Pipelines do however play a key role in strategic considerations. Some considerations are:

- pipelines invariably are designed for a specific commodity, e.g. oil and gas
- they can be subjected to disruption through acts of terrorism
- they can be subjected to political intervention, e.g. Russia with natural gas
- terrain difficulties can be overcome, e.g. the Trans Alaskan pipeline
- operating costs are low.

15.7.4 Maritime

This facet of international supply chain is of great interest to purchasers. There has been very significant growth in freight traffic, occasioned by:

- it being a low-cost mode, strengthened by containerisation
- the growth in globalisation, e.g. retailers in the UK purchasing from the Far East
- movement of energy and mineral cargoes
- technology improvements in terminals.

There are two categories of freight – bulk cargo (commodity cargo), classified as dry or liquid that is not packaged such as iron ore (dry), gasoline (liquid). It often has a single client, origin and destination. Break-bulk cargo (general cargo) is the second category and is packaged in bags, boxes or drums.

Key considerations of maritime transportation include:

- bulk cargo approximates to some 65 per cent of all ton miles shipped
- slow speeds averaging 15 knots
- severe delays in some ports
- significant capital outlay
- economies of scale, particularly with full container loads
- difficulties for the buyer to control transit times
- the operation of conference (formal agreements between companies engaged on particular trading routes).

15.7.5 Air transport

This is a vital aspect of international trade and transportation. It has a significant speed advantage, e.g. moving foodstuffs overnight and access to many geographic locations around the world. Some key considerations are:

- the threat to supply where there is severe weather
- use of airspace and political interventions
- relatively high cost but fast speed and flexibility of routes
- high levels of investment and fixed costs
- possible impact of terrorism and security
- fluctuations in fuel prices which can be circa 30 per cent of operating costs.

15.7.6 Intermodalism

The need for an integrated supply chain management system played a large role in the evolution of intermodalism. Some key considerations are:

- containerisation facilitates a quick turnaround
- relatively low cost
- clients can use one bill of lading to get a through rate
- the TEU (Twenty-foot Equivalent Unit) can move 10 tons of cargo and a 40-foot box circa 22 tons of cargo.

15.8 Freight agents

The freight agent has always played an important role in commerce and international carriage of goods. The freight agent acts as the agent for the cargo owner and in some cases at the same time for the carriers. In modern days the freight forwarder has adopted a new role in which he is not only assisting the parties in the transportation of goods, but in 'undertaking' the carriage by his own means of transport or by making arrangements with other transport providers.[14]

15.8.1 What is a freight agent or forwarder?

A freight agent or forwarder is a person or company, who, for a fee, undertakes to have goods carried and delivered to a destination. The services of freight agents are normally engaged when the carriage of goods involves successive carriers or the use of successive means of transport.

Traditionally, freight agents make contracts of carriage for their principals. Under the principles of the law of agency, a freight agent is under an obligation to the principal to conclude the contract on the agreed terms. Although in civil law freight agents are distinguished from carriers, the latter sometimes also act as freight agents.

15.8.2 The services of freight agents

Foley[15] has identified the services provided by freight forwarders as:

- international freight quotations
- export packing
- providing scheduling of carriers
- booking inland and international freight movements
- containerisation and consolidation of freight
- transshipments
- supervising freight movements (such as loading of goods onto carriers)
- computerised tracking of international freight movements
- export and import documentation
- applying for export licenses
- overseas documentation and foreign government requirements
- preshipment inspections
- marine and air insurance
- warehousing
- overseas logistics strategies such as free trade zones and warehousing
- assisting with insurance claims.

Other services offered by forwarders may include:

- consolidation or groupage – that is, the grouping of consignments from several consignors in a single load
- road haulage, such as the operation of a cargo collection and delivery service to and from sea or airports
- containers – some forwarders may operate container services or lease containers
- provision of warehousing, packing, insurance, financial and market research services
- coordination of the deliveries of multiple consignments.

15.8.3 Freight agents' fees

Freight agents or forwarders are paid a negotiated fee by the shipper or importer depending on the service or documents required. Fees are related to Incoterms in that they depend on the responsibilities undertaken by the different parties. They will be lower, for example, if the responsibilities end FOB at the departure port and increase as responsibilities extend DDP to the destination terminal.

15.8.4 Freight agents and the future

Willmott[16] points out that the development of logistics and supply chain management requires:

> the services of 'logistics practitioners' who can mesh themselves into the overall pattern, not just as suppliers of freight forwarding services but as links that might encompass several business functions.

Such functions are listed by Willmott as being:

- customerisation, or tailoring for individual markets or customers
- sourcing and delivery of raw materials
- allocation of materials and packaging
- manufacturing and capacity planning
- inventory determination and allocation to warehouses
- international movement by sea, road, rail and air
- domestic trunking and primary and multidrop distribution
- order fulfilment, including picking, packing and dispatch/delivery to customers
- e-commerce support of supply chain visibility
- reverse logistics, perhaps involving call centre management and collections for repair or servicing and so on.

Possible developments include:

- establishing 'one stop' entities by merging logistics and forwarding services, providing increased capabilities as suppliers of materials and components, enabling manufacturers to outsource non-core logistic and transport activities
- the secondment of the freight forwarder's staff to major customers to provide on-site freight expertise
- whole supply chains setting up in competition with each other rather than individual companies in that chain doing so, with the consequence that a freight forwarder may become a link in more than one chain.

15.9 Methods of payment

Overseas suppliers (exporters) may be unwilling to release goods until they have received payment. Conversely, buyers may be unwilling to pay before the goods have been delivered. SITPRO[17] (Simplifying International Trade) has produced the payments risk ladder shown in Figure 15.1, setting out some methods of payment and the risks of each to exporters and importers respectively.

Each of the four methods of payment shown in Figure 15.1 is briefly described below. SITPRO also advises that importers and exporters should consider their options carefully and hedge the risks with appropriate insurance and credit checks on overseas suppliers or customers.

Figure 15.1 **The payments risk ladder for exporters and importers**

Exporter	Least secure →	Less secure →	More secure →	Most secure →
	Open account	Bills for collection	Documentary credits	Advance payment
Importer	← Most secure	← More secure	← Less secure	← Least secure

15.9.1 Open account

This is similar to most home transactions. Goods are shipped and documents remitted to the buyer with an invoice for payment on previously agreed terms, such as 'net 30 days'.

15.9.2 Bills for collection

Under this system, the shipping documents – including the *bill of lading* (which is a receipt signed by a ship's master specifying the goods shipped on board and constituting a negotiable bill of title to such goods) are sent to the buyer's bank rather than direct to the buyer. These will be handed to the importer only when payment has been made (documents against payment) or against a promise to pay (documents against acceptance) and, until the documents are received, the title to the goods remains with the exporter. Documents against acceptance are usually accompanied by a *draft* or *bill of exchange* drawn on the buyer. Bills of exchange are the oldest method of payment for goods bought overseas. A bill of exchange (B/E) is defined as[18]:

> An unconditional order in writing, addressed by one person to another, signed by the person giving it, requiring the person to whom it is addressed to pay on demand, or at a fixed or determinable future date, a sum certain in money to or to the order of a specified person or to the bearer.

A cheque is a specialised form of B/E drawn on a bank to pay a specified sum to X on demand.

When a buyer (drawee) agrees to pay on a certain date – say, '30 days from acceptance' – the draft is said to have been accepted. It is against this acceptance that the goods are released to the buyer.

The *bills for collection* process is governed by the 'Uniform rules for collections' (Document 522, published by the International Chamber of Commerce). Over 90 per cent of the world's banks adhere to Document 522.

15.9.3 Letters of credit

With bills for collection, the bank acts only as an intermediary and enters into no payment undertaking. It is therefore a cheaper arrangement than a *letter of credit* (LOC), which is a legal instrument constituting a cash guarantee, obligating the bank to make a payment to a named beneficiary, such as an exporter, within a specified time against the presentation of documents such as the bill of lading, certificate of quality, insurance and origin, packing list and a commercial invoice. The risk of non-payment by the buyer is therefore transferred to the issuing bank. Letters of credit are governed by the ICC rules 'Uniform customs and practice for documentary credits' (Document UCP 500).

An LOC is opened by an importer (applicant) to ensure that the documentation requested proves that the seller has fulfilled the requirements of the underlying sales contract by making such requirements conditions of the LOC.

From the exporter's perspective, apart from cash in advance, an LOC is the most secure method of payment in international trade. The conditional nature of an LOC means that payment will not be made to the exporter unless all the credit terms have been precisely met.

LOCs may be conditional, standby or transactional:

- a *conditional LOC* may require some burden of proof by the owner that the contractor has not failed to perform before the bank will pay
- a *standby LOC* is normally used for open accounts (see section 13.10.1) and deals only with payment of documented sums within a specified period
- a *transactional LOC* applies to one specific transaction.

Most LOCs are irrevocable, which means that both parties must agree to any changes in terms.

While LOCs are a very secure method of payment, the security comes at a price. The security must therefore be weighed against the cost of higher bank charges.

15.9.4 Payment in advance

As shown in Figure 15.1, this is the least secure and most secure method of payment from the standpoint of buyers and sellers respectively. Often this method takes the form of a payment up front of, say, 50 per cent of the selling price, with the remainder payable on agreed credit terms.

15.9.5 What method of payment to use?

SITPRO[19] lists the following factors to bear in mind when deciding which method to choose:

- company policy
- cash flow considerations
- relationship with the overseas supplier
- the market conditions under which the overseas supplier operates
- the buyer's gut feeling.

The effectiveness and expeditiousness of all the processes involved in the exchange of documents and payments has been greatly facilitated by the various electronic means at our disposal.

15.10 Countertrade

15.10.1 What is countertrade?

Yasvas and Freed[20] define countertrade (CT) as:

> a generic term for parallel business transactions, linking sellers and buyers in reciprocal commitments that usually lie outside the realm of typical money-mediated trade.

Essentially, CT is a form of international reciprocal trading in which an order is placed by a purchaser with a supplier in another country (or vice versa) on condition that goods of an equal or specified value are sold or bought in the opposite direction.

CT often, but not necessarily, takes place in less well-developed, more centrally planned economies. The rising price of oil, higher interest rates and foreign debt have meant that many countries are unable to generate sufficient hard-core earnings by means of their exports to service their debts, but desperately need imports. As a result of economic, financial and political forces, CT has become an established feature of modern markets. Estimates vary but approximately 25 per cent of all world trade is accounted for by CT.

15.10.2 Forms of countertrade

Carter and Gagne[21] identify five distinct types of CT.

■ *Barter or swaps* – a one-off, direct, simultaneous exchange of goods or services between trading partners without a cash transaction, such as an exchange of New Zealand lamb for Iranian crude oil. The term 'swap' is used when goods are exchanged to save transportation costs.

Kreuze[22] instances the shipping of Russian oil to Greece rather than Cuba and the sending of Mexican oil to Cuba instead of Greece, thereby saving considerable transportation costs for both nations.

■ *Counterpurchase* occurs when a company in country X sells to a foreign country Y on the understanding that a set percentage of the sale's proceeds will be spent on importing goods produced in country Y. Both trading partners agree to fulfil their obligations within a fixed time period and pay for the major part of their respective purchases in cash.

■ *Buy-back or compensation* occurs when the exporter agrees to accept, as full or partial payment, products manufactured by the original exported product.

Occidental Petroleum negotiated a deal with the former USSR under which they agreed to build several plants in the Soviet Union and receive partial payment in ammonia over a 20-year period.

The main differences between buy-back and counterpurchase are that, in buy-backs:

– the goods and services taken back are tied to the original goods exported, while this is not the case with counterpurchase

– buy-back deals usually stretch over a longer period of time than counterpurchase ones.

The Xerox Corporation sold plant and technology for the production of low-value photocopying machines to the People's Republic of China and contractually agreed to repurchase a large proportion of the machines produced in the Chinese plant.

■ *Switch trading* refers to the transfer of unused or unusable credit balances in one country to overcome an imbalance of money by a trading partner in another country. Country X sells goods of a certain value to country Y. Country Y credits country X with the value of the goods, which X can use to buy goods from Y. Country X, however, does not wish to buy goods from Y. X therefore sells the credits to a third party trading house at a discount. The trading house then locates a country or company wishing to buy goods from Y. In return for a small profit, the trading house sells the credits to the country or company wishing to buy from Y.

- *Offset* – this is similar to counterpurchase, except that the supplier can fulfil the undertaking to import goods or services of a certain percentage value by dealing with any company in the country to which the original goods were supplied.

This can be shown diagrammatically as in Figure 15.2.

Figure 15.2 **Preferred items for export in countertrade transactions**[23]

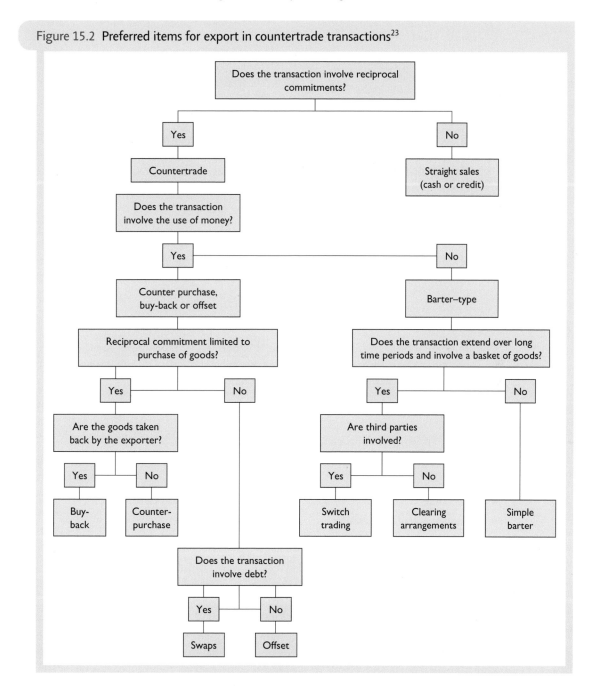

Table 15.5 **Advantages and disadvantages of countertrade**

Advantages	Disadvantages
Acceptance of goods or services as payment can: ■ avoid exchange controls ■ promote trade with countries with inconvertible currencies ■ reduce risks associated with unstable currency values Overcoming the above financial obstacles enables countertrading enterprises to: ■ enter new or formerly closed markets ■ expand business and sales volume ■ reduce the impact of foreign protectionism on overseas business Countertrade has enabled participants to: ■ make fuller use of plant capacity ■ have longer production runs ■ reduce unit expenses due to greater sales volume ■ find valuable outlets for declining products	Countertrade negotiations tend to be longer and more complicated than conventional sales negotiations and must, sometimes, be conducted with powerful government procurement agencies Additional expenses, such as brokerage fees and other transaction costs, reduce the profitability of countertrade deals There may be difficulties with the quality, availability and disposal of goods taken as countertrade Countertrade may give rise to pricing problems associated with the assignment of values to products/commodities received in exchange Offset customers can, later, become competitors Commodity prices can vary widely during the lengthy periods of countertrade negotiation and delivery

15.10.3 The advantages and disadvantages of countertrade

These have been identified by Forker,[24] as shown in Table 15.5.

15.10.4 Problems of Countertrade

The implementation of CT requires special expertise. The problems encountered will fall into one of the following categories: marketing, negotiation ability, attitudinal, managerial, pricing and procurement. Examples include:

■ no control over quality of products traded and possible absence of specification detail
■ pricing decisions and lack of knowledge on cost drivers
■ lack of CT knowledge and relevant expertise
■ difficult, complex and negotiations with multi-participants when there is no common agenda
■ contractual relationships lacking clarity with jurisdictional issues
■ difficulty reselling products
■ added third-party costs
■ unknown and unquantifiable risks.

15.11 The true cost of offshore buying

As indicated in earlier sections of this chapter, while the benefits of buying offshore can be substantial, there are also significant financial costs and risks. It is therefore important that such costs and risks should be evaluated before deciding to source offshore.

Table 15.6 Comparisons of costs of offshore and UK suppliers

Expense category	Costs: areas of expenditure	Offshore supplier	Home supplier
Basic price	Supplier's quoted price per item Packaging Sea/air freight Marine insurance Supplier's final price CIF/destination		
Handling/transportation charges	Handling charges (port of entry) Storage Port costs Internal transport to buyer Freight forwarding fees Insurance		
Customs and associated charges	Customs duties Customs clearance fees		
International financing	Costs of documentation Currency conversion rates Exchange rate fluctuations Bank fees		
Inventory costs	Holding costs of higher inventory Levels at x per cent per annum		
Sourcing costs	Costs of visit to offshore supplier Estimated communication costs Costs of inspection by offshore agent Special fees, such as translation, legal		
Total actual or estimated costs			

Tables such as 15.6 facilitate comparisons between the true costs of buying offshore and from home-based suppliers. They also provide a list of some possible items for negotiation.

Many of the costs shown in Table 15.6 will also attract VAT. Costs will vary according to different weights, sizes and quantities. The effects of such variances are easily computed with the aid of a spreadsheet.

15.12 Global sourcing – Boeing case study

It is always academically and practically better to study actual examples of global sourcing in action. The Boeing 787 Dreamliner project offers a significant learning opportunity. What now follows are selected extracts from a Gudmundsson case.[25] Each extract is followed by the author's comments, designed for learning, not making criticism of

Boeing actions or inactions. Readers should be aware that the Gudmundsson case was published in August 2017 and many things will have changed since then.

By way of background the creation of the Dreamliner was required to strengthen Boeing's Business Model. In June 2003, the name Dreamliner was chosen by online vote. On April 26 2004, the first order for 50 aircraft was placed by Nippon Airways. The delivery date was set for late 2008. The first delivery was made on September 25, 2011.

The Boeing company underlined its embeddedness in the global economy bluntly in 2011 *"U.S. jobs are created by selling airplanes around the world."* It is clear that aircraft manufacturers must offer more work on their aircraft beyond their national borders, not only to risk-share, but also to reduce costs of new technologies and materials aimed at increasing reliability and fuel efficiency of the aircraft. Today's cutting-edge resources, capabilities, and know-how is distributed to a greater extent around the world compared to what it used to be. Every new aircraft put in production requires a new reconfiguration of resources to turn out a competitive product.

This is an example of why procurement must be involved at the global strategy, recognising the impact of new technologies on procurement risk management, cost and selection of global partners.

In the new globalised environment a network of suppliers take on a greater role, contributing to a larger part of each new project, ranging from design to manufacturing of large aircraft sections. Boeing no longer limits its partnerships to the USA, but works with plants all over the world, Japan, China, Italy and France, these partners will assemble major sections of the aircraft, and install everything from electronics to seats, and then haul the sections to Boeing's assembly plants. The role of the integrator is to make sure that the massive parts fit to tight tolerances. In the aerospace industry national borders and language barriers must be overcome as the multinational Airbus has demonstrated by overtaking Boeing as the world's largest aircraft manufacturer.

This highlights the procurement challenges including culture, language barriers and logistical issues. The Boeing procurement team would have to understand the subtleties of partnering behavioural as opposed to adversarial relationships.

Boeing hoped the new partnering model would reduce development time from six to four years and the development cost from $10 to $6 billion. However, this did not materialize and the project cost overrun amounted to 11 billion dollars and the first aircraft was delivered three years behind schedule. Was the partnership network to blame or was it simply the high cost of learning new ways, perhaps benefitting the company greatly on future projects?

The rhetorical question posed by Gudmundsson is very relevant. It is the cost of learning that is also relevant to procurement. There can be no doubt that price and cost management were actively considered before placing contracts. However, the subsequent contract management, technically and commercially would warrant stringent scrutiny.

In negotiations with partners, pricing and risk-sharing conditions were the main hurdles. Along the way some designated partners wanted to exit the consortia if not receiving a higher revenue percentage from Boeing to reflect greater perceived risk in the project. For example, Boeing asked partners to bear the cost of the safety certification of their parts, escalating risk if the certification process called for a costly redesign of parts, they would have to bear.

In the early phases, negotiations with the Japanese partners dragged past deadlines, causing work to go ahead without a signed contract, an act of good will to prevent project delays. However, the lack of contract caused cash-flow problems for the partners as the government backed International Aircraft Development Fund (IADF) in Japan would not grant loans unless there was a signed contract between Boeing and the Japanese partners. *"The cash flow is very severe without government support,"* said Fuji's Norisha Matsuo, explaining problems his company faced working on the project. There were also knock-on effects from the negotiation delays causing partners like Fuji requesting new terms with Boeing to recuperate extra costs. For example, Fuji was unable to invest in the necessary machinery to test the 787's wing section parts, causing it to send the work back to Seattle. Further delays were even caused by U.S. immigration policies refusing visas for Fuji's engineers doing the wing testing work in Seattle.

Elsewhere in this book we emphasise the skill of negotiation. In our view it is still an underdeveloped skill. The Boeing case highlights the range, depth and complexity of negotiations that were required. It also highlights the need for procurement research when dealing with innovative contracts and relationships.

To comprehend the logistics maze of the 787 project, the work division was as follows: The Wichita plant did the nose section; a joint venture of Italy's Alenia Aeronautica and Vought

Aircraft Industries in Dallas did the tail section and the half the fuselage; three Japanese industrial giants, Mitsubishi Heavy Industries, Kawasaki Heavy Industries and Fuji Heavy

Vought Aircraft Industries, build the wing and centre section; finally, a host of smaller suppliers provided everything from air-conditioning systems to the landing gear. Boeing, by involving global partners, is also depending on another dimension, namely government to provide subsidies to the respective partners to carry out their part of the deal. For example, 35% of the 787's airframe is built in Japan, and this work package was supposed to receive at the outset US$1.6 billion in Japanese government aid straight to the suppliers. In this way, government relations also became a direct and indirect element in supply network.

The complexities of a supply chain are demonstrated here. It raises questions regarding integration of products from different suppliers and involvement of governments, who are sometimes known to prevaricate on alleged deals.

The 787 project eventually required Boeing to send its engineers to the various suppliers to solve technical problems that were the chief cause of the 787's development delays. These problems were serious enough for Boeing eventually redesigning the aircraft sub-assembly process, causing additional expenses that were larger than if such support had been included in the project from the beginning.

This situation cannot be a surprise. The liaison between engineers in Boeing and suppliers was central to project success. The author has experience of creating partnering in the nuclear sector and has created co-located engineering teams with access to a joint design IT system.

More partnerships around the globe meant that Boeing had to work across cultures and break down barriers. An example of this is when Boeing sent engineers to Mitsubishi in Nagoya, Japan, to help reduce the number of 787 wing parts. The most straightforward approach was to mix wing specialists from both companies, to come up with ideas and solutions. In the meeting Boeing engineers sat on one side and Japanese engineers on the other side. The Americans started to brainstorm writing notes and sticking them to the wall. However, the Japanese kept their posture and watched the activity on the other side of the room. *"This is new culture for us,"* said Masnori Yamaguchi, a Mitsubishi engineer. *"At this time. . . It's. . . culture shock."* The American style is to attack problems head on, sometimes a wasted effort, but often the process leads to innovative solutions. Contrary wise, the Japanese prefer to plan carefully and create a hierarchy of testable results to arrive at a high-quality solution in the end. The outcome of this cross-cultural partnership was a compromise where Boeing designed the wing box, while Mitsubishi developed a way to minimize defects. The outcome, Jenks said, *"leads to both innovative solutions and ones that are practical in a manufacturing environment."*

This highlights the clash of cultures. This cultural difference is applicable to negotiation and will, typically prolong the negotiations due to many reasons including translation, pace of discussions, involvement of the management hierarchy and so on.

We emphasise the extracts have been selected from a comprehensive case. The Dreamliner project was highly innovative and complex.

15.13 Buying capital equipment offshore

15.13.1 Reasons for buying capital equipment offshore

Capital equipment can be sourced offshore for numerous reasons, including:

- compatibility with existing equipment
- the technology is protected by patents
- to meet stringent 'offset' commitments
- to achieve high quality specifications
- access to 24/365 expert service support
- access to cutting edge technology
- long-term through life support
- high quality operator training and support
- competitive prices of equipment and support
- ability to negotiate stringent contract performance specification and penalties for non-performance.

15.13.2 Technical requirements of equipment bought offshore

Essentially these are listed in section 15.4, although special attention will be given to lifecycle costs and the availability of spares – especially the speed at which they can be provided by air transport or other methods. Other important factors are international standardisation and, with some complex equipment, the provision of assistance with installation and post-purchase maintenance advice and services.

15.13.3 Cultural, contractual and currency factors

The cultural, political, ethical and foreign exchange factors referred to in this chapter apply equally to the purchase of capital equipment.

Legal factors will also need special consideration, especially what legal system is applicable, and the provision for the international settlement of disputes by means of such agencies as the International Chamber of Commerce (ICC). Special clauses may need to be included in the contract, such as an undertaking by the supplier of the equipment to maintain stocks of spare parts for a prescribed minimum number of years.

Currency considerations which need to be taken into account are the same as those referred to in section 15.4.3. In some cases, countertrade may be applicable, especially buy-back arrangements, whereby the country exporting capital equipment undertakes to buy back some of the products made in the buyer's country.

15.13.4 Import factors

These include the most suitable forms of transport and the way in which freight and import agents can provide assistance. All buyers of capital equipment offshore should have a thorough understanding of Incoterms especially FOB, CIF and CFR.

Finally, it is essential to make an evaluation, as shown in section 15.11, of the comparative costs of buying capital equipment from offshore and home sources, when these alternatives are available.

15.14 Factors in successful offshore procurement

The Birou and Fawcett research referred to earlier in this chapter identified the factors listed in Table 15.7.

Other important considerations include ascertaining the total cost of ownership for all significant purchases, using offshore suppliers that practice TQM, providing offshore suppliers with accurate demand forecasts, a boundary-spanning philosophy for supply chain participants, as opposed to a narrow vision of business processes, and sensitivity to the interests and cultures of overseas suppliers. Most procurement professionals can benefit from training in buying offshore, but hands-on experience is usually the best teacher of all.

Table 15.7 Factors influencing success in international sourcing[26]

Rank	Factor	Rating
1	Top management support	5.68
2	Developing communication skills	5.67
3	Establishing long-term relationships	5.65
4	Developing global sourcing skills	5.62
5	Understanding global opportunities	5.13
6	Knowledge of foreign business practices	5.09
7	Foreign supplier certification and qualifications	5.02
8	Planning for global sourcing	5.02
9	Obtaining expert assistance	4.79
10	Knowledge of exchange rates	4.53
11	Use of third-party logistics services	4.12

Note: all ratings are on a seven-point Likert scale, with seven for major challenge

Discussion questions

15.1 What are the potential risks when purchasing offshore, particularly in regard to financial and supply chain considerations?

15.2 Would you prefer to deal with a local agent of an offshore supplier or deal directly with the supplier? What considerations have influenced your response?

15.3 Define countertrade and identify the five distinct types of countertrade.

15.4 If you were selecting a freight agent to represent your business what would be the top six qualities you would be looking for?

15.5 What are the main differences between a Letter of Credit and a Bill for Collection?

15.6 If you purchased capital equipment from a supplier in Japan, how would you guarantee a continuing supply of spare parts?

15.7 Compare and contrast the movement of goods, internationally, by sea and air freight.

15.8 Why should a procurement specialist be concerned about foreign exchange risk and how can this risk be mitigated?

15.9 Name six Incoterms® and explain their strengths and weaknesses from the buyer's point of view.

15.10 What are the dangers of signing a contract subject to a foreign jurisdiction?

15.11 What lessons have you learned from the Boeing Dreamliner case?

15.12 Why should procurement be involved at the earliest stage of determining a global supply chain?

15.13 Other than price, there are few other reasons to purchase offshore. Do you agree? Why?

References

1 Birou, L. H. and Fawcett, S. E., 'International purchasing benefits and requirements and challenges', *International Journal of Purchasing and Supply*, Jan., 1993, pp. 22–5.

2 Trent, R.J. and Monczka, R.M., 'International purchasing and global sourcing: what are the differences?', *Journal of supply Chain Management*, Nov., 2003.

3 Rexta, N. and Miyamo, T., 'International sourcing: an Australian perspective', ISM *Resource Article*, Winter, 2000.

4 Brian Farrington Limited, www.brianfarrington.com.

5 Radical SportsCars Ltd.

6 Hankook Tire Co Ltd.

7 Griffin, R. W. and Pustay, M. W., *International Business. A Management Perspective*. Global Edition. Pearson Education Ltd, Harlow, UK, 2003.

8 Ferraro. G., *The Cultural Dimension of International Business*. Prentice Hall, Upper Saddle River, New Jersey, USA, 2010.

9 Op cit.

10 The World's Religious Make-Up. *The Economist*. 22 December 2012, p. 102.

[11] www.corporatecomplianceinsights.com, 'Incoterms Rules-How they can improve your Company's compliance, reduce your risk and maximise your profit'. 21 January 2013.

[12] 'Incoterms' is a registered trademark of the International Chamber of Commerce.

[13] Obtainable from ICC United Kingdom. The British affiliate of ICC. 12 Grosvenor Place. London, SW1X 7HH.

[14] www.forwarderlaw.com 'Stuck in the Middle: Part A – Functions of the Freight Forwarder'.

[15] Foley, J. F., *The Global Entrepreneur: Taking Your Business International*, 2nd edn, Jamme Press International, 2004.

[16] Willmott, K., 'Understanding the freight business', in as 3 above, pp. 203–4.

[17] SITPRO (Simplifying International Trade) at: www.sitpro.org.uk/trade/paymentmethods.htm.

[18] Bills of Exchange Act 1882, section 3(1).

[19] As 18 above – SITPRO is the UK's Trade Facilitation Agency, supported by the DTI.

[20] Yasvas, B. F. and Freed, R., 'An economic rationale for countertrade', *The International Trade Journal*, Vol. XV, No. 2, Summer, 2001, pp. 127–56.

[21] Carter, J. R. and Gagne, J., 'The dos and don'ts of countertrade', *Sloan Management Review*, Spring, 1988, pp. 31–7.

[22] Kreuze, J. G., 'International countertrade', *Internal Auditor*, Vol. 5, No. 2, April, 1997, pp. 42–7.

[23] https://amfori.org.

[24] Forker, L. B., 'Purchasing's views on countertrade', *International Journal of Purchasing and Materials Management*, Spring, 1992, pp. 10–19.

[25] Svenn Vidar Gudmundsson 'Global Partnering Dilemma: Following in the steps of the Boeing 787 Dreamliner,' Version 1.7 August 2017. Toulouse Business School, Toulouse, France.

[26] Birou, L. H. and Fawcett, S. E., 'International purchasing benefits and requirements and challenges', *International Journal of Purchasing and Supply*, Jan., 1993.

Part 5

Strategy, tactics and operations 3: Negotiation skills, contract management, category and world class procurement

Chapter 16

Negotiation skills, practice and business benefits

Learning outcomes

This chapter aims to provide an understanding of:

- approaches to negotiation
- the content of negotiation
- the negotiator's authority
- the negotiation process
- pre-negotiation
- the actual negotiation
- post-negotiation actions
- what is effective negotiation?
- negotiation and relationships
- negotiation ethics.

Key ideas

- The distinction between adversarial or distributive and collaborative or integrative negotiations.
- Consequences of failed negotiations.
- Methods of influencing others for positive outcomes.
- Substance and relationship negotiating roles.
- Time and location as a factor in negotiations.
- Planning as a key negotiation element.
- The key stages of the negotiation process.
- Pre-negotiation, negotiation and post-negotiation activities and considerations.
- Negotiating interactions and analysis.
- Negotiation reviews and transfer of learning.
- Positional and principled negotiation.
- Ethical aspects of negotiation.

Introduction

Negotiation is a skill required, in abundance, by all procurement specialists. The skill has, in recent years, become more critical. It is a fact that many contracts are becoming long-term. During the term of the contract, many factors will change, making it vital that contracts reflect potential change and, how it will be dealt with. Competition has become global, resulting in negotiations involving social and business practices in conflict between buyer and seller.

There must be specific conditions that pertain before negotiation is used in an attempt to resolve differences between buyers and sellers. These will include any situation where:

- It is believed that a tender or quotation contains cost elements that are uncompetitive when compared with other bidders, or, where there is internal financial and technical expertise to show that bid costs are too high.

- A tender or quotation is unclear on major features, for example, the delivery date is unsupported by a detailed production plan showing key points of manufacture or where service implementation fails to identify milestones. This would require negotiation to probe these key points and to identify how the contract will include the delivery obligations required.

- There is reason to believe that the seller has a high probability of not fulfilling a critical feature of the contract, and where in consequence contractual safeguards are required. An example of this is a failure to mobilise resources on a project.

- IT product support is necessary and different levels, e.g. gold, silver and bronze, are available, and where the proposed cost in use is unclear or unacceptable. This will require negotiation to obtain definitive prices, service levels and understand the consequences of non-performance and to include these in the contract.

- There is good reason to believe that the tenderers are not pricing competitively. This could be through collusive practices, estimating deficiencies or a desire to price in such a way as to make excessive profit.

- The supply market is monopolistic thereby diminishing the normal forces of competition.

- The tenderers are reluctant to explain how they arrived at their price, particularly on high-value contracts. If this situation is also accompanied by circumstances which make it probable that contract changes will be inevitable, negotiation is required to identify the price review mechanism which will operate in the contract.

- The purchase has a unique element, such as a once only purchase in a specialist area where the buyer has little expertise. This can occur in Information Technology procurement where the seller will usually have expert knowledge.

- There is a contractual dispute that requires a detailed understanding of all the circumstances leading to the dispute and seeking a resolution to the dispute.

- The buying company is contemplating a long-term contract such as outsourcing back office services for ten years and, hence, where the decision will involve long-term pricing considerations. In this case negotiation is necessary to ensure appropriate price control mechanisms such as indexation, continuous improvement, price benchmarking and possible incentivisation mechanisms.

- Technology refreshments are to be incorporated as an element of contract performance and where the recovery on investment needs to be specifically identified.

- There is a price increase request from a seller which will have an adverse effect on operating costs, budgets and ability to compete in their markets.

- Supply market research, identifies opportunities to obtain buying company competitive advantages previously denied them. Examples have been provided by outsourcing and offshoring.

- It can be demonstrated that existing contracts are no longer competitive and/or where the technical solution is outdated.

This is not a comprehensive listing, although it identifies reasons why negotiation is frequently necessary.

The most successful negotiations are conducted under circumstances where there is mutual respect between buyer and seller and where both parties perceive that there are valid professional reasons for negotiations taking place. This is not to say that both sides will not pursue their objectives with vigour and persistence.

Definitions of negotiation

There are numerous definitions of negotiation. Three examples are given and commented on below.

> The process whereby two or more parties decide what each will give and take in an exchange between them.[1]

This definition of negotiation highlights:

- its interpersonal nature
- the interdependence of the parties
- the fact that concessions will be necessary.

A formal negotiation is:

> An occasion where one or more representatives of two or more parties interact in an explicit attempt to reach a jointly acceptable position on one or more divisive issues about which they would like to agree.[2]

This definition highlights that negotiation:

- is applicable when two or more parties need to reach agreement
- involves *representatives of the parties* – the buyer, sales executive and legal representatives, for example
- is *explicit* – that is, the process genuinely and deliberately attempts to reach an agreement
- involves *divisive issues* about which the parties would like to agree providing the ensuing business risks are acceptable.

> Negotiation is:

> Any form of verbal communication in which the participants seek to exploit their relative competitive advantages and needs to achieve explicit or implicit objectives within the overall purpose of seeking to resolve problems that are barriers to agreement.[3]

This definition stresses three elements of negotiation:

- it involves communication – that is, the exchange of information
- it takes place in a context in which the participants use their comparative competitive advantages and the perceived needs of the other party to influence the outcome of the negotiation process
- each participant has implicit as well as explicit objectives that determine the negotiating strategies – a seller will explicitly wish to obtain the best price, for example, but, implicitly, will be seeking a contribution to fixed overheads and endeavouring to keep the plant and workforce employed.

Identifying business reasons for negotiation

It is essential that supplier's quotations and tenders are professionally evaluated to identify those aspects which are unacceptable because of the seller's stance, and/or where there has been a non-compliant offer. The procurement specialist will be able to identify those aspects which can be accepted without further discussion and those areas where the attendant risk is unacceptable and where negotiation is a desirable business approach.

It is impossible to be prescriptive regarding everything that may be negotiable but it is possible to predict those aspects which would typically require negotiation effort:

- obtain compliance with the specification
- delivery milestones, completion dates and consequences of failure to meet them
- financial safeguards, e.g. bank guarantees, performance bonds, and parent company guarantees
- pricing of products and services, disclosure of data
- long-term product support, e.g. releases of software and period of supportability
- product guarantee conditions, e.g. repair/replace, then extension to guarantee?
- compliance with statutory regulations, e.g. health and safety at work
- pricing of non-recurring costs, e.g. tooling and software source code development
- seller's requests for enhanced payment terms including advance payments
- seller's exclusion clause proposals
- insurance requirements, e.g. values and whether 'per claim' or 'in the aggregate'
- termination clauses and consequences for both parties
- price review mechanisms on long-term contracts, e.g. indexation
- redetermination of prices for increased quantities
- discount and/or rebate structures
- use of licenses for computer software and payment, e.g. a site licence or user numbers
- hourly rate composition and charges for weekends
- *force majeure* – what is included

- rights to intellectual property in design, copyright, etc.
- use of sub-contractors and flow down of contract conditions
- charges for commissioning, e.g. IT software
- arbitration mediation and dispute resolution rights under contract
- jurisdiction
- mobilisation charges on major projects
- liquidated or unliquidated damages.

Note – these are broad headings only and would require a significant amount of planning to ensure that the detail is dealt with in ensuing negotiations.

Consequences of failed negotiation

There are many potential consequences of failed negotiations, including:

- the loss of a business opportunity
- an irrevocable breakdown in relationships
- excessive costs incurred by misuse resources
- adverse corporate and personal credibility
- in-house mistrust of personnel engaged in the failed negotiations
- defensive posturing on reasons for failure
- in a dispute scenario, the dispute gathers momentum
- very expensive third parties engaged to correct the situation
- potential legal consequences
- impact on long-term business strategy.

16.1 Approaches to negotiation

Approaches to negotiation may be classified as adversarial or collaborative:

- *adversarial negotiation* – also termed *distributive* or *win–lose negotiation* – is an approach in which the focus is on 'positions' staked out by the participants, the assumption being that every time one party wins, the other loses, so, as a result, the other party is regarded as an adversary
- *collaborative negotiation* – also called *integrative* or *win–win negotiation* – is an approach in which the assumption is that, by means of creative problem-solving, one or both parties can gain without the other having to lose and, as the other party is regarded as a collaborator rather than an adversary, the participants may be more willing to share concerns, ideas and expectations than would otherwise be the case.

The characteristics of adversarial and collaborative negotiation are summarised in Table 16.1.

Table 16.1 Adversarial and collaborative negotiation contrasted

Adversarial negotiation	Collaborative negotiation
■ The emphasis is on competing to attain goals at the adversary's expenses	■ The emphasis is on ascertaining goals held in common with the other party
■ Strategy is based on secrecy, retention of information and low level of trust in the perceived adversary	■ Strategy is based on openness, sharing of information and high level of trust in the perceived partner
■ The desired outcomes of the negotiations are often misrepresented so that the adversary does not know what the opponent really requires the outcome of the negotiation to be. There is little concern for or empathy with the other party	■ The desired outcomes of the negotiation are made known so that there are no hidden agendas and issues are clearly understood. Each party is concerned for and has empathy with the other
■ Strategies are unpredictable, based on various negotiating ploys designed to outmanoeuvre or 'throw' the other	■ Strategies are predictable. Whilst flexible, such strategies are aimed at reaching an agreement acceptable to the other party
■ Parties use threats, bluffs and ultimatums with the aim of keeping the adversary on the defensive	■ Parties refrain from threats and so on, which are seen as counterproductive to the rational solution of perceived problems
■ There is an inflexible adherence to a fixed position that may be defended by both rational and irrational arguments. Primarily, the approach is destructive	■ The need for flexibility in the positions taken is assumed. The emphasis is on the use of imaginative, creative, logical ideas and approaches to a constructive resolution of differences
■ The approach is essentially hostile and aggressive – 'us against them.' This antagonism may be enhanced in team negotiations where members of the team may seek to outdo their colleagues in displaying macho attitudes	■ The approach is essentially friendly and non-aggressive, 'We are in this together'. This involves downplaying hostility and giving credit to constructive contributions made by either party to the negotiations
■ The unhealthy extreme of an adversarial approach is reached when it is assumed that movement towards one's own goal is facilitated by blocking measures that prevent the other party from attaining the goal	■ The healthy extreme of the partnership approach is reached when it is assumed that whatever is good for the other party to the negotiation is necessarily good for both
■ The key attitude is that of: 'We win, you lose'	■ The key attitude is, 'How can the respective goals of each party be achieved so that both win?'
■ If an impasse occurs, the negotiation may be broken off	■ If an impasse occurs, this is regarded as a further problem to be solved, possibly by the intervention of higher management or an internal or external mediator or arbitrator

16.1.1 An evaluation of adversarial and collaborative strategies

Adversarial strategies may, on occasion, be appropriate in the following situations:

■ where there is no ongoing relationship or the potential for one does not exist or is not desired – the deal is a one-off

■ to counteract the opposing party's domineering style of negotiation

■ a quick solution to a disagreement is required.

Collaborative strategies, while more time-consuming and difficult to achieve, they have the following advantages:

■ they are more stable and lead to long-term relationships and creative solutions to mutual opportunities and difficulties

■ they may be the only way to obtain agreements when both parties to a negotiation have high aspirations and resist making concessions until they are convinced of the benefits.

16.1.2 Transforming adversarial attitudes

Fisher and Ury[4] suggest five tactics designed to transform an adversarial into a collaborative approach. These approaches are discussed in section 16.10.

16.2 The content of negotiation

In any negotiation, two types of goals should receive consideration. These may be referred to as *substance goals* and *relationship goals*.

16.2.1 Substance goals

Substance goals are concerned with the content issues of the negotiation. The possible content issues are legion and depend on the requirements relating to a situation. Most negotiations will be about high-value/usage items – that is, the 15–20 per cent of items that constitutes the major portion of inventory investment. Negotiation also applies to non-standard items, although a large user will seek, if possible, to negotiate preferential terms for standard supplies. Most negotiation topics affect price (and cost), either directly or indirectly. There are numerous ways in which content issues can be grouped, including overseas buying and buying for construction projects. Groupings may also relate to products, such as IT or commodities. Three typical groupings – shown in Figures 16.1, 16.2 and 16.3 respectively – relate to price, contractual and delivery issues in negotiation. The issues listed are in no way exhaustive and the lists often overlap.

Figure 16.1 The price content of negotiation – some issues

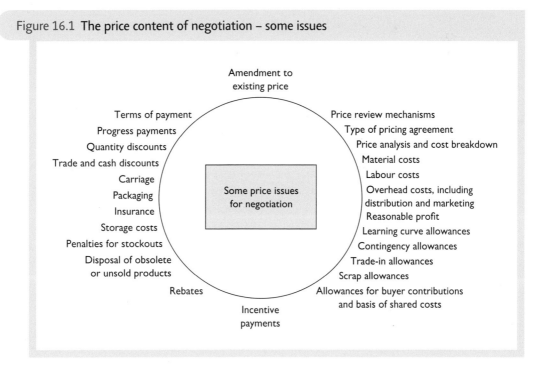

Figure 16.2 The contractual content of negotiation – some issues

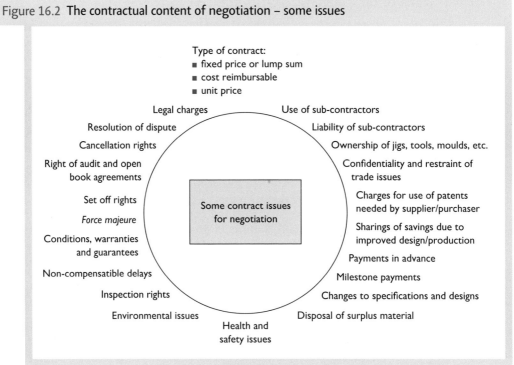

Figure 16.3 The delivery content of negotiation – some issues

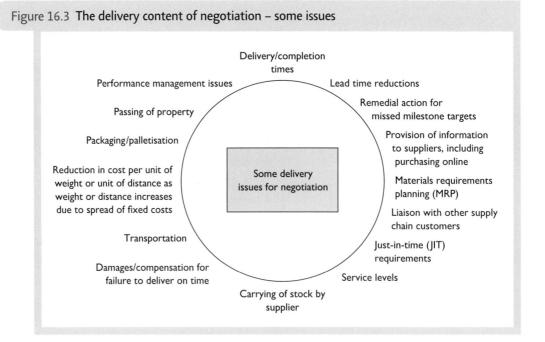

16.2.2 Relationship goals

Relationship goals are concerned with outcomes relating to how well those involved in the negotiations are able to work together once the process is completed and how well their respective organisations or 'constituencies' may work together. Some areas for relationship goals include:

- partnering sourcing
- preferred supplier status
- supplier involvement in design, development and value analysis
- sharing of technology and innovation projects.

16.2.3 Legal implications of negotiations

Some negotiations focus on a single issue, while others are complex with multi-issue discussions taking place. It is quite usual for legal specialists to become engaged in complex negotiations and buyers need to be aware of the legal implications of actions taken during and subsequent to negotiations.

If we assume that an offer has been made by the supplier, either through a quotation or tender, then any attempt to negotiate will amount, in law, to a counter-offer. This puts the seller into a position, by which the counter-offer can be accepted in full, or it can be rejected, or the seller may make a counter-offer. This is simply following the legal rules of formation of a contract through the rules of offer and acceptance.

The buyer must also be aware that the moment the seller's offer is challenged and any term(s) rejected this gives the seller the right to withdraw their bid. That is unlikely to happen except in extreme circumstances, but it could!

The Misrepresentation Act 1967 is relevant to negotiations. Section 2(1) of the Act provides as follows:

> Where a person has entered into a contract after a misrepresentation has been made to him by another party thereto and as a result thereof he has suffered loss, then, if the person making the misrepresentation would be liable to damages in respect thereof had the misrepresentation been made fraudulently, that person shall be so liable notwithstanding that the misrepresentation was not made fraudulently, unless he proves that he had reasonable ground to believe and did believe up to the time the contract was made the facts represented were true.

A classic legal case involving misrepresentation is that of BSkyB Ltd & Anor v HP Enterprise Services UK Ltd & Anor (Rev1) [2010] EWHC 86 (TCC) (26 January 2010)

This is a complex case with more than 2350 pages of a judgment by The Hon. Mr. Justice Ramsey. The detailed allegations of misrepresentation begin at para 552 and deals with 'initial representations' (there are more representations later) relating to resources, time and cost. It is pertinent to note that the evidence presented to the court, involved tender documents, emails, letters and meetings. These are all important facets of the audit trail.

For example, two representations were made, namely, 'We have the resources and ability to deliver the systems and services you require and to meet the financial and budgetary targets that you have set,' and

> 'Ready to start this project as of Monday, 17 July. We have the resources reserved for this project; in fact, we have picked up some additional high level resources that you have worked with previously. These folks come with great experience of these types and size of project.'

The author (regardless of the Judge's findings in the case) now encourages you, the reader to consider what you would do in a negotiation to deal effectively with the two points above.

How would you deal with the statement 'We have the resources?'

It would require some carefully phrased questions, such as:

- Who are the key personnel, by name and position?
- Do you have a comprehensive resource plan for each phase of the project?
- Are the resources based in the UK or do they have to come from another country(ies)?
- What do you mean when you say the resources are 'reserved'?
- Does your company employ the resources or are some sub-contracted?
- What do you mean by 'high-level resources'?
- How can you demonstrate the experience of these types and sizes of projects?
- When you 'start the project' what resources and roles will there be?
- Can you explain the resources plan in relation to the financial and budgetary targets you have set?

You, the reader, will recognise that these questions need to be prepared prior to the negotiation commencing, otherwise the negotiation would be unplanned and probably ineffective.

16.3 The negotiator's authority

In negotiations, it is important for participants to know the extent of their authority to commit the organisations that they are representing as such authority prescribes their options and responsibility for the outcome of the negotiations.

The degree of authority may range from that of an emissary, commissioned to present, without variation, a position determined by his or her superiors to that of a free agent. The buyer must establish at the outset of negotiations that the person(s) who represent(s) the seller do have the authority to commit their organisation on technical, legal, financial issues and commercial. This authority is not necessarily related to job titles. It could be that a person with the title of Key Account Executive has no authority to negotiate all or any aspects of a deal. If it is established that the person has no authority the negotiation should not continue, otherwise the buyer will reveal his position, leaving nothing available in tactical terms, when, and if, the negotiations continue. There must be no embarrassment in asking if the negotiators have the appropriate authority.

There is evidence that the fewer constraints imposed on a negotiator, the greater will be the scope for his or her personal characteristics, such as knowledge, experience and personality to influence the negotiation process. Five sets of conditions prevent negotiators from responding spontaneously to their opposite number when:

- they have little latitude in determining either their positions or posture
- they are held responsible for their performance
- a negotiator has sole responsibility for the outcome of negotiations
- negotiators are responsible to a constituency that is present in the negotiations
- they are appointed rather than elected.

In the above situations, the behaviour of negotiators will be constrained by their obligations. The more complicated and open-ended the negotiations, the greater should be the status of the negotiators.

16.3.1 The negotiating situation

This relates to the strengths and weakness of the participants in the negotiation. The factors identified by Porter as affecting the relative strengths of supplier and buyer groups are outlined in Chapter 2 (see Figure 2.4). There are a number of factors that will impact upon the buyer's ability to negotiate, including:

- knowledge of the supply market and available competition
- technical and other data of the product or service being purchased
- intelligence on supplier's finances, organisation, production capability, etc.
- professional knowledge of buying and interface subjects
- perceived status of buying power
- use of appropriate negotiation skills, including comprehensive planning
- courage of convictions and persistence with demands
- ability to deal with long-term issues and to see the 'big picture'
- ability to handle time constraints imposed by others
- knowledge of past negotiations with seller, their behavioural pattern and concession pattern
- confidence in own ability to negotiate and to create an effective team.

In any negotiating situation, it is important to consider how to manage the process and influence the outcome. Having done so, there must be a concentration on the limited number of methods that can be used to influence others. The ability is recognising which one, and why it is being deployed.

Adversarial – power and coercion

This is, potentially, the most dangerous form of negotiation and is likely to be destructive. Power is never one sided and therefore the person using power invites a similar response. Unquestionably there may be short-term gains for one party but in the longer term it will not engender positive relationships between the parties. Each side may have the upper hand when power is available to them but when market forces change, e.g. when demand exceeds supply the buyer who has used power to achieve their objectives may find supplies impossible to obtain. The large organisational buyer who uses power to drive prices down to uneconomic levels may find the seller withdrawing from the market or directing their output elsewhere. The unsophisticated use of power can often in part, be attributed to those with outsize egos who lack the finesse and ability to act differently.

Attitude change involving emotion

Negotiations based purely on emotion require little planning effort. The success of this approach is largely dependent upon the gullibility, inexperience and weakness of the other party. The experienced negotiator can readily counter such an approach on the basis of using hard facts. The unprepared negotiator will not be in a position to refute the detailed counter attack. Requests based on emotion are easily spotted because they will often be prefixed by anguished pleas such as 'surely you can . . . ' and 'we will all be in trouble if you can't?. . . ' and 'my boss will make me redundant if you don't agree . . . '. There are occasions when emotion may have a place in the negotiation, but it is not the ideal approach.

There are a number of negotiators who adopt a two-person approach, the hard and soft negotiators to stimulate emotions. This is, potentially, a foolish tactic which can be spotted from afar by an experienced negotiator. When faced with this tactic the other party's confidence will be boosted on the basis that if emotion is the basis of their approach it lacks substance. The negotiator who has a sound business proposition should not need to resort to such shallow tactics.

Search for middle ground compromise

It is necessary, in all negotiations, to set targets for outcomes. Such targets may be derived from knowledge, business drivers and personal objectives. Once a target has been made known in a negotiation it must be persevered with until the personal judgment is that it cannot be achieved. At that point, the next demand must be tested at a level close to the original; otherwise the first demand lacks credibility. The buyer who persistently asks for 10 per cent off the price and will settle at 5 per cent is an amateur negotiator. If the negotiator offers in one move to 'split the difference' this should be viewed as a weakness and/or lack of planning.

Concessions may have to be made but it is their scale and timing which require careful thought in the heat of a negotiation.

Trading mutually advantageous concessions

The ability to trade concessions is the hallmark of a professional negotiator. The sales representative is trained to 'trade concessions, never give them away'. The buyer must carefully prepare what can be traded and put a value on those factors. That value must be the value to the other party, not the cost to the buyer. The buyer must get accustomed to making proposals for action in which demands are put on the table. The seller may offer one concession, say a slight reduction in price, providing the buyer agrees to enhanced payment terms and takes a greater quantity. At all times when concessions are being made or accepted a value must be placed upon them.

Logical persuasion

This tactic requires sophisticated research because it depends entirely on detailed, factual knowledge. The buyer who seeks concessions on quotations and tenders through the use of logical persuasion will typically have available:

- comprehensive market knowledge
- a wide range of quotations/tenders
- economic analysis
- product knowledge
- raw material sources and prices
- product or service cost analysis
- supplier financial data
- supplier activity/capacity data.

A skilled negotiator with this extent of knowledge is a formidable opponent. Whatever is said by the other party, the facts opposing that view can be assembled and put forward in a non-emotive manner and a response sought. The remorseless tabling of demands, supported by accurate knowledge will have a positive, conditioning effect. It will also engender confidence and persuade the other party to realise that the particular negotiation can be conducted in a spirit of factual exchange of information. This is the basis for sensible negotiations, leading to contractual agreements which have a high chance of being honoured.

Genuine business objectives

This method of negotiation demands integrity on both sides and accurate exchange of confidential information. It has, as its base, a genuine desire to form long-term trading relationships. It is not the usual type of negotiation which ensues between buyer and seller where each party is 'keeping something up their sleeves'. This is usually evidenced at a late stage in negotiation when one party says, 'let's put all our cards on the table'. The obvious implication being that up to that point something was being withheld, a position that does not inspire trust.

If this style of negotiation is to be pursued it does require an opening statement from the buyer which is quickly supported by action which demonstrates goodwill. When this is reciprocated by the seller the negotiations should then continue with a positive psychology. It is important, however, not to put all your 'cards on the table' until the seller has demonstrated their reciprocal goodwill. The creation of trust is a challenge.

16.3.2 The impact of time on negotiations

Time is a vital consideration when planning negotiations. Procurement specialists must ensure there is an appropriate context to:

- convince all those engaged in a procurement process that sufficient time must be provided to facilitate (if necessary) complex and prolonged negotiations
- prevent the other party engaging in procrastination and delaying tactics to put the buyer against a deadline, thereby preventing negotiation on difficult issues
- ensure that when negotiating overseas the buyer allows sufficient time to make return travel arrangements only when the objectives have been achieved
- ensure that the planned agenda is timed by topic, allowing sufficient time for active debate, review of positions and, for example, reworking cost models or redrafting contract clauses
- allow for respective decision making at executive level. It is not unusual for the outcome of negotiation to have to be approved at a senior level. In the public sector this could add at least a month to the procurement process
- prepare for the intervention of specialist advisers in a negotiation process, particularly lawyers, who are not noted for timely and speedy responses.

16.3.3 Influential factors

The author has modelled the factors influencing a complex Central Government procurement negotiation. This model is shown in Figure 16.4.

Figure 16.4 Factors influencing a complex Central Government procurement

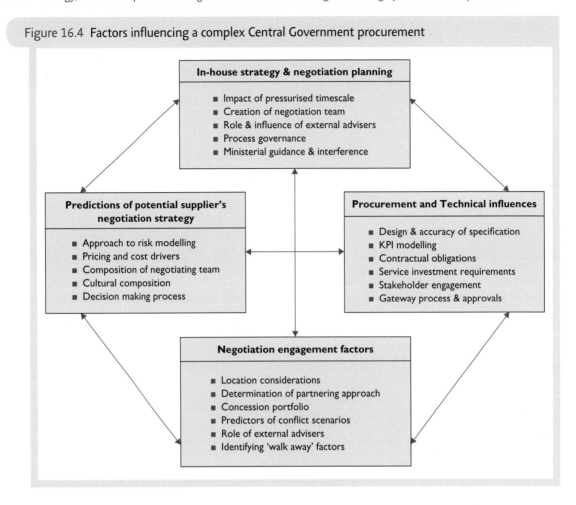

16.4 The negotiation process

Some negotiations concern a single issue and are relatively straightforward. A simple example is that of a product priced at, say, £9.70 each, when the buyer's objective is to purchase it at a price of, say, £8.30. All other aspects of the transaction may be agreed and it is the buyer's task to negotiate the lower price.

As shown by Figures 16.1, 16.2 and 16.3, other negotiations can be far more complicated and give rise to a multiplicity of issues relating to price, cost, contracts and delivery. Whether simple or complicated, however, the negotiation process will involve three phases: pre-negotiation, the actual negotiation and post-negotiation.

16.5 Pre-negotiation

'Cases are won in chambers' is the guiding principle in pre-negotiation – that is, legal victories are often the outcome of the preceding research and planning of strategy on the part of counsel. Buyers can learn much by studying the strategies and tactics of legal, diplomatic and industrial relations and applying them to the procurement field. The skilled negotiator will pay equal attention to all phases of negotiation which impact on the outcome. The early stages of negotiation, will, of course, be very important. The matters to be considered at the pre-negotiation stage include:

- who is to negotiate
- the venue
- intelligence gathering
- negotiation objectives
- strategy and tactics
- rehearsal.

16.5.1 Negotiating agenda

It is inconceivable that serious negotiations could be conducted without an agenda. The agenda serves many purposes, including, it:

- instils discipline into the planning process
- establishes the content of the specific negotiation meeting
- establishes the order in which points will be raised
- assists in control of the meeting
- demonstrates a professional approach
- conditions the attitude and response of the other party
- demands attention to time management
- assists in the clarity of roles when in a team negotiation.

Agendas can be overt and circulated in advance. They can also be covert and used as an aide-mémoire. In the latter situation it has the advantage of not displaying the potential scope of the negotiation. Each party will have their different perceptions, intended structures and objectives for a negotiation. The process must seek to accommodate both; otherwise it runs the risk of being unproductive.

When planning the agenda, the following checklist is relevant:

- Identify the range of subjects to be dealt with.
- Consider the sequence in which subjects will be raised.
- Predict the other party's likely subjects.
- Decide the starting and finishing time (the latter may not be disclosed).
- Predict the possible time each subject will take.
- Plan for breakout sessions.
- Decide who will chair the negotiation (lead negotiator role).
- Decide the specific roles of team members.
- If flexibility is required, how will this be accommodated?
- Do not forget the need to make notes and summarise agreements.
- Permit time at the end for other subjects to be raised.
- Agree the next actions and who is accountable for them.

16.5.2 Who is to negotiate

Negotiations can be between individual representatives or teams representing the buying and selling organisations respectively.

The individual approach

When negotiations are held between two individuals, both should normally have sufficient status to settle unconditionally without having to refer back to a higher authority other than in exceptional circumstances. The other party's authority must be established. If it emerges that they have no negotiation authority the meeting should be terminated, unless key information can be obtained which will later help the buyer.

The majority of rebuy and modified rebuy negotiations are conducted on an interpersonal basis. The challenge for the individual undertaking negotiation is the ability to ask a question, note or document the response and prepare to ask the next question. This is a demanding task.

The team approach

For complex negotiations, where, for example, technical, legal, financial and other issues are involved or for new buy or capital purchases, a team approach is preferred. An individual buyer is rarely capable of acting as sole negotiator in such situations.

In team negotiations it is important to:

- *allocate roles* – typical 'players' include:
  - the *spokesperson*, who actually presents the case and acts as captain of the team in terms of deciding how to respond to the situations arising in the course of the negotiation
  - the *recorder*, who takes notes of the negotiation
  - the *experts*, such as management accountants, engineers or other technical design or production staff, legal advisers, who provide back-up for the spokesperson – it is not essential for every member of the team to speak during negotiations in order to make a useful contribution to the negotiation.

- *avoid disagreement* – there should be no outward disagreement between team members while negotiations are in progress, so any differences should be resolved in private sessions, but the desirability of devising a code of signals, enabling team members to communicate imperceptibly during negotiations, should be considered to avoid having to wait to make a decision.

There are drawbacks to team negotiation. These include:

- *the tendency for groupthink*, that is, for team members to hold illusions of group invulnerability, stereotyped perceptions of perceived opponents and unquestioning belief in group morality
- *the emphasis on win–win* (Cox, A.[5]) is, unless modified by the spokesperson, greater in team negotiations as team members may wish to demonstrate their 'toughness', inflexibility and ability to demolish rather than consider the merits of proposals made by the other side, so the importance of the role of spokesperson on each side in setting the 'tone' of the negotiations cannot be overemphasised.

16.5.3 The venue

Buyers, traditionally expect the seller to attend the buyer's premises. Both parties are comfortable with this arrangement and that may be advantageous. Two other potential locations of the negotiation are the seller's site or a neutral third-party location such as a conference centre. The buyer may learn more about the seller and his operation by visiting his site. It is a tactic worth considering, mindful of time constraints. A neutral location may be appropriate for longer, complex negotiations particularly where the ethos of partnering is being explored – neither party would be on 'home turf'.

16.5.4 Gathering intelligence

This normally involves:

- ascertaining or predicting the strengths and weaknesses of the respective negotiating positions
- assembling relevant data relating to costs, production, sales and other relevant topics
- preparing data that is to be presented at the negotiation in the form of graphs, charts, tables so that it can be quickly assimilated.

Three important negotiation tools are:

1 price and cost analysis (see section 11.7)

2 situational analysis (see section 16.9)

3 value analysis (see section 8.11.3).

16.5.5 Determining objectives

The negotiator/negotiating team must understand the varying interests of participants in a negotiation. The author has used his experience to illustrate the varying interest on a defence contract project. These differing interests are shown in Figure 16.5.

Players in a negotiation process will have both cooperative and competitive characteristics. Sensitivity to the goals of other players by all participants will set the tone of

Figure 16.5 **Varying interests of participants in negotiations relating to defence contract project**

Ministry of Defence	Ministers of the State	Manufacturer	Suppliers/ Contractors	Operational accountability officers
■ Long-term cost ■ Reliability ■ Safety ■ Build milestones ■ Contract obligations ■ Co-located design	■ Publicity ■ Risk of failure ■ Cost ■ Involvement ■ Secrecy ■ Project approval	■ Resources ■ Funding ■ Cash Flow ■ Obligations ■ Profitability ■ Risk profile	■ Project certainty ■ Risk profile ■ Corporate advantage ■ Profit ■ Strategic positioning ■ Positive publicity	■ Availability of spares ■ MTTR/MTBF ■ Operational Support ■ Emergency contacts ■ Environmental ■ Operational cost

negotiations and contribute to planned outcomes, including win-win. A model of bar-gaining applicable to negotiations relating to procurement issues is shown in Figure 16.6. Thus, assuming that the negotiation relates to a pricing issue:

- axis A–B represents the range of positions that the negotiators could take
- IS_B represents the buyer's ideal settlement – the most favourable price that can, real-istically, be achieved in negotiation – that is, £5
- IS_V represents the vendor's ideal settlement which is £13.

(*Note*: In most cases, IS will represent the starting position of each of the negotiators, subject, of course, to the fact that, if there is to be negotiation, the initial demands must not be too far apart to preclude bargaining.)

- RS_B is the buyer's realistic settlement – here, about £8 – or that point of settlement fully justified by bargaining power that would be reached with reasonable skill in negotiation and no adverse, unforeseen circumstances
- RS_V is the vendor's realistic settlement – around £10
- FBP_B is the buyer's fallback position – around £10 – or the price beyond which they will not go; after this point, they break off negotiations or seek alternative means of meeting their requirements
- FBP_V is the vendor's fallback position – around £8
- the shaded portion represents the area of settlement and this model is based on the con-vention that each side will normally be prepared to move from their original positions, so the negotiated price will typically be between £8 and £10, depending on the skills of the negotiators and assuming that the bargaining positions are approximately equal.

Figure 16.6 **A model of bargaining in a purchasing context**

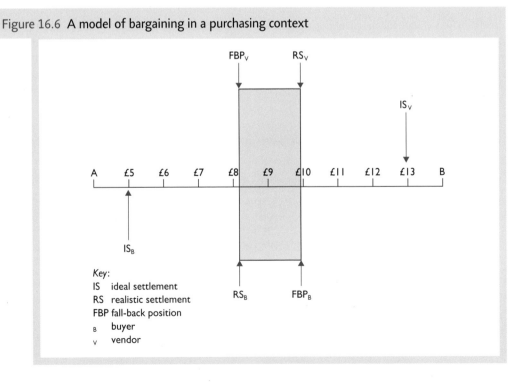

Before commencing negotiations, the buyer should have a clear mandate from his or her superiors to settle at any point not exceeding an agreed fallback position. It is important to stress the importance of determining in advance what a *good* agreement is. Too often, negotiators consider that their goal is to arrive at *an* agreement or even *any* agreement. They should therefore determine what is their own and what is likely to be the other side's BATNA. A BATNA is the 'best alternative to a negotiated agreement' – a concept introduced by Fisher and Ury.[6]

While BATNAs and fallback or reserve positions are similar in many respects, they are not the same. For example, if you are trying to outsource your catering function, the BATNA may be to continue to provide this facility in-house.

16.5.6 Negotiation strategy and tactics

Strategy is the overall plan that aims to achieve, as nearly as possible, the objectives of the negotiation as seen from the perspective of each participant. A *tactic* is a position, manoeuvre or attitude to be taken or adopted at an appropriate point in the negotiation process. Among the tactics to be decided are the following:

- The order in which the issues to be negotiated shall be dealt with.
- Whether to speak first or allow the other side to open the negotiations. Galinsky[7] states that 'substantial psychological research suggests that, more often than not, negotiators who make first offers come out ahead' and suggests that 'making a first offer is related to one's confidence and sense of control at the bargaining table.' The same writer, however, suggests that making the first offer may not be advantageous when the other side has much more information about the item to be negotiated or the relevant market or industry than they do. This situation can be remedied by information gathering prior to the negotiation so that a more level playing field is achieved.
- Whether to build in recesses for discussion. Recesses may cause a negotiation to lose its momentum. Conversely, recesses provide opportunities for reflection on the negotiation so far, for devising new or alternative proposals and sometimes for 'cooling down' and face-saving.
- What concessions to make should the need arise? Some writers suggest that negotiators should only make concessions in return for trade-offs – that is, they should seek to get something in return for everything they concede.
- The timing of concessions.
- What issues can be linked, such as price and quality.
- What the other party's likely reaction will be to each tactic you're thinking of using.
- What tactics the opponent is likely to adopt and how these can be countered.

16.5.7 Rehearsal

Before an important negotiation, it is advisable to subject all arguments, tactics and overall strategies to critical scrutiny. The negotiator will have prepared and indeed may have rehearsed the 'opening speech' which will be made when the negotiation opens. This is a crucial conditioning statement and should include clarity of the benefits of the contract on offer, the fact that the seller must deal with each point as requested and a summary of the contract and its intended operation. The negotiator must prepare and create an environment within which the negotiation will take place. It is possible to create a hostile or relaxed atmosphere, and either party may influence this by actions and words.

16.6 The actual negotiation

16.6.1 Stages

Even with a philosophy of collaborative negotiation, the activities of the participants will change at each stage of the negotiation process. These activities alternate between competition and cooperation. It is useful for a negotiator to recognise this pattern of interaction and the stage that has been reached in a particular negotiation. At this time the following points will be relevant:

- Recap, from time to time, on points that have been agreed and make an appropriate record.
- If there has been a time lapse between negotiations, the negotiator must make a résumé of action points outstanding from the last meeting. If information has not been generated by the other side as agreed, it must be sought, ideally prior to the meeting.
- The negotiator must ensure that there has been no major change in the other party's circumstances since the last meeting. This will require some due diligence and research.
- If the other party tables new information, or retracts previously agreed points, a recess must be called to evaluate the new position but only when the detail is understood.
- If any costs or prices change the buyer must check the new calculations. The seller's interpretation must not be accepted without checking and confirming.
- Take the initiative by making proposals for the other side to consider. If the seller takes the initiative be mindful that it has happened and make counter demands.
- Whenever the buyer makes a concession its value to the other party must be calculated. It should be noted that the value to the other party is not necessarily the cost to the buyer.
- Try to link previously unconnected points. If the seller seeks a contractual concession, the buyer should look for the corresponding price change.
- Know your walk-away point, where you are prepared for the negotiations to cease. This cannot be a bluff!
- If the negotiation is failing with the seller's negotiators, it may be necessary to request a change in personnel to make progress. This can be done by escalating the negotiations to a higher level in the sellers' business.
- Control your emotions at all times. If a negotiation becomes personal there is a danger that there will be a lack of focus.
- Try to recognise when the seller is bluffing and entering into brinkmanship.
- Acknowledge positively concessions made and allow a loss of face. This behaviour may motivate more concessions.
- Be mindful of unwittingly creating contractual agreement.

The stages that occur during negotiation are indicated in Figure 16.7.

Figure 16.7 **The stages in the negotiating process**

> *Introductions, agreement of an agenda and rules of procedure*
>
> *Ascertaining the 'negotiating range'*
> This means the issues that the negotiation will attempt to resolve
> With *adversarial* negotiations, this may be a lengthy stage as the
> participants often overstate their opening positions
> With *collaborative* negotiations, 'openness saves time'
>
> *Agreement of common goals that must be achieved if the negotiation is to reach
> a successful outcome*
> This will usually require some movement on both sides from the original
> negotiating range, but the movement will be less or unnecessary in
> partnership negotiations
>
> *Identification of and, when possible, removal of barriers that prevent
> attainment of agreed common goals*
> At this stage there will be:
> - problem solving
> - consideration of solutions put forward by each
> - determination of what concessions can be made
>
> It may also be useful to:
> - review what has been agreed
> - allow a recess for each side to reconsider its position and make
>   proposals or concessions that may enable further progress to be made
> If no progress can be made, it may be decided to:
> - refer the issues back to higher management
> - change the negotiators
> - abandon the negotiations with the least possible damage to relationships
>
> *Agreement and closure*
> Drafting of a statement setting out as clearly as possible the agreement(s)
> reached and circulating it to all parties for comment and signature

16.6.2 Techniques

Specialist books of negotiation usually list a number of techniques available to negotiators. It is not possible to detail these in this book, although a more detailed description of Fisher and Ury's approach is given in section 16.10. Some general findings include the following:

- In framing an agenda, ensure that the more difficult issues appear later, thus enabling some agreement to be reached early in the negotiation on less controversial matters, smoothing the way to agreement on less straightforward points.

- Questions are a means of both eliciting information and keeping pressure on an opponent and can also be used to control the pattern and progress of the negotiation.

- Concessions are a means of securing movement when negotiations are deadlocked. Research findings show that 'losers' tend to make the first concession and that each concession tends to raise the aspirational level of the opponent, so buyers should avoid a 'pattern of concession' in which they are forced to concede more and more. The convention is that concessions should be reciprocated. While flexibility is essential, there is no compulsion to make a counter-concession and the aim should be to concede less than has been obtained. The outcome tends to be more favourable when the concessions made are small rather than large. An experienced negotiator will often 'throw a sprat to catch a mackerel.'

■ Negotiation is between people, so it is essential to be able to weigh up the personalities of one's opponents and the drivers that motivate them, such as achievement, fear and similar factors.

16.6.3 Deadlocked negotiations

Negotiations sometimes come to an impasse when both sides see no prospect of further movement or concessions. Techniques for resolving such deadlock include those suggested by Fisher and Ury's concept of principled negotiation (see section 16.10).

Other approaches to such situations include:

■ taking a break for each party to refocus
■ lightening the atmosphere by the use of humour
■ breaking down an issue into sub-issues
■ agreeing to 'agree in principle' – if the parties agree in principle, they also agree on objectives
■ considering the consequences of non-agreement for the parties concerned
■ obtaining third-party assistance as they can listen objectively to arguments, clarify issues and, where required, adjudicate.

The degree of third-party involvement can vary.

Not every situation can be negotiated. For example, the decision of a contractor to refuse to work in situations that might put them in breach of Health and Safety Regulations or expose their employees to physical danger, such as from violent protests or terrorists, has to be accepted.

16.6.4 Negotiating behaviour

All negotiations involve interpersonal skills. The negotiating styles that are applicable vary according to the specific situation. Training in negotiation should, therefore, include training in behaviour analysis, which should lead to an understanding of the responses likely to be evoked by particular behaviour. For example, shouting usually causes the other person to shout back, while humour may diffuse a tense situation.

Lee and Lawrence[8] have identified seven categories of behaviour, all of which may be encountered in negotiations (see Table 16.2).

16.6.5 Effects of behaviour on other parties

The main fact that the negotiator can learn from the generalisations given in Table 16.2 is that our outward behaviour must be arranged to have the desired effect on those with whom we are negotiating. The desired effect depends on the negotiator's goals. Thus, development behaviour is more likely than emotional disagreement to persuade the

Table 16.2 Types of behaviour and likely responses to them

Types of behaviour	Likely response
Proposing behaviour Such as suggesting actions: 'Shall we look at sub-contracting?'	Usually elicits either development behaviour in the form of support or reasoned negative behaviour in the form of difficulty solving
Development behaviour Such as building on or supporting proposals made by others: 'Having decided to sub-contract, who shall we approach?'	Usually leads to further development behaviour or, perhaps, a question in return, asking for further explanation
Reasoned negative behaviour Such as disagreeing with others in a reasoned way, stating difficulties with their ideas: 'Price is likely to be a difficulty because their material costs don't attract our quantity discounts'	Tends to evoke similar negative behaviour in response, leading to a downward spiral in terms of communications and emotions. This spiral can be avoided by stating difficulties and identifying differences as reasonably as possible, perhaps by asking further questions
Emotional negative behaviour Such as attacking others, being critical, defending against attacks in the same way: 'Rubbish'	In general, attack begets either attack or defence. It can make resumption of constructive negotiation difficult
Clarifying behaviour Such as checking whether or not people understand, summarising previous discussion: 'As I see it, this is what we agreed'	Tends to lead to supportive development behaviour, although there can be disagreement
Seeking information behaviour Such as seeking facts, opinions, ideas: 'How much discount if we doubled the quantity?' 'What if . . . '	This almost always results in information being given. The certainty of response makes this a powerful shaping behaviour
Giving information behaviour Such as giving facts, opinions, ideas: 'We need to reach a decision today'	This is usually a response to other behaviour, especially seeking information. It is uncertain in its effect, as it depends largely on the content of the statement

other party to accept our viewpoint. Providing and giving information is indispensable to influencing a group. Sometimes it is better to begin a negotiation by asking questions than giving information about the subject matter.

16.6.6 Ploys

A *ploy* is a manoeuvre in a negotiation aimed at achieving a particular result. This is a complex aspect of negotiation, requiring specific application to meet the needs of a particular negotiation. This section deals with some common issues encountered in buyer–seller negotiations.

1 Priority of demands

Having pre-determined the range of demands there is a key decision to be made regarding which one shall be tabled first. It could be argued that demanding a rather simple concession which does not carry great financial burden will persuade the seller to make that concession, whereas if a large concession is sought first this will motivate resistance and, possible, continued intransigence. If there are absolute 'must haves' these should be raised first because if these cannot be agreed everything else is a relative waste of time.

2 Managing timescales

It is imperative that the buyer fully understands all the implications of the timescales being dealt with. There are occasions when a contract must be in place by a specific date, sometimes very urgently. The buyer must ensure that the time and resources are available, on both sides to cope with the timescale. It may require continuous negotiations until agreement is reached.

3 Use of jargon

Every profession has its jargon and sellers will use it to test the buyer's knowledge. It can also be used to undermine the buyer's confidence. It is used as a quite deliberate ploy. If jargon is used and the term is not known, clarification must be sought, although the more times this is necessary by the buyer the more credibility is being lost. As this is being written the author is dealing with a situation where a seller said 'Our EBITDA is very good.' If you were on the receiving end of this statement what would be your response?

4 Use of figures

It is inevitable that many negotiations will relate to cost and related financial data. The buyer must be alert when 'numbers' change in any context. An important rule is to always check figures given by a seller. If they offer a complicated discount structure and say, 'The net effect of this offer is $250,000.' No assumption must be made that this is correct. It is professional to respond by saying, 'Thank you, I will through my own calculations confirm your amount.'

5 Handling objections

The seller will have prepared and rehearsed responses to predictable buyer demands. These will come in the form of objections. The ideal counter from the buyer is a range of tactics which use logical persuasion as the basis for a request, where each demand can be explained in a business-like manner. For example, if the buyer asks for liquidated damages and the seller says 'We do not typically offer that.' The buyer's response could be 'Your company has given us a delivery date, which is acceptable. It is rational for us to be compensated if you do not meet your own date. Do you agree?'.

6 Use of silence

This will cause problems to the inexperienced negotiator. The skilled seller will, upon receiving a demand which he does not wish to accept, fail to respond. The silence can be overwhelming and embarrassing. The danger is that the buyer will break the silence and change the subject or soften the demand. This relieves the seller of a responsibility to respond to the initial demand and weakens the buyer's position. The buyer must cope with silence and be aware that it is being used as a ploy.

16.6.7 Considerations at the concluding stage of negotiations

Depending upon the length of time the negotiations have been in progress, there is the danger of a lack of focus on progress being made. This is a risk because it is precisely at this time that concentration and mental facilities must be at their highest. The following factors are relevant:

- Ensure that progress is related to the objectives that you set. Ensure that the buyer's resolve has not waned due to the seller's conditioning with such tactics as blocking progress and refusing to concede major points.

- Determine and confirm the financial implications of all actions and agreements reached.

- Summarise the total agreement and test this on the other side. If there is a disagreement of fundamental points they must be discussed and resolved.

- Maintain pressure on the other party for any remaining concessions that you require.

- Listen for attempts to 'close the sale' by the seller. This takes courage on their part and usually means they are confident that no more concessions are required.

- Be prepared to make additional demands if an opportunity presents itself, even if they had not been planned.

- When it is appropriate (this is a matter of judgment) make a statement of the buyer's final position.

- Explain the contract award process.

- Explain to the other party that all agreements reached and changes to quotations/tender documents must be evidenced in writing. This may be in the form of a Best and Final Offer.

- Confirm the basis of contract reporting and monitoring.

- Maintain the audit trail of hard and electronic copy of notes of negotiations.

- Arrange for later debriefing of unsuccessful tenderers.

- Undertake a personal evaluation of opportunities lost, successes and mistakes made in the negotiation. Transfer the learning to colleagues for future benefits.

- List the benefits obtained and evaluate if they could be transferred to other sellers and product groups.

16.7 Post-negotiation actions

This involves:

- drafting a commentary detailing as clearly as possible the agreements reached and circulating it to all in-house parties including stakeholders for comment and sign off

- implementing the agreements, such as contract establishment, setting up joint implementation teams, performance review and continuous improvement events through the life of the contract.

- establishing processes for monitoring the implementation of the agreement and dealing with any problems and interpretation that may arise.

16.8 What is effective negotiation?

16.8.1 Characteristics

An effective negotiation may be said to have taken place when:

- substance issues have been satisfactorily resolved – that is, an agreement has been reached that is acceptable to all parties

- working relationships are preserved or even enhanced.

Fisher and Ury[9] have identified the following three criteria for an effective negotiation:

■ the negotiation has produced a *wise agreement* – one that is satisfactory for both sides
■ the negotiation is *efficient* – no more time-consuming or costly than necessary
■ the negotiation is *harmonious* – fosters rather than inhibits good interpersonal relationships.

16.8.2 Negotiation post-mortems

Many organisations hold in-house post-negotiation meetings for the purpose of discussing:

■ *negotiating strategies and tactics* – the extent to which they were satisfactory and how they might be improved
■ *negotiating costs* – the number and duration of negotiating sessions and how these may be reduced
■ *negotiating methods* – the extent to which personal contact was necessary and the use of electronic aids were applied
■ *people considerations* – the impact made by the negotiator(s) and whether escalation was required to more senior people, and, if so, the benefits that accrued
■ *the procurement process prior to negotiation* – for example, the impact on events of the quotation/tender process and resolving genuine clarifications from potential bidders.

16.9 Negotiation and relationships

16.9.1 Situational and institutional approaches

Ertel[10] states that only rarely do companies think about their negotiating activities as a whole:

> Rather they take a situational view, seeing each negotiation as a separate event, with its own goals, its own tactics and its own measures of success. That approach can produce good results in particular instances, but it can be counterproductive when viewed from a higher, more strategic plane. Hammering out advantageous terms in a procurement contract may torpedo an important long-term relationship with a supplier.

16.10 Negotiation ethics

Negotiation ethics is an aspect of the wider subject of procurement ethics, considered in Chapter 19, and relationships, covered above. This topic is considered here because ethical perspectives largely determine whether or not a particular negotiation is adversarial or integrative.

Fisher and Ury[11] distinguish between positional and principled negotiation.

16.10.1 Positional negotiation

Positional negotiation views negotiation as an adversarial or conflict situation in which the other party is the enemy. It is based on four assumptions:

■ we have the correct and only answer to a particular problem
■ there is a 'fixed price'

- opposite positions equal opposite interests
- it is not our responsibility to solve the problems of the other party.

Positions and interests are closely related. Often negotiators will not move from a fixed position because of psychological pressures or needs. A leader of a negotiating team may refuse to consider alternatives for fear of losing face or being seen by team members as backing down.

Positional negotiation has at least two drawbacks:

- it is win–lose – it has only two ways to go, which are forwards to victory or backwards to defeat
- from an ethical standpoint, positional negotiation leads to such questionable tactics as:
  - misrepresentation of a position
  - bluffing
  - lying or deception
  - only providing selected information or being economical with the truth
  - threatening
  - manipulating.

16.10.2 Principled negotiation

Principled negotiation is fundamentally different from positional negotiation. The very term 'principled' has an ethical connotation. Fisher and Ury criticise positional negotiating on four grounds:

- *arguing about positions produces unwise agreements* – compromising, for example, involves both parties giving up something, so neither is completely satisfied with the outcome
- *arguing about positions is unwise* – time is wasted in trying to reconcile extreme positions
- *ongoing relationships are endangered* – anger and resentment result when one side sees itself as being forced to bend to the rigid will of the other
- *positional bargaining is worse when there are many partners* – it is harder to change group or constituency positions than those of individuals.

Fisher and Ury also see principled bargaining as an alternative to 'hard' or 'soft' bargaining. Soft bargainers may make concessions to cultivate or maintain relationships. Hard bargainers demand concessions as a condition of the relationship.

16.10.3 The Fisher and Ury principles

Apart from 'Don't bargain about positions', Fisher and Ury lay down four elements that parties must follow to obtain an ideal settlement:

1 Separate the people from the problem

This involves viewing the problem as the central issue to be resolved rather than regarding the other person as an adversary. Failure to do so can lead to antagonism between the parties. Fisher and Ury put forward 18 propositions under the four headings of perception, emotion, communication and prevention, of which the following are typical.

- *Perception*
  - put yourself in the other party's shoes
  - don't blame the other party for your problem
  - discuss each other's perceptions
  - look for opportunities to act inconsistently with their perceptions.
- *Emotion*
  - first, recognise and understand emotions – theirs and yours
  - allow the other side to let off steam
  - don't react to emotional outbursts.
- *Communication*
  - listen actively and acknowledge what is being said
  - speak about how you feel, not how you feel about them.
- *Prevention*
  - where possible, build pre-negotiation relationships that will enable parties to absorb the knocks incurred in the actual negotiation.

2 Focus on interests, not positions

Positions are symbolic representations of a participant's underlying interests. Each side has multiple needs. To find out about interests, ask 'Why?' and 'Why not?' questions.

3 Invent options for mutual gain

Again, Fisher and Ury classify their approaches under five headings – diagnosis, prescription, broadening options, searching for mutual gain and facilitating the other party's decisions.

- *Diagnosis*

  This includes avoiding:
  - premature judgments
  - searching for a single answer
  - assuming a 'fixed price'.
- *Prescription*
  - separating inventing from deciding
  - engaging in brainstorming, including brainstorming with the other party.
- *Broadening options*
  - look through the eyes of different experts
  - invent agreements of different strengths, such as substantive versus procedural, permanent versus provisional and so on.
- *Searching for mutual gain*
  - identify shared interests
  - dovetail differing interests.

■ *Facilitating the other party's decision*

  – help the other party to sell a decision to his/her constituency
  – look for precedents
  – provide a range of options.

4 Insist on using objective criteria

This requires:

■ fair standards, such as objective criteria, including market value, professional or moral standards, legal criteria, custom and practice

■ fair procedures for resolving conflicting interests

■ reasoning and openness to reasoning

■ never yielding to pressure, only to principle.

16.10.4 Criticisms of principled negotiation

A number of criticisms have been made of principled negotiation, some of which Fisher and Ury recognise. Thus, where the other party has some negotiating advantage, they suggest that the answer is to improve your BATNA. The only reason we negotiate is to produce something better than the results we could obtain without negotiating. BATNAs offer protection against accepting terms that are too unfavourable and rejecting terms that it would be beneficial to accept.

Where the other party will not play or uses dirty tricks, the answer is to insist on principled negotiation in a way that is most acceptable to the competitor. Thus, principled negotiators might ask about the other party's concerns to show that they understand such concerns and ask the competitor to recognise all concerns.

Where the other party refuses to respond, two techniques to try are those of 'negotiation jujitsu', in which, instead of directly resisting the force of the other party, it is channelled into exploring interests, inventing options and searching for independent standards, and using outside intervention or mediation.

McCarthy[12] offers two main criticisms of the Fisher and Ury approach. The first is that it does not provide an adequate analysis of the role of power. The concept of negotiation jujitsu, for example, does not actually turn power back on the other party, but encourages both to ignore dirty tricks and minor power plays. McCarthy holds that the balance of power between the two parties is the key element in determining the limits of a mutually acceptable settlement and concludes 'in the area of collective bargaining at least I know of no set of maxims or principles that will enable any of us to escape from the limits set by a given power situation.'

McCarthy's second point is that Fisher and Ury assume rather than argue that the factors that make for effective negotiation in widely differing situations from domestic quarrels to international disputes are the same. There may be situations in which positional is preferable to principled negotiation.

16.10.5 Can negotiation be ethical?

Arguments that negotiation cannot be completely ethical include:

■ the belief that success in negotiation is enhanced by the use of deceitful tactics, such as bluffing and outright misrepresentation

- negotiators have the responsibility and pressure of obtaining the best results for those they represent
- what is ethical is affected by cultural factors, such as bribery and deception that may be acceptable in some global negotiations, that 'When in Rome, do as the Romans do'
- self-interest is the most powerful of all motivations – few negotiations can be wholly altruistic
- ethical negotiation is an idealistic concept that does not work in practice
- sharing information may put a negotiator at a disadvantage.

Crampton and Dees[13] list a number of reasons for it being possible to gain from deceptive tactics:

- information asymmetry is great – the greater the information disparity between the two parties, the greater the opportunity one has for profitable deception
- verification of such details as long-term maintenance costs and performance is difficult
- the intention to deceive is difficult to establish – it is hard to distinguish it from a mistake or an oversight
- the parties have insufficient resources to adequately safeguard against deception
- interaction between the parties is infrequent – deception is more likely in one-off relationships
- ex-post redress is too costly – the deceived party may, however, prefer to make an effort, even when the costs exceed the expected compensation
- reputable information is unavailable, unreliable or very costly to communicate
- the circumstances are unusual in a way that limits inferences about future behaviour and deceptions are unlikely to damage future negotiations because they occur in distinctly different circumstances
- one party has little to lose (or much to gain) from deception – a negotiator may not be concerned about the prospect of being caught, providing that it does not occur before the deal has been closed.

Crampton and Dees state that they cannot recommend a single strategy that will work effectively to promote honesty in all negotiations, but they make the following suggestions:

- *Assess the situation* – this involves considering the incentives for deception. What incentives are there for suppressing or misrepresenting information? What is known about the principles of the other side? What is the competence and character of the other side?
- *Build mutual trust* – in most cases, the incentive for deception in negotiation is defensive. It arises from the fear that the other party will unfairly exploit any weakness. This also involves building mutual benevolence, creating opportunities for displaying trust and demonstrating trustworthiness.
- *Place the negotiation in a long-term context. Caveat emptor* is reasonable advice for negotiators. Select negotiating partners wisely, verify when you can, request bonds and warranties, get important claims in writing and, where applicable, such as in IT and outsourcing negotiations, it may be advisable to hire a skilled intermediary.

Ethical negotiation can only take place in a climate of trust. Ascertaining whether or not such a climate exists requires negotiators to answer two questions – 'Can the other party trust us?' and 'Can we trust them?' Each party can answer the first question with some certainty, although they should be aware of self-deception. Not until both sides have established a working relationship can a certain answer be given to the second question. In the interim, both sides should show diligence in obtaining information to provide assurance that the other party will negotiate ethically.

Discussion questions

16.1 In a negotiation, each party knows that the other has some power to influence the outcome. What powers have:
   (a) a Council buying a branded IT system?
   (b) an international airline buying aviation fuel?
   (c) a monopoly seller and a customer in a price negotiation?

16.2 If you were asked to negotiate a contract to purchase IT software what would be your top five 'must haves' in terms of contractual obligations on the supplier?

16.3 A supplier refuses to provide a 'fixed price' for a piece of equipment. They insist on an 'ROM' (Rough Order of Magnitude) price that will be finalised when the equipment has been manufactured. How would you plan to deal with this issue in the negotiation?

16.4 Can you identify three reasons why some negotiations fail?

16.5 Who is the best negotiator you know? What are their distinguishing personal qualities?

16.6 How does an effective negotiator ensure they have sufficient time to complete the negotiations?

16.7 You have been asked to negotiate with the second highest priced supplier in a tender process. Their sales director attends the meeting and immediately says, 'Do not even mention the price because we will not change it.' What are your response options?

16.8 The use of 'power and coercion' is a potential negotiation strategy. Under what circumstances could you see it being used?

16.9 Suggest five ways in which to resolve a deadlock in a negotiation.

16.10 Discuss the following statements:
   (a) 'Once you consent to some concession, you can never cancel it and put things back the way they were'
   (b) 'We cannot negotiate with those who say "What's mine is mine, what's yours is negotiable"' (John F. Kennedy)
   (c) 'Flattery is the infantry of negotiation' (Lord Chandos)
   (d) 'Always define your terms' (Eric Partridge).

References

[1] Rubin, J. Z. and Brown, B. R., *The Social Psychology of Bargaining and Negotiation*, Academic Press, New York, USA, 1975.

[2] Gottschal, R. A. W., 'The background to the negotiating process' in Torrington, D., *Code of Personnel Management*, Gower, Aldershot, UK, 1979.

3 Lysons, C. K., Modified version of definition in *Purchasing*, 3rd edn, Pitman, London, 1993.

4 Fisher, R. and Ury, W., *Getting to Yes*, Penguin, London, UK, 1983.

5 Cox, A., *Win-win*, Earlsgate Press, Stratford-upon-Avon, UK, 2004.

6 As 4 above.

7 Galinsky, A. D., *Negotiation Strategy: Should You Make the First Offer?* Harvard Business School, Boston, UK, 2004.

8 Lee, R. and Lawrence, P., *Organisational Behaviour: Politics at Work*, Hutchinson, London, UK, 1988, p. 182.

9 As 4 above.

10 Ertel, D., 'Turning negotiation into a corporate capability', *Harvard Business Review*, May–June, 1999, pp. 55–70.

11 As 4 above.

12 McCarthy, W., 'The role of power and principle in getting to yes', in Breslin, J. W. and Rubin, J. Z., *Negotiation Theory and Practice*, Cambridge University Press, Cambridge, UK, 1991, pp. 115–22.

13 Crampton, P. C. and Dees, J. G., 'Promoting honesty in negotiation', *Journal of Business Ethics*, March, 2002, pp. 1–28.

Chapter 17

Contract management

Learning outcomes

This chapter aims to provide an understanding of:

- the pre-contract award activities impact on contract management
- the contract manager's role, skills and knowledge
- contract management good practice
- contract management plans
- key performance indicators (KPIs) for contract management
- lapses in contract management
- Social Services contract monitoring audit
- contract provisions
- contract clauses and what they mean.

Key ideas

- The importance of contract management to business success.
- The breadth of scope of contract management.
- The skills and knowledge that is required.
- Effectiveness of contract management plans.
- Why specifications are a vital consideration
- Dealing with lapses in contract management.
- Ensuring contract performance is beyond reproach.
- Actions at contract commencement.
- Continuing contract management actions.
- Understanding the provisions of contract clauses.
- Contract management is a disciplined business approach.

Introduction

The emphasis of this chapter is the post contract award actions and decisions that should occur to ensure the contractual obligations are met by the supplier. Contract management, for many reasons to be explored in this chapter, is often an inadequate activity. There are, potentially, many reasons for this including:

- lack of investment in contract management
- a failure to ensure contract managers have appropriate skills and knowledge
- a failure to consider contract management at the pre-contract award phases
- inadequate provision of Management Information by suppliers/contractors
- inadequate contract reviews
- lack of knowledge about Key Performance Indicators
- lack of detailed knowledge of the contract
- a failure to manage contract change
- inadequate supplier relationship management
- lack of attention to risk management
- failure to inculcate a desire for continuous improvement
- lack of engagement with stakeholders
- failure to take decisive action when contract default occurs.

The World Bank[1] states that

> Effective Contract Management is critical for ensuring the supplier/contractor/consultant, and the Borrower meet their contractual commitments to time, cost, quality and other agreed matters. It requires systematic and efficient planning, execution, monitoring and evaluation to ensure that both parties fulfil their contractual obligations with the ultimate goal of achieving VFM and contractual results.

The scope of contract management is shown in Figure 17.1 below:

A careful scrutiny of the scope of contract management demonstrates that the contract manager's role is far more than administration and routine. It requires intellect, high personal values, commitment to detail, business acumen and an astute knowledge of contractual detail.

The four components of contract management[2] are shown in Figures 17.2 and 17.3.

17.1 The pre-contract award activities impact on contract management

Contract management must not be viewed as only commencing when a contract award has been made. The author has engaged in many procurements that have given early procurement process careful thought to the contract management activity, taking into account:

1 *The complexity of the contract.* This is a key determinant of the skills and knowledge required from the contract manager. There may be complex specifications and cost

Figure 17.1 **The scope of contract management**

models, interfaces between contractors, a need for complex relationship management and coping with an array of stakeholders.

2 *The contract performance regime* There may be a demanding contract performance regime involving many KPIs together with a contractor's obligation to deliver continuous improvement. This latter requirement may be linked to incentive payments.

3 *The resources and cost of contract management* Sufficient resources must be allocated to the contract management activity. The cost of contract management will need to be circa 10 per cent of the contract price on complex contracts. It should be recognised that the contractor will allocate sufficient contract management resources because they will be accountable for profit that is derived from the contract, and, in some instances, ensuring the scope and cost of the contract increases.

4 *Managing future contract risks* The tender stage must identify future risks and develop risk mitigation strategies that will have to be constantly reviewed by the contract manager. This must include the risks that are the responsibility of the buying organisation, as set out in their contract obligations.

Figure 17.2 **The four components of contract management**

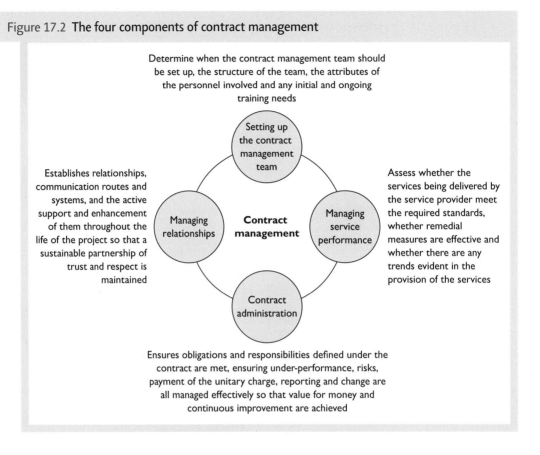

17.2 The contract manager's role, skills and knowledge

The contract manager's role, skills and knowledge were adequately set out by 4ps.[3] The contract manager plays a key role in developing relationships with the service provider and monitoring the service provider's performance, and therefore is a critical appointment. As such, the appointment is likely to be full-time and will take account of the risk and complexity of the project. The contract manager is required to:

■ have clarity of his/her role, levels of delegated authority and reporting lines

■ be empowered to make decisions to enable the contract to successfully operate on a daily basis

■ have the requisite seniority and experience to reflect the level of delegated authority and complexity of the project

■ have the appropriate skills and experience in contract management

■ have the ability to lead a team – which may be multi-disciplinary

■ communicate effectively with all members of the contract management team, Partnering Board, stakeholders, users and the wider community

■ put in place an appropriate contract management methodology and risk register

Figure 17.3 The four components of contract management – key tasks

Setting up the contract management team	Managing relationships	Managing service performance	Contract administration
When should contract management commence?	Identification and development of good partnership working	Why should service performance be monitored and measured?	The payment mechanism
Determine the contract management team structure	Development of partnership protocols and behaviours	The fundamentals of performance measurement	Dealing with disputes
Determining and securing the resources required for contract management	Defining communication protocols, routes and systems	Working with the service provider to mobilise services	Variations to the contract
Job profiles, skills, and competencies required for contract management	Overcoming relationship difficulties	Monthly performance monitoring processes and payment	Benchmarking and market testing
Identifying the initial and ongoing training requirements	Developing successful relationships	Monitoring the provision of the services	Contract administration Checklists

Payment mechanism checklist |
| Ensuring continuity of the contract management function | Practical problem and dispute resolution | Tools for measuring performance – helpdesk | Benchmarking market testing checklist

Dispute resolution checklist |
| Setting up the contract management team checklist | Managing relationships checklist | Managing service performance checklist | Service variation checklist |

- put in place an appropriate performance monitoring and audit system
- oversee and ensure the service provider mobilises effectively and on programme
- keep the output specification and method statements up-to-date
- form a good, long-term, sustainable relationship with the service provider
- ensure that service standards are provided and maintained and have day to day links with the service provider
- monitor the service provider's ongoing performance and service delivery

- agree monthly payments/deductions to the service provider
- ensure Best Value is obtained
- identify key trends in the service delivery and the service provider's performance
- ensure remedial measures for improving service delivery are implemented when required, and monitor the service provider's approach to rectifying non-compliance
- manage changes in legislation within the contract
- manage variations, benchmarking, market testing and change
- monitor and manage risk
- be responsible for the ongoing training requirements of the contract management team
- deal with disputes and default
- ensure the contract remains up-to-date with changes and variations agreed
- provide quality assurance
- undertake business planning with the service provider, looking for opportunities to enhance delivery and improve value for money
- review service specifications on a periodic basis
- network with other local authorities to understand and share best practice
- review exit strategy and handback procedures.

The main skills and knowledge for the contract manager and the contract management team collectively are:
Skills, attitude and experience

- demonstrates strong leadership skills
- has good people skills (interpersonal and management)
- has a partnering 'win: win' ethos for relationship management
- has a positive outlook and attitude and is proactive
- demonstrates effective negotiating skills
- is able to manage relationships successfully and resolve conflict
- is able to manage users and their demands
- is able to work effectively with a team
- is able to plan resource requirements effectively
- exercises good judgment, based on experience and sound analysis
- has experience in managing complex services
- has experience in performing contract monitoring
- can establish processes for monitoring performance
- has the ability to anticipate and respond to future business needs
- possesses well-developed analytical skills
- has good organisational and QA skills
- has a realistic and practical approach to change and innovation
- is able to develop strategies to meet changing contractual needs

- is able to apply contract management procedures
- is able to evaluate and control expenditure.

Knowledge of

- relationship management
- partnership working
- managing a team
- developing a team
- service monitoring processes and the data required to do so
- output specifications and performance measurement systems
- end user requirements (e.g. the requirements of schools)
- procurement processes
- government accounting principles
- benchmarking/market testing
- the private sector and its business drivers
- changes and developments in the relevant service markets.

17.3 Contract management good practice (including VFM)

The World Bank[4] highlights good international practice that organisations with high performance Contract Management programs have typically employed.

Key area	Leading practice
People	■ Organisation has identified contact management 'champions' ■ Contracts can be segregated based on department ownership, vendor types, and spend ■ Contract administrators within all relevant functional groups and aligned enterprise-wide ■ Specific contract information made available to pre-authorise resources
Performance	■ Contract renewal process is performed in a timely manner identifying all required resources prior to the renewal date ■ Implemented contracts are reviewed to verify compliance with changing regulatory environment ■ Periodic meetings are held with top level vendor officials and buyers to discuss vendor performance ■ Customer satisfaction surveys are used to evaluate vendor performance
Process	■ Contracting process is streamlined through use of risk-assessed templates and standard contracting language ■ Creation of vendor contracts is integrated with vendor selection, verification and performance measurements ■ PO templates are pre-populated with approved suppliers and corresponding supplier profile data ■ Standardised process for contract creation across the business and process are standardised companywide

Key area	Leading practice
Policy	■ Terms and conditions are specific to each contract type ■ Vendor reporting requirements are reviewed to identify potential compliance issues ■ There are both standard procedures and defined roles and responsibilities for implementing monitoring, and enforcing contract compliance ■ Common procurement data definitions should be established across the company
Technology	■ Contract information is automatically integrated with vendor information contained in the master file ■ Contract obligations and contract compliance are clearly visible ■ System functionality includes ability to scan images of required documents and attach to master contract ■ System is configured to provide advance notice of contract expiration, insurance expiration and status of resolution

17.4 Contract management plans

17.4.1 Sample procurement – relatively low value – low risk

The following checklist has been adapted from the ANAO 'Example contract management plans'.[5]

This example shows the key elements of contract management for a simple procurement. It could be used by the contract manager as the basis for developing a contract management plan.

Contract management plan

Contractor	Name: Address: Contractor Representative: Position: Telephone: Email: SME: Yes/No Charity Yes/No BME: Yes/No
Contract Deliverable(s):	Summary of deliverables
Contract Manager:	
Contract Sponsor:	
Key stakeholder	
Contract Start Date:	
Contract End Date:	
Contract extension options:	Detail process for managing and assessing possible contract extension options.
Payment Schedule:	
Total Contract Value:	
Payment Arrangements:	Detail how often payments are to be made (e.g. on completion of deliverables, at milestones or monthly).

Invoice Verification:	Who will confirm invoices are correct? (should be Contract Manager). Who will authorise payment of invoices? (should be Contract Sponsor).
Incentive or Penalty Payments:	List any incentive or penalty provisions in the contract
Milestones:	List all milestones and key dates.
Performance Measures:	List performance measures and methods of data collection and analysis.
Reporting Requirements:	Format/Frequency.
Communication Protocols:	How regularly will the entity and contractor communicate and format of communication?
Risk Assessment and Review:	What is the risk assessment at the beginning of the contract? Regularly review the contract to determine if risk status has changed in any significant way.
Contract Review	How will lessons learned be identified and recorded?

17.4.2 Large or more complex procurements – relatively high value – high risk

The following checklist has been adapted from the ANAO 'Example contract management plan for large or more complex procurements'.[6]

This example shows the key elements of a contract management plan for large or more complex procurements. It could be used by the contract manager as the basis for developing a contract management plan. The amount of detail required for any section that is used should be adjusted to reflect the complexity of the contract, the level of risk associated with it and the internal processes of the entity.

Contract Management Plan:	Title and purpose	Insert title of plan and summarise its purpose. Also include details of name and date of the delegate approving the plan, including arrangements for reviewing and updating the plan.
Contract Structure:	Contract summary	Summarise key contract details, for example, contract number, commencement date, contract term, procurement process (e.g. panel, open tender), delegate details, approved users of the contract, estimated contract value, reporting obligations completed (yes/no).
	Background	Provide a brief summary of the procurement process that led to the contract. This may include the purpose, objectives, scope and key deliverables of the contract. Note: information should be detailed enough to allow a person, with no prior involvement in the contract to have a clear understanding of a contract's background.
	Documentation	List all documentation relating to the contract that is held by the contract management team. This may include, for example, transition plans, tender evaluation reports, risk management plans etc., and identification of their location and when they were last updated.

	Contract term and extension options	List contract start and end dates and contract extension options, if applicable.
	Pricing	Total contract value, pricing arrangements and fee variations. If applicable, a fee schedule may also be included.
Roles and Responsibilities:	Contact details	At a minimum, the contract managers for both the acquiring entity and the contractor should be listed with their contact details.
	Identified roles and their descriptions	List key stakeholders, where they come from and their major responsibilities in relation to the contract. In some contracts there will be a number of parties with various levels of contractual, financial and reporting involvement. A map of these relationships may be useful for illustrating these relationships.
	Stakeholder management and communications strategies	Identify key methods to be used for liaison, reporting, signalling issues to, and building relationships with, key stakeholders identified above.
Conditions of the Contract:	General conditions	Identify if any standard form contract is used
	Special conditions	List any special conditions that are not covered elsewhere in this plan. For example, warranties, intellectual property ownership etc.
	Contract variations (price, product/ services or other)	List contract variations and requirements that need to be met to implement a variation. This should be consistent with the provisions in the contract.
	Insurance	Record details of currency and adequacy of insurance certificates and procedures for obtaining evidence from the contractor of future currency.
Financial Considerations:	Payment conditions	Insert any clauses from the contract on payment conditions. The payment schedule should also be described, for example, the schedule may provide for monthly payment, or payment on completion of deliverables.
	Incentives or rebates	Describe any incentive arrangements included in the contract and how they are to be calculated.
	Penalties or disincentives	Describe any penalties that may be included in the contract and how they are to be calculated and applied.
	Invoicing	Detail the invoicing requirements for the contract.
Performance Measurement:	Key performance measures	List key performance measures/indicators to be used for measuring the performance of contract. These should be consistent with the performance measures identified in the tender documentation and the contract.
	Performance incentives/disincentives	List any non-financial performance incentives or disincentives that are applicable to the contract and the key performance indicators that trigger them.

	Performance monitoring	Describe the data collection and analysis methods to be used for monitoring and assessing performance (e.g. user surveys, third party accreditation, benchmarking etc.) Also detail who will undertake performance monitoring including: responsibility for collecting and analysing data; how frequently monitoring will take place; the reporting arrangements; and any processes to review the arrangements.
Contract Administration:	Provider's obligations	Detail all obligations the contractor has under the contract. This may include goods or services to be provided, any other deliverables covered by the contract, timeframes to be met, specified personnel, reporting requirements, provision of equipment and back-up arrangements.
	Product or service standards expected	Detail any requirements included in the contract relating to product or service standards and how they are to be administered.
	Compliance management	Detail relevant procurement connected polices and obligations that the entity and the contractor are required to comply with and how these will be managed. Note: the contract manager is responsible for the management of these obligations. It may be useful to include these as an attachment to the plan.
	Transition	Include here arrangements for managing any transition and attach transition strategies or plans.
	Reporting requirements	List the reporting requirements, for example, what is to be reported and the format/frequency of reporting.
	Audit requirements	Detail any requirements for both internal and independent audits, and the elements of the contract to be audited. The timeframe for the audit, along with resources required (in-house or external) should also be identified.
	Contractor meetings	Detail a schedule of meetings specific to the contract and the process for inviting and reminding relevant parties.
Risk Assessment and Management Strategy:	Procurement Risk Plan	Include details of earlier risk planning conducted for earlier procurement phases and highlight any risks that carry through to the contract management phase.
	Contract Risk Plan	Insert details of contract risk planning, risks and mitigation strategies. Attach the completed contract risk plan to this plan. An example of a contract risk and treatment plan is included in this Guide.
	Issue Register	Record any issues (realised risks) that may arise and how they are to be managed, including by whom.
	Contract Review	Outline regular reviews (for example quarterly, annually). Detail how they will be conducted, including what data needs to be collected and by whom. Outline the trigger point(s) at which contract review becomes necessary due to underperformance.
	Dispute Resolution Process	Detail any clauses specified in tender documents and the contract and detail procedures for addressing the dispute.

	Termination	Detail any clauses in the contract which may give rise to termination and detail the termination process to be followed.
Contract Review:	Renewal or extension	Outline the process to be followed in assessing whether to renew or extend a contract and the steps that need to be followed as the contract nears expiry.
	Contract closure	List the tasks that are required to successfully complete and close the contract. Handover procedures; security and access closure; contract evaluation, including the process and resources required (in-house or external); documentation of lessons learned; and notification to stakeholders.
Attachments:		Depending on the type and scope of the contract a variety of attachments may be required. Examples include compliance management, risk management plans, transition plans, invoicing and payment schedules, service level agreements, and user/client survey questionnaires.

17.5 Key performance indicators (KPIs) for contract management

17.5.1 KPI measures

The World Bank[7] explain that KPIs are measures of contract performance that are aligned to the key outcomes that the procurement approach has been designed to deliver. The World Bank provide examples of KPIs, reproduced in Table 17.1.

KPIs in action – Southwark Council – Housing Repairs Service

There is a very informative report[8] dealing with KPIs. The Council has a stock of 55,000 properties and typically the service delivers around 120,000 repairs per year. The report states at para 1.3

> The quality of the housing repairs service in Southwark has been the subject of controversy for some time. Anecdotal evidence from councillor's casework has suggested serious problems with the quality of the service whilst key performance indicators (KPIs) show very strong performance across a range of areas.

The Council goes on to say at para 2.6:

> when they work well, the reputational impact of key performance indicators can concentrate the minds of contractors and senior officers on improving a service . . . conversely, a serious and damaging situation arises when KPIs show high performance irrespective of the real quality of service being provided.

There are very significant statements in the report that should alert all organisations to the potential inadequacies of KPIs. The statements include:
Para 5.6

> The sub-committee expressed its surprise and concern that so much of the information required to compile the KPIs and calculate payments came from the contractors themselves without being cross-checked or verified. Subsequent investigation found that these concerns were more than justified.

Table 17.1 Examples of KPIs for key performance areas

Key performance area			KPI description	KPI measurement
1. Delivery	a.	On-Time Delivery	Provide contractually obligated deliverables and outcomes on agreed dates	■ On time delivery of contractually obligated deliverables as per mutually agreed plans
	b.	Documentation of Deliverables	Information is managed (shared, stored and communicated) in line with expectations defined in contract or as agreed between the parties	■ Deliverables uploaded to knowledge system according to agreed timeframe. ■ Supporting/working documents uploaded (templates, weekly status reports, minutes of meetings, training manual, project progress etc.)
2. Support	a.	SLA Performance	Successfully meets contractual requirements relating to agreed SLAs.	■ Number of SLA breaches, based on contractually agreed limits (e.g. service/hardware calls are completed on time)
	b.	SLA Documentation	Information is managed (shared, stored and communicated) in line with expectations defined in contract or as agreed between the parties	■ Deliverables uploaded to knowledge system according to agreed timeframe. ■ Supporting/working documents uploaded (templates, weekly status reports, minutes of meetings, training manual, project progress etc.)
3. Quality	a.	Delivery Quality	Product/service meets quality acceptance criteria	■ Number of deliveries that have met acceptance criteria (e.g. Number of defects, functionality of application, User Interface)
	b.	Supplier Personnel	Teams are made up of members with expertise relevant to our business including input from Subject Matter Resource (SMR)	■ Number of people proposed, rejected or replaced due to performance issues or not meeting the expectations ■ Number of key project resources leaving and joining for the contracted services
	c.	Customer Satisfaction	Level of satisfaction received from service recipients/business users	■ Rating received by service recipients/business users
4. Partnership & Innovation	a.	Relationship	Committed to building and maintaining effective relationships with senior executives.	■ Number of no-shows of supplier senior executives in steering committee meetings etc. ■ Number of dedicated supplier account management visits
	b.	Flexibility & Responsiveness	Demonstrates willingness and ability to respond to non-forecasted demand and ensure timely response to sourcing requirements	■ Number of requests met without raising CRs ■ Timely response to sourcing and ad-hoc requirements

Table 17.1 *Continued*

Key performance area		KPI description	KPI measurement
	c. Continuous Improvement and Innovation	Improved processes, products and services that are credible and implementable (quick wins). New product development (services) and innovative ideas for discussion and strategic decision making	■ Number of improvement and innovation recommendations that are accepted ■ Adherence to supplier development plan
5. Governance & Risk	a. Governance	Adheres to supplier performance management principles and meets requirements for governance	■ Number of missed deadlines for inputs (agenda and pre-reads) and outputs (reports) ■ Actions closed from previous review meeting as agreed timeline ■ Disputes resolved amicably as per dispute resolution framework
	b. Risk Management Compliance	Understands and adheres to requirements for risk management. Establishes and implements adequate controls to mitigate risks	■ Risks are communicated as part of governance process. Risks raised with effective mitigation plans: ■ Project-related risks ■ Supplier-related risks
	c. Contractual Compliance	Successfully meets legal contractual requirements and statement of work specification	■ Number of contractual breaches identified
6. Financial	a. Invoicing	Contractually compliant with the time and quality for submission of invoices	■ On time submission of invoices with supporting documents as agreed ■ Number of invoice errors identified in the past period
	b. Cost Transparency	Supplier provides transparency into its cost breakdowns	■ Cost (invoices, financial proposals) is provided with a detailed breakdown of activities, services, products, quantities, etc.
	c. Travel Spend	Amount spent on travel with and/or Partner Airlines.	■ Amount spent on travel using qualified and/or Partner Airlines.
	d. Price Reduction/ Discount/Saving Opportunities	Price reductions/discounts/savings are consistently applied	■ Number of instances of price reductions/discounts/savings and the amount ■ Identified volume discounts and other price reducing options
	e. Penalties	Financial penalties applied due to non-compliance to SLA, delivery schedule, product quality, etc.	■ Number of instances of financial penalties applied and the amount
	f. Change Requests/ Contract Amendments	Number and value of CRs/Contract Amendments initiated since the previous scorecard or over the reporting period	■ Total number of CRs raised/ Contract Amendments, value & scope of each CR/Contract Amendment

In the author's experience, Southwark are not alone in this situation!
Para 8.4

> 32% of the calls we listened to related to missed appointments by the contractor. Again this is at odds with the KPI which consistently reports that 99% of appointments are kept.

One learning point from this is that if inaccurate reporting takes place it is probable that a contractual provision for the payment of damages for non-performance will not be applied.
Para 10.3

> These findings show the pitfalls that arise when so much ownership and control of KPI information is devolved to the contract operatives themselves. There appears to be very little oversight of their reporting activities, even by the management of Morrisons and SBS themselves.

This illustrates one of the key principle roles for contract management, namely, persistently the accuracy of KPI achievement reporting.
Para 13.2

> Through this scrutiny process the sub-committee has discovered that Southwark Council, in agreement with both contractors, has not implemented the financial incentives based on the KPIs. The explanation for this can be seen below. The following quote is taken from an email exchange between the Chair of the sub-committee and an officer involved in the management of the contract. The incentives have not been implemented: 'Because of the difficulty of measuring the KPIs in a way that actually reflects the service being provided we have reported them but have not adjusted payments up or down. I understand that you have come across this problem during your Scrutiny investigation. KPIs are now being measured in a more 'realistic' way. Unfortunately this does not align with the provisions of the contract and it has not been possible to either incentivise or penalise the contractor. There have also been significant difficulties with the integration of the various computer systems used by the Council and the contractors which have rendered some of the KPI almost unachievable.'

This paragraph speaks for itself.

KPIs in action – North Somerset Council – Support Services Contract

In April 2012 KPMG produced a contract management report[9] for North Somerset Council. This stated:

Performance management

> The Council has agreed a set of key performance indicators (KPIs) with the contractor that measure performance across a range of services lines such as customer satisfaction, accuracy of payroll and invoices paid on time. Each of these KPIs sets performance standards which can attract a penalty (service credit) if performance regularly falls below the minimum expected standard, but can also attract an incentive payment if the standard is regularly exceeded.

> In November 2011, of the 22 KPIs that were able to be measured only two were below the expected performance standard, and 11 exceeded the performance standard. Between September and November 2011, performance either improved or remained at the same standard in 91% of cases, with just two KPIs showing a decline in performance over that period.

> The service credit system attached to KPIs has not been applied to the first 18 months of the contract to allow a baseline to be established. However, if it had been applied only one penalty payment on one KPI would have been applicable to date.

> This performance data indicates that the SSP is performing at the level contractually agreed by the Council. However, this positive performance picture does not correspond to the feedback

received from staff during this review, who experienced service quality below their expectations, particularly related to the business as usual (BAU) services.

This suggests two things. Firstly that the KPIs being used to measure the contract are not measuring the right things – the things that are important to service providers and users, and secondly, where they are measuring the right things, the performance standards are set at a level below that expected by the service provider or user. Service users are unclear what service levels have been agreed in the contract. This has not been clearly communicated to them by the client team. The contractor is developing a Partnership Guide to help improve understanding. The Client Team uses a contract summary manual, but this is not available to staff.

Breadth of coverage of KPIs is also not yet comprehensive. The contract sets out a suite of 38 performance indicators to monitor the contract. Currently, 16 are not being reported or have performance standards unassigned while baselines are established or measuring regimes put in place despite the contract being in operation for 15 months. This list of PIs includes particularly important measures such as user satisfaction, and benefits realised versus planned. This means the picture on performance is incomplete.

17.6 Lapses in contract management

The author has used his experience and research to develop the content of Table 17.2. It provides an academic and practical checklist of such lapses.

Table 17.2 Lapses in contract management

Phase of contract management	Failure to:
Actions Post Contract Award	■ Carry out contract handover to contract manager ■ Have a supplier meeting to discuss respective obligations ■ Explain Security and Health & Safety requirements ■ Confirm contract performance KPIs and performance reporting ■ Confirm key personnel engaged in contract deliverables ■ Confirm key contract clauses and impact on contract performance
Delivery milestones & completion of delivery/acceptance	■ Confirm key milestones (if any) ■ Confirm that resources are available to meet delivery obligations ■ Agree reporting mechanism for delivery progress ■ Ensure Acceptance Criteria are fully understood ■ Understand logistics issues to achieve delivery ■ Understand supplier's reliance on third parties for supplies
Contract Review meetings	■ Agree frequency and content of contract review meetings ■ Insist on performance data ahead of meetings ■ Insist on key decision makers attending meetings ■ Document discussions and actions points ■ Manage time effectively to achieve agenda item discussion ■ Consider location for meetings, including supplier's premises
Managing Contract changes	■ Involve procurement in documenting agreed contract changes ■ Determine the cost and delivery implications of changes ■ Determine the quality management implications of specification changes ■ Agree payment mechanism relating to changes ■ Agree inspection regime for changes to specification ■ Consider resource implication associated with changes

Phase of contract management	Failure to:
Managing contractual non-performance	■ Decisively deal with contract delivery slippage ■ Identify potential risks of non-performance ■ Impose damages for late delivery ■ Adequately document non-performance ■ Audit reasons for non-performance ■ In extreme circumstances consider contract termination rights
Payment	■ Have in place a robust mechanism for approving payment ■ Prevent advance payments being made ■ Withhold agreed retention amounts ■ Have proof of deliverables prior to payment approval ■ Ensure discounts/rebates are properly accounted for ■ Audit whether supplier is paying subcontractors in a timely manner
Management of warranty period	■ Create a data base whereby all warranty provisions are documented ■ Understand when specific warranties commence ■ Take decisive action when products fail in warranty period ■ Avoid payment for repairs/replacement in warranty period ■ Understand interface with other products when there is a warranty failure ■ Document when warranty period ends

17.7 Social services contract monitoring audit

The Office of the City Auditor[10] published a report that is indicative of the problems facing contract management. The audit report is included in this chapter to highlight issues that unquestionably apply elsewhere. Concerns had been expressed by the Health & Human Services Department (HHSD) related to contracting policies, procedures and processes. From FY 2009 through FY 2011, there were 82 social services contracts (funded from City revenues), which totalled approximately $54 million. The audit objective was to determine whether the contract monitoring process ensured compliance with contract terms and conditions.

The Audit Report included:

Contract monitoring activities are insufficient and hinder the Health and Human Services Department's (HHSD) ability to provide reasonable assurance that services are delivered according to contract terms and that City funds are not misused.

In general, HHSD has not performed contract monitoring as required by internal policies and procedures, applicable contract requirements, or industry best practices. While issues regarding monitoring were raised in 2009 related to fraud by an HHSD contractor, management did not ensure staff performed contract monitoring duties as required. In addition, most staff members did not have prior contract monitoring experience, and HHSD does not have a training program in place to ensure staff is trained to perform contract monitoring duties. Documentation of monitoring performed is not maintained consistently by staff, and is not maintained consistently by HHSD for official record retention purposes. Further, IT controls over the contract management system used by HHSD do not provide sufficient assurance for security or data reliability.

Finding 1: HHSD has draft policies and procedures for conducting contract monitoring; however, contract monitoring has not been conducted consistently, and HHSD cannot provide assurance that contracted services are provided as purchased by the City.

Contract monitoring is subject to HHSD policy. The draft HHSD procedure manual states that on-site reviews for contracts should be performed on a three-year cycle with invoice verification reviews (IVR) occurring in Year 1, administrative and financial review (AFR) in Year 2, and programmatic reviews (PR) in Year 3. HHSD does not have policies and procedures related to reviews of performance measure reports submitted by contractors; however, according to management, staff is required to review these reports in practice.

Management oversight of and communication with staff is insufficient, and staff are not held accountable for performing contract monitoring duties as required. For example, staff reported that management redirected resources to the development of the new contracting process instead of enforcing expectations related to contract monitoring. Staff also stated they did not conduct on-site visits during the new contracting process out of concern for violating the City's anti-lobbying ordinance, but management stated contract monitoring could be performed without violating the ordinance. In addition, staff reported that policies are in draft form because procedures are changing and have not been finalized by management.

Additionally, staff reported that their job duties also include funding application review, technical assistance, and regular communication with the contractors. Some staff believes this creates conflicts of interest and hinders their ability to conduct objective contract reviews.

Without consistent monitoring, HHSD cannot ensure that services are provided in accordance with contract terms and conditions. For example, during site visits at 9 agencies, auditors found that one contractor, LEAP, could not provide documentation of services provided. Furthermore, HHSD cannot provide assurance that agencies are using City funds as intended.

For example:

■ LEAP was unable to provide documentation to reconcile revenues and expenditures and LEAP commingled City funds. In 2010, HHSD staff notified LEAP of the need to modify its accounting practices.

■ Austin Area Urban League had not paid payroll taxes for several months during our scope period and did not have support for the resulting adjustments made to their HHSD payment requests.

■ The Council on At-Risk Youth did not have documentation to tie their accounting statements to their expenditure reports to HHSD.

Overall, HHSD's contract monitoring practices allowed for payment of invoices without proof of service or verification of invoice validity, and appropriate follow up was not performed to ensure deficiencies identified were corrected.

FINDING 2: HHSD's contract monitoring program does not adhere to best practices, which decreases HHSD's ability to detect fraud, waste, or abuse, identify contract non-compliance, or protect against the misuse of City funds.

According to the best practice guidance offered by the State of Texas Contract Management Guide and the City of Austin Contract Monitoring Guide, contract monitoring programs should include such protocols as:

■ standardizing contract monitoring practices across the division,

■ creating risk-based monitoring plans,

■ reviewing invoices prior to payment,

■ ensuring payment is tied to performance, and

■ establishing minimum expectations for staff training and expertise.

According to staff, not all contract terms are represented in the review process. Notably missing is monitoring to ensure that contractors perform background checks on individuals that work with children, and monitoring to ensure contractor funds are not commingled. We reviewed the processes in place for the contractors who should have conducted background checks and did not note any exceptions. One contractor comingled funds, and although HHSD identified the issue, staff did not follow up to ensure it was corrected. Furthermore, HHSD does not maintain a centralized listing of all grants and contracts, or track grantor audits performed, so there is no mechanism to ensure appropriate monitoring of all contracts under HHSD's purview.

In terms of conducting risk-based monitoring, according to staff, some contractors are subject to additional levels of review as a result of past non-compliance, but these decisions are not documented and clear criteria for additional review levels do not exist.

In addition, best practice calls for reviewing all invoices prior to payment. However, HHSD policy requires invoice verification once every three years, and HHSD does not have a process in place for reviewing or confirming reported expenditures on a more regular basis. For example, we found that invoices were not reviewed prior to payment in two of the five (20%) sampled contracts.

Furthermore, best practice calls for tying payment to performance, but the social services contracts sampled do not include performance requirements. Performance goals are included in the statement of work but are not enforced as part of the contract monitoring process or tied to payment.

Other weaknesses reported by HHSD staff regarding the contract monitoring program include:

- training is not provided,
- most employees assigned to perform contract monitoring duties have limited or no prior contract monitoring experience,
- inconsistent use of the contract management system by staff,
- support documentation is not always submitted by or requested from contractors, and
- inconsistent maintenance and retention of contract documentation.

According to HHSD management, many of the weaknesses noted above are due to a cultural shift Citywide between a contracting approach that focuses on supporting agencies (providing funding with limited oversight) and purchasing services (tying service provision directly to funding.) In addition, monitoring activities are decentralized across the Human Services Division and, as previously noted, are performed by staff who also work closely with contractors in planning and capacity-building roles.

Overall, the weaknesses identified above hinder HHSD's ability to detect fraud, waste, or abuse, identify contractor non-compliance, or protect against the misuse of City funds. Insufficient contractor accountability standards increases the risk that the City will pay for services that were not delivered or pay contractors who did not meet contractual expectations. Failure to confirm background checks potentially jeopardizes client safety. Without an integrated risk assessment process, non-compliant contractors may not receive the necessary level of oversight. These risks are compounded by the lack of centralized tracking of grants and contracts.

FINDING 3: Security and data reliability controls over the contract management system are insufficient, increasing the risk for unauthorized access to data and maintenance of inaccurate contract information.

HHSD's password security procedures for the contract management system do not comply with best practice. Since this system is web-based, it can be accessed from any computer, increasing the risk exposure.

The management system has optional features that would comply with some components of industry best practices, however they have not been implemented. According to staff, the system's password requirements were established to make the system friendly to users (both HHSD staff and contractors), and the contract with the system's vendor does not require the vendor to adhere to best practice.

During our review of data, we also noted that two levels of authorization are required for payment approval, but for 11 out of 53 contractors (21%), the same HHS staff person routinely authorizes payments for both levels.

In addition, we noted that data entered into the management system is not always accurate.

For example, report date entered as a date prior to the date the monitoring was performed, and

■ risk scores[11] are entered via a drop down menu and via manual entry, and 2 out of 10 (20%) of the agencies sampled revealed that the risk scores did not match

The management system produces exception reports for illogical dates, but these reports are not used consistently by staff. There is no process in place to verify the accuracy and completeness of data entered into the system, prevent entry of illogical dates, or enforce segregation of duties for payment approval.

As a result, although we found no instances of unauthorized access during the course of our audit, HHSD's control system is inadequate to provide assurance that such access has not occurred. In addition, we did not identify any inappropriate payments in our audit, but without safeguards for segregated duties, HHSD cannot protect against unauthorized payments to contractors, which could result from collusion between the staff and the contractors to which they are assigned. Inaccurate and incomplete information within the database limits staff's ability to use the information for decision-making, and places the City at risk for housing inaccurate public records.

Recommendations:

The recommendations listed below are a result of our audit effort and subject to the limitation of our scope of work. We believe that these recommendations provide reasonable approaches to help resolve the issues identified. We also believe that operational management is in a unique position to best understand their operations and may be able to identify more efficient and effective approaches and we encourage them to do so when providing their response to our recommendations. As such, we strongly recommend the following:

1 **The HHSD Director should create a complete contract monitoring system that includes the following components:**
   ■ **contract monitoring policies and procedures that comply with best practices, are formally adopted, and communicated to staff;**
   ■ **contract monitoring is performed and documented in accordance with HHSD policies, procedures, and best practices;**
   ■ **review of organizational structure, job duties, and personnel within the contract monitoring function, in order to determine whether changes are needed to ensure objectivity and independence in performing contract monitoring roles and responsibilities; and,**
   ■ **a formal, documented training program specific to training needs that is provided to staff.**

17.8 Contract provisions

Contract provisions vary, widely, depending on the nature of the procurement. A contract will create legal obligations and liabilities for the parties to a contract. Prior to contract award it is probable, on more complex contracts, that procurement, legal advisors, stakeholders and contract negotiators will all play a part in determining the final contract provisions. What cannot be ignored is the fact that the supplier and their legal advisor will leave their fingerprint on the final contract outcome. This is for the obvious business purpose of limiting their liabilities and ensuring their obligations are clear and achievable.

The contract manager must be briefed on the detail of the contract, including schedules to the contract. The intent, application of the clauses and consequences of non-compliance must be clearly understood. The content of this section of the chapter carries a health warning to our readers. **NEVER** interpret a contract clause unless appropriate advice has been received. The purpose of contract management is to avoid disputes.

It is probable that most contract managers will encounter a need to understand the following clauses (and others):

■ Access to premises	■ Key personnel
■ Audit rights	■ Liabilities and indemnities
■ Assignment	■ Milestones
■ Assistance to the supplier	■ Payment and price
■ Confidential information	■ Penalties and incentives
■ Contract change	■ Rejection
■ Contract variations	■ Security arrangements
■ Dispute resolution	■ Securities and guarantees
■ *Force majeure*	■ Step-in rights
■ Guarantees	■ Sub-contracting
■ Indexation of price	■ Termination
■ Inspection rights	■ Transition arrangements
■ Insurance	■ Warranties
■ Intellectual property rights	

17.9 Contract clauses and what they mean

At some stage in the life of every contract manager the question will arise, 'What does this clause mean?' The following worked example is taken from a contract, at Clause 7, 'Performance Indicators'. A good starting point to understand a clause is to bullet point the key provisions, which in our example, are:

■ meet or exceed the Target Performance Level for each Performance Indicator

■ monitoring and reporting performance

■ deduction of service credits

■ rectification plans

■ Material Performance Indicator failure

■ exceptions to service credits as exclusive financial remedy

■ rights of buying organisation for unacceptable KPI failure

■ supplier accepts consequences of unacceptable KPI failure.

The bullet points are the lay person's shorthand for the provisions. The requirement for the contract manager is to drill into the detailed wording and understand it. The provisions are:

Provision	Commentary
Clause 7.1 (a) The supplier shall provide the Operational Services in such a manner so as to meet or exceed the Target Performance Level for each Performance Indicator from the Milestone Date for each relevant CPP Milestone.	All words or phrases that are capitalised should be a defined term – to be found in the Definitions part of the contract. There is no obligation for the supplier to exceed the TPL 'meet or exceed' is the requirement. The contract manager must understand the TPL, PI and CPP Milestones.

Provision	Commentary
Clause 7.1 (b) comply with the provisions of Schedule 2.2 (Performance Levels) in relation to the monitoring and reporting in its performance against the Performance Indicators.	The Schedules to a contract are essential reading for the contract manager. Within Schedule 2.2 it will set out the 'monitoring and reporting' requirements. For example, the frequency and content of reporting is crucial to holding effective contract review meetings.
Clause 7.2 introduces Performance Failures and says 'If in any Service Period (a) a KPI Failure occurs, service credits shall be deducted from the Service Charges in accordance with Paragraph 3 of Part c of Schedule 7.1 (Charges and Invoicing)'.	It should be noted here that there are a number of defined terms, each of which will have a specific meaning. A KPI Failure is important to the contract manager as is the need to deduct Service Credits. There are a form of damages, which if not deducted leave the buying company out of pocket.
Clause 7.2 (b) provides 'if a Material KPI Failure occurs, the Supplier shall comply with the Rectification Plan Process' (in addition to Service Credits accruing in accordance with Clause 7.2 (a).	The contract manager will need to understand what a 'Material KPI Failure' actually means. The word 'Material' usually means something of substance that drives at the heart of a contract. The 'Rectification Plan Process' is very relevant to the work of a contract manager. When has the plan to be submitted? To who? In what format? Who approves it? What happens if the plan after approval isn't met?
Claus 7.2 (c) provides 'if a PI Failure occurs; the Supplier shall notify the Authority of the action (if any) it will take to rectify the PI Failure and/or to prevent the PI Failure from recurring'.	The wording of this clause is loose, note the words 'shall notify'. It doesn't say how! It would, ideally, say in writing to avoid a future situation where the supplier claims to have told someone verbally. The contract manager would need to fully understand any proposed rectification actions. It is important to note that the contact manager's agreement to the rectification actions does not relieve the supplier from performing their obligations under the contract.

The above analysis shows only shows parts of one contract clause, it will show the detail that needs to be understood by a contract manager. It requires an investment of time and guidance on any facets with which the contract manager is unfamiliar or which requires explanation.

Discussion questions

17.1 What is the scope of contract management, and how does contract management contribute to business success?

17.2 Why is it important to create positive relationships with a supplier?

17.3 If you were managing a contract for the supply of catering services to your organisation's Head Office, what monthly information would you require from the supplier to assure you that the contractual obligations are being satisfied?

17.4 Would you agree with the statement that: "Conflict is inevitable between a supplier and a contract manager because the former is intent on maximising their profit?"

17.5 Why is it important for a contract manager to understand all the content of a contract?

17.6 If a contract manager has ascertained that the supplier has removed some Key Personnel, without authority, what remedies are available to a contract manager to correct the situation?

17.7 Is it the contract manager's responsibility to ensure that the contract risk register is continually reviewed and, when necessary, changed? Why?

17.8 Is the contract manager accountable for ensuring that the contact price is not exceeded?

17.9 Can you name six skills that a contract manager should have?

17.10 What events would lead a contract manager to recommend contract termination?

17.11 Name six failings in contract management.

17.12 Do you agree that contract management is generally under-resourced? What factors lead to your conclusion?

References

1 The World Bank, '*Procurement Guidance – Contract Management General Principles*', 1st edition. The World Bank, Washington DC, USA, September 2017.

2 A guide to contract management for PFI and PPP projects. 4ps.

3 A guide to contract management for PFI and PPP projects. 4ps pp16/17.

4 As 1 above.

5 Australian National Audit Office (ANAO) *The Better Practice Guide*. ANAO, Canberra, Australia, 2012.

6 As 5 above.

7 As 1 above.

8 Southwark Council Report of Housing & Community Safety Scrutiny Sub-Committee, February 2011.

9 KPMG.LLP North Somerset Council, 'Review of the Agilisys support services contract'. Final Detailed Report – April 2012.

10 City of Austin (Texas USA) Audit Report 'Social Services Contract Monitoring Audit', October 2011.

11 As noted in Finding 2, HHSD's risk-based decisions are not fully documented. There is also a risk-assessment process as part of contract close-out, which is recorded in the contract management system. However, it does not drive monitoring devices.

Chapter 18

Category and commodity procurement

Learning outcomes

This chapter aims to provide an understanding of:

- defining categories
- illustrations of category management issues
- the talent challenge
- category management – corporate travel
- category management – ICT
- capital investment procurement
- production materials
- raw materials
- futures dealing
- methods of commodity dealing
- procurement of non-domestic gas and electricity
- energy regulation
- energy supply chains in the UK
- markets
- pricing
- procuring energy contracts
- energy consultants and management
- component parts and assemblies
- consumables and MRO items
- construction supplies and bills of quantities
- procurement of services.

Key ideas

- Differentiation of procurement approaches depending on the category and commodity.
- Complexity of capital equipment procurement.
- Sources of relevant data.

- Financing considerations.
- Procurement risk consideration.
- Complexity of energy markets and cost generators.
- Characteristics of construction supplies.
- Commodity dealing.
- Raw material procurement.
- Expert sources of market data.
- Opportunities for procurement expertise to be applied in specialist areas.

Introduction

The CIPS definition of category management is,

> Category Management is a strategic approach which organises procurement resources to focus on specific areas of spends. This enables category managers to focus their time and conduct in depth market analysis to fully leverage their procurement decisions on behalf of the whole organisation. The results can be significantly greater than traditional transactional based purchasing methods.

18.1 Defining categories

CIPS Australia published 'The state of the art of category management' in 2011 and identified the following categories:

- Information & Communications Technology
- Maintenance, Repairs & Overhaul
- Professional Services
- Raw Material & Ingredients
- Travel
- Specific Directs (discreet category or related direct spend categories)
- Other Indirects (multiple unrelated or unspecified indirect categories)
- Facilities Management
- Logistics & Transport
- Capex
- Fleet Services
- Other Directs (multiple or unrelated direct categories)
- Equipment
- Medical
- Print
- Energy
- Recruitment & Labour Hire
- Packaging
- Marketing Services

- Stationery & Office Supplies
- Fuels & Lubricants
- Chemicals
- Other (multiple or unrelated direct and indirect categories).

The nature and range of categories will vary from one organisation to another. So will the emphasis on particular categories. APQC[1] identified 14 compelling category management findings, grouped by the following themes:

Strategic Implications

- Adopt a business – not cost – driven focus
- Balance long-term vision and planning with short-term agility
- Separate strategic pressures from tactical processes
- Recognise supplier segmentation as a foundation for category management
- Engage procurement in the full value chain with a specific focus on customer needs and values.

Resource Commitment and Talent Management

- Empower visible, focused category management teams with diverse membership
- Provide opportunities for career progression and skills acquisition through clearly articulated and differentiated requirements across the procurement organisation
- Seek to incorporate procurement and sourcing early in the new product development process.

Category-Specific Processes and Tools

- Create a standardised category approach to enable working and resourcing across categories and the ability to decide how much to invest by category
- Implement category risk management to monitor external market risks at the market or category level
- Conduct supplier risk assessments as part of the strategic sourcing process and on an ongoing basis
- Maintain an Intranet portal to provide one source for information that all relevant employees can access.

Extending Supplier Relationships

- Invest in building strong suppliers
- Give suppliers tools to succeed and create a symbiotic relationship.

18.2 Illustrations of category management issues

The APQC report is informative, thought provoking and worthy of detailed consideration by those contemplating transforming their approach to category management. Insightful commentary includes actual real-life illustrations of category management issues, including:

- Seeing sourcing through the lens of business success or failure, not just the cost to purchase, helps put the sourcing organisation in alignment with the larger enterprise
- In order of priority, FMC's strategic goals for sourcing and procurement focus on its core strategic areas: safety, quality, delivery and cost

Figure 18.1 Risk and compliance management

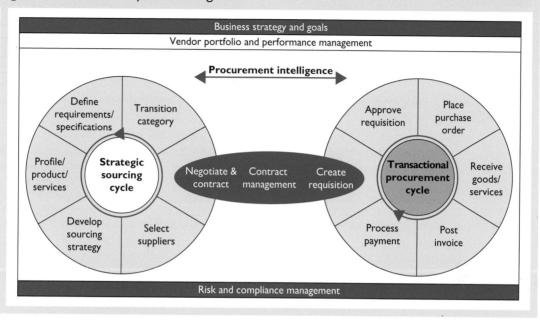

— Changes that can impact category management may come from both inside the organisation (e.g. shifts in strategy or product mix) and outside (e.g. market volatility or supply disruption)

— Strategically, sourcing and procurement focus on leveraging global spend to achieve high-quality products, import product integrity, attain superior cycle times and lower the total cost of ownership.

The APQC report explains that KPMG view of procurement's core value proposition and responsibilities reflects the following organisational construct (see Figure 18.1).

The APQC report sets out the ATMI process for the management of each of its categories that pulls in different functions at various points (see Figure 18.2).

Figure 18.2 ATMI's supplier management process

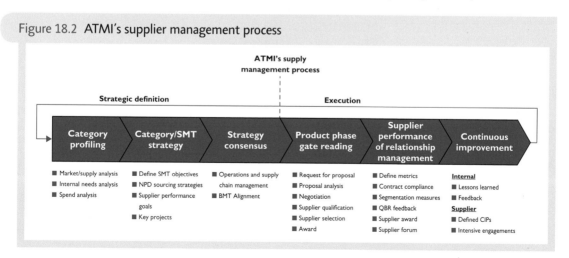

18.3 The talent challenge

The APQC report draws attention to a growing talent challenge across procurement organisations and highlights the key attributes of a strategic business partner that requires significant human capital (see Figure 18.3).

18.4 Category management – corporate travel

GBTA[2] in their KPI Reference Guide aim the KPIs at key stakeholders of corporate travel programmes which includes the travel category manager and procurement, finance and corporate social responsibility managers, as well as the travel programme's suppliers.

The typical programme metrics describing a company's profile include:

■ Travel spend: How much do we spend on travel and related expenses by business unit/ region, etc.?

■ Destinations: Where are we travelling?

■ Travel expense productivity: What is our travel spend compared to the output of our core business (e.g. revenue, sales)?

Figure 18.3 APQC report – Key attributes of strategic business partners

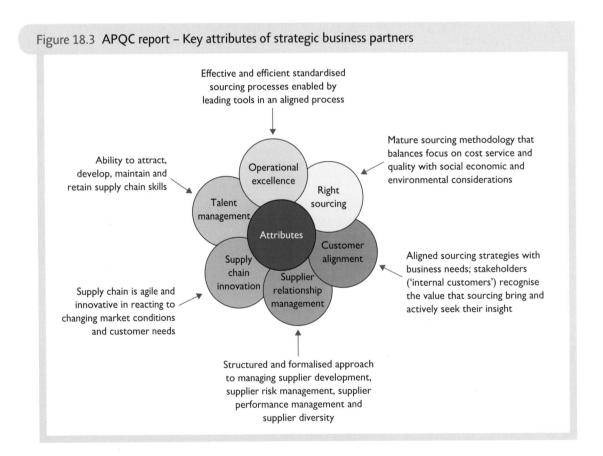

- Spend concentration: How concentrated is our travel spend on specific routes/cities. . . ?
- Prices: What is the trend of spend and pricing per category (e.g. average ticket price, average daily rate) and against the industry?
- Business travel intensity: How much are our employees travelling to conduct business (number of trips, duration, distance, frequency, . . .)?
- Number of frequent travellers: How many frequent travellers do we have?
- Travel risk exposure: How risky are our destinations (security/health/extreme weather)?

The Overview of KPI's determined for key categories are shown in Figure 18.4. GBTA suggest the following KPIs for managing corporate travel see Figure 18.5: The details of three KPI's are shown below:

(1) Booking Visibility (KPI ID 2)

Booking Visibility

Spend and Savings; Behaviour/Policy

Priority 1, Complex

KPI ID 2

Key Question: What share of our travel is booked via the approved Travel Management Company and self-booking tool (Self Booking Tool)?

Why this KPI: Booking Visibility measures the degree to which travellers are using the approved booking channels. It also measures the degree of data visibility one has, as bookings made through approved channels are captured for reporting. Data from bookings made through non-approved channels is not captured and so weakens a managed travel program.

Definition: (Ticketed and Booked Spend) divided by Total Travel Spend.

Buyer must capture the ticketed airfare and rail spend, and the booked hotel and rental car spend (booked rate * room nights or rental days), as reported by the approved Travel Management Company, hotel booking agencies, and Self Booking Tool.

Buyers may choose as the denominator the total travel spend as captured either by their general ledger or by their Expense Reporting System.

Example: 60 percent of our travel spend is booked through the approved Travel Management Companies or our corporate self-booking tool. This means 40 percent of our travel spend is booked in a way that gives us no visibility to that data.

Desired Direction: Higher is better. 100 percent is ideal.

Considerations: Obtaining the numerator should not be difficult. It is the denominator that can get messy due to the noisy and inconsistent data often included in the general ledger and expense reporting data sources.

An alternative form of this KPI is to measure the amount of travel spend booked via approved channels, and ignore the need to calculate a percentage.

Likely Data Sources: General ledger, Expense Reporting System, Travel Management Company, Self Booking Tool

Figure 18.4 Overview of KPIs determined by author for key categories

Spend and Savings	Behaviour and Policy	Suppliers	Process	Traveller Safety	CSR	Data Quality
■ Spend under contract ■ Booking visibility ■ Payment visibility ■ Realised negotiated savings ■ Contract competitiveness ■ Cost of managed travel	■ Cabin non-compliance ■ Lowest Logical Airfare (LLA) non-compliance ■ Advance booking non-compliance ■ Online adoption rate ■ Hotel visibility ■ Hotel quality	■ Traveller satisfaction ■ Contract support	■ Re-booking rate ■ Reimbursement days	■ Location insights ■ Profile completion	■ Carbon visibility ■ Rail vs. air	■ Data quality

Figure 18.5 GBTA KPIs for managing corporate travel

Suggested key performance indicators	
■ Spend under contract	■ Re-booking rate
■ Booking visibility	■ Hotel quality
■ Payment visibility	■ Traveller satisfaction
■ Realised negotiated savings	■ Contract support
■ Contract competitiveness	■ Reimbursement days
■ Cost of managed travel	■ Location insight
■ Cabin non-compliance	■ Profile completion
■ Lowest logical airfare non-compliance	■ Carbon visibility
■ Advance booking non-compliance	■ Rail vs. air
■ Online adoption	■ Data quality
■ Hotel visibility	

(2) Contract Competitiveness - Suppliers KPI ID 5

Contract Competitiveness

Suppliers

Priority 1, Complex

KPI ID 5

Key Question: How good are our negotiated contracts (air, hotel, car, Travel Management Company)?

Why this KPI: Key stakeholders want to know how cost-effective their company's negotiated prices are.

Definition: A supplier's contracted prices need to be compared to the relevant undiscounted fares or rates. Multiply the difference (the price savings) by the unit volume purchased. Sum this amount across all purchases made with the supplier. This is the contract's savings.

Convert all purchases made with the supplier to the supplier's undiscounted (a.k.a., pre-discounted, or gross) spend. This quantifies the amount of pre-discounted spend.

Divide the contract's savings by the supplier's undiscounted spend. This is the contract's savings rate.

Construct a ratio by placing the buyer's savings rate in the numerator, and the benchmarked peer group's average savings rate in the denominator. The result is the Contract Competitiveness Ratio.

Example: Our airline contract produces a 12 percent overall savings rate, compared to our peer group's benchmarked average of 20 percent. Our Contract Competitiveness for this airline contract is 12/20, or 60 percent.

Our airline contract delivers 60 percent of the savings rate achieved by our benchmarked peer group.

Desired Direction: Higher is better.

Considerations: It is very difficult to obtain apples-to-apples price benchmark data. Any such data provided by Travel Management Companies or third parties should be viewed as very rough indicators. Care must be taken to properly calculate the undiscounted (a.k.a. pre-discounted, or gross) spend.

Likely Data Sources: Supplier contracts, Travel Management Company, Self Booking Tool, suppliers (e.g., rental cars)

(3) Carbon Visibility – Sustainability KPI ID 19

Carbon Visibility

Sustainability

Priority 2, Simple

KPI ID 19

Key Question: How well do we measure our travel program's carbon impact?

Why this KPI: Travel managers are often asked about the carbon impact of their travel program. This measure indicates the ability to do that.

Definition: For each category, rate the current quality of measuring CO_2 emissions associated with corporate travel. Use a standard scale across each category, such as:

- Excellent – We use a leading-edge carbon calculator designed for the relevant travel category and we
- collect sufficient data; score of 5 points
- Adequate – We use a GHG Protocol-approved method for estimating the category's emissions (see http://www.ghgprotocol.org/) and we collect sufficient data; score of 3 points
- Inadequate – We don't capture sufficient data or don't have a method in place to estimate carbon emissions for this category; score of 1 point

Example: Our carbon visibility for air travel is excellent (5 points); for hotel stays, car and rail it is inadequate (1 point for each category). We chose to weight air at 70 percent, hotel at 10 percent, car at 10 percent and rail at 10 percent, so our overall score is 3.8 out of possible 5.0, or 76 percent.

Desired Direction: Higher ratings are better.

Considerations: Travel managers should seek guidance from their corporate social responsibility colleagues about how to best estimate a travel program's carbon impact. The Icarus Project is a source of excellent information on this topic. See http://www.icarus.itm.org.uk/

Likely Data Sources: Travel Management Company, Self-Booking Tool, car rental suppliers

18.5 Category management – ICT

ICT is, in many organisations, a significant procurement category. There are many influences on ICT expenditure, including:

- ICT technical specialists lacking commercial and contractual acumen
- absence of a long-term ICT strategy
- some ICT market segments dominated by a few large multinationals
- ownership of intellectual property
- high cost of technology change
- outsourcing actions
- disparate systems in use across corporate bodies

Figure 18.6 **ICT current landscape**

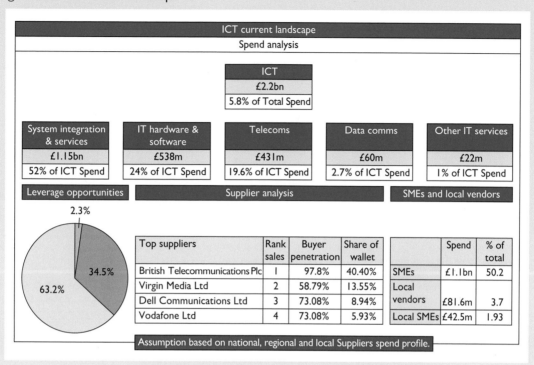

- procurement specialists lacking ICT technical knowledge and expertise
- difficulty negotiating contracts with dominant market leaders
- reputational damage when new systems fail.

In the United Kingdom, the scale of the issues is highlighted in the 'National ICT Commercial Category Strategy for Local Government'. The report includes a spend analysis, included here to give an indication of the scale of the issues and top four suppliers as shown in Figure 18.6.

The South Australia Government published a report in 2013, 'Strategic Procurement of ICT Products & Services', which provides a useful insight into the implementation of a change programme across ICT. In tranche 1 (Table 18.1) the following contracts were included:

Tranche 2 and 3 detail is also included in the report.

18.6 Capital investment procurement

18.6.1 Definitions

Capital equipment has been defined by Aljian[3] as:

> One of the subclasses of the fixed asset category and includes industrial and office machinery and tools, transportation equipment, furniture and fixtures and others. As such, these items are properly chargeable to a capital account rather than to expense.

Table 18.1 Tranche 1 of implementation programme for ICT

Distributed Computing Support Services	Two suppliers, responsible for the provision of server management and support services on agencies distributed server infrastructure
Electronic Messaging Services	A single supplier of electronic messaging services to the State (based on the Microsoft Exchange 2007 application)
Hosting Services	A panel of hosting services, including unmanaged colocation, shared hosting and dedicated hosting
Internet Services Provider	A single supplier of ISP services
Mainframe Computing Services	A single supplier of mainframe computing services, where the mainframe and operating system are owned, managed and maintained by the supplier, and user agencies own, manage and monitor the applications running on the mainframe
Managed Network Services	A single supplier responsible for the management, maintenance and support of the State's central and local data networks
Microsoft Large Account Reseller	A single supplier of Microsoft LAR services to State agencies
Threat Management & Protection Services	State agencies must adhere to the State's Technical Standard for Anti-Virus product (these products include Computer Associates/Total Defence, McAfee and Microsoft)

Alternative terms include 'capital goods', 'capital assets' and 'capital expenditure', which can be defined as follows:

- *Capital goods*

    Capital in the form of fixed assets used to produce goods, such as plant, equipment, rolling stock.[4]

- *Capital assets*

    Assets used to generate revenues on cost savings by providing production, distribution or service capabilities for more than one year.[5]

- *Capital expenditure*

    An expenditure on acquisition of tangible productive assets which yield continuous service beyond the accounting period in which they are purchased.[6]

Of the above definitions, that for capital expenditure is the most useful as it emphasises the three most important characteristics of capital equipment, namely:

- *tangibility* – capital equipment can be physically touched or handled
- *productivity* – capital equipment is used to produce goods or services
- *durability* – capital equipment has a life longer than one year.

18.6.2 Characteristics of capital expenditure

Expenditure on capital equipment differs from that on materials and components in many ways, including the following:

- the cost per item is usually greater and is often a one-off cost

- the items bought are used to facilitate production rather than as a part of the end product, or in a service environment are used to increase efficiency
- capital expenditure is financed by long-term capital or appropriations of profit rather than from working capital or charges against profit
- tax considerations, such as capital allowances and investment grants, have an important bearing on whether or not to purchase capital equipment and the timing of such purchases
- government financial assistance towards the cost of capital equipment may be available, such as where a manufacturing organisation is locating to, or is in a development area
- the procurement of capital equipment can be postponable, at least in the short term
- the decision to buy capital equipment often results in consequential decisions relating to sales, output and labour – in the latter case, consultations with the appropriate unions may be necessary.

Capital equipment procurement requires tailed contract terms and conditions to deal with such matters as guarantees, support services, intellectual property, and output availability, through life cost and installation/testing.

All of these considerations mean that the procurement of capital equipment is usually more complicated than that of materials and components, a large proportion of which can be handled using repeat procedures.

18.6.3 Factors to be considered when buying capital equipment

Apart from the mode of purchase, finance and the required return on the investment, the following factors should be considered when buying capital equipment.

- *Purpose* – what is the prime purpose of the equipment?
- *Flexibility* – how versatile is the equipment? Can it be used for purposes other than those for which it is primarily being acquired?
- *Spares* – cost, lead times, initial purchase of essential spares, Escrow for drawings and length of time spares will be provided.
- *Standardisation* – is the equipment standardised with any already installed in our organisation, thus reducing the cost of holding spares?
- *Compatibility with existing equipment* – is there any compatibility offering financial and/or operational benefits?
- *Life* – this usually refers to the period before the equipment will have to be written off due to depreciation or obsolescence. It is, however, not necessarily linked to the total lifespan of the item if it is intended that the asset will be disposed of before it is obsolete or unusable.
- *Reliability* – breakdowns mean greater costs, loss of goodwill due to delayed deliveries and possibly a high investment in spares.
- *Durability* – is the equipment sufficiently robust for its intended use?
- *Product quality* – defective output proportionately increases the cost per unit of output.

- *Cost of operation* – costs of fuel, power and maintenance. Will special labour or additional labour costs be incurred? Is consultation with the trade unions advisable?
- *Cost of installation* – does the price include the cost of installation, commissioning and training of operators?
- *Cost of maintenance* – can the equipment be maintained by our own staff or will special service support agreements with the vendor be necessary? What estimates of maintenance costs can be provided before purchase? How reliable are these?
- *Miscellaneous* – these include appearance, space requirements, quietness of operation (decibel level), safety and aspects of ergonomics affecting the performance of the operator.
- *Intellectual property rights* – who owns the design? Will the 'as built' drawings be provided?

18.6.4 Financing the acquisition of capital equipment

The acquisition of new or capital equipment may be financed by:

- outright purchase
- hire purchase
- leasing.

18.6.5 Outright purchase

The most obvious acquisition strategy for the purchase of equipment is for the buying organisation to pay the full price to the seller. The relative advantages and disadvantages of this strategy are shown in Table 18.2.

The effect of an outright purchase is to increase fixed (equipment) and reduce current (cash) assets. The capital cost of acquisition and the revenue cost of maintenance may adversely affect the working capital of an enterprise and so must, in the long term, be expected to create a positive return on the investment.

Table 18.2 Advantages and disadvantages of outright purchase of equipment

Advantages	Disadvantages
■ The total cost, particularly in comparison to rental, is low	■ Investment in fixed capital resources will reduce liquidity
■ Equipment may have a residual or second-hand value	■ Obsolescence or market changes may drastically reduce residual or second-hand market expectations
■ User has total control over the equipment (there may, however, be maintenance and software constraints)	■ Long-term commitment to maintenance and software may be necessary to protect the capital equipment investment
■ Capital allowances (normally 25 per cent annually on the reducing balance) may be set against tax	■ Equipment may rapidly become obsolete and the costs of upgrading by means of sale, trade-in or leasing may be expensive

Table 18.3 Advantages and disadvantages of hire purchase for equipment

Advantages	Disadvantages
■ Provides a compromise between straight purchase and leasing. Hire purchase agreements are easily negotiated and available	■ Financing arrangements impose more restrictions than when equipment is purchased outright
■ Subject to such factors as interest rates and the user's rate of return, hire purchase may be more financially effective than outright purchase or leasing	■ Interest rates and the user's rate of return may make hire purchase a less financially effective method than outright purchase or leasing
■ The most up-to-date technology may be hired and used to increase the company's productivity and efficiency	■ There will, in general, be no opportunity to upgrade
■ After all the payments have been made, the user becomes the owner of the equipment, either automatically or on payment of an option to purchase fee	■ The disadvantages of outright purchase as stated in Table 18.2
■ For tax purposes, the user is, from the start, regarded as the owner of the equipment and can claim capital allowance and VAT on the equipment	

18.6.6 Hire purchase

With a hire purchase (HP) agreement, when all the payments have been made, the business customer becomes the owner of the equipment. This ownership is transferred either automatically or on payment of an option to purchase fee.

For tax purposes, from the beginning of the agreement the business customer is treated as the owner of the equipment and can therefore claim capital allowance. This can be a significant tax incentive to invest in new plant and machinery.

HP agreements are different from ordinary credit agreements. With an HP agreement there are certain rules which apply including:

– you may not sell the goods until the money's paid off

– creditors may ask you to return the goods if you don't make regular payments.

The relative advantages and disadvantages of hire purchase of equipment are shown in Table 18.3.

18.6.7 Leasing

Leasing is a contract between the leasing company – the *lessor* – and the customer, the *lessee*.

■ The leasing company buys and owns the asset that the lessee requires.

■ The customer hires the asset from the leasing company and pays rental over a pre-determined period for the use of the asset.

As shown in Figure 18.7, there are two types of leases: finance leases and operating leases. Leasing has both advantages and disadvantages, as listed in Table 18.4.

Other advantages of leasing include easier replacement decisions. Ownership of an asset sometimes has the psychological effect of locking the owner into the use of an asset that should be replaced by a more efficient item of equipment. Leasing is also a hedge against inflation. The use of the asset is obtained immediately. The payments are met out of future earnings and are made in real money terms with the real costs falling over the years.

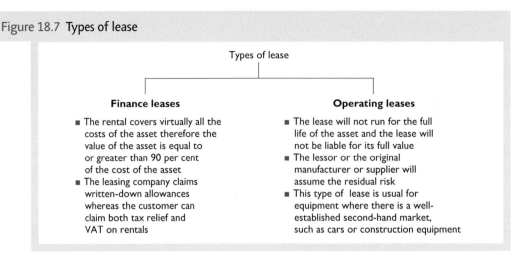

Figure 18.7 **Types of lease**

18.6.8 Leasing or buying

In practice, the decision to lease or buy is complicated, depending on operating, legal and financial considerations.

■ *Operating factors* relate to the advantages of a trial period before purchase, the immediate availability of cost-saving equipment, the period for which the assets are required and the hedges provided against obsolescence and inflation.

■ *Legal factors* are important as the leasing agreements are one-sided in that most risks are transferred to the lessee. The lessee should therefore carefully examine the terms and conditions of the contract, especially with regard to such aspects as limitations on the use of the equipment and responsibilities for its insurance, maintenance and so on. Where possible, improved terms should be negotiated.

■ *Financial factors* are usually crucial in deciding whether to lease or buy. These include:
  – the *opportunity cost* of capital – that is, what the purchase price of the equipment would earn if used for other purposes or invested elsewhere
  – the *discounted cost* of meeting the periodical rental payments over the period of the lease – note that 'flat' interest rates, calculated on the initial amount owing rather than on the average amount owed, can be misleading.

Table 18.4 **Advantages and disadvantages of leasing equipment**

Advantages	Disadvantages
■ Costs are known in advance and cannot be amended without agreement once the lease has been signed	■ Fixed obligation to pay rental may create an embarrassment in depressed conditions
■ Reduced need to tie up capital in fixed assets. Use of an asset can be obtained without capital outlay	■ Does not provide the prestige or flexibility of ownership
■ Leasing is concerned only with rentals and not with grants, allowances, depreciation or other calculations	■ Large organisations may be able to obtain capital or equal terms with lessors and, because of a steady flow of taxable profit, be able to obtain the use of capital allowances for themselves
■ Leasing provides a hedge against the risk of obsolescence	■ The flexibility to dispose of obsolete equipment before the end of the lease may be reduced

Example 18.1

How to work out whether it is best to lease or buy

(Taken from *The Lease–buy Decision*, BIM)

| Cash price of asset £1000 | Leased cost – 20 payments of £75 per quarter over 5 years £1500 | Excess cost of leasing over purchase £500 or 50 per cent | Annual flat rate of interest 50%/5 = 10 |

The true rate, however, is just over 20.4 per cent per annum, as can be seen from the following table.

Quarterly periods	Balance brought forward £	Repayment in advance £	Interest 20.4064% compound £	Balance carried forward £
1	1000.00	−75.00	43.95	968.95
2	968.95	−75.00	42.48	936.43
3	936.43	−75.00	40.94	902.37
4	902.37	−75.00	39.32	866.69
5	866.69	−75.00	37.62	829.31
6	829.31	−75.00	35.85	790.16
7	790.16	−75.00	33.98	749.14
8	749.14	−75.00	32.04	706.18
9	706.18	−75.00	29.99	661.17
10	661.17	−75.00	27.85	614.02
11	614.02	−75.00	25.62	564.64
12	564.64	−75.00	23.27	512.91
13	512.91	−75.00	20.81	458.72
14	458.72	−75.00	18.23	401.95
15	401.95	−75.00	15.54	342.49
16	342.49	−75.00	12.71	280.20
17	280.20	−75.00	9.75	214.95
18	214.95	−75.00	6.65	146.60
19	146.60	−75.00	3.40	75.00
20	75.00	−75.00	0.00	0.00
		−£1500.00	£500.00	

Ignoring tax, the lessee will be indifferent, on cost grounds, about whether to lease or buy if the opportunity cost of capital is about 20.4 per cent. If the cost of capital exceeds 20.4 per cent, however, then leasing will be cheaper in net present value (NPV) terms. If it is less, then leasing will be the most expensive proposition.

Excluding such factors as the time value of money, capital allowances and maintenance and other ownership costs, the simple lease versus buy break-even point can be calculated by using the formula:

$$N = \frac{P}{L}$$

Where:

P = purchase cost of equipment

L = monthly leasing payment

N = the number of months needed to break even

Thus, if the equipment costs £5000 and the leasing payment is £200 monthly, the simple break-even point is 25 months. This indicates that, other considerations apart, owning is preferable to leasing if the equipment is going to be used for more than 25 months.

18.6.9 Selecting suppliers of capital equipment

The decision about which of several possible suppliers to accept, is normally undertaken by an evaluation panel consisting of procurement, technical and financial specialists because the acquisition of capital equipment is a high-risk, high-cost issue.

In general, the greater the technical nature and complexity of an item, the greater will be the influence of the technical staff as both users and deciders. This will apply to both the acquisition of new or used equipment and purchase or lease decisions and, although there tend to be differences between the criteria for outright purchase and leasing, the most important considerations in both cases are technical and cost factors.

18.6.10 Technical factors relating to capital equipment

A matrix for the comparison and evaluation of quotations or tenders received from, say, three potential suppliers on the basis of technical factors is shown in Table 18.5. Points may be awarded to each factor or, alternatively, to a group of factors. The points awarded may be weighted according to the importance of the factor, as shown in Table 18.6.

The example given in Table 18.6 illustrates the difficulties of using a points system of evaluation. Using this system, the equipment supplied by B scores higher than that of A. If the evaluation teams however regarded A as having a greater suitability for use, then clearly the points allocation is flawed or the awarding of points is not based on a correct judgment.

Table 18.5 Capital equipment: technical factors evaluation sheet

Factor	Supplier			Points	Aggregate	Recommendations
	A	B	C			
General suitability for purpose						
Ease of installation						
Convenience of operation						
Ease of maintenance						
Power demand (kVA) ■ Normal running ■ Peak running						
Energy consumption ■ Power (kWh) ■ Fuel						
Other utility consumption ■ Steam ■ Water ■ Compressed air						
Equipment warranties						
Estimated life						
Life of items not subject to equipment warranties: estimates of normal operational wear						
Environmental considerations ■ Noise ■ Pollution ■ Effluent treatment						
Appraisal of ■ Electrical equipment ■ Instrumental and control equipment						

Factor	Supplier			Points	Aggregate	Recommendations
	A	B	C			
Standardisation with existing equipment						
Spare parts to be carried						
Interchangeability of spare parts						
Initial spares or tools to be supplied						
Services to be provided (if any) by supplier regarding: ■ Installation ■ Commissioning ■ Operator training						
Supplier's after-sales service and spare parts availability						
Other relevant factors ■ Delivery time ■ Insurance ■ General reputation or previous experience of supplier						
Totals						

kVA – kilovolt ampere; kWh – kilowatt hour

18.6.11 Cost factors

References to the important financial factors relating to the acquisition of capital equipment are made in sections 18.6.4 and 18.6.12. Some additional cost aspects that apply to the acquisition of capital items are set out in Table 18.7.

18.6.12 Evaluating capital investments

Although this is the province of the finance department, buyers should have an awareness of the methods of appraising expenditure on capital items. Three highly simplified examples of these approaches – payback, average rate of return and two applications of discounted cash flow – are briefly considered below.

Table 18.6 **Weighting factors according to their importance for capital equipment**

Factor	Assigned number of points	Points achieved	
		A	B
Overall suitability for purpose	500	400	300
General quality of technical design	400	300	400
Estimated life	400	300	400
Economy of performance and reliability	300	200	300
Economy of maintenance and after-sales service	300	250	200
Environment factors	300	200	300
General reputation of supplier	200	200	300
Estimated trade-in value at end of life or on disposal	200	20,0	300
Totals	**2600**	**2050**	**2500**

Table 18.7 Factors to be considered in quotations for capital equipment

Factor	Supplier			Notes
	A £	B £	C £	
Ex-works cost of equipment				
Delivery and handling costs				
Cost of insurance				
Additional costs for essential spares				
Installation costs for essential spares				
Installation costs payable to supplier				
Cost of extra work specified by purchaser				
Customs or other duties/tariffs for imported equipment				
Price escalation charges computed by using accepted formulae				
Terms of payment				
Warranty/guarantee payments				
Servicing, if any by supplier				
Less discounts				
Trade-ins				
other deductions				
Less capital allowances				
Final cost				

18.6.13 Payback

This is the time required for cash returns to equal the initial cash expenditure.

Example 18.2

The payback approach

An enterprise buys two machines, each costing £20,000. The net cash flows – after operating costs and expenses but not allowing for depreciation – are expected to be as shown below.

Year	Cash flow machine A (£)	Cash flow machine B (£)
1	5000	4500
2	5000	4500
3	5000	4500
4	5000	4500
5	5000	4500
6	–	4500
7	–	4500
	£25,000	£31,500

$$\text{Payback} = \frac{£20,000}{5000} = 4 \text{ years or } \frac{£20,000}{4500} = 4.4 \text{ years}$$

Example 18.2 shows the principle and fallacy of the payback approach. Machine A has the better payback figure as the initial cost is recovered in less time than for machine B. Machine B has an inferior payback, but the return extends over two further years.

The payback method, because of its simplicity, is probably the most popular method of investment appraisal. With this approach, the emphasis is on risk rather than profitability – that is, the risk with machine B is somewhat greater because it has a longer payback period.

18.6.14 Average rate of return (prior to tax)

This method aims to assess the average annual net profit after depreciation and other cash outlays as a percentage of the original cost. Three simple calculations are required:

1 *The annual rate of depreciation* – this is calculated by the 'straight line' method, namely:

$$\frac{\text{Cost} - \text{Residual value}}{\text{Estimated value}}$$

Assuming that machines A and B each had an estimated residual value of £1000, their annual depreciation rates would be:

$$\text{Machine B} = \frac{£20,000 - £1000}{7} = £2714$$

2 *Deduct depreciation from the average annual profit*

$$\text{Machine A} = £5000 - £3800 = £1200$$
$$\text{Machine B} = £4500 - £2714 = £1786$$

3 *Express net annual profit after depreciation as a percentage of the initial cost*

$$\text{Machine A} = \frac{£1200 \times 100}{£20,000} = 6 \text{ per cent}$$

$$\text{Machine B} = \frac{£1786 \times 100}{£20,000} = 8.93 \text{ per cent}$$

An alternative formula is that of return on capital employed (ROCE):

$$\frac{\text{Average annual profit after depreciation}}{\text{Original capital invested}} \times 100 \text{ per cent}$$

This method shows that the investment in machine B is the most profitable and allows comparison with the returns anticipated from alternative investments.

18.6.15 Discounting

Discounting is the opposite process to compounding. *Compounding* shows the extent to which a sum of money invested now will grow over a period of years at a given rate of compound interest. Thus, £100 invested now at 10 per cent compound interest will be worth £110 in one year's time and £121 at the end of two years.

Discounting shows the value at the present time of a sum of money payable or receivable at some future time. This present value can be obtained by dividing the amount now held by that to which it would have grown at a given rate of compound interest. So:

$$\frac{£100}{£110} = 0.9091 \text{ or } \frac{£100}{£121} = 0.08264 \text{ or } \frac{1}{(1 + r)^n}$$

where r is the rate of interest and n the number of years we are discounting.

These present values are *discount factors* and state that £100 at the end of one year at 10 per cent is worth £0.9091 or £0.8264 at the end of two years. In practice, the discount factors would be obtained from present value tables, which give the following for £1 at 10 per cent and 12 per cent respectively:

Years	10%	12%
1	£0.9091	£0.8929
2	£0.8264	£0.7972
3	£0.7513	£0.7118
4	£0.6830	£0.6355
5	£0.6209	£0.5674
6	£0.5645	£0.5066
7	£0.5132	£0.4523

Net present value and yield methods illustrate two of a number of approaches based on discounted cash flow.

18.6.16 Net present value (NPV)

In this method, the minimum required return on the capital investment is determined. The present value of anticipated future cash flows is that discounted at this rate. If the sum of these discounted cash flows exceeds the initial expenditure, then the investment will be given a higher return than forecast. Using the figures given above and a minimum required rate of 10 per cent, the discounted cash flows for machines A and B would be:

Machine A

Year	Cash return	10% factor	Net present value
1	£5000	0.909	£4545
2	£5000	0.826	£4130
3	£5000	0.751	£3755
4	£5000	0.683	£3415
5	£5000	0.621	£3105
6	–	–	–
7	–	–	–
	£25,000	–	£18,950

Machine B

Year	Cash return	10% factor	Net present value
1	£4500	0.909	£4090
2	£4500	0.826	£3717
3	£4500	0.751	£3379
4	£4500	0.683	£3073
5	£4500	0.621	£2794
6	£4500	0.565	£2542
7	£4500	0.513	£2308
	£31,500		£21,903

Machine A has a total return that is less than the initial expenditure of £20,000 – that is, less than the 10 per cent required. In contrast, machine B will exceed the given figure. This approach is very useful in evaluating which of two alternative investment propositions to adopt.

18.6.17 The buyer and capital investment purchases

Purchasing capital equipment requires extensive liaison between procurement, technical specialists and finance to ensure that when a purchase is made the company/organisation is completely satisfied. So far as procurement is concerned, the following considerations are paramount:

■ It is likely to be a one-off procurement event for which there is no technical, contractual, or commercial precedent.

■ The specification must reflect the performance required, with sufficient allowance for the total capacity that may be required.

■ The detail to be included in the contract must be established. Some facets of the contract include: the right to reject for failure to meet the specification; damages for late delivery; provision of drawings; provision of spare parts and their cost.

■ The price and payment terms (including foreign currency considerations) must be thought out.

■ The lifecycle cost of the equipment must be calculated.

■ Supply market research should be conducted to identify potential suppliers.

■ Disposal of displaced assets should follow a defined process.

18.7 Production materials

Risley[7] has classified materials and parts for use in manufacture under the following three headings:

■ *Raw materials* – primarily from agriculture and the various extractive industries – minerals, ores, timber, petroleum and scrap – as well as dairy products, fruits and vegetables sold to a processor.

■ *Semi-finished goods and processed materials* – to which some work has been applied or value added. Such items are finished only in part or may have been formed into shapes and specifications to make them readily usable by the buyer. These products lose their identity when incorporated into other products. Examples include: metal sections, rods, sheets, tubing, wires, castings, chemicals, cloth, leather, sugar and paper.

■ *Component parts and assemblies* – completely finished products of one manufacturer that can be used as part of a more complicated product by another manufacturer. These do not lose their original identity when incorporated into other products. Examples include: bearings, controls, gauges, gears, wheels, transistors, radio and TV tubes, car engines and windscreens.

18.8 Raw materials

18.8.1 Characteristics of raw materials

Raw materials are:

■ often 'sensitive' commodities
■ frequently dealt with in recognised commodity markets
■ safeguarded in many organisations by backward integration strategies.

18.8.2 Sensitive commodities

Sensitive commodities are raw materials – copper, cotton, lead, zinc, hides and rubber – the prices of which fluctuate daily. Here the buyer will aim to time purchases to fulfil requirements at the most competitive prices.

The main economic and political factors that influence market conditions are:

■ interest rates, such as the minimum lending rate
■ currency fluctuations, such as the strength of sterling
■ inflation, such as the effect of increased material and labour costs
■ government policies, such as import controls or stockpiling
■ 'glut' or shortage supply factors, such as crop failure
■ relationships between the exporting and importing country, such as oil as a political weapon.

18.8.3 Information regarding market conditions

The main sources of information regarding present and future market conditions for a commodity such as copper are as follows:

■ *Government sources* – in the UK, the Department for Business, Innovation and Skills.
■ *Documentary sources* – these may be 'general', such as the *Financial Times*, or specialised, such as *World Metal Statistics*, published by the World Bureau of Metal Statistics, or the *Metal Bulletin* and the *Mining Journal*.
■ *Federations* – the British Non-ferrous Metals Federation or International Wrought Copper Council, Eurometaux – the European Association of Metals.

■ *Exchanges* – these include independent research undertaken by brokers and dealers into metal resources and the short-term and long-term prospects for the commodity and daily prices of commodities dealt with by the exchange.

■ *Analysts* – these include economists and statisticians employed by undertakings to advise on corporate planning and purchasing policies and external units, such as the Commodities Research Unit and the Commodity Research Bureau.

The task of the buyer is to evaluate information and recommendations from sources including the above when relevant, and put forward appropriate policies that fall broadly into two classes: hand-to-mouth and forward buying.

18.8.4 Hand-to-mouth buying

This is buying according to need rather than in the quantities that are most economical. Circumstances in which this policy might be adopted are where prices are falling or where a change in design is imminent and it is desirable to avoid large stocks.

18.8.5 Forward buying

This applies to all purchases made for the purpose of increasing stocks beyond the minimum quantities required to meet normal production needs based on average delivery times.

Forward buying may be undertaken:

■ to obtain the benefit of economic order quantities (EOQs)

■ when savings made by buying in anticipation of a price increase will be greater than the interest lost on increased stocks or the cost of storage

■ to prevent suspension of production, due to occurrences such as strikes, by stockpiling to avoid shortages

■ to secure materials for future requirements when the opportunity arises, for example, some steel sections are only rolled at infrequent intervals.

Forward buying can apply to any material or equipment. A particular aspect of forward buying applicable to commodities is dealing in 'futures'.

18.9 Futures dealing

Futures dealing is an example of dealing in derivatives. *Derivatives* are financial contracts that have no intrinsic value but instead derive their value from something else. They hedge the risk of owning things that are subject to unexpected price fluctuations, such as foreign currencies and sensitive commodities. There are two main types of derivatives: futures and contracts for future delivery at a specified price and options that give one party the opportunity to buy from or sell to the other at a prearranged price.

A commodity such as copper may be bought direct from the producer or a commodity market. The latter provides the advantages of futures dealing. The London markets are divided into two main areas: metals and soft commodities. The six major primary non-ferrous metals dealt with on the London Metal Exchange (LME) are:

- primary high-grade aluminium
- 'A' grade copper
- high-grade zinc
- primary nickel
- standard lead
- tin.

The LME also offers contracts for secondary aluminium and silver. The soft commodities markets dealing in cocoa, sugar, vegetable oils, wool and rubber are the concern of the Futures and Options Exchange. The International Petroleum Exchange covers crude oil, gas, gasoline, naphtha and heavy fuel oil.

18.9.1 Functions of exchanges

Four functions of exchanges are to:

- enable customers, merchants and dealers to obtain supplies readily and at a competitive market price – on the LME, for example, contracts traded are for delivery on any market day within the period of three months ahead, except for silver, which can be dealt in up to seven months ahead
- smooth out price fluctuations due to changes in demand and supply
- provide insurance against price fluctuations by means of the procedure known as 'hedging' (see Example 18.3)
- provide appropriately located storage facilities to enable participants to make or take physical delivery of approved brands of commodities.

18.9.2 Differences between forward and futures dealing

- Futures are always traded on a recognised exchange.
- Futures contracts have standardised terms (see section 18.9.4 below).
- Futures exchanges use clearing houses to ensure that futures contracts are fulfilled. The London Clearing House (LCH), for example, is a professional, international clearing house owned by the six UK clearing banks. The responsibility for completing the execution of trade across the LME ring is transferred from the brokers to the LCH by what is called *novation*. The clearing house is, thus, the buyer and seller of last resort.
- Futures trading requires margins and daily settlements. A *margin* is a cash deposit paid by a trader to a broker who, in effect, lends money to enable the futures contract to be purchased. Traders hope to sell their futures contracts for more than their purchase price, enabling them to repay the broker's loan, have their margins returned and take their profits. No broker may margin a contract for less than the exchange minimum. Each trading day, every futures contract is assessed for liquidity. If the margin drops below a certain level, the trader must deposit an additional, or 'maintenance, margin'. Futures positions are easily closed as the trader has the option of taking physical delivery.

18.9.3 The purpose of and conditions for futures dealing

The purpose of futures dealing is to reduce uncertainty arising from price fluctuations due to supply and demand changes. This benefits both producers and consumers as the producer can sell forward at a sure price and the consumer can buy forward and fix material costs in accordance with a predetermined price. Manufacturers of copper wire, for example, might be able to obtain an order based on the current price of copper. If they think the price of copper may rise before they can obtain their raw materials, they can immediately cover their copper requirements by buying on the LME at the current price for delivery three months ahead, thus avoiding any risk of an increase in price.

For futures dealing to be undertaken, five conditions *must* apply:

1 The commodity must be capable of being stored without deterioration for a reasonable period.
2 The commodity must be capable of being graded for the purpose of providing a basis for description in the contract.
3 The commodity must be capable of being traded in its raw or semi-raw state.
4 Producers and consumers must approve the concept of futures dealing in the commodity.
5 There must be a free market in the commodity, with many buyers and sellers, making it impossible for a few traders to control the market and, thus, prevent perfect competition.

18.9.4 Some terms used in futures contracts

- *Arbitrage* – the (usually) simultaneous purchase of futures in one market against the sale of futures in a different market to profit from a difference in price.
- *Backwardation* – the backwardation situation exists when forward prices are less than current 'spot' ones.
- *Contango* – a contango situation exists when forward prices are greater than current 'spot' ones.
- *Force majeure* – the clause that absolves the seller or buyer from the contract due to events beyond their control, such as unavoidable export delays in producing countries due to strikes at the supplier's plant. Note that there is now no *force majeure* clause in a London Metal Exchange contract. Customers affected by a *force majeure* declared by a producer or refiner can always turn to the LME as a source of supply. Equally, suppliers can deliver their metal to the LME if their customers declare *force majeure*.
- *Futures* – contracts for the purpose of selling commodities for delivery sometime in the future on an organised exchange and subject to all the terms and conditions included in the rules of that exchange.
- *Hedging* – the use of futures contracts to insure against losses due to the effect of price fluctuations on the value of stocks of a commodity either held or to be acquired. Essentially, this is done by establishing a position in the futures market opposite one's position in the physical commodity. The operations of hedging can be described by means of a simplified example, given in Example 16.3.

Example 18.3

Hedging

1. On 1 June, X (manufacturer) buys stocks of copper to the value of £1000, which X hopes to make into cable wire and sell on 1 August for £2000, of which £750 represents manufacturing costs and £250 profit.

2. The price of copper falls by 1 August to £750 so X sells at £1750 – that is, X makes no profit.

3. To insure against the situation in (2), X, on 1 June, sells futures contracts in copper for £1000.

4. In August, if the price remains stable X will buy at this price, thus making a profit of £250 on the futures contract, which will offset any loss in manufacturing. If the price rises to £1250, X will lose on the futures contract, but this will be offset by gains on manufacturing. While trading refers to actual physical copper trading, a futures transaction is really dealing in price differences and the contract would be discharged by paying over or receiving the balance due.

- *Options* – a buyer who expects the price of a commodity to rise may pay option money to a dealer for the right to buy it at a stated future date – a *call option* – or sell at a future date – a *put option*.

- *Spot price* – the price for immediate cash payment.

- *Spot month* – the first deliverable month for which a quotation is available in the futures market.

- *Options contracts* – relate to the sale or purchasing of commodities that will occur at a specified price on a specified future date, but only if the prospective buyer or seller wishes to exercise the option to buy or sell at the predetermined *strike* or *exercise price*. Options, as we saw above, can be either 'call' or 'put'. Buyers of call options are exposed to limited risk as the most they can lose is the amount of the premium or the sum of money paid when the option is purchased. They have, however, an unlimited profit potential. Conversely, writers of put options have unlimited risk but limited profit potential. Mathematically, however, the odds favour the put option writer.

18.9.5 Commodities at the right price

Buying commodities is the province of specialists who have access to current and relevant information. Such specialists use two approaches to determine the right price, namely *fundamental analysis* and *technical analysis*.

- *Fundamental analysis* relies heavily on an assessment, both statistically and in other ways, of supply and demand. Statistics in particular, indicate whether the trend of prices is up or down. In addition to trends, fundamentalists take into account production, consumption and stocks. Thus, an imbalance in production and consumption will affect prices. Prices will rise or fall according to whether less or more of a commodity is being produced than is consumed. Stock figures, according to the mood of the market, may be counted either way. In a *bull*, or rising, *market*, stocks tend to be held by producers or merchants, thus forcing consumers to bid higher for available stocks of the commodity. In a falling, or *bear market*, consumers hive off their stocks and buy less of the commodity than they are using, while producers reduce prices to a level at which they can turn unsold stock into cash. Additionally, fundamental analysis pays attention to news items that affect sensitive commodities, such as wars, weather, natural disasters, political developments, environmental legislation, labour unrest and macroeconomic statistics from major economies.

■ *Technical analysis* claims to be quicker and more comprehensive than fundamental analysis as the market is efficient and the current market price clears the market or brings it into equilibrium. If this is so, it is unnecessary to do more than look at the record of prices to read the future of prices. Technical analysis, therefore, makes great use of chart formations, such as can be obtained from plotting prices on two different timescales, such as daily price movements and the one year rolling average – that is, every day, the latest day's price is added to the list of prices, the oldest year ago price is dropped and a new average for the past year is calculated. Chartists have developed a language of their own for interpreting their charts, such as 'base formation', 'break out', 'overprofit', 'oversold' and so on, to name a few. The results of charting are offered to commodity market makers, often at a considerable charge. The basic concept is that of using the past to predict the future. Chartists, however, are no more able to forecast the effects of news than those who rely on fundamental analysis. In practice, a combination of the two approaches is often used. It has been rightly observed that 'the whole point of having an idea of the 'right price' is to spot when the market price is wrong'. Companies have been forced into liquidation by making long-term forecasts on the assumption that today's price is right when, in fact, it is wrong and vice versa.

18.9.6 Commodity trade financing

There are financing needs of all stages of the supply chain, including producers/exporters, trading companies, processors, importers, end users/distributors.

A Trade Finance example[8] is shown in Figure 18.8.

Understanding the commodity and risk profiling is shown in Figure 18.9.

18.10 Methods of commodity dealing

Dealing in commodities or derivatives is a highly complicated activity, involving the possibilities of heavy gains or losses. In 1995, Barings Bank 'went bust' when one of its employees, Nick Leeson, gambled that the Nikkei 225 index of 225 leading Japanese company shares would not move materially from its normal trading range. That assumption was shattered by the Kobe earthquake on 17 January 1995. Leeson, who attempted to conceal his gamble, lost the bank $14 billion. Warren Buffett[9] said:

> We view them [derivatives] as time bombs both for the parties that deal in them and the economic system . . . In our view derivatives are financial weapons of mass destruction, carrying dangers that, while now latent, are potentially lethal.

An organisation buying large quantities of a commodity will therefore employ a specialist buyer who has made a specialist study of that commodity and its markets.

Figure 18.8 Trade finance example – crude oil from Angola to the US

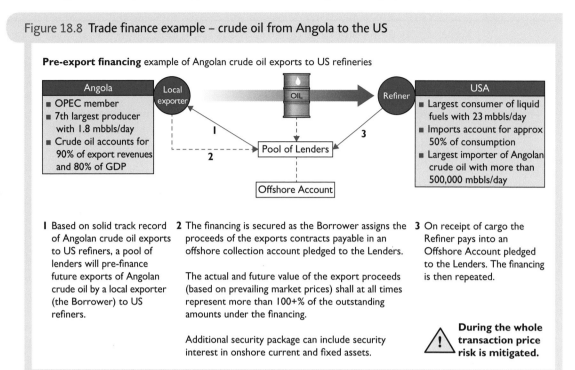

Pre-export financing example of Angolan crude oil exports to US refineries

1 Based on solid track record of Angolan crude oil exports to US refiners, a pool of lenders will pre-finance future exports of Angolan crude oil by a local exporter (the Borrower) to US refiners.

2 The financing is secured as the Borrower assigns the proceeds of the exports contracts payable in an offshore collection account pledged to the Lenders.

The actual and future value of the export proceeds (based on prevailing market prices) shall at all times represent more than 100+% of the outstanding amounts under the financing.

Additional security package can include security interest in onshore current and fixed assets.

3 On receipt of cargo the Refiner pays into an Offshore Account pledged to the Lenders. The financing is then repeated.

⚠ **During the whole transaction price risk is mitigated.**

Figure 18.9 Understanding the commodity and risk profiling

Understanding and mitigating the risks behind a commodity transaction is at the heart of the expertise

Risk	Description	Mitigants
Performance	The risk that an exporter does not deliver the goods in the context of a commercial contract backing a credit facility	**Track record,** contractual terms, capacity and cost analysis
Commodity price	The risk that commodities' price volatility negatively impact the cash flows of a specific transaction or the value of assets	Overcollateralisation, **marked-to-market adjustments** or hedging
Country	The risks inherent to the situation of a particular country that may directly or indirectly negatively affect a transaction	Analysis of **commodity's strategic importance,** offshore repayments, political risk insurance
Corporate	The risk related to the financial health of a counterparty based in most cases on an assessment of the business model, balance sheet and income statements and cash flow analysis	Financial analysis of the company, ownership and strategy. **In-depth liquidity analysis**
Payment	The risk that an importer does not comply with its payment obligation in the context of a commercial contract backing a credit facility	**Track record,** letter of credit or payment guarantee
Damage or loss of goods	Self explanatory	Track record, **insurance**
Quality & quantity	Goods delivered do not comply with contractual specifications in terms of quantity and quality	Track record, Clients–Supplier relationship, **overcollateralisation,** first class inspection companies
FX	Self explanatory	Trade is **back to back in USD,** offshore repayments
Legal	Self explanatory	**Legal opinions** (local and international)

Commodity (Collateral)

Often, commodity buying will be a separate department distinct from other procurement operations. Where quantities or the undertaking are smaller, a broker may be retained to procure commodity requirements – in effect, subcontracting this aspect of procurement.

Other approaches are designed to enable non-specialists to undertake commodity buying with a minimum of risk. These include the following.

18.10.1 Time budgeting or averaging

This is an application of hand-to-mouth buying in which supplies of the commodity are bought as required and no stocks are held. As supplies are always bought at the ruling price, losses are divided, but, of course, the prospect of windfall gains is obviated. This policy cannot be applied if it is necessary to carry inventory.

18.10.2 Budgeting or cost averaging

This approach is based on spending a fixed amount of money in each period – say, monthly. The quantity purchased therefore increases when the price falls and reduces when the price rises.

Example 18.4

The budgeting or cost averaging approach

Assume the monthly requirement for commodity X is 100 tonnes, the average price of which, from experience, is estimated at £100. We therefore budget to spend £100 × 100 = £10,000 monthly. The price fluctuates as shown below.

Date	Cost per tonne	Amount spent	Tonnes purchased
January	£98	£10,000	102.04
February	£97	£10,000	103.09
March	£95	£10,000	105.26
April	£96	£10,000	104.16
May	£95	£10,000	105.26
June	£93	£10,000	107.52
July	£92	£10,000	108.69
August	£95	£10,000	105.26
September	£97	£10,000	103.09
October	£100	£10,000	100.00
November	£102	£10,000	98.03
December	£104	£10,000	96.15
		£120,000	1238.55

$$\text{Average cost per tonne, total cycle} = \frac{£120,000}{1238.55} = £96.89$$

Purchases over the total cycle exceed requirements by 38.55 tonnes. There is thus an average saving of £3.11 per tonne.

18.10.3 Volume timing of purchases

This approach is based on forward buying when prices are falling and hand-to-mouth buying when prices are rising. Its success depends on accurate forecasting of market trends.

Example 18.5

The volume timing approach

Assume that the price of a commodity with a constant monthly requirement of 100 tonnes is between £100 and £120 per tonne. The buyer is authorised to purchase up to three months' supply.

In January, market intelligence is that the current price of £100 is likely to rise over the next three months to £120. An order is therefore placed for 300 tonnes at £100 per tonne.

In early March, intelligence is that, over the next 3 months – April to June – the price of £120 will rise further to £135. A further 300 tonnes are ordered at £120 per tonne. In early June, it is forecast that prices will fall. For each of the months July, August, September and October, therefore, only one month's supply is bought, at £130, £125, £120 and £110 respectively. In September, the forecast is of a further rise to £125. Therefore, a forward order for three months' supply is placed at £110 per tonne.

The savings from forward buying on the upswing and hand-to-mouth buying on the downswing are shown in the table.

Date	Quantity purchased (tonnes)	Price paid per tonne £	Market price per tonne £	Actual cost £	Market cost £
January	100	100	100	10,000	10,000
February	100	100	110	10,000	11,000
March	100	100	120	10,000	12,000
April	100	120	125	12,000	12,500
May	100	120	130	12,000	13,000
June	100	120	135	12,000	13,500
July	100	130	130	13,000	13,000
August	100	125	125	12,500	12,500
September	100	120	120	12,000	12,000
October	100	110	110	11,000	11,000
November	100	110	120	11,000	12,000
December	100	110	125	11,000	12,500
	1200			136,500	145,000

$$\text{Average price paid per tonne over year} = \frac{£136,500}{1200} = £113.75$$

$$\text{Average market price per tonne} = \frac{£145,000}{1200} = £120.83$$

$$\text{Saving over total period} = \frac{\text{Average market price} - \text{Average price paid}}{\text{Average market price}}$$

$$= \frac{£120.83 - £113.75}{120.83} \times 100 = \frac{7.08}{120.83} \times 100$$

$$= 5.86\%$$

18.11 Procurement of non-domestic gas and electricity

The deregulation of energy supply started in the UK with the implementation of the Gas Act 1986. Then the Electricity Act 1989 brought chances and opportunities, risks and complexities for those responsible for the procurement non-domestic energy supplies. To exploit these opportunities and minimise the risks, purchasers of gas and electricity require a knowledge of energy regulation, the relevant supply chains and energy markets, pricing, the process of switching suppliers, the use of online retail energy marketplaces and energy consultants and management.

18.12 Energy regulation

The Office of Gas and Electricity Markets (Ofgem) is the regulator of Britain's gas and electricity. Ofgem was established in 1999 by the merger of the Office of Gas Supply (Ofgas) and Office of Electricity Regulation (Offer); set up under the Gas Act 1986 and the Electricity Act 1989 respectively. Under the Utilities Act 2000, Ofgem ceased to be an independent regulator and now reports to the Gas and Electricity Markets Authority (GEMA) and the Gas and Electricity Consumers Council. The Utilities Act also put Ofgem under the direct control of the Secretary of State for Trade and Industry (now DECC).

Ofgem also has enforcement powers under the Competition Act 1998 and the power to enforce consumer protection law under the Enterprise Act 2002. It can also name and shame companies that it believes are acting against the interests of gas and electricity consumers.

Any organisation seeking to supply gas and electricity to customers has to be licensed by Ofgem, which is one of its powers under the Gas and Electricity Acts. One area it does not licence is the offshore gas industry, which is regulated by the Department of Energy and Climate Change (DECC).

18.13 Energy supply chains in the UK

In 2017 the electricity generated by fuel type was[10]:

Gas	40.4%
Nuclear	20.8%
Hydro	1.8%
Wind & Solar	18.2%
Other renewables	9.4%
Coal	6.7%
Oil and other fuels	2.9%

The total electricity generated was 338.6 TWh.

Ofgem[11] report there are 14 licensed distribution network operators (DNOs) in Britain and each is responsible for a regional distribution services area. The 14 DNOs are owned by six different groups. In addition, there are also a number of smaller networks owned and operated by Independent Network Operators (IDNOs). These are in the areas covered by the DNOs.

Great Britain can receive gas from a diverse range of sources:

a)   Extracted from Great Britain's gas reserves, most of which are located offshore

b)   Five pipelines connected directly to Norwegian offshore gas fields

c)   Two pipeline connections to mainland Europe

d)   Three liquefied Natural Gas (LNG) terminals accessing the global LNG market, with the majority of supply currently from Qatar

e)   Eight storage sites

Great Britain's transmission system is made up of nearly 8000 km of pipelines with gas flowing through them at a typical speed of 38km/hour. After flowing through the transmission system, gas enters the distribution networks. There are twelve different regions, known as local distribution zones.

18.14 Markets

Markets for gas and electricity are both wholesale and retail.

18.14.1 Wholesale markets

Wholesale markets are those in which electricity and gas are traded between parties before being sold to suppliers that, in turn, sell to consumers. In the present context, the parties to the wholesale market are gas producers, electricity generators, transmitters, distributors and suppliers.

The distributors or transmitters are monopolies regulated by price controls based on the RPI – X formula. Using this formula, the prices that transmitters or distributors can charge is limited to the increase in the retail price index less a proportion to drive up transmitter or distribution efficiency. Thus, if the RPI is 3 per cent and X is 2 per cent, prices cannot be increased by more than 1 per cent annually.

The process of balancing is best illustrated by reference to electricity supply. Approximately 24 hours before its physical delivery, suppliers begin to fine-tune their positions to cover any shortfall between their actual positions and that covered by their contracts on the forwards and futures market. Any shortages will be covered by short-term spot trading. Suppliers must declare their positions up to 35 hours before delivery. This is known as *gate closure*. From gate closure to the time of physical delivery, the operator (the National Grid) works to ensure that 'the lights stay on'. This is possible because the UK transmission systems are fully interconnected and the operator can use the bids made on the power exchanges to balance demand and supply.

18.14.2 Retail markets

Retail markets are those in which suppliers sell gas or electricity to consumers.

18.15 Pricing

18.15.1 Gas pricing

Gas was traditionally invoiced in therms, but now, like electricity, is charged in kilowatt hours (kWh). There are approximately 29.3 kilowatt hours to a therm.

UKERC[12] point out that natural gas production in the UK peaked in 2000, and in 2004 it became a net importer. A decade later and the UK now imports about half the natural gas it consumes. Given the nature of the UK's gas balance, two arenas are of particular significance: development in the Northwest European gas market (and the broader EU strategy of gas market integration) and developments in the global liquefied Natural Gas market.

The report then hypothesised that:

> The supply chain approach addresses the shortcomings of the current energy security literature that we consider to be fourfold: first, it tends to be too abstract and fails to engage with the specific characteristics of natural gas; second, it assumes that oil and gas are the same when it comes to assessing energy security; third, it is too state-centric and tends to ignore the crucial role of companies and other stakeholders involved in the gas markets; and fourth, it is overly concerned with upstream physical security of supply.

The price paid for gas comprises:

- operating costs
- other costs (network and environmental/social)
- network costs
- wholesale costs
- profit
- VAT.

The price of gas can vary due to such factors as:

- the season – the price of gas is more in winter than summer
- the annual volume of gas used
- the location of the customer
- the duration of the contract
- whether the contract for the supply of gas is firm or interruptible – a firm supply is guaranteed unless there is an emergency whereas, due to weather or market conditions, interruptible customers may be required to interrupt their use of natural gas either by switching to an alternative fuel source or to curtail their use, but, in return, they enjoy lower rates than firm commercial customers.

18.15.2 Electricity pricing

For a detailed overview of Electricity Distribution Price Control Cost and Revenue reporting see the Ofgem Regulatory Instructions and Guidance: version 3.1 published in March 2014.

A typical invoice for electricity will be broken down into the following elements.

- *Total kilowatts used* – this is known as the *energy charge*. The energy charge along with the profit, are the only negotiable elements. The most important aspect of the energy charge is the time at which the energy is used.

- *Transmission charge* – this is the amount paid to the National Grid (NG) in England and differs according to capacity and location. Such charges, for example, tend to be low in the north and high in the south of England. Suppliers pay three forms of transmission charges:
  - demand charges, based on demand during the three annual peak demand periods (triads), which differ depending on zones
  - energy consumption charges, based on the energy consumed between 1600 and 1900 hours throughout the year
  - charges for non-energy ancillary services, covering reserve generation and standby services to facilitate balancing.
- *Distribution charges* – these also vary according to the customer's regional location and the capacity held for the customer.
- *Meter charges* – these are discussed later.
- *Fossil fuel levy (FFL)* – a charge to reduce consumption of electricity produced by using fossil fuels, such as coal and oil, and increase usage of electricity produced by renewable energy sources, such as wind power and geothermal energy.
- *The Climate Change Levy (CCL)* is a tax on the use of energy in industry, commerce and the public sector. It was introduced in 2001. More information can be found on the Department of Energy and Climate Change website. The current CCL rates can be found on the HM Revenue and Customs website. A general guide to CCL is available at www.hmrc.gov.uk (click on the Environmental taxes' section of 'Excise and other').

18.16 Procuring energy contracts

The procurement of energy contracts is a highly specialised task requiring considerable expertise. The traditional annual tender routine brings with it significant price risks. If the tender process coincides with high market prices the buyer could pay circa 50 per cent more than another buyer whose tender coincides with low prices. Gas and electricity markets are highly volatile and complex.

18.16.1 Price structure

Electricity and gas prices (see Figure 18.10) are made up of the raw energy cost, transmission and distribution costs, data and meter service costs and supplier costs. Price elements are either fixed, such as regulated pass-through costs, or flexible, such as time-to-market decisions (when in the year to buy) or supplier negotiation.

Climate Change Levy (CCL) is the government tax charged on the units of energy and acts as an environmental tax on energy delivered to non-domestic users. Following the government's decision to terminate the Carbon Reduction Commitment Energy Efficiency Scheme (CRC) on 31 March 2019, the CCL would become the UKs only carbon tax on energy bills.

The rates from 1 April 2019 are:

- Electricity (£per kilowatt hour) 0.00847, a 45% increase from 2018
- Natural Gas (£ per KWh) 0.00339, a 67% increase from 2019.

Figure 18.10 Electricity and gas price structures

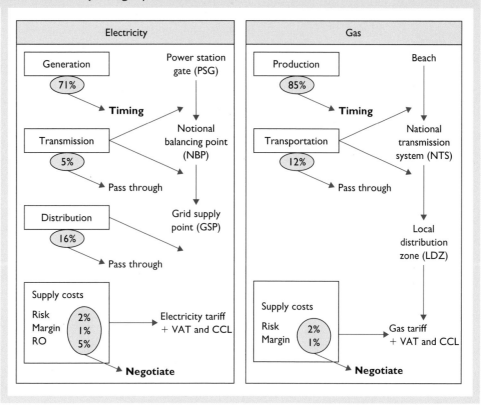

18.16.2 Market analysis

Readers who require this highly specialised data are advised to read the Department for Business, Energy & Industrial Strategy[13] report 'Energy Consumption in the UK'.

18.16.3 Organising to procure energy

Prior to tendering a great deal of information will have to be gathered and collated, including:

- full details of site(s) including activities, addresses and special characteristics
- electricity Meter Point Administration (MPA) number (a 21-digit reference introduced in 1998)
- all MPANs for gas and electricity
- meter serial number
- meter operator
- half-hourly data files for last twelve months
- working days

- shift patterns/hours of work
- details of any planned changes in usage
- agreed supply capacity.

18.16.4 Price risks

So what is the price risks involved?[14] There are four main aspects of price risk in energy contracts, which should be covered in a robust risk management strategy:

- *Volume risk* refers to the change in consumption, either planned or unplanned, which will affect budgets. Other volume considerations such as any minimum or maximum consumption clauses in contracts should also be taken into account in your risk strategy. These can attract high financial penalties and without proper control, they could have a significant impact on the overall costs.

- *Procurement risk* refers to the level of authorisation and expertise of the person making the contract decision. In a stable market, no significant energy procurement expertise is required to choose the time to buy energy. However, in a volatile market, prices can be missed by a lack of necessary authorisation, and any price that is held open for a long period of time attracts a high price premium. Energy market analysis and expertise are therefore essential to ensure an understanding of the price drivers for the short-, medium- and long-term markets.

- *Operational risk* details contingency plans for dealing with problems which may prevent the procurement of energy such as ICT issues or key personnel being unavailable from both the supplier and purchaser side.

- *Value risk* essentially details the price risk and the measures being taken to minimise 100 per cent exposure to the markets. This can be achieved, for example by having stops and targets on time periods or choosing to build up the volume over time.

18.17 Energy consultants and management

Because of the complexity of energy management, companies may outsource both their energy buying and energy management. Gas and electricity brokers such as EnergyQuote undertake both to negotiate the best deals on behalf of clients and provide services beyond the procurement stage, too, such as energy audits, monitoring and bill checking. A register of approved energy consultants is kept by the Energy Institute, Register of Professional Energy Consultants (RPEC). Major EU energy companies and large customers are now required to undertake energy audits under the EU's Energy Efficiency Directive 2012/27/EU. The energy audit is required every four years.

Buyers of gas and electricity can obtain much help from associations of purchasers that share information and expertise in exchange for a fee. Such associations include the Energy Information Centre Ltd, the government's Energy Efficiency Best Practice Programme and, for big companies, the Major Energy Users Council Ltd. There is also the European Council for an energy efficient economy (eceee). Details of these organisations are available on the internet.

18.18 Component parts and assemblies

A *component* is a structure that has parts and connections. The parts are also components and the *connections* are to other components. Essentially, components are proprietary, where the supplier owns the intellectual property, or the buyer's organisation owns the intellectual property.

When buying components there are many considerations, including:

Make *v* buy	There is, sometimes, the option of make or buy to which the buyer should be alert.
Pricing	The price of proprietary components can be negotiated and discounts/rebates applied in specific circumstances.
Tooling	Some components require tooling to be paid for. This may be a one-off charge or amortised over an agreed quantity.
Free issue	The buyer may consider supplying raw materials for conversion into components but will need to consider scrap arising.
Specification	The specification is vital for components, particularly when components have safety critical applications.
Quality	Agreement must be reached about how components will be checked for quality compliance, e.g. tested to destruction.
Quantity	There will be a relationship between price and quantity so it is an important decision to make how many to purchase.
Continuing supply	For proprietary components the buyer must make sure there is a continuing supply available otherwise there will be a resourcing cost.
Availability of drawings	If it is a proprietary item the buyer may consider requesting a copy of the drawings to facilitate supply if the supplier goes into administration or cannot meet an agreed lead time.
Inventory	The buyer may ask the supplier to supply on the basis of consignment stock or to guarantee supply from his own stock.

18.19 Consumables and MRO items

Apart from negotiating the actual procurement of consumables and MRO items, the procurement function can:

- liaise with maintenance staff to ensure that information regarding the cost, availability and delivery times is available, especially for 'critical' items
- advocate a policy of standardisation to avoid holding a variety of 'critical' spares
- suggest alternatives, such as outsourcing of catering and cleaning, which can obviate the need to hold stocks of food and cleaning materials
- minimise administrative and storage costs by the application of small order procedures and direct requisitioning by users against 'call-off' contracts, subject to approved safeguards
- analyse proposed maintenance contracts offered by suppliers and advise whether or not these should be accepted.

18.20 Construction supplies and bills of quantities

18.20.1 Construction supplies

Construction supplies differ in a number of respects from supplies purchased for manufacturing and service organisations.

- Construction supplies are purchased for use on a site that may be distant from the office that placed the orders or even in another country.
- Many construction supplies have a high bulk relative to their value, such as bricks and steel. Because of the high cost of transport, it is desirable that construction supplies are procured as near as possible to the site where they will be used.
- With many construction schemes, the procurement department will probably be asked to negotiate agreements for electricity, gas and water supplies and, occasionally, for sewage or effluent disposal.
- Specification of construction supplies will often be on the basis of:
  - instructions given by the client to an architect or civil engineer
  - architect's specifications.

  These specifications are often stated in the bill of quantities.

- In the interests of security, it is important that purchased supplies are delivered to site as close as possible to the time that they will be used.
- Because of the remoteness of the site from the contractor's office, procedures for recording of supplies received and issued will have to be agreed between the contractor's procurement department and site engineer.
- Some construction supplies may be 'free issue' supplies or 'customer furnished equipment' (CFE) – that is, items provided by the client for use in connection with a construction project that is being undertaken on the client's behalf.
- Sub-contracting is an important aspect of procurement for construction projects. Examples would be contracts for foundations, drainage, air-conditioning, lift installation, ventilation, structural steelwork and so on.
- Some construction supplies involve intra-company procurement. Thus, a construction company may also own stone, sand and gravel quarries that supply other companies within the group.
- Supplies may be transferred from one site or construction contract to another. It is therefore important to know what supplies are available at each site.
- Some discretion must be allowed to the site engineer to arrange for the supply of materials and services, such as hiring plant for particular parts of the project. All such orders should be notified to the contractor's procurement department to ensure that orders are placed and amounts due to suppliers are duly paid.

18.20.2 Bills of quantities

Bills of quantities are documents prepared by quantity surveyors from drawings and specifications prepared by architects or engineers, setting out as priceable items the detailed requirements of the work and the quantities involved.

Bills of quantities are usually formidable documents running to many pages and incorporating schedules of conditions of the contract in addition to the specifications of labour and materials required for the particular construction project. A typical bill of quantities will have the following six sections.

■ *Section 1: Preliminary items and general conditions* – this sets out the terms and conditions of the contract and responsibilities of the contractor, architect and other parties involved in the contract, altogether with provision for the settlement of disputes arising from the contract.

■ *Section 2: Trade preambles* – this sets out the general requirements relating to such aspects of a construction contract as:

  – excavation and earthwork
  – concrete work
  – brickwork and blockwork
  – roofing
  – woodwork
  – structural steelwork
  – metalwork
  – plumbing installation
  – foul drainage above ground
  – holes/chases/covers/supports for services
  – electrical and heating installations
  – floor, wall and ceiling finishes
  – glazing
  – painting and decorating.

■ *Section 3: Demolition and spot items* – Foundation work
■ *Section 4: General alteration and refurbishment work*   } These sections set out
■ *Section 5: Provisional sums and contingencies*   the quantities of work
■ *Section 6: Grand summary*   to be done

Typical extracts from Sections 2 and 4 relating to plumbing installations are shown in Figures 18.11 and 18.12.

The main aims of bills of quantities are to:

■ enable tenderers to show against each item on the unpriced bill of quantities a price per unit covering labour, materials, overheads and profit and, when totalled in the 'grand summary', the items will provide the tender price for the contract

■ enable the quantity surveyor, on receipt of the successful tender, to ensure that the contractor has made no serious errors that could cause complications at a later date

■ avoid the inclusion by the tenderer of a large amount for contingencies

■ assist in verifying the valuation of variations due to changes in design requested or agreed by the client after the contract has been placed.

Figure 18.11 Extract from a bill of quantities

Clause	SECTION 2 Plumbing installation Trade Preambles
R1	**General** Before pricing the specification, contractors tendering are requested to visit the site, peruse the drawings and make themselves fully conversant with the nature of the works for which they are tendering. **HOT AND COLD WATER** **GENERAL INFORMATION/REQUIREMENTS**
R2	**The installation** – Drawing references: See architect's layout – Cold water: Mains fed – Hot water – direct system(s): Unvented direct water storage cylinder Heat source(s): Immersion heaters Control: Thermostat on immersion heater – Other requirements: Remove existing pipework Allow for general builder's work
R3	ELECTRICAL WORK in connection with the installation is not included, and will be carried out by the electrical contractor. Provide all information necessary for the completion of such work.
R4	SERVICE CONNECTIONS are covered elsewhere by a provisional sum.
R5	FUEL FOR TESTING: Costs incurred in the provision of fuel for testing and commissioning the installation are to be included in clause B40 section 1. **GENERAL TECHNICAL REQUIREMENTS**
R6	PIPELINE SIZES: Calculate sizes to suit the probable simultaneous demand for the building and to ensure: – a water velocity of not more than 1.3 m/s for hot water and 2.0 m/s for cold water – suitable discharge rates at draw-off points – a filling time for the cold water storage cistern of not more than 1 hour.
R7	INSTALLATION GENERALLY: – Install, test and commission the hot and cold water systems so that they comply with BS 6700, water supply bye-laws, and the requirements of this section to provide a system free from leaks and the audible effects of expansion, vibration and water hammer. – All installation work to be carried out by qualified operatives. – Store all equipment, components and accessories in original packaging in dry conditions. – Protect plastic pipework from prolonged exposure to sunlight. Wherever practicable retain protective wrappings until practical completion. – Securely fix equipment, components and accessories in specified/approved locations, parallel or perpendicular to the structure of the building unless specified otherwise, using fixing brackets/mountings etc. recommended for the purpose by the equipment manufacturer. – In locations where moisture is present or may occur, use corrosion-resistant fittings/fixtures and avoid contact between dissimilar metals by use of suitable washers, gaskets, etc. – All equipment, pipework, components, valves, etc., forming the installation to be fully accessible for maintenance, repair or replacement unless specified or shown otherwise.

Figure 18.12 Extract from a bill of quantities

```
                              SECTION 4

                                                              Plumbing
                                                              Installations
  Item              PLUMBING INSTALLATION                      £      p
                 GENERAL
  A              Bring to site and remove from site on completion all plant
                 required for the work in this section          } Item
  B              Maintain on site all plant required for the work in this
                 section                                   ...  Item
                 Installation as shown in the following sections to be
                 carried out to the architect's drawings and specifications
  C              Soil and waste pipes                       ...  Item
  D              Hot and cold water supply including all fittings and
                 rising mains                               ...  Item
  E              Dry riser installation                     ...  Item
  F              Sanitary fittings                          ...  Item
  G              Allow for carrying out all builder's work in connection
                 with the plumbing installations as described including cutting
                 and forming chases, cutting and forming holes, forming ducts
                 through walls and floors, timber support battens, all dire
                 stopping to walls and floors and everything necessary to
                 complete the whole of the works to the reasonable
                 satisfaction of the architect                  Item
  H              Allow for testing and commissioning to plumbing installations
                 including obtaining any certificates to be handed to the
                 architect                                      Item
  I              Hand to the architect at practical completion of the works
                 copies of the manufacturer's operation and maintenance
                 instructions together with two sets of 'as fitted' drawings.  Item
                 PLUMBING INSTALLATIONS CARRIED TO
                 SUMMARY FOLIO NO. 4/63

                                                              £
```

18.21 Procurement of services

18.21.1 Procurement and services

In any large organisation, expenditure on services is a major element of total corporate spend. Fearon and Bales[15] in a study of 116 large USA organisations reported that:

- over half of the purchase dollars (54 per cent) were spent on services
- only 27 per cent of the expenditure on services in their sample organisation was handled by procurement staff
- of the total spend, the largest categories were utilities (9 per cent), insurance (82 per cent), sales/promotions (7.2 per cent), health benefit plans (6.1 per cent) and travel – air tickets (58 per cent), and in none of these areas was the procurement department handling more than half the total expenditure

- two explanations for the low involvement of procurement departments in the procurement of services are:
  - the users of services considered that they had greater expertise in the particular area of service buying than procurement department staff
  - the purchase of services involves a closer personal relationship with suppliers than does the purchase of goods, yet Fearon and Bales suggest that 'if a logical procurement process as normally used by procurement professionals was employed substantial savings might be possible regardless of by whom the actual buying is done' and they also concluded that 'the opportunity to increase profits through more effective procurement probably is greater in the buying of services than in the purchase of goods'.

18.21.2 Differences in the procurement of goods and services

Services can be defined as:

> Those procurements that arise within the framework of a project (such as the translation of software) or with regard to regular maintenance of facilities, legal services, audit work and so on.

Characteristics of services are:

- *intangibility* – the result of a service transaction is not a transfer of ownership as with physical goods; a service is a process or act
- *simultaneity* – the actualisation of a service implies the presence of a supplier as well as a customer, both of whom play an active part in the realisation of services.

Intangibility and simultaneity imply two further service characteristics:

- intangibility implies *perishability* – unlike tangible goods, services cannot be stored and used or resold at a future date
- simultaneity implies *heterogeneity* – or the large risk of a service being performed differently depending on such factors as the provider of the service, the particular customer, the physical setting or even the hour of the day.

These differences between services and goods are shown in Table 18.8.

Table 18.8 **Comparison of services and goods**

Services	Goods
■ An activity or process	■ A physical object
■ Intangible	■ Tangible
■ Service is produced and consumed simultaneously	■ Separation of production and consumption
■ Customers participate in production	■ Customer may or may not participate in production
■ Heterogenous	■ Homogenous
■ Perishable – cannot be stored for future use	■ Can be stored for future use or sale

From a procurement perspective, there are other differences.

- Boshoff[16] suggests that, because of their intangibility, services are riskier to purchase than physical products. This enhanced risk is due to:
  - service buyers only knowing what they have bought after the buying decision
  - the high level of human involvement and interaction, which makes the standardisation of a service not only difficult but, over time, almost impossible
  - customers differing in the amount of information they seek before purchasing a service and satisfaction depending on factors such as prior experience and recommendations.
- Boshoff suggests that service guarantees reduce the anxiety and uncertainty of potential service buyers.
  - Specifications for goods are generally more specific than service statements of work.
  - Cost analysis and negotiation are more difficult with services than for goods.
  - Services are likely to become a significant proportion of total spend as many non-core service competences are outsourced.

18.21.3 Segmentation of services

Services can be segmented or categorised in several ways.

- The Kraljic matrix is equally applicable to services as it is to goods.
- Hadfield[17] provides a matrix that categorises services according to their cost and strategic impact on a particular organisation. As applied to a bank, an example of this matrix is shown in Figure 18.13.
- In Figure 18.13 the lower and upper quadrants respectively reflect lower and higher cost services. The left quadrants show services of the commodity type, of less

Figure 18.13 **Hadfield's matrix of services arranged according to their cost and strategic impact for a bank**

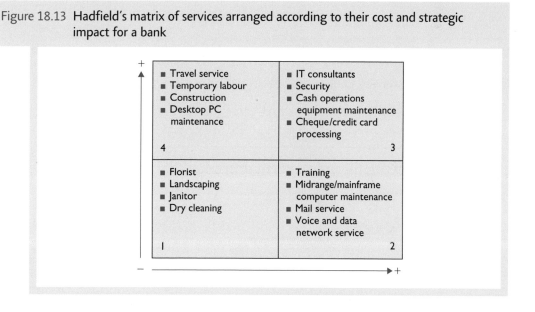

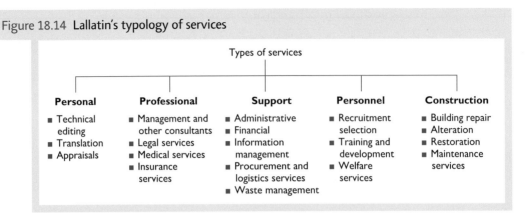

Figure 18.14 **Lallatin's typology of services**

importance to the bank's operations. The right quadrants hold services that are either essential or of strategic importance to the particular bank. Thus, security is of critical importance, dry cleaning is not.

- Lallatin[18] suggests simple groupings of five major types of service – personal, professional, support, personnel and construction – each of which has special characteristics from a purchasing standpoint. Typical examples of each type are shown in Figure 18.14.
- Some services in Figure 18.14 can be categorised under more than one heading. Finance, for example, can be either 'support' or 'professional'.

Segmenting services as described above is essential for the analysis of what to spend and their importance.

From the standpoint of *spend*, such analysis shows:

- *volume aggregation* – that is, the process of collecting and categorising procurement spend to determine what services are being purchased throughout the entire organisation who buys and from which suppliers
- the percentage of spend relating to each category of service
- areas of excessive service spending where control is required.

From the standpoint of importance, such analysis shows:

- where a particular service falls on a Kraljic matrix or a cost/strategy matrix
- whether a service should be provided internally or outsourced.

18.21.4 Processing the procurement of services

This normally involves six steps.

- **Step 1**: Determine the appropriate process for procuring the service
- This involves consideration of:
  - the nature and strategic importance of the service, with reference to the Kraljic matrix – Duffy and Flynn[19] advise:

    In general automate or routinise non-critical and leverage buys; identify a champion for each strategic service and form a team to eliminate bottlenecks

- where procurement of services such as insurance, advertising, transport or energy is done by non-procurement personnel, provide training in specialist procurement techniques.

- **Step 2**: Prepare a statement of work
- A statement of work is defined as:[20]

> A statement outlining the specific services a contractor is expected to perform, generally indicating the type, level and quality of service as well as the time schedule required.

- Much of the information relating to the content and principles of specification writing given in sections 9.4.6 and 9.4.7 applies equally to statements of work. Statements of work should clearly indicate:

  - the services required
  - where, when and to whom the services are to be provided
  - under what conditions
  - standards or levels of performance required
  - period of initial provision and renewal intervals
  - roles, if any, to be undertaken by the purchaser of the service(s), such as assistance with coordination, equipment, staff or research.

- As with specifications, special attention should be given to language, such as the use of mandatory words 'shall', 'will' and 'must' and avoidance of ambiguous words or words with multiple meanings, such as 'adequate', 'necessary', 'as required'.

- **Step 3**: List the statement of work as the basis of a request for proposals (RFP) or quotations (RFQ)

  - Request that potential suppliers suggest their solution(s) for a given requirement.
  - Provide scope for supplier innovation and suggestions.
  - Such documents are useful for locating solutions or sources of supply.

- **Step 4**: Obtain quotations or tenders from potential suppliers

  - Invitations may be advertised generally, thus giving all potential suppliers an equal opportunity to make proposals or quotations. Alternatively, RFPs or RFQs may be restricted to three or four selected suppliers. Reverse auctions are increasingly used as a means of obtaining the lowest price and allowing bidders to see those submitted by competitors. Reverse auctions need the requirements for a service to be clearly specified.

- **Step 5**: Evaluate quotations or tenders

  - Evaluation should be by a cross-functional team. Individual evaluators should rank the offers received. The team should then discuss the individual rankings. The final decision should be on the basis of a consensus rather than a majority vote and should be recorded.

- **Step 6**: Notification and issue of contract

  - Notify the successful and unsuccessful suppliers and issue the contract. Pohlig[21] states that it is critical – to make the contract enforceable – that the statement of work is either incorporated into the contract or included as an appendix.

Discussion questions

18.1   Discuss the reasons why category management offers strategic and operational benefits to an organisation.

18.2   Explain the key facets on the strategic sourcing cycle.

18.3   What is the talent challenge for procurement and how will the challenge be met?

18.4   Discuss six procurement risks associated with energy procurement and how they may be mitigated in the real world.

18.5   Discuss three KPIs for measuring the effectiveness of Corporate Travel procurement solutions.

18.6   Why does procurement find it difficult, in some organisations, to influence ICT expenditure?

18.7   When procurement is involved in buying new capital equipment what specific commercial knowledge and skills can be applied to ensure the best value for money is obtained?

18.8   What criteria would you use to decide if new capital equipment should be purchased as opposed to second hand equipment?

18.9   XYZ is considering whether to lease or buy a machine. The machine will cost £2000 and have a life of three years, at the end of which it will have no residual value. A loan for the purchase of the machine can be obtained for an annual interest rate of 7 per cent, payable at the end of each of the three years. The machine can also be leased from an equipment hire company in return for an annual payment of £762.50, payable at the end of each year.

Ignoring taxation factors, which option will be the lowest-cost solution? What factors might you consider when making a decision?

18.10   Calculate the ROCE from the following figures.

Cost of machine	£160,000
Expected life	5 years
Estimated scrap value	£20,000
Estimated profits before depreciation	
Year 1	£40,000
Year 2	£80,000
Year 3	£60,000
Year 4	£30,000
Year 5	£10,000

Solution

Note: Average profit before depreciation £220,000/5 = £44,000

Total depreciation = £160,000 − £20,000 = £140,000

Average depreciation = £140,000/5 = £28,000

Average annual profit after depreciation = £44,000 − £28,000 = £16,000

$$\therefore ROCE = \frac{£16,000}{£160,000} \times 100\% = 10 \text{ per cent}$$

[Answer: 10 per cent]

18.11 How would you explain hedging to the lay person?

18.12 Why is the price of gas so volatile? What role does the international market play?

18.13 In relation to futures markets, ascertain the meaning of the following terms:
    (a) going long
    (b) going short
    (c) spot market price index.

18.14 What makes procurement for a construction project quite different to buying parts for production assembly?

18.15 If you were asked to purchase a proprietary IT system what would be the major procurement considerations?

18.16 Maintenance & Repair & Operating (MRO) items are typically of low value and do not require the application of procurement expertise. Do you agree? What is your reasoning?

References

1 APQC, *Supplier Category Management – Driving Value Through the Procurement Organization*, APQC, Houston, Texas, 2012.

2 Global Business Travel Association 'Key Performance Indicators for Corporate Travel' – A reference guide development for the Global Business Travel Association 2012.

3 Aljian, G. W., *Purchasing Handbook*, National Association of Purchasing Management, 1958, section 16.1.

4 Van Nostrand, *Dictionary of Business and Finance*, Van Nostrand, London, 1980.

5 Barfield, J. T., Raibon, C. A. and Kinney, M. R., *Cost Accounting*, West Publishing, Eagan, Minnesota, USA, 1994, p. 709.

6 Definition provided by the Inland Revenue.

7 Risley, G., *Modern Industrial Marketing*, McGraw-Hill, New York, USA, 1972, pp. 24–5.

8 Galena Asset Management Zurich.

9 Buffett, W., 'Apocalypse is nigh: Buffett tells Berkshire Faithful', *Money Telegraph*, 4 April 2005.

10 Department for Business, Energy & Industrial Strategy UK Energy in Brief 2018.

11 Ofgem.gov.uk. The GB electricity distribution network. 2019.

12 UK Energy Research Centre. 'The UK's Global Gas Challenge' Research report, November 2014.

13 http://assets.publising.service.gov.uk. Energy Consumption in the UK. July 2018.

14 DUKES 2015 https://www.gov.uk/government/statistics/renewable-sources-of-energy-chapter-6-digest-of-united-kingdom-energy-statistics-dukes.

15 Fearon, M. E. and Bales, W. A., *Purchasing of Non-traditional Goods and Services*, Center for Advanced Purchasing Studies, USA, focus study executive summary, 1995.

16 Boshoff, C., 'Intention to buy a service: the influence of service guarantees: general information and price information advertising', *South African Journal of Business Management*, Vol. 34(1), 2003, pp. 39–43.

17 Hadfield, J. E., 'Purchasing services on the Internet', *Inside Supply Management*, May, 2002, p. 20.

18 Lallatin, C. S., 'How can I categorise my service purchases', *Purchasing Today*, November, 1997.

19 Duffy, R. J. and Flynn, A. E., 'Services purchases: not your typical grind', *Inside Supply Management*, Vol. 14, No. 9, p. 28.

20 ISM, 'Glossary of Key Supply Management Terms': www.ism.ws.

21 Pohlig, H. M., 'Legal issues of contracting for services', *Inside Supply Management*, September, 2002, pp. 22–5.

Chapter 19

World-class procurement to enhance business performance

Learning outcomes

With reference, where applicable, to procurement and supply management, this chapter aims to provide an understanding of:

- innovation and supplier continuous improvement
- innovation
- environmentally sensitive design
- procurement involvement in product development
- supplier development
- procurement research
- procurement performance evaluation
- accounting approaches
- the procurement management audit approach
- benchmarking and ratios
- integrated benchmarking
- procurement ethics
- ethical issues relating to suppliers
- ethical codes of conduct
- procurement and fraud
- cyber security.

Key ideas

- Innovation and supplier continuous improvement.
- The stages of new product development.
- The key considerations for cyber security.
- Procurement contributions to new product development.
- Results and process-orientated supplier development.
- Procurement ethics.
- Procurement fraud.

19.1 Innovation and supplier continuous improvement

Procurement has a significant role to play in influencing strategic suppliers to be innovative and provide continuous improvement. It can be argued that procurement has not yet been successful in the quest to achieve these goals. In the author's opinion there are four dominant reasons for the lack of success:

■ procurement specialists lacking technical knowledge to drive change

■ procurement lacking the commercial imagination to reward suppliers for their innovative developments

■ procurement lacking credibility with technical colleagues and therefore unable to influence change

■ buying organisations unwilling to invest in product/service research and development.

19.1.1 Innovation

Innovation is the process of turning ideas and knowledge into products and services that create a consumer demand within the marketplace.[1]

■ *Product innovation* is the process of transforming technical ideas or market needs and opportunities into a new product (or service) that is launched on to the market.

■ *Process innovation* is the introduction or development of new methods or technology by means of which products or services can be manufactured or delivered more effectively or efficiently. An example of process innovation is the introduction of robots and other forms of automated equipment.

Table 19.1 **Differences between innovation and *kaizen***

Characteristics	Innovation	Kaizen
Focus	Large, short-term, radical changes in products	Small, frequent, gradual improvements over a long time
Expertise	Leading-edge breakthrough	Conventional know-how
Sources	Scientific or technological discovery or invention	Design, production and marketing
Capital requirements	Substantial investment in equipment and technology	Relatively modest investment
Progress	Dramatic breakthroughs	Small incremental steps
Results	Spontaneous	Continuous
Risks	High	Low
Involvement	Corporate activity	Individual or small team
Recognition	Results	Effort

■ *Breakthrough innovation* is completely new or revolutionary products, such as new scientific discoveries in pharmaceuticals. Commonplace products, such as the radio, television and aircraft were once breakthrough innovations.

■ *Incremental innovations* are gradual improvements in a product or service.

19.1.2 *Kaizen*

Kaizen is a Japanese term and means continuous improvement. The concept of *kaizen* is the basis of total quality management (TQM) and is strongly associated with Japanese lean production.

Although analogous to incremental innovation, *kaizen* is, as shown by Table 19.1, generally different from innovation.

Both innovation and *kaizen*, however, share the common objective of enabling an organisation to achieve a sustainable advantage.

Computer-aided engineering (CAE) eliminates entirely some of the traditional steps in the new product development process and allows others to be performed simultaneously. Mileham et al.[2] state that, where used properly, appropriate software can reduce cycle times, costs and risks by 90 per cent.

19.2 Innovation

19.2.1 Concurrent engineering

Definition

> Concurrent engineering is a systematic approach to the integrated, concurrent design of products and their related processes, including manufacture and support.[3]

Typically, concurrent engineering involves the formation of cross-functional teams, which allows engineers and managers of different disciplines to work together simultaneously in developing product and process design. This approach is intended to cause the developers from the outset, to consider all elements of the product lifecycle from concept through disposal, including quality, cost, schedule, and user requirements.

Australia's National Institute for Manufacturing Management[4] has published *A Guide to Introducing Concurrent Engineering in Your Organisation*. They pose a question for companies to ascertain whether concurrent engineering is for them:

'Does my company face any of the following problems in product development?

■ increasing competitive pressure to develop new products

■ product launch delays

■ higher costs in processing and developing products than is acceptable

■ a predominantly internally focused product development process

■ little or no direct knowledge of customer requirements

■ no or low involvement by marketing in the early stages of product development

■ shift in responsibility for product development from one function to another as the project progresses and transfer points often characterised by conflict

■ poor transfer of learning from one product development project to the next.'

A proactive procurement function can positively influence the concurrent engineering process by:

- promoting the logic for the early involvement of suppliers in the design process to ensure the true cost and maintainability of materials and components
- becoming a key member of the concurrent engineering team, through an effective challenge to specifications
- the effective management of the procurement of samples for test and production prototypes
- ensuring that emerging contractual detail includes supplier's obligations for replacing faulty materials and components
- providing training to the concurrent engineering teams on all facets of cost drivers impacting on through life costs
- assisting in networking with other organisations who have successfully implemented concurrent engineering
- ensuring that a rigorous risk assessment process is in place for all facets of supplier engagement
- assisting in overcoming cross-functional team barriers by the application of negotiation skills.

19.3 Environmentally sensitive design

19.3.1 Factors in environmentally sensitive design

Pressures exerted by environmental groups and relevant legislation, such as the UK Clean Air Act 1993, the Radioactive Substances Act 1993 and the Environmental Protection Act 1990, require designers to devise socially responsible products. In the design of such products, special consideration must be given to:

- increasing their efficiency and economy in the use of materials, energy and other resources
- minimising pollution from chosen materials
- reducing any long-term harm to the environment caused by using the product
- ensuring that the planned life of the product is the most appropriate in environmental terms and that the product functions efficiently for its full life
- ensuring that full account is taken of the end-disposal of the product
- specifying packaging that can be recycled easily
- minimising nuisances, such as noise or odour
- analysing and minimising safety hazards.

Attention given to the above factors at the design stage can simplify production, enhance the manufacturer's reputation and prevent investment in products and processes that environmental legislation may make obsolete.

19.3.2 Approaches to environmentally sensitive design

Four important approaches are lifecycle analysis (LCA), design for disassembly (DFD), the use of environmentally preferred materials and guidance by the International Organisation for Standardisation (ISO).

641

Figure 19.1 Product lifecycle

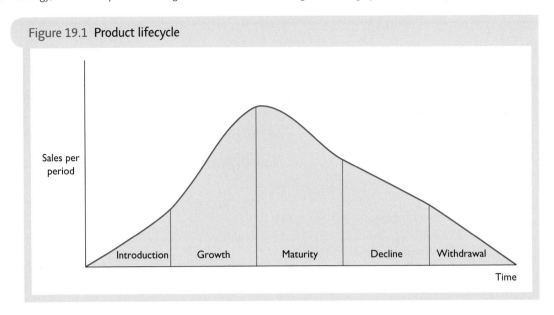

19.3.3 Lifecycle analysis

This is based on the concept that all products have a lifecycle. The product lifecycle, or Gopertz curve, is shown in Figure 19.1.

19.3.4 Design for disassembly (DFD)

This has two aspects:

■ *Recyclability* – this saves both energy and resources. Recycling aluminium, for example, requires 95 per cent less energy than producing aluminium from bauxite ore. Making paper from recycled stock requires 64 per cent less energy than using wood pulp. About 70 per cent of all metal discarded is used only once before it is discarded.

■ *Repairability* – the aim is to prolong the life of products by ensuring that they can be repaired easily at low cost.

19.3.5 Use of environmentally preferred materials

Industrial ecology aims to manage human activity on a sustainable basis by:

■ minimising energy and materials usage

■ ensuring acceptable quality of life for human beings

■ conserving energy and natural resources, such as minerals and forests.

Industrial ecology advocates the application of the following principles when selecting materials for product design:

■ choose abundant, non-toxic materials whenever possible

■ choose materials familiar to nature – for example, cellulose, rather than synthetic materials, such as chlorinated aromatics

- minimise the number of materials used in a production process
- use, where possible, recyclable materials
- where appropriate, use recycled materials.

19.4 Procurement involvement in product development

Wynstra et al.[5] have identified four areas of procurement involvement in product development, each of which has a different time horizon and each involves different activities. These are shown in Table 19.2.

Table 19.2 Areas of procurement involvement in product development

Area of involvement	Associated activities
Development management The higher the level of availability and stability and the lower the level of dependence, the greater the possibilities to 'buy' the technology and leave the development to suppliers	Determining which technologies to keep/develop in-house and which to outsource Policy formulation for supplier involvement Policy formulation for procurement-related activities of internal departments Internal and external communication of policies
Supplier interface management Proactive, continuous research with the aim of identifying suppliers or technologies that may be relevant for the development of new products	Monitoring supplier markets for technological developments Pre-selecting suppliers for product development collaboration Motivating suppliers to build up/maintain specific knowledge or develop certain products Exploiting the technological capabilities of suppliers Evaluating suppliers' development performance
Project management Involves two sub-areas – product planning and project execution	Product planning activities are primarily carried out during or before initial development and include: - determining specific develop-or-buy solutions - selecting suppliers for involvement in the development project - determining the extent of supplier involvement Project execution involves activities during the project and includes: - coordinating development activities between suppliers and manufacturers - coordinating development activities between different first-tier suppliers - coordinating development activities between first-tier and second-tier suppliers - ordering and chasing prototypes

Product management
Directly contributing to the specifications of the new product
	Activities can be divided into two categories:
	
	- extending activities – those aimed at increasing the number of alternatives, including:
	  - providing information on new products and technologies already available or in course of development
	  - suggesting alternative suppliers, products and technologies that can yield higher-quality results
	- restrictive activities – those aimed at limiting the number of alternative specifications:
	  - evaluating product designs in terms of part availability, manufacturability, lead time, quality and costs
	  - promoting standardisation and simplification

19.5 Supplier development

19.5.1 Definition

Supplier development has been defined as:

> Any activity that a buyer undertakes to improve a supplier's performance and/or capabilities to meet the buyer's short-term or long-term supply needs.[6]

Supplier development programmes can be either results-orientated or process-orientated.

- *Results-orientated programmes* focus on solving specific problems for suppliers and normally involve step-by-step changes relating to supplier's costs, quality and delivery. Hartley and Jones[7] identify three characteristics of results-orientated supplier development:

  - the process is standardised and buyer-driven
  - the changes made are primarily technical
  - the process is of short duration and requires limited follow-up.

  With this approach, the supplier improves while the buyer's supplier development team is on site and the achieved level of performance can be maintained after the team has left. The results approach is basically an attempt to transfer an organisation's in-house capabilities across boundaries.

- *Process-orientated programmes* focus on increasing the supplier's ability to make production improvements without hands-on assistance from the buyer. This requires the supplier to learn the problem-solving techniques required for continuous improvements. Such learning is complicated, may require the 'unlearning' of old practices and the encoding of new knowledge in organisational routines.

19.5.2 The steps of supplier development

The actual process may differ according to the organisation and, as stated above, whether the development is primarily results-orientated or process-orientated. There are nine steps in a typical supplier development programme. These are briefly explained as follows:

1 *Identify critical products* – this is done using a portfolio approach, such as that of Kraljic These will be mainly strategic and bottleneck products.

2 *Identify critical suppliers* – this involves consideration of such questions as the following.

   - What is the capability of the suppliers? Sako[8] identifies three levels of capability:

     - *maintenance capability* – the ability to maintain a particular level of performance consistently
     - *improvement capability* – that which affects the pace of performance improvements
     - *evolutionary capability* – the capacity for capability building, which is different from dynamic capabilities in that the emphasis is less on 'adapting, integrating and reconfiguring internal resources in response to changing environments and more on the sustained accumulation of the other two capabilities'.

■ Are the present suppliers capable of meeting future needs?

■ Are the present suppliers worth developing or is it time to source new ones?

3 *Appraise supplier performance*

4 *Determine the gap between present and desired supplier performance* – gap analysis involves identifying the differences between the current and a desired business situation. It is important to recognise that gaps may be considered from a supply-side as well as a demand-side perspective.

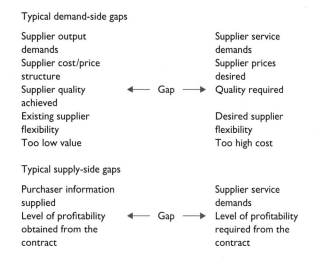

Typical demand-side gaps

Supplier output demands		Supplier service demands
Supplier cost/price structure		Supplier prices desired
Supplier quality achieved	←— Gap —→	Quality required
Existing supplier flexibility		Desired supplier flexibility
Too low value		Too high cost

Typical supply-side gaps

Purchaser information supplied		Supplier service demands
Level of profitability obtained from the contract	←— Gap —→	Level of profitability required from the contract

There may also be combined gaps, such as the level of collaboration or where the level of purchaser–supplier relationships satisfies neither party.

5 *Form cross-functional supplier development team* – this team will be responsible for appraising present and potential suppliers, identifying gaps and negotiating with suppliers to try to devise mutually acceptable resolution of problems.

6 *Meet with supplier's top management team* – meeting with the top management team of the supplier provides an insight into the extent to which a collaborative relationship with the purchaser is required. It also provides an opportunity for both sides to know each other as individuals, discuss areas of cooperation not previously identified, exchange views frankly and build trust. Negotiated improvements can also be minuted and thereby provide an agreed record of decisions made.

7 *Agree how the perceived gaps can be bridged* – approaches may include:

■ seconding purchaser's staff to the supplier

■ seconding supplier's staff to the purchaser

■ purchaser on site audits at the supplier's premises

■ third-party assessment, as is required for ISO 9000 registration

■ loan of machinery and IT hardware

■ granting access to IT systems, such as CAD

■ negotiating improved transportation contracts

■ joint value analysis exercises

■ improved costing approaches

- using the purchaser's leverage to obtain materials and other items for the supplier at cheaper cost
- the offer of incentives.

8 *Set deadlines for achieving improvements* – these should be reasonable, agreed by both parties and strictly enforced. The supplier should understand that failure to effect improvements by the agreed date may lead to loss of business. The emphasis, however, should be on constructive help rather than punitive measures.

9 *Monitor improvements* – even after achievement of the required standards, the performance of suppliers should be carefully monitored. Handfield et al.[9] state that the pitfalls of supplier development fall into three categories: supplier-specific, buyer-specific and buyer–supplier interface. Supplier-specific pitfalls stem chiefly from the supplier's lack of commitment or lack of technical or human resources. Buyer-specific factors derive from a reluctance to commit to supplier development fully when the purchaser sees no obvious potential benefits in so doing, such as a supplier being considered of insufficient importance to justify the investment. The principal buyer–supplier interface pitfalls are due to lack of mutual trust, poor alignment of organisational cultures and insufficient inducements to the supplier. As Handfield and his co-authors state:

> Initiating supplier performance improvement is not an easy task. . . Our findings suggest that such an accomplishment takes time and is only achieved by patient relationship managers who are tenacious enough to pay follow-up visits to suppliers and continually enforce a strong programme of supplier evaluation and performance feedback.

19.6 Procurement research

19.6.1 Definition

Procurement research has been defined by Fearon[10] as:

> The systematic gathering, recording and analysing of data about problems relating to the purchasing of goods and services.

The importance of procurement research has been enhanced by the following:

- rapid changes in technology and economic circumstances are increasing the complexity of procurement
- much procurement is undertaken in conditions of uncertainty so that strategic decisions have to be made involving individuals, organisations and events outside the direct control of the purchasing company
- electronic data processing provides the facility to store and process vast quantities of data that, when processed, can improve decision making
- the increased outsourcing of non-core business functions
- the new focus on partnering and evaluation of the benefits
- e-procurement facilitating real-time ordering and payment by line employees
- procurement as a function is increasingly required to quantify its contribution to profitability and its strategic function in the supply chain.

19.6.2 Areas of research

In selecting topics for research, it should be remembered that the greater the expenditure on an area, the greater is the potential for significant cost savings. Among the most important areas of research are the following:

- *materials and commodities*
  - trends in the requirements of the company for specific materials
  - price and cost analysis
  - substitute materials or items
  - specifications and standardisation
  - value analysis, value engineering
  - usage analysis
  - use of learning curves.

- *procurement policies and procedures*
  - whether or not any policies are in need of revision
  - if it is more economical to make in rather than buy out or vice versa
  - whether or not any opportunities exist for the consolidation of procurement requirements
  - procurement contributions to competitive advantage
  - forms design, distribution and elimination
  - the application of activity-based costing to the procurement function
  - how the information made available by EDP can be used more effectively
  - whether or not the procurement organisation for materials can be improved by regrouping the procurement, stores and other related subsystems, such as by means of materials or logistics management approaches
  - to what extent operational research methods can be applied to procurement
  - internal and external customer satisfaction with the purchasing function.

- *suppliers*
  - supplier appraisal
  - supplier performance
  - the possibilities for supplier development
  - contracting simultaneously with two suppliers to design and build
  - supplier reviews – how often suppliers are changed and how new suppliers are found
  - supply chain – analysis of at least one level back
  - procurement consortium
  - price monitoring after contracting
  - outsourcing the procurement process
  - global sourcing.

- *staff*
  - staff responsibilities
  - staff turnover, absenteeism, morale

- what overtime, if any, is worked
- staff succession
- staff training and development
- staff remuneration, facilities and incentives.

■ *miscellaneous*

- procurement applications of IT
- expert systems and artificial intelligence
- transportation of bought-out items
- securing supplies in conditions of uncertainty
- disposal of scrap and obsolete stores equipment
- terms and conditions of contract
- the measurement of procurement performance
- procurement ethics
- identification and management of supply chain risk.

19.6.3 Organisation for research

Some research is undertaken by all procurement departments, even though this may be only rudimentary, such as consulting trade directories or the Internet to locate possible suppliers of an item not previously bought. A willingness to initiate research is essential to the development of the status of procurement. Unless such an initiative is taken by procurement, the research role will be assumed by other functions, such as design, marketing and production. Procurement research may be formal or informal.

- *Small business units* – these may be unable to allocate resources such as personnel and finance to establish a formal procurement research section. Staff should nevertheless be encouraged to keep up to date by meeting supplier representatives, attending trade exhibitions, attending appropriate short courses, having access to and opportunities for studying journals and other relevant literature, as well as networking with other procurement staff at meetings of professional bodies, such as the CIPS.
- *Research sections* – systematic research requires time and freedom from other distractions. These conditions can be best provided when the organisation is large enough, by establishing a special procurement research section as a centralised staff activity to provide assistance to line members of the procurement function. Experience has shown that companies with formal procurement research arrangements:

  - engage in more research projects
  - do so in greater depth
  - make a significant contribution to profitability and operational effectiveness.

- *Other approaches* – when a specialised research section is not feasible, formalised procurement research may be undertaken by the following groups:

  - *Project teams* concerned with a specific problem or range of problems – probably including staff from outside the procurement function, such as design, production, finance and marketing, as in a value research or engineering project.

- *Supplier associations.*
- *Research consortiums.*
- *Use of specialised outside research facilities*, such as the Commodities Research Unit of the International Monetary Fund.
- *Collaboration with universities* – this may be 'contract' or 'collaborative' research. In contract research, the agenda for a project is set by the industrial partner with a university providing a research service at a commercial price on the same basis as any other supplier, while collaborative research's goals are jointly defined by both company or companies and the university. 'Clubs' or 'networks' are often set up by an individual university or consortium of universities to focus on a particular research topic. Companies wishing to become members usually pay an agreed annual subscription. Thus, the Centre for Research in Strategic Purchasing and Supply at Bath University claims to work, at any one time, with over 100 companies, often organised into 'project clubs'.
- *Support of individuals working for higher degrees* in procurement and supply chain management.
- *Use of consultants* to investigate a specific matter. Some large consultancy organisations also undertake independent research that is made available to the relevant industries at a cost.
- *Professional institutes* – The Institute of Logistics and Transport maintains a logistics research network – a special interest group of academics with some interested practitioner members. The network produces the *International Journal of Logistics Research and Applications*. The CIPS supports chairs in procurement at several UK universities. In the USA, the *Center for Advanced Studies (CAPS Research)* was established in 1986 as a national affiliation agreement between the NAPM (now ISM®) and Arizona State University.

19.6.4 Research methodology

As with all other research, the first step in a procurement or supply chain investigation is to adopt a plan or model of the research, from inception to completion. Sarantakos[11] states that the general assumption made by researchers who employ a research model in their work rests on the belief that:

- research can be perceived as evolving in a series of steps that are closely interrelated and the success of each depends on the successful completion of the preceding step
- the steps must be executed in a given order
- planning and execution of the research is more successful if a research model is employed – a typical one being that shown in Figure 19.2.

19.7 Procurement performance evaluation

19.7.1 Definition

Procurement performance evaluation may be defined as the quantitative or qualitative assessment over a given time towards the achievement of corporate or operational goals and objectives relating to procurement economies, efficiency and effectiveness.

Figure 19.2 A purchasing research model

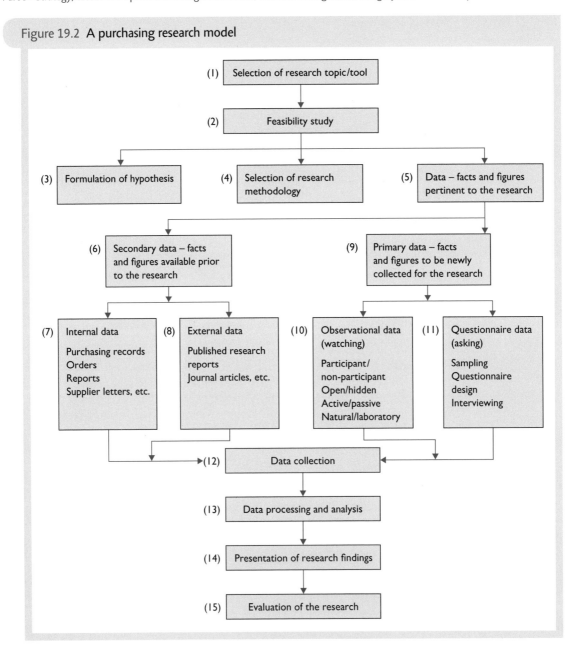

The significant words in this definition are the following:

■ *Quantitative or qualitative* – *quantitative* assessments are objective and measurable, using such measures as numbers of orders placed, reduction in lead times, price savings and reduced administrative costs, and will tend to be used where procurement is regarded as a mainly clerical or transactional activity. *Qualitative* assessments use judgmental impressions regarding the contribution of procurement to suppliers' goodwill, partnership sourcing, value analysis and internal customer satisfaction and is applicable when procurement is regarded as a strategic function.

■ *Performance evaluation* – *evaluation* is a more accurate term than *measurement*. By definition, 'measurement' implies quantification or the expression of a quality or attribute in numerical terms. Although the performance of procurement managers is usually assessed by means of objective, quantified measures such as cost/price reductions and contributions to added value or profitability, performance evaluation frequently uses subjective, qualitative assessment approaches.

■ *Over a given time* – evaluations may relate to long-term (over one year) or short-term performance. Long-term objectives frequently extend several years into the future. Periodical reviews look at progress and outstanding actions needing to be undertaken. Progress can only be measured by reference to what was achieved in a past period and targets set for a future period. For this purpose, evaluations should always relate to specific time intervals.

■ *Corporate or operational goals and objectives* – goals or objectives are basic to performance evaluation: 'If we don't know where we are going, we shall not know when we arrive'. *Corporate objectives* will usually be set at board level. Such goals are relatively permanent, expressed in broad terms and derive from the mission statement of an organisation. Today, most corporate objectives relate to the provision of 'customer satisfaction'.

Organisational goals must be 'congruent' – that is, consistent with corporate goals, not only over time but also vertically and horizontally. *Vertically* means that the objectives should be consistent at all levels of the organisation, *horizontally*, that the objectives set for different activities concerned with delivering value to the ultimate customer, as in a supply chain, must be consistent and integrated.

Corporate objectives – usually expressed in broad qualitative terms – must be turned into specifics for operational purposes. Thus, the general strategy of 'delivering a cost-effective procurement service' may, for the next financial year, require procurement to:

– achieve savings of 10 per cent on purchases
– award contracts for an e-tendering and supplier information database not later than [specify date], subject to availability of funds
– ensure that not less than 70 per cent of procurement staff are working towards an approved procurement qualification.

Operational goals, such as those shown above, can be expressed as quantified (SMART) objectives – that is, they should be **S**pecific, **M**easurable, **A**ttainable, **R**esults-orientated and **T**ime-based.

■ *Economies, efficiency and effectiveness* – *economies* means minimising the cost of resources acquired without loss of quality, which is achieved by spending less. Important tools in achieving economy are value engineering and value analysis.

Efficiency covers the relationship between the output of goods or services and the resources used to produce them, which means spending well. Efficiency and productivity are related as productivity is measured by the following ratio:

$$\text{Productivity} = \frac{\text{Outputs produced}}{\text{Inputs consumed}}$$

Effectiveness covers the relationship between the intended and the actual results of projects and programmes – that is, spending wisely. Economy, efficiency and effectiveness – commonly referred to as the three Es – constitute value for money (VFM). Securing and improving VFM is an important corporate objective and responsibility for its achievement lies primarily with operational managers. The terms efficiency and effectiveness will occur again in this text, but, from the standpoint of performance evaluation, some further aspects include the following:

– Organisations, functions, processes and the people concerned may be efficient but not effective – being the lowest-cost producer of products or services that no one wants is efficient but not effective and, as Kydos[12] observes:

> Nothing is more wasteful than doing with greater efficiency that which is totally unnecessary.

– Conversely, we can be effective without being efficient – using a steam hammer to crack the proverbial nut is effective, but not efficient.

– Managers can delegate efficiency, but must deal personally with effectiveness.

– Efficiency and effectiveness are not mutually exclusive – acceptable performance may reflect a combination of efficiency and effectiveness.

19.7.2 Some difficulties in measuring procurement performance

Van Weele[13] has identified four 'problems' that, he states, 'seriously limit an objective and accurate assessment of the procurement function':

■ *lack of definition* – concepts such as procurement performance, efficiency and effectiveness are often not clearly defined or are used interchangeably

■ *lack of formal objectives and performance standards* – the problem, as we see it, however, is not the lack of standards – which receive considerable attention in textbooks and academic articles – but that many procurement practitioners are either unaware of such standards or unwilling to apply them

■ *problems of accurate measurement* – Van Weele rightly states:

> Procurement is not an isolated function; procurement performance is the result of many activities which, due to their intangible character, are difficult to evaluate. In general, direct input–output relationships are difficult to identify; this seriously limits the possibility of measuring and evaluating procurement activities in an accurate and comprehensive way.

■ *differences in the scope of organisational procurement* – procurement is not a homogenous activity and with such factors as status, responsibilities, organisation, policies and procedures, it differs widely from one enterprise to another and those differences preclude the development of uniform measurement systems, so they also detract from the attention given to procurement performance evaluation.

As stated above, a major problem when evaluating procurement performance is the heterogeneous nature of the procurement activity. In a USA study of the absence of a consistent system for measuring procurement performance, Fearon and Bales[14] report that:

> Anyone who wants a single group of performance measures for procurement activities at every organisation is going to be disappointed. The measures that are important to the individual organisation may not be important to another. Therefore, the measures for procurement performance have to be customised for virtually every organisation.

Measurement of procurement performance is, however, important for all organisations as:

■ if an activity cannot be measured, it cannot be effectively managed, nor can continuous and sustainable improvements be made

■ measurement is critical for maintaining the competitive edge of companies in an increasingly crowded global marketplace.

19.7.3 Approaches to performance measurement

These may be grouped under four main headings:

■ accounting approaches, namely:

   – profit centres

   – activity-based costing

   – standard costing and budgetary control.

■ the procurement management audit approach

■ comparative approaches

   – benchmarking and ratio

   – integrated benchmarking, such as EFQM and balanced scorecards (see sections 19.11.1 and 19.11.2)

■ miscellaneous approaches, such as Six Sigma (see section 8.9.3).

19.8 Accounting approaches

19.8.1 The profit centre approach

In this approach, the procurement function or activity is regarded as the part of the company that controls assets and is responsible not only for expenditure but also income.

The aim of this approach is to demonstrate that the procurement function is a profit rather than a cost centre.

The profit centre approach involves establishing a centralised procurement organisation that controls assets. The profitability of this centralised procurement function is generated by an internal accounting transfer of items and services procured by procurement to other functions at a price above their actual direct cost. In effect, procurement sells to other functions at what is termed a *transfer price*. The executive in charge of procurement is therefore expected to base any decisions, where applicable, on profit criteria and performance is measured in terms of the profits generated by the function. An example of the profit centre approach is given in Example 19.1.

This approach is theoretical rather than practical, although it is advocated on the grounds that it:

■ provides a measure of the efficiency of the supplies function

■ allows supplier managers to control their budgets and spend to save money

■ enhances the status of the supplies function by providing measurable objectives.

Example 19.1

A procurement department treated as a profit centre

		£
Value of assets controlled by the supplies manager		
Inventory		1,500,000
Procurement function's floor space and equipment		250,000
Stores' floor space and equipment		750,000
		2,500,000
Annual rate of return required by the company on assets employed	15%	375,000
Estimated annual operating expenses		
Procurement	£150,000	
Stores	£475,000	625,000
Total expenses and return (a)		1,000,000
Total purchases for year (b)		20,000,000
(a) + (b)*		21,000,000

Transfer cost of supplies to user function (i.e. internal customers) will therefore be 5%, i.e.

$$\frac{£1,000,000 \times 100}{20,000,000}$$

	£
Assume notional supplies profit (1%)	
Therefore profit on turnover of £20,000,000	200,000

$$\text{Return on assets controlled by supplies} = \frac{(£200,000 \times 100)}{£2,500,000} = 8\%$$

To reach the expected return of 15 per cent, other than by increasing the notional profit, the supplies function will either have to reduce the investment in inventory or operating expenses.

19.9 The procurement management audit approach

19.9.1 Definition

An *audit* may be defined, inter alia, as a check or examination. The term *procurement management audit* has been defined by Scheuing[15] as:

> A comprehensive, systematic, independent and periodic examination of a company's procurement environment, objectives and tactics to identify problems and opportunities and facilitate the development of appropriate action plans.

Scheuing states that the operative words in this definition are:

- *comprehensive* – the audit should cover every aspect of procurement
- *systematic* – a standard set of questions should be developed and used respectively
- *independent* – procurement personnel should not evaluate themselves
- *periodic* – audits yield the greatest value if they are performed periodically – annually – thus facilitating comparisons, checks and balances and an evaluation of progress.

19.9.2 The purpose of conducting procurement management audits

A review of some standard procurement texts by Evans and Dale[16] indicated that procurement audits serve four main purposes. They are:

- police the extent to which the procurement policies laid down by senior management are adhered to
- help to ensure that the organisation is using techniques, procedures and methods that conform to best working practice
- monitor and measure the extent to, that resources are used effectively
- assist in the prevention and detection of fraud and malpractice.

19.9.3 Who should carry out the procurement management audit?

Such audits can be carried out by:

- external auditors
- internal auditors
- a corporate procurement function
- a procurement research function (independent of operational decision making)
- external management consultants.

Two principles are suggested to govern who should carry out the audit:

- the auditors should be external to the function or department that is the subject of the audit
- the auditors should have an in-depth knowledge of the procurement function, which will enable them not only to monitor adherence to policies and procedures but also to understand procurement perspectives and problems and make recommendations as to how policies, procedures and practice can be improved, and, if external with specialist knowledge and experience, are likely to carry greater authority and provide greater objectivity in relation to procurement audits.

19.9.4 The content of procurement audits

Suggested headings and typical items for a management – as distinct from a financial – audit of the procurement function are as follows:

- *Procurement perspectives, problems and opportunities*
  - What are the perceptions of a sample of procurement staff of their:
    - status in the organisation
    - involvement in strategic decision making
    - contribution to profitability and competitive advantage?
  - What are the job satisfactions and job dissatisfactions identified by the procurement staff interviewed?
  - What are the main problems encountered by procurement staff in doing their job? To what extent are these problems related to:
    - management
    - colleagues

- internal customers
- suppliers
- information
- resources
- other internal or external factors?
  - What is the level of morale in the procurement function?

- *Procurement organisation*

  - To whom does the person in charge of the procurement function report?
  - What aspects of procurement are centralised/decentralised?
  - Would any centralised aspects of procurement benefit from decentralisation or vice versa?
  - With what other functional activities does procurement interrelate?
  - What are the formal mechanisms for the coordination of procurement activities with other functions?
  - What is the assessment of procurement function performance by its internal customers?
  - On what interfunctional/departmental committees is the procurement function represented or could be represented?
  - How might the internal organisation of the procurement function be improved?
  - How might the integration of procurement with other related functions be improved?

  This information can be obtained from organisational charts and formal/informal interviews.

- *Procurement personnel*

  - How many members of staff are employed in the procurement function?
  - What are their grades, qualifications and respective lengths of service?
  - Has every member of the procurement function an appropriate job description?
  - How do actual duties carried out relate to the job descriptions?
  - Which staff are over/under deployed?
  - Is an attempt made to 'empower' procurement staff?
  - What training and development opportunities are provided for procurement staff?
  - How do salaries and remuneration packages compare with those in similar enterprises/industries?
  - What is the staff turnover as measured by the following formula?:

  $$\frac{\text{Number of leavers in function for a specified period (usually 1 year)}}{\text{Average number of employees in function during the same period}} \times 100$$

  - What is the stability of employment in the function as measured by the following formula?

  $$\frac{\text{Number of staff with 1 year's service or more}}{\text{Number employed 1 year ago}} \times 100$$

  - What staff will reach retirement age within the next five years?

This information can be obtained from job descriptions or specifications, training documents, human resource plans and formal or informal interviews.

■ *Procurement policies*

- What written/unwritten policies apply to the procurement function?
- Is there a procurement manual? How and how frequently is this updated?
- What guidance is provided to procurement staff about:
    ■ the value an individual at a particular grade can commit the enterprise to spending
    ■ supplier relationships, such as disputes, prompt payment
    ■ conflicts of interest, such as gifts and entertainment
    ■ buying from abroad
    ■ environmental policies
    ■ reciprocal, local and intra-company procurement?
- What machinery exists for the investigation and enforcement of reported departures from policy compliance?

This information can be obtained, in the main, from relevant documents, manuals, memoranda, instructions and so on.

■ *Procurement procedures*

- From what sources are requests to purchase obtained?
- How quickly are such requests processed?
- What procedures are laid down for such operational activities as requesting and evaluating quotations, issuing purchase orders, receipt of goods and payment for supplies?
- Are all appropriate procedures computerised?
- To what extent does the procurement function make use of EDI and e-procurement?
- How are small orders processed?
- What procedures/activities add value and which others do not add value?
- How might procurement documentation be improved, simplified or eliminated?
- How much time does procurement staff spend on seeing supplier representatives and engaging in relationship management?
- What are the procedures for the procurement of capital equipment?
- What e-procurement security methods are in place to prevent fraud?

Much of this information can be obtained from trailing a sample of purchase orders through from the receipt of the requisition to receipt of goods and payment of the suppliers and from formal and informal interviews.

■ *Procurement reports*

- What reports are prepared by the procurement function?
- Who prepares each report?
- At what intervals is each report prepared?

- What is the cost of preparing each report?
- To whom is each report sent?
- What use is made of each report by the receiver?
- Is the report really necessary?

Much of this information can be obtained by trailing reports through from their inception to storage or disposal.

■ *Purchases, suppliers and prices*

- What is the procurement expenditure budget – in quantities and value – for the period under review?
- What are the principal purchases?
- Who are the principal suppliers?
- What attempts have been made to achieve single and partnership sourcing?
- How and by what criteria are suppliers appraised?
- Are the results of appraisals communicated to suppliers?
- How do prices paid for samples of purchases compare with what is obtainable in the market?
- In what ways does the procurement function seek to obtain value for money?
- How and by whom are specifications prepared? Is there any procurement involvement?
- What environmental procurement policy/policies are in existence and how successfully are these implemented?
- What savings have been achieved in the period under review and how have these been achieved?

Much of this information can be obtained from the examination of a sample of orders and other procurement documentation and formal and informal interviews.

■ *Inventory*

- Does the company make use of ABC analysis?
- How much inventory are carried, i.e. strategic items, bottleneck items, leverage items and non-critical items?
- What is the rate of turnover of a sample of items under each category?
- What items of inventory have been in stock for more than one year?
- What procedures are in place for the identification of obsolescent, slow-moving or damaged inventory and for the prevention of pilfering?
- What procedures are in place for the disposal of surplus stock, obsolete or scrap supplies or discarded capital items?
- What stockouts have been experienced in the period and why?
- What attempts have the procurement/supplies function made to reduce inventory investment?

Much of this information can be obtained from an investigation of stores records, the physical inspection of inventory and stores procedures and formal and informal interviews. From the above, it can be seen that the main 'tools' used in procurement performance audit include:

- formal or informal interviews
- sampling
- trailing a procedure or document through from its inception to its end or storage or disposal
- observation.

These 'tools' can be supported by such procedures as benchmarking and ratio analysis.

19.9.5 Procurement management audit reports

After compiling the findings into a report with summarised recommendations and supporting reasons, the audit should be presented to senior management. When preparing such reports, auditors should:

- highlight policies, procedures and personnel where efficiency and effectiveness can be improved
- commend good practice and performance
- think beyond simple quantitative measures of performance and consider the full consequences, side-effects and reactions likely to occur when these recommendations are presented
- support constructive proposals made by procurement staff that may receive greater attention if made by an outside source.

19.10 Benchmarking and ratios

19.10.1 Benchmarks

A benchmark may be defined as:

> a measured 'best in class' achievement – a reference or measurement standard for comparison that is recognised as the standard of excellence for a specific business process.

As shown in Figure 19.3 benchmarking may take four main forms.

19.10.2 The benefits and criticisms of benchmarking

Benchmarking offers the following benefits:

- provision of a 'gap analysis' tool – that is, the gap between where we are and 'best in class' organisations
- the opportunity to creatively incorporate the best practice from any industry into an organisation's operations
- decision support for setting objectives and a basis for cost–benefit analysis
- it is motivating as it identifies objectives that have been achieved by others

Figure 19.3 **The four main forms of benchmarking**

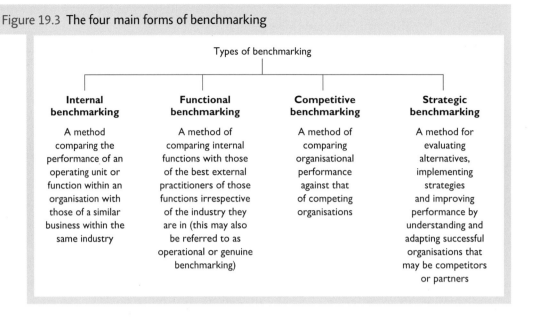

- resistance to change can be diminished when ideas for improved performance come from external sources
- innovations and technical breakthroughs from other industries can be identified earlier and their applicability assessed
- the experience and knowledge bases of employees can be enhanced.

The importance of benchmarking as a basis of comparison is indicated by examples given by Business Link:[17]

- in the top 25 per cent of firms, only 0.5 per cent of suppliers are substandard, whereas those in the lower quartile have six times as many substandard suppliers
- the top 25 per cent of organisations appear to be getting an average of 97 per cent of supplies on time, while in the lower quartile, only an average of 66.5 per cent of supplies are delivered on time
- the upper quartile performers use one ninth (or less) of the number of suppliers used by lower-quartile performers
- the bottom 25 per cent of firms reported an average of eight stock turns per year compared to 32 stock turns achieved by the top 25 per cent of firms in the sample.

There are, however, four main criticisms of benchmarking. These are that:

- benchmarking implies there is only one best method of performing, but there may be approaches other than those chosen as benchmarks that can be better ways of resolving an issue or improving performance
- benchmarking may indicate yesterday's solutions to tomorrow's problems
- price comparisons may be difficult because customised specifications may be unique to the buying institution
- price drivers, such as volume, procurement practices and terms and conditions, may further complicate comparisons.

19.11 Integrated benchmarking

A number of 'frameworks' have been devised to provide a holistic means of evaluating organisational performance and promoting continuous improvement by means of effective and integrated benchmarking. Two of the best-known frameworks are the European Foundation for Quality Management (EFQM) model and balanced scorecards.

19.11.1 The EFQM model

The EFQM model – shown in Figure 19.4 – consists of nine elements, classified into *enablers* and *results*. As a tool for self-assessment, the model allocates 1000 points on a weighted basis between the nine elements, of which 500 points are allocated to enablers and 500 to results. The *enabler elements* are *how* the organisation approaches the criteria of each element. The *results elements* are *what* the organisation has achieved, and, is likely to achieve. The degree of excellence in the results, the extent to which the results are being achieved and the degree to which they address all relevant facets of the criteria all form the basis for the assessment of results.

19.11.2 The balanced scorecard

The balanced scorecard shown in Figure 19.5 was developed in the early 1990s by Robert Kaplan and David Norton of the Harvard Business School. They describe the innovation of the balanced scorecard as follows:

> The balanced scorecard retains financial measures, but financial measures tell the story of past events. An adequate story for industrial-age companies for which investments in long-term capabilities and customer relationships were not critical for success. These financial measures are inadequate, however, for guiding and evaluating the journey that information-age companies must make to create future value through investment in customers, suppliers, employees, processes, technology and innovation.

Figure 19.4 The EFQM business excellence model

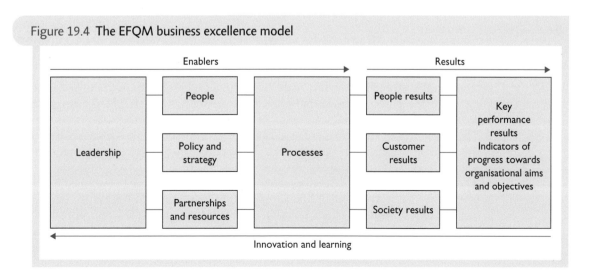

Figure 19.5 **The balance scorecard**

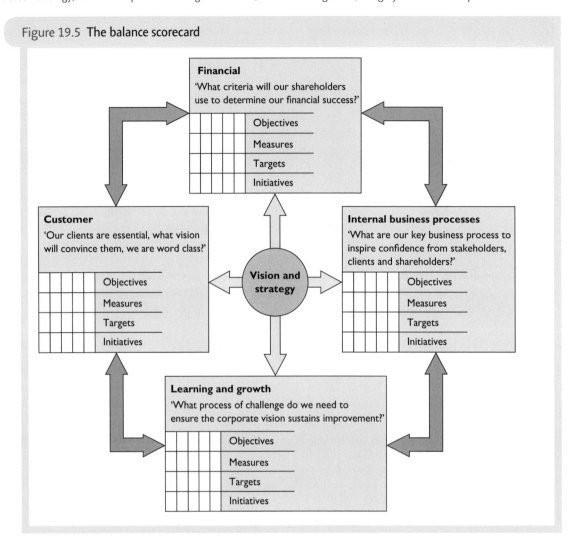

As shown, the balanced scorecard is not only a measurement system but also a framework that enables organisations to clarify their vision and strategy and translate them into action. The balanced scorecard approach suggests that we view the organisation from four perspectives: customer, financial, internal business processes and learning and growth. For each of these perspectives, the scorecard suggests that we should develop metrics and collect and analyse data.

The advantage of the scorecard is that it presents many of the seemingly disparate elements of an organisation's agenda in a single report. It also encourages managers to consider all relevant operational measures at the same time.

The *performance prism* is a development of the balanced scorecard developed by Andy Neeley of the Cranfield School of Management and Chris Adams of Anderson Consulting.

For reasons of space, it is not possible to provide a detailed description of EFQM, balanced scorecards and performance prism approaches here. Further information on the EFQM model can be obtained from the British Quality Foundation.[18] The foundation also publishes *Assessing for Excellence: A Practical Guide to Self Assessment* and *The EFQM Excellence Model*.

Much has been published on the balanced scorecard. A good place to start is with the books by R. Kaplan, D. Norton and A. Lowes – *The Balanced Scorecard: Measures that Drive Performance, Putting the Balanced Scorecard to Work* and *Using the Balanced Scorecard as a Strategic Management System*.[19]

Two other useful books are Paul R. Niven's, *Balanced Scorecard Step-by-Step* and M. C. S. Bourne and P. A. Bourne's, *Understanding the Balanced Scorecard in a Week*.[21]

The Balanced Scorecard Software Report, published by the Centre for Business Performance, Cranfield University, provides evaluations of 28 existing software packages relating to the selection of balanced scorecard software.

The pioneering book on the performance prism is by A. Neeley, C. Adams and M. Kennerley, *The Performance Prism: The Scorecard for Measuring and Managing Business Success*.[22]

19.12 Procurement ethics

19.12.1 Definitions

Procurement ethics is a subdivision of business ethics, which in turn is the application of general ethical principles in a commercial or industrial context. Procurement ethics are also related to professional ethics.

Ethics as a general field of study may be defined as:

> The principles of conduct governing an individual or group; concern for what is right or wrong, good or bad.

Business ethics is just the application of the above definition to the workplace and business relationships specifically.

- *Professional ethics* are guidelines or best practice that embody ideals and responsibilities that inform practitioners as to the principles and conduct they should adopt in certain situations.

19.12.2 Principles

The main principles of professional ethics are:

- impartiality or objectivity
- openness and full disclosure
- confidentiality
- due diligence, competency and a duty of care
- fidelity to professional responsibilities
- avoiding potential or apparent conflicts of interest.

These principles are to be interpreted in the light of the wider fields of personal and global ethics shown in Figure 19.6.[23]

The range of corporate and individual issues relating to business ethics that might be considered under the above headings is infinite.

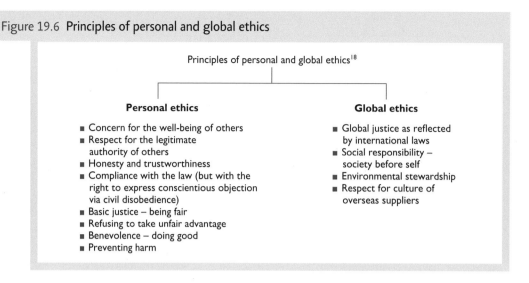

Figure 19.6 **Principles of personal and global ethics**

19.13 Ethical issues relating to suppliers

These are the provision of practical help and advice, prompt payment, honesty and openness, e-ethics and courtesy to supplier representatives.

19.13.1 Provision of practical help and advice

This can take such forms as:

- helping suppliers to procure their own supplies more effectively and economically
- assistance in finding alternative customers to prevent too great a reliance on a single source
- provision of feedback on unsuccessful tenders
- collaboration on design and production
- supplier development
- placing a proportion of orders with local suppliers, thus assisting the prosperity of the community in which the procurement organisation is located.

19.13.2 Prompt payment

The organisation should help suppliers maintain their cash flow by:

- paying invoices on time
- ensuring that both finance and procurement departments are aware of the organisation's prompt payment policy and adhere to it (bearing in mind a failure to pay on time puts the buying organisation in breach of their own contract)
- dealing with complaints as expeditiously as possible so that payments are not needlessly deferred.

Under the UK Late Payments of Commercial Debts (Interest) Act 1998, which is based on an EU directive, bills must be paid within 30 days. The act provides that, after 30 days, small businesses (those with 50 or fewer employees) can claim interest retrospectively.

19.13.3 Honesty and openness

Honesty and openness are the opposite of deception, as defined by Robertson and Rymon:[24] 'one party's intention to create or perpetuate a false belief in another party'.

The same writers identify four types of 'bluffing' that some procurement agents may adopt on the premise that, in negotiations, their responsibility is to obtain the best possible price, quality and delivery and that deception and manipulation of the supplier is an acceptable means of achieving the desired end.

The four examples of deception instanced by Robertson and Rymon are giving a false impression to suppliers that:

- other vendors are aggressively competing for a particular contract
- time limits for the completion of negotiations apply
- a competitor is offering a better deal
- the selling firm is in danger of losing the contract.

From their research, Robertson and Rymon reported that:

- 29 per cent of their respondents admitted to having deceived the seller
- the suggestions that there were other vendors and that the vendors might lose the contract were, respectively, the most and least common forms of deception
- deceptive behaviour is likely to be the outcome of organisational pressure to perform or lack of clear guidance regarding what is permissible, so there is 'ethical ambiguity'
- deception may be a recognised negotiating ploy: 'the buyer may be selling a false deadline but the seller knows that the deadline is false'.

The writers also suggest that the replacement of short-term, arm's length by long-term collaborative procurement arrangements is likely to be conducive to the development of cooperation, interdependence and trust between buyers and suppliers.

19.13.4 E-ethics

The CIPS[25] suggests that the Internet 'is creating a new environment in which unethical behaviour has far greater implications for companies than was previously the case'. In particular, the balance of power in e-trading, as exemplified by e-auctions, is shifting in favour of the purchaser. A typical code of ethics for e-auctions is that of Dow Chemicals:

- Only use an auction when there is a genuine intent to award a contract
- When invitations to participate have been issued, do not seek, negotiate or accept any offers that are in breach of the written brief issued for the auction
- When an auction is complete, no participants or other potential suppliers must be permitted to submit bids outside the auction process

- Document and make available to all participants the detailed auction process, its rules and how non-conformance by participants shall be dealt with

- When necessary provide training to bidders who request training. In doing so, no bidder must be given an advantage

- Document and make available the evaluation mechanism and model for bids received

- Restrict participation to those bidders who can meet the 'product' requirements and auction timescales

- Prevent bids that have no substance and/or which are unsustainable on the data provided

The CIPS further suggests that, with B2B e-commerce, the issues of trust, access, identity, security, privacy, property and confidentiality take on new dimensions.

19.13.5 Courtesy to suppliers' representatives

There is evidence that sales representatives often have a poor opinion of buyers. This is likely to be enhanced where sales representatives are prior to meetings kept waiting unnecessarily. It should be appreciated by procurement staff that, allowing for travelling time and discussions, a sales representative has a relatively short working day in which to fit calls. Unsolicited sales calls tend to be unwelcome before 9.30am, between 12.15pm and 1.30pm and after 4.30pm. If kept waiting, the salesperson's whole programme of visits in a particular area may be disrupted. Other factors to bear in mind when receiving sales representatives should include:

- using a suitable room for interviews
- giving information regarding the times between which representatives will be seen
- providing them with honest information.

While procurement staff should be open to information about new products and suppliers, they should be frank, but courteous, about informing a representative, if there is no possibility of business, to avoid making future calls. Above all, a buyer should never be patronising, rude or supercilious. Such behaviour demeans both the representative and the buyer and is clearly not conducive to establishing supplier goodwill. While there must clearly be an exchange of pleasantries, it should be remembered that 'time is money', for both the purchaser and the supplier.

Kennedy[26] instances 22 different tactics used by unscrupulous buyers when dealing with representatives. Not only are such tactics unprofessional, but they also negate a golden rule – always treat others as you would like them to treat you.[27] This rule is unambiguous and easy to understand. The motives for endorsing it may be altruistic, but are actually a reflection of precautionary, defensive self-interest.

19.13.6 Business gifts and hospitality

Policies with regard to the receipt by members of the procurement staff of gifts from suppliers, especially at Christmas, and hospitality at other times vary widely. The three most common policies for procurement are that members of the procurement staff:

- are forbidden to accept gifts of any kind and those received must be returned
- may retain gifts that are clearly of an advertising nature, such as calendars, diaries, pencils and so on
- are allowed to decide for themselves whether a proffered gift of hospitality is an appreciation of a cordial business relationship or an attempt at commercial bribery.

Our considered view is that the third bullet point of the above policies is the best as it regards staff as responsible individuals, capable of distinguishing a gift or hospitality from a bribe. There is also the fact that the first two policies encourage subterfuge, such as having gifts sent to the buyer's home address. There is, however, the danger that younger, less experienced, lower-paid members of staff are likely to be flattered to receive gifts, the implications of which are not always recognised. For this reason, it is useful for all members of the procurement staff to receive guidance on ethical practice from professional and organisational ethical codes and ethical training.

19.14 Ethical codes of conduct

In Chapter 1, it was stated that one of the essentials of a profession is 'adherence to a code of conduct'. Professions as diverse as medicine, law, accountancy and architecture have issued codes of conduct. Codes of conduct are issued by the Chartered Institute of Procurement and Supply (CIPS) in the UK and Institute of Supply Management (ISM) in the USA.

There are also national and international codes. A good example of a national code is the UK government's *Procurement Code of Good Practice for Customers and Suppliers*. An example of an international code is the *Global Compact*, introduced by the United Nations' secretary general in 1999. This challenges world business leaders to help build the social and environmental pillars required to sustain the new global economy and covers ten principles under four headings on which companies are asked to act.

- Human rights
  - *Principle 1* – businesses should support and respect the protection of internationally proclaimed human rights
  - *Principle 2* – make sure that they are not complicit in human rights abuses.

- Labour
  - *Principle 3* – businesses should uphold the freedom of association and the effective recognition of the right to collective bargaining
  - *Principle 4* – the elimination of all forms of forced and compulsory labour
  - *Principle 5* – the effective abolition of child labour
  - *Principle 6* – the elimination of discrimination in respect of employment and occupation.

- Environment
  - *Principle 7* – businesses should support a precautionary approach to environmental challenges
  - *Principle 8* – undertake initiatives to promote greater environmental responsibility
  - *Principle 9* – encourage the development and diffusion of environmentally friendly technologies.

- Anti-corruption
  - *Principle 10* – businesses should work against corruption in all its forms, including extortion and bribery.

Other international codes are those of the *Ethical Trading Initiative (ETI)* and the *International Labour Organisation (ILO)*.

The ETI is an alliance of companies, non-governmental organisations (NGOs) and trade union organisations. The ultimate ETI goal is to ensure that the working conditions of workers producing for the UK market meet or exceed international labour standards.

The ILO's *Declaration on Fundamental Principles and Rights at Work*, adopted in 1998, covers four areas:

- freedom of association and the effective recognition of the right to collective bargaining
- the elimination of all forms of forced or compulsory labour
- the effective abolition of child labour
- the elimination of discrimination in the respect of employment and occupation.

19.14.1 The benefits of ethical codes

Karp and Abramms[28] suggest that both professional and organisational codes are useful in:

- *providing a basis for working together* – most codes require that people treat each other with respect
- *setting boundaries as to what constitutes ethical behaviour* as determined by organisational human rights and professional values, examples of which are declarations of interest, confidentiality of information, competition, business gifts and hospitality
- *providing a safe environment for all subscribers to the code* – without the guidance provided by a code of ethics, employees are always subject and accountable to the value system of anyone in a higher position
- *providing a commonly held set of guidelines* enabling what is right and wrong in a given situation to be judged on a consistent basis, so they help to dispel 'ethical ambiguity'.

19.14.2 Some criticism of codes

Probably, most procurement people think of ethical codes as being remote from the real world. This may be because pressurised work often leaves little time for reflection. The requirement to maintain an unimpeachable standard of integrity in all business relationships is fine until one questions the meaning of integrity and to whom the duty of integrity is due. The most prominently cited obstacle to managing ethically is when there is a conflict between employees' own or their profession's ethical code and the ethics of their organisation or their immediate superior, employees may have to choose between remaining silent or speaking out and facing the consequences of being seen as disloyal. They may even have to face termination of employment, which, under conditions of redundancy and restructuring, is not to be lightly contemplated. Some comments from Brigley's[29] respondents include:

- high unemployment affects your ethics – cynical but true
- what people say and what people do are very different

- people suppress their own ethical values in order to be generally accepted and get on in business
- the more senior you are, the easier it is to maintain an ethical stance.

The ISM's code of conduct, for example, lays down that subscribers must denounce all forms or manifestations of commercial bribery. What do you do, though, knowing full well what happens to whistle-blowers, if you discover that your boss or colleague is receiving bribes? In summary, it seems that, to be effective, both organisational and professional codes need to be made more relevant to those they apply to and be supported by administrative procedures designed to assist in creating an ethical culture. This in turn means that, to be effective, procurement ethics require appropriate training and education.

19.14.3 Training in ethics

Ethical training sessions for procurement staff can provide a number of benefits. They reinforce the organisation's ethical codes and policies, remind staff that top management expects participants to consider ethical issues when making procurement decisions and clarify what is and what is not acceptable. Such training can include the following:

- the field of ethics
- the feasibility of ethics in business
- how people may rationalise their unethical behaviour

    - 'I was only doing what I was told'
    - 'It's not really illegal'
    - 'It's in everyone's interest'
    - 'Everybody does it'
    - 'No one will ever know'
    - 'The company owes me this because it doesn't pay me enough'

- factors to be considered when receiving a gift or the offer of hospitality, including:

    - the motive of the donor – whether a gift is a token of appreciation or a bribe
    - the value of the gift or the hospitality – when it exceeds what is permissible
    - the type of gift or the nature of the hospitality
    - the manner in which the offer is made – openly or surreptitiously
    - what strings, if any, are attached
    - what impressions the gift or hospitality will make on superiors, colleagues, sub-ordinates, bearing in mind the human propensity to think the worst
    - what the employer's reaction would be if the matter was brought to his or her attention
    - whether the buyer can honestly be satisfied that the gift will not influence his or her objectivity when dealing with suppliers.

If the buyer has doubts about any of the above, the gift or hospitality should be refused.

- double standards – some companies offer gifts to customers' buyers, but refuse permission to their own staff to receive gifts, for example
- what members of the procurement staff should do if they discover a superior, colleagues or subordinates acting contrary to the company's ethical code
- whistleblowing
- what the possible penalties are for unethical behaviour
- fostering ethical standards:

  - dealing with ethical suppliers

  - management support for ethical behaviour.

Badaracco and Webb,[30] in a study of organisational ethics as perceived by younger managers, conclude that ethics as 'viewed from the trenches' is very different from that viewed from the 'general's headquarters':

> The younger managers believed that, in effect, the people who pressured them to act in sleazy ways were responding to four powerful organisational commandments. First, performance is what really counts so make your numbers. Second, be loyal and show us that you're a team player. Third, don't break the law. Fourth, don't overinvest in ethical behaviour.

The researchers also point out:

> In short, a clear pattern of implicit norms and values had taken shape in the minds of many of these younger managers. This pattern is what we have called the fourth commandment. In only a minority of cases did ethics seem to pay. Middle managers who pressed subordinates for sleazy or illegal behaviour went unpunished. Whistleblowing was often a professional hazard and sleazy behaviour didn't hurt or even seemed to accelerate career advancement especially in the short run and sometimes in the long run too.

Two important conclusions from this research are:

- codes of ethics can be helpful, though not decisive, particularly if they are specific about acceptable and unacceptable behaviour
- codes are more likely to be credible if they are enforced and violations of the code are punished.

Brigley[31] considers that codes are easier to introduce and implement in larger organisations. Smaller companies generally prefer an informal approach to ethical issues. Brigley also reports that, within organisations, senior management's attitudes and tactics and conflicts of values with senior management are mainly concerned with pressures arising from harshly competitive climates and the need for a good bottom-line performance.

19.15 Procurement and fraud

19.15.1 What is fraud?

Fraud is defined by the CIMA[32] as:

> Dishonestly obtaining an advantage, avoiding an obligation or causing loss to another party.

The term 'fraud' commonly includes activities such as theft, corruption, conspiracy, embezzlement, deception, bribery and extortion.

The World Bank has identified the following violations that should be referred to their Department of Institutional Integrity:

- contract irregularities and violations of the bank's procurement guidelines
- bid rigging
- collusion by bidders
- fraudulent bids
- fraud in contract performance
- fraud in an audit enquiry
- product substitution
- defective pricing and parts
- cost/labour mischarging
- bribery and acceptance of gratuities
- solicitation and/or receipt of kickbacks
- misuse of bank funds or positions
- travel fraud
- theft and embezzlement
- gross waste of bank funds.

The possibility of procurement fraud is of great concern to all organisations. The three essential ingredients of fraud are intent, capability and opportunity. This situation creates a need to maintain effective communication of accepted behaviour and codes of conduct, thereby clarifying what is and is not acceptable behaviour. Procurement guidelines should always be clearly communicated to all staff, contractors and suppliers.

19.15.2 Distinction between fraud and error

The basic distinction between fraud and error is that of the intention. Any error is unintentional – that is, the person committing the error does not do so knowingly. Errors are accidental and may arise due to negligence, genuine misunderstanding or incompetence. With fraud, however, it is intentional. The person committing fraud does so knowingly, wilfully and with the motive of gaining advantage or benefit by cheating or causing loss or injury to others, acting alone or in collusion with one another.

19.15.3 Indicators of procurement fraud

There are many indicators of potential procurement fraud. They include:

- excessive supplier hospitality to selected staff
- new suppliers continually facing entry 'obstacles'
- budget holders pressurising buyers to place work with named suppliers
- a buyer's lifestyle changing dramatically
- pricing schedules being completed in pencil
- suppliers and contractors being very familiar with senior staff
- specifications favouring a particular supplier

- supplier payments going unchallenged
- the absence of supplier approval data
- no supplier visits or audits.

As indicated in Table 19.3, opportunities for fraud occur at every stage in the procurement process.

19.15.4 E-procurement and fraud

E-procurement clearly provides many opportunities for both input and output fraud. *Input fraud* can take such forms as the opening of accounts for non-existent suppliers who are paid electronically, the payments going into an account designated by the fraudster, over-stating or understating inventory amounts, deleting inventory records, copying of credit card numbers and so on.

Output fraud tends to be comparatively rare. One example is that of sending unauthorised e-mails with intentionally false information.

19.15.5 The prevention of fraud

The threat of fraud can be reduced in four ways.

- *Establish a culture of integrity* – Casabona[33] points out that 85–90 per cent of computer fraud is the result of an insider job. Some computer experts therefore claim that the most effective security system is the integrity of company employees. Much fraud can be eliminated by careful employee selection. Organisations that communicate and support a commitment to integrity will create environments hostile to fraud. When employees leave, organisations should immediately delete all access information of the former worker and inform all relevant people of the termination.
- *Be alert to giveaway signs* – giveaway signs of fraud include:
  - unfolded invoices that have not come through the post
  - too many orders to one supplier, except where single-sourcing applies
  - loss of supporting documentation
  - sudden, unexplained affluence
  - unwillingness of the employee to take holidays or accept a transfer or promotion to other work.

  Evans and Maguire[34] state that the commonest source of discoveries of fraud is outside information. This includes the reporting of fraudulent practices by colleagues and disgruntled mistresses.
- *Take appropriate e-security measures* – technological concerns in e-commerce are usually divided into two broad categories – client server security and data and transaction security. *Client server security* uses various authorisation methods, such as passwords and firewalls, to ensure that only valid users have access to databases. *Data and transaction security* involves ensuring the privacy of electronic messages by using encryption.
- *Recognise the importance of audits* – audits may be internal or external. *Internal audits* in relation to procurement were described in section 17.9. *External audits*, by members of a recognised professional accountancy body approved by the UK

Table 19.3 Fraud at different points in the procurement process

Phase of procurement process	Possible fraudulent activity
1 Establishing need for goods or services	■ Maintaining excessive stock levels to justify purchases ■ Declaring serviceable items as excess or selling them as surplus while continuing to purchase ■ Buying in response to aggressive sales activities ■ Estimates prepared after RFQs requested ■ Failure to develop alternative sources
2 Development of specifications	■ Defining specifications to fit capabilities of a single contractor ■ Defining specifications to fit a specific product ■ Advanced release of information to favoured contractors ■ Selective release of information to favoured contractors ■ Breaking up of requirements to allow rotation of bids ■ Vague specifications that make comparisons of estimates complicated
3 Pre-solicitation	■ Unwarranted sole source justifications ■ Erroneous statements to justify sole source ■ Justification of sole source signed by managers with no authority ■ Technical personnel providing advance information to carefully selected suppliers ■ Invalid restrictions in RFQ documents to limit competition
4 Solicitation	■ Restriction on procurement to prevent/obstruct qualified suppliers ■ Limiting time for submission of tenders so that only those with advance information can respond ■ Improper social contact with supplier representatives ■ Conducting bid conferences in such a way that bid rigging or price fixing is facilitated ■ Discussions with personnel about likely employment with a supplier or sub-contractor ■ Rendering special assistance to a supplier in preparing their bid
5 Bid acceptance	■ Improper acceptance of a late bid ■ Falsification of documents or receipts to get a late bid accepted ■ Change in the bid after other bidders' prices are known ■ Falsification in supplier's qualifications, financial capability, successful completion of previous jobs and so on ■ Submission of the bids by one bidder in a different party's name ■ False certificates, such as insurance ■ Rejection of bids without any valid reason ■ Deliberate loss of bids ■ Exercising favouritism towards a particular supplier during the evaluation process ■ Using biased individuals on the evaluation panel ■ Failing to forfeit bid bonds when a supplier withdraws improperly
6 Post contract award	■ Certifying goods without conducting inspections ■ Action not taken for the non-compliance with contract terms and conditions ■ Double payments for same items/services ■ Contract files are incomplete ■ Substitution of specified goods with used or inferior products ■ Time sheets signed for hours not expended ■ Expenses paid when not incurred ■ Essential spares not delivered but invoiced ■ Invoices settled earlier than contract requires ■ Payment for non-delivered goods/services ■ Unsubstantiated cost growth ■ Charges for skills levels below those contractually agreed

Department of Trade and Industry, are a statutory requirement under the UK companies acts. Contrary to popular belief, it is not an auditor's primary duty to prevent fraud, but, rather, make an independent examination of the books, accounts and vouchers of a business for the purpose of reporting whether or not the balance sheet and profit and loss account show a 'true and fair view' of the affairs and profit (or loss) of the business according to the best information and explanations obtained. An audit may include a physical verification of assets, such as inventory, and the auditors may also make recommendations that can make the business less susceptible to fraud by its customers, suppliers and employees. Where a fraud is discovered, the auditor has a duty to prove that fraud to its full extent, regardless of the amount in question.

19.15.6 Bribery

The Bribery Act 2010 modernised the law on bribery and came into force in the United Kingdom in April 2011. The Act repealed and replaced England's old, much-criticised, laws on bribery with a new comprehensive anti-bribery code. There were a number of Acts repealed or revoked, including:

- Public Bodies Corrupt Practices Act 1889 – The whole Act
- Prevention of Corruption Act 1906 – The whole Act
- Prevention of Corruption Act 1916 – The whole Act
- Scotland Act 1998 – Section 43
- Government of Wales Act 2006 – Section 44

The full list can be found in Schedule 2 'Repeals and Revocations' of the Bribery Act 2010.

There are six principles to guide organisations, namely, proportionality, top level commitment, risk assessment, due diligence, communication and, monitoring and review.

There are far reaching consequences of the new Act, some of which have direct relevance to procurement activities. There are two general offences as follows:

- Paying bribes: it will be an offence to offer or give a financial or other advantage with the intention of inducing that person to perform a 'relevant function or activity' 'improperly' or to reward that person for doing so.
- Receiving bribes: it will be an offence to receive a financial or other advantage intending that a 'relevant function or activity' should be performed 'improperly' as a result.

'Relevant function or activity' includes any function of a public nature and any activity connected with a business. The person performing that activity must be expected to perform it in good faith or impartiality or be in a position of trust.

There is a controversial new offence which can be committed only by commercial organisations (companies and partnerships). It will be committed where:

- a person associated with a relevant commercial organisation (which includes not only employees, but agents and external third parties) bribes another person intending to obtain or retain a business advantage; and
- the organisation cannot show that it had adequate procedures in place to prevent bribes being paid.

There are practical steps that organisations should consider to demonstrate that they have 'adequate procedures'. These steps may include:

- procurement issue guidance to all suppliers and sub-contractors; publish a code of conduct and then monitor and revise it
- establish an internal anti-corruption committee
- corruption training and testing for staff
- prohibitions on facilitation payments
- clear policies on corporate hospitality
- robust screening processes for third-party payments
- conduct due diligence around selection and appointments of suppliers and sub-contractors
- disciplinary measures and remedial action arising from unethical behaviour.

The Bribery Act 2010 raises the maximum jail term for bribery by an individual from seven years to ten years. A company convicted of failing to prevent bribery could receive an unlimited fine.

Figure 19.7 shows the impact on firms of the UK Bribery Act and Figure 19.8 shows an overview of the Bribery Act 2010.[35]

Figure 19.7 UK Bribery Act: Impact on firms

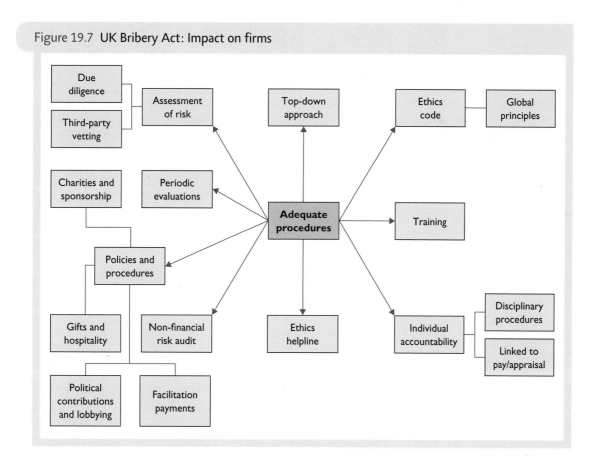

Figure 19.8 UK Bribery Act 2010: An overview

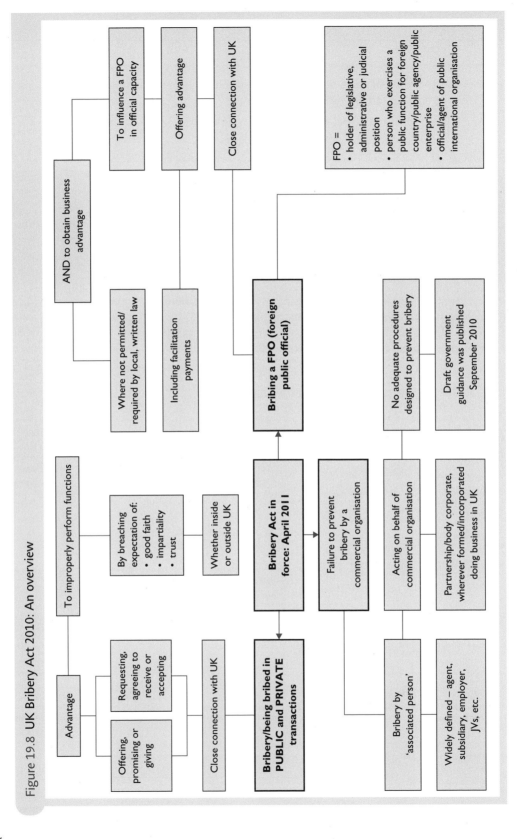

19.16 Cyber security

19.16.1 The challenge for procurement

Cybersecurity has now assumed a vital role in procurement decisions. The indications are that procurement does not adequately fulfil its risk management responsibilities when dealing with cybersecurity as it impacts on suppliers/contractors and the supply chain. Cybersecurity is a complex and technical subject, as this section of the chapter will show, Procurement must have more than a rudimentary knowledge of the subject matter and be capable of liaising effectively with in-house specialists in, for example, IT and Legal Services. Beyond this, there is the need to manage procurement and contract management events with the whole supply chain.

19.16.2 Definitions

The Canadian Centre for Cyber Security[36] define a cyber threat as 'an activity intended to compromise the security of an information system by altering the availability, integrity, or confidentiality of a system or the information it contains.' They then define the cyber threat environment as 'an online space where cyber threat actors conduct malicious cyber threat activity.'

19.16.3 The cyber threat space

Cybersecurity threats were put in sharp focus by the USA Energy Sector Control Systems Working Group (ESCSWG)[37] when they stated, 'Cybersecurity threats, whether malicious or unintentional, pose a serious and ongoing challenge for the energy sector. Today's highly reliable and flexible energy infrastructure depends on the ability of energy delivery systems to provide timely, accurate information to systems operators and automated control over a large, dispersed network of assets and components. A cyberattack on an energy delivery system can have significant impacts on the availability of a system to perform critical functions as well as the integrity of the system and the confidentiality of sensitive information. This, in turn, could impact on national security, public safety, and the economy.'

The Canadian Centre for Cyber Security[38] also put cyber threat activities in clear terms when they stated, 'Cyber threat actors conduct malicious cyber threat activity by exploiting technical vulnerabilities, employing social engineering techniques, or by manipulating social media. A determined and capable adversary will often carefully select the technique most likely to result in successful exploitation after conducting reconnaissance against their target and may use a range of techniques to achieve their goal. The majority of threat actors, however, simply cast a wide net in hopes of exploiting any unsecure network or database.'

19.16.4 Cyber threat – deployment of cyber capabilities

It is very relevant for procurement specialists to become aware of some of the technical nuances of cyber threat. The author is indebted to the Canadian Centre for Cyber Security[39] for permitting the following inclusion of a sample list of common tools and techniques used by threat actors.

Code Injection

Code injection is when threat actors introduce malicious code into a computer program by taking advantage of a flaw in a program's functionality instructions or in the way in interprets data input. Two common code injection techniques are **cross-site scripting (XSS)** and **Structured Query Language (SQL) injection**.

[Distributed] Denial of Service

Denial of service (DoS) is a technique by which a threat actor makes an attempt at disrupting the normal activities of a specific host (e.g., website, server, network, Internet of Things device) by overwhelming it with Internet traffic, also known as requests. The overall objective is to render the host unavailable for legitimate requests from users and render the targeted system dysfunctional. **Distributed denial of service (DDoS)** adds a level of complexity by introducing traffic flooding from multiple sources (e.g., from a botnet). This larger-scale activity makes it much harder to stop and very difficult to distinguish legitimate user traffic from malicious traffic.

Exploits and exploit kits

An **exploit** is malicious code that takes advantage of an unpatched vulnerability. An **exploit kit** is customised to search for specific vulnerabilities and execute the corresponding exploit for the vulnerability it finds. If a user visits a website hosting an exploit kit, the exploit kit will test its repository of exploits against the software applications on the user's device and deploy the exploit that fits the user's vulnerability.

Phishing

Phishing is a common method by which threat actors disguise themselves as a trustworthy entity with the intent to lure a large number of recipients into providing information, such as login credentials, banking information, and other personally identifiable information. Phishing is an example of a social engineering technique and is mainly conducted through email spoofing and text messages. Users become victims when they open malicious attachments or click on embedded links.

Rootkit

Rootkit is a malicious application that is designed to covertly provide a threat actor with 'root 'or administrative privileged access to software and systems on a user's device. A rootkit provides full control, including the ability to modify software used to detect malware. Rootkit installation can be achieved in many ways, including through password cracking social engineering, and leveraging a bug or design flaw that can grant privileged access to a user's system or device.

Spyware

Spyware is malicious software used to track a user's digital actions and information with or without the user's knowledge or consent. Spyware can be used for many activities, including keystroke logging, accessing the microphone and webcam, monitoring user activity and surfing habits, and capturing usernames and passwords.

Typo-Squatting

Typo-Squatting is a technique by which a threat actor registers domain names that have very similar spelling to and can be easily confused with a legitimate domain address.

Typo-squatting is also known as URL hijacking and enables a threat actor to redirect a user who incorrectly typed a website address to an alternative look-alike domain under the actor's control. The new domain can then deliver malware and acquire personally identifiable or other sensitive information. Luring a victim to a hijacked URL an also be achieved through phishing techniques.

Virus, Worm, Payload and Trojan

Malware is commonly delivered through the use of viruses, worms, and Trojans with far-reaching consequences. A **virus** is an executable and replicable program that inserts its own code into legitimate programs with the objective of damaging the host computer (i.e., deleting files and legitimate programs, corrupting storage and operating systems). In its simplest state, a **worm** is a computer program meant to self-replicate and spread to other computers to drain a system's resources. Additionally, just like a virus, a worm has the ability to propagate code that can damage its host. Such code is referred to as a **payload** (e.g., the ability to encrypt files in ransomware and the installation of system backdoors that enable remote access). A **Trojan** is a malicious program disguised as or embedded within legitimate software that has similar objectives to viruses and worms, but, unlike either of them, does not replicate or propagate on its own.

19.16.5 Supply chain risk management practices

The National Institute of Standards and Technology – US Department of Commerce has published the NIST Special Publication 800-161.[40] It is very informative in dealing with many facets of cyber security as it impacts on the supply chain. The overall context is explained in the following manner.

> Commercially available ICT solutions present significant benefits including low cost, interoperability, rapid innovation, a variety of product features, and choice among competing vendors. These commercial off-the-shelf (COTS) solutions can be proprietary or open source and can meet the needs of a global base of public and private sector customers. However, the same globalisation and other factors that allow for such benefits also increase the risk of a threat event which can directly or indirectly affect the ICT supply chain, often undetected, and in a manner that may result in risks to the end user.

> These ICT supply chain risks may include insertion of counterfeits, unauthorised production, tampering, theft, insertion of malicious software and hardware, as well as poor manufacturing and development practices in the ICT supply chain. These risks are associated with an organisation's decreased visibility into, and understanding of, how the technology that they acquire is developed, integrated, and deployed, as well as the processes, procedures, and practices used to assure the integrity, security, resilience, and quality of the products and services. Threats and vulnerabilities created by malicious actors (individuals, organisations, or nation states) are often especially sophisticated and difficult to detect, and thus provide a significant risk to organisations. It should be noted that ICT products (including libraries, frameworks, and toolkits) or services originating anywhere (domestically or abroad) might contain vulnerabilities that can present opportunities for ICTT compromises [This document defines an ICT Supply Chain Compromise as: An occurrence within the ICT supply chain whereby an adversary jeopardises the confidentiality, integrity, or availability of a system or the information the system processes, stores, or transmits. An ICT supply chain compromise can occur anywhere within the system development life cycle of the product or service]. For example, an adversary may have the power to insert malicious capability into a product or to coerce a manufacturer to hand over the manufacturing specifications of a sensitive U.S. system. Note that it is impossible to completely eliminate all risks.

Currently, organisations and many private sector integrators and suppliers use varied and not yet standardised practices, which make it difficult to consistently measure and manage ICT supply chain risks across different organisations. ICT Supply Chain Risk Management (SCRM) is the process of identifying, assessing, and mitigating the risks associated with the global and distributed nature of ICT product and service supply chains.

19.16.6 ICT Procurement – Security Guide

The European Union Agency for Network and Information Security[41] has produced a Security Guide that contains relevant information and guidance relevant, among others, to procurement specialists.

Selective extracts are provided for our readers who are urged to access the Security Guide. Please note that 'provider' refers to electronic communications network and service providers while 'vendor' refers to suppliers of ICT products or outsourcing parties.

SO3: Security roles and responsibilities

Security Risks

Failure to clearly and/or correctly establish key roles and responsibilities regarding security risks management between the provider and the vendor leading to:
- Confusion and misunderstanding between parties in case of threat or incident;
- Incorrect implementation of security requirements;
- Lack of accountability in case of security breaches not recognised within the vendor's organisation.

Security requirements

✓ Clearly define and state responsibilities and roles within the contract to avoid confusion, misunderstanding or abuses.
✓ One person within the vendor's organisation should be accountable during the whole contract lifecycle to ensure that:
  - security risks and requirements are fully understood:
  - appropriate processes are in place and a minimum acceptable level of residual risk is agreed with the provider and duly accepted by each party;
  - security risks are managed and appropriate processes are in place and communicated to the provider;
  - appropriate support is provided to the provider through relevant helpdesk or other as defined by the contract;
  - contractual clauses are respected.
✓ Force Majeure which releases the vendor from its responsibility should be clearly defined to avoid any abuses by the vendor.

SO4: Security of third-party assets

Security Risks

Provider's exposure to additional security threats due to the vendor's use of downstream subcontractors to provide products or services to the provider. These threats include but are not limited to:
- Lack of information regarding the downstream subcontractors;
- Lack of vendor's competent supervision and effective control on its subcontractors:
Failure to enforce security requirements to the vendor's subcontractors

Security requirements

✓ The vendor should provide information regarding existing and/or potential subcontractors used to provide products and services to the provider. This information will be included in the Risk Assessment performed by the provider and should be taken into account in the definition of the security requirements.

Security requirements

✓ The subcontractor must comply with the same or equivalent security measures as the ones applied to the vendor
✓ The vendor should remain solely accountable for all the actions performed by its subcontractors, responsible for manging security within its subcontractors and providing assurance that security requirements operate efficiently to meet the provider's security objectives.

SO6: Security knowledge and training

Security Risks

Vendor's failure to allocate sufficient skilled and trained resources to effectively and efficiently manage security risks.

Security requirements

✓ The vendor's employees should receive appropriate training to implement and operate security requirements applied to the provider.
✓ The vendor should provide sufficient evidence regarding the training program of its employees.
✓ If requested by the provider, the vendor should have the required qualified personnel (e.g., ISO certified).
✓ A designated proportion of the vendor's employees should follow regular training to stay up-to-date in an evolved technological environment with changing security practices.
✓ The vendor should provide sufficient evidence regarding the training program of its employees.
✓ The vendor should carry out its due diligence to ensure that its employees have sufficient security and technical knowledge, skills and qualification, to avoid any unintentional alterations of products or systems. Evidence of the due diligence should be available to the provider for consultation.

19.16.7 Cyber resilience – mitigation strategies

The Australian Cyber Security Centre[42] has compiled a list of mitigation strategies that organisations can use as a starting point to improve their cyber resilience and the technical details of these strategies. They have identified eight essential strategies which should be implemented as a baseline where practicable.

We reproduce, below, four of the eight essential mitigations strategies.

Mitigation strategies to prevent malware delivery and execution

Application whitelisting of approved /trusted programs to prevent execution of unapproved/ malicious programs including .exe, DLL, scripts (e.g., Windows Script Host, PowerShell and HTA) and installers.
Why: All non-approved applications (including malicious code) are prevented from executing.

Patch applications e.g., Flash, web browsers, Microsoft Office, Java and PDF viewers. Patch/ mitigate computer with 'extreme risk' vulnerabilities within 48 hours. Use the latest version of applications.
Why: Security vulnerabilities in applications can be used to execute malicious code on systems.

Configure Microsoft Office macro settings to block macros from the Internet, and only allow vetted macros either in 'trusted locations' with limited write access or digitally signed with a trusted certificate.
Why: Microsoft Office macros can be used to deliver and execute malicious code on systems.

User application hardening. Configure web browsers to block Flash (ideally uninstall it), ads and Java on the Internet. Disable unneeded features in Microsoft Office (e.g., OLE), web browsers and PDF viewers.
Why: Flash, ads and Java are popular ways to deliver and execute malicious code on systems.

19.16.8 Cyber security – contractual safeguards

This part of the chapter must not be interpreted as providing contractual advice. The content is very selective to illustrate some considerations. Legal advice must be sought prior to entering into contractual arrangements for cyber security (or any other contractual arrangements). The extracts below are provided by Bidnet[43] and are subject to Texas jurisdiction.

The selected clauses to inform our readers are shown below:

2. User Security

(a) Account Management: Establish and administer user accounts in accordance with role-based scheme and shall track and monitor role assignment.

(b) Account Management: Automatically audit account creations, modifications, disabling and termination actions with notification to the Department's personnel.

(c) Prevent multiple concurrent active sessions for one user identification.

(d) Enforce a limit of no more than five (5) consecutive invalid access attempts by a user.

(e) Automatically lock the account/node for a ten (10) minute time period unless released by the Department's Administrator.

(f) Prevent further access to the system by initiating a session lock after a maximum of thirty (30) minutes of inactivity, and the session lock shall remain in effect until the user re-establishes access using appropriate identification and authentication procedures.

(g) Ensure all users shall be uniquely identified.

(h) Force users to follow the secure password attributes, below, to authenticate s user's unique ID. The secure password attributes shall:

1 Be a minimum length of eight characters;

2 Not be a dictionary word or proper name;

3 Not be the same as the user ID;

4 Expire within a maximum of ninety (90) calendar days;

5 Not be identical to the previous ten (10) passwords;

6 Not be transmitted in the clear text outside the secure location;

7 Not be displayed in clear text when entered; and

8 Never be displayed in clear text on the screen.

3. System security

(a) Provide audit logs that enable tracking of activities taking place on the system.

(b) Audit logs must track successful and unsuccessful system log-on attempts.

(c) Audit logs must track successful and unsuccessful attempts to access, create, write, delete or change permission on a user account, file, directory or other system resource.

(d) Audit logs must track successful and unsuccessful attempts to change account passwords.

(e) Audit logs must track successful and unsuccessful actions by privileged accounts.

(f) Audit logs must track successful and unsuccessful attempts for users to access, modify, or destroy the audit log.

(g) Provide the following content to be included with every audited event:

1 Date and time of the event;

2 The component of the information system (e.g., software component, hardware component) where the event occurred;

    3 IP address;

    4 Type of event;

    5 User/subject identity; and

    6 Outcome (success or failure) of the event.

(h) Provide real-time alerts to appropriate Departmental officials in the event of an audit processing failure. Alert recipients and delivery methods must be configurable and manageable by the Department's System Administrators.

(i) Undergo vulnerability scan/penetration testing conducted by the Department or the Texas Department of Information Resources. The Contractor shall remediate legitimate vulnerabilities and system/application shall not be accepted until all vulnerability issues are resolved at no cost to the Department.

(j) Notifications shall display an approved system use notification message or banner before granting access to the system. The notification shall state:

    1 Users are accessing a Departmental system;

    2 System usage shall be monitored, recorded and subject to audit;

    3 Unauthorised use of the system is prohibited and subject to criminal and civil penalties; and

    4 A description of the authorised use of the system

(k) The Contractor shall implement and use management and maintenance applications and tools, appropriate fraud prevention and detection, and data confidentiality/protection/ encryption technologies for endpoints, servers and mobile devices. This must include mechanisms to identify vulnerabilities and apply security patches.

(l) The Contractor shall establish and maintain a continuous security program as part of the Services. The security program must enable the Organisation (or its selected third party) to:

    1 Define the scope and boundaries, policies, and organisational structure of an information security management system;

    2 Conduct periodic risk assessments to identify the specific threats to and vulnerabilities of the Organisation due to the Services, subject to the terms, conditions and procedures;

    3 Implement appropriate mitigating controls and training programs, and manage resources; and

    4 Monitor and test the security program to ensure its effectiveness. The Contractor shall review and adjust the security program in the light of any assessed risks.

6. Encryption

The system shall protect the confidentiality of the Department's information. All data transmitted outside or stored outside the secure network shall be encrypted. When cryptography (encryption) is employed within information systems, the system shall perform all cryptographic operations using Federal Information Processing Standard (FIPS) PUB140-2 validated cryptographic modules with approved modes of operation. The system shall produce, control, and distributes symmetric cryptographic keys using NIST- approved key management technology and processes. The key management process is subject to audit by the Department.

(a) Wireless: The following requirements specifies the minimum set of security measures required on WLAN-enabled portable electronic devices (PEDs) that transmit, receive, process, or store PII or confidential information:

    1 Personal Firewall: WLAN-enabled PED shall use personal firewalls or run a Mobile Device Management system that facilitates the ability to provide firewall services.

2 Anti-Virus Software: Anti-virus software shall be used on wireless ECMs-capable PEDs or run a Mobile Device Management System that facilitates the ability to provide anti-virus services.

3 Encryption of PII or confidential data-in-transit via WLAN-enabled PEDs, systems and technologies will be implemented in a manner that protects the data end-to-end. All systems components within a WLAN that wirelessly transmit PII or confidential information shall have cryptographic functionality that is validated under the National Institute of Standards and Technology (NIST) Cryptographic Module Validation Program as meeting requirements per Federal Information Processing Standards (FIPS) Publication 140-2. Encryption shall be a minimum of 128 bit.

4 Data-at-Rest: Data at rest encryption shall be implemented in a manner that protects PII and confidential information stored on WLAN enabled PEDs by requiring that the PED must be powered on and credentials successfully authenticated in order for the data to be deciphered. Data-at-rest encryption shall include the encryption of individual files, portions of the file system (e.g., directories or partitions), or the entire drive (e.g. hard disks, on-board memory cards, memory expansion cards). In recognition of the increased risk of unauthorized access to PII or confidential information in the event that a PED is lost or stolen and the inherently mobile nature of these devices, encryption shall be provided for data-at-rest on all WLAN enabled PEDs that is validated as meeting FIPS 140-2.

5 WLAN Infrastructure: WLAN infrastructure systems may be composed of either stand-alone (autonomous) access points (AP) or thin APS that are centrally controlled by a WLAN controller.

6 Validated Physical Security: APs used in the WLANS should not be installed in unprotected environments due to an increased risk of tampering and/or theft.

(b) Mobile Device Management Requirement. Mobile Device Management (MDM) facilitates the implementation of sound security controls for mobile devices and allows for centralized oversight of configuration control, application usage, and device protection and recovery. MDM shall include the following core features:

1 The ability to push security policies to managed devices;

2 The ability to query the device for its configuration information;

3 The ability to modify device configuration as required;

4 Security functionality that ensures the authenticity and integrity of the transaction in the three categories above;

5 Asset management (track/enable/disable) mobile devices being managed via the MDM server;

6 The ability to manage proxy access to network resources via the connection of the mobile device to the MDM server;

7 The ability to query devices being managed on the status of security policy compliance and to implement a specified mediation function based on compliance status;

8 The ability to download and store mobile device audit records;

9 The ability to receive alerts and other notifications from manage mobile devices;

10 The ability to receive alerts and other notifications from managed mobile devices;

11 The ability to generate audit record reports from mobile device audit records; and

12 Application management (application white list) for applications installed on managed mobile devices.

19.16.9 Cyber insurance requirement

The Contractor will maintain sufficient cyber insurance to cover any and all losses, security breaches, privacy breaches, unauthorised distributions, or releases or uses of any data transferred to or accessed by Contractor under or as a result of this Contract.

a This insurance shall provide sufficient coverage(s) for the Contractor, the Department, and affected third parties for the review, repair, notification, remediation and other response to such events, including but not limited to, breaches or similar incidents under Chapter 521, Texas Business and Commerce Code.

b The Department may, in its sole discretion, confer with the Texas Department of Insurance to review such coverage(s) prior to approving them as acceptable under this Contract.

c The Contractor shall obtain modified coverage(s) as reasonably requested by the Department within ten (10) calendar days of the Contractor's receipt of such request from the Department.

Discussion questions

19.1 Give two examples each of:
   (a) product innovation
   (b) process innovation
   (c) incremental innovation.

19.2 When a company is involved with breakthrough innovation, such as a new drug, what is the role for procurement?

19.3 What is 'concurrent engineering'? What specific roles can procurement play to ensure the success of new product development?

19.4 What are the key areas in which procurement can make a valued contribution to managing cyber security in their organisation?

19.5 Do you believe that cyber security has sufficient visibility in your organisation? What factors have led you to your conclusion?

19.6 'Supplier development is a structured approach to creating additional, competent, sources of supply. In consequence, no buyer should ever be in a position where they are a captive buyer and unable to negotiate.' Do you agree?

19.7 Long-standing barriers between design, production and procurement can be difficult to overcome. Suggest how such barriers might be broken down and what benefits might accrue from replacing conflict with collaboration.

19.8 How should procurement and/or other managers weigh the relative strengths and weaknesses of potential suppliers in areas such as technological knowledge, manufacturing capabilities, length of relationship with the supplier, degree of trust and alignment of technology?

19.9 You have been asked to make a presentation on behalf of procurement to the board of directors of a key supplier. They have a reputation of being old-fashioned, unresponsive to design queries and lacking in customer care. It has got to the point where your engineering director wants you to find an alternative supplier. What points would you make to the board of directors at your supplier?

19.10 Discuss the viewpoints that, in supplier involvement or development:
(a) 'the customer receives most of the benefits and the supplier receives few'
(b) 'cooperative relationships are often cooperative in name and suppliers do more than their fair share of cooperating'.

How might you seek to deal constructively with these objections?

19.11 Comment on the following statements:
(a) Much academic research into procurement is of little practical benefit to practising procurement people.
(b) Much academic research is published in journals that purchasing professionals never read.

19.12 If you were employed as the head of procurement in a private sector, privately owned power station that could not generate electricity competitively and the chief operating officer wanted 15 per cent saved on the total amount of expenditure:
(1) how would you tackle this task?
(2) would you talk to buyers in other power stations?
(3) what would you say to your strategic suppliers?

19.13 In some procurement situations, suppliers own the intellectual property rights in what they supply, including software source codes and patents. What steps can the buyer take to encourage other suppliers to bid for business?

19.14 Benchmarking of procurement performance is rarely done in either the public or private sectors. Why?

19.15 Your head of internal audit has asked you to help her to devise an audit plan to check on the way which purchase prices are agreed and how the process links to accounts payable. What elements of the procurement and payment process would you advise be included in the audit?

19.16 The CIPS policy statement on environmental procurement suggests that products or services should be selected that 'use or emit fewer substances that damage the environment or health'. How can you do this if you are not a chemist and have no specialised knowledge of the chemical content or disposal difficulties of the products or materials you are buying?

19.17 Consider how, from an ethical standpoint, you would react in each of the following cases.
(a) A sales representative telephones you to say that he has left the employment of a supplier from whom you are currently buying large quantities of a component. He knows the price you are paying and states that his new company can undercut your present price by 20 per cent. You have been dealing satisfactorily with your present supplier for a number of years.
(b) You are negotiating on a one-to-one basis with a small machine shop to carry out operations on 100,000 items to relieve capacity in your own production department. You inadvertently mention that you are very pleased with the price and that, subject to discussion with your own production manager, the sub-contractor is likely to receive an order. He then asks, 'Why not let me increase the price by another £1 – 50p for me and 50p for you?'

(c) You can buy cheaper from an overseas supplier, but you know he has starvation levels of pay and the loss of the local order will cause unemployment.

(d) You have negotiated and signed a contract with a supplier. When you arrive home, you find that an expensive piece of jewellery has been sent anonymously to your wife.

(e) You mention to the sales representative of a steel stockist that you are proposing to build an extension to your home. He says, 'Why not let us supply you with the steelwork at cost price?'

(f) On two occasions, a supplier has delivered sub-standard components that can nevertheless be used. You telephone the supplier's production manager to complain. He says, 'Don't write about it because it might affect a promotion I'm expecting. Let's keep it to ourselves and I will put it right'.

(g) You inform a potential supplier that, on average, your company buys 100,000 units of a certain item each year and, as a result, obtain a substantial quantity discount. You know that the average usage is only 50,000 units.

(h) A supplier asks you, in confidence, to give details of competitive quotes, saying that he will beat any price offered and 'that must be good for you'.

(i) A supplier offers you a bribe, saying, 'We do exactly the same for your boss and he has no worries'.

(j) One of your subordinates tells you that, last night, he took his family to a football match and had the use of a hospitality box (including dinner), provided by a company that you know is seeking a share of your business.

19.18 The procurement department is in an ideal position to be accountable for the value of inventory held in a business. That way, procurement and inventory management would be truly integrated. Do you agree, or is there an alternative approach (es)?

References

[1] London Development Agency, *Why Innovate?* www.lda.gov.uk.

[2] Mileham, A. R., Morgan, E. J. and Chatting, J., 'An attribute approach to concurrent engineering', *Proceedings of the Institute of Mechanical Engineers*, Vol. 218, Part B, 2004, pp. 995–1005.

[3] Winner, R. L., Pennel, J. P., Bertrams, H. E. and Slusarczuk, M. M., 'The role of concurrent engineering in weapon system acquisition', *IDA Report R-338*, AD-A203 615, 1988.

[4] Website – www.smartlink.net.au.

[5] Wynstra, F., van Weele, A. and Axelsson, B., 'Purchasing involvement in product development', *European Journal of Purchasing*, Vol. 5, 1999, pp. 129–41.

[6] Handfield, R. B., Krause, D. R., Scannell, T. V. and Monczka, P. M., 'Avoid the pitfalls in supplier development', *Sloan Management Review*, winter, 2000, pp. 37–48.

[7] Hartley, J. and Jones, G., 'Process oriented supplier development', *International Journal of Purchasing and Materials Management*, Summer, 1997.

[8] Sako, M., 'Supplier development at Honda, Nissan and Toyota', *Comparative Case Studies of Organisational Capability Enhancement*, November, 2003.

[9] As 6 above.

[10] Fearon, H., *Purchasing Research, Concepts and Current Practice*, American Management Association, New York, 1976, p. 5.

[11] Sarantakos, S., *Social Research*, Macmillan, New York, 1993, p. 91.

12 Kydos, W., *Measuring, Managing and Maximising Performance*, Productivity Press, Boca Raton, Florida, USA, 1991, p. 17.

13 Van Weele, A. J., *Purchasing Management*, Chapman & Hall, London, UK, 1995, pp. 201–2.

14 Fearon, H. E. and Bales, W. A., *Measures of Purchasing Effectiveness*, Arizona State University, 1997.

15 Scheuing, E. E., *Purchasing Management*, Prentice Hall, Upper Saddle River, New Jersey, USA, 1989, p. 137.

16 Evans, E. F. and Dale, B. G., 'The use of audits in purchasing', *International Journal of Physical Distribution and Materials Management*, Vol. 18, No. 7, 1988, pp. 17–23.

17 Business Link, 'Closing the marketing gap', obtainable from Benchmark Index at Field House, Mount Road, Stone, Staffordshire ST15 8LI (0870 111143) or www.benchmarkindex.com/articles/CTMG.pdf

18 The British Quality Foundation, 32–34 Great Peter Street, London SW1P 2QX (020 7654 5000) or visit www.quality-foundation.co.uk.

19 Published by Harvard Business School Press (*Harvard Business Review*: Sept–Oct 1992; Sept–Oct 1993; Jan–Feb 1996).

20 Niven, P. R., *The Balanced Scorecard Step-by-Step*, John Wiley, Hoboken, USA, 2002.

21 Bourne, M. C. S. and Bourne, P. A., *Understanding the Balanced Scorecard*, Hodder, London, UK, 2000.

22 Neeley, A., Adams, C. and Kennerley, M., *The Performance Prism: The Scorecard for Measuring and Managing Business Success*, Financial Times Prentice Hall, Upper Saddle River, New Jersey, USA, 2002.

23 Adapted from Colera, L., *A Framework for Universal Principles of Ethics* at: www.ethics.ubc.ca/papers/invited/colera.html

24 Robertson, D. C. and Rymon, T., 'Purchasing agents' deceptive behaviour: a randomised response technique study', *Business Ethics Quarterly*, Vol. 11, No. 3, 2001, pp. 455–79.

25 CIPS, 'E-ethics: position on practice guide', prepared by the CIPS Consulting Group: www.cips.org

26 Kennedy, G., *Everything is Negotiable*, Business Books, 1989, pp. 220–5.

27 Matthew 7, verse 12.

28 Karp, H. B. and Abramms, B., 'Doing the right thing', *Training and Development*, August, 1992, pp. 37–41.

29 Brigley, S., *Walking the Tightrope: A Survey of Ethics in Management*, Institute of Management/Bath University, 1994, p. 36.

30 Badaracco, J. L. Jr and Webb, A. P., 'Business ethics – a view from the trenches', *California Management Review*, Vol. 37, No. 2, Winter, 1995, pp. 64–79.

31 As 30 above.

32 CIMA, *Fraud Risk Management: A Guide to Good Practice*, Cima, London, UK, 2008.

33 Casabona, P., 'Computer fraud: financial and ethical implications', *Review of Business*, Vol. 20, Issue 1, Fall, 1988.

34 Evans, E. and Maguire, R., 'Purchasing fraud: a growing phenomenon', *Purchasing and Supply Management*, May, 1993, pp. 24–6.

35 Included by kind permission of Linklaters.

36 Government of Canada.

37 Cybersecurity Procurement Language for Energy Delivery Systems. ESCSWG. April 2014. es-pl@energetics.com.

[38] Canadian Centre for Cyber Security.

[39] As 38 above.

[40] Supply Chain Risk Management Practices for Federal Information Systems and Organisations. April 2015. The publication is available free from: http://dx.doi.org/10.6028/NIST. SP.800-161.

[41] Security Guide for ICT Procurement. European Union Agency for Network and Information Security. December 2014. www.enisa.europa.eu.

[42] Essential Eight Explained. January 2019. https://www.cyber.gov.au/publications/essential-eight-explained

[43] Cyber Security Requirements. 07/25/2014 RFO 405-LES-15-050255 https://www.bidnet.com.

Code of ethics–Your commitment to the profession

Use of the code

Members of CIPS are required to uphold this code and to seek commitment to it by all those with whom they engage in their professional practice.

Members are expected to encourage their organisation to adopt an ethical purchasing policy based on the principles of this code and to raise any matter of concern relating to business ethics at an appropriate level.

The Institute's Royal Charter sets out a disciplinary procedure which enables the CIPS Council to investigate complaints against any of our members and, if it is found that they have breached the code to take appropriate action.

Advice on any aspect of the code is available from CIPS. This code was approved by the CIPS Council on 11 March 2009.

As a member of The Chartered Institute of Purchasing & Supply, I will:

- maintain the highest standard of integrity in all my business relationships
- reject any business practice which might reasonably be deemed improper
- never use my authority or position for my own personal gain
- enhance the proficiency and stature of the profession by acquiring and applying knowledge in the most appropriate way
- foster the highest standards of professional competence amongst those for whom I am responsible
- optimise the use of resources which I have influence over for the benefit of my organisation
- comply with both the letter and the intent of: the law of countries in which I practise agreed contractual obligations CIPS guidance on professional practice
- declare any personal interest that might affect, or be seen by others to affect, my impartiality or decision making
- ensure that the information I give in the course of my work is accurate
- respect the confidentiality of information I receive and never use it for personal gain
- strive for genuine, fair and transparent competition
- not accept inducements or gifts, other than items of small value such as business diaries or calendars

- always to declare the offer or acceptance of hospitality and never allow hospitality to influence a business decision
- remain impartial in all business dealing and not be influenced by those with vested interests.

Advice on any aspect of the code of ethics is available from

CIPS, Easton House, Easton on the Hill, Stamford, Lincolnshire PE9 3NZ, UK Tel: +44 (0)1780 756777 Fax: +44 (0)1780 751610 Email: info@cips.org Web: www.cips.org

CIPS Code of Conduct
(Adopted September 2013)

The purpose of this code of conduct is to define behaviours and actions which CIPS members must commit to maintain as long as they are members of CIPS.

As a member of CIPS, I will:

Enhance and protect the standing of the profession, by:

- never engaging in conduct, either professional or personal, which would bring the profession or the Chartered Institute of Purchasing & Supply into disrepute
- not accepting inducements or gifts (other than any declared gifts of nominal value which have been sanctioned by my employer)
- not allowing offers of hospitality or those with vested interests to influence, or be perceived to influence, my business decisions
- being aware that my behaviour outside my professional life may have an effect on how I am perceived as a professional.

Maintain the highest standard of integrity in all business relationships, by:

- rejecting any business practice which might reasonably be deemed improper
- never using my authority or position for my own financial gain
- declaring to my line manager any personal interest that might affect, or be seen by others to affect, my impartiality in decision making
- ensuring that the information I give in the course of my work is accurate and not misleading
- never breaching the confidentiality of information I receive in a professional capacity
- striving for genuine, fair and transparent competition
- being truthful about my skills, experience and qualifications.

Promote the eradication of unethical business practices, by:

- fostering awareness of human rights, fraud and corruption issues in all my business relationships
- responsibly managing any business relationships where unethical practices may come to light, and taking appropriate action to report and remedy them
- undertaking due diligence on appropriate supplier relationships in relation to forced labour (modern slavery) and other human rights abuses, fraud and corruption
- continually developing my knowledge of forced labour (modern slavery), human rights, fraud and corruption issues, and applying this in my professional life.

Enhance the proficiency and stature of the profession, by:

- continually developing and applying knowledge to increase my personal skills and those of the organisation I work for
- fostering the highest standards of professional competence amongst those for whom I am responsible
- optimising the responsible use of resources which I have influence over for the benefit of my organisation.

Ensure full compliance with laws and regulations, by:

- adhering to the laws of the countries in which I practise, and in countries where there is no relevant law in place I will apply the standards inherent in this Code
- fulfilling agreed contractual obligations
- following CIPS guidance on professional practice.

Use of the code

Members of CIPS worldwide are required to uphold this code and to seek commitment to it by all the parties they engage with in their professional practice. Members should encourage their organisation to adopt an ethical procurement and supply policy based on the principles of this code and raise any matter of concern relating to business ethics at an appropriate level within their organisation. Members' conduct will be judged against the code and any breach may lead to action under the disciplinary rules set out in the Institute's Royal Charter. Members are expected to assist any investigation by CIPS in the event of a complaint being made against them.

Contact us

UK: +44 (0)1780 756777 Africa: +27 (0)12 345 6177 Australasia: +61 (0)3 9629 6000 MENA: +971 (0)4 311 6505 Singapore: +65 6808 8721 +65 6808 8722 Email: info@ cips.org

This code was approved by the CIPS Global Board of Trustees on 10 September 2013. www.cips.org

Definitions, acronyms and foreign words and phrases

Definitions

Acronyms

Foreign words and phrases

Index of names and organisations and some publications mentioned in the text

Subject Index